STERLIN
Test Prep

Bar Exam Review

MBE & State Essay Essentials

Governing Law

3rd edition

3 2 1

ISBN-13: 978-1-9547250-3-4

Sterling Test Prep products are available at quantity discounts.

For more information, contact info@sterling–prep.com.

Sterling Test Prep
6 Liberty Square #11
Boston, MA 02109

Published by Sterling Test Prep
Printed in the U.S.A.

Customer Satisfaction Guarantee

Your feedback is important because we strive to provide the highest quality prep materials. Email us comments or suggestions.

info@sterling–prep.com

We reply to emails – check your spam folder

Thank you for choosing our book!

STERLING
Test Prep

Thousands of students use our study aids to pass the bar!

Passing the bar is essential for admission to practice law and launching your legal career.

This preparation guide describes the principles of substantive law governing the correct answers to exam questions. It was developed by legal professionals and law instructors who possess extensive credentials and have been admitted to practice law in several jurisdictions. The content is clearly presented and systematically organized for targeted preparation.

The performance on individual questions has been correlated with success or failure on the bar. By analyzing previously administered exams, the authors identified these predictive items and assembled the rules of law that govern the answers to questions tested. Learn the essential governing law to make fine-line distinctions among related principles and decide between tough choices on the exam.

We look forward to being an essential part of your bar prep and wish you great success in the legal profession!

210603vgr

Comprehensive Glossary of Legal Terms

Over 2,100 essential legal terms defined and explained. An excellent reference source for law students, practitioners and readers seeking an understanding of legal vocabulary and its application.

Landmark U.S. Supreme Court Cases: Essential Summaries

Learn important constitutional cases that shaped American law. Understand how the evolving needs of society intersect with the U.S. Constitution. Short summaries of seminal Supreme Court cases focused on issues and holdings.

Visit our Amazon store

Table of Contents

EXAM INFORMATION, PREP & TEST-TAKING STRATEGIES *(continued)*

EXAM INFORMATION, PREP & TEST-TAKING STRATEGIES *(continued)*

Essay Preparation Strategies and Essay-Writing Suggestions *(continued)*

CONSTITUTIONAL LAW (*continued*)

CONSTITUTIONAL LAW (*continued*)

CONTRACTS *(continued)*

CONTRACTS (*continued*)

CRIMINAL LAW and CRIMINAL PROCEDURE (*continued*)

CRIMINAL LAW and CRIMINAL PROCEDURE *(continued)*

EVIDENCE (*continued*)

EVIDENCE *(continued)*

REAL PROPERTY *(continued)*

The Estate System *(continued)*

REAL PROPERTY *(continued)*

Title *(continued)*

TORTS (*continued*)

TORTS *(continued)*

CIVIL PROCEDURE (*continued*)

CIVIL PROCEDURE *(continued)*

CIVIL PROCEDURE (*continued*)

Motions (*continued*)

BUSINESS ASSOCIATIONS (*continued*)

BUSINESS ASSOCIATIONS *(continued)*

BUSINESS ASSOCIATIONS *(continued)*

BUSINESS ASSOCIATIONS *(continued)*

CONFLICT OF LAWS *(continued)*

CONFLICT OF LAWS (*continued*)

CONFLICT OF LAWS (*continued*)

FAMILY LAW (*continued*)

FAMILY LAW *(continued)*

TRUSTS AND ESTATES (*continued*)

TRUSTS AND ESTATES (*continued*)

TRUSTS AND ESTATES (*continued*)

The Distribution of the Estate After Death (*continued*)

TRUSTS AND ESTATES *(continued)*

TRUSTS AND ESTATES *(continued)*

SECURED TRANSACTIONS (*continued*)

APPENDIX *(continued)*

Exam Information, Preparation and Test-Taking Strategies

Introduction to the Bar Exam

The Multistate Bar Examination (MBE)

The Multistate Bar Examination consists of 200 four-option multiple-choice questions prepared by the National Conference of Bar Examiners (NCBE).

Of these 200 questions, 175 are scored, and 25 are unscored pretest questions.

Candidates answer 100 questions in the three-hour morning session and the remaining 100 questions in the three-hour afternoon session.

The 175 scored questions are distributed with 25 questions on each of the seven subject areas: Federal Civil Procedure, Constitutional Law, Contracts, Criminal Law and Procedure, Evidence, Real Property, and Torts.

A specified percentage of questions in each subject tests topics in those subjects.

For example, approximately one-third of Evidence questions test hearsay and its exceptions, while approximately one-third of Torts questions test negligence.

Interpreting the MBE score report

Examinees receive a scaled score and not an MBE "raw" score (i.e., the number of correct answers). MBE scores are scaled scores calculated by the NCBE through a statistical process used for standardized tests.

According to the NCBE, this statistical process adjusts raw scores on the current exam to account for differences in difficulty compared to previously administered exams. The scaled score is calculated from the raw score, but the NCBE does not publish the conversion formula.

Since the MBE is a scaled score, equating makes it impossible to know precisely how many questions must be answered correctly to receive a particular score. Equating allows scores from different exams to be compared since a specific scaled score represents the same level of knowledge among exams.

The MBE is curved, so just because a score is "close" to passing does not mean you are close. For example, a 124 may be in the 31st percentile and a 136 in the 62nd percentile. A 12-point difference in scaled scores equates to a 31-point percentile difference. If you are in the 120s, much preparation is needed to increase your score.

For most states, aim for a scaled score of 135 to "pass" the MBE. If you are unsure what score you need, divide the passing score by two. For example, if a 270 is needed to pass the bar, divide 268 by two to yield 135 as a threshold score on the MBE.

The importance of the MBE score

A passing MBE score depends on the jurisdiction. In jurisdictions that score on a 200-point scale, the passing score is the overall score. Passing scores are often approximately 135.

For the July 2020 bar exam, the national average MBE score was 146.1, an increase of 5 points from the July 2019 national average of 141.1.

For comparison, on the July 2018 bar, the national average MBE score was 139.5, a decrease of about 2.2 points from the July 2017 national average of 141.7.

How much the MBE contributes depends on the jurisdiction. Each jurisdiction has its policy for the relative weight given to the MBE compared to other bar exam components.

For Uniform Bar Examination (UBE) jurisdictions, the MBE component is 50%.

Most jurisdictions combine the MBE score with the state essay exam score.

The overall state candidates' performance on the MBE controls the raw state essay's conversion to scaled scores. Achieve a scaled MBE score of at least 135 to pass the bar.

The objective of the Multistate Bar Exam

Working knowledge of the MBE objectives, the skills it tests, how it is drafted, the relationship of the parts of an MBE question, and the testing limitations provide you a substantial advantage in choosing the correct answers to MBE questions and passing the bar.

Knowing which issues are tested and the form in which they are tested makes it more manageable to learn the large body of substantive law. The MBE's fundamental objective is to measure fairly, and efficiently which law school graduates have the necessary academic qualifications to be admitted to the bar and exceed this threshold.

The exam used to accomplish this objective must be of a consistent level of difficulty. The level at which the pass decision is made must be achievable by most candidates.

The MBE tests the following skills:

- reading carefully and critically
- identifying the legal issue in a set of facts
- knowing the law that governs the legal issues tested
- distinguish between frequently confused closely-related principles
- making reasonable judgments from ambiguous facts
- understanding how limiting words make plausible-sounding choices wrong
- choosing the correct answer by intelligently eliminating incorrect choices

Preparation Strategies for the Bar Exam

An effective bar exam study plan

There are a lot of great ideas about how to prepare. Follow through with these ideas and turn them into persistent action for successful preparation.

A detailed and well-planned study schedule has benefits, such as giving you a sense of control and building confidence and proficiency.

Pick a date about 12-14 weeks before the exam (November for the February exam and April for the July exam) and use it as the start of your active study period.

Start a month earlier than many others to have a month to review as final preparation at the end.

Students have found this effective. Use an elongated prep period as a study schedule.

Most examinees prefer at least two weeks before the exam to review the material.

By planning early, you will have more time. You may want three or four final weeks to review subjects, take timed exams, and ensure that you are prepared to take the exam.

A few notes on schedule management:

> Do not *start* memorizing during your initial review period. You should be learning every week from the beginning of your study schedule. This final prep period is for reviewing and taking timed exams.
>
> If you stretch the study schedule over several months, plan review weeks into your schedule. For example, every four weeks, use a few days to review the governing law and take timed exams. This is a practical and fruitful approach as you will be more likely to retain the information.

Pick specific dates for specific tasks; this makes it more likely you will complete them.

Make sure the tasks are measurable. (e.g., practice two essays).

Be realistic about the tasks, time, energy, and your ability to complete the items listed as tasks in preparation for the exam.

Remember to take some scheduled breaks from studying.

Exercise, sleep and take care of your physical and mental health.

If you are not in the right mental state preparing for the exam, you will likely be ineffective when studying and are less likely to pass the exam.

Focused studying

Some people are better at multiple-choice questions; others do better with essays. The multiple-choice portion and the essay portion are weighted equally. Doing poorly in one section means it will be challenging to achieve a passing score.

Identify weaknesses early in the preparation process and focus on them. If you struggle with multiple-choice questions, dedicate extra time to practicing MBE questions. If you struggle with writing, focus on completing essays and complete MPT practice materials.

By reviewing your performance on released multiple-choice practice tests, be concerned if you consistently miss questions that are most answered correctly.

If you have problems with questions and perform below 50%, you lack the fundamental knowledge necessary to pass the MBE.

When reviewing your answers to practice questions, it is essential to review all questions and answers, even those you got right.

Make sure you got that correct answer for the right reason.

Reviewing the questions and answers is critical for success on the exam.

Spend time reviewing those basic principles and working deliberately on the straightforward (and easy) questions that supplement learning.

Advice on using outlines

As a user of this governing law book, several of the following points are moot. They are included, so you can be confident that you are using the proper resources to prep for the bar.

Having a useful governing law study guide (such as this book) is critical.

Without effective resources, it is challenging to understand, learn and apply the governing law to the facts given in the question.

Some students use outlines that make learning difficult.

A few common mistakes about outlines:

- Learning outlines that are too long (e.g., more than 100 pages per subject) or too short (e.g., a seven-page Contracts outline). You will be overwhelmed by information or never learn enough governing law.
- Spending too much time comparing several outlines for the same subject.

  For example, using different Contracts outlines and needlessly comparing them. This confusion results in an undue focus on insignificant discrepancies.

- Outlining every subject. If you are not starting to study early, this consumes too much study time. Do not attempt to outline all subjects. It may be a good idea to outline a select few problematic subjects.

Using a detailed and well-organized governing law outline (e.g., this book) is essential; it saves time, organizes concepts, reduces anxiety, and helps you score well and pass the bar.

Easy questions make the difference

Limitations on the examiners lead to the first important insight into preparation for the exam – the kind of questions that decide whether you pass.

Performance on specific questions correlates with success or failure on the bar.

By analyzing statistics, questions predicting success or failure have been identified.

In general, the most challenging questions were not particularly good predictors of failure because most people who missed them passed the bar.

However, many of the straightforward questions were excellent predictors of success.

The median raw score ranges from about 60% to 66% correct on the MBE.

The National Conference of Bar Examiners (NCBE) writes, "expert panelists reported that they believed MBE items were generally easy, correctly estimating that about 66% of candidates would select the right answer to a typical item."

Depending on the exam's difficulty, in most states, scoring slightly below the median (miss up to 80 questions) still passes.

The most important questions to determine if you pass are not the exceedingly challenging ones but the easy ones where 90% of the examinees answer correctly.

The easy questions usually test a basic and regularly tested point of substantive law.

The wrong choices (i.e., the distracters) are typically easy to eliminate.

Your first task in preparing for the MBE is to get easy questions correct.

Study plan based upon statistics

These statistics show that an excellent performance on either the MBE questions (approximately 67% correct) or the state essays (4s on essays) assures you a passing score.

If you fail the MBE by 9 points or the essays by 5 points, the probability of passing the bar is in the single digits.

Put effort into performing well on the MBE questions for the following reasons.

- The questions are objective, and there are enough questions that are predictable concerning content and structure that it is possible, through reasonable effort, to answer 67% of the questions correctly.
- Studying the MBE first has the added advantage of preparing the necessary substantive law for state essays.
- The essays cover several subjects, the precise topic tested is unpredictable, and the answers are graded subjectively by graders who work quickly.

You had three years of law school practice with essays and less experience with multiple-choice questions.

Master the MBE before spending time preparing for the essays.

Factors associated with passing the bar

Based on an analysis of statistics from students' performance, the following factors predict the likelihood of passing the bar:

LSAT score

First-year Grade Point Average (GPA)

LSAT scores are a significant predictor of success on the bar because the LSAT requires similar multiple-choice test-taking skills as the MBE.

The LSAT tests many of the types of legal reasoning tested on the MBE.

A lower LSAT can be overcome by a comprehensive study of the MBE governing law, but these students must work harder.

Most of the subjects tested (e.g., constitutional law, civil procedure, contracts, criminal law, real property, torts) on the MBE are taken in the first year of law school.

First-year GPA measures mastery of subjects, preparedness for exams, and the ability to understand legal principles and apply them to given fact patterns.

The MBE measures the same factors but in a multiple-choice format instead of essays.

Pass rates based on GPA and LSAT scores

Past statistics indicate that law students with LSAT scores above 155 and a first-year GPA above 3.0 are reasonably assured of passing the bar.

They should study conscientiously and take practice MBEs to perform at the level needed, but they have little cause to panic.

Students with LSAT scores between 150 and 155 and a first-year GPA between 2.5 and 3.0 are in a bit more danger of failing and need to undertake rigorous preparation.

They must achieve a scaled score of 135 and take released practice exams and understand the reasons for incorrect choices. They should prepare for state essays by learning the governing laws in this book.

Students with LSAT scores between 145 and 150 and a first-year GPA between 2.2 and 2.5 have a moderate chance of passing the bar from deliberate efforts.

These students should not rely on ordinary commercial bar reviews and need intense training, particularly on the MBE component of the bar. They must devote 50-60 hours per week for seven weeks to prepare for the bar by learning the format and content of substantive law tested on the MBE. They should take released practice exams under exam conditions and conscientiously study the questions missed.

Students with LSAT scores below 145 and a GPA below 2.2 have had a failure rate of approximately 80%.

They must prep faithfully and conscientiously beyond the advice above and must engage in a rigorous course of study, more than is demanded by a traditional bar review course.

Learning and Applying the Substantive Law

Knowledge of substantive law

The fundamental reason for missing a question is 1) a failure to know the principle of law controlling the answer or 2) failure to understand how that principle is applied.

You must know and apply the governing law to pass the bar. If you do not know the governing law, you will not apply it to answer correctly.

Many students *think* they understand the governing law but do not know the nuances. Do not assume that you understand the governing (i.e., substantive) law. It is prevalent for students not to know the governing law well.

Re-learn the substantive and procedural law taught in first-year courses.

A major mistake is not to memorize the governing law outlined in this book.

The multiple-choice and essay portions test nuances and details of governing law. It is essential to analyze the governing law as it is applied in the context of the question.

On the multiple-choice section, many questions require fine-line distinctions between similar principles of law.

Several multiple-choice answers will *seem* correct, given the limited time to answer. If your knowledge of the governing law is suboptimal, you will not make these subtle distinctions and will have to guess on many questions.

For the essay to be developed, you must know the governing law and apply it to the issues within the call of the question.

If you do not know the governing law, you will not state the correct rule in your essay. You will be unable to apply the correct rule to the fact pattern.

Where to find the law

The questions must be related to the subject matter outlined in the bar examiners' (NCBE) materials.

While the NCBE outline is broad and ambiguous, years of experience with the exam delineate the scope of material you must learn.

The governing law covered in this book is foundational to the exam. The governing law statements were compiled by analyzing questions released by the multistate examiners. The analysis revealed a limited number of legal principles repeatedly tested.

Review these principles before taking practice exams and understand how they are applied to obtain the correct answer.

The property questions are probably the most difficult. The fact patterns are usually long and involve many parties in complex transactions.

In preparing for the exam, learn basic property principles and apply them. However, extensive studying into property law's crevices is not necessary to score well on these questions.

Feel confident that you do not have to go beyond the information provided in this book to find the governing law.

Controlling authority

The examiners have specified the sources of authority for the correct answers.

In Constitutional Law and Criminal Procedure, it is Supreme Court decisions.

In Criminal Law, it is common law.

In Evidence, the Federal Rules of Evidence controls.

In Torts and Property, it is the generally accepted view of United States law.

The UCC is the controlling authority in sales (Article 2) questions.

The NCBE released questions, and the published answers determine the controlling law through deduction.

Recent changes in the law

The exam is prepared months before it is given because of logistical requirements. Therefore, the examiners cannot incorporate recent changes in the law into the questions.

Recent changes in the law will not form the basis for correct answers.

If a recent change makes an answer initially designated as the correct answer to be incorrect, the examiners will credit more than one answer.

The recent holding of a Supreme Court case will not be tested for about two years since the decision was published.

Lesser-known issues and unusual applications

Some of the challenging exam questions are based on obscure principles of law.

Missing the most challenging questions will not cause you to fail the exam if you have a solid understanding of the governing law. You can learn these principles and answer the question correctly, thereby improving your overall performance.

There are instances where the correct answers are different from the usual rules.

For example, hearsay evidence inadmissible at trial is admissible before a judge hearing evidence on a preliminary question of fact (e.g., Federal Rules of Evidence 104(a)).

Practice applying the governing law

Some students know the governing law but have problems *applying* it to the facts.

The exam is as much about testing skills as it is about testing the governing law.

Therefore, knowledge of the governing law is not enough to pass.

You must practice answering multiple-choice questions and writing well-organized, coherent, and complete essays where you apply the governing law to the given facts.

Know which governing law is being tested

A typical wrong answer (i.e., distracter) on a question is an answer which is correct under a body of law other than the governing law being tested.

An example is a question governed by Article 2 of the Uniform Commercial Code (UCC), where an offer is irrevocable if:

1) it is in writing,

2) made by a merchant, and

3) states that it is irrevocable.

One of the wrong answers states the correct rule under the common law of contracts, where an offer is revocable unless consideration is paid (i.e., an option) for the promise to keep it open.

Answers which are always wrong

Some commonly used distracters are always wrong and can be eliminated quickly.

For example, a choice in an evidence question says, "character can only be attacked by reputation evidence." This choice is wrong because both opinion and reputation evidence is admissible under the Federal Rules of Evidence when character attacks are permissible.

Honing Reading Skills

Reading skills are critical. The basic level is reading to understand the facts, identify the issue and keep the parties distinct. A mistake at this juncture results in answering incorrectly, no matter how much law is known.

Understanding complex transactions

If the question involves a transaction with many parties, diagram the transaction before analyzing the choices.

The diagram should show the relationship between the parties (e.g., grantor-grantee, assignor-assignee), the transaction date, and the person's relationships in the transaction (e.g., donee, *bona fide* purchaser).

Impediments to careful reading

Two reasons candidates fail to read carefully are:

1) hurrying through a question,

2) fatigue due to a lack of sleep or strain caused by the exam.

A careful test taker maintains a steady, deliberate pace during the exam. Practice in advance and be well-rested on the test day.

Reading too much into a question

The examiners are committed to designing questions, which are "a fair index of whether the applicant has the ability to practice law." Psychometric experts ensure that they are fair and unbiased.

Even though you must read every word of these carefully drafted questions, do not read the question to find some bizarre interpretation.

The examiners must ask fair questions and not rely on "tricks." Reading too much into a question and looking for a trick lurking behind every fact leads to the wrong answer often.

It is the straightforward questions that determine whether you pass, not the occasional challenging question that tests some arcane principle of law.

Therefore, take questions at face value.

Read the call of the question first

Before reading the facts, read the call of the question because it indicates the task for selecting the correct answer. This perspective focuses your attention before reading the facts.

The question contains many *words of art*, such as "most likely," "best defense," or "least likely," which govern the correct answer.

The call is often phrased positively; the "best argument" or "most likely result."

Read answers for consistency with the question and eliminate inconsistent choices.

Negative calls

When the call of the question is negative, asking for the "weakest argument" or asking which of the options is "not" in a specified category, examine each option with the perspective that the choice with those negative characteristics is the correct answer.

After reading and understanding the question stem, read the call of the question again before reading the choices.

Analyze each choice with the requirements specified in the call of the question.

Read all choices

Never pick an answer until carefully reading all the choices. The objective is to pick the best answer, which cannot be determined until comparing the choices.

Sometimes the difference between the right and wrong answer is that one choice is more detailed or precisely sets forth the applicable law. You do not know that until reading all the answers carefully.

Broad statements of black letter law may be correct

When reading an answer, do not rule out choices with imprecise statements of the applicable *black letter* law.

If the examiners always included a choice that was precisely on point, the questions would be too easy. Instead, they often disguise the wording used in the correct answer.

For example, the Federal Rules of Evidence contain an elaborate set of relevancy rules that limit the right to introduce evidence of repairs after an accident. If there was a question where the introduction of that evidence was permissible, and no choices specifically cite the exception to the general rule of exclusion, an answer phrased with the general rule of relevancy "Admissible because its probative value outweighs its prejudicial effect," would be the correct answer.

Multiple-Choice Test-Taking Tactics

Determine the single correct answer

Increase the odds of picking the correct answer based on technical factors independent of substantive (governing) law knowledge.

The examiners' limitation is that every question must have one demonstrably correct and three demonstrably incorrect answers, limiting how the examiners write the choices.

From the question's construction, this limitation may give clues about the answer.

Process of elimination

Answering a multiple-choice question is not finding the ideal answer to the question asked but instead picking the best option.

Eliminate choices and evaluate the remaining choice for plausibility.

Eliminate choices that state an incorrect proposition of law or do not relate to the facts.

If you eliminate three options and the remaining one is acceptable, pick it and move on.

Elimination increases the odds

It takes about 125 correct answers to pass the MBE. An important strategy in reaching that number is intelligently eliminating choices.

If you are sure of the answer to only 50 of the 200 questions on the exam and confidently eliminate two of the four choices on the remaining 150 questions. Guess between the two remaining choices, and the odds predict 75 correct.

Those 75 correct, coupled with 50 questions you were confident of the answer, produce a raw score of 125 on the MBE and a scaled score above the benchmark 135.

Unfortunately, you cannot avoid guessing on questions, but intelligent methods reduce options to only two viable choices.

Sometimes you might not be able to eliminate the wrong answers just because you are sure of the answer to one of the choices. Eliminating with confidence even one choice increases the probability of correctly answering the question.

Eliminating two wrong answers

Specific questions on the MBE are challenging because of distinguishing between two choices when selecting the best answer.

A typical comment from examinees leaving the exam is, "I could not decide between the last two choices."

The positive side of that problem is eliminating two of the four choices.

Pick the winning side

The most common choice pattern is the "two-two" pattern – two choices state that the plaintiff prevails, and two that the defendant prevails.

The best approach for this type of question is to rely on your knowledge of the law or instinctive feeling to which conclusion is correct.

In a question with two choices on one side and two on the other side of a court's decision, first, pick a choice on the side you think should prevail.

Distinguish between the explanations following this conclusion and pick the choice that best justifies it.

Distance between choices on the other side

If the justifications following the conclusion for the side you chose seem indistinguishable, look at the explanations for the choices on the other side.

If the reasons for the choices on the other side are readily distinguishable, and one appears reasonable and the other incorrect, reconsider your initial conclusion.

Remember, the examiner is required to provide a distinguishable reason why one explanation of a general conclusion is correct, and the other is wrong.

That obligation does not exist if the general conclusion itself is incorrect.

Suppose choices (A) and (B) on one side look correct; that is, they are reasonable and consistent with the fact pattern. One of the choices with the opposite conclusion, answer (C), seems incorrect or inconsistent with the facts, and answer (D) with the same general conclusion sounds reasonable. From a strictly technical viewpoint, the best choice is answer (D).

Questions based upon a common fact pattern

There are several instances where two or more questions are based on the same facts.

Look at the second question's wording to guide the first question's correct answer. When asked to assume an answer to a first question from a fact pattern to answer the second question, the probability is high that the answer to the first question follows that assumption.

For example, if the first question has two choices beginning with "P prevails" and two with "D prevails," and the second question starts with "If P prevails," it is likely one of the "P prevails" choices is correct for the first question. If you picked "D prevails," think carefully before selecting it as the final answer.

Multiple true/false issues

In addition to true/false questions, the exam sometimes states three propositions in the root of the question and tests characteristics of those propositions in the call of the question.

The choices list various combinations of propositions.

The difference between this type of question and the double true/false question is that only four of the eight possible combinations fit into the options. It is possible to answer correctly even if you are not sure of all propositions' truth or falsity but are sure of one.

Correctly stated, but the inapplicable principle of law

The task of the examiners is to make the wrong choices look attractive. A creative way to accomplish this is to write a choice that impeccably states a rule of law that is not applicable because of facts in the root of the question.

For example, in a question where a person is an assignee, not a sublessee, one of the choices may correctly state the law for sublessees, but it is inapplicable to the fact pattern.

Therefore, these answer choices with inapplicable law can be confidently eliminated.

"Because" questions

Conjunctions are commonly used in the answers. It is essential to understand their role in determining whether a choice is correct.

The word "because" connects a conclusion and the reason for that conclusion with the facts in the body of the question.

There are two requirements for a question using "because" to be correct:

1) the conclusion must be correct,

2) the reasoning must logically follow based upon facts in the question, and the statement which follows "because" must be legally correct.

If the "because" choice has the correct result for the wrong reason, it is incorrect.

"If" questions

The conjunction "if" requires a much narrower focus than "because."

When a choice contains an "if," determine whether the entire statement is true, assuming that the proposition which follows the "if" is true.

There is no requirement that facts in the root of the question support the proposition following "if." There is no requirement for facts in the question to support the proposition that such a construction be reasonable.

"Because" or "if" need not be exclusive

There is no requirement for the conclusion following "if" or "because" to be exclusive.

For example, if a master could be liable in tort under the doctrine of *respondeat superior* or because the master was *negligent*, a choice using "if" or "because" holding the master liable would be correct if it stated either reason, even though the master might be liable for the other reason.

Exam tip for "because"

Notice that in an answer that would have been correct, the word "because" limits the facts you could consider to those in the body of the question containing specific facts.

The difference between the effect of "if" and "because" controls the answer.

Identify those limited situations (e.g., where the appropriate standard is strict liability) and distinguish them from those that are satisfactory (e.g., if the standard is negligence).

"Only if" requires exclusivity

Sometimes the words "only if" are used to distinguish between the two "affirmed" choices to make one wrong.

When an option uses the words "only if," assume that the entire proposition is correct as long as the words following "only if" are true.

The critical difference, where "only if" is used, is that the proposition cannot be true except when the condition is true. If there is another reason for the same result to be reached, the choice is wrong.

"Unless" questions

The conjunction "unless" has the same function as "only if," except that it precedes a negative exclusive condition instead of a positive exclusive condition.

It is essentially the mirror image of an "only if" choice.

For an option using "unless," reverse and substitute the words "only if" for "unless."

Limiting words

Choices can be made incorrect with limiting words that require that a proposition be true in all circumstances or under no circumstances.

Examples of limiting words include *all*, *any*, *never*, *always*, *only*, *every*, and *plenary*.

Making Correct Judgment Calls

Applying the law to the facts

Most questions give a fact pattern and ask which choice draws the correct legal conclusion required by the call of the question.

The first skill required is to draw inferences from facts given to place the conduct described in the question in the appropriate legal category.

The second skill is to apply the appropriate legal rule to conduct in that category and choose the option which reaches the appropriate conclusion.

The process of drawing inferences from a fact pattern and placing conduct in an appropriate category often requires judgment.

Bad judgment equals the wrong answer

To make the questions difficult, the examiners often place the conduct near the border of two different legal classifications.

Decide which side of the demarcation the conduct falls on. Inevitably, reasonable people can differ on these judgments.

If your judgment does not match the examiners, you will likely answer the question incorrectly, no matter how much law you know.

Mitigate this problem by reviewing released questions involving judgment calls where the examiners have published correct answers (i.e., their judgment call).

For example, a death occurring because the parties played Russian roulette is considered *depraved heart murder*, not *involuntary manslaughter*.

Judgment calls happen

Difficult judgment calls occur several times on the exam, and you are likely to make some close judgment calls incorrectly.

While this adds to the frustrations of multiple-choice tests, it is part of the exam.

By narrowing judgment call questions to two choices and guessing, you will get approximately half of them correct.

You will not fail the exam solely because you were unlucky on judgment calls.

The examiners remove many judgment calls by procedural devices.

The importance of procedure

The question may not ask what a jury should find on the facts.

The answer may be controlled by the procedural context of the criminal prosecution.

For example, it is given that the jury has found the defendant guilty of murder, and the only question on appeal is whether the judge should have granted a motion to dismiss at the end of hearing evidence. This is because a reasonable jury looking at the facts and inferences most favorable to the prosecution should not have found the defendant guilty of murder.

The same procedural issues exist when the question asks if a motion for summary judgment should be allowed or if the court should direct a verdict.

Exam Tips and Suggestions

Timing is everything

The time given to complete the exam is usually adequate if you practiced enough questions to improve speed and efficiency to the required level.

As you get closer to the test date, just doing practice questions is not enough.

You need to time your practice. Take previously released exams in two three-hour periods on the same day. Since these practice exams are approximately the same length as the exam, you will know if you have a timing problem.

If you do not practice under timed conditions, you risk exhausting time on the exam before answering all the questions.

Practice your timing under test-like conditions to know if the timing will be an issue. If you cannot complete the practice exam, you will have trouble with the exam.

If time is an issue, adjust your pace and continue practicing.

All questions do not require the same amount of time.

An approach for when time is not an issue

If you can complete 100 questions in three hours, use this strategy. At the start of the exam, break the allotted time into 15-minute intervals and write them down.

Set an initial pace of 9 questions every fifteen minutes.

Check your progress at each 15-minute interval.

If you completed 18 questions in the first half-hour, 36 in the first hour, 72 in the first two hours, and 90 in the first two and a half hours, you are on target to complete the exam on time. At this pace, you should complete 100 questions in two hours and forty-six minutes.

This leaves 14 minutes to check the answer sheet, revisit troublesome questions, or use the time to go a little slower on the last questions when fatigue impairs acuity.

If you find that your careful pace is faster than the budgeted 9 questions every 15 minutes, work at a faster pace, but use the extra time on the more challenging questions or in rechecking your work at the end.

Do *not* change the original answer choice unless you have a specific reason.

It is unwise to leave the exam early.

An approach for when time is an issue

During practice, continue answering questions to complete the section even after the time for self-paced exams has expired. Note which question you completed within the allocated time. Strive to complete the questions within the allotted time during your final exam prep.

If you learn from taking the practice test that you may not finish the questions in the allotted time on the actual exam, skip those questions with a long fact pattern followed by only one question. Keep your place on the answer sheet by skipping the row.

Return to those questions at the end and complete as many as time permits. Before turning your exam in, guess at the rest to reduce the number of random guesses.

Answer every question, even if you have not read the question, since wrong answers do *not* count against you.

Difficult questions

If you do not know the answer, do not spend a disproportionate amount of time on it since each question counts the same. Mark it in the test booklet, make a shrewd guess within the budgeted time and come back if time allows.

Do *not* leave questions unanswered. No points are deducted for wrong answers.

Minimize fatigue to maximize your score

The mental energy required to answer all the multiple-choice questions under stress produces fatigue (even with a lunch break).

Fatigue slows processing questions effectively and impairs reading comprehension. You may process questions more slowly at the end of each session and more quickly at the beginning before fatigue sets in.

Take at least two released exams under timed conditions to know how significantly fatigue affects your performance.

Be sure to arrive at the exam site on time. If necessary, stay at a nearby hotel rather than getting up early and risking a long drive the morning of the exam.

Relax during the lunch break and do not discuss the morning session with others.

You should know enough about your metabolism to eat the correct foods during the exam and reinforce appropriate caffeine levels if appropriate.

Proofread the answer sheet

As you decide on each correct answer, circle the corresponding letter in the exam book, and mark the appropriate block on the answer sheet.

The answer sheet is the only document graded by the examiners.

At the pace of 9 questions per 15 minutes, about 14 minutes should remain. Spend that time proofreading the answer sheet. Verify the answers circled to be certain that you marked the appropriate block on the answers.

Ensure that there are no blanks, and no questions have two answers.

Do *not* use this time to change an answer already selected unless you have a particularly good reason to change it.

If you have erased, ensure the erasure is thorough, or the computer may reject the answer because it cannot distinguish between marked answers.

If you have time after proofreading, review the problematic questions, and re-think the answers chosen. However, even after careful thought, hesitate to change an answer.

Do not leave any section of the exam early; use the allotted time wisely.

Intelligent preparation over a sustained period

There is no easy way to conquer an exam as challenging and comprehensive as the MBE, except through practice and an investment of time and effort well before the exam.

By diligently preparing, practicing questions, and intelligently assessing why questions were answered incorrectly, your skills for the exam will improve substantially.

Continue to improve those skills by following the advice given herein until reaching a proficiency level enabling you to pass the bar. This proficiency is accurately measured in multiple-choice format questions.

Some students will have to work harder to achieve the required proficiency.

The tools are in this study guide, and any law school graduate can be successful in passing the bar if they invest the required time and effort to be prepared.

Essay Preparation Strategies and Essay-Writing Suggestions

Memorize the law

Do not make the mistake of waiting too long before memorizing the governing law. Start learning the governing law early to be better prepared and pass the exam.

Memorize essential principles and focus on highly tested governing law.

Focus on the highly tested essay rules

Do not treat all subjects the same when you prepare for the essay portion of the exam.

Some governing law topics are tested more than others. It is crucial to focus on the highly tested topics (e.g., torts, contracts. property, civil procedure).

Know and apply enough governing laws to pass the bar – focus on commonly tested governing laws (e.g., negligence) provided in this book.

Practice writing essay answers each week

Practicing is crucial to a high score on essays. Practice regularly and avoid procrastination for this essential component of bar prep.

Incorporate practicing essay writing into your exam study schedule. To reduce procrastination, schedule time for writing practice essays each week.

For the MPT, practice by drafting full MPTs. Most examinees procrastinate on preparing for the MPT; there is nothing to memorize.

Do not make the *fatal mistake* of not practicing. The MPT portion is worth 20% of the UBE score.

Know the format and *practice that format to* increase your UBE score. This practice will increase your score and the probability of passing the bar.

Add one essay-specific subject each week

Depending on the jurisdiction, state essay exam subjects include the 7 MBE subjects plus subject of Business Associations (Agency, Partnerships, Corporations, and LLCs), Conflict of Laws, Family Law, Trusts and Estates, and Secured Transactions (UCC Article 9).

Combine highly tested subjects (e.g., torts) with less-tested subjects (e.g., secured transactions) and complex topics (e.g., contracts) with easier topics (e.g., business associations).

From preparation, know which subjects you struggle with and require a focused effort to master the essential governing law.

Make it easy for the grader to award points

Your answer to a question will probably be read in less than five minutes by a grader with a checklist to find that you have seen the issues and discussed them intelligently. Writing organized and clear answers makes it easy for the essay grader to award points.

Use headings for each of the major issues.

If the question suggests a structure for the answer because it is divided into parts or because the facts present a series of discrete issues, use the structure of the question, which is probably the structure of the checklist.

Use the IRAC method for the essay questions: state the issue, state the Rule. Apply the rule to the facts and conclude. IRAC seems simple, but following this approach makes it easier for the grader to know that you identified and addressed every issue and applied the law to the facts given.

IRAC results in more points during the exam.

Do not spend time trying to formulate eloquent issue statements. The question often outlines the issues, so an eloquent issue statement is redundant, and issue statements do not earn extra points.

Many examinees spend too much time developing an impressive issue statement and omit other essentials of their analysis (e.g., truncated analysis section).

An issue statement "Torts" or "Is the defendant liable for negligence?" is enough.

Do not waste time arguing both sides. There are no "two sides" for many essays to argue on bar essays because these are not law school essays.

Apply the law to facts and conclude unless asserting each party has good arguments.

Conclusion for each essay question

Points will be lost unless you conclude for each issue identified in the facts or are asked to address it in the call of the question.

Use caution starting the essay with the conclusion unless confident it is correct.

Many sample answers provided by the National Conference of Bar Examiners start with a definite and strong conclusion. Use caution to start with a conclusion unless confident (e.g., NCBE sample responses) your conclusion is correct.

Starting with a conclusion that is not correct draws attention to an incorrect conclusion at the start, which may influence the grader disproportionality. The grader may lose faith in your answer from the onset, and it is advisable to have a neutral heading rather than a firm conclusion that is wrong.

Tips for an easy-to-read essay

Use paragraph breaks between the Issue, Rule, Analysis, and Conclusion. Paragraph break makes it easy for the grader to read and score your essays. Additionally, this approach makes the answer appear longer and more complete.

Emphasize keywords and phrases. Underline key phrases so the grader notices that you addressed the governing law and applied it to the facts given.

After graders score several essays on the same topic, they scan essays for specific phrases that they expect to locate within a complete essay.

Think before you write

Read each question carefully to understand the facts and their necessary implications thoroughly and accurately.

After skimming the question, spend time on the focus line at the end of the question. Review the facts with the call of the question in mental focus.

Write a short outline of the issues raised. Outline in your mind the issues; state to yourself the tentative conclusions; test each conclusion from the standpoints of law and common sense; revise, as necessary.

Decide on a logical, orderly, and convincing arrangement for the response. Until then, you are not ready to write the answer.

Of the time allotted to each essay, spend about two-fifths of the time on issue spotting and organization and about two-fifths of the time on writing the answer.

The ability to think and communicate like a lawyer

The Board knows that you have completed law school, under competent instructors, and have passed law school exams. The bar does not challenge the results of your law school courses.

The exam tests the ability to apply what you have learned to facts that might arise in practice and which, in some instances, involve several fields of law. The value of an answer depends not only on the correctness of the conclusions but on displaying essential legal principles and thinking like a lawyer.

Conclude on each issue presented. If a conclusion is derived from fuzzy facts, construct a well-reasoned argument supporting your conclusion to receive full credit regardless of if you conclude the same as the examiners.

If the correct answer depends on a provision of substantive law, which you are not familiar with, you can obtain a passing answer to the question by reaching a well-reasoned conclusion applying general law principles.

Do not try to limit the question to a particular subject area. Many questions combine traditional subjects, and you must be prepared to answer the question applying principles you learned across various subjects.

Do not restate the facts

The examiners know the facts; there is no time to waste. Do not restate the facts but use them to apply and integrate legal principles in writing the essay.

Do not fight the facts, particularly the focus line of the question.

For example, if the facts state that A executed a valid will, write about valid wills. If the question asks you to argue on behalf of A, do not argue on behalf of B because B has a prevailing argument. However, raise potential arguments which could be made on behalf of B and counter them in arguing on behalf of A.

Do not state abstract or irrelevant propositions of law

It is usually undesirable to begin an answer with a legal proposition. If the proposition is applicable, it will be more appropriate later to indicate the reason for your conclusion. If it is not applicable, do not state a surplus fact or legal principle.

Although it is seldom necessary to state an applicable rule of law in detail, make a sufficient reference to it so that the examiner appreciates your knowledge of the principle and conditions when it applies.

Do not, by speculating on different facts, nor in other ways, work into your answer some point of law with which you happen to be familiar, but which does not apply to the answer. Importantly, the examiners are not interested in knowing how many rules of law you know, but your ability to apply the applicable rules to the facts.

If the question says that A and B in the above hypothetical are unrelated, do not talk about the results which would occur if they were husband and wife.

Use the principles of law applicable to the call of the question and the facts. You must state the principles of applicable law to demonstrate to the examiner that you know the elements of the rule and how they apply to these facts.

For example, if the facts said that A transferred to B (a non-relative) the money necessary for B to purchase Blackacre from C and asks who owns Blackacre, you would say, "Since A furnished the consideration for the purchase of Blackacre and B took the title to the property in their name, B holds title to Blackacre in a resulting trust for A.

Do not detail the black letter law of resulting trusts since you have shown your knowledge by properly applying the facts to the law of resulting trusts.

Do not fight the facts and address a contrary fact not presented. The examiners may take points away if you make that mistake because you are not focused on the issues presented.

Discuss all the issues raised

A grasp of all the issues is essential.

For example, if there are three issues in a question, a discussion of only one issue, no matter how masterly, if coupled with omitting the others, could not result in 100% credit. It would probably result in a score of 33%.

The exam includes many issues in most questions so it can be graded mechanically. This maintains consistency across a group of several graders for each exam question.

The grader has a checklist of issues and awards most points for the examinee that identifies issues and intelligently discusses each.

Failure to see and discuss enough issues intelligently is probably the biggest reason for failure on the essay portion of the exam.

Methods for finding all issues

Use all the facts presented. Failure to discuss facts probably means that you missed important issues.

If you must decide in the early part of the question (e.g., does the court have jurisdiction) and you decide that issue so the remaining facts become irrelevant, make an alternative assumption ("If the court does have jurisdiction") and answer the question in the alternative using facts which would otherwise be irrelevant.

Do not avoid issues because you are not sure of the substantive law. If the examiners stated that X's nephew helped X escape after a crime, discuss the nephew's status as an accessory after the fact. If you do not know whether he is a close enough relative to be exempt under the statute, answer this issue by making alternative assumptions.

Indicators requiring alternative arguments

Ambiguous terms – if there are words in the fact pattern that are neutral or ambiguous such as "put up," the examiners look for possible interpretations of these terms.

Language in quotes – language placed in quotes is almost always ambiguous and must be construed as part of the answer.

Avoid ambiguous, rambling statements and verbosity

Generally, do not use compound sentences. Two separate sentences are preferred.

Complex sentences are particularly useful to apply the facts of the question to the applicable principle of law.

For example, in the previous resulting trust hypothetical, write, "Since B purchased Blackacre and took title in their name with money furnished by A, A holds title to Blackacre in a resulting trust, even if B has not signed a memorandum."

Avoid undue repetition

If the same principle of law and conclusion apply to two parts of an answer, state it once in detail, and refer back for the second part.

For example, if you have discussed A's liability and now must discuss B's liability, say, "B is also guilty of murder for the same reasons as A. (see discussion above)."

Avoid slang and colloquialism

The examiners judge your formal writing style.

If the examiner shows humor with names and events, do not show your sense of humor.

Use the standard abbreviations:

P for Plaintiff

D for Defendant

K for Contract

BFP for *Bona Fide* purchaser

Write legibly and coherently

Printing is usually easier to read than handwriting.

Use all the pages, and do not crowd your answer.

Plan your answer so that you do not have to use inserts and arrows.

Timing strategies

You have some flexibility with time limitations as questions are not of the same difficulty. But be careful about not going over the time limit on the first question because this will require a readjustment of your timing for the entire session. If you miss the deadlines, re-divide your remaining time so that you will have an equal amount of time on each question.

Stay focused

Do not start by reading the entire exam. Answer the questions in order and do not consider more than one question at a time.

After answering, put it out of your mind and not worry about your response. Keep your mind clear to focus on the next question.

Proofread your answers as time permits.

Best wishes with your preparation!

Notes for active learning

Notes for active learning

Constitutional Law

Constitutional Law is divided into governmental powers and individual rights. On the MBE, both categories are tested equally. Constitutional Law essay questions may be combined with another subject, such as Civil Procedure. Issues tested repeatedly are the commerce clause, equal protection, free speech, separation of powers, judicial review, and nation-states relations. Be well versed in these highly tested topics to maximize your score.

The statements herein were compiled by analyzing released Constitutional Law questions and setting forth the principles of law governing the correct answers. Review these principles before preparing answers to practice Constitutional Law questions. Memorize this governing law and understand how it applies to the correct answer.

Per the National Conference of Bar Examiners, the terms "Constitution," "constitutional," and "unconstitutional" refer to the U.S. Constitution unless indicated otherwise.

Constitutional Law – Overview

1. Creates a national government – allocates power among three branches
2. Controls the relationship between federal and state governments (federalism)
3. Limits government power – protecting individual rights
4. Constitutionalism

Issues of constitutional law: Historically, important decisions (e.g., *Marbury v. Madison*, *Dred Scott v. Sanford*, *Brown v. Board of Education*) and current cutting-edge issues.

The issue is usually about *who* gets to decide the merits (executive, legislative, judicial branches – federal or state)

Decisions by a single, multi-justice court: US Supreme Court

Effects of judicial philosophies and personnel changes

Methods of Constitutional decision-making are based on the Constitution's text, original intent, precedent, policy considerations, or current societal needs.

The Constitution addresses the essential characteristics of our system of government:

Separation of Powers

Limited Powers (or Plenary/Exclusive Powers)

Bicameralism

Checks & Balances

Federalism

Protection of Civil Rights/Individual Freedoms

Judicial Review of Legislative & Executive Branches

Notes for active learning

Nature of Judicial Review

Federal and state court systems

The most important constitutional bases of federal court jurisdiction are federal question jurisdiction and jurisdiction based upon diversity of citizenship.

States and agencies of a state are not citizens of a state for diversity jurisdiction.

A claim based upon the U.S. Constitution presents a federal question conferring jurisdiction on the federal courts.

A claim that an agency whose activities constitute state action discriminates by race raises a federal question arising under the Constitution.

If no basis of federal jurisdiction is present, the federal court must dismiss the suit.

A statute creating a right of action under federal law can require state courts to grant jurisdiction to litigants pursuing that action.

Eleventh Amendment

The Eleventh Amendment bars a suit in federal court against a state by a resident of that state or resident of another state for damages against a state.

The Eleventh Amendment does not bar suits permitted by the state in state court.

A private citizen can challenge a state statute's constitutionality in federal court by suing a state officer to enjoin the statute's enforcement because it is unconstitutional.

Under *Ex Parte Young* (1908), such a suit is not barred by the Eleventh Amendment.

Municipalities can be sued in federal court because they do not have Eleventh Amendment protection.

Congress can constitutionally authorize a suit by a citizen against a state without violating the Eleventh Amendment if it acts according to the Fourteenth Amendment.

Supreme Court jurisdiction and review

The Supreme Court may not review a decision by a state court decided on *independent and adequate state grounds*, even if the state court has decided on an issue under federal law, which is not essential to the case's outcome.

If the state court decides on an issue controlled by state law and declares that it is deciding that federal law issue, the Supreme Court may review that decision because the state ground is not independent of federal law.

In addition to suing to vindicate a proprietary state interest, a state may sue another state under the Supreme Court's original jurisdiction on behalf of its citizens on claims affecting citizens. This right is the *parens patriae* doctrine (e.g., Sherman Antitrust Act, Environmental Protection Agency).

A litigant may not appeal directly from a federal district court's decision holding an act of Congress unconstitutional to the Supreme Court.

If a state court acting under applicable state law renders an advisory opinion interpreting federal law or the Constitution, there is no right to appeal the decision to the Supreme Court because there is no case or controversy, as required by the Constitution for federal court jurisdiction.

Congress cannot expand or contract the U. S. Supreme Court's original jurisdiction.

Congressional control over jurisdiction: Article III Courts

Under Article III of the Constitution, Congress controls the lower federal courts' jurisdiction within constitutional limitations and can establish or abolish them.

Once it has created a federal court, Congress cannot interfere with its inherent judicial functions by legislation.

Congress can alter the Supreme Court's appellate jurisdiction according to its authority under Article III but cannot remove appellate jurisdiction from the court to interfere with the Court's constitutional function preserving constitutional order and the separation of powers.

For example, Congress cannot pass an unconstitutional statute that provides the Supreme Court with no jurisdiction to review its constitutionality.

Under Article I powers, Congress can establish courts such as the United States Tax Court.

Judges serving in Article I courts are not guaranteed life tenure and other constitutional protections given to Article III courts' judges.

To be constitutional under the Due Process Clause, a matter decided by an Article I tribunal or an administrative body must have an ultimate appeal to an Article III court.

The Supreme Court, and not Congress, has the ultimate power to determine the Equal Protection Clause's substantive content.

Case or controversy requirement

Under Article III of the Constitution, federal court jurisdiction extends only to *cases and controversies* (i.e., lawsuits based upon existing, not hypothetical facts). The court has the power to enter a binding judgment in a dispute between litigants.

Standing

Federal taxpayer standing is available only in a suit challenging legislation authorizing federal expenditures on the grounds that those expenditures violate specific constitutional limitations on the spending power, such as the Establishment Clause.

Standing cannot be maintained to litigate a case where the plaintiff has a philosophical, ethical, or intellectual interest in the outcome but not an interest that personally affects them (i.e., cognizable harm).

Standing exists in a party whose interests are not directly affected by litigation but have a close relationship to the party injured if the injured party is unlikely to assert their rights successfully.

A person whose interests are affected by the litigation's outcome is likely to have standing.

Mootness

If the passage of time or changes in the facts or law resolve a controversy so that a party who originally had the standing to bring the lawsuit no longer has a stake in the outcome, the case will be dismissed as moot.

If a case by its nature becomes moot before it can be fully litigated, and the issue would consistently evade review because of mootness, the case will not be dismissed.

Ripeness

Cases that raise material issues that have not yet occurred will be dismissed as unripe because no *case or controversy* exists when the suit is filed.

The federal courts lack the power to entertain a suit that is not ripe for adjudication because such a suit does not present a "*case*" or "*controversy*" within the meaning of Article III, Section 2, Clause 1 of the Constitution.

Abstention

If a state court's decision on an issue of state law, which is pending in a federal court, might eliminate the need for the federal court to decide a federal constitutional issue, the federal court has the discretion to abstain from deciding the issue of constitutional law until the state court has decided the issue of state law.

If a state criminal prosecution has begun in a state court, a federal court will abstain from an action in the federal court, asking for an injunction against the state proceeding and asking that the state statute be declared unconstitutional.

Justiciability: political questions

The political question doctrine requires the dismissal of suits when the court determines that the Constitution commits the final decision on the matter raised in the suit by another branch.

For example, individuals' qualifications to be members of the House of Representatives are determined by the House of Representatives.

The conduct of foreign relations is finally vested in the Office of the Presidency.

Burden of proof in constitutional litigation

The burden of proof is on the state to show a compelling state need or meet a similarly phrased burden and to show that no less burdensome method would achieve that objective.

Constitutional litigation on matters assigned *strict scrutiny* level of equal protection include (but not limited to) 1) the denial of highly protected personal substantive due process rights, 2) the deprivation of the right of free speech based upon content, and 3) some cases involving the free exercise of religion.

If it is not clear that discrimination requiring *strict scrutiny* (or the *intermediate standard* of review) exists, the plaintiff has the initial burden of showing discriminatory purposes before the state has the burden of showing a compelling state interest and compliance with strict scrutiny or the intermediate standard of review.

For example, gender discrimination (*intermediate scrutiny*) shifts the burden on the state to show that its classification is designed to achieve an important governmental interest and is closely tailored to achieve those objectives.

For rational basis review, the plaintiff must prove that the government's actions are not "rationally related" to a "legitimate" government interest.

For rational basis, the burden of proof is on the plaintiff to show a lack of a rational basis in constitutional litigation involving economic regulation and other matters such as due process or equal protection under the Fifth or Fourteenth Amendment.

The plaintiff never has the burden of proof in cases involving highly protected rights (i.e., Constitutional fundamental rights) or when a suspect or quasi-suspect group is involved).

The state never has the burden to prove a *rational basis*.

Separation of Powers

Congressional Commerce Power

Congress has almost unlimited power to regulate commerce in the United States, both interstate and local, under its power to regulate interstate commerce. It may regulate purely local commerce if it affects interstate commerce.

For example, Congress can restrict private individuals from discriminating by race on the theory that such discrimination affects interstate commerce.

Congress could not achieve this result under the Fourteenth Amendment because the private individual's activities would not constitute state action.

The current limitation on Congressional commerce power is expressed in *United States v. Lopez* (1995), which held that, where Congress regulates intrastate activities because of their relation to or effect on interstate commerce, the relationship must be substantial.

The Court did not find such a substantial interstate commerce relationship to ban guns around local schoolhouses.

Congressional Taxing and Spending Power

If a taxing statute does not violate a specific limitation on Congress's power, and it has the effect of raising revenue, there is no limitation on Congress's taxing power.

Congress cannot require state governments to enact legislation.

Congress may constitutionally condition the right to receive appropriations upon the states' performance or individuals of actions that Congress could not require them to perform through regulatory action.

The only limitations on the congressional spending power are the specific constitutional limitations on Congress's power (e.g., prohibiting the establishment of religion).

To *tax and spend for the general welfare* is given to Congress as an enumerated power of the Constitution (Article I, Section 8).

Congress cannot regulate directly through the General Welfare Clause; it can influence behavior through a taxing statute, constitutional if to raise revenue.

Congressional Property Power

Article IV vests in Congress the power to control the United States' property.

Rather than the Commerce Clause, property power is the most appropriate source of congressional power to oversee property owned by the federal government.

The executive branch does not have inherent rule-making authority over public lands.

Article I, Section 8, Clause 17 gives Congress the power to regulate such lands.

Congressional power over territories

In territories, Congress can regulate activities reserved for state legislatures of states.

Judges authorized to perform the function like state court judges in U.S. territories are authorized under Article I of the Constitution and are thus not entitled to the lifetime tenure enjoyed by Article III judges.

Congressional investigative powers

Congress has the power to investigate to obtain information for potential legislation.

Congress can subpoena witnesses and documents.

Congress may question members of the executive branch about the performance of their duties to gather the information that might help propose legislation.

Privilege, either executive privilege or against self-incrimination, would be the only practical reasons for refusal to answer.

An individual can defend against a contempt of Congress charge for failing to answer a question from a congressional committee by successfully claiming the privilege against self-incrimination or showing that the question was beyond the scope of the powers delegated by Congress to the committee seeking the information.

Speech and Debate Clause

A member of Congress has absolute immunity for any speech on the floor of either house of Congress, which relates to a legislative function.

An aide to a member of Congress acting in support of such a member would have the same immunity as a Congress member if they were performing a legislative function.

States' Police Power

There is no grant of police power to Congress; police powers (i.e., regulations for health, safety, welfare, aesthetics, and morals) are a source of state power.

Congressional powers enforcing the 13th, 14th and 15th Amendments

Under the Thirteenth Amendment, Congress has the power to regulate individual conduct and state activity but only to eradicate slavery or the effects of slavery.

According to the authority to eradicate the effects of slavery, it can affect individual conduct detrimental to the African Americans.

Congressional power under the Fourteenth Amendment is limited to "state action" as defined hereafter, which abrogates the rights guaranteed by that Amendment.

Congress has the power under the Fifteenth Amendment to directly regulate voting procedures in the states to ensure that persons have the right to vote and that their votes are appropriately counted.

Courts can invalidate legislative apportionment statutes if their effect deprives minorities of having their votes effectively counted.

Powers of the President

The President has the discretion to refuse to spend funds that Congress has authorized unless the authorizing legislation directs the President to spend the funds.

The President's power to pardon federal crimes, whether or not there has been a conviction, is plenary and cannot be limited by Congress.

The President and aides have the absolute executive privilege to refuse to answer questions about defense and foreign policy matters.

Disclosure of confidential communications between the President and advisors concerning other areas in which the President operates are presumptively privileged.

That presumption of privilege can be overcome only if a specific communication is subpoenaed and a substantial governmental interest outweighs the President's interest in nondisclosure.

The President has the power to enter into executive agreements according to the power to conduct foreign policy.

State actions or legislation inconsistent with the executive agreement are unconstitutional because of the Supremacy Clause.

The Constitution reserves acts of foreign relations to the President. Ordinarily, the President does not have authority to direct persons outside the executive branch unless Congress authorizes it.

As the chief executive officer, the President has the authority to direct federal executive agencies' actions, so long as the directives are not inconsistent with an Act of Congress.

Unless legislation explicitly limits the President's authority, the executive power conferred on the Office of the Presidency by the Constitution gives the officeholder latitude to initiate action relative to domestic affairs.

Inter-branch checks on power

By enacting a law by the procedure for enactment set forth in the Constitution, passage by a majority vote of each house of Congress and either a signature by the President or passage over a presidential veto, legislation has the right to delegate, with appropriate standards, the rule-making power to administrative agencies.

Once delegated, the only way that Congress can nullify a rule made by that administrative agency according to the grant of authority is to pass a new law nullifying the rule.

It cannot reserve a legislative veto over an administrative rule by vesting in itself the power to negate that rule by the vote of the entire Congress or by a congressional committee.

Only the President has the right to appoint officers of the United States. An attempted appointment by Congress renders an Act establishing the office unconstitutional.

The final authority to decide an issue can be vested in a federal government branch other than the Supreme Court (e.g., Congress has the authority to determine its members' qualifications).

While the Supreme Court has the ultimate authority to determine which branch has the right to make a final decision on a matter, it will not decide an issue reserved for another branch of the government. It designates such an issue as a political question.

The Advice and Consent Clause gives the Senate the right to confirm judicial appointments and other presidential appointments.

Except for recess appointments, advice and consent are conditions precedent to such appointees holding federal office. However, the President can remove federal executives without congressional authorization.

According to their obligation to execute the United States laws, the President must execute provisions of law if Congress makes obligation mandatory instead of discretionary.

Congress can delegate to the President and the executive branch of government authority to determine how a law should be implemented.

If there are general guidelines, such delegation is constitutional. Congress may delegate rule-making authority to federal agencies through statutes that provide an intelligible principle governing the exercise of authority.

The Relation of the Nation and States

Intergovernmental immunities

States may not impose taxes on property owned by the United States.

States and their subdivisions can impose nondiscriminatory taxes on owners of buildings leased to the federal government and contractors doing business with the federal government.

Congress, by specific legislation, can exempt such individuals from taxation.

The federal government has the right to tax and regulate the state government's instrumentalities and employees.

Under the Supremacy Clause of the Constitution, a federal agency's lawful actions may not be regulated by a state or municipality in a manner that impedes its functions without the consent of Congress.

The federal government does not have the power to require state government officers to enforce federal laws.

In *New York v. United States* (1992), the Court held that the federal government could not commandeer state governments' mechanisms to accomplish federal policies.

The federal government cannot tax essential state governmental functions and cannot single out the states for specialized taxes.

Authority reserved to the states

Except rarely, the Tenth Amendment as the basis to justify state action is the wrong answer to constitutional law multiple-choice questions.

The Commerce Clause (Article I, Section 8, Clause 3 of the Constitution) gives Congress the power to regulate commerce among the states and, by negative implication, restricts the states' regulatory power concerning interstate commerce.

Any state law that substantially affects interstate commerce must not be protectionist or impose an undue burden on interstate commerce.

A protectionist law benefits in-state interests at the expense of out-of-state interests. A state law that discriminates against interstate commerce is protectionist unless it serves a legitimate local interest that cannot be served by non-discriminatory legislation.

State activity authorized by a provision in a state constitution rather than an act of the state legislature is irrelevant in determining its constitutionality.

A state's regulation or taxation of interstate commerce is unconstitutional because of the Commerce Clause's negative implications if that regulation discriminates in favor of local commerce or against interstate commerce.

For example, a state statute requiring state natural resources to be sold only to in-state buyers or permitting disposal of refuse in-state landfills only for trash generated in-state is unconstitutional.

A state's interstate commerce regulation is unconstitutional if the Commerce Clause's negative implications deem that regulation, even if nondiscriminatory, unduly burdens interstate commerce.

In determining the validity of such a regulation, the court balances the state's police power to provide for its citizens' safety against the extent of the harm caused by the regulations to interstate commerce.

An important consideration in weighing that balance is whether the state used the least restrictive means to achieve a legitimate state objective.

As a purchaser or seller of goods and services (as distinguished from the state as a regulator), the state is not subject to the negative implications of the Commerce Clause; it may discriminate in favor of in-state entities.

Congress is the holder and ultimate arbiter of a state's power to discriminate in favor of local commerce.

Congress can expressly authorize such discrimination, even if that discrimination has been held unconstitutional by the courts because of the Commerce Clause's negative implications.

Federal power to override state authority

The Supremacy Clause (Article VI, Section 1, Clause 2) invalidates state action contrary to federal law.

The Supreme Court holds state statutes, actions, or decisions unconstitutional under the Supremacy Clause if they conflict with the Constitution, laws, or treaties of the United States or acts done in furtherance of them.

For example, the Supremacy Clause's application invalidates a state or municipal law in conflict with a federal regulation applicable to federal office buildings.

A state may not regulate interstate commerce if the regulation is contrary to specific federal policy or Congress has expressly or impliedly forbidden state regulation in a particular field.

The Supremacy Clause is a vehicle for invalidating state actions but is not a source of congressional power.

As a general principle, when there is a federal action regulated by the state, the federal government wins.

State legislation or decisions contrary to a federal policy expressed in an executive agreement between the President and a foreign country are invalid.

Foreign policy is the exclusive province of the federal government. States may not act in foreign policy.

Preemption

Congress occupies the entire field by enacting a comprehensive regulatory scheme in an area.

When it has occupied the field, any state regulation (even if complementary to the federal legislation) will be invalid unless Congress intended to allow state regulation.

Congress can permit state activity in areas in which it has legislated as long as the state regulation is not contrary to federal policies.

In many instances, such as civil rights, Congress has permitted states to enact stricter regulations than the Congressional legislation.

Privileges and immunities

The Privileges and Immunities Clause of the Fourteenth Amendment has been narrowly construed to apply only to citizenship privileges.

The Privileges and Immunities Clause is usually the wrong answer to a multistate question.

The Privileges and Immunities Clause of Article IV operates like the Commerce Clause's negative implications.

It renders unconstitutional a state statute or action which discriminates on a matter of fundamental interest in favor of the state's citizens and against citizens of other states.

Precedent under the negative implications of the Commerce Clause where a state governmental entity is permitted to discriminate in favor of local commerce acts as a market participant rather than a regulator. The Privileges and Immunities Clause of Article IV applies to governmental entities when acting as market participants.

The Privileges and Immunities Clause of Article IV applies to discrimination against out-of-state residents and discrimination by a subdivision of the state against non-residents of that subdivision.

When there is an abridgment of a fundamental right of a non-resident, the Privileges and Immunities Clause does not automatically hold the governmental action unconstitutional.

If there is a tight fit between the discrimination against out-of-town residents and the evil which the limitation on non-residents is designed to remedy, the action is constitutional.

Higher fishing and hunting license fees for out-of-staters do not violate the Privileges and Immunities Clause of Article IV.

Full Faith and Credit Clause

The Full Faith and Credit Clause (Article IV, Section 1) prohibits state courts from re-litigating cases in which another state's courts have rendered final judgment.

The Full Faith and Credit Clause requires a state to enforce a sister state's final judgments in its courts if the sister state had the jurisdiction to render that judgment.

Individual Rights

State action

The Due Process Clause of the Fifth Amendment applies only to the Federal Government.

The Fourteenth Amendment guarantees individual liberties applicable to state action and does not apply to private individuals' actions unless they perform a governmental function, or the activity is so entwined with the state that it is deemed state action.

The fact that a state taxes or regulates a private activity does not in itself cause the activity itself to become "state action."

The act of permitting private organizations to use public facilities on a non-discriminatory basis without additional factors does not constitute state action, causing the organization's activity to be subject to Fourteenth Amendment scrutiny.

State aid to a segregated facility that benefits that facility to an extent greater than general governmental services constitutes forbidden state action.

The governmental activities of a political subdivision of a state or state agency constitute state action.

If a state is an economic partner in a facility, its activities constitute state action.

A one-time state subsidy to a private project does not provide a sufficient nexus to constitute state action.

The activity of an entity that performs a governmental function, such as performing municipal services, can constitute state action.

Activities in a privately owned shopping center do not constitute state action.

Fourteenth Amendment applies to state action

The Fourteenth Amendment applied many protections against the federal government contained in the Bill of Rights (e.g., free speech, searches) to the states.

From Supreme Court holdings, the Fourteenth Amendment incorporates most of the specific provisions of the first eight Amendments to the Constitution.

The basis on which specific Amendments are incorporated is "whether they are essential to an ordered system of liberties."

Substantive due process

The rational basis standard of review applies to economic regulations when such regulations violate substantive due process.

While the substantive Due Process Clause will not invalidate economic regulation, it can be used to invalidate the regulation of fundamental privacy interests unless the state shows a compelling state need.

Examples of regulations held invalid are banning contraceptives, zoning regulations limiting the right of an extended family to live together, and abortion rights.

Abortion

The Substantive Due Process Clause protects fundamental personal rights. *Griswold v. Connecticut* (1965) held that the right to access and use contraceptives is a fundamental right.

Roe v. Wade (1973) held that a woman has a constitutionally protected right to an abortion until the fetus becomes viable.

The state cannot prohibit a woman's right to an abortion before the fetus becomes viable.

A state can prohibit abortions at state facilities if there are reasonable alternatives for abortion at private facilities, and the state does not interfere with the alternative facilities.

In *Planned Parenthood v. Casey* (1992), the Supreme Court held that parental notification requirements violate a minor's rights unless there is a satisfactory judicial bypass procedure.

Such a procedure must allow a court to approve an abortion for a minor without parental notification if the court finds:

1) the minor is sufficiently mature and informed to make an independent decision, or

2) the abortion would be in the minor's best interest.

Takings

Requiring the dedication of interest in the property as a condition of a building permit when there is no proportionality between the interest requested and the permit's adverse impact constitutes a taking.

The government's acquisition of property is sufficient but unnecessary to establish a taking (i.e., eminent domain) under the Fifth Amendment, as applied to States by the 14th Amendment.

A government regulation that eliminates the investment-backed expectation and economic value of an individual's property is a taking for which the government must pay just compensation.

A government ordinance requiring private property owners to dedicate a portion of their building for permanent physical occupation (e.g., cable wires) is a taking.

Imposition of the death penalty

A court can only order the death penalty when the defendant has committed an act of murder.

When there is a felony murder where several conspirators participated in the felony, the death penalty can only be administered to the individual who caused the death.

A statute that mandates the death penalty for a specific crime is unconstitutional because a jury must have the opportunity to impose the death penalty only after considering mitigating factors.

The death penalty can only be imposed by a jury.

A judge can not impose it after the jury has convicted the defendant of the substantive crime.

Procedural due process – applicability

The Due Process Clause is contained in the Fourteenth Amendment; the requirements of procedural due process do not apply to the actions of private individuals unless those individuals are engaged in "state action."

Procedural due process applies only when a state or an entity whose activities constitute state action deprives an individual of life, liberty, or property without due process of law.

The Due Process Clause of the Fourteenth Amendment generally prohibits states from taking property from an individual without; 1) a hearing and 2) an opportunity to be heard.

In the context of a government job, where state law provides that state employees can be fired only for a good cause, a person has a legitimate claim of entitlement to, and thus a property interest in, their government job.

When an individual is dismissed from government employment, the right to a hearing depends upon whether the individual has been deprived of a property right.

In the field of education, tenure, or a contract that is either continuing or which the individual has an express or implied right to renew is the type of property interest that cannot be taken away without notice and a hearing.

If the government action is dismissal from an individual's employment possessing property rights, the hearing must be held before the employee is terminated.

Unlike the rule when there is suspension from protected government employment, procedural due process is satisfied in the license revocation when the licensee is afforded an appropriate hearing within a reasonable time after the suspension has occurred.

Due process clause

The minimum government action necessary to satisfy due process whenever procedural due process is required is 1) notice of the action taken and 2) an opportunity for the person affected by the action to be heard by the governmental entity taking action.

Greater governmental procedural steps are necessary to satisfy due process if the interests infringed are substantial, or there is a substantial likelihood that the governmental actions will be erroneous.

A court assesses the government's burden in providing an additional process in determining if that additional process is required.

The initial burden in a constitutional challenge to lack of procedural due process in discharge cases is upon the employee to show a property right in their employment.

Once the employee shows a constitutionally-protected property interest, the government agency would have to demonstrate that it did not violate procedural due process by how the employee was discharged.

If government employment was terminated after an employee exercised their free speech rights, the government must demonstrate that the employee was fired for reasons other than the exercise of free speech even if the employee does not have a property right in their employment.

Criminal statutes so vague and imprecise that they do not give a fair warning of the criminal conduct are unconstitutional under the due process clause.

The judicial construction of a vague statute that defines the criminal action under that statute more precisely renders that statute constitutional concerning persons charged after the judicial decision, but not for any person charged before the judicial decision was published.

Equal Protection Classifications

Sources of civil rights

- Due Process Clause of the 14th Amendment
- Equal Protection Clause of the 14th Amendment
- Congressional Legislation – the Interstate Commerce Clause

Amendment XIV (1868)

"No State shall... deny any person within its jurisdiction the equal protection of the law."

The Equal Protection Clause of the XIV Amendment prohibits the states from denying similarly situated persons the equal protection of the law.

It applies only to public/state action and not to private conduct.

The Equal Protection Clause of the XIV Amendment applies only to state (as opposed to Federal) action.

The 5th Amendment to the Constitution, which applies to Federal action, has been interpreted to include the right to equal protection.

The following test helps determine if the equal protection clause may be successfully invoked to challenge the constitutionality of a statute, rule, or regulation.

When looking at a statute, rule, or regulation, ask the following questions to decide whether the Equal Protection clause is triggered.

Equal protection analysis

Is a governmental classification treating similarly situated persons differently?

Is the classification discriminatory *or* benign on its face? If yes, what is the nature of the classification; is it a *suspect classification* or a *protected class*?

Nature of classification

1) Classification based on race, national origin, or ethnicity is considered suspect.

For a protected class, use *strict scrutiny.*

Is the statute narrowly tailored to further a compelling government interest?

Burden: *government holds the burden.*

2) Classifications based on gender are considered quasi-suspect.

For a protected class, use *intermediate scrutiny*.

Is the statute substantially related to an important government interest?

Burden: *government holds the burden.*

3) Classifications based on sexual orientation, cognition, age, or poverty are not considered suspect.

For a *not* protected class, use *rational basis test* (i.e., minimum scrutiny):

Is the statute rationally related to the legitimate public interest?

Burden: *plaintiff challenging the law holds the burden.*

When a governmental classification implicates a fundamental right or interest guaranteed by the Equal Protection Clause, apply strict scrutiny (regardless of protected or suspect classification).

Fundamental rights have been held to include:

1. voting,
2. appeals to criminal and quasi-criminal proceedings, and
3. travel.

The Equal Protection Clause fundamental interest pedigree of cases mandates "equal access" to the right or interest.

Levels of scrutiny

	Standard of review	Purpose of statute	Satisfies *least restrictive* analysis	Burden of proof	Likely prevailing party
Rational basis test	*Rationally* related	*Legitimate* purpose	No	Plaintiff	Government
Intermediate scrutiny	*Substantially* related	*Important* purpose	Unlikely	Government	Often plaintiff
Strict scrutiny	*Necessary*	*Compelling* purpose	Yes	Government	Plaintiff

The Equal Protection Clause

Applicability

There is no constitutional provision guaranteeing citizens equal protection of the laws against action by the federal government; the Equal Protection Clause's substance is applied to the federal government through the Due Process Clause of the Fifth Amendment.

Fundamental rights

If the state classification involves a fundamental right, the highest tier of equal protection, *strict scrutiny*, applies.

The right to travel

The right to travel is a fundamental right subject to strict scrutiny in Equal Protection Analysis.

Discrimination by the state for those newly arrived in the state because they have exercised their fundamental right to travel must be justified by a compelling state need.

To satisfy the legitimate need for voters to be *bona fide* residents, states may impose limited residency requirements on the right to vote.

A two-month residency requirement has been upheld, while a one-year residency requirement has been held unconstitutional.

The right to vote and have that vote counted

The right to vote is a fundamental right and subject to strict scrutiny in equal protection analysis.

The state may deny that right only if it can show a compelling state need and that the method chosen is the least restrictive means of achieving that need.

The right to vote includes the right to a vote count on an equal basis with other votes.

To accomplish this goal, legislative districts for congressional, state legislative, and municipal bodies must contain approximately equal numbers of voters.

This requirement is popularly known as the one-person-one-vote rule.

The election of members of a district whose primary function is to manage land or water resources can constitutionally be limited to property owners, an exception to the one-person-one-vote requirement.

Ballot access

While the right to be a candidate is at the highest tier of equal protection, to protect against frivolous candidacies, the state may impose reasonable requirements for an individual to appear on the ballot.

These include collecting filing fees, residency requirements, and gathering petition signatures to achieve ballot access, which may be less stringent for nominees of parties who have demonstrated substantial support in previous elections.

Suspect classifications

The state's classifications as suspect invoke the highest level of equal protection review.

The state must show that the classification is necessary to satisfy a compelling state need.

The initial burden in a constitutional challenge for violating rights under the Equal Protection Clause is upon the plaintiff to show a purposeful classification warranting increased scrutiny.

Once the plaintiff shows purposeful discrimination, the burden shifts to the government to satisfy the higher tier of equal protection standards.

Classification by race

No governmental entity can classify by race or nationality except for a compelling state need.

The Equal Protection Clause applies to a regular pattern of discrimination in the enforcement of a statute and discrimination on the face of the statute.

A regulation or decision that classifies based on race to remedy specific past racial discrimination satisfies a compelling state need and is constitutional.

A system of racial quotas by itself does not satisfy the compelling state need standard.

A governmental classification based upon a racially neutral principle such as residence, which indirectly discriminates by race, is only unconstitutional if the classification is made to discriminate by race.

In drawing legislative districts, a state may not deliberately use race as a criterion to dilute the voting power of racial minorities.

The drawing of compact districts that follow existing municipal boundaries rebuts the inference that race was misused.

Classification by alienage

Alienage is not a suspect classification for the federal government.

The federal government may constitutionally discriminate based on alienage in the furtherance of foreign policy.

A state can discriminate against non-citizens in elective governmental positions and non-elective governmental jobs that formulate or execute public policy.

Otherwise, states cannot discriminate against non-citizens.

Classification by gender

Gender-based classification is valid only if it serves an important governmental purpose and is substantially related to achieving that purpose.

Classification by legitimacy

The state cannot deny workers' compensation, wrongful death, or intestacy benefits based upon illegitimacy where the parent-child relationship was adjudicated or acknowledged.

The state can classify by legitimacy, where proof of the parent-child relationship is tenuous.

The rational basis standard

In all cases, except where fundamental rights or suspect classifications are involved, such as economic regulation, the court applies the rational basis standard.

In rational basis cases, the plaintiff must show no rational basis for the classification in the legislation.

The right to be free from poverty is not a fundamental right, so classifications by states discriminating against poor people are ordinarily judged by the rational basis standard.

The right to work is not a fundamental right, so classifications that deprive individuals of employment (e.g., age classifications) are judged by the rational basis standard.

Level of scrutiny – litigation

If constitutional litigation involves the strict scrutiny tier of equal protection, the denial of substantive due process rights which are highly protected, or the deprivation of the right of free speech or freedom of religion, the state must show a compelling state need (strict scrutiny) and that no less burdensome method would achieve that objective.

If constitutional litigation involves sexual discrimination, the state must show that the classification has an important governmental objective and is substantially related (intermediate level scrutiny) to achieving those objectives.

If constitutional litigation involves matters other than those described above, the plaintiff must prove that the legislation lacked a rational basis.

The state (defendant) never has the burden of proof for rational basis analysis.

The plaintiff never has the burden of proof when highly-protected rights (or suspect class) are involved.

Obligations of contract

The Obligations of Contracts Clause is a limitation on states but not the federal government.

State laws or activities which render unenforceable a valid executory contract are invalid unless 1) there is a valid police power for the legislation or 2) it only alters the remedies for breach of contract and other feasible remedies are available.

The provision applies to contracts between private individuals and contracts in which the state is a party.

The Contracts Clause (Article I, Section 10, Clause 1 of the Constitution) does not forbid state laws affecting prospective contractual relations between private parties so long as they are reasonably related to a legitimate state interest.

Courts typically defer to state regulations of prospective private contracts as reasonable.

Bills of attainder

A bill of attainder, a legislative punishment for specific actions, is unconstitutional.

This clause applies to the state and the federal government.

Legislation, which withholds appropriations for a specific job if a named individual holds that job is a bill of attainder.

Ex post facto laws

An *ex post facto* law is a legislative enactment that punishes acts as criminal, which occurred before the law became operative.

Such a law is unconstitutional and cannot supply the basis for a conviction based upon that conduct.

First Amendment Rights

Freedom of religion

When an individual defends against a criminal charge on the basis that the statute unconstitutionally restricts their freedom of religion (e.g., claim to resist the draft because of conscientious objection), the courts have a right to examine the sincerity of their religious belief, but not the belief itself.

Because of the Free Exercise Clause, courts do not have the right to determine the truth or falsity of religious beliefs in litigation, including litigations dealing with the title to church property, even if that determination is necessary to decide the case.

The government may impose non-discriminatory time, place, and manner restrictions on religious activity when they are designed to serve vital public interests.

A compelling state interest need not justify a statute or rule by the state, which has an incidental effect of burdening a particular religious practice but is religiously neutral and generally applicable.

Establishment of religion

Displays on state property that are solely religious violate the Establishment Clause of the First Amendment.

Officially sponsored prayers as part of public high school commencement ceremonies violate the Establishment Clause.

From *Lemon v. Kurtzman* (1971), state activity in aid to religions is constitutional if it satisfies each part of the following three-part test.

1) such aid must reflect a secular purpose,

2) have a primary effect which neither advances nor inhibits religion, and

3) there must be no excessive entanglement between church and state.

Even though state activity aid does not discriminate between religions, it violates the Establishment Clause if it violates any part of the three-part *Lemon* test.

State statutes requiring that the Biblical account of Creation be taught in public schools violate the Establishment Clause.

State statutes or activities that discriminate between established and non-established religions violate the Establishment Clause.

Rights of the press to trials

Absent a compelling state need, the press, as a representative of the public, has the right to attend trials even if the prosecution and defense want the trial to be closed.

Regulation of speech content

The First and Fourteenth Amendments limit states and the federal government's right to regulate protected speech content unless the government can show a compelling state need.

All speech is protected speech for content regulation purposes except fighting words, defamatory speech, and obscene speech.

Protected speech can include action, which substitutes for words.

Even if action is intended as symbolic speech, it can be regulated to protect a legitimate government interest divorced from the symbolic speech's content.

For example, the federal government can ban the burning of draft cards on public safety grounds.

The state can proscribe the content of protected speech, which is directed toward inciting immediate lawless action and is likely to incite that action.

A threat communicated with the intent to intimidate the recipient is not constitutionally protected speech.

Commercial speech does not enjoy the same degree of constitutional protection as non-commercial speech.

It is subject to reasonable governmental regulation to prevent it from being misleading to protect consumers and other legitimate government interests.

The outright prohibition of commercial speech is unconstitutional. Commercial speech regulation must be narrowly tailored to achieve a substantial governmental interest.

There must be a reasonable fit between the interests that the governmental entity desires to protect in commercial speech regulation and the means chosen to advance it.

The state is unconstitutionally regulating the content of speech if it requires an individual to display a message prescribed by the state.

The state has an affirmative obligation to protect a speaker before an audience. However, the speaker can be required to stop speaking if there is a genuine likelihood of immediate violence, which the state cannot prevent.

Meeting rooms at public institutions made generally available for student use are a limited public forum.

Students have a First Amendment right to use such a limited public forum for expressive activity consistent with the purpose they are made available.

A denial of using a limited public forum based on the content of the expression proposed for that forum must be tested by strict scrutiny, which requires the institution to prove that its denial was necessary to serve a compelling governmental interest.

Obscene speech

Speech is obscene and subject to prohibition if it:

1) appeals to the prurient interest of an average person applying contemporary community standards,
2) depicts or describes sexual activity in a patently offensive way, and
3) taken as a whole, lacks serious literary, artistic, political, or scientific value.

Child pornography is unprotected speech.

Even if the communication is not pornographic, portraying nudity or sexual activity can be regulated based on its content concerning the time, place, and manner of its exhibition.

For example, a zoning ordinance can limit the areas in which sex-oriented businesses are allowed to operate, provided alternative sites are available.

Regulation of time, place and manner of speech

If the regulation is not based upon the content of the speech, the state can regulate the time, place, and manner in which free speech rights are exercised in public forums such as streets and parks.

The regulations limiting speech must be narrowly drawn and limit public officials' discretion in administering the regulation.

Speech rights cannot be banned in a public forum.

Free speech rights in semi-public forums such as schools, courthouses, and libraries can be limited to prevent interference with governmental functions conducted at those forums.

In government-owned property closed to the public, such as jails, military bases, and private offices, the state may prohibit the exercise of free speech rights completely.

Unless the operation of private property is the equivalent to state action, such as the operation of a company town, but not a shopping center, the owner of private property can regulate the exercise of free speech on that property even according to content and can prohibit the exercise of free speech on that property.

Procedural problems

If a court issued an injunction banning the exercise of free speech rights, the constitutional issues raised by the injunction cannot be litigated in a contempt prosecution for violating the injunction.

An overly broad statute (e.g., prohibits protected speech and properly regulated speech) or vague (e.g., a person of ordinary intelligence cannot distinguish permitted from prohibited activities) is unconstitutional on its face. The statute can be successfully challenged even by those regulated if the statute was clear and narrowly drawn.

An individual is entitled to 1) notice and 2) a right to be heard at a hearing before an injunction is granted, limiting the time, place, and manner of expression unless there is a genuine emergency justifying an *ex-parte* application.

Freedom of association

A public employee cannot be fired for exercising their right of free speech for public concern matters or merely joining an organization deemed subversive.

If employment is terminated after exercising the rights of free speech or association, the public employer has the burden of demonstrating that the exercise of their free speech rights or joining an organization was not the reason for termination.

A public employee can be fired for speech indicating they are not performing their job.

The state can condition employment on an employee taking a loyalty oath, which requires the employee to agree to adhere to constitutional processes.

Constitutional Law – Quick Facts

1. Action having the purpose and effect of altering the legal duties, rights, and relations of persons, **including executive branch officials**, *must* be subjected to a **presidential veto.**

2. The Constitution prohibits the impairment of **contractual obligations** by a state *except* in certain *narrow circumstances*; a self-interest choice to reduce the State's contractual burdens generally does *not* constitute such an exception.

3. The 11th Amendment does *not* bar suits against state officials **unless retroactive relief** is sought.

4. Congress's **general welfare power** relates to **Congress's spending power** (i.e., right to expend federal tax revenues).

5. Congress's power to regulate **interstate commerce** is plenary. Congress has the right to completely ban the transportation of "harmful" substances in commerce channels.

6. Statutes violate the **Privileges and Immunities of Citizens** of Art. IV—prohibits discrimination against nonresidents concerning essential activities—*unless* 1) the discrimination is closely related to a substantial state purpose, *and* 2) less restrictive means are *not* available.

7. Congress's power to **regulate commerce** has been construed *broadly* so that it *may* regulate ***any activity, local or interstate***, that either or in combination with other activities has a substantial economic effect on interstate commerce.

8. The **police power** – the power to adopt regulations for citizens' health, safety, morals, aesthetics, and general welfare – belongs to the states.

   A police power conflicting with federal law is **invalid** under the **Supremacy Clause**.

9. For practical purposes, the power to **regulate foreign commerce** lies exclusively with Congress; therefore, a state adopting legislation requiring private vendors to favor the U.S. over foreign products may be acting outside the scope of its powers.

10. The **Property Clause** (Art. IV § 3) gives Congress the power to make needful rules and regulations respecting the territory or other property belonging to the U.S., which permits Congress to acquire and dispose of *all* kinds of property and to protect its property with relevant laws.

11. The states have *no* power to regulate the federal government's activities *unless* Congress consents; thus, the federal government's instrumentalities and agents are **immune from state regulations** that interfere with their federal functions.

12. The **media** may *not* be punished for publishing a fact once it is lawfully obtained from the public records or otherwise released.

13. Supreme Court has held, at least for criminal cases, that **trials and pretrial proceedings** can be closed *only* if necessary to preserve an overriding interest, and the closure order is *narrowly tailored* to serve the overriding interest.

14. Congress may *not* appoint members of a body with **administrative or enforcement powers**.

15. Congress *may* vest the appointment power of **inferior officers** in the federal courts.

16. Congress has the power to levy taxes under Art. II § 2 and a tax measure will usually be upheld *if* it bears some **reasonable relationship** to revenue production *or* if Congress has the power to regulate the taxed activity.

17. **Supremacy Clause** – whenever a valid federal law conflicts with state law, the state law is inapplicable, and the federal law controls.

18. Supreme Court uses a **balancing test** in determining whether a regulation of the electoral process is valid. If the **restriction** on 1st Amendment activities is severe, the regulation will be upheld *only* if it is **narrowly tailored** to achieve a **compelling state interest.**

    For example, requiring a political candidate to obtain a percentage of voter signatures to run probably qualifies as a severe 1st Amendment restriction.

19. The **13th Amendment's** prohibition against **servitude** and **involuntary servitude** is *not* limited to proscribing state action, allowing Congress to adopt legislation regulating private parties.

Resolving constitutional questions

Legislative branch	Executive branch	Judicial branch	State or local government	Private (non-governmental)
1) Does Congress have the legislative authority to act? 2) Has Congress violated the limit on its constitutional powers?	1) Has the President or executive branch exceeded the scope of executive powers? 2) Has the President or executive branch violated the limit on its constitutional powers?	Does the federal court have subject matter or personal jurisdiction to hear and adjudicate the issue?	Has the state or local government violated the limit on its mandated powers?	1) Is there state or governmental action? *If so* 2) Does the state or governmental action violate the Constitution?

Relationship matrix

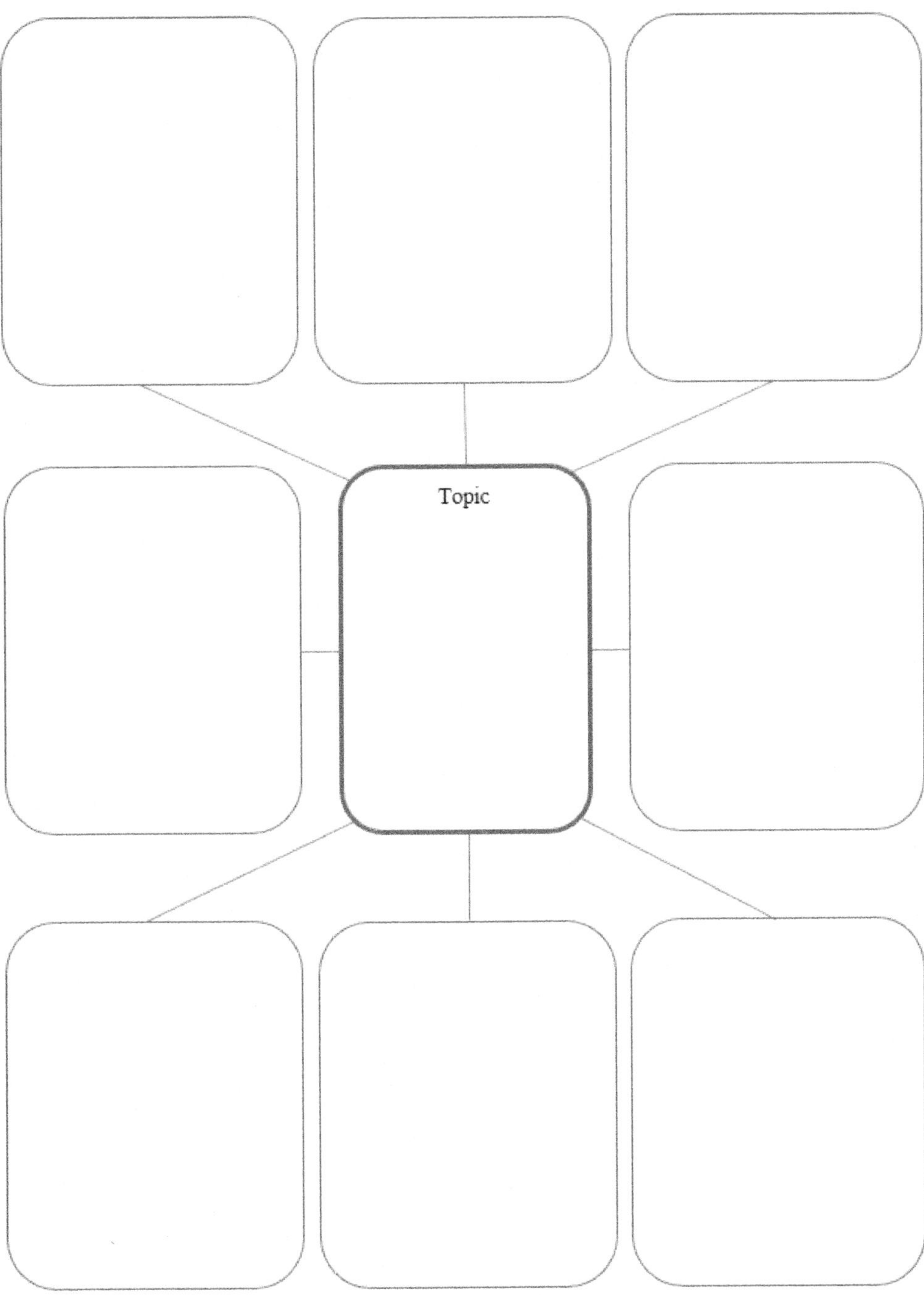

Notes for active learning

Contracts

Contracts is a stand-alone topic testing common law principles and the sales of goods (UCC Article 2). To maximize your score, focus on the frequently tested topics of contract formation, performance, breach, discharge of obligations, contract enforceability, third-party rights, parol evidence, interpretation, damages, and contract remedies.

The statements herein were compiled by analyzing released Contracts questions and setting forth the principles of law governing the correct answers. Review these principles before preparing answers to practice Contracts questions. Memorize this governing law and understand how it applies to the correct answer.

Per the National Conference of Bar Examiners (NCBE), assume the Official Text of Articles 1 and 2 of the Uniform Commercial Code (UCC) has been adopted.

Contract Law – Overview

Definition of and parties to a contract

A *contract* is an agreement that is enforceable by a court of law or equity.

Second Restatement on Contracts: a contract is a promise or a set of promises for the breach of which the law gives a remedy or the performance of which the law recognizes a duty.

Parties to a contract:

Offeror – the party who makes an offer.

Offeree – the party to whom the offer is made.

Requirements of a contract

To be an enforceable contract, the following four basic requirements must be met:

- Agreement – there must be an agreement between the parties.
- Consideration – a *bargained-for* consideration must support the promise.
- Contractual capacity – the parties must have the capacity to contract.
- Lawful object – the object of the contract must be lawful.

Agreement is the manifestation by persons of the contract's substance.

Acceptance is the *manifestation of assent* by the offeree to the terms of the offer.

Acceptance of the offer creates a contract.

Consideration is the thing of value given in exchange for a promise.

Gift or gratuitous promises are unenforceable because they lack consideration.

An *illusory promise* is not enforceable due to a lack of consideration. For example, a promise *to paint a house if time permits.*

Contractual capacity – parties must have mental capacity to be bound by a contract.

Lawful object. The object of the contract must be lawful. A contract to perform an illegal act is void.

Contracts contrary to public policy are illegal (e.g., murder, theft).

Requirements of the offer

The offeror must objectively intend to be bound by the offer.

The terms of the offer must be definite or reasonably certain.

The offer must be communicated to the offeree.

Termination of the offer

A counteroffer simultaneously terminates the offer and creates a new offer.

A contract may be either express or implied.

Express contracts are stated in oral or written words.

Implied-in-fact contracts are implied from the conduct of the parties.

Executed contract has promises made and completed immediately (e.g., product purchase at a store).

Executory contract has promises made but not entirely performed immediately (e.g., apartment lease, painting contract).

Capacity to contract

The law presumes that the parties to a contract have the requisite contractual capacity.

Minors do not always have the maturity, experience, or sophistication needed to enter into contracts with adults.

The infancy doctrine allows minors to disaffirm most contracts with adults.

The minor has the option of choosing whether to enforce the contract.

The contract is voidable by a minor.

Minors are obligated to pay for the necessities of life for which they contract.

Mentally incompetent persons

The law protects people suffering from mental incapacity from enforcing contracts against them.

Intoxicated persons

Most states provide that contracts entered into by intoxicated persons are *voidable* by that person.

The Statute of Frauds – writing requirement

All states have enacted a Statute of Frauds.

Generally, for contracts covered by the Statute of Frauds, an executory contract not in writing is not enforceable.

Contracts must be in writing to be enforceable under the Statute of Frauds (see discussion elsewhere).

Contracts requiring a writing:

1) Land contracts – transfers of ownership interests in real property must be in writing.
2) One-year rule – contracts that cannot bc completed within a year (assuming unlimited money and human resources). For example, singing at a person's birthday party in 18 months from contract formation
3) Contracts for the Sales of Goods over $500.
4) Contracts to be responsible as a surety for another's debts.
5) Contracts in consideration of marriage.
6) Contracts by the executor of a will to pay a debt of the estate from their monies.

The formality of the writing requires a signature.

Fraud

Material Misrepresentation of Fact

Intent to deceive

Reliance on the misrepresentation

Injury to the innocent party

Notes for active learning

Formation of Contracts

Offer

To form a contract, there must be an offer that is accepted.

A person makes an "offer" to enter into a bilateral contract by communicating to another person a proposed exchange of promises between the parties. The recipient of the communication reasonably believes that they can enter into a binding contract by accepting that proposed exchange of promises.

The more precise the communication, the more likely it will be characterized as an offer.

Communication is an offer for a unilateral contract if it sets forth valid consideration in exchange for a proposed action by the addressee, in such a manner that the person to whom it is directed reasonably believes that they can enter into a binding contract by performing the requested action.

UCC rule: A sale of goods contract may be made in a manner sufficient to show agreement even though the moment of its making is undetermined.

Acceptance

While rules govern how an offer is accepted in the absence of specific conditions of acceptance set forth in the offer, the offeror has a right to specify the manner of acceptance and make the usual rules inoperative.

If the offeror does not specify conditions for acceptance, an offer may be accepted at a reasonable time and in a reasonable manner.

If the offer is one for a unilateral contract, it may be accepted only by the performance of the act requested, not by a return promise.

Unless the parties have had a course of dealing where the offeree has accepted offers from the offeror by doing nothing, an offeror will be unsuccessful in arguing that silence by the offeree constitutes acceptance.

Unless the terms of an offer or course of dealing permit the offeree to accept by doing nothing, an offeree will be unsuccessful in arguing that they accepted an offer by silence.

For contracts controlled by common law and not the UCC (i.e., common law contracts), the offeree can only accept an offer by communicating acceptance of the terms of the offer before the time the offer expires, is terminated, or revoked.

Unless the offeror requires a different acceptance method in the offer, an offer is accepted when the letter of acceptance is mailed.

Words of the offeree which the offeror can reasonably believe an acceptance will cause a contract to be formed, even if those words do not include the term "accept."

UCC rules: Under § 2-206, an offer to buy goods for prompt shipment is accepted when the seller ships the goods, and a binding contract is formed at that time.

Unless otherwise unambiguously indicated by the language or circumstances,

(a) an offer to make a contract shall be construed as inviting acceptance in any manner and by any medium reasonable in the circumstances, and,

(b) an order or another offer to buy goods for prompt or current shipment shall be construed as inviting acceptance, either by a prompt promise to ship or by the prompt or current shipment of conforming or non-conforming goods.

Such a shipment of non-conforming goods does not constitute an acceptance if the seller reasonably notifies the buyer that the shipment is offered only as an accommodation.

Where the beginning of a requested performance is a reasonable mode of acceptance, an offeror who is not notified of acceptance within a reasonable time may treat the offer as having lapsed before acceptance.

UCC rules: Under § 2-207(1), a definite and reasonable expression of acceptance or a written confirmation sent within a reasonable time operates as an acceptance even though it states terms additional to or different from those offered or agreed upon unless acceptance is expressly made conditional on assent to the additional or different terms.

Under § 2-207(2), the additional terms are to be construed as proposals for an addition to the contract.

Between merchants, such terms become part of the contract unless:

(a) the offer expressly limits acceptance to the terms of the offer,

(b) the additional terms materially alter the offer, or

(c) notification of objection to the terms is given within a reasonable time after notice of them is received.

If the proposed additional term materially changes the original offer, there is still a contract, but the additional term is not included.

Under § 2-207(3), conduct by both parties, which recognizes the existence of a contract is sufficient to establish a contract for sale. The writings of the parties do not otherwise establish a contract.

The terms of the contract consist of those terms on which the writings of the parties agree, with supplementary terms incorporated under any other provisions of this Act.

If a seller under the UCC ships non-conforming goods in response to an offer and indicates that they have not accepted the original offer, the shipment of the non-conforming goods is a counteroffer. The seller is not in breach of contract for shipping the non-conforming goods.

If the buyer accepts the non-conforming goods and the counteroffer, they must pay the full contract price.

Revocation of offers

At common law, an offer is revocable by the offeror at any time, even if the offeror promises to keep the offer open for some time.

At common law, an offer is irrevocable if the agreement to keep it open for a specified period is supported by consideration.

Such an offer is an option contract.

The offeror may not revoke an offer for a unilateral contract if the offeror knows that the offeree has commenced substantial performance.

To be effective, the revocation must be communicated to the offeree before the offeree accepts the offer.

A revocation need not be in the express language.

Any communication, such as "I have sold it to someone else," which reasonably indicates to the offeree that the offer has been withdrawn, is a revocation.

A revocation need not be a direct communication between the offeror and the offeree.

If the offeree learns from a third party that the offer has been revoked before the offeree has accepted the offer, the revocation is effective.

An offer for a unilateral contract which occurs when the owner of real estate hires a broker and agrees to pay a commission when and if the broker finds a buyer ready, willing, and able to purchase the property, is automatically revoked without notice if the owner accepts another offer to purchase the property.

A written offer required by the Statute of Frauds can be revoked orally.

The death of the offeror terminates an offer.

If a contract has been formed, either party's death does not terminate the contract unless a party's death makes the contract impossible to perform.

UCC rules: A "merchant" means a person who deals in goods of the kind, or otherwise by their occupation holds themself out as having knowledge or skill peculiar to the practices or goods involved in the transaction, or to whom such knowledge or skill may be attributed by their employment of an agent, broker, or another intermediary who by occupation holds themself out as having knowledge or skill.

"Between merchants" means a transaction for which both parties are chargeable with the knowledge or skill of merchants.

An offer by a merchant to buy or sell goods in a signed writing, which by its terms gives assurances that it will be held open, is not revocable, for lack of consideration, during the time stated, or, if no time is stated, for a reasonable time.

In no event may such period of irrevocability exceed three months.

The offeror must separately sign a term of assurance on a form supplied by the offeree.

An offer by a non-merchant for the sale of goods under the UCC is revocable in the same manner as an offer at common law.

An oral offer by a merchant for the sale of goods is revocable in the same manner as an offer at common law.

A merchant's written offer, which states that the offer remains open for more than three months, remains irrevocable for three months.

Rejection

If at common law, the offeree purports to accept an offer but changes the terms of the offer in any way, the communication is a counteroffer, and no contract is formed.

This rule is qualified for the sale of goods by § 2-207 discussed above.

An offer is terminated by rejection or by a counteroffer. After that, the offeree cannot accept the original offer even if the time to remain open has not expired.

If the offeror has made a multipart offer that can be accepted in part, such as "I will sell you any one of these five lots for $5,000 apiece," acceptance of part of the offer can be considered as a rejection of the remainder of the offer.

An inquiry concerning the offer by the offeree about the offeror's precise terms or willingness of the offeror to modify the terms of the offer is not a rejection.

Mistake, fraud and duress

The defense of unilateral mistake is available when one party's mistake was so apparent that the other party should have known the mistake when the offer was accepted.

Unilateral mistake is grounds for avoiding a contract if the first party is mistaken about a material fact. While not mistaken about that fact, the second party is aware that the first party is mistaken about that material fact.

Mutual mistake is grounds for avoiding a contract if both parties relied on an untrue material fact at the time of contracting.

There is no meeting of the minds, an essential requirement for a contract's existence if each party to the contract without fault has a different understanding of the meaning of the words they agreed to.

If the contract involves the ship "Peerless," but each party innocently and honestly thinks of a different ship named "Peerless," there is no meeting of the minds and no contract.

If the parties orally agree on terms of a contract, which is reduced to writing and the scrivener makes an error in setting out the terms of the contract, either party can reform the written contract to conform to the actual oral understanding of the parties.

Indefiniteness and absence of terms

UCC rule: A contract is not void for indefiniteness if there is no price agreed to. Under UCC, there is a valid contract for a reasonable price.

Capacity to contract

A person who has entered into a contract while a minor can disaffirm that contract, even one that has been completed, except a contract for necessities, within a reasonable time of reaching the age of majority.

If a minor, after reaching majority, agrees to make a payment on a contract they had a right to disaffirm, for an amount which is less than the full contract price, the agreement is only enforceable without new consideration to the extent of the promise made after reaching majority, not for the full contract price.

Implied-in-fact contracts

An implied-in-fact contract arises out of the conscious action of a party.

Without words spoken or written, a contractual obligation can be implied from a party's action. For example, accepting services from someone in providing those services creates an obligation to pay those services' fair value.

If a landowner watches another party perform work on their land, which they know is not intended to be gratuitous and says nothing, the landowner has entered into an implied-in-fact contract to pay for the fair value of the work.

Implied-in-law contracts

An implied-in-law contract arises even though a party has not acted in word or deed to incur contractual liability.

The law will imply a contractual liability to pay for necessary services rendered to an individual when they lack the mental capacity to request such services or agree to be contractually bound to pay.

Quasi-contracts

If parties entered or attempted to enter into a contractual relationship, but the contract is not enforceable because of the Statute of Frauds or other reasons, and one party conferred a benefit on the other, the party conferring the benefit can sue in quasi-contract for the fair value of the benefit conferred. Contract measures of damages do not apply.

A person who has a right to pursue a remedy under an enforceable contract does not have the right to sue in *quantum meruit* (i.e., a reasonable sum of money) for a benefit conferred.

Pre-contractual liability based upon detrimental reliance

If the owner of property puts a construction contract out to bid to general contractors, and a subcontractor submits an offer to perform a subcontract for the general contractor, with the knowledge that the general contractor is relying on the bid when bidding for the general contract, the subcontract's bid is treated as an option contract.

The general contractor's detrimental reliance is a sufficient substitute for bargained-for consideration so that the subcontractor cannot revoke their bid. The general contractor has a reasonable time after they become the successful bidder to accept the bid.

However, since the subcontractor's bid is an offer, there is no contract between the general contractor and the subcontractor until the general contractor accepts the bid.

Unconscionability

Unconscionability arises when there are unfair terms coupled with an unfair bargaining process.

A contract is unconscionable, and a court can refuse to enforce such a contract if one of its provisions was oppressive at the time of the contract's execution.

The concept of unconscionable is part of the UCC and applied with increasing frequency to common law contracts.

Notes for active learning

Consideration

Bargain and exchange

The concept of the bargain is the essence of consideration.

A promise by one party to perform an act or refrain from acting, in exchange for a counter-promise by the other party to perform an act or refrain from acting, constitutes valid consideration, making the promises enforceable.

For valid consideration, the party making the bargain need not be the person benefiting.

An agreement is supported by consideration if the person benefited is a third party for whom the benefit was requested.

If a party promises to do something that they are not legally obligated to, they have given consideration even though the performance of that obligation is not burdensome.

A promise that does not limit a party's rights is an *illusory promise* that does not constitute valid consideration because the promisor possesses a unilateral right to avoid an obligation made in the promise.

"I promise to pay you one dollar for that apple if I choose to" is an illusory promise.

If a promise is illusory because its enforceability is subject to a condition precedent that is entirely within one party's control, a valid contract forms once the condition is satisfied.

The promise to undertake a minor burden imposed on the recipient of property in what is essentially a donative transaction does not transform that burden into consideration.

For example, an aunt's statement to her nephew, "I will buy you a jacket for your birthday if you stop by the store to pick it up," creates a donative transaction because the aunt is not bargaining with her nephew about picking up the jacket.

Adequacy of consideration

In determining whether a contract is supported by consideration, courts do not measure the value of what a party promises compared to what they receive.

An agreement to settle a meritless claim is not valid consideration.

Suppose an agreement is supported by consideration so that a valid contract exists. According to its terms, a party who performs their side of the bargain is entitled to enforce the contract even if they get far more than given.

Detrimental reliance

Even if an agreement is not supported by bargained-for consideration, such as a promise to make a gift, it may be enforceable if there is a substitute for bargained-for consideration; promissory estoppel.

If an agreement is supported by bargained-for consideration, the promissory estoppel elements are irrelevant and the wrong answer to a multiple-choice question.

An agreement not supported by bargained-for consideration, such as a promise to make a gift, is enforceable if promissory estoppel (the substitute for bargained-for consideration) is present.

Promissory estoppel is present if:

1) one party knows that their promise induces substantial reliance by the promisee, and

2) failure to enforce the promise causes substantial hardship, and

3) injustice can be avoided only by such enforcement.

Moral obligations

A service that has already been gratuitously rendered is not valid consideration for a later promise to pay because the bargain element (i.e., the essence of consideration) is absent.

Even though there is no new bargain, a unilateral promise in writing to pay a debt barred by the statute of limitations (SOL) is enforceable without new consideration.

If the new promise differs from the original, the contract is only enforceable to the extent of the new promise.

A contract that was initially voidable because of age is enforceable against that party without new consideration if the minor makes a new promise after reaching majority.

If the new promise differs from the original promise, the contract is only enforceable to the extent of the new promise.

Modification of contracts and pre-existing duty rule

An agreement to rescind an existing executory contract is supported by consideration since each side is bargaining to give up the rights they previously had under the contract.

The common-law rule is that fresh consideration (a different obligation than already agreed to) must support contract modification. The agreement to modify is unenforceable if one party's promises are unmodified and the other party's promises are more burdensome.

A contract can be modified at common law if each gives new consideration for modification.

Consideration is not an issue if one party to an existing contract modifies its promises in exchange for the other party's promise to modify its promises.

Modern common law contract cases hold that an agreement to modify an existing contract without fresh consideration is enforceable when the modification is made in good faith. An example of good faith is when the circumstances under which the contract is to be performed changed through no fault of the parties when the contract was executed.

The traditional common-law rule was that if a party to a contract agreed with the other party to perform an act that they were already obligated to perform because of contractual relations with a third person, the agreement was unenforceable as not supported by consideration.

Under modern contract principles tested, the contractual obligation to a third party to perform the act does not prevent the promise to perform the act from being adequate consideration.

UCC rule: An agreement modifying a contract needs no new consideration to be binding.

Compromise and settlement of claims

Forbearance, a promise not to assert a right, is not valid consideration if the agreement forbears asserting a frivolous claim that the party knows is invalid.

Forbearance is valid consideration if the person seeking to enforce the contract reasonably believes that they have a valid legal claim.

When there is a dispute concerning the amount owed, and one party tenders a check as payment in full, which the other party cashes, there is a discharge of the contractual obligation.

If the claim's amount and validity are undisputed, the cashing of the check does not bar a suit for the remainder.

If there is no dispute concerning either the validity, collectability, or amount of the claim, an agreement to settle the claim for a lower amount is not supported by consideration.

Output and requirements contracts

Output and requirements contracts are not invalid on the grounds of indefiniteness or lack of consideration.

Output and requirements contracts are specifically enforceable if the non-breaching party will have difficulty obtaining substitute performance.

UCC rules: A quantity term expressed as a manufacturer's requirements is enforceable.

UCC § 2-306 provides that "a term which measures the quantity by the . . . requirements of the buyer mean such actual . . . requirements as may occur in good faith . . ."

The definiteness of quantity requirement is satisfied if there is an available objective method for determining the quantity, and the requirements of a manufacturer would generally satisfy that need.

No quantity unreasonably disproportionate to any stated estimate, or in the absence of a stated estimate, to a standard or otherwise comparable prior output or requirements, may be tendered or demanded.

A lawful agreement by either the seller or the buyer for exclusive dealing in the kind of goods concerned imposes, unless otherwise agreed, an obligation by the seller to use best efforts to supply the goods and the buyer to use best efforts to promote their sale.

Third-Party Beneficiary Contracts

Intended beneficiaries

Third-party beneficiary contracts arise when the performance of one of the parties' contractual obligations benefits a person, not a party to the contract, instead of the party who furnished the consideration necessary for that obligation to arise.

Thus "A" and "B" enter into a contract whereby A furnishes consideration to B, who is contractually obligated to render performance to "C," not A.

If two parties contract a service that each intends to benefit a designated third party, the third-party beneficiary and promisee are entitled to sue upon the promisor's breach.

The victim of a breach is entitled to recover only those damages which could not reasonably have been avoided.

Failure to take reasonable steps to mitigate damages defeats a claim for consequential damages.

No contractual rights vest in an intended third-party beneficiary unless the promisor and promisee parties conclude a binding contract.

Third-party beneficiaries are intended beneficiaries when the contracting parties either explicitly or implicitly direct the contract's performance for their benefit.

A *creditor beneficiary* is a type of intended beneficiary where the contract's performance for the benefit of the beneficiary, C, is designed to relieve the party who furnished the consideration, A, from a legal obligation.

A *donee beneficiary* is another type of intended third-party beneficiary where the original contracting party, A, satisfies no legal obligation by entering into a contract designed to benefit C.

Since one of the contracting parties, A, has furnished the consideration which obligated B to perform, the third party, C, need not provide consideration to be able to sue on a third-party beneficiary contract.

A third-party creditor beneficiary, C, does not give up their rights against the contracting party who furnished the consideration, A, which required that performance be rendered to them until the party obligated to render performance, B, completes their obligation.

Intended third-party beneficiaries need not know that a contract has been made for their benefit when they become a third-party beneficiary to have the right to sue.

If a party to a third party beneficiary contract, B, is obligated to render performance to an intended third-party beneficiary, C, in exchange for performance by A., they are relieved of that obligation if A does not perform their obligations to B.

Therefore, B has a valid defense in a suit by C if A fails to perform its obligations to B.

Incidental beneficiaries

An incidental beneficiary, a person benefited if a contract between two other parties is performed but is a person that the original contracting parties did not intend to benefit, has no right to enforce a third-party beneficiary contract.

Modification of the third-party beneficiary's rights

The two original parties to a third-party beneficiary contract, A and B, can modify or rescind their contract to the detriment of the intended beneficiary, C, up until the time that C's rights in the contract become vested.

They become vested when C either assents to the contract at a party's request, sues on the contract, or changes position in reliance on it.

Assignment and Delegation

Assignment of rights

An assignee succeeds in a contract as the contract stands at the time of assignment.

Once a party has fully performed obligations under a contract, their right to return performance, including the right to sue for breach of the other party's obligations, can be assigned to a third party even if the contract prohibits assignment.

A party to a contract can assign the benefits of the contract, which accrue without obligating the assignee to assume the burdens of the contract.

An assignee of a contract only obtains rights under it, which are limited by defenses that the original contracting party has against the assignor.

The rule is contrary to the rule when the assignment is a negotiable instrument.

The assignee, known as a *holder in due course*, takes free of the personal defenses that the other party to the negotiable instrument has against the instrument's assignor.

If a contracting party pays a second contracting party an amount due on the contract before receiving notice that the second party assigned their interest under the contract, the first party is not obligated to an assignee, even though the assignment took place before the payment.

If the first party has been notified of the assignment before making payment, they can only discharge their contract obligation by paying the assignee.

UCC rule: Unless otherwise agreed, all rights of either seller or buyer can be assigned except where the assignment would materially change the duty of the other party, increase materially the burden or risk imposed by contract, or impair their chances of obtaining return performance materially.

Unless the circumstances indicate the contrary, a prohibition of the contract assignment is to be construed as barring only the delegation to the assignee of the assignor's performance.

Delegation of duties

A contractual provision forbidding delegation is valid and enforceable.

A party may perform their duty through a delegatee unless:

1) it is otherwise agreed, or
2) the other party has a substantial interest in having the original promisor perform, or
3) the party wishing to delegate possesses unique characteristics (e.g., a singer), so the performance by a delegatee materially alters the bargained-for performance.

No delegation of performance relieves the party delegating duty to perform or liability for breach.

If the parties enter into a novation so that one original contracting party agrees to look solely to the delegatee for performance in exchange for releasing the other original party from the contract's obligations, the original party is no longer liable if the delegatee breaches the contract.

UCC rule: An assignment of "the contract" or "all my rights under the contract" or an assignment in similarly general terms is an assignment of rights and duties.

Unless the language or the circumstances (e.g., an assignment for security) indicate to the contrary, it is a delegation of the duties of the assignor's performance.

The acceptance of the assignee's assignment constitutes a promise to perform those duties.

The promise is enforceable by the assignor or the other party to the original contract.

Statute of Frauds

The exemption of contracts for less than $500 from the Statute of Frauds requirements applies only to contracts for the sale of goods governed by UCC-2.

Memorandum

The Statute of Frauds applies to specific types of contracts discussed below. The contract itself need not be in writing to satisfy the statute.

There need only be a memorandum that contains the essential terms of the contract signed by the party to be charged.

The memorandum sufficient to satisfy the statute need not be written when making the promise, nor need it to be writing addressed to the promisee.

Contract cannot be performed within one year

In measuring the one year to determine if the Statute of Frauds is applicable, the period starts when making the contract, not at the commencement of performance.

The Statute of Frauds applies to an eleven-month personal services contract made on January 1 with work starting on April 1, since the contract will not terminate until March 1 of the following year.

The possibility that death could prematurely terminate a personal services contract for more than a year does not cause the Statute of Frauds to be inapplicable.

The Statute of Frauds does not apply to a personal services contract for the life of the party because the natural termination of that contract could occur within a year.

Land contracts

See Property Law for the Statute of Frauds as it applies to land contracts.

A real estate brokerage contract is enforceable even if there is no memorandum signed by the property owner sufficient to satisfy the Statute of Frauds.

General rule for the sale of goods

UCC rules: Except as otherwise provided, a contract for the sale of goods for the price of $500 or more is not enforceable by action or defense unless there is a writing sufficient to indicate that a contract for sale had been made between the parties.

This writing must be signed by the party against whom enforcement is sought or by their authorized agent or broker.

A writing is not insufficient because it omits or incorrectly states a term agreed upon, but the contract is not enforceable beyond the number of goods shown in such writing.

A memorandum satisfies the Statute of Frauds if it indicates a contract; it contains a description of the goods, quantity and is signed. It does not need to contain the price.

Exceptions for sale of goods

UCC rules: Between merchants, if within a reasonable time a writing in confirmation of the contract and sufficient against the sender is received, and the party receiving it has reason to know its content, it satisfies the requirement of the Statute of Frauds against such party unless written notice of objection to its contents is given within ten days after it is received.

A contract that does not satisfy the general rule, but which is valid in other respects is enforceable if:

1) the goods are to be specifically manufactured for the buyer and are not suitable for sale to others in the ordinary course of the seller's business, and the seller, before notice of repudiation is received and under circumstances which reasonably indicated that the goods are for the buyer, has made either a substantial beginning of manufacture or commitments for their procurement, or

2) the party against whom enforcement is sought admits in pleadings, testimony, or in court that a contract for sale was made, but the contract is not enforceable under this provision beyond the number of goods admitted, or

3) for goods for which payment has been made or accepted or which have been received or accepted.

If, as modified, a UCC contract involves a sale of goods for more than $500, it requires compliance with the Statute of Frauds.

Suretyship

An oral promise to pay another's debt is usually unenforceable because of the Statute of Frauds.

If the primary purpose of the promise to pay another's debt is to further the promisor's goals, the promise is enforceable even if there is no memorandum signed by the promisor sufficient to satisfy the Statute of Frauds.

In addition to the writing required by the Statute of Frauds, a party seeking to collect from a surety must give reasonable notice to the surety that they have extended credit to the other party to the contract.

The suretyship provisions of the Statute of Frauds are inapplicable unless there is:

1) a contractual relationship between the creditor and the party who is to benefit from the services, and

2) the creditor knows that the defendant is acting in a suretyship capacity rather than in a direct contractual capacity.

Notes for active learning

Parol Evidence Rule

The *parol evidence* rule bars evidence of prior or contemporaneous statements that contradict the terms of a written contract.

If the written contract is integrated, evidence of prior or contemporaneous agreements between the parties is inadmissible.

Exceptions to the parol evidence rule

However, *parol evidence* for the terms of a contract is admissible:

1) to prove that there is a condition precedent to a contract's coming into existence;

2) to explain an ambiguity;

3) to show that the parties used words in a nontraditional manner or spoke in code;

4) to prove a mistake in reducing the terms of an oral agreement to writing;

5) to prove contract modification by evidence of conversations after contract formation.

   At common law, a provision in a written agreement that a writing can only modify a contract is not valid;

6) to prove, for an oral contract which is not integrated, subjects not covered by the written contract.

UCC rules: The terms to which the confirmatory memoranda of the parties agree, or which are set forth in writing intended by the parties as a final expression of their agreement may not be contradicted by evidence of prior or contemporaneous oral agreement but may be explained or supplemented by:

1) *course of dealing*, *usage of trade*, or *course of performance*, or

2) evidence of consistent additional terms unless the court finds the writing was intended as a complete and exclusive statement of the terms of the agreement.

When inconsistent with usage of trade, a course of dealing trumps usage of trade and controls the interpretation of the contract.

Unlike the rule at common law, under the UCC, a signed agreement that excludes modification or rescission except by a signed writing cannot be modified or rescinded.

Except for between merchants, such a requirement on a form supplied by the merchant must be separately signed by the other party.

Although an attempt at modification or rescission does not satisfy the UCC provisions for the Statute of Frauds or *parol evidence* rule, it can operate as a waiver.

Notes for active learning

Interpretation of Contracts

Employment-at-will

The primary goal in interpreting a contract is to carry out the intent of the parties.

Permanent employment means employment-at-will.

In an employment-at-will relationship, either party can terminate the agreement at any time without termination being a breach unless the termination violates public policy.

> When parties attach significantly different meanings to the same material term, the meaning that controls is that "attached by one of them if at the time the agreement was made . . . that party did not know of any different meaning attached by the other, and the other knew the meaning attached by the first party." Restatement (Second) of Contracts § 201.

UCC course of dealing and usage of trade

UCC rules: A *course of dealing* is a sequence of previous conduct between the parties to a particular transaction, which is reasonably regarded as establishing a common basis of understanding for interpreting their expressions and other conduct.

A *usage of trade* is a practice or method of dealing with such regularity of observance in a place, vocation, or trade to justify an expectation that it will be observed for the transaction in question.

The existence and scope of such usage are to be proved as facts.

If it is established that such a usage is embodied in a written trade code or similar writing, the interpretation of the writing is for the court.

A course of dealing between parties and usage of trade in the vocation or trade in which they are engaged, or of which they are or should be aware, shall give meaning to, and supplement or qualify, terms of an agreement.

The express terms of an agreement and an applicable *course of dealing* or *usage of trade* shall be construed wherever reasonable as consistent with each other.

When such construction is unreasonable, express terms control both the course of dealing and usage of trade, and the course of dealing controls usage of trade.

Notes for active learning

Conditions

Express conditions

If the obligation of one party to a contract to perform under that contract is subject to an express condition precedent, the other party seeking to establish a breach must either show compliance with an express condition or that the other party was in bad faith for the condition, thereby excusing compliance with the condition.

A contract condition that performance be satisfactory to the purchaser means that an objective standard will be applied, and performance must be satisfactory to a reasonable person.

If the contract involves personal taste, the performance must be subjectively satisfactory to the purchaser.

Even when the subjective standard is applied, the purchaser must act in good faith.

If one party assumes an obligation and the size of which at the time of contracting is unknown, they are entitled to be paid the consideration promised, even if the obligation is substantially smaller than anticipated.

If a certificate of completion by the architect is a condition of completing a construction contract, the builder cannot collect in full under the contract until that certificate is obtained unless they prove that the architect failed to provide it because of bad faith.

If it is clear that the purpose of the condition was to benefit or protect one of the parties, that party may waive the condition and insist that the other party perform.

Constructive conditions of exchange

If no order of performance is specified in the contract, each party must perform its obligations under the contract as a condition for demanding performance from the other.

For example, in a sale of goods contract, the buyer must pay for the goods, and the seller must deliver the goods simultaneously. Such mutual conditions precedent is constructive conditions of exchange.

The parties to a contract can make the performance by one party a condition precedent to the performance by the other.

Absent a special provision concerning partial payment in the contract; a party has no right to be paid until they complete the required performance.

If the time for performance is not made of the essence, a party may perform in a reasonable time.

Divisible contracts

A divisible contract occurs when performance by one party of less than the full contractual obligation gives that party a right to require partial performance of the other party's obligation.

For example, if A is employed by B for one year, B will ordinarily have an obligation to pay A a portion of their yearly salary periodically.

If a contract is divisible, one divisible portion's performance permits the plaintiff to demand performance from the defendant for that separable portion, even if the plaintiff is in breach of another separable portion.

For example, if A, the employee on an annual salary with monthly pay periods, works for one month, they are entitled to be paid for that month's work, even if they do not complete the full year's employment.

Contract law acknowledges the fact that parties sometimes embody obligations that are, in most respects, separable into a single document or agreement.

Rules for damages permit the separable parts to be treated separately.

Though the contract has separable components for damages, it is still a single contract permitting the damages suffered by each side to be litigated in a single lawsuit.

If the contract requires one party to perform a single task (e.g., building a structure), the fact that the contract requires periodic payments does not make it a divisible contract.

Immaterial breach and substantial performance

Under the common law, the plaintiff can sue for breach of contract and collect contract damages if they have substantially performed the contract, even if there is an immaterial (non-willful) breach.

If the plaintiff has not fully performed the contract, the defendant can successfully assert a counterclaim for damages caused by the plaintiff's failure to perform fully.

UCC rule: The UCC does not recognize the doctrine of substantial performance. Instead, it follows the rule of *perfect tender*.

Except for an installment contract, the seller must tender the correct amount of conforming goods at the time specified, or the buyer can reject the goods without liability and sue the seller for damages.

Installment contracts

UCC rules: An installment contract is one where the seller does not have an obligation to deliver all the goods to be sold under the contract at one time.

If a contract is determined to be an installment contract, the rule of perfect tender, which permits the buyer to reject non-conforming goods if all goods are to be delivered at one time, is inapplicable.

The buyer can reject a nonconforming shipment only if it substantially impairs the installment value and cannot be cured.

A failure by the seller to deliver the appropriate quantity of conforming goods on time for one installment of an installment contract is a breach of the total contract only if the nonconformity substantially impairs the entire contract's value.

UCC rule – implied warranty of merchantability

All merchant sellers give implied warranties of merchantability.

UCC § 2-314(2) defines the implied warranty of merchantability:

1) goods, to be merchantable, must at least pass without objection in the trade under the contract description; and
2) in the case of fungible goods are of a fair average quality within the description; and
3) are fit for the ordinary purpose for which goods are used; and
4) run within the variations permitted by the agreement, or even kind of quality and quantity within each unit and among all units involved; and
5) are adequately contained, packaged, and labeled as the agreement may require; and
6) conform to promises or affirmations made on the container or label, if any.

UCC rule – warranty of fitness for a particular purpose

Under UCC § 2- 315, a warranty of fitness for a particular purpose arises whenever the seller has reason to know of any particular purpose for which the goods are required. The buyer is relying upon the seller's skill to select suitable goods.

Constructive condition of cooperation

A condition of cooperation is implied in every contract.

A party who wrongfully hinders the other party's performance breaches the contract.

Each party to a contract has an implied duty to cooperate with the other party in achieving the objects of the contract.

Obligations of good faith and fair dealing

Each party to a contract has an implied duty to act in good faith.

Acting in bad faith can constitute a breach of contract and give the other party a defense to a suit for breach of contract.

Suspension or excuse of conditions by waiver

A waiver occurs when a party to a contract affirmatively represents to the other party that it will not act on or enforce a known right.

A waiver is revocable unless the other party relies on the waiver to their detriment, or the waiver is an agreement supported by consideration.

The conduct of a contracting party in failing to insist on full performance for some time can constitute a course of dealings and a waiver of the right to full performance during the remainder of the contract if relied upon by the other party to their detriment.

If the certification of a condition's performance is placed in a third party to benefit one of the contracting parties, that contracting party can waive the certification.

UCC rule: A party who had made a waiver affecting an executory portion of the contract may retract the waiver by notification to the other party so that strict performance of terms waived will be required unless the retraction would be unjust due to a material change of position in reliance on the waiver.

Remedies

Rescission

When a seller induces a buyer's consent to a contract through a material misrepresentation, the resulting contract is voidable at the election of the buyer.

In some cases, a failure to independently inspect property might constitute a defense to a claim of misrepresentation.

The buyer is entitled to rely on the truth of the seller's material representations and need not conduct independent tests to see whether the seller is lying.

Buyer's and seller's obligations unless terms are specified

UCC rule: The seller must tender conforming goods at their place of business at the specified time, and the buyer has a concurrent obligation to pay the purchase price at that time.

Cure

UCC rules: Where tender or delivery by the seller is rejected because it is non-conforming and the time for performance has not yet expired, the seller may timely notify the buyer of the intention to cure and within the contract time make a conforming delivery.

Where the buyer rejects a non-conforming tender which the seller had reasonable grounds to believe to be acceptable with or without money allowance, the seller may, if they seasonably notify the buyer, have a further reasonable time to substitute a conforming tender.

Rights of the non-breaching party

UCC rule: If a party to a contract has committed a material breach, the non-breaching party is excused from further performance of the contract.

Demand for assurances

UCC rule: A contract for the sale of goods imposes an obligation on each party that the other's expectation of receiving due performance will not be impaired.

When reasonable grounds for insecurity arise concerning either party's performance, the other may in writing demand adequate assurance of performance. Until receiving such assurance, if commercially reasonable, the requesting party may suspend performance for which they have not already received the agreed return.

Acceptance of improper delivery or payment does not prejudice the aggrieved party's right to demand adequate future performance assurance.

After receipt of a justified demand, failure to provide within a reasonable time, not exceeding thirty days, such assurance of due performance is adequate under the case's circumstances and is a repudiation of the contract.

Anticipatory repudiation

Anticipatory repudiation occurs when a party to the contract gives unequivocal notice to the other party that they will not perform their obligations at the time set for performance.

If the non-repudiating party has not relied on anticipatory repudiation by canceling the contract or materially changing their position, the repudiating party may retract the repudiation, providing they give adequate assurances.

The non-repudiating party has no right to sue for a breach before the time of scheduled performance.

UCC rule: When either party repudiates the contract concerning a performance not yet due, the loss of which will substantially impair the value of the contract to the other, the aggrieved party may:

1) for a commercially reasonable time await performance by the repudiating party; or
2) resort to a remedy for breach even though they have notified the repudiating party that they would await the latter's performance and has urged retraction; and,
3) in either case, suspend their performance or proceed following this article's provisions on the seller's right to identify goods to the contract notwithstanding the breach or salvage unfinished goods.

Risk of loss

UCC rules: The risk of loss is initially on the seller.

The risk of loss shifts to the buyer when the seller completes delivery obligation for goods that meet the contract's quantity and quality specifications.

If nothing is said about the place of delivery or the contract specifies that delivery is at the seller's place of business, the risk of loss shifts to the buyer when the seller places conforming goods on a common carrier with instructions shipped to the buyer.

If the contract requires delivery at the buyer's place of business, the risk of loss does not shift to the buyer until conforming goods arrive at the buyer's place of business.

If the goods shipped are non-conforming, the seller retains the risk of loss until accepted.

If the buyer initially accepts the goods and rightfully revokes acceptance, the risk of loss is on the buyer only to the extent that the buyer's insurance covers the goods.

Rights of *bona fide* purchasers

UCC rule: A *bona fide* purchaser of goods from a person in the business of selling those goods takes superior title to the true owner of those goods.

Seller's remedies in the event of buyer's breach

UCC rules: The standard measure of damages for non-acceptance or repudiation by the buyer is the difference between the market price at the time and place for tender and the unpaid contract price, together with incidental damages but less expenses saved in consequence of the buyer's breach.

If the measure of damages provided in the preceding paragraph is inadequate to put the seller in as good a position as performance would have done.

The measure of damages is the profit (including reasonable overhead), which the seller would have made from the buyer's full performance, together with incidental damages provided in this article, due allowances for costs reasonably incurred, and due credit for payments or proceeds of resale.

As a limited alternative remedy, the seller may make the goods available to the buyer and sue for the contract price if the goods cannot be sold in the seller's ordinary course of business.

Buyer's remedies in the event of seller's breach

UCC rules: The buyer may seek damages – the difference between the market price and the contract price.

The buyer may fix damages by purchasing the goods elsewhere and collect the difference between the price they pay and the contract price; this remedy is *cover*.

The buyer may tender the full purchase price and seek an order requiring the seller to deliver the goods if they are unique.

Measure of damages

Expectancy damages are the standard measure of contract damages, i.e., the amount of money that would put them in the same position as if the breaching party had performed their obligations under the contract.

The amount of a non-breaching party's expectancy damages on a contract where the non-breaching party has not expended money towards their obligated performance is the profit they would have made had the contract been performed.

If the non-breaching party has expended money in the performance of their obligations under the contract, they are entitled to recover those sums plus profit.

If expectancy damages are too speculative and cannot be recovered, the non-breaching party is entitled to reliance damages, the amount expended to perform the contract, whether or not those expenditures benefited the breaching party.

If payments on a contract are due in installments and there is no acceleration clause, the non-breaching party can only sue for the unpaid installments.

If a party voluntarily incurs additional expenses toward the performance of the contract after they know that the other party is in breach, they may not recover those additional expenses.

A non-breaching party has a duty to mitigate damages by taking steps to avoid damages they should have foreseen and could have avoided without undue risk, expense, or humiliation.

For example, if the employer breaches an employment contract, the employee must use reasonable efforts to seek substitute employment during the remainder of the contract period.

If they fail to mitigate, the fair value of what they would have received if they had found other employment is deducted from their expectancy damages.

If incurred to mitigate damage after the breach, reasonable expenses are recoverable as incidental damages, even if expenses are not connected to a successful mitigation attempt.

The victim of a breach is entitled to recover only those damages which could not reasonably have been avoided.

Failure to take reasonable steps to mitigate damages defeats a claim for consequential damages.

Consequential damages

Consequential damages are limited to those damages that were reasonably foreseeable by the parties when the contract is made.

Liquidated damages

A provision fixing liquidated damages is unenforceable unless the amount fixed is reasonable compared to the damages that the parties could anticipate when making the contract or the damages incurred.

Specific performance

The buyer and seller are entitled to sue for specific performance of enforceable land contracts.

Specific performance requiring the defendant to perform is not available to remedy a personal services contract.

A negative injunction can be granted by the standards for granting injunctions, preventing the defendant from working for a person other than the one to whom contractually bound.

Restitution damages (*quantum meruit*)

If a party is prevented from suing on the contract because the contract is unenforceable (e.g., Statute of Frauds) or because they committed a material breach, they are limited to restitution damages.

Restitution (or *quantum meruit*) damages are the fair value of the benefit conferred on the other party.

An unjust enrichment claim cannot exceed the contract price when all the work giving rise to the claim has been performed, and the only remaining obligation is the payment of the price.

Restitution damages cannot be greater than the recoverable damages if the contract were enforceable.

Notes for active learning

Impossibility and Frustration

Impossibility of performance

If events after the formation of a contract make the performance by one party illegal or impossible, the doctrine of impossibility is applicable, and the parties are discharged from their contractual obligations.

The doctrine of impossibility applies at common law when the contract's subject matter is destroyed, or a party to a personal service contract dies.

The destruction of an existing structure renders a contract to repair it impossible, terminating the contract.

The contractor has the right to collect for the fair value of the work done in *quantum meruit* but cannot sue for contract damages because the contract obligations have been discharged.

A party may not rely on the defense of impossibility if they expressly assume the risk of performing an objectively impossible obligation.

Excused performance under the UCC

UCC rules: Under the doctrine of impracticability, performance is excused when:

1) goods identified to the contract are destroyed,

2) performance becomes illegal,

3) performance is prevented by a non-foreseeable event, the nonoccurrence of a basic assumption of the contract.

Under § 2-615, when a contract specifies produce to be grown on a specific farm and the crop is destroyed by natural forces beyond the farmer's control, the farmer is excused from performance to the extent of the damage.

Relationship matrix

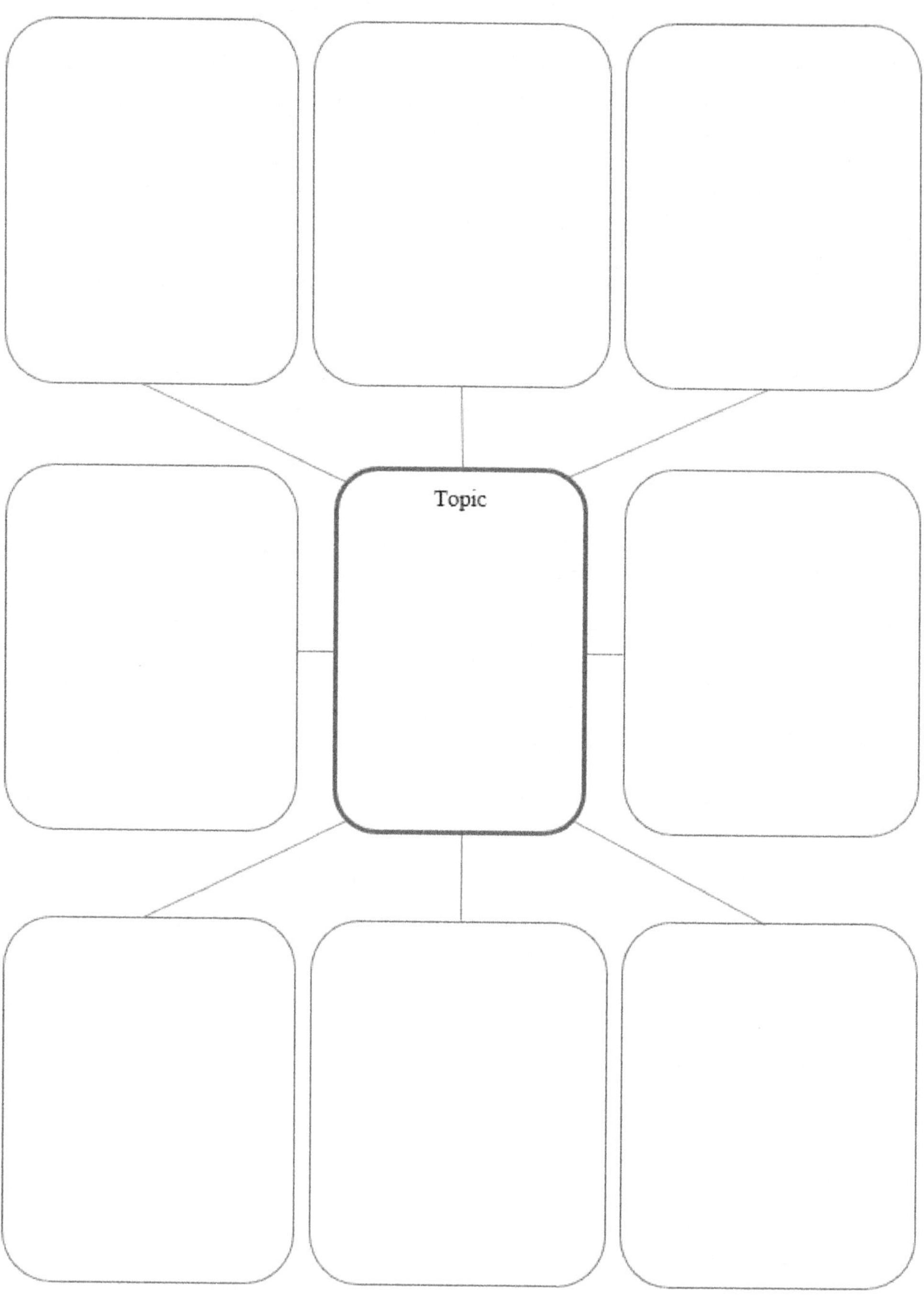

Contract Law – Quick Facts

1. A **gratuitous assignee** has rights under a contract that *may* be enforced against the **obligor** *until or unless* the assignment is revoked.
2. Where there is a **delegation of duties**, the delegator *and* the delegate are *liable* for the performance of the agreement.
3. Under UCC, a **crop failure** resulting from an unexpected cause excuses a farmer's obligation to deliver the full amount if they make a fair and reasonable allocation among their buyers, which could be allocated *pro-rata* between buyers.

   The buyer may accept the proposed modification *or* terminate the contract.
4. The general rule is that a **contractor** is responsible for destroying the premises under construction *prior to completion*; once the residence is complete, the **risk of loss** shifts to the owner.
5. **Performance is excused** where it is prevented by the **operation of law**, despite stipulations to the contrary; governmental interference makes the contract's performance illegal. The party may be excused from the performance.
6. A **detriment** exists whenever a promisee gives up the **legal right** to do something, regardless of whether they would have done otherwise.
7. Under UCC, a **written confirmation** is sufficient as an acceptance even though it states additional terms *unless* the acceptance is **expressly made conditional on assent** to the additional terms.
8. An **implied-in-fact** contract is formed by *mutual manifestations of assent* (i.e., conduct) other than oral or written language. Even if there is no mutual assent, the parties are bound if their conduct objectively manifests contractual intent.
9. **Assignment and delegation** are prohibited where they would substantially alter the obligor's risks, such as an **exoneration clause**, which effectively holds the obligor accountable (liable) for the obligee's actions.
10. A **novation** substitutes a new party for an original party to the contract—requires the assent of *all* parties and completely releases the original party.
11. **Despite reliance**, a third-party **donee beneficiary** has *no* cause of action against the promise because the promisor's act is gratuitous. The promisor may *not* be held to it *unless* they have directly created the reliance by personally informing the beneficiary.
12. Where there is an **oral condition precedent**, evidence of the condition falls outside the *parol evidence rule*.

Notes for active learning

Criminal Law and Criminal Procedure

Criminal Law and Criminal Procedure are tested about equally. Criminal Procedure may be combined with another topic, such as Evidence. Heavily tested topics include homicide (causation is often tested with homicide), the defense of insanity, Fifth Amendment, Fourteenth and Sixth Amendments, unreasonable searches and seizures.

The statements herein were compiled by analyzing released Criminal Law and Criminal Procedure questions and setting forth the principles of law governing the correct answers. Review these principles before preparing answers to practice Criminal Law and Procedure questions. Memorize this governing law and understand how it applies to the correct answer.

Homicide Crimes

For criminal homicide, the prosecution must show that the defendant's act was the proximate cause of the victim's death.

Murder

When the test uses a word like "murder" or "robbery" and provides no further definition of the crime, it refers to the common law crime.

Know the elements of common law crimes and apply them to specific facts.

If the question wants a definition of a crime different from the common law, they will either define the crime in the question or use a term such as "under modern law."

Definition of malice for common law murder

The mental state required for common law murder is malice.

Murder has four separate definitions.

1) Intent to kill.
2) Intent to do great bodily harm.
3) A death occurring in the course of a felony.
4) Willful and wanton disregard of an unreasonable risk (i.e., depraved heart killing).

A person under a duty to aid another because of a contractual or familial relationship is guilty of involuntary manslaughter if death occurs because of unreasonable failure to give that aid.

An intent to kill constitutes malice (*mens rea* for common law murder).

A defendant must have a mental state of *malice* when acting to end the victim's life to be guilty of murder.

Murder – intentional killings

Intent to kill has two definitions:

1) the desire to accomplish a specific result.

2) engaging in such actions that the result is inevitable even though not explicitly desired.

The motive behind that intent is irrelevant in establishing intent.

The killing of a terminally ill patient who pleads with a person to end their life is murder at common law because it is an intentional killing.

The consent of the victim is not a defense to intentional killing.

The doctrine of transferred intent makes the killing of an unintended victim an intentional killing if it occurs due to an intent to kill the victim.

If a person employs a mechanical device that kills a person when activated, the intent to set up the device is equivalent to the intent to activate it.

If there are no mitigating circumstances or defenses to the killing, the person setting up the device is guilty of murder.

An intentional killing by a person threatened with death if they do not complete the killing is murder; there is no defense of duress to murder.

Murder – intent to do great bodily harm

Inflicting severe bodily harm on a victim that was not likely to cause death constitutes murder if the victim dies due to the infliction of that serious bodily harm.

A single blow administered by a fist would not ordinarily give rise to an inference that the actor intended severe bodily harm; a severe and prolonged beating or kicking a victim indicates such intent.

The infliction of a wound with a gun or a knife or other weapon would ordinarily give rise to the inference that intent to do great bodily harm was present.

The victim must die from injuries inflicted with the intent to do serious bodily harm before this malice becomes the malice needed for murder.

Felony murder

Felony murder occurs only when the defendant is committing or attempting to commit a felony, which qualifies as a felony supporting felony murder.

If the defendant is not guilty of the underlying felony, they are not guilty of felony murder. Often this is the best defense to the charge of felony murder.

A person is not guilty of felony murder if the underlying felony has not commenced or is not completed when the death occurs.

Mayhem, **R**ape, **B**urglary, **A**rson, **K**idnapping, **E**scape and **R**obbery (acronym MR. BAKER) are common law felonies that support felony murder.

Manslaughter and assault and battery, even though common law felonies, cannot be the underlying felony for felony murder.

Neither intent to kill, nor intent to commit serious bodily harm, is an element of the malice necessary to support felony murder.

An intentional killing during a felony provides two bases of malice for common law murder.

A death that occurs during a conspiracy to commit a MR. BAKER felony constitutes felony murder, imputed to all conspirators when the killing occurs unless the killing was beyond the scope of the conspiracy (e.g., rape by one actor during a bank robbery).

The killing of a co-felon in the course of a felony by a third person does not sustain a felony murder charge against the surviving felon because, under the Redline rule, the killing is justifiable homicide.

Depraved heart murder

A defendant is guilty of murder if they engage in conduct involving a wanton and willful disregard of unreasonable human risk, resulting in death.

The reckless conduct must involve a substantial degree of risk to human life.

The risk involved is to be assessed considering what the defendant knows, and the risk taken must be unjustifiable under the circumstances.

Examples of conduct that constitute the malice for malignant heart murder (depraved heart murder) if death occurs because of the action are:

- firing bullets in a confined space, through a wall, or into an urban area for confusing police;
- playing Russian roulette;
- deliberately and unjustifiably driving a car onto a crowded sidewalk;
- using deceit to convince an individual to take action likely to get them killed.

Homicide exam questions

The wording of a question may require discarding the standard pecking order of analysis of homicide crimes.

Typically, felony murder is considered first-degree murder and more serious than murder under the depraved-heart doctrine.

A question may suggest that murder under the depraved-heart doctrine is more serious than killing during a common law felony in a specific situation.

It is crucial to carefully read the question and be prepared to suspend the standard principles of black letter law if the question reads that way.

Degrees of murder

Since there are no degrees of murder at common law, a question concerning degrees of murder will set forth a statute that controls how degrees of murder are calculated.

Many statutes define first-degree murder as killing with deliberate, premeditated malice aforethought, limiting first-degree murder to planned, intentional killings.

When the malice for murder intends to do great bodily harm or with the recklessness which constitutes depraved heart murder, the murder is usually classified as second-degree murder.

Voluntary manslaughter

To reduce a murder crime where the malice was either the intent to kill or intent to do great bodily harm, to voluntary manslaughter, there must be:

(a) adequate provocation to inflame a reasonable person into the heat of passion, and

(b) the defendant must have been in such a state, and

(c) the killing must have taken place at a time when the passions of a reasonable person would not have cooled, and those of the defendant did not cool.

Where the malice for murder is felony murder or depraved heart murder, there is no reduction of the murder crime to manslaughter.

A violent battery, witnessing or learning about spousal infidelity, mutual affray, and an illegal arrest satisfy the adequate provocation element of voluntary manslaughter.

Mere words, no matter how insulting, are not adequate provocation for violence.

A second basis for reducing murder to voluntary manslaughter is when the defendant has the right to self-defense or defend another. However, such a defense will not result in an acquittal because it was not properly perfected.

For example, a defendant only had a right to use non-deadly force to defend themself but used deadly force, or a defendant failed to retreat where the retreat doctrine was applicable.

Under the doctrine of *transferred intent*, the killing will be reduced from murder to manslaughter if the defendant killed the victim mistakenly when trying to kill another whose death would have resulted in manslaughter rather than a murder conviction.

Involuntary manslaughter

Willful, wanton conduct is behavior slightly less egregious than the conduct which forms the basis of malice in depraved heart murder.

A death caused by willful, wanton, but not the defendant's intentional conduct, is involuntary manslaughter.

If death occurs while the defendant is engaged in a misdemeanor, which is morally wrong (a misdemeanor *malum in se*), he/she is guilty of involuntary manslaughter.

Generally, there is no affirmative duty to aid a person in peril and no criminal liability on the person in a position to give aid who fails to provide aid.

A person is under a duty to aid if they have a contractual obligation to do so, their actions (or inactions) put the victim in peril, or there is a parent-child or other family relationship between the defendant and the victim.

In such circumstances, if the failure to render aid results in death, the refusal to give aid can constitute willful, wanton conduct, causing the defendant to be guilty of involuntary manslaughter.

A defendant must act in a willful, wanton manner in performing the act, ending the victim's life to be guilty of involuntary manslaughter.

An unreasonable belief concerning the defendant's threat of harm is not justification for engaging in willful, wanton conduct.

Elements for murder statutes

Note the terms of the statute given in the question, which separates murder into degrees.

Intentional killings and felony murder are two elements of malice classified as first-degree murder.

Intention to do great bodily harm and depraved heart murder are two elements of malice classified as second-degree murder.

For an intentional killing, determine if the intent was formed due to deliberate premeditation and whether circumstances reduce the crime to voluntary manslaughter or provide a total defense to the murder crime such as self-defense.

Self-defense

Deadly force is likely to cause death, whether or not death occurs in a particular instance.

Non-deadly force is not likely to cause death, even though death occurred.

A defendant who uses deadly force can successfully raise *self-defense* to a homicide charge if they reasonably believe they are in danger of death or great bodily harm, even if not actually in such danger.

A defendant who uses deadly force can successfully raise a defense if they used that deadly force to apprehend a dangerous felon or to prevent a dangerous felony from being committed

The defense is successful for misdemeanor crimes if the force used is non-deadly.

If a jurisdiction requires a person to retreat before using deadly force in self-defense, a retreat is not required if the person believes that there is no reasonable method of retreat or if attacked in their home.

Even though they are in danger of death or serious bodily harm, a defendant does NOT have the right of self-defense if:

- they are in the commission of a felony,
- a police officer lawfully arrests,
- they were the original aggressor, except when the original aggressor attacks with non-deadly force and is met with deadly force or unless they:
    1) completely terminates their status as an aggressor, and
    2) make that known to the person attacked.

Defense of property does not justify deadly force.

If a person has a valid right of self-defense against A and kills B by mistake, they have a defense to a charge that they murdered B because that killing is justified under the doctrine of *transferred intent.*

Defense of others

A person using deadly force to defend another, in the belief that the person defended has the right to use deadly force in self-defense, has a valid defense in a criminal prosecution, even if the person defended does not have the right of self-defense because the person defended was the original aggressor.

A person has the right to use the same force, defending others as they do defend themself.

The right to use the same force is not limited to family members.

Other defenses to homicide crimes

Justifiable homicide is a killing permitted by law, such as the killing by the executioner in a death penalty case or the killing by soldiers on the battlefield.

Justifiable homicide is not criminal homicide.

Duress occurs when an individual commits an act against their will because of a fear of death or substantial bodily harm threatened by another human being.

Necessity relates to coercion by nonhuman elements, such as natural forces threatening an individual's life.

Neither duress nor necessity is a defense to a homicide crime.

In a felony murder case, duress or necessity can be a defense to the underlying felony, thereby eliminating an essential element of felony murder.

Notes for active learning

Other Crimes Against the Person

Assault and battery

A criminal battery is the unlawful application of force, either by direct contact or indirect physical contact, to a person or recognized extension.

The force may be direct physical touching or using a gun (or another weapon) applied either against the body of the victim or something closely associated with the victim.

Intent or conduct amounting to criminal negligence forms the *mens rea* for battery.

A person has the right to use non-deadly force in self-defense if attacked with non-deadly force.

A defendant using non-deadly instead of deadly force in self-defense against an aggressor does not have to retreat.

The retreat doctrine only applies in limited circumstances to the use of deadly force against the aggressor.

Whether actual or implied, consent is a defense to assault and battery.

Rape

Consent to intercourse would be a defense to rape even if the defendant committed fraud in inducing the victim to have intercourse.

If the defendant commits fraud in the *factum* instead of fraud in the inducement, the victim does not realize they are having intercourse; their consent is not a valid defense.

Penetration, no matter how slight, is the *actus reus* for rape.

At common law, a husband could not be guilty of raping his spouse.

The underage participant in intercourse cannot be found guilty as a conspirator to commit statutory rape or as an accessory to statutory rape.

In most jurisdictions, the mistake of the underage participant's age is not a defense to statutory rape.

A mistake of age is a defense to the crime of attempted statutory rape.

Kidnapping

Two elements to simple kidnapping:

false imprisonment, and

asportation (carrying away).

Demand for a ransom is a necessary element of aggravated kidnapping but not an element of simple kidnapping.

For the false imprisonment element of kidnapping, the perpetrator must confine the victim against their will, and the victim must be aware of the confinement.

Any movement of the victim of false imprisonment without their consent from the place where imprisoned satisfies the asportation element of kidnapping.

Property Crimes

Common law theft crimes

The three common law theft crimes are:

larceny

embezzlement

obtaining property by false pretenses.

Since these crimes are mutually exclusive, many questions require distinguishing them.

Larceny requires a trespassory taking; the defendant cannot have the rightful possession when the property is removed from the victim.

Embezzlement is when the defendant had rightful possession when the conversion occurred.

Obtaining property by *false pretenses* occurs when the defendant obtains the property's title and possession due to a fraudulent act.

Larceny

Larceny is the trespassory taking and asportation (carrying-away) of another's personal property, with the intent to deprive the possessor of the property permanently.

An intent to destroy the property is equivalent to permanently deprive the possessor.

Any movement of the property of another, no matter how slight, satisfies the asportation element of larceny.

The specific intent necessary for larceny (i.e., to permanently deprive the person entitled to possession of the property) is missing if the defendant intended to return the property when they committed the trespassory taking.

If the property is unintentionally destroyed while in possession of a defendant who took it with the intent to return it, the defendant is not guilty of larceny.

If the defendant does not intend to steal because they mistakenly think, either reasonably or unreasonably, that the property belongs to them, they are not guilty of larceny.

The trespassory taking element of larceny is satisfied if an innocent agent takes the property at the defendant's direction.

A person holding title to property can be guilty of larceny if they wrongfully take that property from a person entitled to possession of it.

If a lower-level employee is in physical possession of their employer's property, the employee only has custody of it.

Embezzlement

Embezzlement is completed when a person in rightful possession of property converts it to their use to permanently deprive the property owner.

Without "possession" of the goods, the crime is larceny, not embezzlement.

An offer to return the property later does not negate the crime.

Embezzlement only occurs when the defendant in rightful possession of the personal property of another converts it to their use.

If a defendant converts property to their use and intends to steal, they are guilty of the crime of larceny, not embezzlement.

If a bailee, who has possession of the totality of the goods entrusted to them by the bailor, breaks into the container holding goods and takes a portion, they are deemed only to have custody of the goods taken.

Obtaining property by false pretenses

To constitute the crime of obtaining property by false pretenses:

1) There must be a false material fact.
2) The defendant must know that it is false; an honest but unreasonable belief that the statement is true is not enough to constitute guilt.
3) The victim must rely on the statement of material fact.
4) The defendant must obtain title to the property. If the property is cash and is deliberately delivered to the defendant, the defendant's possession would equal title.
5) The defendant must intend to deprive the victim of the property permanently.

An honest belief in the truth of the defendant's representation, even if that belief is unreasonable, negates the specific intent necessary for the crime of obtaining property by false pretenses.

Larceny by trick

Larceny by trick is a form of larceny which occurs when the defendant obtains possession of the property by fraud.

Since the defendant does not have rightful possession of the property when they form the intent to steal, there is a trespassory taking, and the crime is known as larceny by trick.

Even though the defendant has physical possession of the property, this is not a conversion from one in possession, so the crime is not embezzlement.

Receiving stolen goods

A belief, either reasonable or unreasonable that the goods possessed by the defendant were not stolen is a defense to the crime of receiving stolen goods.

The property must have the characteristic of being "stolen goods" when the defendant possesses them for a conviction to occur.

If goods, once stolen, are recovered by the police, restored to their rightful owners, and offered to a defendant, the defendant cannot be convicted of receiving stolen goods.

Robbery

The underlying crimes of larceny or attempted larceny are essential elements of the crimes of robbery and attempted robbery.

For the crime to be robbery and not larceny, the trespassory taking must occur from the person through force or intimidation.

The element "from the person" means property within the person's control.

The force and intimidation must coincide with the larceny.

If all elements of robbery are present, the underlying crime of larceny and (if present) the underlying crimes of assault and battery merge into the crime of robbery.

If the defendant has stolen property, the use of force or intimidation to retain possession of it does not constitute the crime of robbery.

The threat to use force in the future and obtaining property through the use of that threat is the crime of extortion, not robbery.

The victim must be intimidated for the crime to be robbery.

Burglary

Common law burglary is defined as breaking and entering the *dwelling of another* (burglary cannot be committed in your own house) in the *nighttime* to *commit a felony therein*.

Modern statutes redefined burglary to eliminate the nighttime requirement and include all buildings.

The breaking and the entering elements of burglary need not coincide.

To be guilty of burglary, the defendant must have the specific intent to commit a felony on the premises at the moment of the entering. There is no requirement for the intended felony to be successful.

If a person enters through an open door, the breaking element of burglary is not present.

Burglary is committed if the defendant breaks and enters a dwelling house, even if the defendant does not break when they first enter the dwelling.

Breaking and entering need not occur by force.

If the defendant obtains entry to the property through fraud, the breaking and entering elements are present.

Since the common law definition of burglary requires that the property be the dwelling house of another, a person cannot commit burglary by breaking and entering their own home.

There is no breaking when entering through an open window/door or when the premises are open to the public.

A defendant in a space open to the public can be guilty of burglary if they break and enter into an adjoining space not open to the public.

There is no breaking and entering if the defendant opens personal property (e.g., a chest) while the property is open to the public.

A defendant is not guilty of burglary if committing larceny on premises open to the public.

If the original entry to the property was not breaking and entering, the defendant could be guilty of burglary if they break into a portion of the real estate once on the premises.

A defendant is not guilty of burglary by entering a commercial establishment while open to the public, hiding until after closing time, stealing, and breaking out of the property.

Arson

At common law, arson is the intentional burning of the dwelling house of another.

The definition has statutorily been expanded to the burning of a building, including one's own dwelling house, to defraud an insurer.

Arson has been committed if an act was done under circumstances where there was a direct and strong likelihood that a fire would result even if the defendant did not desire it, or if the fire resulted from reckless conduct by the defendant.

Since the common law definition of arson requires that the property involved be the dwelling house of another, a defendant cannot commit common law arson by burning their house.

Most jurisdictions have enacted statutes to include burning one's home as arson.

For the defendant to be guilty of arson, there must be combustion of a portion of real property.

The burning of personal property alone is insufficient to constitute arson.

Starting a fire accidentally does not constitute the *mens rea* for arson.

However, if the defendant lets an accidental fire continue to burn even though they could have easily put it out, the decision to let it burn is sufficient *mens rea* for arson.

Forgery

Forgery is the fraudulent making of false writings that have legal significance.

Notes for active learning

Inchoate Crimes

An inchoate (i.e., incomplete) crime is preparing to commit another crime (e.g., attempt).

Attempts

A person cannot be guilty of the crime of *attempt to commit* a crime unless they intend to commit the crime.

This applies to crimes, including strict liability offenses, where intent to commit the completed crime is not required.

The crime of attempt merges with the substantive crime if the defendant completes the substantive crime.

If the act which the defendant intends to perpetrate is not a crime, they cannot be guilty of attempt at any stage of their action, even if they think their act is a crime and intends to be engaged in criminal conduct.

An attempt requires substantial preparation to commit a substantive crime. Substantial preparation requires proximity to the place and time of the execution of the target crime.

Attempt is likely to be found where the acts required for the crime have been completed.

Attempt is likely to be found where the defendant has progressed so far that they would be unlikely to stop without outside interference.

Factual impossibility is a defense to an attempted crime if and only if the defendant did not know that the commission of the crime was inherently impossible.

Conspiracy

Conspiracy is defined as an agreement by two or more individuals for an unlawful purpose.

The agreement among conspirators necessary for that combination can be inferred from the parties' actions and need not be expressed.

To be a conspirator, a defendant must intend to agree with other conspirators and intend to accomplish the conspiracy objective.

Conspiracy is a separate crime from the substantive offense; the object of the conspiracy.

The crime of conspiracy does not merge with that substantive offense if the conspiracy accomplishes its objective.

A conspiracy is a completed crime at common law, even if no conspirator has committed an overt act in pursuance of the conspiracy.

The crime is not complete under federal law until an overt act occurs.

At common law, a conspiracy starts at the time of the agreement.

In a jurisdiction in which there must be an overt act to complete the crime of conspiracy, the conspiracy commences when the overt act takes place.

The conspiracy ends when the conspiracy objectives are accomplished or when abandoned.

A person who is a conspirator is guilty not only of the crime of conspiracy but of substantive crimes committed by co-conspirators according to the conspiracy if they are within the scope of the conspiracy and are committed while the conspiracy existed.

To be guilty of conspiracy, the defendant must combine with at least one other who is not necessary to the substantive crime to commit an unlawful or lawful act by unlawful means.

There must be as many conspirators as there are persons needed to commit the substantive offense plus one.

Ordinarily, two or more persons are needed for the crime of conspiracy.

For example, if two persons are needed to commit the substantive crime (e.g., the crime of adultery), there must be three conspirators.

A member of a legislatively protected class (e.g., a minor involved in statutory rape) cannot be counted as a conspirator.

If all possible conspirators other than the defendant are acquitted of conspiracy, the defendant must be acquitted.

A person who has committed the crime of conspiracy is not guilty of the other conspirators' substantive crimes if they *withdraw* from the conspiracy before the substantive crimes are committed.

To *withdraw from* the conspiracy, a conspirator must disaffirm the conspiracy's goals and inform the co-conspirators of the withdrawal.

Withdrawal is not a defense to the conspiracy crime.

If persons combine to perform a lawful act, they are not guilty of conspiracy even if they believe that the act they are to perform is illegal.

The impossibility of accomplishing the purpose of the conspiracy is not a defense to the crime of conspiracy.

A person is guilty of conspiracy only if they intend to join with another to commit a crime.

Solicitation

The act of asking another person to commit a crime with the intent that the person asked should commit that crime is a sufficient *actus reus* and *mens rea* for the crime of solicitation.

Once a person solicited agrees to commit the crime, there is a conspiracy between the solicitor and the person solicited.

The crime of solicitation is merged into the conspiracy so that the solicitor is no longer guilty of conspiracy.

Parties to crimes

The person who knows that the principal is committing a crime and intends to help the principal is guilty as an accomplice.

A person, even though they intend to help with the commission of an illegal act, is not guilty as an accessory if the act which they are helping the principal commit is, in fact, not a criminal act.

Presence at the crime scene without assisting or encouraging the principal does not incur accomplice liability.

If a person present at a crime scene encourages the principal to commit the criminal act, they are guilty as an accomplice.

Supplying goods or services which have criminal and non-criminal uses to a person, with the knowledge that they will be used in a crime, can cause the supplier to be guilty of accomplice liability.

Supplying goods that can only be used for criminal purposes without precise knowledge of their intended use can be the basis for accomplice liability if the recipient uses those goods to commit a crime.

An essential element of the crime of accessory after the fact is that the defendant must have aided the felon to hinder the felon's capture or conviction.

Notes for active learning

General Principles

General intent crimes

There must be a coincidence of the intent to accomplish the *actus reus* with the actual accomplishment of the *actus reus* for a defendant to be guilty of a general intent crime.

Intent for criminal law is when a person desires a result, and that result occurs.

Intent is present even though the person thought the end would be accomplished by different means.

Specific intent crimes

To be guilty of a specific intent crime, the defendant must have the required specific intent, which is more than an attempt to accomplish the *actus reus* when accomplishing the *actus reus*.

For example, in the specific intent crime of larceny, the defendant must have the intent to deprive the possessor of their property when they engage in the trespassory taking.

The mental state of maliciousness is associated with an intentional act, but it can be present where the defendant acts recklessly.

Strict liability

If a statute does not include language requiring fault, a court may impose liability without fault (i.e., strict liability) after considering factors, such as:

legislative history,

severity of the punishment for the crime,

seriousness of harm to the public created by the criminal activity,

defendant's opportunities to be informed of the facts which lead to an offense,

difficulty of proving *mens rea*,

number of violations,

likelihood that prosecution is likely to occur.

No mental state is required for the defendant to be guilty of a strict liability offense.

A defendant is guilty of strict liability if they accomplish the *actus reus*.

A principal can be guilty of a strict liability offense for an act performed by their agent, which is within the scope of authority.

Specifically, forbidding such an agent to perform an illegal act is not a defense.

To be guilty of an attempt to commit a strict liability offense (distinguished from the guilt of the crime itself), the defendant must have the specific intent to commit the offense.

Mistake of fact and law

Neither a mistake of law nor a mistake of fact, whether reasonable or unreasonable, is a defense to a strict liability offense.

A reasonable mistake of fact is a defense to a general intent crime.

Neither a mistake of law nor an unreasonable mistake of fact is a defense to a general intent crime.

A reasonable and unreasonable mistake of fact and a mistake of law that prevent the specific intent from being formed are valid defenses to a specific intent crime.

If a crime requires the specific intent of "knowing," and the defendant subjectively does not know that their actions are criminal because they relied on the erroneous advice of a lawyer, the defendant is not guilty of the crime.

Insanity

If the individual knows what they are doing and knows that it is a crime, delusions caused by mental illness will not establish the defense of insanity under the *M'Naghten* test.

The *M'Naghten* test of insanity does *not* include the irresistible impulse test.

Intoxication

Generally, voluntary intoxication is not a defense to a crime.

However, if voluntary intoxication prevents the specific intent necessary for a specific intent crime from being formed, the defendant is not guilty of the specific intent crime.

If the crime of first-degree murder requires deliberate premeditation and voluntary intoxication prevents the defendant from premeditating, the defendant would be guilty of second-degree murder.

Causation

If the defendant sets in motion actions that cause the victim's death, the fact that the victim would have died sooner if they had not set those actions in motion is not a defense to the homicide crime.

A defendant is not guilty of murder, even though they inflict serious bodily harm, which will eventually result in death if the victim dies from an independent cause.

If a defendant inflicts serious bodily harm on the victim, which would not cause death if the victim received proper medical treatment, the defendant is guilty of murder when the victim dies from their injury due to lack of proper medical treatment.

The improper medical treatment is not an independent cause relieving the defendant of liability.

Justification

A police officer is not criminally liable if they used deadly force to apprehend a person when they reasonably believe that they are committing or escaping from a dangerous felony.

A police officer is not justified in using deadly force to arrest a person for a non-dangerous felony or a misdemeanor.

A person who assists a police officer in apprehending a criminal has the same right to use force as the police officer they are assisting.

Notes for active learning

Constitutional Protections

Arrest

An arrest warrant is required to validly arrest an individual in their home, except if the arrest occurs while the arresting officer was in *hot pursuit.*

If the person commits a misdemeanor in a police officer's presence, the officer has the right to arrest without a warrant.

A police officer who has a reasonable belief that a person has committed a felony has the right to arrest without a warrant at any place except in the defendant's home.

The fact that the defendant was unlawfully arrested is not a defense to subsequent criminal prosecution for the offense for which they were arrested.

However, evidence seized as the result of an unlawful arrest is inadmissible in court.

Definition of a search

Only searches by governmental authorities, persons acting as agents, or under their direction and control, are governed by the Fourth and Fourteenth Amendments' exclusionary rule.

The exclusionary rule does not foreclose evidence obtained by searches by private parties.

Searches that require warrants or an exception to the warrant requirements to be valid are closely tied to the concept of a reasonable expectation of privacy.

While a homeowner has a reasonable expectation of privacy from ground-level intrusion in the fenced-in backyard of their home, they have no reasonable expectation of privacy from aerial surveillance.

A homeowner is protected from searches by advanced devices measuring heat escaping from their home.

The person, desk file, and file cabinets in a private office at work, a changing room in a clothing store, and containers of personal effects are protected areas.

An individual does not have a reasonable expectation of privacy in open fields beyond the home's curtilage. Warrantless searches beyond the curtilage of homes are permitted.

The government can obtain financial records in the custody of banks, accountants, or other third parties by a subpoena on the third party without obtaining a search warrant.

There is no search and seizure if the object taken is in plain view from a place where the law enforcement agent has a lawful right to be.

Search procedure – standing

An individual only has standing to object to searches that violate their reasonable expectation of privacy, not that of third persons.

Ordinarily, the claimant must show a possessory interest in the items seized and a legitimate expectation of privacy in the areas searched.

A search's validity cannot be challenged in a grand jury proceeding.

The proper way to raise the validity of a search is by a pre-trial motion to suppress.

An objection to the admission of improperly seized evidence at trial is available only when the search facts are unknown to the defendant beforehand.

A defendant has the right to establish standing without admitting the seized evidence was under their control and without that admission being admissible at trial.

A guest in a home has standing to challenge a search of that home.

Search incident to a valid arrest

The police may search a defendant's person and the area in their immediate control incident to a valid arrest.

To protect safety, police may, incident to a lawful arrest, search the premises in which the arrest took place to find other persons who may have been present and involved in the crime.

The search must immediately follow or be contemporaneous with the arrest.

Objects seized in a warrantless search made according to an invalid arrest are inadmissible.

Objects seized in a search before there is a valid ground to make an arrest are inadmissible unless there is another ground than a search incident to an arrest to justify their admissibility.

Consent searches

Consent must be by either the owner or the person entrusted with the property.

A person other than the defendant can give valid consent to search areas over which they have access jointly with the defendant.

Consent obtained by fraud or duress is invalid.

The consent given by an individual to search their property must be voluntary, but the suspect need not be warned that they do not have to consent.

The superintendent of an apartment house complex or the manager of a hotel does not have the authority to validly consent to the search of an apartment or room in a hotel rented to persons occupying the premises.

Automobile searches

There is a lesser expectation of privacy in a motor vehicle than in a person's home, and therefore greater latitude to permit warrantless searches.

A non-owner passenger does not have standing to object to the search of an automobile.

If police engage in the random stopping and searching of motor vehicles, the search is invalid.

The police may conduct a valid search of vehicles at a fixed checkpoint, at the border, or the functional equivalent of a border.

If the police have probable cause to stop a motor vehicle, including a stop for a traffic violation, the police may validly search the automobile (including the trunk and containers in the automobile) without a warrant.

The search need not take place immediately. If the motor vehicle is impounded, the police may conduct an inventory search.

Regulatory search

A regulatory search may be made without a warrant, even if the search is to obtain evidence of criminal activity.

Regulatory searches are confined to businesses and premises that must be licensed to operate legally (e.g., gambling establishments, businesses serving alcoholic beverages) and businesses selling merchandise where criminal activity is likely (e.g., pawn shops).

Other warrantless searches

A "stop and frisk" pat-down search is constitutionally valid even if there are no grounds for a valid arrest, as long as there is reasonable suspicion of criminal behavior.

The search is limited to a "pat-down" search but may be extended to a more intrusive search if the *pat-down* uncovers an object which reasonably could be a weapon.

A search of school lockers without a warrant is permissible.

Searches under a search warrant

Police or anther investigatory agencies may not issue a search warrant.

A search warrant may only be issued by a judge or other neutral magistrate based upon probable cause set forth in the warrant application.

The application for a search warrant does not require independent evidence on the basis for the search and the reliability of the informant.

The magistrate can issue a valid warrant based upon the totality of the circumstances.

The application for the search warrant must state, with particularity, the place to be searched and the objects of the search.

If, when executing the warrant, the police find evidence not explicitly mentioned in the warrant, they may validly seize it.

If the application for a search warrant is not sufficient to establish probable cause, but the magistrate nevertheless grants a search warrant, and the police execute it believing in good faith that the search warrant is valid, the property seized according to the search is admissible.

If the police are granted a search warrant based upon information that they know is false, evidence obtained according to that warrant is inadmissible because the search is invalid.

Fruits of an illegal search

If a search is illegal and information obtained from that illegal search is used to conduct further searches that would otherwise be proper or to obtain admissions from a defendant, which they would otherwise not have obtained, the information or the evidence obtained will be excluded from evidence as *the fruits of an illegal search.*

Coerced confessions

If either the police or a private individual obtains a confession or admission by coercion (either physical or psychological), the statement made is inadmissible for any purpose.

This rule against admission by coercion applies even if the defendant was given the Miranda warning and waived it.

If a coerced confession is improperly admitted, the conviction will not be overturned on appeal if the admission of the confession constitutes a harmless error.

Miranda warning

The *Miranda warning* is applicable only when there is interrogation by the police while the defendant is in custody.

An individual is in custody if their freedom to leave the police's presence is restricted.

A statement made to a private individual not working in concert with the police is not subject to Miranda rights limitations.

Volunteered statements are not the products of interrogation.

If the police engage in conduct other than questioning the defendant designed to elicit a statement, that statement is considered the product of interrogation.

Statements made by a defendant in custody due to interrogation are inadmissible at a subsequent trial unless the defendant is informed of Miranda rights and waives them.

If the defendant exercises their Miranda rights by demanding a lawyer, statements made in response to questioning after that demand and before a lawyer is present are inadmissible.

Further questioning can occur only after the defendant consults with their lawyer and agrees to further questions.

A statement given in violation of the defendant's Miranda rights is admissible to impeach their credibility if they take the stand in their trial and testify in a manner inconsistent with the statement previously given.

If the defendant exercises their Miranda right to remain silent while in custody, that silence in the face of accusations made to them that they committed the crime cannot be used in the trial as an adoptive admission.

The police need not inform the defendant of the charge they are investigating to obtain a valid waiver of Miranda rights.

If a defendant waives their Miranda rights and agrees to submit to interrogation, they may be questioned about more subjects than the crime, which is the primary object of the police interrogation.

Once a defendant is indicted or otherwise formally charged with a crime, the right to counsel accrues. The defendant cannot be interrogated by the police except in the presence of counsel, even if given Miranda warnings and waived their Miranda rights.

Lineups and other forms of identification

A right to counsel at a lineup only after the criminal process (i.e., indictment) has occurred.

The fact of a lineup identification without counsel present after an indictment is not admissible at trial, but the victim can still make an in-court identification.

Testimonies about lineup identification and subsequent in-court identification are inadmissible if the pre-trial identification offends due process standards.

Due process is violated when the likelihood of proper identification is so remote because the victim could not observe the criminal or because the lineup, whether pre-indictment or post-indictment, is very prejudicial.

Right to counsel

A conviction is invalid if the defendant has not had the opportunity for the assistance of counsel in the trial of felonies and misdemeanors for which the defendant is incarcerated, or the penalty on conviction includes the possibility of incarceration.

A defendant has the right to refuse to have counsel appointed and act as their lawyer.

If they act as their lawyer, they cannot later raise inadequacy of representation or being denied the right to counsel.

A defendant has the right to have counsel provided to prosecute only one appeal.

A defendant's conviction will be reversed even if they had a lawyer if the representation is ruled inadequate.

An attorney representing a defendant who represents a co-defendant may have a conflict of interest, which is so severe that they cannot render effective assistance of counsel.

Public trial

The public's right to a public trial can be enforced by the news media even if both prosecutor and defendant object.

The court has the discretion to ban or limit the public at a trial if there is a substantial likelihood of prejudice to the defendant or a need to limit access to ensure an orderly proceeding.

Fair conduct by the prosecutor

A prosecutor has an affirmative obligation to disclose to the defendant material known or in possession of the prosecutor's office, which is exculpatory.

Speedy trial

The beginning point to measure a defendant's right to a speedy trial is when criminal proceedings commence, not the time that the crime is committed.

The prosecution can wait until the day before the statute of limitations expires to indict and start the clock on the right to a speedy trial.

The passage of time alone does not give the defendant the right to dismissal for lack of a speedy trial.

The defendant must show prejudice from the delay.

Jury trial

In a criminal case, the defendant is entitled to a jury trial if the greatest possible sentence can exceed six months in jail.

The defendant is entitled to be tried by a jury chosen from a venire in which there is no systematic racial, ethnic, or gender exclusion.

There is a right to challenge the jury's racial makeup, even if the defendant is not a member of the race excluded.

When selecting a petit jury, neither the defendant nor the prosecutor may use peremptory challenges to systematically exclude individuals of one race or gender from the jury.

The state may constitutionally try a defendant before a petit jury, which contains no members of the defendant's minority group if the procedure for selecting the jury venire was proper. There was no systematic exclusion of jurors through the exercise of peremptory challenges.

A judge must take some procedural steps before accepting a guilty plea; otherwise, the plea will not satisfy the process standard that the plea is voluntary and intelligent.

The judge must inform the defendant that they:

need not plead guilty,

has a right to a jury trial.

The judge must explain:

1) the elements of the crime with which the defendant is charged, and

2) the maximum possible legal penalty.

Confrontation

The prosecution has satisfied the defendant's right to confront the witness if the witness appeared at a preliminary hearing where the defendant had the right to cross-examine, and there is a valid excuse for the witness's failure to appear at trial.

Then, the evidence given at the preliminary hearing is admissible under the prior testimony exception to the hearsay rule.

A criminal defendant does not have the Sixth Amendment constitutional right to confront their accuser at a preliminary hearing.

If the accuser is a child who might suffer substantial emotional damage by appearing in the same room as the defendant, the accused's right to confront the witness is satisfied by watching the testimony electronically.

Severance

When two individuals are charged with the same crime and one has given a confession that implicates the other, the non-confessing defendant has the right to have their trial severed from that of the confessing defendant unless the statements in the confession implicating the non-confessing defendant can be excised.

When a confession is admissible against the confessing defendant but is inadmissible against the non-confessing defendant, severance is not required under *Nelson v. O'Neil* (1971) if the confessing defendant testifies at trial because the non-confessing defendant has the right to cross-examine about the truthfulness of that confession.

Standard of proof

To satisfy its burden of proof in a criminal case, the prosecution must prove *all elements of the offense beyond a reasonable doubt.*

In a murder case, the burden of proof includes showing that the elements which would reduce murder to manslaughter are not present.

If state law so provides, the defendant can be given the obligation to plead affirmative defenses and prove them by a preponderance of the evidence.

Unless the state has shifted the burden of proof of insanity to the defendant, once a criminal defendant has raised the defense of insanity, the prosecution must prove that the defendant is sane beyond a reasonable doubt.

In a voluntary manslaughter prosecution, lack of justification is an element of the crime and must be proven by the prosecution beyond a reasonable doubt.

Imposition of the death penalty

A court can only order the death penalty if the defendant has committed murder.

When there is a felony murder where several conspirators participated in the felony, the death penalty can only be administered to the individual who caused the death.

A statute mandating the death penalty for a specific crime is unconstitutional because a jury must have the opportunity to impose the death penalty only after considering mitigating factors.

The death penalty can only be imposed by a jury.

A judge can not impose the death penalty after the jury has convicted the defendant of the substantive crime.

Fair trial – post-trial stage

The appellate court may constitutionally vacate a sentence and order a new trial if it determines that the verdict is against the weight of the evidence.

While the prosecution cannot, except in rebuttal, introduce a defendant's criminal record in a criminal trial, the judge can review the record for purposes of deciding the appropriate sentence.

Double jeopardy

Jeopardy attaches to the double jeopardy clause in a criminal jury trial when the jury is sworn.

In a jury-waived trial, the double jeopardy clause becomes operational when the first witness begins to testify.

The defendant does not have the defense of double jeopardy when the judge declares a mistrial to benefit the defendant or appellate court orders a new trial from the defendant's appeal.

The prosecution has the right to appeal a criminal judgment of not guilty only if the appeals court's judgment will have the right to reinstitute a guilty verdict, and there will be no new trial.

If a defendant is tried and convicted of a criminal offense of assault and battery, and the victim later dies, the defense of double jeopardy does not apply to a subsequent homicide prosecution for the death arising out of the acts which constituted the assault and battery.

The statute of limitations on criminal activity starts to run when the last act, an element of the crime, occurs.

Double jeopardy prevents prosecution in a subsequent case for any crime with an essential element of the crime prosecuted earlier.

Double jeopardy does not prevent prosecution for a crime that coincided with but was not an essential element of the crime which was first prosecuted.

Collateral estoppel

Under the collateral estoppel (issue preclusion) branch of the double jeopardy clause, the prosecution may not constitutionally litigate issues that have been litigated and decided in favor of the defendant in a previous criminal case.

Notes for active learning

Guilty Pleas and Plea Bargaining

Plea colloquy

The plea conversation between a judge and a criminal defendant has four requirements:

nature of the charge,

maximum authorized sentence and mandatory minimum,

defendant's right to plead not guilty and go to trial, and

by pleading guilty, a defendant is waiving trial, and the case proceeds to sentence.

The court must ask the defendant if they understand each of these points and receive a voluntary affirmative response.

Failure by the court to advise the defendant of any of the above supplies grounds for a collateral attack of the plea.

If such an attack is successful, the guilty plea will be withdrawn, and the defendant will be allowed to enter a new plea.

A defendant may withdraw a guilty plea after sentencing if:

problem with a colloquy,

jurisdictional defect,

defendant prevails if deprived of effective assistance of counsel, and

prosecutor fails to fulfill their agreement.

Fifth Amendment privilege against compelled testimony

Anyone can assert the privilege in *any* proceeding where an individual testifies under oath.

Must be asserted *at the first opportunity,* or else it is lost.

Privilege against compelled testimony:

protected from compelled testimony only, does not apply to the state's use of a person's biological samples, and

prosecutors cannot comment on the assertion of the privilege.

Eliminating privilege against compelled testimony

There are three methods to eliminate the privilege against compelled testimony.

1) Immunity grant for the use and derivative use of testimony. The prosecution cannot use the defendant's testimony, or anything derived from it to convict.

   However, a defendant can be convicted based on evidence obtained before a grant of immunity.

2) Defendant takes the stand and waives the Fifth Amendment right against self-incrimination as to anything properly within the scope of cross-examination.

3) The statute of limitations has run on the underlying crime because of no criminal prosecution.

Punishment

Eighth Amendment prohibits:

1) Criminal penalties *grossly* disproportionate to the seriousness of the offense.
2) Death penalty statute that creates an automatic category for imposition.
3) Juries must be allowed to hear *all potentially mitigating evidence.*
4) Death penalty *prohibited* for a mentally disabled person, presently insane or was under 18 at the time of the offense.

Criminal Law and Procedure – Quick Facts

1. **Attempting**, even *with* criminal intent, to do an act that is *not* itself a crime is *not* a conviction that is likely to be upheld.

2. **Larceny** – the **taking** and **asportation** (i.e., carrying away) of another's personal property by *trespass* and with **intent to permanently deprive** the person of their interest in the property.

   For example, the moving of a refrigerator (e.g., by salesclerk) to the loading dock constitutes a taking and carrying away; since the clerk did *not* have permission to move merchandise in this way, it was trespassory. Since the clerk intended to permanently deprive the store of an interest in the refrigerator when they moved it, their subsequent *change of heart* was **too late**.

3. The element of **carrying away** (i.e., **asportation**) is satisfied when there is a **movement** of the property as **a step** in carrying it away.

4. The **continuing trespass doctrine** renders continued possession of the property to be trespassory.

   So, if the trespasser later develops the intent to steal, the actions are considered **larceny**.

5. **Attempted murder** is a *specific intent* crime, though a defendant can be found guilty of murder when their actions demonstrate a very high degree of recklessness.

   If the charge is **attempted murder**, it *must* be shown that the defendant committed an act with the **intent** to kill someone.

6. The Fourth Amendment is *not* violated by a statute authorizing warrantless searches of a **probationer's home** with reasonable grounds to believe contraband is present.

7. If a statute is intended to **protect members of a limited class from exploitation**, members of that class are presumed to be immune from liability, even if they participated in the crime in a manner that would otherwise make them liable.

8. The defendant has a legitimate defense where the **statute** under which charged was ***not* published or made reasonably available** before the conduct.

9. For an **affirmative defense** (e.g., insanity), it is permissible to impose the **burden of proof on the defendant**.

10. **Larceny by trick** occurs when property **possession** is obtained by **misrepresentation.**

11. **Pretenses** are the appropriate offense when the misrepresentations have prompted the victim to **convey title** of the property to the defendant.

Relationship matrix

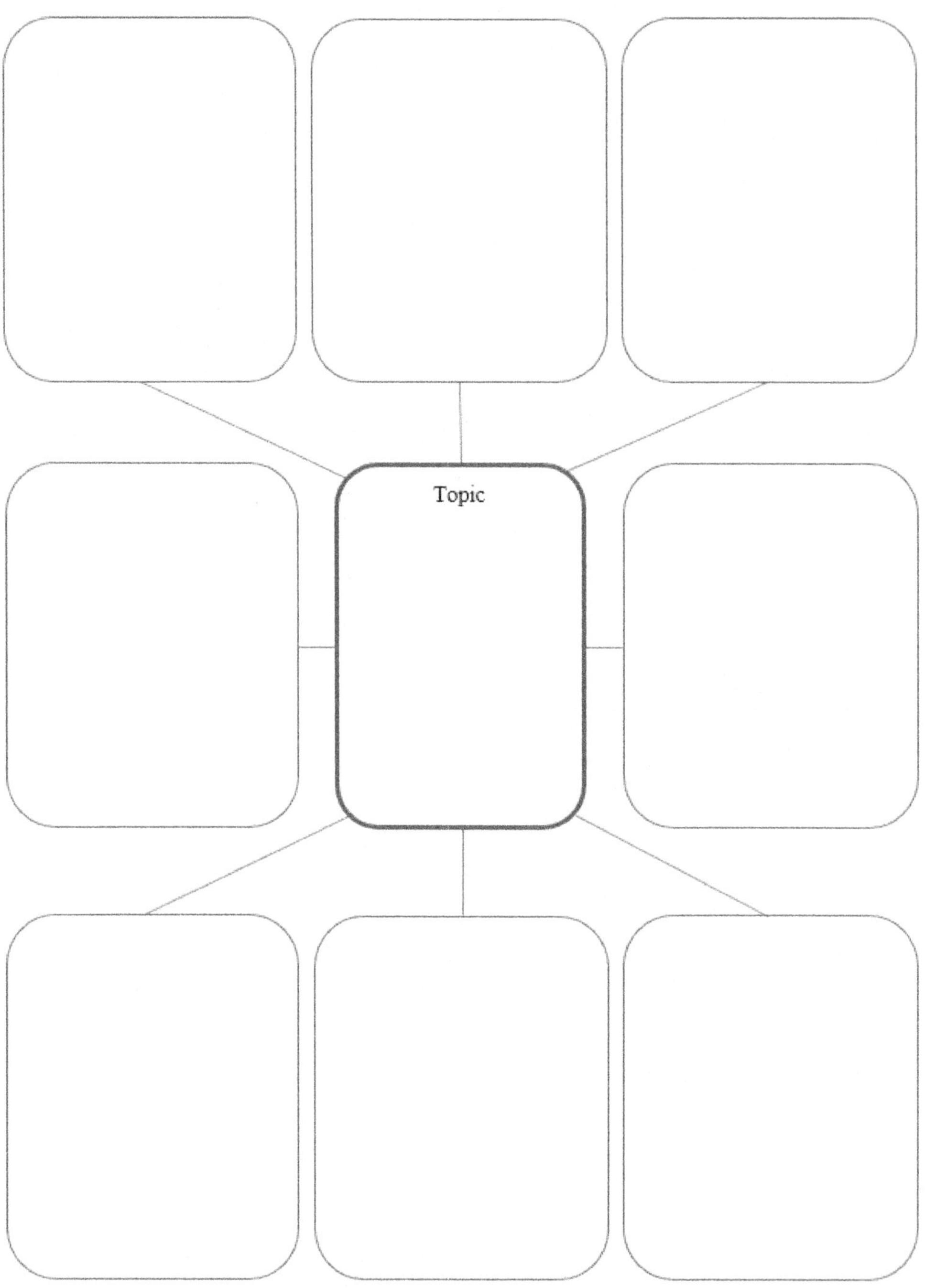

Notes for active learning

Notes for active learning

Evidence

Evidence topics tested on the exam are relatively predictable. However, it is a complex subject to master. Evidence topics frequently tested are hearsay and its admissibility, impeachment, relevancy, reasons for excluding evidence, presentation of evidence, privileges, and policy exclusions. Other issues tested include character evidence, witness testimony, writings, recordings, and photographs. On the essay section, Evidence generally is not combined with other topics. However, it may be tested with Criminal Law and Procedure (e.g., hearsay and *Miranda*).

The statements herein were compiled by analyzing released Evidence questions and setting forth the principles of law governing the correct answers. Review these principles before preparing answers to practice Evidence questions. Memorize this governing law and understand how it applies to the correct answer.

Per the National Conference of Bar Examiners (NCBE), evidence questions should be answered per the Federal Rules of Evidence, as currently in effect.

Presentation of Evidence

Personal knowledge

A witness must testify from *first-hand knowledge*, except when testifying to statements defined out of hearsay or come within exceptions to the hearsay rule.

Expert witnesses are an exception to the requirement of first-hand knowledge.

Under Federal Rule of Evidence 612, if a witness uses a writing to refresh their memory for testifying, either while or before testifying, if the court in its discretion determines it is necessary for the interests of justice, an adverse party is entitled to have the writing produced at the hearing to inspect, cross-examine, and introduce into evidence those portions relating to the testimony of the witness.

Leading questions

Leading questions are permitted on direct examination if a trial judge declares the witness hostile.

Leading questions are permissible on cross-examination and direct examination concerning preliminary matters, young children, and when the witness's memory is exhausted.

A lawyer for a party called by the opponent cannot examine by cross-examination on new matters with leading questions.

Argumentative questions

No questions are permitted on direct or cross-examination where the examiner argues with the witness.

Refreshing recollection

If the memory of a witness is exhausted, the examiner is permitted to show documents or make suggestions to revive their memory so that they once again can testify from personal knowledge.

When a witness testifies from present memory, even if it is refreshed by reference to a document, testimony from present memory based upon their knowledge is not hearsay.

Since the evidence offered is the witness's present knowledge, the document itself need not be admissible.

If it is not possible to refresh the memory of a witness, but, when their memory was fresh, the witness recorded that memory, the record of that past recollection is admissible as an exception to the hearsay rule if it satisfies the requirements for the admissibility of a writing.

Under Federal Rule of Evidence 803 (5), the document itself is not admissible, but the contents may be read to the jury.

If a witness refers to a document immediately before testifying or brings it to the witness stand, opposing counsel can examine it during cross-examination.

Offers of proof

If on direct examination that the judge sustains an objection to a question, the party conducting the examination must state for the record what the answer to the question would be (i.e., make an offer of proof) if they intend to appeal based on the trial judge erroneously excluding the question from evidence.

An offer of proof is not required if a question is excluded from cross-examination.

Preservation of issues for appeal

Counsel must object to evidence when it is offered if claiming on appeal that it was improperly admitted.

If counsel only files a general objection to the admissibility of evidence, which is overruled and evidence admitted, an appeal fails if that evidence is admissible for any purpose.

Preliminary questions

The court shall determine preliminary questions concerning a person's qualifications to be a witness, the existence of a privilege, or the admissibility of evidence.

In making its determination, the judge is not bound by the rules of evidence except those concerning privileges.

Thus, hearsay evidence that would be inadmissible at trial is admissible before a judge hearing evidence on a preliminary question of fact (Federal Rule of Evidence 104 (a)).

Hearings on preliminary questions of fact must be held by the trial judge out of the jury's audible range when the interests of justice require it.

When the relevance of evidence depends upon the fulfillment of a condition of fact, the court shall admit it upon or subject to the introduction of evidence sufficient to support a finding of the fulfillment of the condition.

For example, if the issue is whether the person making a contract was an authorized agent of a principal, the court will admit the evidence of the purported agent's conduct concerning the contract on the condition that proper evidence of agency is introduced.

Federal Rule of Evidence 104(d) provides that the accused, by taking the stand on a preliminary matter, does not become subject to cross-examination on other issues. A waiver of the right of self-incrimination is limited to the subject matter of direct examination, not a general waiver.

Lay opinions

A witness who is not qualified as an expert can give an opinion on matters in which laypersons are competent to form opinions, provided the opinions are based upon the witness's knowledge and is helpful to the trier of fact.

A lay witness who forms an immediate opinion based upon observations to which they testify can testify to the opinion based upon their recent perception.

Expert witnesses

An expert in a subject may be qualified and testify as an expert if scientific, technical, or other specialized knowledge will assist the trier of fact.

Even if qualified as an expert by the trial judge, an expert witness can be cross-examined about specific matters in their background bearing on their qualifications as an expert. Such testimony affects the weight that a jury should give to the expert's opinion.

An expert witness is not required to testify from personal knowledge.

An expert witness may draw inferences from out-of-court facts and may rely on other experts' opinions if it is customary to do so in the field of expertise.

Federal Rule of Evidence 703 allows an expert to rely on hearsay to conclude, so long as other experts in the field would reasonably rely on such information.

Rule 703 distinguishes between expert *reliance* on the hearsay and *admitting* the hearsay at trial for the jury to consider.

Generally, hearsay will not be admissible when offered only because the expert relied upon it.

An expert witness may testify to a hypothetical question and give their opinion using hypothetical questions.

For hypothetical questions, the assumptions in that question must contain all relevant facts.

Facts (or data) otherwise inadmissible shall not be disclosed to the jury by the proponent of the opinion or inference unless the court determines their probative value assists the jury in evaluating the expert's opinion and substantially outweighs its prejudicial effect.

An expert witness can give an opinion on the ultimate issue in a case, except for an opinion on a criminal defendant's mental state.

The expert may testify in the form of an opinion and give reasons without prior disclosure of the underlying facts unless required.

The expert may be required to disclose the underlying facts or data supporting that opinion on cross-examination.

Qualifications and competence of witnesses

Under the Federal Rules of Evidence, witnesses who understand the obligation to testify truthfully are competent.

Generally, the Federal Rules of Evidence apply to matters of competency of witnesses and privilege in cases tried in federal courts.

An exception occurs where jurisdiction is based upon diversity of citizenship or where state law provides the basis for a federal court decision.

In those cases, the law of the state whose substantive law is applicable would determine the evidentiary rules to be applied for competency and privilege.

A juror may testify at a hearing on post-trial motions that the jury considered material from outside sources not properly introduced into evidence.

Judicial notice

In civil cases, a jury is bound to take as facts matters which have been judicially noticed.

Under Federal Rule of Evidence 201(g), a judge may not instruct a jury to find a fact in a criminal case, even if it is a fact that is subject to judicial notice.

Such an instruction to the jury to find a fact in a criminal case would violate the accused's Sixth Amendment right to a trial by jury on elements of the crime.

A judicially-noticed fact in a criminal case allows the court to instruct on a permissible inference, but nothing more.

A court can take judicial notice on its authority, even if not requested by any party.

A party is entitled, upon timely request, to be heard on the propriety of judicial notice and tenor of the matter noticed.

In the absence of prior notification, the request may be after judicial notice has been taken.

Judicial notice may be taken at any stage of the proceeding.

A jury in a criminal case is not bound to take judicially noticed matters as facts.

Cross-examination

A witness's testimony on the direct examination will be stricken if effective cross-examination is denied, either because the witness does not appear for cross-examination or refuses to answer questions relevant to the direct examination.

The striking of the testimony on direct examination is applicable even if a claim of privilege justifies that refusal.

If one party succeeds in admitting a portion of a document, the other party is entitled to introduce the remainder of the document even though there is no independent basis for admitting it. In fairness, it ought to be considered in conjunction with the portion of the document already admitted.

An out-of-court declarant whose testimony is received through admissible hearsay may be impeached by the same methods used to impeach a witness who testifies on the witness stand.

Exculpatory evidence elicited during its case-in-chief does not bind the government.

Impeachment of a witness

A witness's credibility may be attacked by *any* party, including the party calling them.

A witness's character for truthfulness cannot be introduced until that character trait has been attacked.

In a criminal case, the defense can offer either opinion evidence or reputation evidence of the criminal defendant's character traits inconsistent with the alleged criminal activity.

Impeachment by prior inconsistent statements

Unless a prior inconsistent statement qualifies as an admission, a hearsay exception, or was given under oath, it is admissible only to impeach the credibility of the witness who made it and not for the truth of the matters contained in it.

Under Federal Rule of Evidence 613(b), extrinsic evidence of a prior inconsistent statement is inadmissible to impeach credibility unless the witness's attention is called to the statement on cross-examination or unless the witness is subject to recall.

This provision does not apply to a party opponent's admissions as defined in Federal Rule of Evidence 801(d)(2).

Impeachment by bias

Evidence that suggests why the witness might be testifying in a manner that is either favorable or hostile to either party's position is admissible to impeach a witness.

Evidence of bias is considered important and generally admitted liberally.

Extrinsic evidence can be introduced to prove bias.

If relevant on the issue of bias, evidence of the defendant's insurance coverage and prior criminal convictions are admissible.

Impeachment by convictions

Evidence of prior convictions of a criminal defendant is only admissible to impeach their credibility and therefore is not admissible unless they testified.

A party calling a witness with a criminal record can anticipate criminal convictions to impeach by introducing evidence of those convictions during direct examination.

The court must admit evidence of a conviction less than ten years old for misdemeanors or felonies involving dishonesty or false statement against any witness, including the defendant.

The court must admit evidence of a conviction less than ten years old for a non-fraud crime punishable by death or at least one-year imprisonment of a witness other than the defendant unless the objecting party shows that the prejudicial effect of the impeachment substantially outweighs the probative value of the evidence.

The standard is reversed for the criminal defendant.

Evidence of such crimes is admissible against the accused only if the impeaching party shows that the probative value outweighs its prejudicial effect.

The court *may* admit evidence of a conviction more than ten years old for any witness only if the impeaching party first shows that the conviction's probative value substantially outweighs its prejudicial effect.

Federal Rules of Evidence 609(c) permits the introduction of a juvenile conviction of a witness other than the accused in a criminal case if the conviction would be admissible to attack the credibility of an adult and the trial judge determines that admission of the evidence of the conviction is necessary for a fair determination of guilt.

Evidence of convictions for misdemeanors not involving dishonesty or false statement is always *inadmissible* to impeach credibility.

Impeachment by prior bad acts

Under Federal Rule of Evidence 608, a witness can be cross-examined about specific instances of conduct that show fraudulent conduct to impeach credibility.

If the bad acts bear on other character traits, the probative value of the acts as to credibility is substantially outweighed by the risks of prejudice, confusion, and delay and would be excluded under Federal Rule of Evidence 403; the examiner must take the answer given on cross-examination and cannot introduce extrinsic evidence to rebut the answer.

Impeachment by reputation for veracity

The character of a witness for veracity can be impeached by the introduction of extrinsic evidence, either,

1) as an opinion by a person who knows them to be untruthful, or
2) by evidence of a person who knows of the witness's reputation for veracity and that their reputation in the community is poor.

The character of a witness for veracity can be established in the same way it can be attacked. However, such evidence is only admissible for a witness whose character for veracity has been attacked.

The reputation of a person's character among associates or in the community is admissible as an exception to the hearsay rule when it is admissible to prove character.

A criminal defendant's reputation for veracity cannot be attacked unless they testified.

Expert testimony on credibility is usually found inadmissible because credibility issues are for the jury and not for an expert's imprimatur.

Impeachment by contradiction

Extrinsic evidence can be used to impeach a witness by contradicting a material issue.

However, it cannot be introduced to contradict a witness on a collateral matter.

Impeachment of the hearsay declarant

When a hearsay statement or an admission has been admitted in evidence, the declarant's credibility may be attacked and, if attacked, may be supported by evidence admissible for those purposes if the declarant testified as a witness.

Evidence of a statement or conduct by the declarant inconsistent with the declarant's hearsay statement is not subject to any requirement that the declarant may have been allowed to deny or explain.

Rehabilitation and redirect examination

A judge is required to admit a question asked on redirect examination only if it relates to matters first raised on cross-examination or is designed to rehabilitate a witness's credibility in the way that credibility was attacked on cross-examination.

For example, evidence of good character concerning credibility is admissible only if evidence was introduced, showing bad character for credibility.

Evidence of lack of bias is admissible only if a witness's credibility for bias was introduced.

At their discretion, a judge can permit other evidence on redirect examination or rebuttals, such as evidence that should have been present in a direct examination or the case in chief.

Presumptions

A party seeking the benefit of a presumption does so by introducing evidence on basic facts.

For example, to use the presumption concerning the mail's regularity, a party introduces evidence that a letter is properly mailed.

Once a party activates a presumption by introducing credible evidence on the basic fact, and the opposing party produces no evidence on the presumed fact, the jury is obligated to find the presumed fact if they find the basic fact.

For example, the jury must find that a letter is received if they find that it was mailed unless the opposing party introduces evidence of non-receipt.

Once the party against whom the presumption operates introduces evidence on the presumed fact, the artificial procedural effect disappears.

However, the jury can draw appropriate inferences from the basic fact to find the presumed fact's existence.

For example, if one party proves that a letter was mailed, and the other party denies it was received, a presumption is not operative. The jury can infer that the letter was mailed, received and that the evidence of non-receipt is not credible.

Application of federal law

The Federal Rules of Evidence apply in cases in the Federal Court except in diversity cases, where the evidentiary issue is:

1) the application of rules of privilege,
2) the competency of witnesses, or
3) the effect of a presumption.

In these three limited instances, the court will apply the governing state evidentiary rule.

Notes for active learning

Privileges and Exclusions

Spousal communications

Under the witness-spouse rule, a witness-spouse can refuse to take the witness stand and testify in a case where the criminal defendant is the spouse at the time of trial.

The defendant's spouse cannot prevent the witness-spouse from testifying if she/he voluntarily waives the right to refuse to testify.

Confidential communications between individuals who are at the time of the communication married to each other are privileged, even if the spouses are not married at the time of trial.

Each spouse is the holder of the privilege and can prevent the other spouse from testifying confidential communications.

The confidentiality necessary for the privilege is destroyed if the conversation takes place in the presence of third parties capable of understanding the conversation unless that third party is an eavesdropper whose presence is unknown to the spouses.

Attorney–client privilege

The attorney–client privilege claim applies only to confidential communications between a "client" and an "attorney" regarding legal advice.

The terms client and attorney have expanded meanings to define the privilege.

If a person consults with whom they reasonably believe to be an attorney to obtain legal advice, the privilege applies even though the person consulted is not, in fact, an attorney.

The privilege applies to conversations between a person seeking to hire an attorney and the attorney, even if the prospective client does not hire the attorney.

The attorney–client privilege belongs to the client, who can waive it.

The attorney has an affirmative obligation to assert the privilege in the absence of a waiver by the client.

Communications made to an attorney in the presence of third parties such as secretaries or investigators, who are reasonably necessary for either the attorney or the client to perform their duties, do not destroy the confidentiality required for the privilege to be applicable.

The attorney–client privilege protects communications between a client and a person working for the lawyer to provide the client's legal services.

Disclosure made in the presence of persons not necessary for either the attorney or client to perform their duties destroys confidentiality and the applicability of the privilege.

If two clients consult an attorney jointly concerning a common legal problem, the communications in the presence of clients and attorneys are privileged in a suit with a third party concerning the common legal problem.

Communications between the typical clients and the attorney in each other's presence are not privileged in litigation between the two clients.

An admission of a past criminal act by a client to an attorney is privileged. However, the privilege is inapplicable if the client's purpose of the communication were to commit fraud or engage in criminal conduct in the future.

If the client knows that the purpose of the communication was to assist in the commission of fraud or future criminal conduct, there is no privilege even if the lawyer was not aware of the purpose of the communication.

The privilege is inapplicable if the client or a disciplinary body calls the attorney's conduct into question, and the attorney must reveal the confidential communication to defend themself.

Before the commencement of an attorney–client relationship, documents in existence do not become privileged merely because they are delivered to an attorney.

Written communication to an attorney seeking legal advice and written communications from the attorney to the client containing legal advice are privileged.

The attorney–client privilege protects communications from counsel to a corporation, including in-house counsel to the corporation's employee concerning legal matters relevant to the corporation's business.

Physician–patient privilege

Federal Rules of Evidence do not recognize physician–patient privilege.

In states where it is applicable, the physician–patient privilege applies to confidential communications made to a physician and the physician's observations made for diagnosis or treatment purposes.

The confidential nature of the communications or observations required for the physician–patient privilege to be applicable is not destroyed by the presence of third persons necessary to perform the physician's duties.

A patient is the holder of the physician–patient privilege.

The patient waives the privilege when introducing evidence on their physical condition or suing the physician.

Self-incriminating statements

The privilege against self-incrimination only gives a person the right not to incriminate themself through testimony.

The privilege against self-incrimination does not give an individual a right to refuse to exhibit physical characteristics, give samples of bodily fluids, or try on clothing.

The privilege against self-incrimination does not give an individual the power to suppress a statement already made, except for a coerced confession or a statement is made in violation of Miranda rights.

A defendant who testifies on a preliminary matter in a criminal case retains the right to refuse to testify in the trial on the merits.

In a preliminary hearing in a criminal case, a defendant who testifies cannot be asked cross-examination questions beyond the scope of the issues at the preliminary hearing.

A defendant's admission of ownership of the property to establish standing in a preliminary motion to suppress evidence does not carry over as an admission of ownership for purposes of a trial on the merits.

When a defendant testifies after being granted immunity, neither their testimony nor evidence derived from their testimony can be used in a criminal prosecution against them.

If a witness at a hearing claims the privilege against self-incrimination, the judge must sustain the claim of the privilege if the witness reasonably believes that they might incriminate themself.

Other privileges

By statute, some jurisdictions recognize:

priest–penitent privilege,

social worker–client privilege,

privilege not to disclose one's vote,

newsperson's sources privilege, and

government secrets privilege.

The Federal Rules of Evidence do not recognize such privileges.

Notes for active learning

Relevancy and Its Counterweights

Probative value

Evidence is not admissible unless it is relevant to a material issue in the lawsuit or the impeachment of a witness.

Under Federal Rule of Evidence 403, the trial judge may exclude otherwise relevant evidence if its probative value is substantially outweighed by:

1) the danger of unfair prejudice,
2) confusion of the issues,
3) misleading the jury,
4) considerations of undue delay,
5) waste of time, or
6) needless presentation of cumulative evidence.

The admissibility of a rape victim's sexual conduct is limited to two circumstances, providing the judge determines that the probative value of the evidence outweighs its prejudicial effect:

1) if it involves other sexual conduct between the alleged perpetrator and the alleged victim, or;
2) it involves sexual conduct with a person other than the defendant at the time of the alleged rape.

Use of character to prove actions

In cases in which a person's character trait is an essential element of a charge, claim, or defense, character is "an issue."

That character trait can be proved by evidence of reputation, opinion, or specific acts.

In defamation cases, character concerning the alleged defamation evidence is relevant to whether the plaintiff has a particular character and the extent of damages.

In a civil case, evidence of a character trait to show a propensity to act following that trait is always inadmissible.

In a criminal case, the defense can offer either opinion evidence or reputation evidence of the criminal defendant's character traits inconsistent with the alleged criminal activity.

If the defense offers such evidence, the prosecution can rebut with a similar reputation or opinion evidence consistent with the alleged criminal activity.

If the alleged crime does not involve fraud or deceit, character evidence concerning the defendant's honesty is admissible only if they take the stand.

Then, the prosecution can introduce character evidence concerning dishonesty, and the defendant can rebut that evidence with character evidence showing honesty.

If the defendant has raised the defense of self-defense in a homicide case, the prosecution may introduce character evidence of the victim's peaceful nature, and the defense can introduce character evidence of the victim's quarrelsome nature.

Otherwise, the prosecution cannot initiate the proof of character in a criminal case.

Federal Rule of Evidence 405 prohibits evidence of specific acts indicative of a person's character when that character evidence is offered to prove that a person acted by the character trait on occasion in question at trial.

On cross-examination of a character witness for a criminal defendant, the examiner may inquire into the witness's knowledge of specific instances of the defendant's conduct to show that the witness's assessment of the defendant's character is not credible.

Courts require that the cross-examiner must have a good faith belief that the event occurred before inquiring into the act on cross-examination.

Evidence of the past sexual history of a rape victim is inadmissible except for prior sexual conduct with the defendant on the issue of consent or evidence that the defendant was not the person who engaged in the sexual conduct, which constituted the rape.

Past sexual crimes are admissible in sexual assault and child molestation cases.

Evidence of other crimes

Under Federal Rule of Evidence 404(a), evidence of other crimes, wrongs, or acts is not admissible to prove a person's character to show actions in conformity.

Under Federal Rule of Evidence 404(b), prior bad acts can be admitted to prove the defendant's conduct if offered for some purpose other than to show that a defendant is a bad person. For example, it shows that the defendant tends to engage in particular activities that set them apart from others.

Evidence of prior bad acts is admissible to prove motive, opportunity, intent, preparation, plan knowledge, identity or absence of mistake, or accident.

There must be something unique about the crime to be probative on the defendant's identity.

Proof of other crimes or acts is permitted by introducing substantial evidence that the defendant committed them.

Convictions need not have occurred or be proven.

If the defendant raises the defense of entrapment, evidence that the defendant has committed other crimes is admissible to negate the inference that the police induced the commission of the crime.

Under Federal Rule of Evidence 414, in a criminal case where the defendant is accused of child molestation, the defendant's commission of another offense or offenses of child molestation is admissible. It may be considered for its bearing on any matter for which it may be relevant.

Habit, custom and routine practice

Under Federal Rule of Evidence 406, evidence of habit of a person or the routine practice of an organization, whether corroborated and regardless of eyewitnesses' presence, is relevant to prove that the person or organization's conduct conformed with a habit or routine practice.

Subsequent safety measures

Evidence of subsequent remedial measures (e.g., making repairs after the accident or posting warning signs) is not admissible to prove negligence or culpable conduct.

Evidence of subsequent remedial measures is admissible to prove ownership or control of the premises where the accident occurred if the defendant has raised the issue.

Evidence of a change in the design of a product after an accident has occurred is not admissible to show that the change could have been made earlier.

Offers of settlement

Offers made to settle a disputed claim and statements made in such a context of the settlement negotiations, even if they are admissions of liability, are not admissible to prove liability.

An offer in compromise before the opposing party has made a claim is not made inadmissible by this rule because, until the other party has made a claim, no disputed claim exists.

Evidence of an offer in compromise accepted is admissible in a suit in contract to enforce it.

Federal Rule of Evidence 408 does not require excluding evidence otherwise discoverable merely because it is present during compromise negotiations.

Federal Rule of Evidence 408 does not require exclusion when the evidence is offered for another purpose, such as proving bias or prejudice of a witness, negating a contention of undue delay, or proving an effort to obstruct a criminal investigation or prosecution.

Payment of medical expenses

Under Federal Rule of Evidence 409, an offer to pay medical expenses, even one made before a dispute exists, is not admissible to show liability.

A statement connected with an offer to pay medical expenses is admissible as an admission.

Criminal proceedings

If a criminal action has not commenced, an offer made to avoid criminal proceedings and a statement made in connection is admissible in a subsequent trial.

Once the criminal process has begun, evidence of an attempt to compromise in the form of an offer to plead guilty to a lesser offense or plead guilty in exchange for a lighter sentence was rejected, and statements made in connection are not admissible in a subsequent criminal trial.

Liability insurance

Evidence that a person was or was not insured against liability is not admissible upon the issue of whether the person acted negligently or otherwise wrongfully.

Federal Rule of Evidence 411 does not require the exclusion of evidence of insurance against liability when offered for another purpose, such as proof of agency, ownership, control, bias, or prejudice of a witness.

Similar happenings and transactions

Evidence of events or circumstances similar to the material events in the lawsuit is not admissible to prove the relevant event unless the probative value is compelling.

For example, proof that many people eating the same food at the same restaurant became sick with the same symptoms would be admissible on the cause of food poisoning.

However, proof that a driver had many accidents like the one involved in the litigation would not be admissible.

Experimental and scientific evidence

Evidence of a scientific test that is carefully designed to represent a relevant event fairly is admissible even if the opposing party had no notice of the test and did not participate in conducting the test.

Demonstrative evidence

The judge has the discretion to exclude relevant demonstrative evidence, which is highly inflammatory when the less inflammatory material is available to prove the same point.

Writings as Evidence

Authentication: chain of custody, voice & proof of signatures

Objects which do not have identifying characteristics (e.g., cocaine or heroin) must be authenticated by proving a chain of custody from the point at which the object became relevant to the time of trial.

If the objects are sealed in an identifying container, such a chain of custody proof is unnecessary.

If someone is familiar with the image shown on a photograph and testifies from personal knowledge that it fairly and accurately depicts a relevant event, the photograph is admissible even though the person authenticating the photograph is not the photographer.

A witness may authenticate a voice, whether heard first-hand, through mechanical or electronic transmission or recording, by giving a lay opinion based upon hearing the voice at any time under the circumstances connecting it with the alleged speaker.

Telephone conversations can be authenticated by evidence that a call was made to a number assigned by the telephone company to a person or business, if:

1) in the case of a person, circumstances, including self-identification, show the person answering to be the one called, or
2) in the case of a business, the call was made to a place of business, and the conversation related to business reasonably transacted over the phone.

A person who receives a telephone call cannot authenticate the voice on the other end of the conversation if they are not familiar with that voice, even though the voice on the other end of the conversation identifies itself.

If a lay witness testifies that they are familiar with a signature, even though that familiarity was the product of a brief encounter in the distant past, the testimony of that lay witness is sufficient to authenticate the signature.

A handwriting expert can authenticate a signature by giving an opinion based upon comparing the disputed signature with an admittedly genuine signature.

A lay witness cannot authenticate a signature by comparison.

If there is an admittedly genuine signature available, a jury may compare that signature with a disputed signature and conclude on the disputed signature's genuineness without expert testimony to guide it.

An item can be authenticated by circumstantial evidence of how the police obtained possession of it.

Certified copies of official records are self-authenticating, and their contents, if required to be kept, are admissible as a hearsay exception.

Best evidence rule

The original is not required to prove the content of a writing or recording, consisting of letters, words, numbers, or equivalent, set down by handwriting, electronic recording, and other forms of data compilation (e.g., photograph, X-ray films, videotapes).

Other evidence of the contents of a writing or recording is admissible if:

1) all originals are lost or have been destroyed (unless the proponent lost or destroyed them in bad faith), or no original can be obtained by judicial process, and
2) when an original was under the control of the party against whom offered, that party was put on notice by pleading or otherwise that the contents would be a subject of proof at the hearing and that party does not produce the original at the hearing.

Secondary evidence proving a collateral matter is admissible despite the best evidence rule.

If a witness has first-hand knowledge of an event and has made a record of their actions when they obtained that first-hand knowledge, they can testify about the event without producing the record.

The best evidence rule does apply in this situation.

For example, a doctor who performs an autopsy can testify about it without producing the autopsy report.

The best evidence rule only applies when a party wants to introduce the content of a writing or recording.

Hearsay

Definition of hearsay

Hearsay is a statement that is an oral assertion, written assertion, or the nonverbal conduct of a person intended by the person as an assertion, offered in evidence to prove the truth of the matter asserted.

Assertive statements made by the declarant while testifying at the trial or a hearing are not hearsay.

Nonverbal conduct would be hearsay only if the person intended to make an assertive statement by the conduct.

For example, if a witness at a lineup points to the person they believe is the perpetrator of the crime, the act of pointing is assertive nonverbal conduct and hearsay.

A triage officer who separates the living from the dead at the scene of an accident is not making an assertive statement that a particular individual is dead or alive.

If the words of the out-of-court declarant must be believed for their testimony to be relevant, that testimony is hearsay and must either be:

1) defined as non-hearsay by the rules, or

2) come within an exception to hearsay to be admissible in court.

If an out-of-court statement is hearsay and contains within it another out-of-court statement which is also hearsay, there must be a hearsay exception permitting the admissibility of each level of this totem pole of hearsay (see below) before the statement within the statement is admissible.

Evidence used circumstantially as non-hearsay

Out-of-court statements relevant, even without the need to believe that the words in them are true, are only used circumstantially and are not hearsay.

Examples of non-hearsay include statements demonstrating knowledge or state of mind of either the declarant or the recipient of the statement or the meaning to the parties of the words involved in the statement.

Non-hearsay – prior inconsistent statement given under oath

Under Federal Rule of Evidence 801(d)(1)(A), the prior inconsistent statement given under oath of a witness who testifies is defined as non-hearsay admissible for the truth of the matters contained in that prior inconsistent statement.

Unless a prior inconsistent statement of a witness on the stand:

1) qualifies as an admission,
2) qualifies under a hearsay exception, or
3) was given under oath,

it is admissible only to impeach the credibility of the witness who made it and not for the truth of the matters contained in it.

Non-hearsay – prior consistent statement

If a person testifying on the witness stand has made an out-of-court statement consistent with their testimony, that statement ordinarily is inadmissible as hearsay.

The prior statement is admissible for the truth of the matters stated in it if the purpose of offering the prior consistent statement is to show that the testimony given on the witness stand is not a recent contrivance after the opposing party has impeached the credibility of the witness by use of a prior inconsistent statement.

It is admissible when used to rebut an inference of bias, as long as the prior consistent statement occurred before the bias arose.

In other instances, a prior consistent statement is inadmissible hearsay.

Non-hearsay – prior out-of-court identification by a witness at trial

Testimony of prior, out-of-court identification of the criminal defendant by a witness is admissible if the witness is on the stand and testifying subject to cross-examination.

Non-hearsay – admissions by a party

An out-of-court statement of a party to the lawsuit can be introduced by the opposing party as an admission, even though the statement was in the party's interest when made and the party had no personal knowledge of the statement's facts.

Evidence of actions inconsistent with the position a party is taking in a case is admissible as an admission by conduct.

Non-hearsay – adoptive admissions

Through actions, if a party adopts a statement of another, it is admissible as an admission.

Adoptive admissions usually occur when a party remains silent when a statement is made in their presence by another, which they would deny if it were false.

Statements are not admissible as adoptive admissions when made in the defendant's presence at a time when entitled to remain silent because they are in custody and have Miranda rights.

A party may adopt a statement of another without knowing the precise nature of the statement if indicating that its author is a reliable person concerning the statement's subject matter.

Non-hearsay – vicarious admissions

Statements made by an authorized agent within the scope of agency, a partner for partnership matters, or a predecessor in the title for issues of title are admissible as vicarious admissions.

The contents of a statement by a purported authorized agent are admissible to prove that an agency existed, but independent evidence is needed before the agency relationship is established.

Non-hearsay – statement by an employee

Even though it is not admissible as a vicarious admission because the employee is not authorized to speak on behalf of their employer, an employee's statement when employed concerning matters within their employment is admissible as an admission against the employer.

Non-hearsay – statement made by a conspirator

When a conspiracy exists, a co-conspirator's statements are admissible against another co-conspirator if they are made within the scope and in furtherance of the conspiracy.

A conspiracy terminates at the time the conspirators are arrested.

The contents of a statement by a purported conspirator are admissible to prove the existence of the conspiracy but by themselves are insufficient to establish it.

Inadmissible hearsay

Evidence that is hearsay and does not come within a hearsay exception is inadmissible except when offered on a preliminary question of fact.

Totem pole hearsay

If an assertive out-of-court statement contains within it another assertive out-of-court statement made to the first out-of-court declarant, the evidence contains totem pole hearsay.

Each out-of-court statement must come within an exception to the hearsay rule for admissible evidence.

Hearsay Exceptions Requiring Declarant Be Unavailable

Definition of unavailability

Federal Rule of Evidence 804 exceptions, those statements made in contemplation of impending death, declarations against interest, former testimony, and statements of personal and family history are admissible only if the out-of-court declarant is unavailable.

The other exceptions, Rule 803 exceptions, do not require unavailability.

"Unavailability of a Witness" includes situations in which the declarant

1) is exempted by ruling of the court on the ground of privilege from testifying concerning the subject matter of the declarant's statements, or
2) persists in refusing to testify concerning the subject matter of the declarant's statement despite a court order to do so, or
3) testifies to lack of memory of the subject matter of the declarant's statement, or
4) is unable to be present or to testify at the hearing because of death or existing physical or mental illness or infirmity, or
5) is absent from the hearing, and the proponent of a statement has been unable to procure the declarant's attendance by process or other reasonable means.

A declarant is not unavailable as a witness if exemption, refusal, a claim of lack of memory, inability, or absence is due to the procurement or wrongdoing of a statement's proponent to prevent the witness from attending or testifying.

Prior testimony

If the parties in a civil case where former testimony is offered are not identical to the parties who gave the testimony, the prior testimony is admissible only if the opposing attorney in the first trial had an opportunity and the same motive for cross-examination as the party against whom the statement is offered in the second trial.

Testimony given at a deposition is admissible as former testimony if the deponent is unavailable, or the rule of civil procedure authorizing the deposition does not require that the deponent be unavailable.

For former testimony to be admissible in a criminal trial, the testimony must have been given in a case where the defendant was a party.

Testimony given at a preliminary hearing in a criminal case where the defendant had a right to cross-examine qualifies as former testimony.

Declaration against interest

A statement made by an unavailable out-of-court declarant is admissible as an exception to the hearsay rule if at the time it was made it:

1) was contrary to the declarant's pecuniary or proprietary interest, or
2) would likely subject them to criminal or tort liability, or
3) would likely render invalid a claim which possess.

If a declaration against interest is offered to exonerate a criminal defendant by showing that the out-of-court declarant committed the crime, the evidence must be corroborated before it is admissible.

The declaration against interest exception does not apply to a statement or confession offered against the accused, made by a codefendant or another implicating themself and the accused.

Statement made with impending death

A statement made with knowledge of impending death concerning the impending death circumstances is admissible only in civil cases and criminal homicide prosecutions.

There is no requirement that the declarant dies for the statement to be admissible in civil cases.

The out-of-court declarant must know death was imminent when the statement was made.

Forfeiture exception

Under Federal Rule of Evidence 804(b)(6), a statement is admissible as a forfeiture for wrongdoing when it is offered against a party that has engaged in wrongdoing that intended and did procure the unavailability of the declarant as a witness.

Limitation on hearsay exceptions in criminal cases

Even though evidence may be admissible under a hearsay exception recognized by the Federal Rules of Evidence, the out-of-court statement will be inadmissible in criminal cases because of the confrontation clause, unless the out-of-court statement would have been admissible as a hearsay exception recognized at the time the Sixth Amendment was adopted.

Catchall exception

Evidence is admissible under the catchall exception if 1) prior notice is given, 2) it is offered on a material fact that is more probative on the issue than other evidence, and 3) its admission serves the purpose of these rules.

Hearsay Exceptions Not Requiring Unavailability

Present sense impressions

If an out-of-court declarant makes a statement describing or explaining an event while it is happening or immediately after, the statement is admissible as a present sense impression.

A person on the witness stand may testify to a declarant's present sense impression even though that witness could not observe the facts related by the declarant.

Excited utterance

An excited utterance is a statement relating to a startling event or condition made while the declarant was under the stress of excitement caused by the event or condition.

A present sense impression must be more contemporaneous with the prompting event than an excited utterance but does not require an *exciting* event.

Statements of mental or physical condition

A statement of present mental intention is admissible as an exception to the hearsay rule.

An inference that the person who possessed a present mental intention carried out that intent can be used to prove actions in accordance with that mental state.

A statement of present physical condition is admissible as an exception to the hearsay rule. Anyone hearing such a statement can testify to it.

A statement of past physical condition is admissible as an exception to the hearsay rule only if made to a doctor or other health care professional to obtain a medical diagnosis or treatment.

Past recollection recorded

A statement is admissible as past recollection recorded only if the person whose recorded recollection is offered is on the witness stand and testifies that they have no present memory of the recorded matter.

When a document is admissible as past recollection recorded because the witness on the stand had testified that they had a present memory of the contents when made but do not have a memory presently, the document may be read to the jury, but it is not admissible.

Business records

A memorandum or record of acts, events, opinions, or diagnoses is admissible as a business record (provided it was kept in the custody of the regular custodian of those records) if it:

1) made at or near the time of the matter;
2) made by, or from information transmitted by, a person with knowledge;
3) kept in the course of a regularly conducted business activity, and;
4) was the regular practice of that business activity to make this memorandum report, record, or data compilation.

A statement in a document does not come within the business records exception to the hearsay rule if the statement was outside of the scope for records about and kept by the business.

Statements in business records prepared for litigation are not admissible under the business records exception to the hearsay rule.

A record is admissible under the business records exception to the hearsay rule if made by a person who transcribed the record in the ordinary course of business and received the information transcribed from a person who obtained it in the ordinary course of business.

Absence of business records

Under Federal Rule of Evidence 803(7), a certification offered to prove the absence of a business record in business record reports is admissible to prove the nonoccurrence if the matter were of a kind which the business record would ordinarily contain.

Public records

Under Federal Rule of Evidence 803(8), records, reports, statements, or data compilations in any form of public offices or agencies

1) setting forth the activities of the office or agency, or
2) matters observed according to a duty imposed by law as to which matters there was a duty to report, excluding reports of matters observed by police officers in criminal cases, qualify as exceptions to the hearsay rule.

Absence of public records

Under Federal Rule of Evidence 803(10), a certification offered to prove the absence of a public record qualifies as an exception to the hearsay rule.

The certification must be prepared by a public official and must, on its face, indicate that a diligent record search was conducted to be admissible.

Learned treatise

A learned treatise is a writing established by an expert as authoritative on a particular subject on which expert testimony is offered.

The treatise's authoritative nature can be established by cross-examining an expert whose credibility is sought to be impeached by the treatise or can be established by another expert.

Under Federal Rule of Evidence 803(18), the learned treatise exception applies only after an expert relies on the treatise upon direct examination, or the treatise is called to the attention of the witness on cross-examination and the authoritative nature of the treatise is established.

The learned treatise exception allows statements from a treatise to be read into evidence when the treatise is "established as a reliable authority by the testimony or admission of the witness or by other expert testimony or by judicial notice."

The learned treatise exception allows statements from a treatise to be read into evidence where the treatise is "called to the attention of an expert witness" and is found to be reliable by the court. The rule does not require that an expert *relies* on the treatise.

When a learned treatise is admitted as an exception to the hearsay rule, the passage in the learned treatise is admitted not only to impeach an expert's credibility but is also admitted substantively.

The treatise is not admitted as an exhibit, but relevant passages can be read to the jury.

Family history

Family records and reputation concerning family history, contained in documents such as family Bibles, are admissible to prove family relationships without proving the unavailability of the author of that history.

If the declarant is unavailable, their statement concerning personal history is admissible as an exception to the hearsay rule.

Ancient documents

As long as they are held in custody in a place where such documents are customarily kept, statements contained in documents more than 20 years old are admissible under the ancient documents exception to the hearsay rule.

Relationship matrix

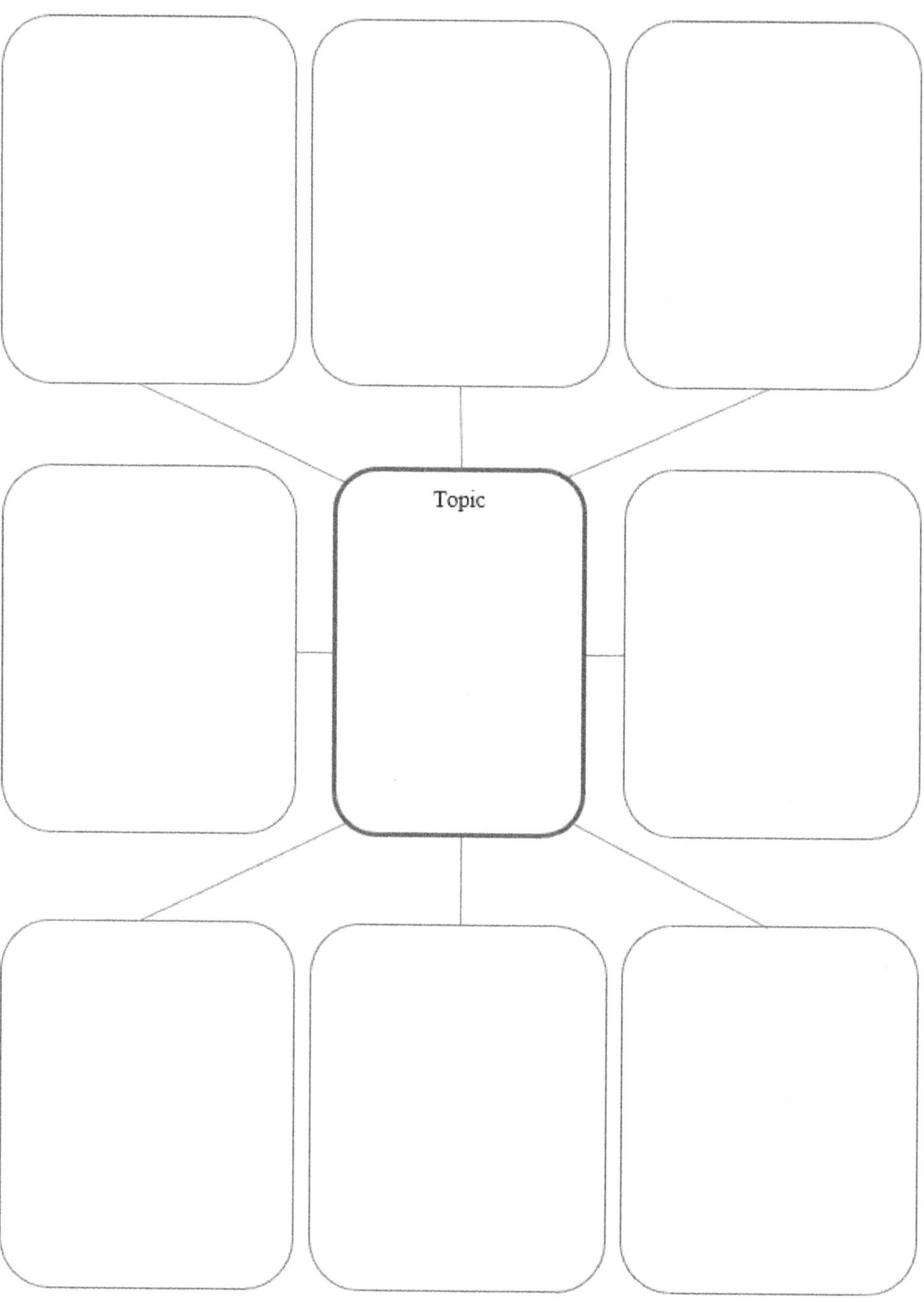

Evidence – Quick Facts

1. The record on appeal *must* show that a **timely, specific objection** was made during the trial and the challenged evidence was inadmissible on that ground before the trial court's action can be considered an **error**.
2. The court is *never* required to state the **reason for overruling an objection**.
3. The Federal Rules of Evidence have abolished the Common Law requirement that a witness can explain **prior inconsistent statements** *before* extrinsic evidence of the statement can be admitted.
4. The witness's opportunity to explain prior inconsistent statements may be provided *after* the introduction of the statement.

Notes for active learning

Real Property

On the essay section, Real Property generally is not combined with other topics. Real Property is a difficult subject, so focus on the highly tested issues: real estate contracts and deeds, ownership and title to property, recording acts, mortgages and security devices, leases, and rights in land. Know the essential terminology such as mortgagor, mortgagee, warranty deed, quitclaim deed, wild deed, assignment, joint tenancy, sublease, easement, merger, equitable conversion, and adverse possession.

The statements herein were compiled by analyzing released Real Property questions and setting forth the principles of law governing the correct answers. Review these principles before preparing answers to practice Real Property questions. Memorize this governing law and understand how it applies to the correct answer.

Real Property Law – Overview

Personal Property: goods or chattels that are not real property

Tangible property: physically defined property, such as goods, animals, and minerals

Intangible property: represents rights not reduced to physical forms (e.g., stock certificates).

Choice of categories

At common law, found property is categorized in five ways:

Abandoned property – the owner has discarded or voluntarily forsaken to terminate their ownership without vesting ownership in another.

Lost property – the owner has involuntarily and unintentionally parted with it through neglect or carelessness and does not know its location.

Mislaid property – the owner has intentionally set it down to retrieve it and forget where they put it.

Treasure trove – a category exclusively for gold or silver in coin, plate, bullion, or paper money equivalents, found concealed in the earth, a building, or another private place. Treasure trove carries thoughts of antiquity (i.e., the treasure has been concealed for so long as to indicate that the owner is probably dead or unknown).

Embedded property – personal property that has become part of the natural earth. Examples include pottery, the sunken wreck of a steamship, or a sack of precious gems buried in the ground). Possession of embedded property goes to the owner of the land on which the property was found.

Under these doctrines, the finder of lost property, abandoned property, and treasure trove acquires a right to possess the property against the entire world, except the rightful owner, regardless of the place of finding.

The finder of mislaid property is required to turn it over to the owner of the premises, who has a duty to safeguard the property for the true owner.

One of the major distinctions between these categories is that only lost property necessarily involves an element of involuntariness.

The four remaining categories involve voluntary and intentional acts by the owner in placing the property where another eventually finds it.

Despite not being lost or abandoned property, the treasure trove has the right to possession recognized to be in the finder rather than the premises' owner.

Law of finders for personal property

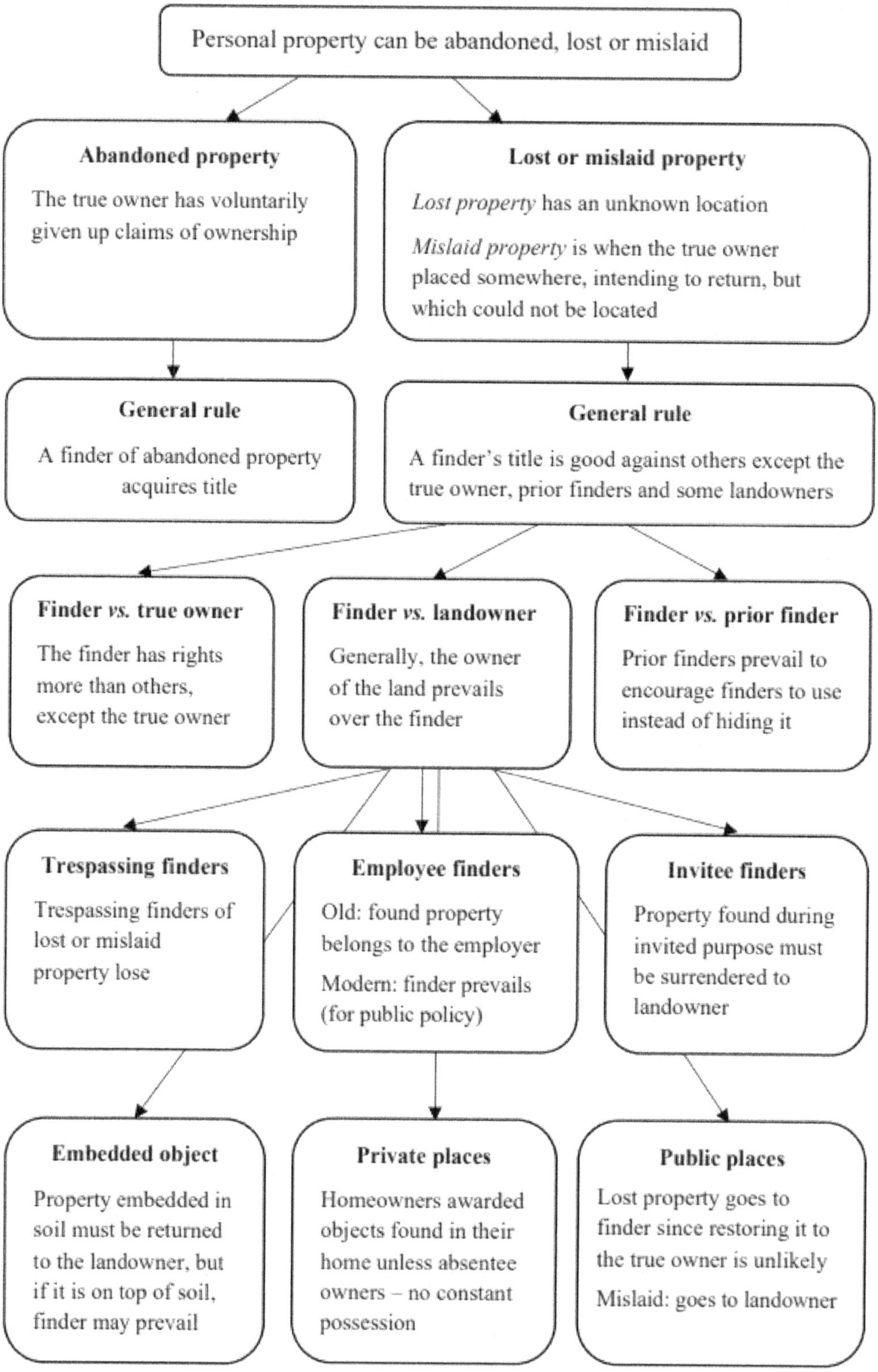

Personal property can be abandoned, lost or mislaid

Abandoned property

The true owner has voluntarily given up claims of ownership

Lost or mislaid property

Lost property has an unknown location

Mislaid property is when the true owner placed somewhere, intending to return, but which could not be located

General rule

A finder of abandoned property acquires title

General rule

A finder's title is good against others except the true owner, prior finders and some landowners

Finder *vs.* true owner

The finder has rights more than others, except the true owner

Finder *vs.* landowner

Generally, the owner of the land prevails over the finder

Finder *vs.* prior finder

Prior finders prevail to encourage finders to use instead of hiding it

Trespassing finders

Trespassing finders of lost or mislaid property lose

Employee finders

Old: found property belongs to the employer

Modern: finder prevails (for public policy)

Invitee finders

Property found during invited purpose must be surrendered to landowner

Embedded object

Property embedded in soil must be returned to the landowner, but if it is on top of soil, finder may prevail

Private places

Homeowners awarded objects found in their home unless absentee owners – no constant possession

Public places

Lost property goes to finder since restoring it to the true owner is unlikely

Mislaid: goes to landowner

The Estate System

Fee simple

A conveyance from owner to "A" or to "A and their heirs" creates a fee simple interest in A and no interest in A's heirs.

Fee simple determinable

A fee simple determinable is created by a conveyance that limits the fee by the grant's words such as "so long as."

The grantor's interest following a fee simple determinable is a possibility of reverter, a reversionary interest not subject to the rule against perpetuities.

In the case of a fee simple determinable, when and if the event is a limitation on the fee occurs, the present interest holder's interest is automatically terminated. The title goes to the grantor as the holder of the future interest.

A right given to a third person after the termination of a fee simple determinable (to A, so long as the premises are used for church premises and if they are not so used, then to B) creates an executory interest in B, which is subject to the rule against perpetuities.

That executory interest is invalid unless any right in the third party must occur within the period of the rule (lives in being plus 21 years) if it will ever occur.

If an invalid executory interest fails, the grantor takes it because they retain the possibility of reverter.

Fee simple subject to condition subsequent

A fee simple subject to condition subsequent is created by a conveyance which grants a fee simple interest and then terminates it if a contingency occurs, usually with the words "but if."

The grantor's reversionary type interest is called a "right of entry for condition broken" and is not subject to the rule against perpetuities.

If the right of entry is given to a person other than the grantor, that right is an executory interest subject to the rule against perpetuities.

If the executory interest is invalid after a right of entry for a condition broken, the grantor takes nothing, and the grantee holds in fee simple.

A fee simple determinable or a fee simple subject to a condition subsequent are the only devices that will allow a seller who retains no land in the vicinity of the property conveyed to control the property's use.

While the possibility of reverter becomes possessory automatically upon the breach of the condition, a person holding a right of entry for condition broken must bring a court proceeding to enforce that right before obtaining ownership.

Future interests

A *reversion* is a future interest in the grantor, consisting of any interest that does not convey.

A reversion is considered vested and is not subject to the rule against perpetuities.

A *remainder* is a future interest created in a party other than the grantor in the same instrument as the prior possessory interest and capable of taking effect at the prior interest termination.

A remainder is vested if it is ready to take in possession whenever the previous possessory interest terminates.

For example, in conveyance "to A for life and then to B," the remainder is vested because either B or B's heirs or devisees own the property upon the termination of the life estate in A.

A remainder is contingent if a condition precedent must be satisfied before the interest becomes possessory.

For example, in the conveyance to "A for life and then to B if B survives A," neither the remainderman, B, nor heirs take if B predeceases A.

A remainder is contingent if the holders of the interest, such as heirs of a living person or unborn children, are unascertained.

A *contingent remainder* becomes vested once the condition precedent is satisfied, or the indefinite beneficiaries (e.g., heirs of a living person) become identified when that person dies.

If a fee simple interest is conveyed subject to a condition precedent, title and possession remain in the grantor.

The grantee does not take until the condition precedent has been satisfied.

While a remainder interest to the "children of A, a living person" is contingent if A has no children, interest is classified as vested subject to open if A already has one or more children.

The interests of the existing children are reduced as the class expands to include afterborn children of A.

The grantee of a contingent remainder takes nothing if the condition precedent is never satisfied.

An executory interest is an interest in land to a third person after a fee simple subject to divestment.

If an interest in land is a contingent remainder and cannot become possessory immediately upon termination of the prior estate because the condition precedent has not been satisfied, the interest is transformed into an executory interest, which will take possession when the condition precedent to its taking is satisfied.

In the meantime, there is a reversion in the grantor.

Class gifts

If there is a class gift, one to individuals bearing a family relationship to a named individual, such as the "grandchildren of A," afterborn members of the class can join the class until the class closes.

If the grantor does not indicate otherwise, the class closes when any member of the class can take possession of the gift.

For example, if the gift is "to my grandchildren when they reach age 21," the class closes when the first grandchild is eligible to take the interest by reaching age 21.

A future interest, whether vested or contingent, can be alienated before its becoming possessory.

Notes for active learning

Life estates

At the termination of a life estate's measuring life, the property reverts to the grantor unless the grantor has deeded a remainder interest after the life estate, title vests in the remainderman.

A life estate that is limited by an event such as remarriage is a determinable life estate and terminates either on the holder's death or upon the event's happening, whichever occurs sooner.

Waste is an action of the life tenant, which reduces the value of a future interest in the property.

If the life tenant takes an action that increases the value of the remainder, that action is ameliorating waste, and the life tenant is not liable for destruction, which occurs in the process of increasing value.

Vested and contingent remaindermen have standing to enjoin a life tenant from committing waste.

The holder of a possibility of reverter, a right of entry for condition subsequent, or an executory interest after a fee simple subject to a condition subsequent does not.

When a mineral extraction activity had commenced before the property was divided between a life tenancy and a remainder interest, the life tenant can continue that extraction activity without being liable for waste without having to account to the remainderman.

If a person holds a life estate *pur autre vie*, the measuring life is a person other than the holder of the possessory interest. The estate terminates at the death of the person who is the measuring life, not upon the death of the person in possession.

When a grantor conveys property subject to a mortgage to a life tenant and remainderman, the life tenant must pay the interest on the mortgage and current real estate taxes if the property generates income sufficient to make such payments, and the remainderman must make principal payments.

Neither life tenant nor remainderman is personally liable on the mortgage note.

If the property generates no income, the life tenant is not personally liable to the remainderman for interest and taxes paid by them.

If the grantor deeds a life estate to a grantee, the grantee's life is the measuring life.

If the grantee sells their life estate, the grantee's life, not the purchaser's life, remains the measuring life.

The rule against perpetuities (RAP)

The common-law rule against perpetuities (RAP) provides that no interest in land is valid unless it must vest, if it ever vests, within 21 years of lives in being at the creation of the interest.

The rule against perpetuities does not apply to reversions retained by the grantor and reversionary type interests such as reverter and rights of entry for conditions subsequent, or to the grantee who holds such a reversionary interest because of a conveyance from the grantor.

The rule against perpetuities does apply to future interests created in persons other than the grantor.

Those interests are the remainder, executory interests, and first refusal rights.

The validity of the interest to which the rule against perpetuities applies depends on whether the interest must vest, or in some circumstances, must become possessory within the statutory period set by the rule.

The first issue in determining the validity of interest is when the period established by the rule starts to run.

If a will creates an interest in land, the period starts to run at the testator's death. Individuals alive at that time are eligible to be measuring lives.

If an *inter vivos* conveyance creates an interest in land, the period starts to run at the time of conveyance. Individuals alive at that time are eligible to be measuring lives.

If an *inter vivos* conveyance creates the interest in land to trust, and if the trust is irrevocable, the period starts to run at the time of the conveyance.

If the trust is initially revocable, the period starts to run when the power to amend or revoke the trust is terminated through the death of the person with the power to amend or terminate it or the relinquishment of the power thereof.

A child conceived but not born at the time of the commencement of the rule will be considered a life in being.

Thus, if a father dies before his child is born, that child will be considered a life in being at the father's death.

The period during which interest must vest under the rule is a minimum of 21 years from when the period begins to run.

That period is extended by the lives in being at the time of the creation of the interest so that the maximum period for vesting is extended to 21 years after the death of a life in being at the creation of the interest, otherwise known as a measuring life.

An interest vests when all persons taking the interest have been ascertained, and no condition precedent prevents their interest from becoming possessory whenever the preceding interest terminates.

If an interest must vest within 21 years when the rule starts to run, it is valid without considering any measuring lives that might extend the period during which the rule runs.

The 21-year period does not make it so that persons born within 21 years of the time that the running of the rule commences constituting measuring lives.

Remainders that may remain contingent beyond the period of the rule, executory interests that may not become possessory during the period, and rights of first refusal that may not become operative during the rule are invalid because of the rule against perpetuities.

Under the common-law rule against perpetuities, a person's ability to have children until death is irrebuttable. If the presence of that possibility prevents an interest from becoming vested during the period of the rule, that interest is invalid.

Under the common-law rule against perpetuities as applied to class gifts, the entire disposition is invalid if any member of the class's interest is invalid.

When an interest is invalid because of the rule against perpetuities, the following rules determine the construction of the conveyance:

If the conveyance has multiple alternative dispositions and only one is invalid, the disposition is construed with the invalid gift deleted.

If the invalid interest is the will's residuary clause, the testator's heirs take. Those heirs under the modern law are determined as if the testator died when the last valid interest terminated, not at the time of the testator's death.

If a conveyance creates an invalid interest, the grantor or the grantor's heirs take by reversion.

Powers of appointment

A power of appointment permits the holder of the power either during that holder's lifetime or in the holder's will to direct the disposition of assets set up in trust by the grantor of that trust containing the power.

A power of appointment is special if the potential beneficiaries of the exercise of that power are limited and general if the holder of the power can direct the assets to anyone.

Jurisdictions are split on whether a will's residuary clause, which does not explicitly refer to a general power of appointment, exercises that power in favor of the residuary beneficiary.

The period of the rule against perpetuities does not start to run until the holder's power of appointment is either exercised or expires.

The period for the rule against perpetuities for a special power of appointment starts to run when the trust becomes irrevocable.

Restraints on alienation

A right reserved by the seller to repurchase the property at the same price, which the owner could obtain from a third party, a right of first refusal, is not an invalid restraint on alienation.

If such a right can be exercised in a time which extends beyond the operative time for the rule against perpetuities, it is invalid, even during the fixed 21-year period of the rule.

A prohibition in a conveyance by the grantor of a grantee's right to alienate property or a provision forfeiting an interest if the grantee attempts to alienate property is invalid.

If an owner of property enters into a contract restricting their right to alienate property, that contract is valid.

Restraints on alienation are invalid only when imposed on the grantee of property by the grantor.

Characteristics of co-tenancies

There is no right of survivorship when parties own property as tenants in common.

Joint tenancy is not devisable or inheritable and cannot be severed by a will.

A co-tenant who makes improvements to the property cannot charge co-tenants for contribution to the cost of the improvements. However, those improvements can be considered in a partition proceeding.

When the property is partitioned, it is accompanied by an accounting between co-tenants concerning payments of expenses and collection of rents.

A co-tenant occupying the property they own as a co-tenant does not owe rent to co-tenants.

Co-tenants holding as joint tenants or tenants in common have an inalienable right to partition.

A tenancy by the entirety can be partitioned by joint deeds of the two co-owners or if the entirety is converted to a tenancy in common by divorce.

The preferred method of partition is a physical division of the property.

When a physical division is not feasible or cannot be accomplished so that each party is fairly treated, the partition is accomplished by a sale at auction and a division of the proceeds.

When parties hold property in joint tenancy or tenancy by the entirety, one tenant's death triggers the complete title vesting in the surviving tenant.

Furthermore, an involuntary lien placed against the interest of the dead co-tenant does not burden the surviving co-tenant.

If one joint owner mortgages their interest in the property and later dies, the interest passes to the other joint tenant free of the mortgage.

One tenant in common owes a fiduciary duty to permit the other co-tenant to maintain proportionate property ownership by paying their proportionate share of debt if one co-tenant acquires the property at a foreclosure sale.

Co-tenancy between spouses

A tenancy by the entirety can only be created between spouses.

Neither party can terminate the tenancy by the entirety using a unilateral act during the marriage.

If one spouse attempts to convey their interest, the conveyance is void, and the spouses still hold the title as tenants by the entirety.

If two persons who are not married take title as tenants by the entirety, they hold the title as joint tenants.

Conversion of joint tenancies into tenancies in common

One joint tenant's conveyance of their interest to a third party converts the title to tenancy in common rights between the other original joint tenant and the third-party grantee.

The joint tenancy is terminated even if the third party reconveys to the original joint tenant.

If a mortgage on the property only creates a lien under state law, one joint tenant granting a mortgage does not terminate the joint tenancy.

If granting a mortgage under state law vests title in the mortgagee subject to a right of redemption, granting a mortgage by one joint tenant terminates the *joint tenancy* and transforms it into a *tenancy in common* between the original joint tenants.

Two joint tenants' simultaneous death creates an undivided one-half interest as a tenant in common in each joint tenant's estates.

If A and B, who hold the entire fee in a parcel of land, jointly convey an undivided one-third interest in the property to C, A and B still hold an undivided two-thirds interest as joint tenants, not as tenants in common. C holds their interest as a *tenant in common* with A and B.

Rights and liabilities of adjoining landowners

The owner of land in its natural state can successfully sue an adjoining landowner who disturbs the support that the adjoining land provides on a strict liability theory without showing negligence.

The owner of improved land can successfully sue an adjoining landowner who disturbs that support only if they prove that the adjoining landowner is negligent.

Rights in Land

Express easements

An *express easement*, or easement by grant, must be in writing and signed by the grantor of the burdened land to be valid.

If permission is oral by the landowner to use land, a license, not an easement, is created.

The *license* is terminable at the will of the owner of the land.

Express easements are interests in land subject to the recording system.

An easement by a grant must be recorded to burden *bona fide* purchasers of the burdened (i.e., servient) land.

An express easement is subject to superior rights existing on the servient estate when it is recorded.

If a mortgage on the property is foreclosed, the purchaser at the foreclosure sale is not burdened by the easement.

An easement is appurtenant if it burdens one parcel of land, the servient estate, for another parcel's specific benefit, the dominant estate.

A conveyance of a parcel of land, which has the benefit of an appurtenant easement, automatically transfers to the grantee the rights in that appurtenant easement even if it is not mentioned in the conveyance.

If the benefits of an easement are appurtenant to one parcel of land, the owner of that land cannot use the easement to benefit an adjacent parcel they own.

The easement is deemed to be "overburdened."

A holder of an appurtenant easement can only transfer the benefits of that easement by transferring the ownership interest in the benefited estate.

An attempted alienation of the easement rights to a person who does not own the benefited estate destroys the easement.

The holder of an easement has the right to make repairs to property within the easement they have a right to use (e.g., stairs, pipes, roads) but does not have an obligation to repair unless they agree.

A person cannot have an easement on land which they own in fee simple.

If the benefited estate holder acquires the servient estate fee simple, the easement is destroyed by merger.

If the two estates are separated later, the deed to the dominant estate creates an easement over the servient estate only if the easement right is expressly granted in the deed.

This principle is not applicable unless the holder has identical interests in the dominant and servient estates.

Even though an oral agreement will not create an easement, if a landowner induces a neighboring landowner to substantially rely on them not assert their property right, the owner is estopped asserting property rights they said would be waived.

Overuse of an easement can be prohibited by an injunction but does not destroy the easement.

When the exact location of an easement is not specified, the servient estate owner has the right to reasonably locate the precise right-of-way.

Once the right-of-way location is established, the easement's location becomes fixed and cannot be moved without the owners of the servient and dominant estates' consent.

An express easement can be terminated by adverse possession if the landowner affirmatively bars the easement holder from using the easement for the statutory period.

Failure to use an easement right, by itself, is insufficient to terminate an easement.

An express easement is valid for an indefinite time unless its duration is limited in the grant itself or subsequently limited in time by the dominant estate holder.

The end of the reason for creating an express easement does not terminate an express easement.

Profit-a-prendre

A *profit-a-prendre* (French, *right of taking*) combines an easement right to enter the land of another and the right to sever interests (e.g., timber, minerals) from the land and remove them.

Because a *profit-a-prendre* incorporates an easement right, it is an interest in property that must be created and recorded with the same formalities as an express easement and unlimited in time unless a time limit is specified.

A *profit-a-prendre* can give the holder an exclusive right to sever property from the land so that the land's fee simple owner no longer has that right.

If the holder has an exclusive right, they can divide that right and assign portions to others.

If the *profit-a-prendre* is not exclusive, the holder cannot apportion it.

Easements by necessity and implication

Easements by necessity and implication arise out of the presumed intent of the parties to a conveyance.

If the document states explicitly there is no intent to create an easement right, neither an easement by necessity nor implication will arise.

An easement by necessity arises only where the parcel is being severed by a conveyance of part of a larger parcel is landlocked and has no legal access of any kind.

The easement is an easement by reservation if the grantor is the party retaining the landlocked parcel of land.

An easement by implication (a situation where a *quasi*-easement exists at the time of the separation of the dominant and servient estates) will be created as long as the easement is reasonably necessary to serve the dominant estate.

An easement by necessity or implication arises only when there is no express easement.

An easement by necessity or implication can only be created during the division of a commonly owned parcel.

If a parcel later becomes landlocked because of an eminent domain taking or otherwise, there is no easement over the larger parcel of land from which the landlocked parcel came.

An easement created by necessity ends when the necessity ends.

For example, if the government provided access to a formerly landlocked parcel, the easement by necessity once held over the adjoining land would terminate.

An easement for light and air or view can only be created by an express easement; such an easement does not arise by necessity or implication.

An easement by necessity or implication need not be recorded to be effective against *bona fide* purchasers.

Adverse possession

Title by adverse possession is obtained if the possessor is in continuous, open, and notorious adverse possession and has exclusive possession for the statutory period.

The method of calculating the statutory period is:

The period for adverse possession does not start to run while the true owner is a minor or is adjudicated mentally incompetent.

If the adverse possessor initially goes into possession while a competent adult owns the property, the subsequent transfer of ownership to a minor or a person with a disability does not interrupt the running of the statutory period.

If the true owner transfers title to the property while the adverse possessor is in possession, the running of the statutory period is not interrupted.

The adverse possessor is entitled to aggregate their time in possession against successive owners to achieve adverse possession for the required statutory period.

The consensual transfer of possessory rights from one adverse possessor to a subsequent adverse possessor permits the subsequent adverse possessor to include the time in which their predecessor was in possession to achieve adverse possession for the required statutory period.

The requirement of continuous and exclusive possession states that:

If the true owner possesses the property in common with the adverse possessor at any time during the required statutory period, the adverse possessor is no longer maintaining continuous, exclusive possession and must start the statutory period again once the true owner leaves.

The actions necessary to satisfy the exclusive and continuous requirements depend upon the type of property involved.

The requirements are less strict for an uninhabited rural or seasonal property than for urban property.

Fencing in the adjacent property or placing all or part of a building on the property adjacent to the property owned satisfies the continuous and exclusive requirements.

The requirement that possession be adverse states that:

Because a co-tenant has a right to occupy all the property they hold as a co-tenant, open, notorious, and exclusive possession by one co-tenant for the statutory period will not establish adverse possession unless explicit notice was given to the other co-tenant at the beginning of that period.

Such notice is usually in the form of a co-tenant barring another from using the property.

Unless it is established that the possession was permissive, possession by an individual where nothing concerning permission is established is considered adverse.

An adverse possessor need not know that they possess the property of another to obtain the property by adverse possession.

Fencing in property belonging to a neighbor in the mistaken belief that the adverse possessor is fencing in their property is sufficient to establish adverse possession.

Title by adverse possession can be obtained to airspace by projections from a structure that overhangs the abutting property.

After an adverse possessor's actions have enabled them to obtain title by adverse possession, the interruption of their exclusive possession by anyone, including the true owner, will not defeat the adverse possessor's title.

Neither title by adverse possession, nor an easement by prescription, need be recorded to be valid against the record titleholder or purchaser.

If two persons act together to obtain title by adverse possession, the adverse possessors hold as tenants in common, not joint tenants.

If one of two adverse possessors dies, their interest in the property goes to their heirs or devisees, not to the surviving joint adverse possessor.

Easements by prescription

The difference between the conduct necessary to achieve an easement by prescription and that needed to obtain title by adverse possession is that possession need not be exclusive to obtain an easement by prescription.

How the property is used during the period necessary to acquire an easement by prescription defines the easement scope after the prescriptive period.

Once the conduct necessary to obtain an easement by prescription continues for the time necessary to achieve the easement, continuous use of the easement after that is not necessary to maintain it.

An easement by prescription can be obtained even if the person acquiring an easement by prescription uses the property without communicating that the use is adverse.

If the use of property commenced as a permissive use, notice to the owner that its character had changed and was adverse would be required to obtain an easement by prescription.

The holder of an easement by prescription has no obligation to keep it in repair.

Fixtures

Upon default, the holder of a properly recorded purchase money security interest can remove a fixture over the objection of a real estate mortgagee if the property subject to the interest is removable, even if the mortgage date preceded the date of the security interest.

A tenant for a fixed term has the right to remove personal property (i.e., trade fixtures) that they attached to the real estate for the lease term, even though the attachment of the property might cause it to be characterized as real property,

A person having an estate of uncertain duration (such as a life estate) who plants crops on that land can enter the land and remove the crops at the end of the growing season even if the possessory property right has terminated.

A person having an estate of uncertain duration who attaches fixtures to the real estate, which can easily be removed without damage to the real estate, can remove them within a reasonable time after the estate terminates.

In a life estate, the personal representative can remove the fixtures.

The mortgagee cannot prevent the mortgagor from removing portions of the real estate secured by their mortgage if removing the structure would leave adequate security for the mortgagee, and removal is reasonable and proper in the prudent management of the business.

Covenants

Covenants run with the land and bind successor owners if:

- they are in writing and formed a contract between the original parties;
- they touch and concern the land;
- the burdened party has notice of the covenant, either actual notice or constructive notice, through recording;
- privity exists between the party initially imposing the restriction and the party enforcing it;
- privity exists between the party initially burdened by the restriction and the party against whom it is being enforced.

The person who imposes a covenant running with the land cannot enforce that covenant against a subsequent purchaser of the burdened land unless at that time they are the owner of the land which was intended to be benefited by the covenant.

Zoning ordinances do not automatically override a private restrictive covenant.

Whichever is stricter (i.e., zoning ordinance or covenant) will prevail.

To be binding, a restrictive covenant must be placed on the property at the time when it is conveyed.

The burden cannot be attached to a parcel of land later by someone who has no interest in that parcel of land.

Although the Statute of Frauds applies to covenants, the recording of a deed containing a covenant running with the land by a grantee of land burdened by the covenant is a satisfactory substitute for a memorandum signed by the grantee.

Covenants running with the land can be enforced with injunctive relief.

Common schemes

If the grantor consistently imposes similar covenants on a group of lots in a subdivision, they have created a common scheme.

Two effects of the creation of a common scheme that is not true of covenants, in general, are:

1) the owner of lots burdened by the covenant restrictions can sue the owner of any other lot burdened by the covenant to enforce the restrictions.

2) the grantor can be required to impose similar restrictions on the remaining lots in the subdivision, even if they had not promised in writing to do so.

If there is no common scheme, persons owning lots not owned by the person imposing the restriction when it was imposed cannot enforce the restriction.

Mortgages

Once the property owner validly gives a mortgage, it remains a lien on the property until the obligation securing it is paid in full and the mortgage is discharged, or the holder of the mortgage voluntarily gives a discharge before being required to do so.

If the mortgagor agrees not to transfer the property subject to the mortgage without the mortgagee's consent, the transfer without the mortgagee's consent constitutes a breach of the mortgage, permitting the mortgagee to declare the entire amount of the mortgage note immediately or to foreclose.

The following rules apply when a mortgage is foreclosed.

If a mortgage foreclosure sale brings more than enough to satisfy the outstanding encumbrance, the balance is paid to satisfy the holders of junior encumbrances, and any remaining balance is paid to the mortgagor.

A judgment lien is a junior lien to existing mortgages on property held by the debtor when the mortgage lien is filed.

If the mortgage foreclosure sale brings less than the amount necessary to satisfy the mortgage note and foreclosure expenses, the mortgage note holder may collect the remaining balance on the note from the mortgagor or purchasers from the mortgagor, depending upon the terms of the mortgage and the subsequent transfer of the property.

The title of a mortgage foreclosure purchaser is not subject to encumbrances placed on the land after the mortgage.

For example, if O gives a mortgage to A and subsequently gives a mortgage to B, P may take the property free of the mortgage to B if they purchase at the foreclosure of the mortgage to A.

The foreclosure of a prior mortgage does not eliminate a junior encumbrance unless notice of the mortgage foreclosure is given to the junior encumbrance holder.

The junior encumbrance holder may still redeem the property from the foreclosing prior mortgagee or still foreclose the mortgage.

A mortgagee has the right to take possession of the property to preserve it if the mortgagor is in default by failing to make the required payments or breaching other mortgage covenants.

When a mortgagee takes possession, they assume the tort liabilities of the equitable owner.

When a second mortgage is foreclosed, the purchaser at the foreclosure sale must continue to pay the first mortgage, which remains a valid prior encumbrance on the property.

If the mortgagor has given the mortgagee a mortgage on several parcels of land and has, after that, transferred some of the parcels without discharge of the mortgage, and the mortgage is in default, the mortgagee must first foreclose on the remaining parcel owned by the mortgagor.

Furthermore, if they are not satisfied in full by that foreclosure, they may foreclose on the remaining parcels in the inverse order in which the mortgagor alienated them.

The following rules apply when the property owner who has given a mortgage transfers property without discharging the mortgage.

It the buyer agrees to assume and pay the mortgage, the buyer is primarily liable on the mortgage, and the original mortgagor is only secondarily liable on the mortgage.

If the mortgagor is required to pay the mortgage note, they may collect the amount paid from the buyer who purchased the property.

If the buyer takes subject to the mortgage (i.e., without agreeing to pay the debt), the buyer is not liable for a deficiency judgment on the mortgage note in the event of foreclosure but can lose the property through foreclosure if they do not pay the mortgage.

The original mortgagor is still primarily liable for any deficiency judgment on the mortgage notes.

If the mortgagor, buyer, and mortgagee enter into a novation at the time of transfer of the property, the buyer is liable to the mortgagee on the mortgage note, and the mortgagor has no liability on the mortgage note.

The following priorities apply when there are multiple security interests on the property.

A mortgage given by the purchaser to the former owner as a part of the property's purchase price, which is recorded immediately after the deed, takes precedence over other liens placed on the property at the time of the conveyance.

The holder of a valid personal property security interest has the right to remove that property on default over a mortgagee's objections who held a valid lien on the real estate when the personal property was affixed to the land.

The following rules apply to equitable mortgages, which occur when the property owner gives a deed rather than a mortgage to secure a debt, with the understanding that the creditor will deed the property back to the debtor when the debt is paid.

Neither the *parol evidence rule* nor the *Statute of Frauds* prevents the debtor from proving by oral evidence that a mortgage transaction rather than a sale was intended when the debtor gave a deed to the creditor.

When the debt has been repaid, the debtor can require a reconveyance of the property if the title is held by the creditor or someone knowing the deed constituted an equitable mortgage.

If the creditor has transferred title to a *bona fide* purchaser, the debtor cannot obtain the property's reconveyance but can obtain damages from the creditor.

If the debtor defaults on the payment of the debt secured by an equitable mortgage, the creditor is not the property's automatic owner but must foreclose the mortgage under state law.

The mortgagor of a property may do such acts on the mortgaged property, including removing part of the building, which is part of the mortgaged premises during good husbandry.

When there is an outstanding mortgage on real estate when the testator dies and devises it, the devisees take the property subject to the mortgage unless the testator requires the executor to discharge the mortgage with other assets of the estate.

Other security devices

Other security devices (e.g., installment sales contracts), where the purchaser is given possession of the property but does not receive a deed until all installments are paid, are treated as a mortgage by a court.

Appropriate procedures required for foreclosure and redemption to protect the owner's equity are required if the property's possessor defaults on their obligation.

Choice of property devices

Covenants that run with the land are the most useful property devices to control land use without harming the title's marketability.

Covenants require that the person enforcing them must own the benefited land.

Easements are useful when limited use of a parcel is desired for an indefinite period.

A conditional fee simple, which takes the title away from the party in possession if they breach their obligations, is useful only where the marketability of the possessor's property interest is not an issue.

The holder of the residuary interest who will take if the condition is broken need not be the owner of any benefited land.

Zoning and other forms of governmental control are limited because they are subject to change by the political process.

Water rights

Under the common law, each landowner through whose land a watercourse flows have the right to make reasonable use of the water.

In determining reasonable use, domestic uses such as drinking water and water for toilets and washing are superior to artificial uses such as irrigation.

In states where riparian rights are governed by the doctrine of *prior appropriation*, the first riparian user to appropriate water for use has the right to continue to use that quantity of water even to the detriment of other riparian owners.

Water from melting snows and rain is diffuse surface water. A landowner may impound diffuse surface waters if they do not do so maliciously.

Notes for active learning

Vendor and Purchaser

Statute of Frauds

An action for specific performance of a land contract must ordinarily satisfy the Statute of Frauds.

The Statute of Frauds is satisfied if a memorandum signed by the party to be charged contains the essential terms of the agreement, namely, the price and an adequate description of the property.

The requirement of a memorandum signed by the party to be charged is not applicable if there are actions that constitute a part performance.

A deposit is not necessary to make a written purchase and sale agreement enforceable, which satisfies the Statute of Frauds.

The Statute of Frauds applies to an agreement among co-owners to change how they hold the property (e.g., change from a tenancy in common to joint tenancy).

An oral agreement to waive the application of the Statute of Frauds is not effective.

The Statute of Frauds is not satisfied by a memorandum creating a brokerage contract.

Payment of the purchase price by the buyer and acceptance by the seller is not sufficient part performance to take an oral agreement out of the Statute of Frauds.

Part performance

If there is no written agreement, a court of equity can specifically enforce an oral agreement to convey if the part performance doctrine is satisfied.

In all cases, there must be an oral agreement to purchase the land relied upon by the purchaser to their detriment.

Part performance is satisfied in many jurisdictions if the seller engaged in equitable fraud.

In other jurisdictions, the court will order a conveyance only if the conduct of the parties unequivocally proves that an oral agreement to convey existed.

This test is ordinarily satisfied when the purchaser pays the purchase price, has possession of the land with the seller's permission, and improves the land.

This test is known as the *unequivocal referability* theory.

Enforceability of purchase and sale agreements by specific performance

Buyers and sellers have the right to specifically enforce purchase and sale agreements for land as well as the right to a damage remedy.

Rights under a purchase and sale agreement survive the deaths of the seller or buyer and may be enforced by the executors of their respective estates.

Equitable conversion

Because buyer and seller have the right to specific performance of a contract to sell land, the doctrine of equitable conversion fixes the time of the property transformation from personalty to realty when a binding purchase and sale agreement is executed by buyer and seller.

Where the doctrine is applicable, upon the execution of a binding purchase and sale agreement, the buyer's interest is immediate in realty, and the seller's interest is immediate in personalty.

The risk of loss is on the buyer when a binding purchase and sale agreement is executed.

A binding purchase and sale agreement recorded serves as notice to any subsequent purchaser from the seller, preventing them from becoming a *bona fide* purchaser.

Time of closing

If a purchase and sale agreement contains a provision that "time is of the essence," the seller and the buyer are in default if they do not close or tender performance on the date specified in the agreement.

If a purchase and sale agreement does not contain a provision that "time is of the essence," each party must close within a reasonable time, and neither is in default if they fail to close on the date specified in the agreement.

Marketable title

A seller need not own the property or have marketable title to it when entering into a purchase and sale agreement for the agreement to be valid.

If a purchase and sale agreement is silent concerning the title to be conveyed, the seller is required to deliver a marketable title.

The title of the holder of a fee simple determinable or a fee simple subject to a condition subsequent is not marketable.

The title is not marketable if an undivided interest is not being conveyed or an encumbrance is not to be discharged.

The limitation placed by a zoning ordinance on the property's future use does not render the title unmarketable.

If the property violates a zoning ordinance at the time set for closing, the title is unmarketable.

If the title would expose a potential buyer to litigation, which is not frivolous, the seller's title is unmarketable.

A person who has obtained title to the property by adverse possession does not have marketable title unless the title has been confirmed in a judicial proceeding.

A seller's obligation to deliver marketable title occurs at the time of the closing. The seller can use portions of the purchase price to pay off encumbrances, which would otherwise destroy marketable title.

Survival of covenants in the purchase and sale agreement

If the buyer accepts a deed to fulfill the seller's obligations under a purchase and sale agreement, the covenants in the purchase and sale agreement are no longer enforceable unless the agreement states that they survive the closing.

Nevertheless, the buyer has the right to sue for a breach of warranty of the deed's covenants.

Failure to disclose hidden defects

Failure by the seller to disclose a latent material defect that could not be discovered by inspection will give the buyer a right to sue for damages or rescind the transaction.

Notes for active learning

Title

Delivery and validity of a deed

To be valid, the grantor must sign a deed, adequately describe the property to be conveyed, and adequately describe the grantee.

Consideration is not needed for a deed to be valid.

Consideration is necessary to enforce a promise to convey property.

A fraudulently altered release, a forged deed, or an undelivered deed stolen is null and conveys no title.

Even if the instrument is recorded, a *bona fide* purchaser who relies on it in good faith is not protected.

If a deed is placed into escrow as part of a commercial real estate transaction and the transaction is completed, the transfer of title is when the deed was delivered into escrow.

The recording does not deprive a grantor of a cause of action to rescind a conveyance against their immediate grantee.

The recording system protects only an innocent purchaser from the immediate grantee.

Title to real estate is transferred from the grantor to the grantee when the grantor delivers a validly executed deed to the grantee, even if the deed is not recorded.

Handing the deed to the grantee or their agent raises a rebuttable presumption of delivery.

The fact that a deed has been recorded raises a presumption that it has been delivered.

The original deed's subsequent redelivery, which has not been recorded from the grantee to the grantor, does not retransfer title to the grantor.

A new deed signed by the grantee to the grantor is required to revest title in the grantor.

A valid transfer of title requires the delivery of a valid deed, which the grantee has accepted.

Acceptance is presumed if the gift is beneficial.

The title has not been transferred if the grantee has affirmatively indicated that they have not accepted the deed.

The existence of a grantee who is identifiable with certainty is a requirement of a valid deed.

A deed delivered with the grantee intentionally left blank is valid and authorizes the person receiving the deed to fill in the grantee's name.

A deed to a grantee who is dead at the time of conveyance does not convey title to the grantee or their estate.

Unless a deed specifies a lesser interest (e.g., a life estate), a deed conveys a fee simple interest.

A gift *causa mortis* may only be made of personal property.

A gift may be made of real estate.

A deed is required as an element for a gift.

Description of property

The property must be described with reasonable certainty to satisfy the condition that the property conveyed be reasonably identified in a deed.

A reference in a deed to a survey or plan is sufficient to identify the property, even if the survey or plan is not recorded.

If the deed description can not determine the exact location of the property conveyed, *parol evidence* is admissible to clarify the parties' intent.

If it is not possible to describe the property conveyed from the contents of the deed itself or with the aid of ancillary procedures, the deed is invalid.

For a *metes and bounds* description of the property, a conflict between distances set forth in the deed and monuments on the ground, the monuments prevail over distance.

If a property boundary describes a private way, the owner owns to the midpoint of the way.

If the deed to property understates the acreage that the parties intended to convey, the grantee is entitled to have an equity court reform the deed to reflect the correct acreage conveyed.

If abutters, uncertain of their exact boundary, fix a line by agreement, either oral or written, and abide by the boundary line, the agreement is valid and enforceable in fixing the boundary even though the boundary is fixed by their respective deeds may be different.

Covenants of title

A quitclaim deed contains no covenants so that the grantee has no claim under the deed against the grantor if the title is defective.

A warranty deed contains present covenants, such as a covenant with no encumbrances on the property, which run only to the grantee and not to their successors.

Present covenants are breached, if at all, at the time of conveyance and thus are limited by a statute of limitations which starts at the time of the conveyance.

A warranty deed contains future covenants that run to the grantee and successors.

The future covenant of quiet enjoyment is breached when the grantee or successor in title is ousted from possession from all or part of the land by one having a superior title.

The covenants of title in a warranty deed do not carry the obligation to pay for a title defense.

There is no requirement that a grantee who receives a deed with covenants need be a *bona fide* purchaser to sue the grantor for breach of warranty if the covenants are not true.

Estoppel by deed

Estoppel by deed applies to validate a deed (e.g., warranty deed) executed and delivered by a grantor who had no title to the land at that time but who represented that they have such title and who after that acquired such title.

For example, A gives a warranty deed of Blackacre to B when A does not own it, and A later acquires title from O, the true owner. B is the property owner without the delivery of a new deed when A acquires title from O.

Operation of the recording system

A deed or other instrument delivered need not be recorded to be effective for the original parties to the transaction.

A *bona fide* purchaser (BFP) who is a subsequent grantee prevails over a prior grantee who fails to record their deed.

A *bona fide* purchaser takes free of encumbrances on the property given by the grantor, which has not been recorded.

A mortgage lien does not automatically have priority over a judgment lien.

A mortgagee who loans money after a judgment lien is recorded is considered to have constructive notice of the judgment lien and cannot be a *bona fide* purchaser and does not have priority over judgment liens.

If O, the owner of the property, delivers a deed to a grantee A and A records immediately, but O then subsequently delivers a deed of the same property to another grantee B, B loses in an action against A because they cannot be a *bona fide* purchaser with respect to a deed that has been properly recorded.

The issue of if grantee prevails does not turn on whether the first grantee is a *bona fide* purchaser.

The inquiry of a *bona fide* purchaser is relevant only for the second grantee.

If A receives and promptly records a deed to the property as a gift and is thus not a purchaser, A prevails in an action by B, a subsequent grantee, even if B paid O for an interest in the property.

The act of recording a valid purchase and sale agreement establishes the purchaser's order of priority in determining rights against subsequent grantees or subsequent lien holders.

The recording system does not protect *bona fide* purchasers who acquire from a person who appears to have good record title but who obtained title by a forged deed.

Bona fide purchasers who acquire from a person who has good record title but who has lost the title by adverse possession are not protected by the recording system and will lose to the person acquiring title by adverse possession.

For example:

The following scenario demonstrates a deed recorded out of order in the chain of title in the recording system:

1) A deeds to B with a warranty deed, but A does not own the property.

2) B records.

3) O, the true owner, deeds to A.

Under the doctrine of estoppel by deed, the deed passes immediately to B.

The deed from A to B is valid even though it is recorded before A had title.

In this case, someone searching the title would not find the deed from A to B, which made B the property owner if they were searching O's name in the grantor index. A search would find the deed from O to A.

The same problem occurs, in the following scenario, when the grantee records late:

1) O deeds to A.

2) A fails to record promptly.

3) O deeds to B as a gift. B records.

4) A records.

In this case, B prevails as the owner over A. Someone searching title would not find the deed from O to A in the grantor index if they searched A's name until O alienated the property by deeding to B.

In each case, a subsequent purchaser can be a *bona fide* purchaser and prevail over the true owner because the deed recorded out of order is not constructive notice to a subsequent *bona fide* purchaser.

If a subsequent *bona fide* purchaser obtains title, the prior grantee has no further interest in the property.

For example, if O deeds to A who does not record and then deeds to B, a subsequent *bona fide* purchaser, and B then deeds to C, who knows of the deed from O to A, C will prevail over A because B prevails over A.

Characteristics of a *bona fide* purchaser

Not all persons who might have an interest in property are "purchasers" who have the protection of the recording system.

Judgment lien holders are frequently denied protection.

A statute frequently used in multistate questions provides:

> *"Any judgment properly filed shall, for ten years from filing, be a lien on the real property then owned or subsequently acquired by any person against whom the judgment is rendered."*

If such a statute is in effect, the judgment lien, even though recorded, does not prevail against an owner who took from the person against whom the judgment was rendered but did not record their deed before the judgment was recorded.

A person who takes a conveyance in satisfaction of a prior debt is considered a purchaser in most jurisdictions.

A person need not search title and rely on the registry records to qualify as a *bona fide* purchaser, although they would be charged with the notice that such a search would provide.

If the subsequent grantee has actual knowledge of the deed to the prior grantee, they cannot prevail even if the prior grantee's deed is not properly recorded.

Facts that would be discovered by an inspection of the property and lead to a further inquiry can destroy a buyer's status as a *bona fide* purchaser.

Even though a donee is not a purchaser and will not prevail over a prior grantee who has not recorded, a *bona fide* purchaser from the donee prevails over a prior grantee if the prior grantee has not properly recorded at the time that the purchaser from the donee accepts the deed and records.

Types of recording systems

There are two principal types of recording systems:

1) The standard notice type recording statute provides:

"No conveyance or mortgage of real property shall be good against subsequent purchasers for value and without notice unless the same be recorded according to law."

2) The standard race-notice recording system provides:

"No unrecorded conveyance or mortgage of real property shall be good against subsequent purchasers for value without notice, who shall first record."

The following transactions illustrate the difference between the standard notice and standard race-notice systems:

1) O, the owner of Blackacre conveys to A.

2) O, then conveys to B a purchaser for value who has no notice of the deed to A.

3) A records.

4) B records.

B prevails in a notice jurisdiction because A had not recorded at the time B paid consideration and received a deed.

In a race-notice jurisdiction, A prevails even though B is a *bona fide* purchaser because A recorded before B.

Landlord–tenant relationship

A landlord-tenant relationship arises when the owner, or possessor of property, grants a party the exclusive use of the property for some time.

A lessor who knows of a hidden defect in the premises must warn the tenant about that defect.

If a landlord denies a tenant the beneficial use of the property and the tenant moves out, the former tenant is not liable to pay rent because the denial of that beneficial use is a constructive eviction.

Under the doctrine of retaliatory eviction, a landlord cannot lawfully terminate a month-to-month tenancy or bring eviction proceedings at the termination of a lease if this action is a retaliation for the tenant's exercise of their legal rights (e.g., reporting building code violations).

The landlord, not the tenant, is the beneficiary of a covenant not to assign a lease and has a right to waive the covenant.

Types of tenancies

A periodic tenancy arises when there is no written lease, and the tenant occupies the property and pays rent periodically.

A periodic tenancy occurs when the tenant continues to occupy at the end of the lease term.

The duration of a periodic tenancy is determined by the length of the period between rent payments.

A periodic tenancy is terminated by notice from one party to the other, given before the commencement of a rental period.

A term for years is a tenancy of a fixed duration. Except for short-term leases of less than one year, the Statute of Frauds applies to a term for years.

A term for years is terminated at the end of the term without notice by either party.

If the tenant holds over, a periodic tenancy is created when the landlord accepts rent after the lease term.

A tenant at sufferance occurs when a tenant has entered the property under either a term for years or a periodic tenancy, and that tenancy has been terminated.

A landlord may bring immediate eviction proceedings against a tenant at sufferance.

Assignment and subletting of tenancies

The tenant must pay rent during the entire term because of the lease contract unless the landlord, tenant, and assignee enter into a novation, in which case the assignee has the contractual obligation to pay rent, and the tenant is no longer liable for the rent.

If the lease is silent, the tenant may assign their lease and sublet the property.

A covenant against assignment does not prevent a tenant from subletting the property.

An assignee is a person who has received from a tenant an assignment of their entire remaining leasehold interest.

A person can become an assignee and entitled to possession even if they have not contractually assumed the obligations of the lease.

Even if not contractually obligated on the lease, an assignee is obligated to pay rent to the landlord during the leasehold property's possession because they are in privity of estate with the landlord.

If an assignee is no longer privity to an estate because they further assigned the lease, they are not obligated to pay rent unless they have contractually assumed the lease obligations.

When a tenant validly assigns a lease, and the assignee assumes the lease, the assignee, and the landlord (or the landlord's successors) are bound by the covenants in the lease running with the land.

Examples include a covenant to pay taxes or a covenant granting the tenant a right to purchase the property.

If the tenant enters into a subtenancy, leasing the property for a term less than the remaining term, there is a new leasehold between the tenant, who is in effect a landlord, and the subtenant.

Where a subtenancy is created, there is no privity of estate between the subtenant and the landlord, and the subtenant is not obligated to pay rent to the landlord unless they agree explicitly.

Licenses

A *license* is permission to use the land of another.

It may be oral, written, or implied.

A license is revocable and is not subject to the Statute of Frauds.

Licenses are created when the occupier of land does not have an exclusive right of possession.

In contrast to a lease, a license permits the holder of a license to occupy the property but creates no property interest in the occupier.

If they hold the license according to a contract, they cannot specifically enforce the contract.

For a license to be irrevocable because of estoppel, the holder of the license must have justifiably incurred a detriment, such as the expenditure of funds to upgrade the property subject to a license in reliance upon an agreement not to revoke it.

Real Property – Quick Facts

1. A proposed use (or improvement) of an **express easement** must *not* exceed the scope of the express burden.
2. A **plat** is *only* a representation of a physical survey made of the land. The plat is like a certified copy of an instrument *controlled by the original*. A survey made and marked upon the ground *prevails* if it conflicts with the plat.
3. In a **partial condemnation**, the landlord-tenant relationship continues, as does the tenant's obligation to pay rent for the remaining lease term.
4. **Landlord-tenant** law traditionally refuses to recognize the *frustration of purpose* as grounds for terminating a lease.
5. Where **joint tenant** A informs joint tenant B that they can do something with a portion of the land, and joint tenant B reasonably relies on those statements to their detriment, joint tenant **A is estopped** to its effect.
6. The Statute of Frauds prevents the enforcement of an **oral agreement** concerning an interest in land.
7. **Reasonable Use Doctrine**—concerning underground water use—permits land use that is *not* merely malicious or a waste of water.
8. **Special Exception to Rule Against Perpetuities** for ***options to purchase attached to leaseholds***—when the one who holds the option is the current lessee, RAP does *not* apply.
9. If at the time a lease is entered into, the **landlord knows of a dangerous condition** that the tenant could not discover upon reasonable inspection, the landlord has a **duty to disclose** the dangerous condition. The landlord's failure to disclose imputes liability for injury resulting from the condition.
10. When a **tenant continues in possession *after* the termination** of their right to possession, the landlord has *two* choices of action:

    a) treat the holdover as a trespasser and evict under an unlawful detainer statute; or

    b) in their sole discretion, bind the tenant to a new **periodic tenancy**, in which case the **terms and conditions** of the expired tenancy apply to the new tenancy.
11. **Marketable title** is a title **reasonably free from doubt**, which generally means free from encumbrances and good record title.

    Easements are generally considered encumbrances that render title unmarketable. However, courts hold **beneficial easements visible or known** to the buyer are *not* an encumbrance.

12. **Reformation** may be available for a **mutual mistake**.

13. In general, courts presume that **time is *not* of the essence** in land contracts.

14. The **doctrine of equitable conversion** holds that once an enforceable contract of sale for real property is executed, the purchaser's interest is in *real property*. The seller's interest (i.e., right to proceeds) is *personal property*.

Relationship matrix

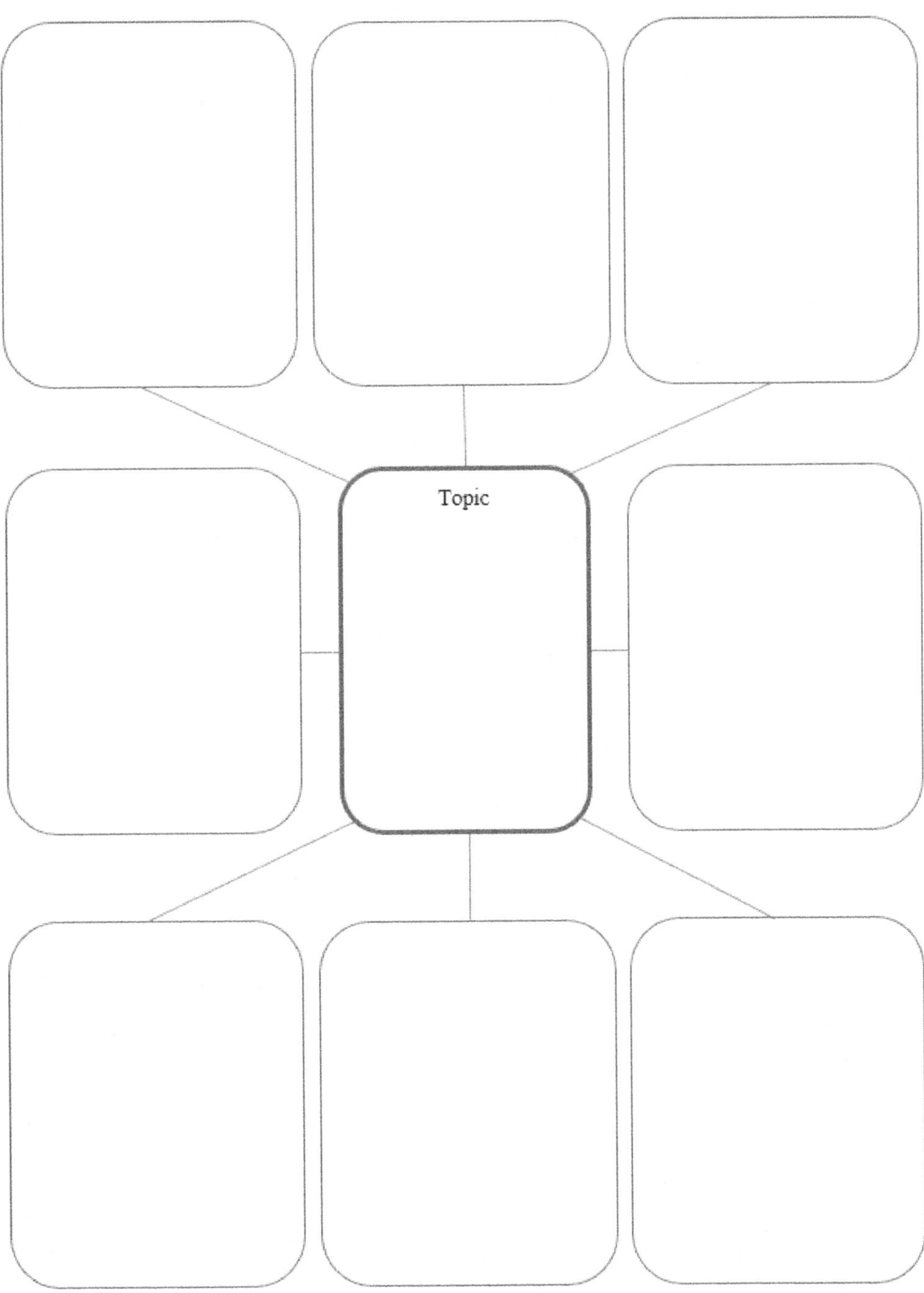

Notes for active learning

Torts

Torts topics tested on the exam are predictable. Master the principles to excel on Torts questions. The most frequently tested Torts issues are negligence (including duties of children), intentional torts, strict liability, products liability, premises liability, vicarious liability (may be coupled with Agency). On the essay portion of the exam, Torts generally is not combined with other subjects. However, it may be combined with Business Associations (e.g., Agency and vicarious liability).

The statements herein were compiled by analyzing released Torts questions and setting forth the principles of law governing the correct answers. Review these principles before preparing answers to practice Torts questions. Memorize this governing law and understand how it applies to the correct answer.

Per the National Conference of Bar Examiners (NCBE), assume that survival actions and wrongful death claims are available. Joint and several liability, with pure comparative negligence, is the relevant rule unless otherwise indicated.

Tort Law – Overview

Definitions

Tort – a non-contractual civil wrong.

Tortfeasor – one who commits a tort.

Personal injury – lawsuits for money damages for injuries; the most common personal injury cases involve automobile accidents.

Cause of action – the basis upon which a lawsuit may be filed in court.

Workers' compensation applies to those injured in the course of employment.

Punitive damage – money awards meant to punish and discourage such behavior.

Intentional torts

An intentional tort is one in which the party committing the tort intends to do the *act* (*knowing* – or with a substantial certainty that – it will cause an injury).

In situations where the same act is a tort and crime, the cases will be handled separately (civil and criminal court proceedings) within the legal system.

Intentional torts against persons

Assault – apprehension of imminent harm

Battery – unlawful contact with another

False imprisonment

Defamation of character

Misappropriation of the right to publicity

Invasion of the right to privacy

Intentional infliction of emotional distress

Intentional torts against property

Trespass to land

Trespass to and conversion of personal property

Unintentional torts (negligence)

Elements of Negligence

1) *Duty* – defendant owed a duty of care to the plaintiff.
2) *Breach* – defendant breached the duty of care.
3) *Causation* – defendant's negligent act caused the plaintiff's injury.
4) *Damages* – plaintiff suffered an injury.

Special Negligence Doctrine

Negligent infliction of emotional distress

Negligence *per se* (i.e., violates a statute or regulation)

res ipsa loquitur (Latin, *the thing speaks for itself*)

Strict (absolute) liability – liability without fault

Defective products (e.g., product liability)

Ultra-hazardous activities (e.g., blasting activities)

Dangerous animals (e.g., wild animals)

Intentional Torts

Children under the age of 7, while not liable for negligence as a matter of law, can be liable for intentional torts if they possess the requisite intent.

Assault

To render a defendant liable for assault, the plaintiff must prove that the:

1) defendant intended at the time of the act to commit a harmful or offensive bodily contact or instill apprehension of such contact, and
2) plaintiff was placed in apprehension of such imminent bodily harm.

No actual damages must be proven to complete the tort of assault.

Intent to cause apprehension of the offensive bodily contact is the state of mind required for assault.

Intent to make actual contact is not required.

The apprehension must be that the contact will be immediate.

A conditional threat of harm in the future does not constitute an assault but could constitute intentional infliction of emotional distress.

The tort of assault cannot be accomplished by words that create the required apprehension unless there is an actual or apparent ability to cause offensive contact.

Where the defendant intends to commit an assault, but not a battery, and the conduct causing the assault results in a battery, the intent to commit the assault fulfills the battery's intent requirement.

There is a privilege to commit an assault in self-defense, defense of others, and to eject trespassers.

These privileges exist if the actor reasonably believed that the circumstances called for the conduct necessary to use an assault in one of these privileged circumstances, even if the actor was mistaken.

Battery

There are four elements for the tort of battery:

1) there must be an intent to cause a touching,

2) there must be a touching,

3) there must not be "consent" to the touching, and

4) the touching must be harmful or offensive.

Proof of actual damages is not required.

The intent element

If the defendant lacks the mental capacity to know that they engaged in touching, they are not liable for battery.

If a party intended only to assault the plaintiff (placing in fear of imminent danger) and instead caused a touching, the intent to commit the assault is the intent necessary for the tort of battery.

Reckless or even willful conduct does not provide the mental intent for battery.

The consent element

Even if consent to physical contact is given during an athletic contest, an intentional force beyond the scope of that consent will result in an actionable battery.

The touching element

Ordinarily, the defendant commits battery by touching the actual person of the plaintiff.

The touching of an object close to the plaintiff, such as an item of clothing or a horse on which the plaintiff is riding, satisfies this element of the tort.

Placing in motion events that will cause an offensive contact constitutes the offensive contact necessary for a battery.

The defense of privilege

There is a privilege to use reasonable force to commit a battery in self-defense, defense of others, and eject trespassers.

These privileges exist if the actor reasonably believed they acted in the circumstances giving rise to the privilege and that the force was reasonable, even if there was a mistake.

An unreasonable belief will not sustain the privilege.

If a party is privileged to commit a battery on a third party, unintentional touching of the plaintiff will not give the plaintiff a cause of action in battery.

However, the plaintiff may have a cause of action in negligence.

An individual has the privilege to commit a battery if the battery prevents an actual injury to the plaintiff, and the actor reasonably believes that the plaintiff is in danger of receiving an actual injury.

False imprisonment

The tort of false imprisonment contains the following elements:

1) confinement (generally, knowledge by the confined)
2) intent to confine
3) lack of consent to the confinement

Since false imprisonment is an intentional tort, no actual damage must be proved as an element of the tort.

Confinement

Confinement occurs when the plaintiff's ability to move from their location is restricted.

Physical force to restrict that movement is unnecessary.

Confinement requires the plaintiff to be aware of the limitation on movement. If the plaintiff knows of a reasonable alternate route to avoid the limitation of movement, they are not confined.

Intent for false imprisonment

The defendant's intentional act must cause the plaintiff's confinement.

Privilege as a defense for false imprisonment

A shopkeeper has the privilege to use reasonable force to detain someone reasonably suspected of shoplifting for a limited time, only to determine if that person has engaged in shoplifting.

A citizen has the right to arrest, which constitutes confinement if they reasonably believe a felony has been committed and reasonably believe that the person detained was the felon.

A police officer has the right to arrest if executing an arrest warrant or arresting for a felony or misdemeanor committed in their presence.

Therefore, a person who has the right to arrest is privileged to confine and has a defense against a claim for false imprisonment.

A wrongful arrest constitutes false imprisonment.

The fact that the person arrested was not guilty of the crime for which they were arrested does not automatically give rise to a cause of action for false imprisonment.

Trespass to land

If the defendant intends to occupy the space they physically occupy, a mistaken belief that the land occupied is not the plaintiff's land will not be a defense to trespass.

Actual damages are not necessary for an action of trespass to land.

Nominal damages can be recovered.

If the defendant is unintentionally placed upon the plaintiff's land, there is no trespass.

However, there could be an action in negligence if the defendant is unintentionally placed upon the plaintiff's land. The negligence action requires damage to the plaintiff's land.

Nominal damages are not sufficient in a negligence action.

Whether express or implied, the consent of the landowner to the defendant's presence on the property is a defense to trespass.

A person may be privileged under emergency circumstances to enter upon another's property to protect the person or property.

An entry under such circumstances will not constitute a trespass.

The person using the property must pay the owner or possessor for damage done to the property.

A property owner has a right to use reasonable means to bar people from their land (through fences or obstructions) and has a privilege to use reasonable force to eject a trespasser but does not have the right to commit battery on the trespasser not connected with the ejection.

A landowner is not liable to a trespasser for ordinary negligence but is liable if they could have prevented the injury after becoming aware of it.

Conversion

Conversion requires *substantial interference* with the plaintiff's personal property.

If the defendant has wrongfully appropriated the plaintiff's personal property and substantially damaged or lost it, or if the defendant refuses to return it after demand, the plaintiff has an action in conversion for the full value of the property at the time when the defendant first appropriated it.

Trespass to chattels

The tort of trespass to chattels (i.e., personal property), unlike trespass to land, requires proof of damage or actual interference with the plaintiff's possessory rights to the personal property.

Trespass to chattels occurs when there is interference with chattels, which is not substantial enough to constitute conversion.

The damages recoverable for trespass to chattels are limited to the diminution in the chattels' value and compensation for the plaintiff's lost use of the chattels.

Intentional infliction of emotional distress

The tort of intentional infliction of emotional distress is composed of the following elements:

1) extreme and outrageous conduct by the defendant,
2) intent of the defendant to cause severe emotional distress.

The plaintiff must suffer emotional distress but need not suffer physical harm to collect damages for embarrassment and mental anguish.

The defendant's conduct must ordinarily be so extreme or outrageous that it would likely cause emotional distress in a person of ordinary sensibilities. However, conduct can be extreme or outrageous if the defendant knows of the plaintiff's unusual sensibilities and tailors conduct to cause the plaintiff's emotional distress.

The defendant who commits an intentional tort might be liable for intentional infliction of emotional distress to a family member of the victim if the defendant knew that a family member was a witness to that intentional tort.

Negligent infliction of emotional distress

If the defendant's negligence causes damage to an individual, a person who does not suffer physical injury as a direct result of the negligent conduct can recover for negligent infliction of emotional distress only if they:

1) experience some actual physical harm as opposed to embarrassment or mental anguish, from the defendant's negligence, and,

2) are within the zone of danger or,

3) witness harm to a family member.

The plaintiff could recover for negligent infliction of emotional distress only if the defendant's conduct were sufficient to cause emotional distress in a person of standard sensitivities.

Once this objective test is met, the plaintiff can recover for emotional harm suffered, even if the harm is unusual.

Negligent infliction of emotional distress caused by negligence in handling a loved one's remains is compensable without proof of physical harm.

If the plaintiff only suffers property damage, as opposed to a personal physical injury caused by the defendant's negligence, damages for emotional distress cannot be recovered.

Once a plaintiff suffers physical injury caused by the defendant's negligence, mental distress is an element of damages. The distinct elements of the tort of negligent infliction of emotional distress need not be met for the plaintiff to recover.

Nuisance

Private nuisance

Nuisance is a theory of tort liability independent of intentional torts and negligent torts.

A plaintiff has a cause of action in nuisance when the defendant's use of neighboring land unreasonably interferes with the use and enjoyment of their land.

If there is an actual physical invasion of the plaintiff's land by the defendant's use of neighboring land, the cause of action is for trespass rather than a nuisance.

Nuisance is applicable when there is detrimental use but not a physical invasion of the plaintiff's land.

A nuisance is a private nuisance if it unreasonably interferes with only a limited number of neighbors' use and enjoyment of their land.

Those neighbors have a cause of action for private nuisance.

Unreasonable interference

Land use before a neighbor arrives is a factor but not dispositive when considering if a use unreasonably interferes with the neighbor's land.

If the neighbor claiming unreasonable interference uses their land in a manner requiring freedom from regular neighborhood activity, they are unlikely to prevail in a suit with a landowner who has been conducting such regular activity before the plaintiff moved into the neighborhood.

The more objectionable the use of the defendant's land, the more likely that an adjoining landowner, even a newcomer, will prevail in nuisance.

The fact that a particular use is permitted on the offending land by local land-use regulations does not per se establish that the use is not a nuisance. However, it is evidence of the reasonableness of use.

Courts can impose injunctive or damage remedies in nuisance cases.

The social utility of land use, which affects neighboring land, such as an operation that recycles material, influences the court's choice of remedy, and may result in the denial of injunctive relief.

Public nuisance

A nuisance is a public nuisance if it interferes with the use and enjoyment of a large area of neighboring land.

In general, only public agencies have standing to pursue the public nuisance cause of action.

A private plaintiff has standing to sue for public nuisance if the harm affects the plaintiff's land more directly and intensely than it does to the larger area affected.

Strict Liability

Product liability for manufacturers

To prevail on a strict liability theory, a plaintiff must prove the product:

1) was defective when it left the defendant's hands,
2) was rendered unreasonably dangerous by that defect, and
3) caused the injury.

The defendant's exercise of utmost care in manufacturing or handling the product will not defeat the plaintiff's strict liability claim if the product was defective, dangerous, and caused an injury.

A product could be defective because it is unreasonably dangerous, even if the manufacturer did not know the danger and even if a regulatory authority approved its distribution.

The plaintiff must prove the defective product was causally related to the plaintiff's injuries.

Suits against users of a product that causes injury must be based upon negligence, not strict liability.

Defenses for manufacturers

If the product was not defective when it left the manufacturer's or vendor's possession, alteration of the product after it left their possession is a defense to the plaintiff's strict liability action.

Plaintiffs can sue on a strict liability theory for harm from unavoidably unsafe drugs (including blood) only if the supplier does not notify the physician of the dangers.

Assumption of the risk is a defense in strict product liability actions.

In jurisdictions that recognize comparative negligence for product liability, the defense of assumption of the risk merges into that defense.

In those jurisdictions, the plaintiff's damages can be reduced but not eliminated when they assumed the risk or is negligent.

The plaintiff's misuse would not be a complete defense unless that misuse were unforeseeable. However, it can be the basis of negligence in a comparative negligence jurisdiction to reduce damages.

The following are NOT defenses to a strict liability action:

1) Privity between the plaintiff and the manufacturer is not a condition that must be satisfied in a strict liability case against the manufacturer or seller of a product.

   Liability extends to foreseeable users and bystanders injured.

2) Negligence in using a product by the product owner, which harms a third party, is not a defense in product liability cases brought by the third party but might be the basis for contribution among joint tortfeasors.

3) Jurisdictions that retain contributory negligence as a defense in negligence do not recognize it as a defense in strict liability actions.

Failure to warn

Failure of the product's label to warn of dangers of a specific use can cause the product to be defective for product liability purposes when used in a way the manufacturer should have warned against, even though the product is not dangerous if used in other ways.

If the basis of product liability is a failure to warn about a dangerous product, the dangerous or defective nature of the product is not the relevant issue.

If the defect consisted of a failure to warn, the plaintiff must show that the injury would not have occurred if the warning had been made.

Product liability for subcontractors

An assembler of a dangerous product is liable on a product liability theory if the product's dangerous nature was caused by the defective parts supplied by a third party, included in the finished product.

If a product is dangerous because of a defect in a component, the finished part manufacturer and the defective component manufacturer are jointly liable in strict product liability.

The manufacturer of the component would be required to indemnify the finished product manufacturer if the finished-product manufacturer is required to pay the judgment.

Product liability for vendors

Strict liability in tort applies to a seller who is not the manufacturer when:

1) the seller is engaged in the business of selling the type of product involved,

2) the product is expected to and does reach the user without substantial change in condition in which it was sold, and

3) such a seller would have a claim for indemnification from the manufacturer if the manufacturer caused the defect.

Claims in negligence

Plaintiffs have the right to sue manufacturers and retailers for negligently manufacturing or selling products that cause harm.

In such suits, the defendant's evidence of due care in manufacturing the product or the retailer in inspecting the product is relevant.

In jurisdictions that retain contributory negligence, it is a defense in a product liability action based on negligence.

A manufacturer is not liable for negligence if it used reasonable care to inspect the parts assembled into a finished product.

Abnormally dangerous or ultra-hazardous activities

Ultra-hazardous activity is that which:

1) is not common in the area and
2) involves a risk of serious harm to others, which cannot be eliminated by the exercise of utmost care.

Blasting is an ultra-hazardous activity.

Defendants are liable in strict liability for abnormally dangerous operations.

A person hiring an independent contractor to engage in an ultra-hazardous activity is vicariously liable for torts.

A plaintiff can recover in strict liability for damage caused by the defendant permitting substances (commonly liquids) to escape from their land onto the neighbor's land.

If the person engaging in the ultra-hazardous activity warns of the danger, and the victim ignores the warnings and deliberately stays in the danger zone, the victim has assumed the risk and cannot recover.

Wild and domesticated animals

Owners of wild animals (e.g., reptiles, insects) are strictly liable for the harm caused by them.

Owners of domesticated animals (e.g., dogs, cats, farm animals) are only liable for their negligence regarding the animals' care and control.

An owner of a domestic animal is liable in negligence for harm caused by failure to restrain an animal, which they knew had a propensity to cause harm.

Notes for active learning

Negligence

In negligence actions, the plaintiff must prove actual, as opposed to nominal, damages caused by the defendant's negligence to prevail.

Duty to rescue

To be liable for negligence, the defendant must be under a duty to the plaintiff to avoid the risk of harm that occurred.

Generally, one has a duty to act reasonably but does not have a duty to act affirmatively to come to someone's aid from a danger that they did not create.

A duty to come to the aid of a person in danger applies for:

1) the creator of the peril,
2) someone under a contractual obligation to protect (e.g., lifeguard),
3) a close family member (e.g., parent), or
4) a nascent rescuer (i.e., initiation of rescue must reasonably continue).

Even though a person does not have an affirmative duty to come to the aid of a person in peril, once one undertakes to rescue, they must act with reasonable care.

Good Samaritan statutes in many jurisdictions exempt or limit liability, except where the defendant is grossly negligent.

A defendant who endangers themselves is liable for negligence to anyone who tries to rescue them from their misconduct.

If the defendant is not negligent in placing the victim in danger, they are not liable to an injured rescuer.

A police officer has a duty to intervene to protect citizens from criminal activity and does not have a cause of action against the citizen whose negligent conduct gave rise to the need for intervention.

General standard of conduct

Except in the circumstances prescribing a different standard of care (e.g., the standard for a minor or a skilled professional), the standard of care applicable in negligence actions is that the person must act like a reasonable adult in the circumstances.

Evidence that the defendant complied with the customs established for a customer's reasonable care is admissible but does not warrant a directed verdict for the defendant.

Statutory standard of conduct

Violation of a statute is negligence *per se* or evidence of negligence, depending on the rule in the jurisdiction, if it can be shown that:

1) the plaintiff was a member of the class whom the statute was intended to protect,
2) the harm was the type of hazard the statute was designed to protect against, and
3) the violation contributed to the harm.

While violation of a statute may be negligence *per se* or evidence of negligence, compliance with an appropriate statute is not conclusive proof of the absence of negligence.

The fact that the defendant did not possess a license required to perform the act legally is irrelevant to the proof of negligence.

Even if the defendant has violated a statute and is negligent *per se*, the defense of contributory or comparative negligence is available.

Some jurisdictions impose a gross negligence standard for a gratuitous guest suing the driver.

Standard of conduct for classes of persons

As a matter of law, children under the age of seven cannot be found to be negligent.

Parents can be held liable for the torts of their child when they fail to exercise *due care* in raising or supervising the child.

Persons acting in the role of parents can be liable for negligent supervision of children.

Method of proving fault

In tort actions based upon negligence, the trier of fact must find that the defendant is negligent by a preponderance of the evidence.

That standard of negligence is by a preponderance of the evidence is met if the plaintiff shows a probability that the defendant was negligent but is not met when the evidence only shows the possibility that the defendant was negligent.

Negligence can be proven by other means than by direct evidence.

Enough evidence concerning negligence can be proven by inference or circumstantial evidence to warrant sending the issue to the jury.

If the plaintiff died because of the defendant's conduct, and there are no living witnesses to the accident other than the defendant, the plaintiff has met their burden of producing evidence of negligence by showing that the defendant might have been negligent in causing the plaintiff's death.

To satisfy their burden of producing evidence on negligence, a plaintiff must produce expert testimony only if the jury cannot determine, based on everyday knowledge and experience, whether the defendant was negligent or whether the defendant's negligence was the cause of the plaintiff's harm.

Res ipsa loquitur

Res ipsa loquitur (Latin, *the thing speaks for itself*) is a doctrine that permits a plaintiff to offer proof that the defendant was negligent by circumstantial evidence.

If the plaintiff can offer evidence on the elements necessary to establish *res ipsa loquitur*, they have satisfied their burden of producing evidence on negligence and avoid a directed verdict.

The elements which must be proven to establish *res ipsa loquitur* are:

1) the injury to the plaintiff would not ordinarily occur in the absence of negligence and
2) the defendant was in control of the instrumentality, which caused the injury.

The plaintiff can prevail without direct proof of the defendant's negligence if they prove (or the circumstances alone indicate) that they would not have been harmed if the defendant had not been negligent.

The plaintiff need only show that it is more likely than not that the defendant was negligent and that there is a causal connection to the plaintiff's harm.

The defendant can negate the inference, which comes from the doctrine of *res ipsa loquitur,* by showing that it is just as likely that someone else's negligence caused the plaintiff's harm.

If the plaintiff attempts to prove negligence by *res ipsa loquitur*, the defendant can introduce direct evidence that they were not negligent.

Res ipsa loquitur is inapplicable in product liability cases.

Causation

The plaintiff cannot recover in tort unless the defendant's conduct is the *proximate* (i.e., legal, sufficiently related) cause of the injury.

The first issue in causation is "*but-for*" (cause-in-fact) causation.

Except in rare instances, for the plaintiff to prevail, they must prove that the harm incurred would not have occurred if the defendant had not acted in a tortuous manner.

Even if the plaintiff proves *but-for* causation, proximate cause must be proven.

The determination of proximate cause is usually a factual question for the jury to be determined by some broad guidelines.

If there is *but-for* causation, but it is determined that a separate *but-for* cause is a superseding cause, the defendant's tortious conduct is not the proximate cause of the plaintiff's harm, they cannot recover.

If the separate *but-for* cause were foreseeable by the defendant, it is not considered a superseding cause, and the plaintiff recovers.

For example, an injured plaintiff will require medical treatment.

It is foreseeable that the plaintiff will suffer additional injury from negligent medical treatment. The defendant is liable for the additional harm caused by that treatment.

The original defendant is not liable for the harm caused by a superseding intervening cause.

The original defendant is liable for harm that would have occurred if not for the superseding cause.

If the defendant has tortiously injured a plaintiff in a manner that includes a permanent disability, the plaintiff is entitled to be compensated for those injuries but not for subsequent injuries that would not have occurred if the plaintiff did not have that permanent disability.

A subsequent tortfeasor is not liable for the injuries which occurred before the time they committed the tort.

In tort actions involving damages caused to a child because of drugs taken by the pregnant mother, or in cases involving a long period between the ingestion of the dangerous substance and the injury, the ordinary tort rule that the plaintiff must prove the defendant's product caused the harm is relaxed.

Each defendant drug manufacturer will be liable for damages in proportion to the market share of the pharmaceutical the defendant had when the plaintiff consumed the item.

Allocation of liability among joint tortfeasors

Defendants are joint tortfeasors when their concurrent tortious actions combine to injure the plaintiff, and it is not possible to reasonably allocate portions of the plaintiff's injury to separate defendants.

In question where a plaintiff and defendants are alleged to be joint tortfeasors, use the following process.

1) Determine how the plaintiff's negligence affects the total amount of the award.
2) Determine how much the plaintiff can collect in damages from each defendant.
3) Determine the rights of the defendant who pays damages to collect from other defendants.

Effect of the plaintiff's negligence on damages

For *contributory negligence* jurisdictions, the plaintiff loses if negligent in any degree.

For *pure comparative negligence*, the plaintiff prevails if a defendant is negligent. However, the defendant's percentage of negligence reduces the award. A plaintiff can be 99% negligent, and the defendant 1%, the plaintiff recovers.

For *modified comparative negligence*, the plaintiff prevails *only* if the defendant's negligence is *greater* than the plaintiff's. However, the plaintiff's recovery is reduced by the percentage of their negligence.

Comparative negligence does not change the rule of jointly and severally liable between joint tortfeasors.

Amount collected from the defendant

Under common law, joint tortfeasors are jointly and severally liable for the entire judgment of the plaintiff.

If the common law has been modified, so joint tortfeasors are severally (individually) but not jointly (mutually) liable, the plaintiff can collect from each joint tortfeasor the judgment amount they are liable for.

Relations between joint tortfeasors

Under common law, a joint tortfeasor who pays more than their equal share of judgment is entitled to seek contribution from the other joint tortfeasors in the amount of any excess paid.

If the jurisdiction provides that joint tortfeasors are only liable in proportion to their percentage of negligence, a joint tortfeasor who pays more than their allocated share of the judgment is entitled to seek contribution from the other joint tortfeasors for the excess paid.

If a person is responsible for vicarious liability, they can seek indemnification from the party who is ultimately liable and collect from them the entire amount paid.

A negligent defendant is only entitled to contribution (not complete indemnification) from a negligent joint tortfeasor. A negligent tortfeasor is entitled to indemnification if a joint tortfeasor has committed an intentional tort.

Liability of owners and occupiers of land

A landowner owes a business invitee a duty to use reasonable care to prevent injuries while on the premises.

An individual is a business invitee when entering the premises intending to conduct business, whether or not they conduct it.

A landowner owes a business invitee a duty to use reasonable care to prevent the invitee from suffering from third parties' criminal acts while on the premises.

A person's status on the premises depends on the area where the injury occurs and whether the public has been invited to that area.

If the issue is the defendant's negligence because of the condition of the premises, evidence of occurrences similar to the accident in issue due to the same condition is admissible if relevant to prove that the defendant had notice of the dangerous condition.

Without incurring tort liability, a landowner can construct a legally permitted building on their land to deprive the adjoining land of light and air and remove a building on their land, which exposes the neighbor's land to sunlight.

At common law, a licensee (social guest) is only owed a duty to *warn of dangers known* to the owner or occupant but not apparent to the licensee.

Many jurisdictions have changed this rule to permit a licensee to pursue a tort claim if the landowner is negligent.

A landowner is not liable to a trespasser for ordinary negligence but is liable if they could have prevented the injury after becoming aware of the danger to the trespasser.

Attractive nuisance

At common law, a trespasser is only owed a duty to avoid gross negligence or wanton, willful misconduct.

A possessor of land is subject to liability for physical harm to children trespassing thereon caused by an artificial condition upon the land if:

1) the possessor knows or has reason to know that children are likely to trespass in the dangerous location (attractive nuisance),
2) the possessor knows or has reason to know that the condition will involve an unreasonable risk of death or serious bodily harm to such children,
3) the children, because of their youth, do not discover the condition or realize the risk involved,
4) the utility to the possessor of maintaining the proper condition and eliminating the danger is slight compared to the risk to the children involved, and
5) the possessor fails to exercise reasonable care to eliminate the danger or otherwise protect the children.

If an attractive nuisance applies, the landowner owes a duty of reasonable care to the infant trespasser(s).

The children do not need to be attracted to the land by the nuisance.

The doctrine is not applicable if the nuisance would only be attractive to those old enough to recognize its hazards.

Vicarious liability

Employers are vicariously liable for the torts of their employees committed within the scope of their employment.

An employer-employee relationship exists where the person contracting for services controls how the job is accomplished.

Indicia of an employer-employee relationship are periodic payments to the worker rather than payment by the job and ownership of the contractor's tools rather than by the worker.

The intentional tort of an employee would be within the scope of their employment if it were committed to further the master's (i.e., employer's) business even though the employer expressly forbade the conduct.

In addition to being held vicariously liable on a *respondeat superior* theory, an employer can be held liable for negligence in hiring or supervising employees.

A plaintiff injured by a servant may sue the servant and the employer.

A defendant, who has not been personally negligent and has been held vicariously liable, has a right to recover the entire amount of the judgment by indemnification from the party whose negligence caused the vicarious liability.

Parents are not vicariously liable for their children's torts but can be held liable for negligence in raising or supervising them.

Joint enterprise liability

When two persons join in accomplishing a task labeled a joint enterprise, such as participating in an automobile race, each is liable for torts committed by the other within the scope of the joint enterprise.

Liability for independent contractors

The person hiring an independent contractor is not liable for the torts of the independent contractor with the following exceptions:

The person hiring a contractor is liable for ultra-hazardous activity (e.g., blasting, pile driving) undertaken by them.

If a person has a non-delegable duty of safety for an ultra-hazardous activity, they cannot relieve tort liability by hiring an independent contractor.

A different theory of liability is that a person who hires an independent contractor can be held liable for negligence in hiring an unfit contractor.

Assumption of the risk

The assumption of the risk would be a valid defense only if the plaintiff had actual, subjective knowledge of the risk, which caused the harm, and voluntarily assumed it.

The defense of assumption of the risk will not be applicable if a defendant is in a difficult situation that they did has not cause and take reasonable effort to extricate.

The assumption of the risk is not available in product liability cases where the jurisdiction has adopted a comparative negligence doctrine applicable in product liability cases.

The assumption of the risk is combined with comparative negligence to reduce the total amount of the plaintiff's recovery.

Last clear chance

While contributory negligence bars the plaintiff's recovery, that doctrine is not applicable if the defendant had the last clear chance after the plaintiff's negligence occurred to avoid the accident.

Attribution of a related party's negligence

One party's negligence will not ordinarily be attributed to another, even for related parties.

Thus, the negligence of a minor child is not attributed to the parent, but the parent can be liable for negligent supervision of their child.

A decedent's negligence will be attributed to their executor in a wrongful death case.

Elements of tort damage

The plaintiff cannot recover in negligence without proving damage.

If an element of tort damage is future medical expenses, the plaintiff must produce expert testimony to prove the expenses expected to be incurred.

If a court determines that the defendant's tortious conduct proximately caused damages and the plaintiff's damages were not foreseeable by the defendant, this is not a valid defense.

If a tort victim is especially prone to injury, the tortfeasor must pay damages incurred because a tortfeasor takes their victim as they find them.

Economic loss to third parties caused by injuries to the defendant is not compensable as an element of tort damage.

If a tort committed on a mother before conception causes damage to a later-born child, the child could recover damages. However, there is a doubt that the child's damages are an element of the mother's damages.

Even though an employee's recovery against their employer is limited to worker's compensation, they may pursue tort claims against third parties who contributed to their injuries.

Notes for active learning

Defamation

Elements of defamation

The plaintiff must prove fault by the defendant in publishing an untrue, defamatory statement about the plaintiff.

If the plaintiff is a public figure, public official, or person well known in the field in which the defamation occurs, the plaintiff must prove that the defendant acted with *malice*; the defendant knew the statement was untrue or published it with a reckless disregard of the truth.

If the plaintiff is not a public figure, they must prove the defendant was negligent in publishing the untrue, defamatory statement.

A statement is defamatory when it might lower the esteem, in the eyes of a reputable segment of the community, of the person who is the subject of the statement.

Publication requirement

Publication of the defamatory statement is an essential element of a defamation action.

The plaintiff must prove that the defendant intended or acted in a way that it is reasonably certain that at least one person other than the plaintiff heard and understood the statement.

The publication element was satisfied even if the person receiving the defamatory statement did not believe it was true.

If a statement by the defendant is directed only to the plaintiff but is overheard by a third person, the publication issue is determined by whether the defendant should have reasonably known that the statement would be overheard.

A defendant can be liable in defamation by republishing a defamatory statement made by a third party.

Libel

Libel *per se* is a defamatory statement to anyone receiving the communication with no other information concerning the plaintiff.

Libel *per quod* is a defamatory statement only when taken in conjunction with facts known by those to whom the libel is published.

If the defamation is a writing or permanent communication (e.g., a recording), the plaintiff may prevail without proving special damages (e.g., lost profits) due to the defamation.

Humiliation, shame, or emotional distress are sufficient.

Slander

Defamation, in the form of oral communication, is slander.

An essential element of the cause of action for slander is the requirement that the plaintiff proves special damages in the form of a monetary loss caused by the defendant's defamatory statement.

The requirement of special damages is not applicable if the slander states that the plaintiff has committed a crime, has a loathsome disease, has engaged in sexual misconduct, or is incompetent in business.

Truth as defense

If the words of the communication are true as those words are reasonably construed, the defendant has a complete defense to a defamation action even if the words are not true.

Privilege as defense

Relevant statements made in a judicial proceeding are absolutely privileged, but those given in an administrative proceeding only have a qualified privilege.

Statements made by a former employer to a prospective employer concerning an employee enjoy a qualified privilege.

The defendant is liable even with a qualified privilege if they make a statement they know is false or makes a statement with reckless disregard of the truth.

Liability standard for defamation

Plaintiff	Liability standard	Damages	Burden of proof
Public official	Malice	Compensatory and punitive	Plaintiff must prove falsity of the assertion
Public figure	Malice	Compensatory and punitive	Plaintiff must prove falsity of the assertion
Private figure, (*matter of public concern*)	Negligence *and* injury	Compensatory; punitive damages require malice	Plaintiff must prove falsity of the assertion
Private figure, (*matter of private concern*)	Negligence	Compensatory; punitive damages do *not* require malice	Defendant must prove truth of the assertion

Privacy

Four invasions of privacy

The tort of invasion of privacy consists of four separate torts involving interference with a person's right to be left alone.

The four invasions of privacy torts are:

1) Unreasonable intrusion on the plaintiff's seclusion.

   The publication is not an element of this invasion of privacy.

2) Appropriation of the plaintiff's name or likeness for commercial purposes.

   The plaintiff's consent to having a picture taken does not constitute consent to use the photo for commercial purposes.

3) Unreasonable publication of the plaintiff's private life.

   The material published must be highly offensive to a reasonable person.

   Truth is not a defense to this invasion of privacy, but newsworthiness of the event in the plaintiff's private life is a defense.

   Publishing information in the public record cannot generally be considered an unreasonable invasion of the plaintiff's private life.

4) Publicity unreasonably placing another in a false light.

   The information published need not be defamatory to give rise to this form of invasion of privacy if it is untrue.

Notes for active learning

Deceit

Misrepresentation of a material fact

For the plaintiff to recover in common law deceit, there must be a misrepresentation of material fact by the plaintiff, relied upon by the defendant to their detriment.

A statement of opinion is not a misrepresentation of a material fact.

Actual damages are an essential element of a cause of action in deceit.

Failing to make a disclosure is the basis for a cause of action in deceit when there is a legal or fiduciary duty to make a disclosure.

The plaintiff must sustain more than nominal damages to have a cause of action for misrepresentation.

Third parties cannot sue for negligent misrepresentation unless the purpose of the information were to permit third parties to rely on it.

Notes for active learning

Torts – Quick Facts

Negligence:

1) Duty – the defendant owed a legal duty to the plaintiff
2) Breach of duty – the defendant breached a legal duty by acting (or failing to act) in a certain way.
3) Causation – the defendant's action (or failure to act) caused the plaintiff's harm.
4) Damages – the plaintiff was harmed or injured due to the defendant's actions (or inactions).

   A cause of action for negligence requires measurable harm to the plaintiff.

1. The swearing of a proper complaint at the time may not serve as a basis for a **false imprisonment action** despite the failure to cancel the complaint.

2. A landowner generally owes *no* duty to an undiscovered trespasser.

   If a landowner discovers *or* should anticipate the presence of a trespasser, the landowner ***must*** exercise **ordinary care** to warn the trespasser *or* make safe the concealed, unsafe, or artificial conditions *known to the landowner* that involves a risk of death or serious bodily harm.

3. A **private nuisance** action requires a showing that the defendant's interference with the use and enjoyment of the plaintiff's property was *unreasonable.*

   A characterization of unreasonable requires that the severity of the inflicted injury *outweigh the utility* of the defendant's conduct.

4. **Commercial invitees** are owed the duty to be warned of non-obvious dangerous conditions, and the defendant must make reasonable inspections to *discover* dangerous conditions and make them safe.

5. The tort of **conversion** does *not* require that the defendant damage or permanently deprive the owner of the chattel – it required that the defendant's volitional conduct results in a serious invasion of the owner's chattel interest.

6. A **bailee** is liable to the owner for conversion *if* the bailee uses the chattel in a manner that constitutes a material breach of the bailment agreement.

7. A plaintiff can recover for defamation where there was **negligent communication** of the defamatory statements to third persons.

8. A defendant will *not* be liable to a child's parents by showing that the child ***appreciated the risk*** of the activity causing injury.

9. Doctors, dentists, and healthcare professionals owe their patients a duty of **informed consent** to provide the patient with information about the risks of a proposed course of treatment, surgical intervention, alternative modalities, or the election to abstain from treatment to enable the patient to make an informed decision (i.e., informed consent).

   Even if there is a **breach of duty**, there *must* be **damages.**

Relationship matrix

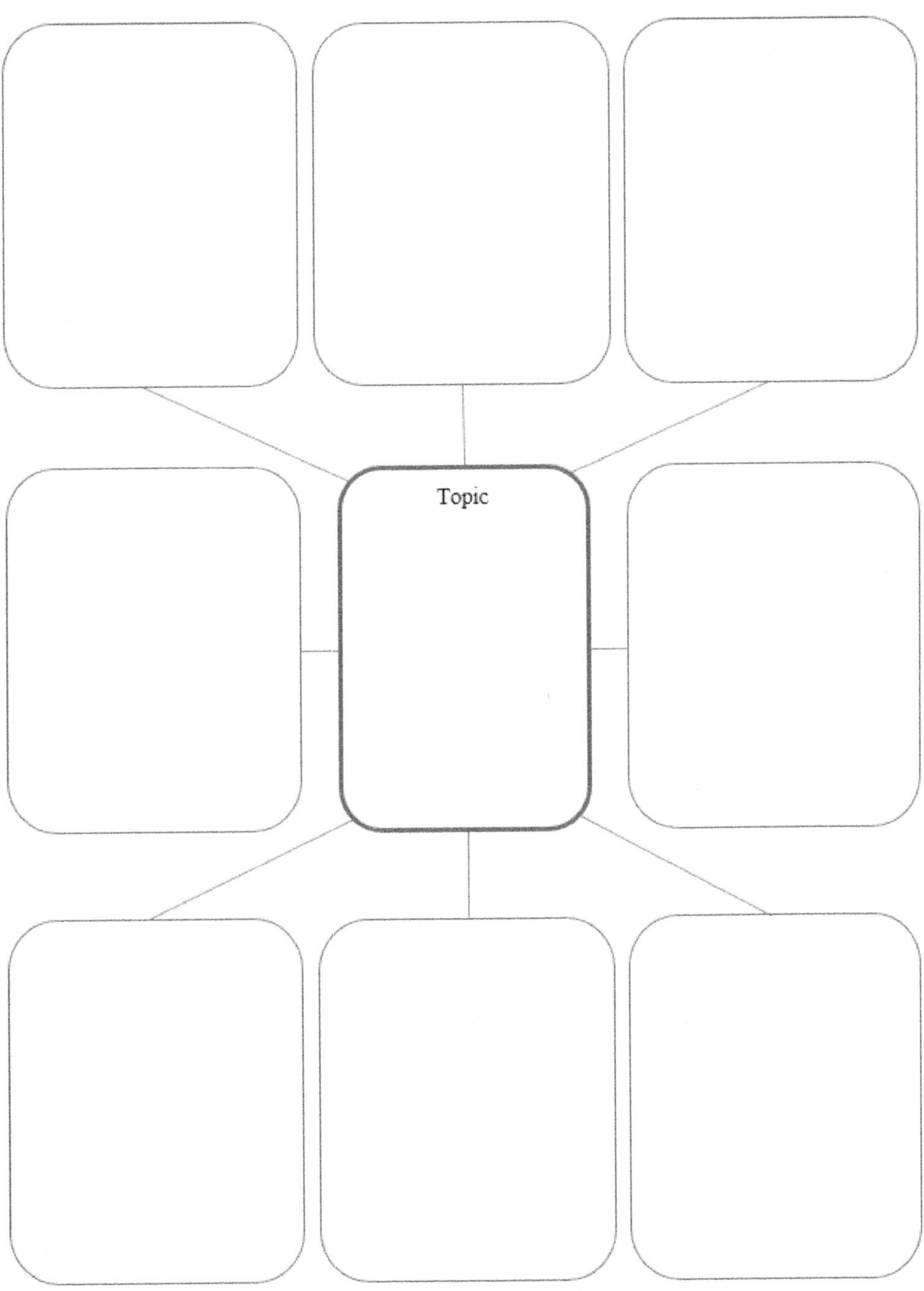

Notes for active learning

Civil Procedure

(Federal Rules of Civil Procedure)

The NCBE often tests the same Civil Procedure issues, so master these topics to maximize your test score. Focus on subject matter jurisdiction (diversity jurisdiction, federal question, supplemental jurisdiction), personal jurisdiction, venue, service of process, discovery, pretrial procedures, motions. Other issues tested include jury trials, verdicts and judgments, appeals, and review. Approximately two-thirds of the Civil Procedure questions cover jurisdiction and venue, pretrial procedures, and motions.

The statements herein were compiled by analyzing released Civil Procedure questions and setting forth the principles of law governing the correct answers. Review these principles before preparing answers to practice Civil Procedure questions. Memorize this governing law and understand how it applies to the correct answer.

Per the National Conference of Bar Examiners, assume the application of 1) the Federal Rules of Civil Procedure as currently in effect and 2) sections of Title 28 of the U.S. Code pertaining to trial and appellate jurisdiction, venue, and transfer.

Federal Jurisdiction

Original and appellate jurisdiction of the Supreme Court

Article III, Section 2 of the Constitution provides that:

> "*In all cases affecting ambassadors, other public ministers and consuls, and those in which a state shall be a party, the Supreme Court shall have original jurisdiction.*"

Within the judicial power of the United States,

> "*the Supreme Court shall have appellate jurisdiction, both as to law and fact, with such exceptions, and under such regulations as the Congress shall make.*"

Cases and controversies

The judicial power extends to "*cases*" and "*controversies.*"

Factors considered in determining when a case or controversy exists include mootness, standing, ripeness, whether the case involves a political or administrative question, whether a case is collusive or whether the parties are seeking a merely advisory opinion.

Article III – Judicial Branch

Article III of the U.S. Constitution establishes the federal government's judicial branch.

Under Article III, the judicial branch consists of *The* Supreme Court of the United States and lower courts created by Congress.

Article III defines judicial power as resolving "*cases and controversies.*"

Article III prohibits advisory opinions.

The Constitution does not articulate the power of the judicial courts.

The judicial review authority was established in *Marbury v. Madison* (1803), where the court created the authority for federal judicial review of legislative and executive actions.

Marbury declared "*that it's the province of the judicial department to say what the law is.*"

The court sets limits on federal judicial power.

Whether the plaintiff is the proper party to bring a matter to the court for adjudication (i.e., justiciability doctrine) has four requirements:

standing,

ripeness,

political question, and

mootness.

These doctrines render a controversy "*nonjusticiable*" if a court decides that any of the four essential elements are absent.

1) Standing: a party's ability to demonstrate to the court sufficient connection and harm from the action challenged to support that party's participation in the case.

   The plaintiff must allege and prove actual or imminent injury.

   The plaintiff may assert only personally suffered injuries:

   Sierra Club v. Morton (1971): Disney wanted to build a ski resort. The Sierra Club sued to stop construction, and the Supreme Court ruled the Sierra Club lacked standing.

2) Causation and redressability: the plaintiff must allege and prove that the defendant caused the injury so that a favorable court decision is likely to remedy the injury.

3) No third party standing: a plaintiff cannot represent the claims of others not before the court (i.e., must be a personal injury).

   There is an important exception where third-party standing is allowed.

   A plaintiff who meets the other standing requirements and one of the following exceptions may bring a suit with proper standing.

   A close relationship between the plaintiff and the injured third party.

   Plaintiff represents the third party adequately.

   Doctor–patient relationship: laws limiting abortion that inflicted injuries on the doctors (e.g., loss of business), so doctors chose to represent the patient's rights.

   The Supreme Court ruled that a father lacked standing to represent his daughter for the "under God" in school because he did not have legal custody, and the mother did not want the suit to proceed.

   Third-party standing is allowed if the injured party is unlikely to assert their rights (the party cannot appear in court); the plaintiff who meets the other requirements may represent the claims of the aggrieved.

4) No generalized grievances.

A cause of action is not a generalized grievance because many people (or everyone) are affected by the injury.

The plaintiff must not be suing solely as a citizen or taxpayer.

The plaintiff sues as a citizen (or general taxpayer) → generalized grievance → no standing.

Exception: taxpayers may challenge government expenditures according to a federal statute as violating the *establishment clause*.

The Supreme Court has held that the establishment clause was a limit on Congressional spending power.

There is a narrow exception to no generalized grievances. The Supreme Court has held that taxpayers do not have standing for government expenditures of property (money) to religious institutions under a specific federal statute.

Flast v. Cohn (1968): federal government adopted a statute that provided textbooks, instructional and library materials for religious and sectarian schools.

Flast had standing. The majority opinion by Chief Justice Earl Warren established a "*double nexus*" test for taxpayer standing.

(a) Plaintiff must "*establish a logical link*" between status (e.g., taxpayer) and the legislative enactment being challenged,

(b) Plaintiff must show that the challenged enactment exceeds specific constitutional limitations upon the exercise of the taxing and spending power and *not* merely beyond the powers delegated to Congress by Article I, Section 8.

Only when both nexuses have been satisfied may the petitioner have the standing to sue.

Notes for active learning

Jurisdiction of Federal Courts

Subject matter jurisdiction

The Constitution limits the subject matter jurisdiction of the federal courts to:

1) suits involving a federal question (e.g., Constitution, federal statutes),

2) suits between citizens of different states for *over* $75,000 (diversity jurisdiction),

3) cases involving ambassadors,

4) admiralty and maritime jurisdiction, and

5) cases where the United States is a party.

Congress has implemented the constitutional provision by imposing additional restrictions on the jurisdiction which federal courts are permitted to exercise, such as the amount-in-controversy requirement.

Subject matter jurisdiction may not be conferred by agreement or consent of the litigants.

The defense of lack of subject matter jurisdiction may be raised at any point in the trial and may be first raised on appeal.

Notes for active learning

Federal Question Jurisdiction

The meaning of "arising under"

A right or immunity created by the Constitution or federal law must be an essential element of the plaintiff's cause of action for the federal district court to have "arising under" jurisdiction.

The fact that the defendant can raise federal law as an affirmative defense in their answer does not confer federal jurisdiction.

Federal question must appear in the complaint

The federal question or constitutional issue must be properly pleaded in the complaint.

The anticipation of a defense based on federal law is insufficient for federal question jurisdiction by the court.

Concurrent and exclusive federal jurisdiction

Absent congressional intent to confer exclusive jurisdiction on the federal courts, both federal and state courts have jurisdiction to try claims based upon federal law.

Congress has granted the federal courts exclusive jurisdiction in:

bankruptcy proceedings,

patent,

copyright cases,

actions against foreign consuls,

admiralty and maritime cases,

antitrust cases,

cases under the Securities Exchange Act of 1934, and

actions where the United States is a party.

Notes for active learning

Diversity Jurisdiction

The requirement of complete diversity

Congress has not conferred on the federal district courts the jurisdiction of cases between citizens of different states that the Constitution allows it to confer.

The lawsuit must have complete diversity between the parties on each side of the controversy for the court to have jurisdiction. Each plaintiff must be from a state different from each defendant, or one must be a citizen of a state and the other an alien.

The exception is an action for *statutory interpleader*, where parties on each side of the controversy can be citizens of the same state if two states are represented among the parties.

For determining whether the statutory requirements for jurisdiction are met, diversity is determined as of the date the action is commenced; diversity need not have existed when the cause of action arose.

If the defendant impleads a third party whose citizenship is the same as the plaintiff, diversity is not destroyed.

However, while a defendant may be brought in by a third-party complaint by a party with the same citizenship as the plaintiff, the plaintiff may not amend the complaint to add such a person as a party defendant.

Citizenship

Citizenship of a natural person for purposes of determining diversity means the state of that party's domicile.

A person's original domicile is the domicile of their parents.

When reaching adulthood, a person can change domicile by being physically present in a place they select as their fixed residence.

Domicile can subsequently be changed by physical presence in the new domicile with the intent to remain there indefinitely.

The citizenship of a corporation for diversity purposes is:

1) the state of incorporation and

2) the state in which it has its principal place of business.

A partnership, labor union, or other unincorporated association as a party has each member's citizenship determine diversity.

If a deceased person's estate is a party, the decedent's citizenship controls for diversity.

The citizenship of the executor or administrator is irrelevant.

In an action on behalf of a trust, the trustee's citizenship (not beneficiary's) controls.

For diversity purposes in class actions, the named representatives' citizenship controls.

Realignment or substitution of parties

Diversity may be created or destroyed by a realignment of the parties according to their interest in the dispute.

If a party is named a plaintiff and is a defendant, they are classified as a defendant when determining if complete diversity exists.

The initial party's citizenship governs the substitution of parties because of death, incompetence, or public office succession.

Amount-in-controversy requirement

The plaintiff's complaint determines the amount in controversy.

For a federal court to have jurisdiction in a diversity suit, the amount in controversy, as measured by the damages the plaintiff sought in good faith when the suit commenced, must be greater than $75,000.

Recovering less than $75,000.01 does not retroactively destroy jurisdiction.

The dollar value for the amount in controversy requirement of injunctive relief is the value of the right protected or injury to be prevented.

Aggregation of claims

A single plaintiff suing a single defendant may aggregate claims to achieve the jurisdictional amount.

Thus, a claim for personal injury and property damage could be added to exceed $75,000.

If a single plaintiff has claims against several defendants, claims can be aggregate only if the defendants are jointly liable.

Thus, if defendant A and defendant B were joint tortfeasors and the plaintiff's total claim was more than $75,000 against each, the right of contribution might reduce the total amount paid by a tortfeasor to less than $75,000.01 is not relevant for jurisdiction purposes.

Several plaintiffs' claims against a single defendant cannot be aggregated except where several plaintiffs have an undivided right, title, or interest in the claim.

Each member's claims in a class action cannot be aggregated, making it less likely that class action cases based upon state causes of action can be brought in federal court.

Jurisdictional amount in counterclaims

If the jurisdictional amount is satisfied by the plaintiff's complaint, a compulsory counterclaim not meeting the jurisdictional amount is permitted.

The amount of a counterclaim cannot be aggregated with the plaintiff's claim to satisfy the amount-in-controversy requirement.

Structure of the United States court systems

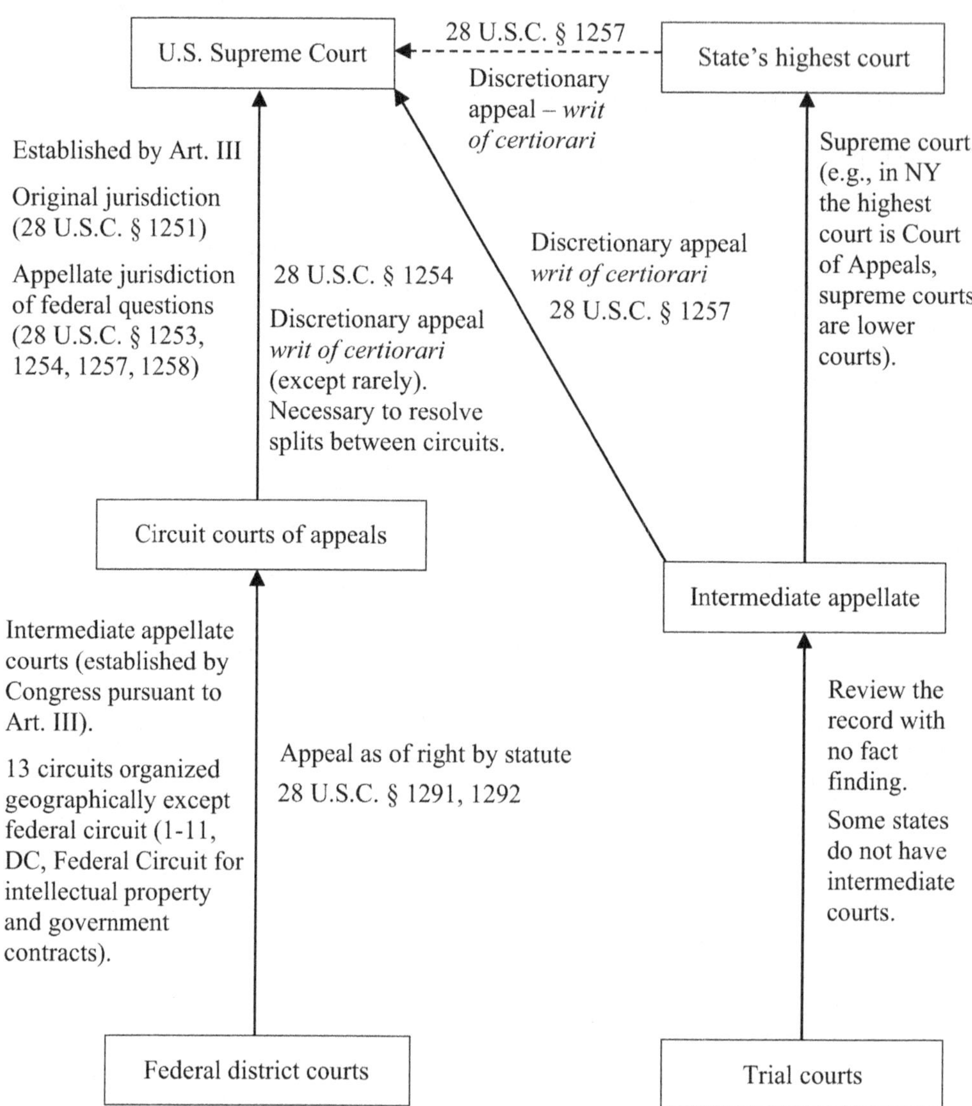

Trial courts (established by Congress pursuant to Art. III). Each state has one or more federal districts.

Jurisdiction (Art. III § 2) based on federal question or diversity of citizenship for disputes greater than $75,000.

In most instances, a state's supreme court is the final arbiter on a legal matter. A matter may be appealed from a state supreme court to the U.S. Supreme Court when it involves an interpretation of the U.S. Constitution. The U.S. Supreme Court does not resolve state constitutions.

Supplemental Jurisdiction

Supplemental jurisdiction rules

Under 28 U.S.C. § 1367(a), a federal district court generally has supplemental jurisdiction over claims related to the claim upon which federal jurisdiction is founded, which form part of the same *case or controversy*.

Thus, a claim under state antitrust law could be brought in the federal court as a count in the same complaint, which alleges a claim under the federal antitrust law.

The federal court can try a state claim under supplemental jurisdiction even if the count brought under the federal claim is dismissed.

Under *Gibbs*, the federal district court has the discretion to exercise supplemental jurisdiction under 28 U.S.C. § 1367 if:

1) there must be a federal claim (i.e., Constitution, a federal statute, or treaty) and
2) the non-federal claim arises from a "common nucleus of operative fact" such that a plaintiff would ordinarily be expected to try them in one judicial proceeding.

Exceptions to supplemental jurisdiction

1367(b) is an exception to 1367(a): no supplemental jurisdiction if the jurisdiction was a diversity case.

If jurisdiction establishing a claim is a diversity claim, a second claim cannot be brought even if part of the same case or controversy.

The reason for exceptions to supplemental jurisdiction is because 1367(b) should not undermine the complete diversity rule & *Strawbridge*.

1367(c): federal district court can decide not to exercise supplemental jurisdiction if:

1) it raises a complicated question of state law,
2) the claim substantially predominates over the claim or claims over which the district court has original jurisdiction,
3) the district court has dismissed all claims over which it has original jurisdiction, or
4) in exceptional circumstances, there are other compelling reasons for declining jurisdiction.

Notes for active learning

Removal Jurisdiction

Prerequisites to removal – federal subject matter

If the plaintiff could have brought the action in federal court originally, the defendant may remove a civil action brought in a state court to the federal district court.

A federal question raised in defense or counterclaim is not a basis for removal.

The court looks only to the complaint to determine if federal question jurisdiction is present.

The pleadings determine the question of federal jurisdiction, which gives the right to remove as of the time of filing the petition for removal.

If diversity is the basis for federal jurisdiction, the diversity must exist when the original action was filed in state court *and* when the petition for removal was filed.

Only the defendant can remove

Once filing suit in state court, a plaintiff cannot change their mind and remove the case to federal court.

The right to remove is vested only in the defendant.

Diversity cases are not removable if any defendants are citizens of the state in which such action is brought.

For example, if a plaintiff of state A sues a defendant of state B in a state B state court, B may not remove the case to federal court if there is no federal question.

A suit involving a federal question is removable even by a resident defendant.

Separate and independent claim

If an otherwise non-removable state claim is joined with a removable separate and independent federal claim in the state court action, the entire case may be removed to the federal district court.

In its discretion, the federal court may determine all issues or may remand the non-removable claims if state law predominates.

Procedure for removal

Plaintiff may bring suit in the court of their choice if jurisdiction and venue are proper.

Removal is an exception since it provides the defendant with an option to remove a case from state to federal court.

Only the defendant can remove a case.

All defendants must agree to remove the case (i.e., unanimity).

Note, there are strict limitations in the statute and case law regarding which cases may be removed and to which court.

Removal is a one-way street: it only goes from state to federal.

The defendant must file a verified petition for removal in the federal court within 30 days after the case becomes removable and must serve all state court parties with that petition.

The proper venue for a removed action is the district where the state action is pending.

28 U.S.C. § 1447(c): a motion to remand the case from a defect (other than subject matter jurisdiction) must be made within 30 days after the notice of removal has been filed.

A motion to remand may be brought for lack of subject matter jurisdiction at any time during litigation before a final judgment is entered.

Once a case has been removed to federal and remanded back to the state, the motion to remand cannot be appealed.

A plaintiff can file a motion to remand based on the federal court lacking subject matter jurisdiction OR requirements for proper removal were NOT followed.

28 U.S.C. § 1446(b): the notice of removal shall be filed within 30 days from the defendant's receipt of the initial complaint.

If the case stated by the initial pleading is not removable, a defendant may file a notice of removal at any point during the litigation that the case becomes removable.

The defendant shall have 30 days to file a notice of removal from the date the case became removable.

28 U.S.C. § 1446(d): once a case has been removed from state to federal court, the state court shall proceed no further unless and until the case is remanded.

Judgments and orders issued by the state court continue to be in force.

Remand

If the case does not qualify for federal court, the federal court can remand to state court.

The federal court must remand the case to the state court if, before final judgment, it appears that the case was removed improvidently and without jurisdiction.

Jurisdiction Over Persons and Property

Statutory limits of jurisdiction

The issue of *personal jurisdiction* is present in litigation in federal courts.

Generally, such courts have the same personal jurisdiction as the state courts in the state where the federal court is located.

For example, in statutory interpleader actions, jurisdiction extends to the entire United States.

Relationship between defendant and forum state

Personal jurisdiction can be based on the four relationships between the defendant and the forum state:

1) domicile,
2) consent,
3) physical appearance (or service on agent),
4) minimum contacts.

Notes for active learning

Service of Process and Notice

Summons and complaint

Federal Rules of Civil Procedure specify the delivery of the summons and complaint.

Every paper must be served on the opposing party.

Rule 5 governs the delivery of later papers (usually first-class mail).

The *complaint* is the assertion of legal claims.

A *summons* is a court-issued document asserting the court's authority over the defendant.

Adequate notice

Rules for the first delivery are more stringent because the plaintiff must provide the defendant with adequate notice of the pending lawsuit.

Even if service is proper, the court will likely be sympathetic to the defendant and not enforce the *default judgment.*

Mullane (1950) establishes what is necessary for adequate notice for judicial proceedings.

Just because a newspaper advertisement satisfies the statute does not mean it is constitutionally sufficient.

The plaintiff should notify the trustee so they can protect the common interests of beneficiaries.

If it is unreasonable to contact unknown trustees, a paper advertisement is adequate.

Rule 4(c)(2) permits a person over 18 and not a party to the case to deliver the summons.

Rule 4(d) allows the defendant to waive personal service.

Personal and corporate service

Rule 4(e)(2) permits personal service by leaving a copy at the usual place of abode with some person of suitable age who resides therein or delivering it to an agent authorized by appointment or by law to receive service of process.

Service to a corporation can be by personal service to an appointed agent, officer, or managing agent.

Notes for active learning

Venue, *Forum Non Conveniens* and Transfer

Purpose and waiver

Venue rules fix the proper place for the trial of an action over which several courts could exercise jurisdiction.

Venue rules are based on convenience and an effort to distribute cases among trial courts.

Improper venue must be raised affirmatively by the defendant by 1) a motion to dismiss or 2) an answer to the complaint. If not, the right is waived.

Venue rules

In diversity and federal question cases, proper venue in the federal court exists in any district in which either:

1) a defendant resides, if all the defendants reside in the same state, or
2) a "substantial" part of the events or property, which are the basis of the claim or can be found, respectively.

In diversity cases, the venue is proper in any district in which "*the defendants are subject to personal jurisdiction at the time the action commenced.*"

In federal question cases, the venue is proper in any district "in which any defendant may be found," but only "if there is no district in which the action may be otherwise brought."

This situation occurs when the defendants do not reside in the same state, and there is no state in which a "substantial" part of the claim arose.

Residence for venue purposes

For venue, *residence* is the state where the plaintiff is a citizen.

Some courts consider venue proper in a state where a second home is located.

An alien may be sued in any district and cannot use the defense of lack of venue.

The venue for a corporation is in any judicial district that can constitutionally assert personal jurisdiction.

The venue for an unincorporated association (e.g., a partnership) is wherever it is doing business.

Transfer – improper venue

If an action is commenced in the wrong district, the court can dismiss the case according to a motion to dismiss under rule 12(b)(3).

If it is in the interest of justice, the court may transfer the case to any district in which it could have been brought.

The court can transfer an action where it lacks *in personam* jurisdiction over the defendant to a court with such jurisdiction.

Venue is proper for convenience

Even though venue is proper in the district where an action is brought, the court may, in its discretion, transfer the suit to any district "*where it might have been brought...for the convenience of parties and witnesses, in the interest of justice*." 28 U.S.C. § 1404(a).

The phrase "*where it might have been brought*" limits transfer to a district where the plaintiff could have brought the action when the suit was initiated.

Forum non conveniens

Forum non conveniens allows dismissal by a court if it would be an unfair or inconvenient forum.

An action will be dismissed for *forum non conveniens* if the appropriate forum is a state court or a court in a foreign country.

Law Applied by Federal Courts

Vertical choice of law

In federal court diversity cases, state law applies unless the Constitution or Congressional Statute contradicts this principle.

State law could include statutes, common law, state constitution.

In the absence of a federal statute, state common law applies when a federal court is sitting in diversity jurisdiction.

In the absence of a federal statute or a contrary provision in the Constitution, federal courts must follow state law in diversity cases.

State law was defined to include state common law (*Erie Railroad Co. v. Tompkins,* 1938); *Erie* relies on the 10th Amendment.

Erie established the current foundation of diversity jurisdiction in federal district courts.

If there is a conflict between a federal statute (or US Constitution) and state law, the federal court in a diversity case must use federal law (i.e., Supremacy Clause).

Congress passed the rules enabling act (i.e., Federal Rules of civil procedure), federal courts generally follow the federal rules in diversity cases even if there are contrary state procedures.

Horizontal choice of law

Addresses which law applies to different state laws.

For torts, the federal district court uses state law where the injury occurred.

For contracts, the federal district court uses state law where the contract was signed.

A court in another jurisdiction (federal courts or another state court) looks at the lower court decisions and *predicts* how the state's supreme court would rule.

Certification is the process where a federal district court has the state supreme court certify the law by resolving questions from other lower courts in the jurisdiction.

Federal courts and other state courts can request the state supreme court to answer how they would resolve the law.

Some states will only certify requests from Federal Appeals Courts.

Notes for active learning

Pretrial Procedures

Preliminary injunctions and temporary restraining orders

A party may seek a preliminary injunction before a trial on the merits.

Rule 65(a) requires that a preliminary injunction may not be issued without notice to the adverse party.

A temporary restraining order (TRO) is granted by a court when necessary to prevent irreparable harm or injury arising before a preliminary injunction hearing.

Interlocutory injunctions

An injunction is an equitable remedy by which a person is ordered to act (or refrain from acting) in a specified manner.

Interlocutory injunctions are granted to maintain the status quo until a trial on the merits.

Pleadings

Rule 3 pertains to the commencement of a civil action by filing a complaint.

Historically, the rules were strict with pleadings, and if different in court than the pleading, the case was dismissed (variance).

Notice Pleading does not have to allege all facts, but the facts of the cause of action being alleged need to support the cause of action.

The pleading alleges sufficient facts to put the defendant on notice of the claim against them.

Rule 8 requires that the complaint sets out the allegation of facts in numbered paragraphs.

Rule 8(e)(2) allows the plaintiff to plead more than one version of the claim because of the lack of time to discover facts and develop applicable legal theories.

Three Requirements for Federal Complaints (Rule 8):

1) Jurisdictional allegations—subject matter;

2) A "*short and plain statement of the claim showing that the pleader is entitled to relief*" (*notice pleading*) – the complaint only needs enough details to put the defendant on notice;

3) Demand for judgment (e.g., monetary damages).

Special Pleadings (fraud or mistake) are covered by 9(b): the complaint must identify a specific individual who said the fraud or mistake and what they said.

An allegation of fraud needs specificity because it is easy to allege, difficult to defend because the defendant needs to disprove a negative, and it is a damaging accusation,

In response to a complaint, within 21 days of service of process, Rule 8(b) requires the defendant to prepare an answer (also a pleading) by numbering the responses to the allegations and responding to each averment:

1) Affirmative defense: statute of limitations would appear in the answer, and at the end of the answer, the defendant would list affirmative defenses.
    (a) Counterclaim: at the end of the answer, assert counterclaims and list the Answer and Third-party complaints.
    (b) Bring in other parties as defendants.
    (c) A third-party complaint is when a defendant sues another not listed in the complaint
    (d) Cross-complaint is one defendant suing another defendant.
2) Motion to dismiss: filed alleging the lack of grounds for personal, subject matter jurisdiction, or venue.

Rule 12(b) defenses may be raised by motion or answer:

1) lack of subject matter jurisdiction (raised at any time),
2) lack of personal jurisdiction (waivable; must be pleaded in the first response),
3) improper venue (waivable; must be pleaded in the first response),
4) insufficiency of process (waivable; must be pleaded in the first response),
5) insufficiency of service of process (waivable; must be pleaded in the first response),
6) failure to state a claim (may be raised at any time during trial), and
7) failure to join an indispensable party (may be raised at any time during trial).

Counterclaims and crossclaims

Counterclaim is a claim against an opposing party (other side of the *v.*), filed as part of the defendant's answer.

Compulsory counterclaim arises from the same transaction or occurrence as the plaintiff's claim. Must be filed in the pending case or waived.

Permissive counterclaim does not arise from the same transaction or occurrence as the plaintiff's claim.

Crossclaims are claims against a co-party (same side of the *v.*).

A crossclaim filed by one defendant against another will not defeat diversity because the exception to the rule applies only to claims filed by plaintiffs.

Amended and supplemental pleadings

Rule 15(a) entitles a party to amend pleading (complaint or answer) once before the responsive pleading is served.

If the pleading is one to which no responsive pleading is permitted, and the action has not been placed on the trial calendar, the party may amend it within 20 days after it was served.

A party shall plead in response to an amended pleading within the time remaining for a response to the original pleading or within 10 days after service of the amended pleading, whichever period is longer.

The plaintiff may amend a pleading after the defendant filed a motion to dismiss under Rule 12(b)(6) as a motion and not an answer.

The defendant must respond to the amended complaint within 10 days or the time remaining before the pleading was amended

The defendant has a right to amend the answer because it is a pleading to which no responsive pleading is permitted, and the party has 20 days to correct it.

If a party waits too long to amend, the party must file a motion to ask the court's permission to amend the complaint.

Rule 15(c) addresses the statute of limitations and joining a new party or adding a new claim.

Rule 15(c)(2): an amendment to add a claim after the statute of limitations expired relates back only if it illuminates factual details, changes the legal theory, or adds another claim arising out of the same transaction, occurrence, or conduct.

Relation back is denied for those amendments based on entirely different facts, transactions, or occurrences.

Rule 15(c)(3): an amendment to add a new party after the statute of limitations has run.

This amendment is only allowed after the statute of limitations expires if the defendant would not be prejudiced and should have known that, but for a mistake, the party would have been named a defendant.

Rule 15(d): supplemental pleadings set forth events occurring after a pleading is filed for events that occurred after the original pleading was filed.

Supplemental pleadings do not include facts that occurred before the original filing but which were discovered after filing.

Supplemental pleadings update the dispute by bringing such new facts to the court's attention even if they change the relief sought or add additional parties.

Supplemental pleadings are allowed only with the court's permission.

Rule 11 – Ethical Restraints in Pleadings

Veracity of pleadings

Rule 11 (the veracity of pleadings) requires attorneys (or *pro se* litigants) to sign all papers (except discovery documents) certifying:

the paper is not for an improper purpose (e.g., harass, cause unnecessary delay, needlessly to increase the cost of litigation),

legal contentions are warranted by law or by a nonfrivolous argument for extending, modifying, reversing existing law, or for establishing new law,

factual contentions and denials have evidentiary support, and

the denials of factual contentions are warranted on evidence.

Rule 11 applies to pleadings, motions, and paper representations submitted to the court.

Certification is continuous, so if an attorney argues a point plead, they re-certify the above.

Nonfrivolous claims

A party cannot bring a claim certain they cannot win (challenging a Supreme Court decision).

However, this is not frivolous after a judicial turnover, or the previous bench decision was narrow. Must identify allegations of support likely from discovery *vs.* those already supported.

Sanctions for violations

Sanctions (monetary or non-monetary) may be levied to deter repeated bad conduct.

Safe Harbor Rule: if the other party violates rule 11, a motion can be filed for sanctions on the party and request correction before filing the motion with the court.

There is no safe harbor requirement when the court itself initiates sanctions.

Notes for active learning

Pretrial Motions

Rule 12 pre-answer motions

Rule 12(a)(4): if the pre-answer motion is denied, the respondent has 14 days to file an answer (unless the court sets a different time).

If the pre-answer motion is accepted, an answer may not be required.

After filing the pre-answer motion, there is an ongoing duty to answer until motion is decided.

Rule 12(b) and the special appearance rule require a prompt challenge to personal jurisdiction.

Rule 12(b) allows other defenses to be raised at the same time while a special appearance consents to the jurisdiction of the court.

A defendant can make these motions before filing an answer.

Rule 12(b)(1): dismiss for lack of subject matter jurisdiction – when the court lacks the statutory or constitutional power to adjudicate the case.

Rule 12(b)(4): object to process (e.g., the summons).

Rule 12(b)(5): insufficient service (e.g., manner the summons was served).

Rule 12(b)(6): goes to the merits of the case (i.e., failure to state a claim), and the law does not provide a remedy.

Amending the complaint

Then, the plaintiff can probably amend the complaint.

Rule 12(b)(6): modern version of *demurrer*: even if all facts as pleaded are true, the law supplies no relief.

The court will only look at the complaint and assume facts are true and ask what remedy is available; if none, motion granted

Rule 12(b)(7): failure to join an indispensable party (i.e., cannot adjudicate without violating the rights of a third party).

Many of the above deficiencies are curable (e.g., the court can instruct the plaintiff to serve properly, add the third party).

Motions do not suspend discovery.

However, motion can be made to stay discovery until the motion is decided.

If a motion is made for lack of personal jurisdiction, the litigation proceeds through discovery until the motion is decided.

Most jurisdictions require a brief (i.e., reasons for motion) with the pre-answer motions.

Removal is not a responsive pleading.

After removal, pre-answer motions available are still at the beginning of the suit.

Joinder

Rule 8: joinder of claims for parties

Rule 8 governs counterclaims: pleadings for claims for relief with counterclaims and crossclaims.

Joinder of claims for parties:

1) Some common questions of law or fact.
2) Arising from the same transaction or occurrence.

Counterclaims

Rule 13(a) compulsory counterclaim: from the same set of events.

Rule 13(b) permissive counterclaim: if arising from different events.

Rule 13(b): once a defendant has been sued with a crossclaim, the defendant can invoke compulsory and permissive counterclaims.

Crossclaims

Rule 13(h): additional parties to a crossclaim for related claims.

Rule 18(a): plaintiff or defendant asserting a claim may join claims, even if unrelated to underlying facts, against an opposing party.

Once a proper crossclaim is done, additional unrelated crossclaims can be added without violating subject matter jurisdiction.

Rule 18(b): joinder of contingent claims.

A party may join two claims even though one is dependent on the disposition of the other.

Joinder of parties

Rule 19: pertains to the joinder of parties. Requires individual defendants must be ordered by the court to be added into a suit.

This motion for joinder may be raised in a pre-answer motion.

Rule 20(a): joinder of parties from common questions or facts in the occurrence of the action, the defendant and plaintiff can be joined.

Proper joinder under Rule 20(a), Rule 18 permits adding unrelated claims.

Rule 42(b) authorizes a judge to do separate trials for unrelated claims. If the claim is a diversity claim, and a non-diverse party's joinder destroys diversity, the court decides if the party is necessary and, if so, if a party is indispensable and still a remedy exists for the plaintiff (in state court).

Discovery

Automatic disclosure

Discovery is a lawyer-driven process to investigate a claim and compel documents.

Rule 26(a)(1) pertains to initial disclosures.

Rule 26 requires disclosure without waiting for a discovery request.

Opposing counsel must turn over at the beginning of litigation.

1) witnesses that support a position in the case
2) any document that will be used to support the case
3) describe the adversary nature of damages
4) insurance agreements to determine the policy limits

Rule 26 requires parties to disclose all information "*then reasonably available*" that is not privileged or protected as work product.

Rule 26 has provisions allowing stipulation of the parties (or court order) to modify some disclosure requirements.

Before making disclosures, a party must make a reasonable inquiry into the facts.

Privileges exist as recognition that it is more important to protect this communication than reveal this information.

Courts have discretion, so the Appellate level standard for review is an *abuse of discretion.*

For a good cause shown, a court can allow the discovery of any matter "*relevant to the subject matter*" involved.

Information need not be admissible to be discoverable if it is "reasonably calculated *to lead to* the discovery of admissible evidence"—evidence might lead you to admissible evidence.

Rule 33 allows a party to provide access to files, but there could be privileged information in these files.

Common objections of discovery

Rule 26(b)(1): discovery regarding any matter not privileged is relevant to any party's claim or defense.

Not all relevant information is admissible but may lead to admissible evidence.

The broader the pleadings in the complaint, the broader is discovery.

If it is allowed for the opposing side to inspect all documents, privileged and work product are waived.

Rule 26(b)(2): the court can limit discovery.

Parties can object and receive protective orders.

Limitations on discovery include:

1) unduly burdensome
2) cumulative
3) available elsewhere

Rule 26(b)(3): pertains to documents and tangible things.

For example, work product (e.g., notes on preparing for litigation, legal judgments, strategies) is protected.

Rule 26(b)(5): must articulate why using privilege as much as possible (i.e., not disclosing).

Discovery sanctions

Rule 26(g): discovery (including discovery responses) must be:

> Consistent with the rules and warranted by existing law or good faith extension, modification, or reversal of existing law.
>
> Not interposed for any improper purpose (e.g., to harass, cause unnecessary delay, increase litigation costs).
>
> Not unreasonable or unduly burdensome or expensive given the needs of the case.

Rule 26(g)(3): failure to comply with discovery requests can result in sanctions against the attorney or party, including payment of the opponent's expenses (i.e., attorneys' fees) due to violations.

Depositions

Rule 30 covers depositions: witness testimony under oath.

Depositions can be taken from anyone.

Advantages of depositions: uncoached testimony, can ask follow-up questions, and observe a person's reaction to the questions.

Disadvantages of depositions: expensive, difficult to plan, have to study the case to do effectively (a reason why depositions are usually taken late in the case).

Sometimes depositions are taken early in the case before the witness knows enough about the case to be aware of what information to hide.

Usually, a witness comes to trial, but when this is not possible, a videotape of the deposition may be used after being screened for objections.

At deposition, objections are noted, but answers must be given.

The deponent can refuse to answer privileged questions.

Rule 30(d)(4): prohibits harassing or embarrassing questions.

Interrogatories

Rule 33: interrogatories are written questions (limited to 25 interrogatories unless the court approves more).

Interrogatories must be answered from memory or records (e.g., files).

Interrogatories are valuable to determine whom to depose (e.g., determine the identity of people that may have information).

Interrogatories are often written by lawyers and answered by lawyers under oath.

Interrogatories elicit facts (e.g., names and addresses of witnesses, doctors' bills).

Interrogatories are limited in number, so multi-part questions are problematic.

No follow-up questions are permitted.

Interrogatories are for parties of the suit and not for witnesses.

Often, the sequence is interrogatories first, document requests, and depositions after evaluating earlier information.

Production of documents

Rule 34 covers requests for the production of documents sent to parties in the case.

Requests for the production of documents require a subpoena for non-parties.

Witnesses and documents can be obtained by subpoena.

If in a foreign language, the producing party must translate.

Physical and mental exams

Rule 36: covers physical and mental exams.

A court order is needed for the physical or mental exams of a party.

Personal injury cases permit the physical exam but may be limited in scope.

Physical exams for witnesses are excluded, but records may be subpoenaed.

Request for admissions

Rule 36: requests for admissions: to avoid litigating specific points.

Rule 37(a): when someone fails to comply with a motion to compel.

37(a)(2)(b): applies in the context of a motion to compel.

A motion to compel is filed after an opponent has failed to comply with discovery.

Must confer with an opponent before filing the motion to compel.

The court may award fees to the party who successfully pursues or defends against such an action.

Rule 37(b)(2): does not allow sanctions for interfering with discovery until there is an effort to work it out since the defendant may resist if the item requested is too burdensome.

Adjudication Without a Trial

Voluntary dismissal

Rule 41 covers dismissals.

Plaintiff may dismiss an action without a court order by filing:

i) a notice of dismissal before the opposing party serves an answer or a motion for summary judgment; or

ii) a stipulation of dismissal signed by parties who appeared.

Unless specified otherwise, the dismissal is without prejudice.

If the plaintiff previously dismissed a federal- or state-court action based on or including the same claim, a notice of dismissal operates as an adjudication on the merits.

Except as provided in Rule 41(a)(1), a plaintiff's action for dismissal is only by court order, on terms the court considers proper.

If a defendant has pleaded a counterclaim before being served with the plaintiff's motion to dismiss, the action may be dismissed over the defendant's objection only if the counterclaim can remain pending for independent adjudication.

Involuntary dismissal

If the plaintiff fails to prosecute or to comply with these rules or court order, a defendant may move to dismiss the action.

Unless the dismissal order states otherwise, a dismissal operates as an adjudication on the merits, except:

lack of jurisdiction,

improper venue, or

failure to join a party under Rule 19.

Dismissing counterclaims, crossclaim or third-party claims

A claimant's voluntary dismissal under Rule 41(a)(1)(A)(i) must be made:

1) before a responsive pleading is served, or

2) if there is no responsive pleading before evidence is introduced at a hearing or trial.

If a plaintiff who previously dismissed an action in any court files an action based on or including the same claim against the same defendant, the court:

1) may order the plaintiff to pay some costs of the previous action; and

2) may stay the proceedings until the plaintiff has complied.

Pretrial Conference and Order

Pretrial conferences

The court may hold pretrial conferences to expedite the trial and encourage settlement.

Pretrial Disclosures: at least 30 days before trial, a party must disclose to the other parties and file with the court a list of:

witnesses to be called at trial,

witnesses that may be called if the need arises,

witnesses whose testimony will be presented by deposition

transcript of pertinent portions of the deposition, and

documents or exhibits they expect to offer if needed.

Evidence or witnesses that would be used solely for impeachment need not be disclosed.

Within 14 days after this disclosure, a party may serve objections to the use of the depositions at trial and the admissibility of disclosed documents and exhibits.

Such objections are waived if not made at this point, except for objections that the evidence is irrelevant, prejudicial, or confusing under Federal Rules of Evidence 402 and 403.

Rule 16(b): scheduling conference: the court must (except in classes of cases exempted by local rule) hold a scheduling conference among the parties or counsel.

The conference may be held by telephone, mail, or suitable means.

Within 90 days after the appearance of a defendant and within 120 days after the complaint has been served on a defendant, the court must enter a scheduling order limiting the time for joinder, motions, and discovery.

Rule 26(f) Conference of Parties when planning for discovery: as soon as practicable, and at least 21 days before a scheduling conference is held or the scheduling order required by Rule 16(b) is due, the parties must confer to consider:

their claims and defenses,

the possibility of settlement,

initial disclosures, and

a discovery plan.

The parties must submit to the court a proposed discovery plan within 14 days after the conference addressing:

the timing and form of required disclosures,

the subjects on which discovery may be needed,

the timing of and limitations on discovery, and

relevant orders that may be required of the court.

The order may include dates for pretrial conferences, a trial date, and appropriate matters.

A final pretrial conference is held as close to the trial as reasonable.

A final pretrial conference formulates a trial plan, including the admission of evidence.

At least one of the lawyers for each side conducting the trial and unrepresented parties should attend the final pretrial conference.

After a pretrial conference, an order must be entered that controls the subsequent course of events in the case.

Thus, the final pretrial conference order is a blueprint for the trial:

listing witnesses to be called,

evidence to be presented,

factual and legal issues needing resolution.

The final pretrial conference supersedes the pleadings and may be modified only *for good cause.*

Jury Trials

Right to a jury trial – demand

The right of trial by jury as declared by the Seventh Amendment—or as provided by federal statute—is preserved to the parties inviolate.

On issue triable of right by a jury, a party may demand a jury trial by:

1) serving the other parties with a written demand—which may be included in a pleading—no later than 14 days after serving the last pleading; and

2) filing the demand per Rule 5(d).

Rules 38 and 39 govern the demand for a jury trial.

In its demand, a party may specify the issues tried by a jury; otherwise, it is considered to have demanded a jury trial on all issues triable.

If the party has demanded a jury trial on only some issues, within 14 days after being served with the demand or within a shorter time ordered by the court, any other party may serve a demand for a jury trial on issues triable by jury.

A party waives the right to a jury trial unless its demand is properly served and filed.

A proper demand may be withdrawn only if the parties consent.

These rules do not create a right to a jury trial on issues in a claim that is an admiralty or maritime claim under Rule 9(h).

Selection and composition of juries

Rule 47 addresses selecting jurors.

The court may permit the parties to examine prospective jurors or may itself do so.

If the court examines the jurors, it must permit the parties or their attorneys to make further inquiry it considers proper or must ask additional questions it considers proper.

28 U.S.C. § 1870 requires the court to allow some peremptory challenges (e.g., three for civil trials).

During trial or deliberation, the court may excuse a juror *for good cause.*

Number of jurors, verdict and polling

Rule 48 pertains to the number of jurors, verdict, and polling

A jury must begin with at least 6 and no more than 12 members, and each juror must participate in the verdict unless excused.

Unless the parties stipulate otherwise, the verdict must be unanimous and must be returned by a jury of at least 6 members.

After a verdict is returned but before the jury is discharged, the court must, on a party's request (or may on its own), poll the jurors individually.

If the poll reveals a lack of unanimity or lack of assent by the number of jurors that the parties stipulated to, the court may direct the jury to continue deliberating or order a new trial.

Jury instructions

At the close of the evidence or at an earlier reasonable time that the court orders, a party may file and furnish to every other party written requests for the jury instructions it wants the court to give.

After the close of the evidence, a party may:

1) file requests for instructions on issues that could not reasonably have been anticipated by an earlier time that the court set for requests; and

2) with the court's permission, file untimely requests for instructions on an issue.

After the close of the evidence, the court:

1) must inform the parties of its proposed instructions and proposed action on the requests before instructing the jury and before final jury arguments,

2) must allow the parties to object on the record and out of the jury's hearing before instructions or arguments are delivered, and

3) may instruct the jury at any time before the jury is discharged.

Instructions to the jury for objections

A party who objects to an instruction (or failure of instruction) must do so on the record.

The record must include the matter precisely objected to and the grounds for the objection.

An objection is timely if:

1) a party objects at the opportunity provided under Rule 51(b)(2), or

2) a party was not informed of instruction or action on a request before that opportunity to object, and the party objects promptly after learning that the instruction or request will be, or has been, given or refused.

Instructions to the jury preserving a claim of error

A party may assign as error:

1) an error in an instruction given if that party properly objected; or

2) a failure to give an instruction if that party properly requested it and—unless the court rejected the request in a definitive ruling on the record—also properly objected.

A court may consider a plain error in the instructions that have not been preserved as required by Rule 51(d)(1) if the error affects substantial rights.

Notes for active learning

Motions

Pretrial motions

The sequence of events at trial:

Opening Statements

Plaintiff's case in chief: the plaintiff has the burden of proof.

Defendant's case: support position of no liability.

Closing Argument

Deliberation

Summary judgment

Rule 56 pertains to Summary Judgment.

Motions for Summary Judgment takes place after discovery, uses evidence from discovery, and tries to get the case disposed of.

Motion granted if evidence does not show plausibility for a jury to find for one party.

The question for summary judgment: is there a genuine issue of material fact?

Convincing Clarity Standard—the more difficult the case is to prove at trial, the more challenging it to survive a summary judgment motion.

The moving party for summary judgment must demonstrate an absence of evidence to support the nonmoving party's case.

If the moving party establishes a lack of evidence, a non-moving party must present specific facts showing a genuine trial issue.

Summary judgment may be granted on parts of the case.

If the defendant prevails on one element of the case, the plaintiff prevails because the plaintiff has the burden of proof on all elements.

If the plaintiff prevails on one element, that element is not at issue during trial.

The plaintiff may plead a legally sufficient case (i.e., survives a Rule 12(b)(6) Motion), but the defendant may have facts that eliminate an essential element.

In such a case, the defendant can file a motion for summary judgment, attach admissible evidence, and a brief explaining the legal meaning.

The plaintiff has a chance to respond to the motion that shows contradicting evidence to establish a factual dispute requiring a jury.

In some cases, sides agree on the facts, and each submits a motion for summary judgment to get a ruling on the legal implication of those facts.

Rule 56(e): when a motion is made, an adverse party cannot just rely on allegations in the complaint.

If an adverse party does not respond, summary judgment will be granted, if appropriate.

If the evidence presented by an opposing party still makes a conclusion doubtful, summary judgment is not appropriate.

Summary Judgment is based on the papers before trial (e.g., motions, briefs, affidavits).

Declaratory judgment

Rule 57 addresses declaratory judgment (i.e., a binding judgment from a court defining the legal relationship between parties and their rights in a matter before the court).

The existence of another adequate remedy does not preclude a declaratory judgment that is otherwise appropriate.

A court may order a speedy hearing of a declaratory judgment action. Declaratory Judgment is a mechanism for a party to bring suit to itself to determine its liabilities and rights.

If the party expects to be sued, they can bring the matter to the court to hear its opinion on how it would rule if they were sued if they performed in a particular manner.

Courts only grant declaratory judgments when there is an immediately focused controversy between the parties.

Directed verdict – judgment as a matter of law (JMOL)

Rule 50: *Motions of Judgment as Matter of Law* (JMOL): a motion made by a party during the trial, claiming the opposing party has insufficient evidence to reasonably support its case.

Rule 50(a): *Directed Verdict*: verdict rendered by a jury upon instruction by the judge that they must bring in that verdict because one of the parties has not proved their case as a matter of law.

The JMOL has replaced directed verdicts in federal courts.

Direct Verdict motion is raised after a party has had an opportunity to present their case. The non-moving party has presented all evidence:

must be made before the case presented to the jury, and

must specify the basis for the motion.

A motion for judgment as a matter of law (JMOL) may be made at any time before the case is submitted to the jury.

Seventh Amendment considerations

How can this be balanced with the Seventh Amendment?

1) Right to a jury trial shall be preserved as existed in 1791,

2) Juries determine the facts, and if there are no facts to decide, then not taking anything away from the jury.

The plaintiff cannot make the motion immediately after presenting their case because the defendant has no chance to present the case yet, but the defendant could since the plaintiff had their chance to plead their case.

A plaintiff suing several different defendants because not sure which one is liable; the plaintiff puts on evidence that 2 of 3 defendants are liable.

However, the third defendant may move for a directed verdict because the plaintiff has not proved anything for that defendant to be liable. No reasonable jury could find for the plaintiff.

The court grants a motion for a directed verdict (i.e., JMOL) if no reasonable jury could find in favor of the nonmoving party (federal approach).

If the court does not grant a motion for judgment as a matter of law made under Rule 50(a), the court is considered to have submitted the action to the jury subject to the court's later deciding the legal questions raised by the motion.

Why would a judge grant a motion before going to the jury?

1) Preserve the Seventh Amendment by not reexamining the jury's findings; just renew the decision on the motion as a matter of law.

2) Allows a party to fix the problem with the case.

The plaintiff can reopen the case to present new evidence.

Standards of review

Standards of review are the same under Rule 50(a) and Rule 50(b).

Scintilla test: even if only little (*scintilla*) evidence in support, it goes to the jury.

Plaintiff's evidence standard: assessing whether a jury can hear the case, only look at the plaintiff's evidence.

Federal Standards: viewing the plaintiff's case in a most favorable light *and* considering all uncontradicted evidence of the defendant (inferences to favor the plaintiff).

A judgment as a matter of law is reviewed *de novo* on appeal.

More deference is given to the lower court, which conducted the entire trial.

In a bench trial, a motion is made under Rule 52.

Under Rule 52, a fundamentally different argument that evidence has not met the burden of proof (judge is fact finder).

JMOL motion is before the jury so that the other side can address issues.

JMOL is a judgment because the court heard the merits of the case.

Judgment notwithstanding verdict (JNOV)

Rule 50(a) requires the JMOL to be filed *first*.

After the verdict, the JMOL can be renewed.

Rule 50(b): *Judgment notwithstanding the verdict* (JNOV).

The *difference* between a judgment as a matter of law (JMOL) / directed verdict is that the motion for the judgment notwithstanding the verdict (JNOV) is made *after* the jury renders a verdict.

For example, the case goes to the jury, and the jury finds for the other party.

The moving party asks the judge to overrule what the jury concluded.

The standard to issue a JMOL is whether a reasonable jury decided this way. If a reasonable jury could not have decided like this, the judge might enter a JNOV.

Rule: only where there is a complete absence of probative facts to support the conclusion reached does a reversible error appear.

If there is an evidentiary basis for the jury's verdict, the jury is free to disregard whatever facts are inconsistent with its conclusion.

Plaintiff appeals and review is *de novo*; if reversed, the matter goes to a new jury.

If the plaintiff wins, the judge orders a new trial.

If the appeals court agrees, the case is remanded to reinstate the judgment on the original verdict.

If the jury gives excessive damages, the judge can ask the plaintiff to reduce (i.e., remittitur) some of the damages.

If not, the court orders a new trial on damages.

If damages too low, the court asks the defendant to pay more (i.e., additur); a new trial might award more.

The reason for the JNOV is to avoid a new trial.

Scenario 1: Judge grants motion before a jury hears the case (JMOL or directed verdict); if reversed on appeal, the case must be tried again.

Scenario 2: Motion for JMOL/directed verdict; judge denies or defers. The case goes to jury; the defendant renews the motion (JNOV) after the jury presents findings; the judge grants the defendant's motion.

If appealed and reversed, judgment entered on the jury's verdict.

Motions for a new trial

If procedural problems (e.g., jury hearing inadmissible evidence) or clear error, a motion for a new trial will be sustained. For example,

1) Procedural Issues: if a judge makes a prejudicial mistake like inadmissible evidence, improper jury instructions, improper contacts with the jury, an improper argument to the jury.

2) Verdict is clearly wrong; the judge deems seriously erroneous result.

Not deprivation of the Seventh Amendment because it just goes to another jury

Piesco (1990) granted summary judgment and reversed it.

A judge granted Rule 59 motion for a new trial, so no final judgment allowed and no interlocutory appeal.

Must wait for the second trial. If a disfavorable outcome, the plaintiff can appeal the Ruling on the Rule 59 motion, and if reversed, the first trial judgment will be entered or denied, and judgment entered on the second trial

A new trial may be ordered for one defendant (e.g., issue of damages).

The judge could award *remittitur* in which the plaintiff has the option to take less money than the jury granted or go to a new trial.

Instead of saying that no reasonable jury could have rendered this way, the judge decides that it is against the manifest of evidence.

Juries can draw inferences from the evidence, but they must be drawn according to the law.

If inferences are not correctly drawn, despite the manifest of evidence, a new trial can be granted.

Can do partial mistrial – new trial on specific issues.

No later than 28 days after the entry of judgment—or if the motion addresses a jury issue not decided by a verdict, no later than 28 days after the jury was discharged.

The movant may file a renewed motion for judgment as a matter of law and may include an alternative or joint request for a new trial under Rule 59.

In ruling on the renewed motion, the court may:

1) allow judgment on the verdict if the jury returned a verdict;

2) order a new trial; or

3) direct the entry of judgment as a matter of law.

Granting the renewed motion

If the court grants a renewed motion for judgment as a matter of law, the court must conditionally rule on any motion for a new trial by determining whether a new trial should be granted if the judgment is later vacated or reversed.

The court must state the grounds for conditionally granting or denying the motion for a new trial.

Conditional ruling on a motion for a new trial

Conditionally granting the motion for a new trial does not affect the judgment's finality; if the judgment is reversed, the new trial must proceed unless the appellate court orders otherwise.

If the motion for a new trial is conditionally denied, the appellee may assert an error in that denial.

If the judgment is reversed, the case must proceed as the appellate court orders.

Verdicts and Judgments

Findings and conclusions by the court

Rule 52 pertains to Findings and Conclusions by the Court.

In an action tried on the facts without a jury or with an advisory jury, the court must find the facts specially and state its conclusions of law separately.

The findings and conclusions may be stated on the record after the close of the evidence or may appear in an opinion or a memorandum of the court's decision.

Judgment must be entered under Rule 58.

In granting or refusing an interlocutory injunction, the court must similarly state the findings and conclusions that support its action.

The court is not required to state findings or conclusions when ruling on a motion under Rule 12 or 56 or, unless these rules provide otherwise, on any other motion.

A master's findings, to the extent adopted by the court, must be considered the court's findings.

A party may question the sufficiency of the evidence supporting the findings, whether or not the party requested findings, objected, moved to amend them, or moved for partial findings.

Whether based on oral or other evidence, findings of fact must not be set aside unless *clearly erroneous*.

The reviewing court must give due regard to the trial court's opportunity to judge the witnesses' credibility.

Amended or additional findings

On a party's motion filed no later than 28 days after the entry of judgment, the court may amend its findings (or make additional findings) and amend the judgment accordingly.

The motion may accompany a motion for a new trial under Rule 59.

Judgment on partial findings

If a party has been fully heard on an issue during a nonjury trial, and the court finds against the party on that issue, the court may enter judgment against the party on a claim or defense that, under controlling law, can be maintained or defeated only with a favorable finding on that issue.

A court may decline to render a judgment until the close of the evidence.

A judgment on partial findings must be supported by findings of fact and conclusions of law as required by Rule 52(a).

Entering judgment

Judgments NOT on merits: subject matter, jurisdiction, personal jurisdiction, venue, improper service of process, failure to join a party.

Judgments on merits:

summary judgment,

directed verdict,

Rule 12(b)(6) (get chance to amend complaint), or

dismissal for failure to prosecute.

In a state with 12(b)(6) motions not barring the second suit, the suit brought in federal district court will apply the same principles.

The court will probably not grant Rule 60(b) relief as an attempt to avoid *res judicata*.

Rule 58 pertains to entering judgment.

Every judgment and amended judgment must be set out in a separate document, but a separate document is not required for an order disposing of a motion:

1) for judgment under Rule 50(b),

2) to amend or make additional findings under Rule 52(b),

3) for attorney's fees under Rule 54,

4) for a new trial under Rule 59,

5) to alter or amend the judgment under Rule 59, or

6) for relief under Rule 60.

Subject to Rule 54(b) and unless the court orders otherwise, the clerk must, without awaiting the court's direction, promptly prepare, sign, and enter the judgment when:

1) the jury returns a general verdict,

2) the court awards only costs or a sum certain, or

3) the court denies relief.

Subject to Rule 54(b), the court must promptly approve the form of the judgment, which the clerk must promptly enter, when:

1) the jury returns a special verdict or a general verdict with answers to written questions; or

2) court grants other relief not described in this subdivision.

For purposes of these rules, judgment is entered at the following times:

1) if a separate document is not required, when the judgment is entered in the civil docket under Rule 79(a), or

2) if a separate document is required, when the judgment is entered in the civil docket under Rule 79(a), and the earlier occurs:

(a) it is set out in a separate document, or

(b) 150 days have run from the entry in the civil docket.

A party may request that judgment be set out in a separate document per Rule 58(a).

Ordinarily, the entry of judgment may not be delayed, nor the time for appeal extended to tax costs or award fees.

If a timely motion for attorney's fees is made under Rule 54(d)(2, the court may act before a notice of appeal has been filed and become effective to order that the motion has the same effect under Federal Rule of Appellate Procedure 4(a)(4) as a timely motion under Rule 59.

Relief from a judgment or order

Rule 60 pertains to Relief from a Judgment or Order.

The court may correct a clerical mistake or a mistake arising from oversight or omission whenever a mistake is found in a judgment, order, or another part of the record.

The court may do so on motion or its own, with or without notice.

After an appeal has been docketed and pending, a mistake may be corrected only with the appellate court's leave.

On motion and just terms, the court may relieve a party or its legal representative from a final judgment, order, or proceeding for the following reasons:

1) mistake, inadvertence, surprise, or excusable neglect,
2) newly discovered evidence that, with reasonable diligence, could not have been discovered in time to move for a new trial under Rule 59(b),
3) fraud (whether intrinsic or extrinsic), misrepresentation, or misconduct by an opposing party,
4) the judgment is void,
5) the judgment has been satisfied, released, or discharged; it is based on an earlier judgment that has been reversed or vacated, or applying it prospectively is no longer equitable, or
6) any other reason that justifies relief.

Claim preclusion – *res judicata*

A plaintiff cannot bring the second cause of action based on the same facts and evidence after an original cause of action has been litigated.

Federal Rules of Civil Procedure are flexible to get the whole case heard *but* very strict about providing a second chance to try the case.

Four requirements for *res judicata*:

1) final judgment,
2) on the merits,
3) claims must be the same,
4) parties must be the same.

Federal district court uses claims about the same transaction or series of transactions like joinder (same set of historical facts).

Therefore, a plaintiff must present all claims in one lawsuit.

An exception applies to cases that statutes direct the subject to federal court (e.g., patents).

For example, if the defendant pleads *res judicata*, it will not prevail because the patent claim could not have brought in state court.

If the plaintiff may sue on the claim in the first suit – *res judicata* applies.

If the court in the first suit never reached merits (no judgment), *res judicata* does not apply.

If suit 1 is in federal court and suit 2 is in state court, suit 2 will be barred if it could have been added to the federal docket under supplemental jurisdiction.

However, if it did offer the suit and it was denied, it will not be barred.

Win or lose, the plaintiff is barred from a second lawsuit on the claim.

If the plaintiff wins, the claim is merged with the judgment.

If the plaintiff lost, the claim becomes barred.

For analysis, consider the same parties as before and claims from the same underlying transaction – focus on the underlying events/facts.

For an error in the first case, appealing the first judgment is the remedy.

If the defendant sues the plaintiff after the plaintiff sued the defendant, it is barred based on the same underlying facts.

Compulsory counterclaim rules are based on *res judicata*.

If a counterclaim is permissive, then not barred.

If crossclaim is permissive, then not barred.

If the defendant impleads a third party, then the defendant sues the third party on the same underlying facts; it is barred because the defendant should have asserted all claims when impleading the third party.

If the plaintiff did not pursue a lawsuit, then barred by failure to prosecute barred by that judgment or dismissal; had a chance to litigate merits and did not pursue – no second chances.

If the defendant defaults, barred because they ignored the merits.

If the law changes, they still cannot litigate because they would still be suing on the same underlying facts.

Federal courts: (majority rule for state courts): when it arises from the same cause of action—transaction, occurrence, or event—it is part of the same claim and cannot litigate it again.

Minority rule (for state courts): if one cause of action gives rise to two different claims, the second claim is not precluded. Claims are different if the nature of the harm done is different (e.g., property damage *vs*. personal injury).

Determine whether subsequent cases involve the same claim.

1) Type of damages: used in a minority of states.
2) Single occurrence (federal courts).
3) Sameness of evidence: to establish liability.
4) Common nucleus of operative facts: restatement definition.

Parties are identical or in privity with the same configuration (parties bound in the dispute).

Privity: whatever benefits the first plaintiff would get from the first lawsuit would benefit the second plaintiff, so the claim precluded. For example, a trustee brings a claim for the beneficiary's benefit; the beneficiary cannot bring the same claim against the same defendant.

Privity: rights were already exhausted because the previous plaintiff already exhausted them; For example, trying the same case again with a different person standing in.

Class action: person part of a class action, even though not named, cannot bring a claim independently; the legal relationship between litigant and party, not a litigant.

The same configuration of parties: the plaintiff must be the same in the second case.

The plaintiff must be the one to sue the defendant in both cases; it is not the same configuration if the defendant initiates a suit.

Valid final judgment: valid unless no jurisdiction or venue issues; it becomes a final judgment after the trial court is done with the matter.

On the merits – had the opportunity to have the substance heard:

1) summary judgment (SJ),
2) judgment as a matter of law (JMOL),
3) judgment notwithstanding the verdict (JNOV).

If dismissed for lack of jurisdiction, cannot impose claim preclusion because the issue was not tried on the merits.

Dismissed because of other elements not due to merits, have not had a day in court.

Rule 12(6) motion to dismiss for *failure to state a claim*: court dismisses the claim with prejudice (after the amended complaint).

Some states hold that dismissal for failure to state a claim is on the merits because no claim was stated.

Issue preclusion – collateral estoppel

Prevents litigation of particular issues that were litigated and determined in the first case.

If the first case argues A, B, C, and D, and the second case argues A, X, Y, and Z, defendant A cannot be sued again since they were included in the prior suit.

Elements of analysis:

Was the same issue litigated and determined in the first case?

Was the issue essential to the judgment in the first case?

Was the holding on that issue embodied in a valid, final judgment on the merits?

Is the preclusion being exercised against an appropriate party?

Is the preclusion being asserted by an appropriate party (mutuality issue)?

Notes for active learning

Appeals and Review with Government as a Party

Appeal as of right

Rule 4 applies to Appeal as of Right.

In a civil case, except as provided in Rules 4(a)(1)(B), 4(a)(4), and 4(c), the notice of appeal required by Rule 3 must be filed with the district clerk within 30 days after entry of the judgment or order appealed from.

Any party may file the notice of appeal within 60 days after entry of the judgment or order appealed from if one of the parties is:

1) the United States;
2) a United States agency;
3) a United States officer or employee sued in an official capacity; or
4) a current or former United States officer or employee sued in an individual capacity for an act or omission occurring in connection with official duties (including instances in which the United States represents that person when the judgment or order is entered or files the appeal for that person).

An appeal from an order granting or denying an application for a writ of error *coram nobis* (i.e., *a fundamental error of manifest injustice*) is an appeal in a civil case for purposes of Rule 4(a).

A notice of appeal is filed after the court announces a decision or order but before the entry of judgment or order is treated as filed on the date of and after the entry.

If one party timely files a notice of appeal, any other party may file a notice of appeal within 14 days after the date when the first notice was filed or within the time prescribed by Rule 4(a), whichever period ends later.

Notes for active learning

Appeals and Review for Civil Cases

Effect of a motion on a notice of appeal

If a party files in the district court any of the following motions under the Federal Rules of Civil Procedure – and does within the time allowed – the time to file an appeal runs for all parties from the entry of the order disposing of the last remaining motion:

1) for judgment under Rule 50(b);
2) to amend or make additional factual findings under Rule 52(b), whether or not granting the motion would alter the judgment;
3) for attorney's fees under Rule 54 if the district court extends the time to appeal under Rule 58;
4) to alter or amend the judgment under Rule 59;
5) for a new trial under Rule 59; or
6) for relief under Rule 60 if the motion is filed no later than 28 days after the judgment is entered.

If a party files a notice of appeal after the judgment – but before the court disposes of motions listed in Rule 4(a)(4)(A) – the notice becomes effective to appeal a judgment or order, in whole or part, when the order disposing of the last remaining motion is entered.

A party intending to challenge an order disposing of any motion listed in Rule 4(a)(4)(A), or a judgment's alteration or amendment upon such a motion, must file a notice of appeal or an amended notice of appeal – in compliance with Rule 3(c) – within the time prescribed by this Rule measured from the entry of the order disposing of the last such remaining motion.

No additional fee is required to file an amended notice.

Motion for extension of time

The district court may extend the time to file a notice of appeal if:

1) a party so moves no later than 30 days after the time prescribed by this Rule 4(a) expires; and
2) regardless of whether its motion is filed within the 30 days after the time prescribed by Rule 4(a), that party shows excusable neglect or good cause.

A motion filed before the expiration of the time prescribed in Rule 4(a)(1) or (3) may be *ex parte* unless the court requires otherwise.

If the motion is filed after the prescribed time expiration, notice must be given to the other parties per local rules.

No extension under Rule 4(a)(5) may exceed 30 days after the prescribed time or 14 days after the date when the order granting the motion is entered, whichever is later.

Reopening the time to file an appeal

The district court may reopen the time to file an appeal for 14 days after the date when its order to reopen is entered, but only if the following conditions are satisfied:

1) the court finds that the moving party did not receive notice under Federal Rule of Civil Procedure 77(d) of the entry of the judgment or order sought to be appealed within 21 days after entry;

2) the motion is filed within 180 days after the judgment or order is entered or within 14 days after the moving party receives notice under Federal Rule of Civil Procedure 77(d) of the entry, whichever is earlier; and

3) the court finds that no party would be prejudiced.

Entry defined

A judgment or order is entered for purposes of this Rule 4(a):

1) if Federal Rule of Civil Procedure 58(a) does not require a separate document when the judgment or order is entered in the civil docket under Federal Rule of Civil Procedure 79(a); or

2) if Federal Rule of Civil Procedure 58(a) requires a separate document when the judgment or order is entered in the civil docket under Federal Rule of Civil Procedure 79(a) and when the earlier of these events occurs:

    (a) the judgment or order is set forth on a separate document, or

    (b) 150 days have run from the entry of the judgment or order in the civil docket under Federal Rule of Civil Procedure 79(a).

A failure to set forth a judgment or order on a separate document when required by Federal Rule of Civil Procedure 58(a) does not affect the validity of an appeal from that judgment or order.

Appeals and Review for Criminal Cases

Effect of a motion on a notice of appeal

In a criminal case, a defendant's notice of appeal must be filed in the district court within 14 days after the later of:

1) the entry of the judgment or the order being appealed; or
2) the filing of the government's notice of appeal.

When the government is entitled to appeal, its notice of appeal must be filed in the district court within 30 days after the later of:

1) the entry of the judgment or order being appealed; or
2) the filing of a notice of appeal by any defendant.

A notice of appeal filed after the court announces a decision, sentence, or order – but before the entry of the judgment or order –is treated as filed on the date of and after the entry.

If a defendant timely makes any of the following motions under the Federal Rules of Criminal Procedure, the notice of appeal from a judgment of conviction must be filed within 14 days after the entry of the order disposing of the last remaining motion or within 14 days after the entry of the judgment of conviction, whichever ends later.

The above provision applies to a timely motion:

1) for judgment of acquittal under Rule 29;
2) for a new trial under Rule 33, but is based on newly discovered evidence, only if the motion is made no later than 14 days after the entry of the judgment; or
3) for the arrest of a judgment under Rule 34.

A notice of appeal filed after the court announces a decision, sentence, or order – but before it disposes of any of the motions referred to in Rule 4(b)(3)(A) – becomes effective upon the later of the following:

1) the entry of the order disposing of the last motion; or
2) the entry of the judgment of conviction.

A valid notice of appeal is effective – without amendment – to appeal from an order disposing of motions referred to in Rule 4(b)(3)(A).

Motion for extension of time

Upon a finding of excusable neglect or good cause, the district court may – before or after the time expired, with or without motion and notice – extend the time to file a notice of appeal not to exceed 30 days from the expiration of the time otherwise prescribed by Rule 4(b).

The filing of a notice of appeal under Rule 4(b) does not divest a district court of jurisdiction to correct a sentence under Federal Rule of Criminal Procedure 35(a), nor does the filing of a motion under 35(a) affect the validity of a notice of appeal filed before entry of the order disposing of the motion.

The filing of a motion under Federal Rule of Criminal Procedure 35(a) does not suspend the time for filing a notice of appeal from a judgment of conviction.

A judgment or order is entered for purposes of this Rule 4(b) when it is entered on the criminal docket.

Appeal by an inmate confined in an institution

If an institution has a system designed for legal mail, an inmate confined must use that system to benefit from Rule 4(c)(1).

If an inmate files a notice of appeal in a civil or criminal case, the notice is timely if it is deposited in the institution's internal mail system on or before the last day for filing and:

The notice of appeal must be accompanied by:

1) a declaration in compliance with 28 U.S.C. § 1746 – or a notarized statement – setting out the date of deposit with prepaid first-class postage; or

2) evidence (such as a postmark or date stamp) showing that the notice was so deposited, and that postage was prepaid; or

The court of appeals exercises its discretion to permit the later filing of a declaration or notarized statement that satisfies Rule 4(c)(1)(A)(i).

If an inmate files the first notice of appeal in a civil case under this Rule 4(c), the 14-day period provided in Rule 4(a)(3) for another party to file a notice of appeal runs from the date when the district court dockets the first notice.

When a defendant in a criminal case files a notice of appeal under this Rule 4(c), the 30-day period for the government to file its notice of appeal runs from the entry of the judgment or order appealed from or from the district court's docketing of the defendant's notice of appeal, whichever is later.

Mistaken filing in the court of appeals

If a notice of appeal in a civil or criminal case is mistakenly filed in the court of appeals, the clerk must note on the notice the date when it was received and send it to the district clerk.

The notice is considered filed in the district court on the date noted.

Relationship matrix

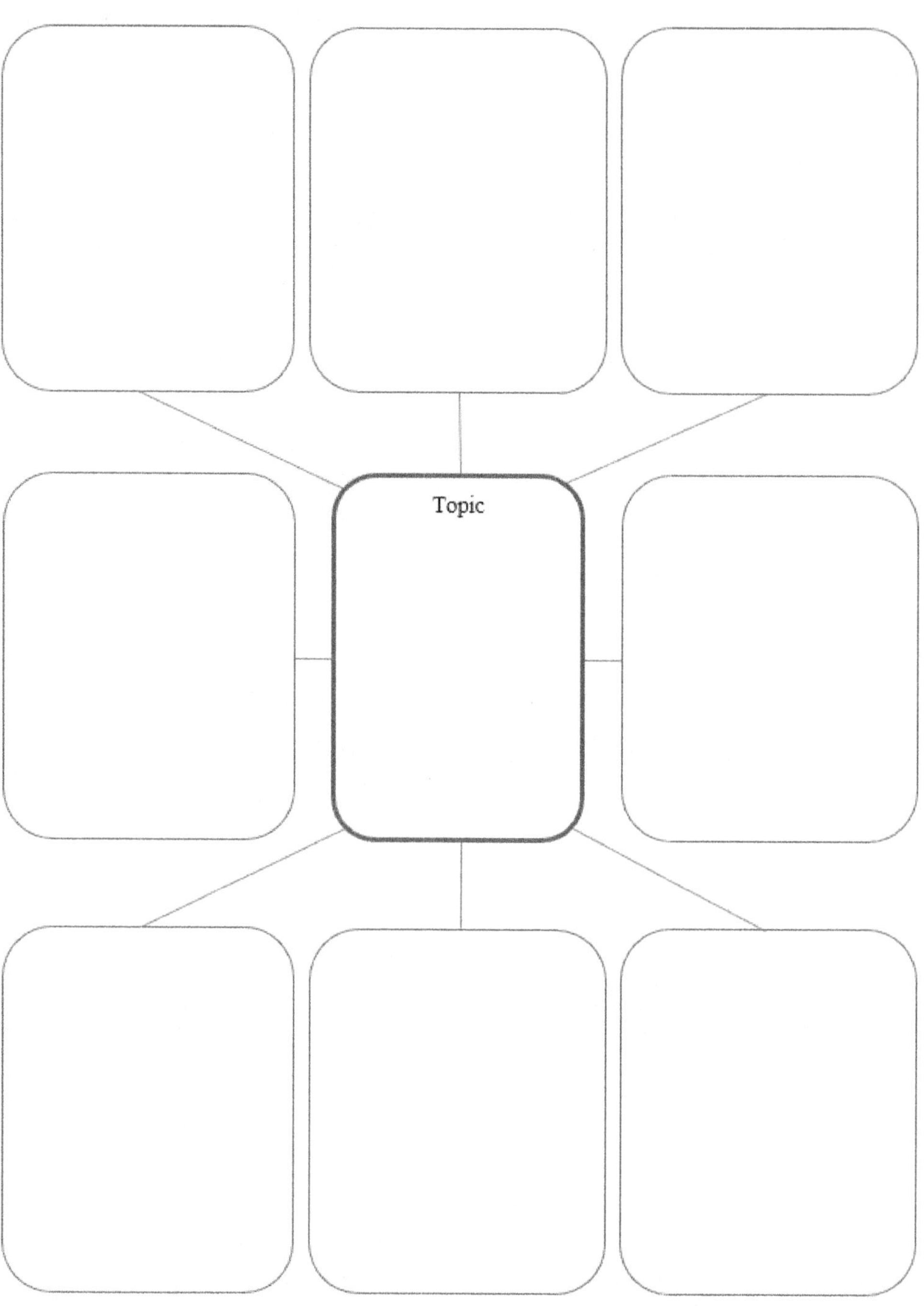

Civil Procedure – Quick Facts

American courts: basic principles

1. Every state has its court system.

   Statutes enacted by the state legislature generally establish the court system's structure and the types of cases courts within a state court system may hear.

2. The Constitution provides for a **separate federal court system**.

   Article III, § 1 of the Constitution creates the **Supreme Court** and authorizes Congress to create other federal courts below the Supreme Court.

   Congress has created **federal trial courts** (i.e., federal district courts) and **intermediate appellate courts** (i.e., federal circuit courts of appeals), and a few specialized courts (e.g., U.S. Tax Court).

3. The structure of the state and federal court systems is similar.

   Like the federal system, the state courts have a set of trial courts and a state supreme court at its court system's apex.

   Many state court systems have intermediate appellate courts analogous to the federal courts of appeals (i.e., Circuit Courts).

4. Most disputes are litigated in *state courts*.

   Every state has trial courts with **broad subject matter jurisdiction**.

   Most states have several specialized (e.g., juvenile) trial courts.

5. The cases that federal courts can hear with **subject matter jurisdiction** are limited.

   The broadest categories authorized in article III § 3 are 1) cases arising under **federal law**, 2) cases between **citizens of different states**, 3) cases between **citizens and aliens**, and 4) **admiralty and maritime cases**.

6. Generally, state courts have **concurrent jurisdiction** over cases that federal courts are authorized to hear.

   For example, cases that arise under federal law usually can be brought in state court, even though general courts are authorized by Article III to hear such cases.

   If a case may be filed in either system, the **plaintiff chooses where** to file.

7. The exception to concurrent jurisdiction is that Congress, when authorizing lower federal courts to hear a particular type of case, may provide such jurisdiction is ***exclusive of the states' courts***.

   It has done so for some types of cases (e.g., patent, copyright, bankruptcy).

Diversity jurisdiction

1. Article III § 2 of the Constitution authorizes federal courts to hear cases *between citizens of different states*, commonly referred to as **diversity jurisdiction**.

2. The constitutional grant in article III § 2 is satisfied as long as there is **minimal diversity** between the parties.

   Under the statutory grant, no plaintiff may be from the same state as any defendant (*Strawbridge v. Curtis*) (1806): no opposing parties may be from the same state. Thus, at least one plaintiff is from a different state than one defendant.

3. Federal district courts do not have **diversity jurisdiction** because the Constitution authorizes it. Congress must convey it by statute.

   The diversity statute, 28 U.S.C. § 1332 does not convey all diversity jurisdiction to the federal district courts.

   The diversity statute imposes an **amount in controversy requirement** (i.e., more than \$75,000). The plaintiff must have a good faith belief that, if they prevail at trial, they might recover more than \$75,000 (e.g., \$75,000.01).

4. For individuals, federal cases hold that a person is a citizen of the state where **domiciled**.

   To establish domicile, a person must reside in a state with the *intent* to remain indefinitely.

   To be a state citizen for diversity purposes, they must be citizens of the United States (or permanent resident).

5. **Corporations are held to be state citizens** for diversity purposes.

   A corporation is a citizen of the state where 1) it is *incorporated* and 2) it has its *principal place of business*.

Arising-under jurisdiction

1. The constitutional grant *arising under* jurisdiction in Article III § 2 is liberally construed.

   If a case involves a non-frivolous federal law issue, whether raised in the original complaint or a defendant's answer, a federal court may be authorized to hear it.

2. The power of Congress to create lower federal courts includes the power to define their jurisdiction by statute.

   Article III § 2 sets the outer limit. Within the scope of Article III § 2, Congress may choose to grant federal trial courts all, some, or none of the jurisdiction authorized by the Constitution.

Thus, Congress has the power to authorize federal district courts to hear some cases that arise under federal law but not others.

3. As with diversity jurisdiction, Congress has never granted the full scope of **arising under jurisdiction** to the lower federal courts.

   In the early days of the republic, only a narrow grant of jurisdiction over claims arising under statutes, such as the patent statute, was granted.

4. Court jurisdiction is more limited than constitutional scope under 28 U.S.C. § 1331.

   Per *Mottley* (1908), a **well-pleaded complaint rule** instructs the court to refer to the *plaintiff's claim* in determining whether a case arises under federal law.

5. In most cases, the *Holmes test* (i.e., *a suit arises under the law that creates the cause of action*) determines if a case satisfies the *Mottley* requirement.

   If federal law creates the cause of action the plaintiff seeks to enforce, the federal court has jurisdiction.

   A case may arise under federal law even though the plaintiff seeks recovery on a state law claim.

   The Supreme Court has recognized that sometimes a plaintiff must establish an important federal law proposition to prove an element of a state law claim.

   A court may find that cases in this category arise under federal law so that a federal district court has jurisdiction over the case.

6. The statutes granting appellate jurisdiction to the Court are much broader than 28 U.S.C. § 1331. Consequently, many state court cases involving federal law issues may be appealed to the Supreme Court, even though the federal issue was not raised in the plaintiff's complaint so that the case could not have been filed initially in federal district court.

Removal to federal court

1. Many cases that may be brought in federal court may be filed in state court if the plaintiff prefers.

   If the plaintiff files such a case in state court, the federal removal statutes allow **defendants to remove** to federal court.

2. The standard for removal in 28 U.S.C. § 1441 allows cases to be removed to federal court **if they could have been filed originally** in federal court.

   The exception is the forum rule, which bars the removal of a diversity case **if any defendant resides in the state where the suit is brought**.

3. If a removable case is filed in state court, defendants must remove within thirty days or remain in state court.

   If a case becomes removable, the defendants have thirty days after notice.

4. **Removal is automatic**. If the defendant removes a non-removable case, it is pending in federal court once the notice of removal is filed and the state court is notified.

   Any party who believes the case was **improperly removed** or not within the federal court's subject matter jurisdiction should **move in federal court to remand** the case.

5. Motions to remand for **lack of subject matter jurisdiction** may be made **at any time before final judgment**.

   Motions for problems must be raised within thirty days of removal.

The evolution of personal jurisdiction

1. Under *Pennoyer v. Neff* (1878), which reflected nineteenth-century jurisdictional precepts, courts typically only had ***in personam*** (particular defendant) jurisdiction over a person if the defendant was personally served with the complaint within the forum state.

   Courts have ***in rem*** (*power in or about the thing*) jurisdiction over property if the property was attached before adjudicating the claim and located within the forum state.

2. *Pennoyer's* rigid doctrine was ill-equipped for an increasingly mobile society and increased interstate corporate activity.

   In *International Shoe* (1945), the court shifted its focus from the strict requirement of an in-state presence to allow jurisdiction based on a **defendant's contacts with the state.**

3. Courts have several ways to establish *in personam* jurisdiction.

   If the claim arises from the defendant's contact, a court has **specific jurisdiction** over the defendant.

   If the claim does not arise out of the defendant's contact, but the defendant has **continuous and systematic contacts with the state**, the court has general jurisdiction.

4. The Supreme Court recognizes several bases for constitutionally sufficient jurisdiction.

   A person is subject to **personal jurisdiction** where **domiciled**.

   A defendant not otherwise subject to personal jurisdiction in a state may **waive** objection or **consent to jurisdiction**.

5. A court may only exercise jurisdiction over a defendant if doing so satisfies the constitutional requirements for **personal jurisdiction**.

   The state legislature must authorize courts to exercise personal jurisdiction in the state's long-arm statute or other jurisdiction-granting statute or rule.

Long-arm statutes

1. A court can usually exercise personal jurisdiction only if: 1) a **long-arm provision authorizes it,** and 2) **constitutional.**

   "Tag" is an exception as part of a court's common law authority even when no long-arm provision authorizes it.

2. Courts often interpret the scope of the applicable long-arm statute.

Basic venue

Litigation is restricted to **convenient courts**, given the **facts** and **location of the parties.**

Notes for active learning

Business Associations

The subject matter outline for Business Associations is divided into four sections: Agency, Partnerships, Corporations, and Limited Liability Companies. The exam often tests either Corporations and LLCs or agencies and partnerships, though occasionally it includes both. Maximize your score by mastering the governing law on these highly tested topics.

For Agency and Partnerships, the principles of the Uniform Partnership Act (UPA), the Revised Uniform Partnership Act (RUPA), or the Restatement (Second) of Agency are generally applied. The commonly tested Agency issues include actual authority, apparent authority, vicarious and direct liability, and principal and agent liability for contracts entered into by the agent. For Partnership, frequently tested items are formation, fiduciary duties, Limited Liability Partnerships (LLPs), Limited Partnerships (LPs), creditors rights, dissolution, and termination.

For Corporations, the principles of the Model Business Corporation Act (MBCA) and the Revised Model Business Corporation Act (RMBCA) apply. The commonly tested Corporations items include fiduciary duties and shareholder (i.e., derivative) lawsuits. LLCs may be tested instead of Corporations. The frequent LLC questions pertain to piercing the LLC veil and fiduciary duties. Many of the same principles apply to partnerships, corporations, and LLCs.

Agency: Relationships

Agency

An agency relationship occurs when one person (the agent or servant) acts on behalf of another (the principal or master).

The legal ramifications that occur because of these acts are delineated in the law of agency.

The five types of agents are general agent, special agent, subagent, agency coupled with an interest, and servant (or employee).

Creation formalities – capacity

An agency relationship is consensual.

An agency relationship can be created without a writing showing an agreement to create an agency relationship.

A minor may act as an agent, even lacking the capacity to contract.

A principal must have the capacity to enter into contractual transactions before they can employ an agent to do the same on their behalf.

Proof of agency

To prove an agency relationship, the party with the burden of proof must show the principal and agent's intent to enter the relationship.

An agency relationship does not automatically arise because of a kinship relationship between the purported agent and principal.

For example, a person who owns the property as a co-tenant is not automatically the other co-tenant's agent.

The person desiring to establish an agency relationship can introduce the alleged agent's testimony from which an agency may be found.

The alleged agent cannot testify to the conclusion that they entered a principal agency relationship.

Presumption of agency

In actions arising out of a motor vehicle accident, evidence that an automobile was registered in the defendant's name *is prima facie* evidence that it was being operated by a person whose conduct the defendant is legally responsible for.

The defendant may prove the absence of such responsibility.

Such proof of legal responsibility is the basis for using the insurance policy covering the motor vehicle to satisfy tort claims arising out of the accident.

Termination of agency for at-will of parties

An agency relationship is terminable at will by the principal or agent except when it is coupled with an interest.

An agency is coupled with an interest if the agent has legal rights in the agency's subject matter.

For example, a liability insurer has the right to defend the insured because of its interest in the litigation

Even though the relationship is terminable, a contract creating the agency has an effect beyond the termination. If the termination constitutes a breach of contract, the non-breaching party can sue for damages but cannot sue to enforce the contract specifically.

Termination by operation of law

Except for agency relationships created by a law authorizing durable powers of attorney and except when an agency is coupled with an interest, an agency is terminated by the principal's death, insanity, or bankruptcy.

Durable powers and powers coupled with an interest are not terminated by the principal's death, insanity, or bankruptcy.

Notice of termination of agency

Notice must be given to persons who dealt with the principal through the agent when an agency relationship is terminated.

If notice is not given, the principal may be held liable on subsequent contracts on the theory of apparent authority of the agent.

Where persons have not dealt with the agent, notice by publication is sufficient.

Notice is not required when the agency is terminated by death, insanity, or bankruptcy of the principal.

Agency: Vicarious Liability of Principal for Acts of Agent

Tort liability

The law of agency imposes liability for tortuous acts the agent (servant) commits upon the principal (master).

The first step in imposing vicarious liability for another's torts is to determine if a principal–agent relationship existed.

Right to control

The *right to control* the tortfeasor (agent) acts is the critical element determining if a master–servant (principal–agent) relationship exists.

If the tortfeasor has the right to control performance and only general goals are specified, the tortfeasor is more likely to be classified as an independent contractor.

Although no test is conclusive in determining if the purported master has the right to control:

1) details of the work assignment (direct boss *vs.* general job description), factors such as:

    (a) the method of payment (hourly wage *vs.* fee for entire job), and

    (b) length of employment (short term is consistent with independent contractor relationship),

2) distinct business (favors independent contractor relationship),

3) degree of supervision (the greater the supervision, the more likely that the relationship will be classified as employer-employee),

4) skills of the actual tortfeasor; the higher the skill level, the more the relationship is deemed an independent contractor).

An *employer can* be *vicariously liable* for an employee's negligence but *will not* be *liable* for intentionally wrongful or criminal acts (e.g., assault, murder) unless the employee's intentionally wrongful acts were *required* by the employment or *foreseeable.*

Case law classified the following special agent-principal relationships.

Borrowed servants

A person who borrows the services of a tortfeasor and controls their activity will be vicariously liable for torts while the servant is on loan to the master.

Temporary servants

A person may be a servant for the commission of a single act, and vicarious liability will be imposed upon the person who has a temporary master's role.

Sub-servants

If an employee in an employer–employee relationship employs a sub-servant to perform tasks usually assigned to the employee, the employee is only liable for the torts of a subservient committed while engaged in work performed with express or implied authority.

Master–servant relationship: *respondeat superior*

Respondeat superior is Latin for "let the master answer."

Vicarious liability is imposed upon a master for the negligent torts of their servant committed while performing on the master's business and acting within the scope of their authority.

The acts of a servant pursuing their personal business when the tort occurred will not be imputed to the master.

Nor will the master be vicariously liable in tort if the servant has substantially deviated from an authorized route.

Use of force by the servant

If the servant commits an intentional tort (e.g., assault and battery) in doing the master's work, the master will be held vicariously liable.

If an employee of a public carrier injures a customer through misconduct while engaged in the performance of a contract of carriage, the company is vicariously liable.

Independent contractors

A person who uses due care in hiring an independent contractor is not liable for negligence, except when the independent contractor is engaged in:

1) inherently dangerous activities (e.g., blasting);

2) creates a nuisance;

3) where the premises worked on are in dangerous disrepair; and

4) where a nondelegable duty is imposed upon the person hiring the independent contractor.

Principal–agent tort liability

A principal is liable for nonphysical torts such as deceit, defamation, and interference with contractual or advantageous relations if the act was expressly, impliedly, or apparently authorized.

Procedural Considerations

The master and servant are not joint tortfeasors.

A master is entitled to indemnification from their servant if the basis of liability is *respondeat superior*.

Notes for active learning

Agency: Contract Liability

A disclosed agent, acting within the scope of their authority, which enters a contract creates a contract between the principal and the other contracting party.

The agent is not liable on that contract.

Actual authority

The most crucial form of authority which will cause an agent to bind a principal is actual authority.

Such authority may be expressed, implied by a course of dealings, or incidental as necessary to accomplish an act expressly authorized.

When the principal is unavailable, an agent is impliedly authorized to take reasonable measures in an emergency.

Apparent authority

If a person has by acts or words indicated to a third party that a particular individual has the authority to act, they will be liable for contracts made on their behalf by the purported agent even if there is no actual authority if the third party reasonably relies to their detriment on the purported principal's representations.

General and special agents

A *general agent* is employed to transact the principal's business and has the authority to conduct that type of business without a specific grant of authority for each transaction.

A *special agent* is employed for a specific transaction and cannot bind the principal beyond the specific authority conferred.

A party who has the authority to complete a transaction has the implied authority to perform the acts incidental to their primary mission.

Secret limitations on such incidental powers do not provide a defense to a principal on the issue of authority unless the third party dealing with the agent becomes aware of them before making the contract.

Imputed knowledge

If an issue in litigation is whether the principal had knowledge and whether that knowledge was imparted (or notice given) to the agent, knowledge (or notice) is imputed to the principal even if the agent does not communicate what was learned while representing the principal.

Ratification

Ratification is an additional process to hold a principal liable for contracts made by an agent without authority.

Words, conduct, or silence may prove ratification.

If a principal ratifies an unauthorized agent's act, they must ratify all conduct and accept burdens and benefits.

Valid ratification occurs only when the following conditions are met:

1) the principal must have knowledge of material facts regarding the transaction;

2) the agent must have intended to represent the principal at the time of the unauthorized act; and

3) the ratifying party must have been in existence at the time of the act.

A corporation cannot ratify pre-incorporation contracts.

Valid ratification is retroactive to the time that the purported agent acted.

Once ratified, the contract is irrevocable unless voidable for fraud, duress, illegality, or lack of capacity.

Agency: Fiduciary Duties Between Principal and Agent

Fiduciary duties

The agent owes the principal duties in two categories:

fiduciary duties (care and loyalty), and

a set of general duties imposed by agency law.

These general duties are not unique to agency law; they are duties owed by an employee to the employer.

The *agent's duties* include:

1) to act on behalf of and be subject to the control of the principal,

2) act within the scope of authority or power delegated by the principal,

3) discharge duties with appropriate care and diligence,

4) avoid conflict between their interests and those of the principal, and

5) promptly tender to the principal monies collected on the principal's behalf.

The *principal's duties* include:

1) to compensate the agent as agreed, and

2) indemnify the agent against claims, liabilities, and expenses incurred in discharging duties assigned by the principal.

Rights and liabilities between agent and principal

A fiduciary *duty of care* is imposed on the agent to avoid acts or omissions, which could be reasonably foreseen to injure or harm other people.

The agent owes a fiduciary *duty of loyalty* to the principal, which stands for the principle that corporate directors and officers make decisions in their capacities as fiduciaries and act without personal economic conflict.

The *duty of obedience* means that the agent must obey reasonable directions concerning the manner of performance.

The agent can be sued for breach of these duties.

An agent is required to act in the manner specified by the agreement creating the agency.

If the agent acts contrary, they can be sued for breach of the agency contract.

The principal is typically required to pay compensation to the agent for services, either the amount in the agency contract or the services' fair value if no amount was agreed.

If a person has acted as a double agent for parties with conflicting interests without informing both, they are barred from recovering compensation from either.

An agent is entitled to indemnification for expenses and liabilities incurred in the performance of their duties.

If held liable on a contract they negotiated as an agent for an undisclosed principal, and the agent and principal are each liable on such contracts, the agent is entitled to indemnification from liability by the principal.

Agent, principal and third-party rights and liabilities

If an agent is disclosed and makes a contract within the scope of their authority, the agent is not personally liable on the contract.

If the principal is undisclosed, the third party may elect to sue the agent instead of the principal.

To bar the third party from suing the person not sued when the election was made, the election to sue the agent or the principal must be made with knowledge that the agent acted for the undisclosed principal.

The principal is not liable for the payment of a judgment obtained against the agent.

If the contract is in the form of a negotiable instrument, only the agent who is the signatory to that instrument can be sued.

An agent may be liable to the third party in a deceit action, but not on the contract, nor any breach of warranty of authority theory if the agent enters into a contract on behalf of a disclosed principal beyond the agent's scope of authority.

The third party is not able to prevail against the principal.

The agent may be held liable to the principal for breach of fiduciary duty or contract if a principal is held liable in the contract because the conduct of the agent acted beyond the express authority granted.

Partnerships: Creation of Partnerships

Formation of a partnership

A partnership is a business entity created when two or more people associate to carry on a business and do not choose another form of business entity (e.g., corporation, limited liability company).

The key test of whether a partnership has been formed is the parties' intent to join efforts to undertake some business enterprise.

No formal documents are required to form the partnership.

No written partnership agreement is required, nor must there be an oral agreement.

The conduct of the parties can form a partnership with a set of common law attributes.

The capacity needed to enter a partnership is the same as the capacity to contract.

An appropriate answer to many business entity questions includes an analysis of whether the conduct of the parties is sufficient to warrant a finding that a partnership has been created.

The factors of whether a partnership has been formed are:

1) Did the parties agree to share the profits of an enterprise?

   A countervailing analysis is that payment to one of the parties is a loan, repayment of a debt, or payment for services rendered rather than a share of the profits.

2) Are the parties sharing gross returns?

3) Do the parties own property jointly?

   A countervailing analysis is that ownership of property by itself does not cause the co-owners to be partners.

   Partnership requires participation in the management of the business.

Partnership by estoppel

A person can incur partnership liability by holding themself out to be a partner or permit someone to represent to others that they are a partner even without a partnership relationship.

> That conduct renders liability for the debts of the partnership to a creditor who has relied on those representations.
>
> If those representations were made privately, only recipients of the representations could sue.
>
> If made publicly, liability extends to anyone who has knowledge of the representations and relied upon them.

A person held out as a partner is an agent of those consenting to the representation and can bind them as if a partner.

For example, placing a lawyer's name on letterhead with other lawyers can constitute a holding out that the other persons on the letterhead are partners.

Partnerships: Power and Liability of Partners

Fiduciary relationship among partners

Each partner owes other partners a *fiduciary duty of loyalty* and the utmost *good faith*.

Unless partners agree, a partner must not compete with the partnership within its business scope or take a business opportunity that could be performed by the partnership for its benefit.

A partner must account to the partnership for their profits, or a court could impose a constructive trust to hold the business opportunity for the benefit of the partnership.

Partners must disclose material facts relating to the partnership business to other partners.

If a partner uses partnership property for their private gain, they must account for the profits of the partnership.

Partner's right to an accounting

A partner is entitled to a formal accounting to determine the partnership's profits and losses and each partner's share:

1) if partners wrongfully exclude them from the partnership business;
2) if the partnership agreement provides for an accounting;
3) when another partner has breached their fiduciary duty to the partnership;
4) whenever it is just and reasonable, each must be given an accounting.

Each partner is entitled to access the partnership books, which must be kept at the partnership's principal place of business.

Rights and duties of partners

If no partnership agreement provides otherwise, each partner is entitled to an equal share of the partnership profits.

If a partnership is being liquidated, each partner is entitled to be repaid their capital contribution after partnership debts have been satisfied.

After capital contributions have been repaid, each partner is entitled to their share of partnership profits.

Those shares will be equal among the partners unless the partnership agreement provides differently.

If there are partnership losses, they will be shared equally by the partners unless the agreement provides a different arrangement.

Ordinarily, if one partner is entitled to more than a pro-rata share of profits, they will be required to pay the same share of the losses.

A partner has a right to be reimbursed by the partnership for payments made and liabilities reasonably incurred in the ordinary and proper conduct of the partnership business or for expenditures made to protect and preserve partnership property.

Unless the partnership agreement provides otherwise, a partner is not entitled to interest on their capital account.

A partner who makes a payment or advances beyond the amount they agreed to contribute is entitled to interest from the date of the payment or advance for that additional amount.

A partner is not ordinarily entitled to a salary for services rendered to the partnership, absent an agreement.

A surviving partner is entitled to reasonable compensation for winding up the partnership.

Unless the partnership agreement provides otherwise, each partner has an equal right in business management and conduct.

Ordinarily, a vote of the majority of the partners is necessary to decide any matter.

No act in contravention of an agreement may be done without the partners' consent.

No person can become a partner in an existing partnership unless existing partners consent.

Partners cannot sue each other for damages in an action at law for partnership matters.

The proper remedy is an equitable lawsuit for an accounting.

Partnerships: Partnership Property and Property Rights

Partnership property

When funds of a partnership are used to acquire property, the property is "partnership property" even if title to the property is taken in the name of an individual partner.

Each partner is a co-owner with partners of partnership property, holding as tenants-in-partnership.

A partner has the right to use partnership property for partnership purposes but cannot use it other than for partnership purposes without the consent of the partnership.

A partner cannot assign their interest in partnership property unless the partners consent.

A partner's interest in partnership property cannot be attached or sold pursuant to execution unless the attachment is based on a claim against the partnership.

Upon death, partnership property vests in the surviving partners and is not an asset of the partner's estate.

The claim of the estate against the partnership is for an accounting.

The partnership interest

A partner's interest consists of their share of the profits and surplus of the partnership.

Unlike specific partnership property, a partner's interest is assignable.

The assignment of a partnership interest by a partner does not dissolve the partnership.

The assignee has rights in the asset assigned (i.e., profits and surplus).

The assignee is not a partner and has no partnership rights.

The assignee is only entitled to receive the profits due to the assignor.

If the partnership is dissolved, the assignee receives the assignor's interest.

A judgment creditor cannot sell the partnership interest to satisfy a claim until the other partners have the opportunity to redeem the partner's interest in the partnership.

Management of the partnership

A partner has the right to manage the partnership where matters are decided in the absence of an agreement by a majority vote of partners.

No person can become a partner without the unanimous consent of the partners.

Conveyance of real property

A partner who has been authorized by the partnership can convey real property owned by the partnership by executing a deed in proper form.

Partnerships: Relationship of Partners to Third Parties

Agency

The act of a partner within the scope of the partnership binds the partnership, except when the partner lacks authority to perform the act, and the third party knows of that lack of authority.

A statement by a partner acting within their authority is admissible as an admission in evidence against the partnership.

There are specific limitations on a partner's authority unless granted by the partners.

The *specific limitations on the authority* of any partner are:

1) assign partnership property in trust for creditors or on the assignee's promise to pay the partnership's debts;

2) dispose of the business's goodwill;

3) do anything which would make it impossible to carry on its ordinary business;

4) confess a judgment;

5) submit a partnership claim or liability to arbitration or reference.

Notice to partner as notice to the partnership

A notice given to one partner or knowledge acquired by one partner on a matter related to partnership affairs is imputed to the partnership unless fraud is committed on the partnership by or with that partner's consent.

Liability of partners for general partnerships

In a general partnership, as opposed to a limited liability partnership, partners are jointly liable for the partnership's liabilities to the extent of their personal and partnership assets.

When a partnership as an entity is sued, at least one partner must be named a defendant.

Because a general partnership obligation is joint, each partner is individually liable for the entire amount of the obligation.

If a partner pays a partnership debt, they are entitled to be reimbursed from the partnership if there are partnership assets available for reimbursement.

If a partner pays more than their pro-rata share of a partnership debt and cannot recover from the partnership, they are entitled to recover from their co-partners the amount which they paid above their partnership share.

A dormant partner (i.e., partner not active in partnership affairs) is liable for partnership obligations in a general partnership.

A person who joins a partnership already in existence is liable for partnership obligations arising before joining the partnership only to the extent of their investment in the partnership.

Liability of partners for Limited Partnerships (LP)

In a limited partnership, a limited partner who has no voice in the partnership management is liable on partnership debts and obligations only to the extent of their interest in the partnership.

General partners are jointly liable for partnership obligations, and their assets can be reached to satisfy the partnership debt.

Liability of partners for Limited Liability Partnerships (LLP)

Common law partnerships can become Limited Liability Partnerships by registering as Limited Liability Partnerships.

When a partnership becomes a Limited Liability Partnership, the partnership property remains liable to satisfy partnership obligations.

Joint and several liability is assessed against the partners only for partners' wrongful acts according to the partnership and money misapplied by the partnership.

A partner in a registered Limited Liability Partnership is not personally liable directly or indirectly for debts, obligations, and liabilities of the partnership except for matters arising in whole or in part from the partner's negligence, wrongful acts, errors, or omissions.

A partner must carry a designated amount of liability insurance prescribed by that profession's regulatory body to benefit from a Limited Liability Partnership rendering professional services.

The limited liability partnership's name must end with the designation *Registered Limited Liability Partnership* or *Limited Liability Partnership* or their abbreviation LLP.

Most general partnerships are now Limited Liability Partnerships.

Partnerships: Dissolution

Causes of dissolution of partnerships

A common law partnership is dissolved within the terms of the partnership agreement by:

1) termination of the term or undertaking;

2) the action of a partner, including death or bankruptcy in a partnership at will;

3) agreement of the partners; or

4) expulsion of a partner.

Winding up is a process whereby all company assets are realized and used to pay off the liabilities and members.

A partnership is terminated when all partnership affairs are wound up.

Dissolution puts an end to the life of the partnership after winding up.

Any partner may dissolve the partnership in contravention of the partnership agreement, and the partner who wrongfully causes a dissolution is liable for damages to any partner injured.

When a partnership is wrongfully dissolved, the remaining partners can continue the business.

Any partner may sue for dissolution on the grounds of a partner's:

1) insanity or incapacity;

2) conduct prejudicial to business; or

3) willful breach of the agreement or conduct rendering the business impracticable.

A dissolution decree is available if the partnership's business can only be carried on at a loss or if other circumstances render a dissolution equitable.

Effect of dissolution on partner's authority

In the process of dissolution, a partner only has the authority to bind the other partners concerning winding up partnership affairs and completing unfinished transactions.

Under agency principles, the partnership is bound on new obligations after dissolution incurred by a partner acting under the following circumstances.

If a partner does business within the apparent scope of the partnership business with a third party who had extended credit before dissolution, the partnership is liable if the third party did not know of the dissolution and the notice of dissolution has not been properly published.

Winding up the partnership

All partners who have not engaged in the partnership's wrongful dissolution have an equal right to wind up the partnership.

Partners may delegate exclusive power to one or more partners.

A partner who engages in winding up the partnership must pay debts, complete unfinished contracts and transactions, collect debts, dispose of partnership property, and close the business.

Continuance of partnership after dissolution

If wrongfully dissolved, the remaining partners can continue the partnership.

The partners must settle the dissolving partner's claims but can deduct damages for breach.

If they continue the business, the continuing partners must indemnify the dissolving partner against partnership liabilities.

Partners may continue the partnership's business when a partner is expelled, retires, dies (if they or their representative consents), or the partnership agreement provides continuation.

If the retiring partner or deceased partner's estate does not settle with the continuing partners, they have the option of receiving either the value of the dissolution shares plus interest or in place of interest, the profits attributable to the use of their right in the firm property from the time of dissolution to settlement.

When the partners continue the partnership business, the original partnership's creditors become creditors of the continuing partnership.

Distribution of partnership assets

If the business is not continued, the partners must wind it up by liquidating its assets if necessary, settling its obligations, and distributing the remaining assets to the partners.

Assets include partnership property and, if necessary, any partners' contributions needed to pay obligations to creditors.

Assets are distributed in the following order of priority:

1) debts to non-partner creditors;

2) debts to partner creditors;

3) return of capital contributions of partners;

4) payment of profits to partners.

Partnerships: Limited Partnerships

Formation of Limited Partnerships

A limited partnership (LP) can carry on any business that a general partnership can and is formed by filing with the Secretary of State a signed certificate, detailing the incidents and composition of the business, the name, including the words limited partnership, and the names and business addresses of the general partners.

A limited partnership is composed of:

1) one or more general partners, who manage the business and are personally liable without limitation for partnership obligations; and
2) one or more limited partners contributing capital and sharing in profits but have no control or management of the business; limited partners' liability is limited to their contribution.

Profits and losses of a limited partnership and distributions of assets are allocated following the written partnership agreement.

If the agreement is silent, profits and losses are distributed based on a partner's contribution.

Obligations of limited partners

A limited partner is obligated to the partnership to perform the promise they made to obtain the limited partnership interest.

Rights and powers of limited partners

A limited partner has the right to inspect and copy the required partnership records and tax returns, obtain from the general partners and full information about the financial condition and state of the business, and such other information as is just and reasonable.

The partnership agreement may grant voting powers to all or some limited partners upon any matter.

General partners

A general partner in a limited partnership is the equivalent of a general partner in a general partnership.

Assignment of Limited Partnership interests

A limited partnership interest is generally assignable.

While an assignee is entitled only to receive the distributions to which the assignor would have been entitled, an assignee may become a limited partner if:

1) the assignor gives rights per authority granted in the partnership agreement, or

2) absent such authority, all partners consent.

Distributions of Limited Partnership interests

A partner is entitled to receive interim distributions following the terms of the partnership agreement.

Upon withdrawal, the withdrawing partner can receive distribution to which they are entitled under the agreement or, absent such provision, the fair value of their partnership interest.

Dissolution of Limited Partnership interests

A limited partnership is dissolved at the time or upon the events specified in writing in the partnership agreement or upon all partners' written consent.

A court may decree dissolution on application by a partner whenever it is not reasonably practicable to carry on the business in conformity with the partnership agreement.

Business Trusts

Business trusts as unincorporated associations

A business trust is an unincorporated business association created by a trust instrument, which transfers the business property to trustees who hold and manage it to benefit the trust certificate holders.

The trust provides limited liability for the beneficiaries unless they retain too much control.

The beneficiaries can neither elect nor remove the trustees.

If the trust instrument vests such control in the beneficiaries that the trustees are merely their agents, the trust will be deemed a partnership, and beneficiaries will be personally liable.

Factors indicating *too much control* of the business trust include:

the power to elect trustees,

to remove trustees and fill vacancies,

to instruct trustees,

to amend the trust, or

terminate the trust.

Beneficiaries may petition the court to remove a trustee for violating their fiduciary duty.

A majority vote of the trustees binds the trust.

Trustees are personally liable on contracts unless the contract provides otherwise.

However, if the trustee has not exceeded their authority, they are entitled to reimbursement from trust assets.

An unsatisfied creditor may reach and apply trust property by being substituted for the trustee to the extent of indemnification right.

Notes for active learning

Corporations: Nature of Corporate Existence

The corporation as a separate entity

A corporation is created by filing appropriate incorporation documents with the Secretary of State and paying the appropriate fee.

A corporation is a legal entity separate and distinct from its owners, the shareholders.

Its owners are not ordinarily personally liable for its liabilities.

The status of the corporation in the constitution

A corporation has constitutional protection *as a person* under:

Fifth and Fourteenth Amendment due process clauses,

Equal protection clause of the Fourteenth Amendment, and

Fourth Amendment search and seizure clause.

It is *not a person* under:

Fifth Amendment clause against self-incrimination, and,

Privileges and Immunities clause of Article IV § 2.

Subordination of shareholder debt

If an inadequately capitalized corporation becomes insolvent and shareholders hold substantial corporate debt, a court can subordinate the shareholder's debt to other unsecured debt paid before the shareholders.

For an inadequately capitalized corporation, shareholders lose payment priority on their debt.

Shareholders are not personally liable for the corporation's debt.

Notes for active learning

Corporations: Organizing the Corporation

Duties and liabilities of promoters during pre-incorporation

Before incorporation papers are filed, persons joining to form the corporation are *promoters*.

The promoters' relationship is a joint venture or partnership whereby each owes the other a fiduciary duty of *full disclosure* and *fair dealing*.

Promoters are agents of each other, having the power to bind promoters to contracts made by one.

Until they form the corporation, they are personally liable for obligations incurred.

Once the promoters file the corporation papers (i.e., articles of incorporation) and have the status of incorporators, but before the corporation issues shares, the incorporators may exercise the powers of shareholders.

The organizational meeting

One or more persons at least eighteen years of age may act as incorporators.

A corporation may act as an incorporator.

At the organizational meeting, the incorporators adopt by-laws, elect directors and officers, and prepare and sign the articles of incorporation (*articles of organization* for an LLC).

The *articles of incorporation* and the filing fee are tendered to the Secretary of State to create a corporation.

The articles of incorporation

The *articles of incorporation* (articles of organization for an LLC) are the highest source of authority in the corporation's internal documents.

In the event of a conflict with the by-laws or directors' actions, the provisions in the articles of incorporation prevail.

The articles of incorporation must contain:

1) name of the corporation (or include Inc., Incorporated, or words which indicate the entity as a corporation);

2) number of shares the corporation is authorized to issue and required description of additional classes or series of shares;

3) names and addresses of the incorporators who form a corporation.

The articles of incorporation may contain provisions concerning:

1) the purposes for which the corporation was organized,

2) managing the business and regulating the corporation's affairs, defining, limiting, and regulating powers of the corporation, board of directors, and shareholders.

The articles of incorporation contain provisions that must be included to be effective.

The articles of incorporation may contain exculpatory provisions concerning directors, but they cannot eliminate the liability of a director for:

1) breach of the *duty of loyalty* to the corporations or its shareholders,

2) acts not in *good faith* involving intentional misconduct,

3) improper distributions, or

4) transactions from which the director derived an improper personal benefit.

In general, the articles must contain (but not as a permanent part of the articles) the corporate office's postal address, the names, residence and postal addresses of the directors and president, treasurer, and clerk, the fiscal year, and the name and business address of the resident agent.

Corporations: Exceptions to Liability Protections

Exceptions to the rule of limited liability

A creditor may enforce corporate liability against a shareholder in two situations.

Defective incorporation

If the incorporators fail to comply with the incorporation statute's mandatory requirements, individual owners are liable for corporate debts.

The Secretary of State's approval of the incorporation is conclusive evidence of a corporation's lawful existence.

The incorporation statute provides that persons purporting to act as or on behalf of a corporation knowing that was no incorporation shall be jointly and severally liable for liabilities created while so doing.

Piercing the corporate veil

There are circumstances when actions of a legally created corporation or its shareholders become the basis for permitting a creditor of the corporation to hold the shareholders or corporations created by those shareholders liable for the debts of the corporation.

Factors relevant to holding shareholders of a corporation liable for corporate debts are:

1) intermingling corporate and personal assets,

2) failing to keep corporate records, and

3) inadequately capitalizing the corporation.

Common ownership of several brother-sister corporations is not alone enough ground for piercing the corporate veil.

If brother-sister corporations intermingle corporate accounts, fail to keep adequate records of each corporation's distinct existence, have shared employees, are inadequately capitalized, or do not hold out each corporation to the public as separate enterprises, the court may find joint liability among a group of corporations.

Notes for active learning

Corporations: Control and Management in the Corporation

Exercise of corporate purposes and powers

The incorporation statute provides a corporation with an extensive group of express and implied powers, including the power to guarantee a parent, subsidiary, or affiliated corporation's debt.

These powers shall be possessed by any corporation incorporated unless the articles of incorporation expressly disavow those powers.

The articles of incorporation do not require an enumeration of corporate powers.

Ultra vires

Because corporations have broad powers, an act of the corporation is rarely in excess of those powers and not *ultra vires* (i.e., acting beyond legal authority).

The *ultra vires* nature of a corporate act can only be challenged in a proceeding by a shareholder against the corporation to enjoin such act, a proceeding by the corporation against a present, former director or officer alleging they acted beyond the powers of the corporation or in a proceeding brought by the attorney general.

Allocation of power between shareholders and directors

The articles of incorporation (articles of organization for an LLC) are the ultimate internal governing document, limited only by the State's corporation statute.

By-laws are the third source of authority and are operative if not in conflict with the statute or articles of incorporation.

The incorporation statute ordinarily provides the power to manage a corporation is vested in the board of directors even though the shareholders as a group own the corporation.

Individual directors and the board of directors, as a body, are independent of the shareholders.

The directors owe a separate fiduciary duty to the corporate entity.

Corporate officers are ordinarily elected by the board of directors, and the chief executive officer reports to the board of directors.

The incorporation statute provides an alternative for the management of nonpublic corporations.

By unanimous agreement of shareholders, incorporated into the articles of incorporation or by-laws of a corporation, a corporation can:

1) eliminate the board of directors or restrict its powers;
2) modify the requirement that distributions be proportionate to share ownership;
3) modify the rules for creating the directors and officers of the corporation;
4) alter the voting power by or between the shareholders and directors;
5) transfer to one or more shareholders or another person part of the authority to exercise corporate powers or manage the business;
6) require the dissolution of the corporation at the request of one or more shareholders upon the occurrence of a specified event or contingency.

The existence of such an agreement must be noted conspicuously on the front or back of shares of the corporation.

Absent an agreement, the shareholders' fundamental power base is their ability to elect and remove directors (under some circumstances).

Fundamental corporate changes such as mergers, acquisitions, and amendments to the articles of incorporation must be approved by the shareholders, usually by a majority vote.

Shareholders have the power to make, amend, and repeal the by-laws unless this power to amend the by-laws is vested in the board of directors by the articles or by-laws.

The shareholders could amend the articles to vest power to amend the by-laws in the shareholders and then amend them.

Corporations: Requirements of Directors

Directors of the corporation

Except as provided in the incorporation statute, a corporation must have as many directors as shareholders but only needs a minimum of three directors if there are more than three shareholders.

Directors need not be stockholders.

Incorporators appoint the initial directors.

After the incorporators appoint the initial directors, they are elected at the annual meeting of stockholders, usually for one year or until their successors are elected and qualified.

Directors may be elected for staggered terms up to three years, but at least one staggered term must end each year.

The incorporation statute provides that the shareholders or the remaining directors may fill the vacancy under the articles or the by-laws.

Election of directors

Unless another method is set forth in the articles of incorporation or bylaws, directors are elected by a plurality of the votes cast by the shares entitled to vote in the election at a shareholders' meeting at which a quorum is present.

This shareholder voting method permits the holders of a majority of voting stock to elect the directors.

This procedure permits each class to secure representation on the board of directors.

The articles of incorporation may permit voting by the class of stock.

Amendments to the articles of incorporation relating to classification can be made only with the approval of a majority of the shares in the affected class.

Removal of directors

A director, including a director appointed by the other directors, may be removed without cause by a vote of the majority of the shares entitled to vote for directors.

A director elected by a class may only be removed by a vote of the majority of the shares in the class, which elected them.

If cumulative voting is authorized, a director may not be removed by the shareholders if the number of votes sufficient to elect with cumulative voting vote against their removal.

A director may be removed for cause by other directors after reasonable notice and an opportunity to be heard.

Operation of the board of directors

Regular meetings of the board of directors may be held without notice if the time and place are fixed by the by-laws or by a director resolution.

Notice is required for a special meeting of the board of directors.

However, directors can waive notice.

An objection based on lack of notice of the meeting is waived if a director attends the meeting and does not object to the lack of notice.

Directors' meetings of the corporation can be held outside of the resident state.

Unless the by-laws prescribe a different percentage, a majority of the directors then in office constitute a quorum.

A majority of those present at a validly called meeting is an act of the board of directors if a quorum is present.

Directors can bind the corporation to contractual obligations beyond the directors' terms.

Each director must vote on matters based on independent judgment at the time of the meeting.

Before a meeting, a director may not enter into a binding agreement to vote a specific way on an issue.

A director must vote in person, although they can attend a meeting through telephone or other electronic means.

Proxy voting by directors is not permitted.

Directors may act without a meeting if all directors consent in writing with a document filed with the clerk of the corporation.

Directors serve without compensation unless there is an agreement by the directors that they shall be compensated.

Delegation of directors' powers

Even though the board has the statutory power to manage the corporation, it usually delegates the authority to run day-to-day operations to the officers whom it elects.

The board can delegate some authority to committees of directors constituted by the board.

However, the board must make major decisions of the corporation (e.g., corporate distributions, propose to issue stock or pay dividends, remove directors, amend by-laws, or buy back stock).

The fact that directors delegated an issue to a committee does not relieve the directors of their fiduciary duty of care.

General standards for directors and officers

A director and officer shall discharge their duties as a director, member of a committee, or as an officer:

1) in good faith;
2) with the care that a person in a like position would reasonably believe appropriate under similar circumstances; and
3) in a manner which the director or officer reasonably believes to be in the corporation's best interests.

A director may consider the interests of the corporation's suppliers, creditors, customers, economy of the state, region, country, and long- and short-term interests of the corporation and its shareholders in determining the best interest of the corporation.

In discharging their duties, directors may rely on information, opinions, reports, or statements of employees, legal counsel, public accountants, and committees of the board of directors if they do not have knowledge that makes such reliance unwarranted.

A director is not liable for action (or failure to act) if they performed their duties following these standards.

Director's conflict of interest

A conflict-of-interest transaction is where a director of the corporation has a material direct or indirect interest.

An indirect conflict occurs if the director has a material financial interest in the other party to the transaction.

A transaction is not voidable solely due to the director's interest if any of the following is true.

1) The material facts of the transaction and the director's interest were known to the board or a committee, and the board/committee approves/ratifies the transaction.

   Approval or ratification occurs if the transaction receives the affirmative vote of a majority of the disinterested directors' votes.

   Disinterested directors on the board/committee have no direct or indirect interest in the transaction, but the transaction may not be authorized/ratified by a single director.

2) The material facts of the transaction and the director's interest were disclosed or known to the shareholders, and the shareholders approved the transaction.

   Approval or ratification occurs if it receives the affirmative vote of a majority of shares entitled to vote who have no direct or indirect material interest in the transaction.

3) The transaction was fair to the corporation.

Loans to directors

A corporation may not loan to or guarantee a loan of a director of the corporation unless:

1) the loan or guarantee is approved by a majority of votes of the outstanding shares of all classes except for the shares owned by the benefited director, or

2) the board of directors determines that the loan or guarantee benefits the corporation and either approves the specific loan or a general plan of loans or guarantees.

Specific liabilities of corporate directors

Unless they have a good faith defense, directors and officers are jointly and severally liable by statute if they cause or authorize the corporation to engage in any of the following acts:

1) improperly issue stock;

2) make a dividend distribution prohibited by statute;

3) wrongfully deny shareholders information.

If a director pays more than their pro-rata share of a judgment, the director is entitled to contribution from the other negligent directors.

Officers of the corporation

The officers of a corporation required by statute are the president, clerk, and treasurer.

The clerk must reside in the state of formation unless a resident registered agent to receive service of process is appointed.

These officers and other offices described in the by-laws are appointed by the board or by such persons as the board delegates its appointing authority.

Authority of officers

An officer is an agent of the corporation.

Each officer has the authority and shall perform the duties set forth in the by-laws or to the extent consistent with the by-laws, the duties prescribed by the board of directors, or the direction of an officer authorized by the board of directors to prescribe the duties of other officers.

An officer can possess implied authority to act because of the general custom or practice of the company or because it is reasonably necessary to accomplish matters specifically delegated.

The president of a corporation or its general manager has implied authority to accomplish any act on behalf of the corporation in the usual and ordinary course of its business.

The treasurer has the authority to receive funds, make approved disbursements, and execute notes.

The clerk or secretary is authorized to keep the corporate books, records, and seal, certify resolutions and keep minutes of corporate meetings.

The president and treasurer acting together have the authority to execute a deed conveying real estate owned by the corporation without a specific corporate vote authorizing the conveyance.

The board of directors can ratify unauthorized acts of an officer.

The agency rules concerning apparent authority apply to corporate officers.

Vacancies and removal of board members

The board of directors may remove an officer at any time with or without cause.

Notes for active learning

Corporations: Fiduciary Duties of Officers and Directors

Corporate opportunity

A director or officer breaches their fiduciary duty of loyalty to the corporation if they purchase a corporate opportunity for personal use without first offering it to the corporation if reasonably foresee that the corporation would be interested in acquiring that opportunity.

To qualify as a business opportunity, the prospective business must be related to the corporation's existing business or a field that the corporation expressed interest in entering.

The prospective business would be a business opportunity if the board of directors expressed an interest in acquiring a business like the prospective business or had acquired such businesses in the past.

An important determinant of whether a particular transaction constitutes a business opportunity is whether the prospective seller approached the officer or director because of their status as an officer or director or whether the offer was made to the officer or director for reasons unrelated to their corporate position.

If a prospective acquisition is a business opportunity, the officer or director may not acquire it for their account until they offer it to the corporation and a disinterested majority of directors.

If there is no disinterested majority and a disinterested majority of shareholders, waive their rights to acquire the business.

If a corporation successfully shows an acquisition by an officer or director was a breach of the fiduciary duty of loyalty, the most common remedy is to hold that the officer and director hold the business in a constructive trust for the corporation's benefit.

Competing with the corporation

Unless a director or officer has entered a contract with the corporation that prohibits it, they may engage in a business in competition with the corporation provided the conduct competes with the business in good faith.

The following activities would be a breach of the officer or director's fiduciary duty to conduct the competing business in good faith:

1) hiring employees of the corporation for the competing business;

2) using corporate facilities to conduct the competing business;

3) planning or conducting the competing business during periods when paid to work for the corporation;

4) use of corporate assets; or

5) use of customer lists of the corporation or confidential information obtained while working for the corporation.

The remedies available to the corporation for breaches of fiduciary duty are damages or a constructive trust.

Unless a corporate officer has signed a non-competition agreement and they did not use corporate assets while working for the corporation to help launch their new business, they are not precluded, upon the termination of their employment, from:

1) competing with their former employer, or
2) from using the intangible knowledge and skill acquired while employed.

Shareholders

Concerning the management of the corporation, shareholders have the right to elect directors, amend the by-laws, and approve fundamental corporate changes; and ratify the director's actions when there is a conflict of interest.

Shareholders' meeting

A shareholders' meeting of a corporation shall be held annually inside or outside of the resident state per the by-laws to elect directors and conduct business specified in the notice of the meeting.

Special meetings of shareholders can be called by the board of directors, the president, or by holders of 10% of the corporation's stock and 40% of a public corporation.

Shareholders of record must be given at least seven days' written notice of the time, place, and purposes of the meeting, but notice may be waived in writing before or after the meeting.

Unless the articles of incorporation or by-laws provide, the quorum requirement for a shareholders' meeting is satisfied if there are a majority of shareholders present in person or by proxy entitled to vote on the matter.

If a class vote is required, the majority quorum required applies to shares in the affected class.

Shareholders may take corporate action without a meeting either by a unanimous vote of shareholders or if permitted by the articles of incorporation by shareholders having not less than the minimum number of votes necessary to act at a meeting at which all shareholders entitled to vote on the action are present and voting.

Shareholder voting

At a shareholder meeting, shareholders of record on the corporate books on the specified record date are the only shareholders entitled to vote.

The board of directors may fix a record date not more than 70 days before a meeting.

If no record date is set, the record date is the close of business on the day before the notice of the meeting is given, or if no notice is given, then the day before the meeting.

Unless the articles of incorporation provide that specific classes of shares hold disproportionate voting power, each share is entitled to one vote.

The articles of incorporation may deny voting rights to a particular class of stock or limit the matters on which the class is entitled to vote.

Holders of non-voting stock have the right to vote on amendments to the articles of incorporation that would adversely affect the rights of non-voting stock.

Stock on which there are unpaid overdue subscriptions may not vote.

Proxy voting

Shareholders may vote by written proxy, which designates an agent to vote their share per their instructions.

A proxy is an agency agreement.

Therefore, it is freely revocable unless coupled with an interest.

One joint owner may execute a proxy on behalf of all joint owners unless the co-owner affirmatively objects.

A proxy is not valid for more than six months and terminates at the end of the meeting for which it is given.

Shareholder voting trusts

Shareholders may arrange to vote their stock collectively by using shareholder voting trusts.

A voting trust is an arrangement by which shareholders transfer legal title to their shares to a trust known as a voting trust.

The trustee of that trust has the power to vote the stock following the voting trust agreement.

The trustee issues voting trust certificates to the shareholders as evidence of their equitable ownership of the share transferred and deposits them with the corporation.

The voting trust certificate holders are entitled to dividends and all other rights, except voting.

A voting trust agreement is valid for the period set by the voting trust agreement and may be extended by shareholders.

Voting trust certificates are freely transferable.

Shareholder voting agreements

A contract among shareholders by which each agrees to vote their shares in a designated fashion is valid and specifically enforceable if it is in writing and signed by the participating shareholders.

A voting agreement is valid for such a period as is specified in the agreement.

Shareholder's right to information

A shareholder has the statutory right to inspect minutes of shareholders' and directors' meetings, the articles of incorporation, the by-laws, and the stock and transfer records, including the names, addresses, and holdings of shareholders.

The corporation may defend against a shareholder's request for information by arguing that the shareholder's purpose is to sell the information or use it for a purpose not in their interest as a shareholder, such as acquiring more stock in the company.

A shareholder has additional rights based upon common law to inspect account books and other corporate records.

To exercise their common law right, the shareholder has the burden of proving the proper purpose and good faith.

Under the incorporation statute, a corporation shall furnish to its shareholders upon request annual financial statements that include a balance sheet and income statement.

Corporations: Special Problems of Close Corporations

Close corporations

Bar exam questions frequently test the specific rules applicable to close corporations.

The following characteristics define a close corporation:

1) a small number of stockholders;

2) lack of a ready market for the corporate stock; and

3) a substantial majority of stockholder's participation in the corporation's management, direction, and operations.

The articles of incorporation of a close corporation frequently contain provisions designed to protect the rights of minority shareholders.

A high quorum requirement for a director's meeting or a shareholder's meeting permits a minority shareholder/director to block action by refusing to attend meetings.

Provisions requiring supermajorities to pass specific resolutions permit a minority director to block action.

Classification of stock permits a class holder to preserve representation on the board of directors.

A provision giving stockholders pre-emptive rights to purchase their pro-rata share of new stock issues protects the minority shareholder from dilution.

Stock transfer restrictions for close corporations

Unless there is a provision in the articles of incorporation or by-laws or an agreement among shareholders restricting the transfer of shares, the shares are freely transferable.

The transfer of shares of a close corporation may be restricted by the articles of incorporation, bylaws, or an agreement among shareholders.

A stock transfer restriction must be noted on the certificate or sent to a shareholder holding stock without a certificate.

Unless noted, a transfer restriction is not enforceable against a person without knowledge of the restriction.

Restrictions on the transfer of shares are authorized to maintain the corporation's status under tax laws such as subchapter S, preserve exemptions under federal or state securities law, or other reasonable purpose.

A valid stock transfer restriction can

1) obligate the stockholder to first offer the restricted shares to the corporation or another person before selling them;
2) require the corporation or another person to acquire the restricted shares;
3) require the approval of the corporation or another person before the shares are transferred if that approval is not manifestly unreasonable; or
4) prohibit the transfer of restricted shares to designated persons or classes of persons if that prohibition is not manifestly unreasonable.

Fiduciary duty of close corporation shareholders

Shareholders in a close corporation owe a duty of the utmost good faith and loyalty.

Majority stockholders must demonstrate a legitimate business purpose for any action harming the minority shareholders.

Even if there is a business purpose, the minority shareholders are entitled to show that the corporations' objective could have been achieved through a less harmful alternative.

The fiduciary duty of shareholders in close corporations extends to minority shareholders and prohibits them from harming the corporation by vetoing necessary actions.

For example, a minority shareholder used the veto power over corporate action given in the articles of incorporation to prevent the declaration of dividends (e.g., this refusal led to substantial tax penalties for which the minority shareholder was held liable).

The majority shareholder's fiduciary duty to the minority shareholders has been applied to require the corporation to extend the same stock repurchase option to minority shares as was given to the majority shareholder.

The fiduciary duty of the majority shareholder to the minority shareholders has been used to prevent an unfair advantage from being given to the majority shareholders in the sale of assets or a merger (e.g., prevented the termination of a minority shareholder's employment with the corporation).

Ordinarily, a breach of fiduciary duty to the corporation in a close corporation must be brought by a shareholders' derivative action.

Where a derivative suit is inadequate, a direct suit by a shareholder who has been harmed by a breach of fiduciary duty by another shareholder has been permitted.

Duties of the controlling shareholders

Controlling shareholders in corporations owe a fiduciary duty to minority shareholders and cannot use their control to exploit the corporation or minority unfairly.

This duty is most apparent when the controlling shareholder sells its shares, which carries the right to manage the corporation.

If the controlling shareholder fails to exercise due care in picking a buyer and sells control to a party who uses control of the corporation to steal from it or another improper purpose, the selling controlling shareholder will be liable in a direct suit by harmed minority shareholders.

If the controlling shareholder merges the corporation with another corporation, the terms of the merger and related agreements that benefit the controlling shareholder (e.g., employment, consulting agreements) will be scrutinized to determine if the controlling shareholder received consideration from these collateral agreements.

Notes for active learning

Corporations: Securities Regulations

Improper trading in securities – state law

When a person with information derived from private, non-public sources within the corporation uses that information to profit on the corporation's stock, that activity may constitute a breach of fiduciary duty.

The corporation could sue to impose a constructive trust on profits derived from trades based upon such information.

This cause of action belongs to the corporation and requires no suit by the buyer or seller.

Federal law: Sections 10(b) and 16 and Rule 10b-5

There are extensive federal laws, notably Sections 10(b) and 16 of the Federal Securities Act of 1934 and Rule 10b-5, which implements Section 10(b), that regulate the use of inside information in the purchase and sale of securities.

Uniform Securities Act

The Uniform Securities Act prohibits fraud in the purchase or sale of securities or related advisory activities.

Broker-dealers and their agents must register with the Secretary of State.

Non-exempt securities must be registered with the Secretary of State before being sold or offered for sale.

Notes for active learning

Corporations: Shareholders and Member Litigation

Direct suits

If a shareholder is harmed in their capacity as a shareholder, they can bring a suit directly against the corporation.

For example, a holder of preferred stock could bring a suit to compel a dividend if the corporation failed to make payment when the terms of the preferred stock made such a payment mandatory.

If the remedy sought is for the corporation's benefit rather than the shareholder in their individual capacity, a direct suit is not permitted.

Derivative suits

A shareholder's capacity to bring derivative suits is heavily tested.

A shareholder files a derivative suit on behalf of the corporation to pursue a legal remedy that the corporation itself has failed to pursue.

A derivative suit is usually brought in the form of a class action on behalf of the plaintiff and other shareholders similarly situated.

Conditions precedent to commencing suit

A shareholder may not bring a derivative suit unless satisfying the following conditions.

1) The plaintiff must have been a shareholder at the time of the transaction, which is the subject matter of the suit, or own shares as the result of the operation of law (e.g., inheritance from a contemporaneous shareholder) and must fairly and adequately represent the interests of the corporation in enforcing their rights.
2) The plaintiff shareholder must make a written demand upon the corporation and wait 90 days to take suitable action.

If the directors refer the demand to the shareholders, the plaintiffs must wait 90 days after the shareholder demand is made.

Stay of the proceedings

If the corporation commences an inquiry into the allegations made in the demand or the complaint, the court can stay the proceedings for such time as it considers appropriate.

Dismissal

A shareholder derivative suit shall be dismissed if the demand required of directors or shareholders has been rejected and the vote to reject the demand was:

1) by a majority vote of the independent directors which constituted a quorum; or
2) a majority vote of a committee consisting of 2 or more independent directors, whether they constituted a quorum; or
3) the vote of the holders of a majority of the shares entitled to vote, not including shares of the shareholder whose wrongdoing is alleged.

A director is not disqualified as an independent director solely because they were nominated or elected by a person who is a defendant in the derivative proceeding or because they have been named a defendant in the derivative proceeding.

As part of a motion to dismiss, the corporation must file with the court a document showing the requisite votes and independence of the directors or shareholders casting them.

The plaintiff can challenge the document.

Discontinuance or settlement of a derivative suit

Court approval is required to discontinue or settle a derivative suit.

If the settlement substantially affects shareholders, the court can direct notice be sent to shareholders affected.

Upon termination of the suit, the court can order the corporation to pay counsel fees for the plaintiff and the defendant.

Other shareholders may move to intervene on the ground that they have an interest relating to the property or transaction; the outcome might impair their ability to protect that interest.

The request for intervention will be denied if the interest of the other shareholder is already adequately represented.

Indemnification of officers and directors

If the articles of incorporation or the By-laws adopted by the shareholders' permit, the corporation may indemnify present or former directors, officers, employees, or agents for the expenses related to defending themselves against shareholder suits for damages awarded against them or paid as a result of a settlement.

The corporation cannot indemnify such a defendant adjudicated not to have acted in good faith in the reasonable belief that their action was in the corporation's best interests.

Indemnification for the expenses of the lawsuit may be provided before the suit is finally adjudicated if the defendant undertakes to repay the advance if not entitled to it.

Corporations may take out an insurance policy to protect officers and directors from such lawsuits regardless of their power to indemnify them.

Notes for active learning

Corporations: Corporate Financial Structure

Debt securities

A debt security is a corporation's contractual obligation to repay borrowed money.

If designated a debenture, the obligation is unsecured.

A debt designated as a bond is usually an obligation secured by a security interest in specific corporate assets.

The debt instrument defines the holder's rights to interest repayment security and, in some cases, the right to convert the debt into specified equity securities.

Equity securities

Equity securities represent the ownership interest in the corporation.

The holders are entitled to profits and bear the economic burden of losses.

Each class of equity securities carries such voting rights, dividend rights, and liquidation rights as are delineated by the articles of incorporation.

Common stock

Its common stock represents the residual ownership interest of the corporation.

Its rights on liquidation are in the corporation's assets after debts have been paid, and the holders of all classes of stock having a liquidation preference have been satisfied.

Voting rights are usually vested in the holders of the common stock.

Common stock may be classified so that the voting rights of classes are differentiated.

Common stockholders have no right to dividends.

If there are classes of preferred stock, common stock dividends ordinarily cannot be paid until the dividend obligations to the preferred stock are satisfied.

Common stockholders are not entitled to a dividend unless declared by the directors after paying preferred stock dividends.

Preferred stock

Holders of preferred stock are entitled to receive a fixed dividend before common stockholders are paid.

Some preferred shares carry additional dividend rights, which permit those shares to participate in further dividend distributions.

Preferred stock may carry the right to a mandatory dividend if there are sufficient earnings.

Preferred dividends are usually cumulative so that back preferred dividends must be paid before holders of common stock are entitled to a dividend.

Ordinarily, preferred stock does not carry voting rights. The liquidation rights of preferred stock are ordinarily a fixed sum, representing par value.

Issuance of shares

Shares cannot be legally issued unless the articles of incorporation authorize them.

Once authorized, the stock may be issued by a vote of the shareholders or the board of directors if the board is authorized to issue stock by the by-laws or shareholders.

Stock subscriptions

A stock subscription is an offer by a prospective shareholder to purchase stock.

A stock subscription offer is irrevocable for six months unless the subscription agreement prescribes a different period.

The agreement is not binding on the corporation until accepted by the directors after the corporation is formed.

In accepting a stock subscription offer, directors can establish the payment terms.

If a subscriber fails to pay the demanded amount within 30 days after the due date, the corporation may auction their subscription rights and hold them liable for the difference.

In the alternative, the directors can specifically enforce the subscription contract by tendering the stock and suing for the amount due.

The corporation can accept payment for shares in cash, by a promissory note, by property transferred to the corporation, as services to the corporation which have already been performed, and contracts for services to be performed.

Before they issue shares, the directors must determine that the consideration to be paid for the shares is adequate. That determination, once made, is conclusive.

The concept of par value as the minimum amount which may be received for shares has been abolished even if shares state a par value.

Pre-emptive rights

Shareholders do not have pre-emptive rights, which entitle them to maintain their proportionate share of a corporation's stock in the event more stock is issued, unless pre-emptive rights are authorized by the articles or in a by-law adopted by and subject to amendment only by the shareholders.

Even if pre-emptive rights do not exist, if the directors vote to issue stock to deprive an existing shareholder of substantial rights, it is possible to enjoin that issuance because the directors are breaching a fiduciary duty to the plaintiff shareholder.

This is a likely result in a close corporation.

Share certificates

The shares of a corporation may be represented by certificates or held in electronic form.

The record of stock ownership is kept with the books of the corporation.

Unless the corporate by-laws specifically provide that no transfer of stock is effective until:

1) that transfer is recorded on the records of the corporation, or
2) unless there is a provision in the articles of incorporation or by-laws, which requires corporate approval before a shareholder can transfer their stock.

A transfer of stock is effective when a stockholder delivers their stock to a transferee with an appropriate endorsement authorizing a transfer on the books of the corporation.

A certificate will state the number of shares and the class to which the shares belong.

If the corporation has more than one class, the characteristics of that class must be noted on the certificate or refer to a description of these rights in the articles of incorporation.

If there are restrictions on stock transferability, for that restriction to be effective, it must be conspicuously noted on the certificate, or the stockholder must have actual notice of the restriction at the time they acquired the stock.

Notes for active learning

Corporations: Corporate Distributions

Corporate dividends – mechanics of payment

A dividend is a transfer of cash, property, or the corporation's stock from the corporation to shareholders in proportion to their stock ownership.

The directors ordinarily have uncontrolled discretion regarding the time and amount of a dividend payment.

Directors may be compelled to pay dividends by a direct suit by a shareholder against the corporation if the governing corporate documents or contractual obligations make the payment mandatory or if the directors have acted in bad faith.

Once the directors vote to pay a dividend, and that declaration is announced to the shareholders, the corporation is contractually obligated to pay the dividend.

When the directors declare a dividend, it is payable to shareholders who own the stock on a particular date, known as the record date, which may be fixed by the articles, by-laws, or resolution on a date no more than 60 days before payment.

Limitations on the payment of dividends

If a corporation would not be able to pay its existing and reasonably foreseeable debts when they become due, or the corporation is insolvent in that its total assets would be less than the sum of its total liabilities, it may not pay a dividend

A corporation cannot pay a dividend if the articles of incorporation forbid the payment.

Liability of directors for improper payments of dividends

Directors are jointly and severally liable for an illegal dividend paid unless they relied in good faith upon corporate financial records.

A director liable for an illegal dividend is entitled to contribution from other negligent directors.

A shareholder must repay an illegal dividend to the corporation.

Redemption of shares

Holders of some classes of stock, usually preferred stock, can be compelled to sell their shares to the corporation for a specific price at the option of the corporation.

This forced sale is a *right of redemption* and must be stated when the stock class is described in the articles of incorporation.

If the corporation decides to redeem only a portion of the stock eligible for redemption, it must redeem pro-rata.

Once a corporation votes to redeem stock and notifies the shareholder, a contract to purchase has been formed, and the shareholder can sue for the redemption price.

Repurchase of corporate shares

If the corporation is solvent, and the repurchase will not render it insolvent, and it is not contractually prohibited for doing so, a corporation can contract with its shareholders to repurchase its shares at a mutually agreeable price.

In a close corporation, the controlling shareholders have a fiduciary duty to repurchase shares from minority shareholders to the same extent and at the same price at which they are repurchasing shares from the majority shareholders.

Reacquired shares are treated as authorized but unissued shares and can be reissued in the manner that unissued stock can be issued.

The concept of treasury stock has been abolished.

Corporations: Fundamental Corporate Changes

Amendment of the articles of incorporation

Articles of amendment must be submitted to the board of directors and approved by them.

The articles of incorporation can be amended by the addition or deletion of provisions. The articles as reconstituted are still valid by a two-thirds vote of the shareholders and a separate two-thirds vote of a specific class of stock if that class of stock is adversely affected.

The articles of amendment must be filed with the Secretary of State within 60 days of the shareholders' vote.

The amendment takes effect on filing unless a later date within 30 days of the filing is specified.

The following amendments only require a majority vote:

an increase or reduction of an authorized class,

changes in par value, or

a change of corporate name.

If an amendment is adopted, which adversely affects a stockholder's rights, they are entitled to be paid for the appraised value of their stock before the amendment.

Appraisal and redemption rights are triggered by:

1) the alteration or termination of a preferential or pre-emptive right; or
2) creation, alteration, or termination of redemption rights or transfer restriction; or
3) the termination of any voting right.

Mergers and consolidations

A merger occurs when one of two existing corporations is absorbed by another.

If two corporations combine into one new corporation, the result is a consolidation.

A merger (or consolidation) requires each corporation's agreement to adopt a merger plan (or consolidation).

Unless the surviving corporation owns 90% of the stock of the acquired corporation, or unless the surviving corporation is issuing less than 15% of its outstanding shares in the merger, written notice must be given to shareholders of both corporations, whether or not entitled to vote, at least 20 days before the shareholder's meeting. Two-thirds of each class entitled to vote must approve the plan.

A class adversely affected is entitled to vote and must be approved by a two-thirds vote.

If the articles of incorporation permit it, a vote of fewer than two-thirds of the shareholders is enough to approve a merger as long as a majority of shareholders approve.

Once the articles of the merger are approved, they must be filed in the Secretary of State's office and in the registry of deeds in each district in which real property is located.

Dissenting shareholders are entitled to appraisal rights (below).

Sale of all corporate assets

Shareholder approval by a two-thirds vote is required for a corporation to sell or lease, but not to mortgage or pledge, substantially all its assets.

A dissenting shareholder is entitled to appraisal rights.

Appraisal rights

A shareholder of a corporation merging or selling its assets is entitled to appraisal rights.

To qualify for the rights, an eligible shareholder must file a written objection to the merger or sale with the corporation before the shareholders' meeting is called to approve the transaction.

This shareholder cannot vote in favor of the plan.

If a shareholder has complied with these conditions, they must make a written demand on the corporation to purchase their shares at fair value within 20 days after notice of shareholder approval of the plan.

Within 50 days from the meeting date, the corporation must pay a fair value of their stock.

If the corporation and dissenter disagree on the stock value, either may file for a judicial determination of value within four months after the expiration date required for payment.

Dissenting shareholders are made parties to that litigation.

The court determines the shares' value on the day preceding the vote approving the action and adds interest to the award.

Dissolution of the corporation

Dissolution terminates the existence of a corporation. Corporate existence continues for three years after the dissolution to settle matters concerning the corporation.

Judicial dissolution is granted in response to a petition by a majority of stockholders or 40% of the stockholders if:

1) the directors are deadlocked, and the shareholders cannot break the deadlock, or

2) the shareholders are deadlocked and have not elected successors for directors whose terms have expired, and dissolution is in the shareholders' best interests.

A corporation can voluntarily dissolve by filing with the Secretary of State articles of dissolution approved by a two-thirds vote of each class outstanding and entitled to vote thereon.

The Secretary of State will involuntarily dissolve a corporation:

which has not filed required reports or taxes for two years, or

if the State Secretary is satisfied that it is inactive, or

if its dissolution would be in the public interest.

The Secretary of State may revive a dissolved corporation irrespective of the time elapsed or dissolution method.

Takeover bids

The incorporation statute limits a person's right to carry out a hostile takeover of a corporation by acquiring stock in that corporation without the approval of management.

A person attempting a takeover must file information with the company and the Secretary of State and provide public notice before attempting to gain control of more than ten percent of any class of securities of a target company.

The offer must be on the same terms and conditions to all shareholders.

Any shareholder holding at least five percent of a corporation's voting stock is prohibited from carrying out a merger, consolidation, sale of at least ten percent of corporate assets, recapitalization, or certain other business combinations with the corporation if the shareholder has been such an interested shareholder for less than three years unless the board approved the shareholder's acquisition of a five percent interest or such a business combination before the shareholder became interested.

Conflict of laws

Internal corporate affairs are governed by statute regardless of where a suit may arise.

Professional corporations

Persons incorporate to render professional services such as legal or medical services.

Only licensed professionals can hold stock in such a corporation.

Tax status of the corporation

The tax status of a corporation occurs if it has three of the following four characteristics:

1) continuity of life;

2) centralization of management;

3) liability for corporate debts limited to corporate property; and

4) free transferability of interest.

Limited Liability Company (LLC)

Limited Liability Companies

The Limited Liability Company Act authorizes the limited liability company (LLC).

The LLC is a combination of a corporation's characteristics and a limited partnership.

Like stockholders of a corporation, the LLC members enjoy limited liability.

The organization is taxed as a partnership rather than a corporation taxed under subchapter C of the Internal Revenue code.

Limited liability companies have been held to lack continuity of life and free transferability of interest and can be taxed as a partnership.

Limited Liability Company formation

An authorized person must execute the certificate of organization (i.e., articles of organization) and deliver it to the Secretary of State to form an LLC.

The articles of organization are for an LLC, like the articles of incorporation (i.e., corporate charter) are for a corporation.

The certificate of organization must contain the information required in the articles of a corporation (e.g., name, purpose, address, agent).

If there is a date when the company will be dissolved, it must be stated.

The articles of organization must state if the company is to be managed by managers and set forth their names and addresses.

If managed by members, their names and addresses must be listed.

The words limited liability company (or LLC) must be the last words of the name.

Powers of the Limited Liability Company

A limited liability company has the power to carry on any lawful business (same manner and same extent) as a business corporation.

Management of the Limited Liability Company

In the absence of an operating agreement, the management of a limited liability company shall be vested in its members.

An LLC is like a general partnership, except that if an operating agreement does not provide for members' voting rights, the decision of members of the limited liability company who own more than fifty percent of the unreturned contributions shall be controlling.

The statute defines unreturned contributions as the agreed value, as stated in the company's records of each member's contributions to the extent the company has received them.

An operating agreement governs the affairs of a limited liability company in most cases.

The operating agreement may designate the managers of a limited liability company and set out their powers, their terms of office, and how they are elected.

The operating agreement may prescribe the rights and obligations of classes of members and how they vote in the same manner as the articles of incorporation (corporate charter) address these issues for corporations.

Contributions of capital to the Limited Liability Company

The capital contributions to an LLC are like stock subscriptions in a corporation.

A member's contributions to the company's capital may consist of cash or other property, services rendered, or a promissory note or other obligation to contribute cash or property or perform services.

If the member fails to contribute the cash or property promised, the defaulting member can be required to pay cash in place of the property or services, is personally liable to creditors who rely on the promise to contribute capital and can be stripped of their interest in the LLC.

Limited Liability Company property

A limited liability company is an entity much like a corporation.

A limited liability company has the power to own, manage, and transfer property.

Instruments relating to the company's real property are binding upon the company if executed by a person identified in the articles of organization as a person authorized to execute such documents on behalf of the company.

Distribution of property

Like a corporation pays dividends, the limited liability company may, from time to time, distribute property to the members upon the basis stipulated in the operating agreement.

Nature and transferability of member's interest

Much like an interest in the stock of a corporation, a member's interest in a limited liability company is personal property.

The operating agreement can provide how the members transfer or assign interests.

A member's interest in a limited liability company can be transferred like transferring a partnership interest.

Unless members who are not disposing of their interest approve of the proposed transfer (or assignment) by unanimous written consent, or there is compliance with a procedure provided for in the written operating agreement, the transferee of a member's interest has no right to participate in the management or become a member in the company.

The transferee is entitled to receive only the share of profits or income compensation and the return of contributions to which that member otherwise would be entitled.

Liability of the LLC member to the company

A member is personally liable to a limited liability company for:

1) the difference between contributions to capital which have been made and the amount stated in the articles of organization as having been made; and

2) unpaid future contribution to capital, which they agreed in the articles to make with conditions stated in the articles.

A limited liability company can reduce or cancel a member who fails to contribute.

These liabilities may be waived or compromised only by the consent of all members.

However, even if the members execute a waiver, the right of a creditor of the limited liability company to enforce the liability is unaffected if the creditor extended credit or if their claim arose after the filing and before cancellation or amendment of the articles.

Liability for company's obligation

A limited liability company offers members similar limited liability protection as a corporation to the shareholders.

Parties to actions

Concerning litigation, a member of an LLC is similar as a shareholder of a corporation.

The LLC member is not a proper party in litigation for or against the company except when the object enforces a member's right against or liability to the company.

Process against the company may be served as if the company were a partnership or upon the registered agent at their business address.

Comparing an LLC with a subchapter S corporation

A limited liability company is like an S Corporation as closely held corporations can elect to avoid taxation as a corporation if they comply with limitations.

A limited liability company avoids these limitations.

In an S corporation, there can be no more than seventy-five shareholders; a limited liability company has no limitation on the number of members.

Only U.S. citizens or resident aliens can be shareholders in an S corporation.

Foreign nationals who are not resident aliens can be members of a limited liability company.

An S corporation shareholder may write off depreciation losses and other deductions only to the extent of their basis in the stock.

In a limited liability company, losses can be claimed more than the investment.

Dissolution of a Limited Liability Company

A limited liability company is dissolved in substantially the same manner as a corporation.

Relationship matrix

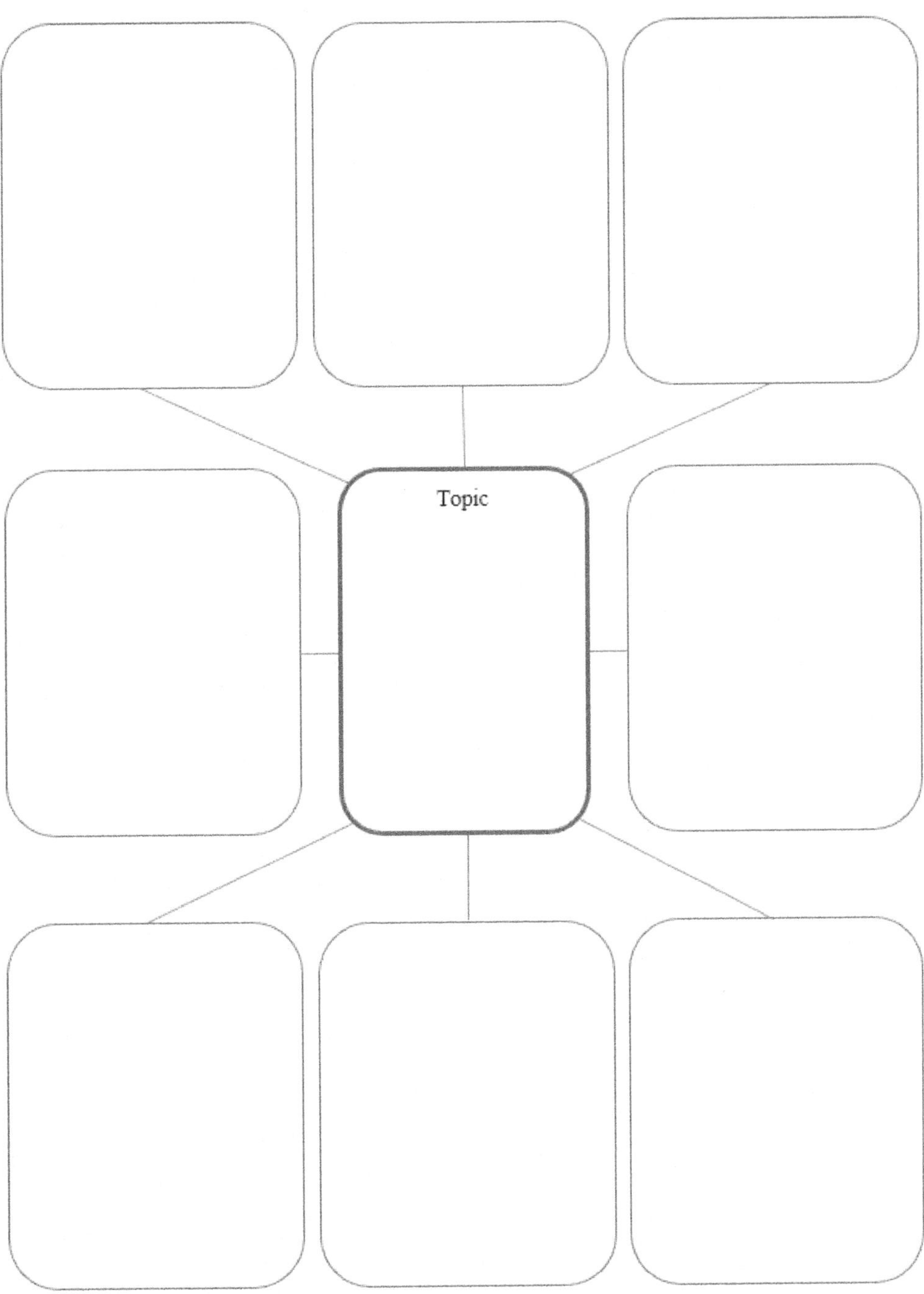

Notes for active learning

Conflict of Laws

Conflict of Laws arises when there is a difference between the laws of two or more jurisdictions connected to the case. Conflict of laws considers what law should be applied to the case before the court. The outcome depends on which jurisdiction's law is used to resolve the issues in dispute. The process by which a court determines what law to apply is "characterization" or "classification."

The conflicting legal rules may come from U.S. federal law, state law, or the laws of other countries. Conflict of laws entails domicile, jurisdiction of the courts, choice of law, and recognition and enforcement of foreign judgments.

Conflict of Laws is not tested as a separate subject. It is generally tested on Civil Procedure and Family Law, and to a lesser extent on Trusts and Estates (decedent's estates specifically). Focus on highly tested Conflict of Laws issues to maximize your score. Frequently tested topics include the Klaxon doctrine, transfer of forum, recognition of marriage, full faith and credit, personal and real property within a decedents' estates.

Domicile

Privileges and immunities clause – citizens of each state are entitled to the privileges and immunities afforded the citizens of the state.

Full faith and credit – the courts of other states will honor the judgment of another court.

Recognition of judgment: analyzing the effect of a judgment in one jurisdiction rendered by another jurisdiction.

Establishing domicile

A person can have only one domicile (i.e., legal address).

2nd Restatement of Conflicts § 17 "Presence Under Compulsion" – people compelled to reside in a location (e.g., prisoners, military personnel) retain their prior domicile unless they intend to make the residence their domicile.

Legal capacity – needed to make a domicile of choice.

Standard: the ability to fend for oneself.

Individuals: physical presence and intent.

Corporations: state of incorporation.

Two tests to establish domicile:

1) physical presence in that state (can be for a short time),
2) intent to remain for the foreseeable (indefinite) future.

Hague Convention – "domicile" is defined in terms of a person's permanent residence.

Objective standard – it does not focus on the party's intent.

Problematic since some people cannot reasonably be said to have a permanent residence (e.g., college students).

Intent for domicile

Residence (i.e., full- or part-time presence) is not synonymous with domicile.

Domicile is kept until another one is acquired.

Common law – must intend to remain indefinitely.

2nd Restatement and modern cases use intent to make the place home for some time (not forever).

The motive is irrelevant when determining the establishment of a new domicile except that it may supply evidence of intent.

Declarations of intent are not dispositive.

A defendant is always subject to the general jurisdiction of a court of domicile (i.e., nexus to government benefits, taxes, legal protections).

Domicile for legal proceedings

The domicile determines intestate succession to personal property.

The decedent is most familiar with the laws of their domicile.

Attorney consultations would most likely be conducted in the domicile.

The domicile state bears the burden of intestate distribution.

The domicile of the decedent is used to choose the law to be applied to determine the intestate succession of personal property.

Domicile at death determines which state gets estate taxes.

The law of the *situs* determines intestate succession to real property.

Conflicting domicile determinations – the states apply their standards for determining domicile and may separately rule that a party was domiciled in their respective state (a legal impossibility).

Dorrance v Martin et al. (1935) – two states imposed estate taxes after deciding that the decedent was domiciled in their respective state.

The imposition of multiple state estate taxes violates the due process clause only if the taxes exceed the value of the estate. To avoid additional tax, an intent to change domiciles should be done thoroughly and quickly.

Diversity actions – the parties must have different domiciles when the action is filed.

The courts may not recognize a change in domicile if it was done to create diversity or for tax advantages (only an artificial difference; no real intent).

Diversity jurisdiction aims to protect non-resident defendants from forum prejudice (a person who has artificially changed domiciles is not prejudiced).

Judicial jurisdiction

The definition of domicile may depend upon the purpose in a proceeding (e.g., statute).

Consider if the results achieved under traditional domicile rules are equitable and according to the statute's intent or other action.

Illegal immigrants acquire a new domicile for government benefits but not necessarily for family law matters (e.g., divorce).

Domicile by operation of law

If a person has no legal capacity to acquire a domicile of choice, they will be assigned a domicile by operation of law.

A person has one domicile at a time and does not lose it until they acquire a new one.

Being without a domicile anywhere is a legal impossibility.

2nd Restatement– a person can simultaneously have different domiciles for different purposes.

Domicile may be the headquarters of the person's personal and professional life.

The law of the forum determines domicile.

Original domicile: a person is presumed to have the domicile of their parents.

New domicile by choice

Establishing a new domicile requires legal capacity, physical presence, and a state of mind.

A person retains their domicile until a new one is perfected.

A mere intent to relinquish domicile without being present in the new one is insufficient.

English rule – one who gives up their domicile of choice regains their domicile of origin until a new one is attained.

American rule – a person retains their domicile until they acquire a new one.

Physical presence: the person must be present, even if briefly.

Domicile of child

Domicile by operation of law – imputed by statute regardless of the party's intent (e.g., parent/child).

An infant lacks the capacity to choose their domicile.

A child will have the domicile of their parents if they cannot make a choice.

If parents are divorced, domicile is that of a parent who has physical custody.

Married spouse

Marriage: domicile is the place of *celebration rule.*

Domicile of a spouse provides subject matter jurisdiction for a divorce.

Common law: a wife has the same domicile as a husband.

Modern view: each spouse may establish a domicile of choice.

Under common law, a husband's domicile was attributed to his wife, but it is only a presumption under modern law.

Jurisdiction of Courts

Types of jurisdiction

Legislative (prescriptive) jurisdiction is the outer limit of a state's power to apply its law, whether statutory or judge made.

Each court has the power to decide if it has jurisdiction over the parties & subject matter.

Recognition of judgment: analyzing the effect of a judgment in one jurisdiction rendered by another court.

Judicial jurisdiction – the power of a court to hear a dispute and render a valid judgment recognized by other courts.

Judicial jurisdiction requires:

personal jurisdiction,

subject matter jurisdiction, and

in rem jurisdiction (authority over the thing)

Personal jurisdiction involves analyzing a court's assertion of the judicial power over parties.

Specific jurisdiction requires minimum contacts with the state. The suit arises out of or related to the defendant's contact with the forum state.

General jurisdiction involves suits not arising out of or related to the defendant's contacts with the forum state.

General jurisdiction requires sufficient contact with the state, which amounts to a continuous and systematic activity in the forum state.

Personal jurisdiction in state court

A defendant's contacts with the forum are such that the court may render a personal judgment against the defendant creating a judgment debt that other states may enforce under full faith and credit.

Personal jurisdiction requires minimum contacts with the state (e.g., the suit *arises out of* or *related to* the defendant's contact with the forum state).

Lack of personal jurisdiction is the classic form of a collateral attack.

Personal jurisdiction in federal courts

Absent congressional creation of federal jurisdiction (e.g., admiralty), a federal court is limited to the state court's jurisdictional reach where it sits.

The federal district court's power to assert personal jurisdiction is the same as the state court's power to assert personal jurisdiction where the federal district court sits.

For example, the District Court for Eastern TX analyzed the defendant's contact with Texas.

Traditional methods for courts to establish personal jurisdiction

Personal jurisdiction is established if the defendant is personally served in the forum state while voluntarily present in the state (purposely availing themselves to the benefits of the forum); no minimum contacts with the forum are required (transient jurisdiction).

Tag jurisdiction encourages forum shopping and could result in unfairness.

The defendant is domiciled in the forum state.

The rationale for jurisdiction – the defendant avails themself to the forum state's benefits.

The defendant consents to the court's exercise of personal jurisdiction.

A plaintiff consents to counterclaims by filing an action.

Forum selection clauses bind the parties to litigate in a forum (must be reasonable).

Consent to jurisdiction clause – vests a court with jurisdiction.

Waiver – the defendant fails to challenge jurisdiction.

The defendant appears specially but argues the merits – waives jurisdictional challenge.

Modern requirements for personal jurisdiction

Minimum contacts – the defendant must have minimum contacts with the forum state (e.g., *International Shoe*).

Foreseeability – the defendant should foresee being hauled into court in the forum.

Purposeful contacts or actions directed toward the forum.

Initiation – the defendant-initiated contact with the forum.

The greater the defendant's forum activities, the lower the need for the relatedness of the claim to the forum.

The defendant adjusted their primary conduct considering the forum's laws (usually applies to insurance cases).

The defendant derived benefits from the forum.

Fair play and substantial justice – subjecting the defendant to jurisdiction within the forum must meet with traditional notions of fair play and substantial justice:

the interest of the forum state in hearing the case (involving its citizens),

contrast *Asahi Metals* (1987), where the controversy was an indemnification action between two Japanese companies.

Overall fairness and reasonableness of exercising jurisdiction in the forum (defendant's burden of defending in the forum).

The plaintiff's interest in having the litigation in the forum (difficulty in bring suit elsewhere, availability of evidence, witnesses).

The interest of the interstate judicial system in obtaining the most efficient resolution to controversies and public policy.

Domestic corporations – a corporation is a resident of the forum if:

1) it is incorporated in the forum, or
2) it has its principal place of business in the forum.

Foreign corporations are subject to the jurisdictional requirements above.

Due process and federalism – the restriction on personal jurisdiction is the due process clause and its protection of individuals.

The sovereignty and rights of states outside the forum do not limit personal jurisdiction.

If federalism were an independent restriction, a defendant could never waive jurisdiction since individuals cannot waive states' rights.

Failure to comply with discovery orders aimed at a jurisdictional issue may be a waiver of jurisdiction.

Defamation – publication meets minimum contacts if the publisher avails itself of the market in a state (includes writers and editors).

Minimum contacts are evaluated in terms of specific or general jurisdiction.

Specific jurisdiction

The non-resident defendant has sufficient contacts with the forum, and those contacts are substantially related to the controversy (the cause of action arises out of the defendant's contact with the forum).

Injury within the forum alone is insufficient to establish jurisdiction over a non-resident defendant unless the defendant directed acts toward the forum and could reasonably expect to be hauled into court there (*World-Wide Volkswagen v. Woodson*, 1980).

All the defendant's contacts with the controversy do not have to be with the forum state so long as enough contacts are with the forum (*Burger King Corp. v. Rudzewicz,* 1985).

Merely placing a product into the stream of commerce may be insufficient unless the defendant has purposefully availed themself of the market (*Asahi Metals* – the court was fractured 4/4 on this issue; the unfairness of requiring the defendant to defend in California was determinative).

Brussels Convention – tort jurisdiction is at the place of acting or the location of the injury.

General jurisdiction

The non-resident defendant has extensive contacts with the forum justifying jurisdiction, and there are no contacts related to the controversy between the defendant and the forum.

The cause of action does not arise out of contact with the forum state.

Exercise of state court jurisdiction is discretionary based upon local court rules or statutes.

Suit not arising out of or related to the defendant's contacts with the forum state.

Sufficient contacts with the state amount to *continuous and systematic activity* in the state.

The minimum contacts threshold is significantly higher than the specific jurisdiction.

Individuals are subject to general jurisdiction in their domicile jurisdiction.

Continuous, systematic and substantial contact requirement

Helicopteros Nationales de Columbia v. Hall (1984) – purchasing equipment, using a bank for those purchases, and training pilots were insufficient forum activities to maintain a cause of action *arising out of* an accident in Columbia (court did not consider specific jurisdiction).

Brussels Convention – general jurisdiction exists only where a defendant is domiciled, incorporated, or has its corporate headquarters.

Piercing the corporate veil – asserting jurisdiction over a parent corporation requires a close relationship with the subsidiary (e.g., board of directors' overlap, direct involvement).

Alternatively, it requires misuse of the corporate identity.

Service of process is complete when served upon the subsidiary.

Partnerships – service on one partner or officer does not impute jurisdiction over property outside the state.

In rem jurisdiction

In rem: the subject of an action is some item of property ("*rem*") located in the forum and the action determines an interest in *rem* against the world:

> adjudicate questions concerning the ownership and control of the property (value of the judgment is limited to the "*rem*"),
>
> acts upon the thing itself rather than the rights of an individual (artificial distinction),
>
> minimum contacts established by the presence in the forum and notice.

Quasi in rem: The plaintiff asserts a preexisting interest in a dispute against specific named individuals only, and the judgment affects only those parties.

The value of the judgment cannot exceed the value of the "*rem*."

Land – a forum has jurisdiction over property located within the *situs*, and *in rem* judgments rendered will be subject to full faith and credit.

If a court only has *in rem* jurisdiction and issues a personal judgment (personal obligations), the judgment will be invalid.

Intangibles – the *situs* of an intangible determines jurisdiction.

A debtor's obligation accompanies them wherever they go and is subject to attachment provided there are minimum contacts.

Minimum contacts must be established to assert personal jurisdiction based upon attachment. The mere presence of unrelated property alone will not provide jurisdiction over persons (*Shaffer v. Heitner*, 1977 – shareholder derivative action failed minimum contacts).

Competence of the court

Subject matter jurisdiction refers to a court's power to hear and decide on an issue.

The parties cannot waive subject matter jurisdiction.

The court must address a lack of competence in its motion (even if parties do not challenge).

Parties cannot confer subject matter jurisdiction upon a court by agreement.

Full faith and credit does not apply to judgments rendered by courts that lack competence.

Continuing jurisdiction – once a court has jurisdiction over a defendant or their property, it retains that jurisdiction for proceedings which arise out of the original cause of action. Plaintiff may not add new claims without a jurisdictional basis. Irrelevant if the initial basis for jurisdiction no longer exists.

Domestic relations cases – a court may refuse to hear a case if the parties have moved elsewhere, and a convenient forum has jurisdiction over the defendant.

Obligation to provide or refuse a forum

A court must entertain a transitory cause of action that arises elsewhere

Refusal to hear a case because it arose under the law of a different state threatens interstate harmony (goal of full faith and credit).

The interests of the law-giving state should be considered unless the forum has substantive law to the contrary.

A forum is entitled to apply its statute of limitations to a transitory cause of action provided it is not discriminatory (state interest in not hearing stale claims).

Limits on the Exercise of Jurisdiction

Traditional limits for jurisdiction

Limitations imposed by contract – forum selection and consent to jurisdiction clauses

Prima facie valid and should be enforced unless unreasonable or unjust, procured by fraud, violative of public policy, or exceptionally inconvenient

Agreement denied effect when the parties and the incident were domestic, and the forum was a foreign country.

Clauses permit sophisticated parties to select the forum to resolve their disputes, and the courts show great deference to freedom of contracts in jurisdiction matters.

Bremen v. Zapata (offshore towing contract/forum selected) – influential factors included: international contract freely negotiated at arm's length, sophisticated parties, and the chosen forum was neutral.

Some courts have interpreted *Zapata* as creating a federal common law standard in diversity cases regardless of state standards.

Brussels' Convention – forum selection clauses vest exclusive jurisdiction in a member nation's court (one of the contracting parties must be from a member nation).

Fraud, force and privilege

A court will not exercise jurisdiction nor grant full faith and credit over a defendant or their property if the jurisdiction has been obtained by force or fraud.

Service of process achieved by tricking the defendant into entering the forum will be invalid.

Privilege – immunity from service applies to foreign sovereigns, defendant appearing specially, and a defendant who enters the forum to participate in civil litigation.

These limitations do not apply to a criminal defendant who will be subject to jurisdiction in the forum on civil matters once there.

Forum non conveniens

Forum non conveniens dismissal permits a court to refuse to exercise jurisdiction if it is an exceptionally inconvenient forum for the action, and a more convenient forum is available to the plaintiff.

Procedurally – motion is only available to the defendant.

The application depends upon the trial judge's sound discretion, who must consider the litigants' and the public's interests.

Litigant's interests – proximity and accessibility of evidence, availability of a compulsory process for unwilling witnesses, travel costs, ability to view the scene, and enforceability of a judgment.

Public interests – caseload pressures if litigation is shifted to popular forums, burden of jury duty, and the local interests of having cases decided where they arose.

The dismissal may be conditioned on submission to jurisdiction or waiver of the statute of limitations. However, it may not be conditioned on unilateral submission to U.S. discovery rules or supervision of a foreign action by a U.S. court.

A due process challenge against a foreign country judgment may be made when the plaintiff brings an enforcement action in a U.S. court.

An unfavorable change in the law is not grounds for the denial unless the remedy provided in the alternative forum is so inadequate that it is no remedy at all.

A presumption favoring the plaintiff's forum is more significant when the plaintiff is an American and the alternative forum is a foreign country.

Race to judgment – a defendant may initiate parallel litigation as a preemptive strike in a competent forum to prevent full faith and credit from binding him:

Most federal circuits follow the "first-filed rule" to decide which judgment has an effect.

State court or federal court with diversity jurisdiction – state law determines if the second forum action will be dismissed or stayed.

State injunction against parallel litigation – penalties available in the first state, but recognition and enforcement are not required in the second state.

Federal Transfer – for the convenience of the parties and witnesses, in the interests of justice, a district court may transfer a civil action to another district where it may have been brought.

A district court may not dismiss under *forum non conveniens* when there is an available district to transfer to

The district court has broader discretion to transfer than under a *forum non conveniens* dismissal.

Court where suit "may have been brought" refers to the defendant's ability and not the plaintiff's capacity (transferee court must have personal and subject matter jurisdiction).

The transferee district court must apply the state law of the transferor court (*Klaxon* rule).

Other jurisdictional limits imposed by the forum

2nd Restatement of Conflicts § 53 – a person will be ordered to act in another state when … required by the demands of justice and convenience. The defendant will not … be ordered to do an act that violates the law of another state.

A court can exercise its discretion and not require an action it has jurisdiction over if it will cause the party to violate the laws of a foreign forum.

It requires a balancing of interests.

Includes criminal laws, substantial sanctions equivalent to criminal penalties, or public policy as expressed in legislation.

Prospective civil liability is insufficient.

Foreign countries concerned with liberal U.S. discovery policy have enacted blocking statutes; however, a U.S. court with jurisdiction does not have to recognize such a statute.

Inability to grant relief – when relief is sought outside the framework of the local court system, the suit must be dismissed.

Slater v. Mexican National Railroad (1904) – the plaintiff was seeking a type of relief under Mexican law (revisable judgment for damages similar to a pension), which the local court was unable to grant.

Commerce clause – dismissal is mandatory when an action in a local court would impose an *unreasonable burden* on interstate commerce.

Statutes requiring general consent to jurisdiction before doing business in a state or consent to service by assignment of one ticket agent in a state are undue burdens on commerce.

The burden must be unreasonable since every transitory cause of action against a foreign corporation imposes some burden on trade.

Most of these cases can be decided on personal jurisdiction or *forum non conveniens* grounds without resort to the commerce clause.

A federal cause of action created by a constitutional act supersedes state law.

States cannot dismiss causes of action because the federal law is against the state's public policy (e.g., increases liabilities).

The principle applies when state and federal courts have concurrent jurisdiction.

Notes for active learning

Constitutional Limitations

Constitutional limitations for the jurisdiction of courts

The "Due Process" clause (5th and 14th Amendments) mandates that the exercise of personal jurisdiction meet the requirements of due process (*Pennoyer v. Neff,* 1878 – service by publication was ineffective for an action to determine the rights and obligations of parties).

Due process requires:

1) substantive due process (jurisdiction) – power over the person or property to assign liability, and
2) procedural due process (notice) – notice and an opportunity to be heard.

The state chosen must have significant contact with the parties or the subject matter of the litigation, which gives it a legitimate interest in seeing its law applied.

Courts do not have to weigh the interests, but if it meets the test.

Situations when the Pennoyer test is not met:

1) after the event in question, someone moves to a new state, and move creates only contact with that state; they cannot apply state law, or
2) if the only contact with the parties or the litigation is that the suit is brought in a state, they cannot apply state law.

Jurisdiction of courts for the choice of law

It is a violation of the due process clause for a forum to apply its law to the controversy when the only contact with the litigation is as the forum.

Home Insurance Co. v. Dick (1930) – the action involved an insurance contract on a tugboat where all the contacts were in Mexico, yet the Texas court applied its contract law (Supreme Court reversed).

If all contacts are with another state, the forum cannot constitutionally refuse to refer to foreign law.

If an actual conflict involves constitutional issues, it is ultimately for the Supreme Court to decide what is procedural and substantive, regardless of forum-applied labels.

The presumption that the law of the place of making determines the validity of a contract.

A forum must have enough contact with and interest in the dispute, so the application of its laws is neither arbitrary nor patently unfair.

De minimis contacts are not enough.

For example, in *Phillips Petroleum Co. v. Shutts* (1985), a small percentage of the plaintiff's gas leaseholds in the forum were insufficient for a nationwide class action.

Multi-state transactions – the forum will not be prevented from applying its law even though it conflicts with the other involved states provided it has a relationship to the action (e.g., injury to a domiciliary in the forum).

Foreseeability that an insured may end up in another justified state application of subsequent forum law to the contract.

Choice of Law

Choice-of-law concepts

Many cases are international or interstate:

The case has factual ties to two or more jurisdictions.

The case involves laws from two sources within the same jurisdiction.

Conflicts-of-law rules mitigate forum shopping and uphold the notions of fairness.

Principal courts decide what body of law to apply to a case; this determination of classification must be made following the law of the forum.

Courts faced with a choice-of-law issue generally have two choices:

1) a court can apply the law of the forum (*lex fori*) -- which is usually the result when the question of what law to apply is procedural, or
2) a court can apply the law of the site (*lex loci*) of the transaction or occurrence that gave rise to the litigation; usually, the controlling law selected when the matter is substantive.

Legal characterization of choice of law

Choice of law: choosing among competing legal principles by analyzing the law of applicable jurisdictions.

Vertical conflicts – conflicts between state and federal government.

Horizontal conflicts – conflicts between state governments.

2nd Restatement § 6: a court, subject to constitutional restrictions, will follow a statutory directive of its state on the choice of law.

If there is no such directive, the factors relevant to the choice of the applicable law include:

1) the needs of the interstate and international systems,
2) the relevant policies of the forum,
3) the applicable policies of other interested states and the relative interests of those states in the determination of the issue are the protection of justified expectations, the basic policies underlying the field of law to ensure certainty, predictability, and uniformity of result,
4) ease in the determination and application of the law to be applied.

Party autonomy to choose the applicable law

Fraternal organization internal affairs doctrine – the strong public policy of uniform application of laws governing a fraternal organization necessitates recognizing the law of the forum of incorporation.

Full faith and credit does not permit a state to legislate across state lines, and any state with a substantial interest in the matter can apply its law constitutionally.

Public acts are afforded full faith and credit, including statutes and case law of sister states.

2nd Restatement § 187 choice-of-law clauses

Struggles to reconcile the principle of party autonomy with the prerogative of the state to regulate contracts.

§ 187(2): issues parties could not have resolved by an explicit provision in their agreement, usually issues of contract validity (e.g., illegality, acceleration provisions, unenforceable based on forum law).

Limits on party autonomy – choice of laws is enforceable unless:

> state chosen must have a substantial relationship to the parties or the transaction, or
>
> there needs to be some other reasonable basis for selecting that state.,
>
> choice-of-law provisions are "unreasonable."

The fact that the choice of law would validate the contract is not enough of a reason.

Considerations include domicile, residence, nationality, place of incorporation, and place of business of the parties.

The forum state must have concern for the fundamental policy which the contractual choice of another state's law subverts.

The forum state must have a materially greater interest in the matter than the state whose law the parties have chosen.

Forum selection clauses

Forum selection clauses generally go with a choice-of-law clause and select the same jurisdiction.

§ 6 of Conflicts: the court will follow the directive of its state.

Without a directive, consider (not exclusive, and not listed in order of importance):

> needs of the interstate and international system,
>
> relevant policies of the forum,
>
> applicable policies of other interested states,
>
> justified expectations of the parties (not applied in tort cases)
>
> basic policies of law (the interested states' policies are essentially the same, but there are minor differences).

Courts apply local law to achieves underlying policies:

> certainty, predictability, and uniformity,
>
> discourage forum shopping,
>
> administrability.

Klaxon (1941) – federal district court in diversity must apply the choice-of-law rule of the state where it sits.

Van Dusen (1964) – transfer from a federal district court to another, the court to which case is assigned applies the law of the state from which it is transferred.

Notes for active learning

The Constitution and Choice of Law

Limits of legislative jurisdiction

The Constitution provides a baseline for rulings on due process or equal protection.

Constitutional protections for choice of law:

reduce interstate friction,

prevent unfair treatment to parties and promote individual fairness, or

limit states' legislative ability.

Minimum contacts for due process is a more challenging test than for personal jurisdiction.

It does not dictate the choice of law unless the law of the state has insufficient contacts.

State interests and the constitution

Full faith and credit *vs.* due process (individual convergence) – the Supreme Court applies the following tests arbitrarily:

due process,

fairness prong (unfair surprise),

quid pro quo (benefits and associated burdens),

state interest must be legitimate as implicated in the facts of the case,

minimum contacts,

choice of law.

Obligation to provide a forum – if one state provides a cause of action, another state must provide a forum.

Full faith and credit clause overrides state laws that promote a state objective by preventing foreign action when the statute gives more deference to substantive rights.

Limitations on the rule:

forum non conveniens,

avoid burdens on forum courts,

equal protection.

States may define substantive rights differently; if the forum has a legitimate interest (public policy conflict), it may apply its law.

Withholding from state courts the power to entertain claims based on the other states' laws is directly at odds with full faith and credit and must be subject to strict scrutiny and specific justification narrowly tailored to fit the rationale.

Renvoi and depecage

Renvoi (French for "send back" or "return unopened") is the principle of whether to apply the foreign state's "whole law" (including choice-of-law rules) or "internal law" (substantive).

This approach is generally rejected in the US except for questions of:

title to land,

questions concerning the validity of a decree of divorce, and

settlement of estates.

Property entirely and exclusively within the sovereign of the state in which it is situated:

estates can involve property in foreign countries,

marital status be treated uniformly throughout the country,

rights spring into existence in the jurisdiction where the property is located, so should use the property's locale for the choice-of-law rules.

Use renvoi whenever the objective of the choice-of-law rule is that the forum reaches the same result on the facts involved as would the courts of another state. It occurs when the other state has a dominant interest.

Remission – if renvoi is accepted and the state whose choice-of-law rules are examined refers the case back to the law of the forum state.

Partial remission – foreign choice of law refers to the internal law of the forum state.

1st Restatement – forum should ignore the foreign choice-of-law rules, except for the title of land and validity of a divorce decree, in which the whole law was accepted.

2nd Restatement – presumption that the choice of law refers to internal law unless uniformity considerations- unless it would trigger renvoi.

Depecage (French for "break into smaller pieces") is the treatment of an issue in a case by referring to the laws of more than one state (characterize or divide issues).

Under the vested rights approach, this dual reference was made to contract issues (e.g., place of making and performance).

Maryland Casualty Co. v. Jacek (1957) – the NJ court held that the issue of immunity was a tort issue and controlled by NY law, and the contract construction issue should be determined by NJ law (the place of the making).

By combining the law of the two states, the court frustrated the policy of each (prevention of collusion) without advancing the interests of either.

Depecage recognizes that a multi-state problem should not necessarily be decided the same way as a purely domestic case and can be used to accommodate the interests of several states.

Notice and proof of foreign law

Courts will take judicial notice of a sister-state and federal law.

The law of a foreign country is a fact, which must be pleaded and proved.

If foreign law cannot be determined, the resident state will apply the resident state law if there is no injustice.

The first response must tell the court what law should be applied.

Some courts assume laws are the same if not proven.

A court can take judicial notice of a sister state's law, but foreign law is unusual in this jurisdiction.

There are statutes authorizing courts to take judicial notice in pleadings or reasonable notice.

Foreign law must be pleaded like other facts, in conformity with the evidence, decided by a trier of fact, subject to only limited appellate review.

FRCP 44.1: the court may take judicial notice as a matter of law, therefore taking the decision of foreign law out of the jury's purview; limits review on appeal.

Notes for active learning

Choice-of-Law Theories

Traditional approaches to conflicts of law

Traditional theory uses a territorial approach (1st Restatement, Beale, vested rights); *lex loci* or law of the place.

History of conflicts of law – European common law historically used a territorial approach (Justice Story – 1st Restatement of Conflicts).

Currently, the interest of states has evolved from dissatisfaction with rigidity.

Vested rights approach (Beale) – localize events of multi-state, place in one state.

Pinpoints the jurisdiction where the parties' rights vest.

Law of the place uses where the last liable event occurred.

For contracts, the law of the location is of contracting.

For property, the law of the place where the property is located.

Party autonomy

Interpretation – intent of the parties determines the parties' expectations under the contract.

Validity affords an artificial device to encourage forum shopping.

For the intention to prevail, the choice of laws must be *bona fide* and in good faith.

The law chosen must have some relation to the agreement.

It cannot be contrary to evade U.S. policy.

No existence of a contrary statute.

2nd Restatement §187 – party autonomy may not be respected even if parties may not have been able to resolve by explicit provisions unless:

1) chosen law is contrary to the fundamental policy of the state, which has a materially more significant interest than the chosen state,
2) absent a contrary intent, reference is to the law of the chosen state.

Modern approaches to conflicts of law

The mere fact that a suit is brought in a state does not make it appropriate to apply the state's substantive law.

For a foreign suit, although the act complained of had no force in the forum, it gave rise to an obligation, which follows the person, and may be enforced where the person may be found.

Domestic rule of the foreign state when a forum case comes to the forum, it should apply its law but adopt and enforce as its law a rule of decision identical or highly similar to a rule of decision found in the law of the state.

UCC rule: a court must characterize issues to select the appropriate choice-of-law provision.

UCC rule: when a transaction bears a reasonable relation to this state and another state or notion, the parties may agree that the law of this state or the other governs the rights and duties; applies to transactions bearing a reasonable relation to the state.

Most significant relationship

Modern approach – 2nd Restatement uses the most significant relationship test.

Issues are separated, and the law of the state with the most significant relationship is applied.

The state as the center of gravity is the popular approach to conflicts because of manipulation, presumptions, and principles.

Judges favor it because of the enormous discretion given.

Interest analysis approach to choice of law

Babcock approach – list the factual contacts with the state.

Note the different state laws and find policies underlying each state law by consulting legislative history and court decisions.

Determine which state law would favor the plaintiff and which would favor the defendant.

Relate the facts to the policy to see if the state is interested in seeing its law applied.

The state has an interest if the party favored by a state's law resides in that state.

Apply the law of the state with the most significant governmental interest in the outcome.

Government interests analysis

General rule: the forum state's law applies unless the party requests another law to apply.

The forum should fundamentally follow its law through a series of steps.

First, the courts should look to policies expressed by the legislature in each jurisdiction.

If a party requests another law, identify the competing laws' policies by "the ordinary processes of construction and interpretation."

Identify the contacts of the parties considering the policies.

False conflicts: if only one state has an interest in having its law applied, the forum court should apply the law of the jurisdiction with interest in the outcome of the litigation.

True conflict: if two or more states are interested in the litigation, one of them is the forum state.

For true conflicts, the presumption is that the forum state's law applies unless the other state's interest is more significant.

If a conflict is unavoidable, the court should apply the law of the forum state.

Criticism challenges defining policy; courts can define policy to reach the desired results.

Allows for forum shopping because forum law is the default law applied to the case.

If the forum court is disinterested, but two or more states have legitimate competing interests, dismiss according to *forum non conveniens*.

Forum court uses its judgment on what law is appropriate or applies the law most closely resembling its own.

If no state has an interest, the court can dismiss the case or forum law governs.

Statutes directed to the choice of law

A court, subject to constitutional limitations, must follow the directions of its legislature.

The court must apply a local statutory provision directed to the choice of law if it would be constitutional to do so.

An example of a statute directed to the choice of law is the Uniform Commercial Code (UCC), which provides certain instances for applying the law chosen by the parties; in some other cases, apply the law of a particular state.

Another example is the Model Execution of Wills Act, which provides that the testator will subscribe to a written document shall be valid as to matters of the form if it complies with the local requirements of several enumerated states.

There are comparatively few statutes that expressly direct the choice of law.

Intended range of application of the statute

A court will rarely find that the statute explicitly covers a question of choice of law.

A court will rarely be directed by statute to apply the local law of one state rather than the local law of another in the decision of an issue.

The court questions whether the issue is within the intended range of the statute.

The court should give a local statute the range of application intended by the legislature when these intentions can be ascertained and constitutionally be given effect.

If the legislature intended that the statute be applied to the out-of-state facts involved, the court should apply it unless constitutional considerations forbid.

If the legislature intended that the statute be applied only to acts within the state, the statute should not be given a full range of applications.

Sometimes, a statute's intended range of application will be apparent on its face, as it expressly applies to citizens of a state, including those living abroad.

When the statute is silent about its range of application, the legislature's intent on the subject can sometimes be ascertained by the interpretation and construction.

Provided that it is constitutional to do so, the court will apply a local statute in the manner intended by the legislature even when another state's domestic law of another state would be applicable under general choice-of-law principles.

Rationale for choice of law

Legislatures usually legislate, and courts typically adjudicate for the locality.

Judges rarely consider the extent to which the laws they enact, and the common-law rules they enunciate, should apply to out-of-state facts.

When there are no adequate directives in the statute or the case law, the court considers the factors below determining the state whose local law will be applied to resolve the issue.

This list of factors is not exclusive, and a court considers other factors in deciding a question of choice of law.

It is not suggested that the factors mentioned are listed in order of their relative importance.

Varying weight will be given to factors in different areas for choice of law.

Favoring policies of the state with a dominant interest have predominant weight.

Transfers of interests in land are governed by the law the *situs*.

However, the policies in favor of protecting the parties' justified expectations and effectuating the basic policy underlying the field of law are essential.

Subject to certain limitations, the parties can choose the law to govern their contract and in the rules which provide, subject to certain restrictions or the validity of a contract against the charge of commercial usury.

The policy favoring uniformity of result gives rise to the rule that succession of interests in movables is governed by the law applied by the state courts where the decedent was domiciled at the time of their death.

Often, some of the factors point in different directions in all but the simplest case.

Hence any rule of choice of law, like other common-law rules, represents an accommodation of conflicting values.

2nd Restatement – the "most significant relationship."

Two-step process:

start with an applicable presumptive rule,

use § 6 with § 145 to determine which state has the most significant relationship.

§ 6 provides judges with a list of relevant factors (not an exclusive list):

needs of the interstate and international systems,

relevant policies of the forum,

relevant policies of other interested states and the relative interests of those states in the determination of the issue,

protection of justified expectations,

basic policies underlying the field of law,

certainty, predictability, and uniformity of result,

ease in the determination and application of the law to be applied.

§ 145 highlights some contacts that matter:

the place where the injury occurred,

the place where the conduct causing the damage occurred,

domicile, residence, nationality, place of incorporation and of business of the parties,

place where the relationship, in any, between the parties, is centered.

Courts consider five principles that inform the forum's ultimate decision.

1) Predictability of results: respect what parties intended (e.g., contract cases).
2) Maintenance of interstate and international order: the forum should not "ruffle feather" by being too unseemly in the disregard of foreign law.
3) Simplification of the judicial task: often results concluding that the forum can apply forum or foreign law with equal ease (at least in domestic cases; foreign country law might be harder).
4) Advancement of the forum's governmental interests: what courts have done and what courts can be expected to do.
5) Application of the better rule of law (something more than different).

Statute of Limitations

Statutes of limitations and repose

Classic approach (*Wells v. Simonds Abrasive Co.*, 1953, Vinson): full faith and credit does not require applying another state's statute of limitations (SOL).

States are free to apply forum statute of limitations.

Not compelled to use the statute of limitations of the state whose substantive law applies.

Constitutional restraints (*Sun Oil v. Wortman*, 1988, Scalia): does not violate the full faith and credit to apply the longer local statute of limitations.

The Constitution is permissive as to applying the forum's substantive statute of limitations.

Choice-of-law approaches to limitations issues: states are free to make their own choice-of-law rules on limitations.

Borrowing statutes direct the forum to dismiss claims under foreign statutes of limitations in appropriate circumstances.

Tolling statutes suspend the running of the SOL against out-of-state defendants.

Uniform conflict of laws – limitation act

For claims substantively based upon the law of another state, the SOL of that state applies.

If a claim is substantively based upon the law of more than one state, the limitation period of one of those states chosen by the law of conflict of this state applies.

The limitation period of the forum state applies to all claims.

2nd Restatement § 142 statute of limitations

2nd Restatement §142 – the forum will apply its statute of limitations barring a claim unless exceptional circumstances of the case make such results unreasonable.

The forum applies its SOL barring the claim if the forum's statute of limitations is shorter.

A state will not give longer life to a cause of action arising in another state than its own.

The forum applies its SOL permitting the claim if the forum's SOL is longer, unless:

1) maintain the suit would serve no substantial interest in the forum, and
2) a suit would be barred under the statute of limitations of a state having a more significant relationship to the parties and occurrence.

Borrowing statutes: if action accrued elsewhere, cannot use forum's statute of limitations.

Tolling rules and statute of limitations

Savings statutes preserve a cause of action that would usually be barred (e.g., file in district court on diversity), the statute of limitations tolls, and no subject matter jurisdiction. The plaintiff can refile in the state for one year after dismissal.

Statute of repose: suit barred from the date of some specific event.

Etheridge v. Genie Industries, Inc., Ala. (1994): statutes of repose are procedural unless they are inextricably bound in a statute creating the right or cause of action.

Because the statute of repose existed in a different section than the cause of action and contained a list of other causes of action to which it applied, the statute was not sufficiently connected to the cause of action; therefore, not substantive.

Application in Specific Areas

Choice of laws for specific areas

The traditional system for choice of law was based on the vested rights theory in the 1st Restatement of Conflicts.

Vested rights – the forum is to apply the law of the state in which the rights of the parties vest (where they are created).

The forum must first characterize the cause of action (e.g., torts, contracts, property).

Approximately one-third of the states still use traditional rules.

Under the 1st Restatement, the forum does not consider the scope or policy of the substantive rule of law until after the state is chosen.

Torts – law of the place where the accident occurred.

1st Restatement § 378: the law of the place of the wrong determines if there is a legal injury.

The instant the cause of action (COA) arises, the plaintiff's rights vest.

Apply the law of the place where the injury or place of wrong occurred.

This may not be the place of negligence (or other wrongs) but the place of injury.

Place of wrong – use the law of the state of consequences, not original wrong / negligence where the force impinged on the plaintiff's body.

Each state has legislative jurisdiction to determine the legal effects of acts done or events caused within a territory.

Laws of the state are intended to possess exclusive sovereignty and jurisdiction within its territory, and persons who are residents and contracts made and acts done within it:

compensate the plaintiff for the harm they suffered,

provide predictability protecting reasonable expectations of the parties,

provide uniformity and administrability,

discourage forum shopping.

Where harm is done to the person's reputation, the place of wrong is where the defamatory statement was communicated.

Invasion of privacy uses the law of the jurisdiction where the plaintiff was when their feelings were wounded.

Exceptions to the place of the wrong test:

1) if the wrong depends on the application of the standard of care, that standard should be taken from the law of the location of the actor's conduct;

2) a person required, forbidden, or privileged to act under the law of the "place of acting" should not be held liable for consequences on another state.

Problems with the territorial approach:

determine where the injury occurred by looking at the localizing event (e.g., reputation, trademark, mass tort case),

unfairness potential,

characterization or escape devices,

renvoi.

Rights under a contract vest at the moment the contract is made.

Apply the law of the place of the making of the contract.

Clear rules but may lead to a state with no policy interest in the outcome of the litigation.

American rule: the place of contract for specific issues (e.g., validity, capacity).

The place of contract determines capacity.

Place of performance for other issues

Old law: the law only if there is a connection.

If a contract is completed in another state, it makes no difference whether the person goes in person, sends an agent, or writes a letter across the boundary lines between the states.

English rule: parties' intent, if unclear, is the "closest and most real connection."

Rome Convention eliminated "mandatory rules," replacing them with "overriding mandatory provisions."

Party autonomy – parties may choose but be limited by "mandatory rules" of the country where the contract was made.

A court can apply its law if it considers the law "overriding," providing much discretion.

Default rule (absent choice) § 4 – "most closely connected."

Presumption (closest connection) § 4(2) – "characteristic performance."

A contract's validity is to be decided by the law of the place where the contract is made unless it is to be performed in another country.

If the contract is to be performed in another place as intended by the parties, the validity, nature, obligation, and interpretation are governed by the location of performance.

Freedom of contract dominates in most states, with some restrictions (2nd Restatement).

Juenger – parties should be free to select their own rules that reflect commercial practice and the best law without regard for the desires of sovereigns.

Place of contracting

Special rules determine where the contract is made depending on the type of conflict.

§311 Place of contracting: principal event necessary to make a contract occurs.

§312 Formal contract: effective on delivery, place of contracting is where delivery is made.

§323 Informal unilateral contract: where the event takes place that makes it binding.

§325 Informal bilateral contract: where the second promise is made in consideration of the first promise.

§326 Acceptance from one state to another: if acceptance is sent by an agent of the acceptor, the state where the agent delivers it or from which acceptance is sent.

§332 Validity and effect of the contract: the law of the place where the contract was made (capacity, necessary form, consideration, requirements to make a promise binding, time, and place where the promise is to be performed, the character of the promise).

§358: performance handled with the place where a contract is to be performed (i.e., manner, time, locality, parties involved, sufficiency, an excuse for non-performance).

Justifiable expectations of parties are enforceable.

Property

Law of *situs* – the place of the property is to govern as to the capacity of the testator. Also determines marriage, property, mortgages, etc.

Immovables are of the most considerable concern: exclusive jurisdiction to the state in which they are situated.

Leaseholds are considered immovable.

Pragmatic concerns – recording system for land interests.

Movables – the law of the *situs* does not always apply as there are many exceptions.

Situs is determined at the time of possession.

Location during litigation to avoid forum shopping.

For distribution between spouses, apply the place of marital domicile.

The Restatement for the choice-of-law issues states the rules in which the courts have evolved in accommodation with specific factors.

For property, such rules are sufficiently precise to permit them to be applied in the decision of a case without explicit reference to the factors which underlie them.

Wills and intestate succession

For land, the law of the *situs* applies.

Movable property – law of the *situs,* but issues arise (e.g., the *situs* of stock certificate).

Personal property – the domicile of the decedent at death.

The policy governs the status of property *vs*. determining who takes under a will (*situs* rule fractionalizes estate but might be consistent with expectations).

For wills, it might be better to look at domicile at the time of execution.

Intestate succession is determined by domicile. Domicile is determined by the law of the forum and requires physical presence and intent to remain indefinitely.

Modern rule – domicile depends on the issue (old rule: unitary).

White v. Tennant (WV 1888) (moved from PA to WV but for less than one day): domicile was established upon arrival.

Estate of Jones (Iowa 1921) (Lusitania): death in transit uses the previous domicile until "new domicile is secured."

Family law

Marriage is valid where the wedding was celebrated or performed.

Exception: marriage would violate the state's public policy; then, it may not be recognized even though it was valid where performed.

Marriages void where performed are void everywhere.

Exception: if marriage is void because of failure to comply with the technical requirement of the state where it is performed, it can still be recognized in the resident state if it would have complied with the resident state rule.

Wilkins v. Zelichowski (NJ 1959); NJ statute for marriage by an underage woman is void if not confirmed. The statute demonstrated "strong public policy" against recognizing marriages of minor women in other states.

2nd Restatement: most significant relationship to spouses and marriage (usually the place of celebration unless it violates another state's policy with the most significant relationship).

Divorce is governed by the law of the plaintiff's domicile.

Domicile (judicial construction, as opposed to the residence) is a legislative term usually meaning without intent to stay.

A person has one domicile and only one domicile.

Domicile requires the coexistence of physical presence and intent to remain.

A person may not have enough relationship with their domicile unless they have been there for a significant time.

In the modern approach, domicile shifts depending on the burden (i.e., taxes *vs.* intestate succession). If there is a rupture in marital relations, one spouse may acquire their domicile even if they are the party at fault.

1st Restatement said that a spouse could not change their domicile without going there first, but 2nd Restatement provides that the other spouse's presence may serve as a substitute.

If a home straddles the border, it could be the principal entrance or where the person sleeps.

A person cannot (1st Restatement) or does not usually (2nd Restatement) acquire a domicile by the presence in a place under physical or legal compulsion.

1st Restatement: marriage is valid everywhere if legal in the state where celebrated.

Notes for active learning

Additional principles for application in specific areas

Torts – *lex loci delicti commissi* [Latin, *the law of the place where the tort was committed*] controls.

Lex loci [Latin, *the law of the place*] applies even though the significant contacts, including the negligent act, occurred in another state.

Vicarious liability is determined by the place of the wrong only if the defendant authorized the tortfeasor to act for them in the state.

Lex loci determines the character and measure of the damages, the standard of care, causation, contributory negligence, master-servant rule, defenses, and survival of actions.

Contracts – *lex loci contractus* ("*law of the place where the contract is made*") applies.

Issues concerning performance are governed by the law of the place of performance.

The forum decides where the contract was made.

The state whose law is applied to the dispute may have no interests at stake (other than being the place of contracting).

Where the contract is made is subject to interpretation based upon the nature of the modern commercial transaction.

The issue may be characterized as one of performance to apply different laws and achieve the desired result. In *Louis-Dreyfus v. Paterson Steamships, Ltd* (1930), each state favored limiting liability, but the *lex loci* rule did not. To advance the interests of the involved states, the court characterized the dispute as performance.

Contracts – party expectations may determine the choice of law.

A court may ignore the *lex loci* law and apply the law of the place of performance to resolve a contract dispute if it determines that the parties entered into their obligation because of that law (contract is invalid under *lex loci* law but enforceable in place of performance)

An adhesion contract (steamship ticket) may designate the law to be applied regardless of *lex loci* if the forum selected has some connection to the agreement.

Usury – courts tend to apply whichever law upholds the validity of the contract if there is a reasonable relationship to the transaction and the parties were in equal bargaining positions.

2nd Restatement § 203 usury – a contract is enforceable if its interest rate is permitted in a state with a substantial relationship to the contract and does not significantly exceed the price allowed by an interested state.

The presumption of validity is necessary to promote the free flow of commerce; otherwise, lenders may be reluctant to lend money.

For real property, the law of the *situs* determines the disposition and succession of real property. This is necessary to administer and ensure the accuracy of title records.

Only courts of the *situs* can directly affect title to land in that state because states have a strong interest in the property within their borders.

Hague Convention and Civil Law countries use law of the possessor's domicile and not *situs*.

Forum law is traditionally applied to domestic, workman's compensation, and criminal matters regardless of the choice-of-law rules.

Applying choice-of-law rules to specific issues

For contracts, the difficulties and complexities involved have prevented the courts from formulating precise rules, which provide satisfactory accommodation of the underlying factors in situations that may arise.

Courts state the general principle, such as applying the local law "of the state of the most significant relationship," to provide perspective about the correct approach but this approach does not furnish precise answers.

The courts must look at the underlying factors to arrive at a decision.

A statement of precise rules in choice of law is complicated by the variety of facts and issues.

Many of these issues have not been thoroughly explored by the courts. These rules represent general statements frequently used by the courts in opinions and the rationale of the decisions in more recent opinions.

Substance *vs.* procedure

Forum determines whether procedural rules or substantive law applies.

Pros of applying forum law (i.e., characterizing as procedural):

administrative convenience,

courts would have to read pleadings for substance (e.g., determining deadlines),

administration of justice (e.g., rules of evidence),

advance policy, but focus on adjudication, not determining the rights of parties,

courts apply their evidence rules for judicial efficiency.

1st Restatement (§ 390) – when foreign law is applicable, it governs the substantive law; the laws of the forum govern the procedure.

The court of the forum decides the procedure.

The assumption is that the rule will be manipulated. It offers little or no guidance on why one type of characterization is better.

Criteria for distinguishing:

characterization in statute or precedent,

outcome determinative.

The remedy is procedural, and the right is substantive.

The court of the forum applies the rules of a foreign system until it becomes inconvenient.

Needs of the interstate and international systems

The function of choice-of-law rules is to make interstate and international systems work well.

Choice-of-law rules should seek to further harmonious relations between states and facilitate commercial intercourse.

In formulating rules of choice of law, a state should regard the needs and policies of other states and the community of states.

Choice-of-law rules for policy are likely to commend other states and be adopted by them.

Adopting the same choice-of-law rules by many states furthers the needs of the interstate and international systems and the values of certainty, predictability, and uniformity of results.

Relevant policies of the state of the forum

Two situations should be distinguished.

The state of the forum has no interest in the case apart from the fact that it tries the action. The relevant policies of the state of the forum will be embodied in its rules relating to trial administration.

The state of the forum has an interest in the case apart from the fact that it is the place of trial. The relevant policies of the forum state may be embodied in rules that do not relate only to trial administration.

Whether embodied in a statute or a common-law rule, every rule of law was designed to achieve a purpose.

A court should consider these purposes in determining whether to apply its rule or the rule of another state in deciding the issue.

If the purposes sought to be achieved by a local statute or its application to out-of-state facts furthers the common-law rule, this is a weighty reason for such a claim.

The court is under no compulsion to apply the statute or rule to such out-of-state facts since the originating legislature or court had no ascertainable intent on the subject.

The court must decide whether the purposes sought to be achieved by a local statute or rule should be furthered at the expense of the other choice-of-law factors mentioned.

Relevant policies of other interested states

In determining a question of choice of law, the forum should consider its relevant policies and the applicable policies of the interested states.

The forum should seek to reach a result achieving the best accommodation of these policies.

The forum should appraise the relative interests of the states involved in the determination of the issue.

In general, the state with interests most deeply affected should have its local law applied.

The state of dominant interest may depend upon the issue involved.

If a person injures their spouse in a state other than that of their domicile, it may be that the state of conduct and injury has the dominant interest in determining whether the conduct was tortious or whether the injured spouse was guilty of contributory negligence.

The spouse's domicile state is the state of dominant interest regarding whether the person who caused the injury should be held immune from tort liability to their spouse.

The relevant local law rule may determine whether this state has the dominant interest.

For example, applying a state's statute or common-law rule, which absolves the defendant from liability, could not be justified based on this state's interest in the welfare of the injured plaintiff.

Protection of justified expectations

The justified expectation is an essential value in law, including the choice of law.

It would be unfair and improper to hold a person liable under the local law of one state when they had justifiably comported conduct to conform to the requirements of another state.

Partly because of this factor, the parties are free within broad limits to choose the law to govern the validity of their contract and that the courts seek to apply a law that will sustain the validity of a trust of movables.

There are occasions, particularly in negligence, when the parties act without giving thought to the legal consequences of their conduct or to the law that may be applied.

In such situations, the parties have no justified expectations to protect and are not factored into the decision of a choice-of-law question.

Basic policies underlying the field of law

Basic policies underlying jurisprudence are important when the policies of the interested states are mostly the same, but there are minor differences between relevant local rules.

In such instances, there is a good reason for the court to apply the local law of that state, which achieves the policies underlying jurisprudence.

For example, courts seek to apply laws that sustain the validity of a contract against the charge of commercial usury or the validity of a trust of movables against the charge of violating the rule against perpetuities.

Predictability and uniformity of result

Predictability and uniformity are essential values in law.

To the extent that they are attained in choice of law, forum shopping will be discouraged.

These values can, however, be purchased at too high a price.

In a rapidly developing area, such as the choice of law, it is often more important than ethical rules developed for predictability, and uniformity of result should be assured through continued adherence to existing rules.

Predictability and uniformity of results are essential in areas where the parties are likely to preemptively consider the legal consequences of their transactions.

Parties are permitted within broad limits to choose the law that will determine the validity and effect of their contract.

The law applied by the courts of the state of the *situs* determines the validity of transfers of interests in land.

Uniformity of result is important when transferring an aggregate of movables situated in different states.

The law applied by the courts of the state of a decedent's domicile at death determines the validity of their will for movables and the distribution of movables in the event of intestacy.

While courts consider the ease of determining and applying the law, it is not overemphasized since producing predictable and uniform results is of greater importance.

The policy does provide a goal for which to strive.

Reciprocity

In formulating common-law rules of choice of law, the courts are rarely guided by reciprocity considerations.

Private parties should not suffer from the courts of the state from which they consider the interests of the state of the forum.

The satisfactory development of choice-of-law rules can best be attained if each court considers other states' interests without regard to whether the courts of one or more of these other states would do the same. For example, whether reciprocity is a condition to recognize and enforce a judgment of a foreign nation.

States sometimes incorporate a principle of reciprocity into statutes and treaties.

They may do so to induce other states to take specific actions favorable to their interests or the interests of their citizens.

Many states have enacted statutes that provide that a suit by a sister state for the recovery of taxes will be entertained in the local courts if the sister state courts would consider a similar lawsuit by the state of the forum.

Additionally, some states provide by statute that an alien cannot inherit local assets unless their citizens, in turn, would be permitted to inherit in the state of the alien's nationality.

A principle of reciprocity is sometimes employed in statutes to permit reciprocating states to obtain by cooperative efforts what a single state could not achieve through the force of its law.

Federal courts applying state law

Federal courts apply different rules than state courts because federal jurisdiction is limited to what has been enumerated in the Constitution.

In a case based on diversity of citizenship, a federal court determines the conflict-of-law issue as if it were the highest court in the state in which it is sitting.

The rules that federal courts must obey regarding which laws to apply are complex.

Federal courts apply choice-of-law rules instead of the law of the forum to discourage forum shopping. This could result in courts applying their law to cases with no connection to the forum.

Parties have expectations about how and which law governs.

Notes for active learning

Defenses Against Application of Foreign Law

Escape mechanisms to forego applying a state's law

Exception for other transactions (2nd Restatement): allow the choice-of-law clause unless the chosen state has no substantial relationship with the parties or transaction and no other reasonable basis for the parties' choice.

A court can apply a law that has a materially more significant interest in the dispute.

Choice-of-forum clauses designate the court where the dispute will be resolved.

Parties can agree that the litigation should be conducted in another forum but must be reasonable at the time of litigation.

Substance *vs*. procedure:

procedure rules govern the conduct of litigation,

substance rules govern out-of-court conduct,

procedural law applies to the forum state.

Characterization

When characterizing a hybrid transaction (e.g., a land sale contract), characterize it as a "property" case to get the *situs* rule.

Examiners prefer the *situs* rule due to the statute of limitations and borrowing statutes.

A court should apply the shorter of two competing statutes of limitations.

Public policy

Courts refuse to apply foreign law if it is contrary to a strong public policy in the forum state.

A court must carefully consider the decision concerning public policy.

Public policy is a part of the conflict of laws, difficult to reconcile with vested rights.

It must be a dramatic departure from the court's idea of justice or fairness.

1st Restatement § 612 precludes suits upon a cause of action created in another state, the enforcement of which is contrary to the forum's public policy.

The court should look to determine public policy based upon legislative debates, constitution, and public opinion.

Application of public policy exception: penal and tax laws of another jurisdiction will not be enforced, as they are intimate notions of another state's identity.

Penal laws award a penalty to the state, public officer, or member of the public suing in the community interest to address a public wrong.

Criminal law does not include wrongful death or corporate director's misconduct because they satisfy a pre-existing claim of right.

Applying state law in diversity cases

A federal court must apply the state's choice-of-law rules in which it sits; *Klaxon Co. v. Stentor Mfg. Co.* (1941).

Courts prefer uniform administration, although Congress is not constitutionally barred from creating federal choice-of-law rules.

Forum non conveniens avoids state conflict-of-laws issues.

Private interest factors include sources of proof, witnesses, practical problems with ease of trial (e.g., impleading third parties).

Public interest factors include a jury's duty with deciding a case, local interest in dealing with the matter, a judge's familiarity with local law, and the interest of the state.

The effect of transfer

§ 1404 permits transfer within federal courts instead of dismissal but uses the same though less rigid factors in deciding transfer.

§ 1404(a) is the codification of *forum non conveniens*: exists when a federal court cannot transfer to the better forum (foreign or state court).

Under §1404(a) (*forum non conveniens*): the transferee court will apply the law of the transferor court (*Van Dusen v. Barrack,* 1964). Use the same factors as *forum non conveniens* in deciding to transfer. It is meant as a transfer of courts for convenience, not for law.

Proper enforcement of the forum selection clause is through § 1404(a) and not § 1406(a).

Van Dusen rule (the choice of law should be that of the state where the case was filed initially) does not apply because it cannot ignore the agreed-to forum's law.

Gulf Oil (1947) analysis changes:

plaintiff's choice merits no weight because they agreed to the forum by contract,

no private interest factors because already decided based on contract,

may consider argument about public-interest factors only.

Constitutional Constraints on Choice of Law

Judicial discretion

The courts can generally apply whatever law they see fit so long as their choice is neither arbitrary nor fundamentally unfair.

Two constitutional provisions limit a court's ability to apply choice of laws if:

> there are no plausible or cognizable connections, or
>
> a party could not reasonably have anticipated the application of forum law.

Due process (14th Amendment) – application of a law is so unconnected to a party it could deprive that party of property without due process.

Full faith and credit (4th Amendment) goes beyond respecting judgments; states must recognize the acts of other states.

Early cases trended towards constitutionalizing choice-of-law principles.

Application of forum law where the forum has no connections or minimal connections to the dispute violates due process (*Home Insurance Co. v. Dick,* 1930, Brandeis) is still good law.

Rights created by contract in the state must use contracting state's law or violates full faith and credit (*Bradford Electric Light Co. v. Clapper*, 1932, Brandeis).

Analysis of full faith and credit and due process seem to have merged; no distinction between the two for determining the constitutionality of choice-of-law rule application.

Choosing forum law

Choosing forum law when other state does not have a significantly greater interest than the forum does not violate full faith and credit (*Alaska Packers Ass'n v. Industrial Accident Commission,* 1935, Stone).

Prima facie – every state is entitled to enforce in its courts its statutes, lawfully enacted.

Full faith and credit clause does not require the forum state to apply the other state's law when the policies of two states conflict in the form of conflicting statutes, and the interest of the non-forum state is not superior to that of the forum state.

It is constitutionally sufficient that the forum has a plausible or cognizable interest in applying its law to the dispute (*Pacific Employers Ins. Co. v. Industrial Accident Board*, 1939).

Like *Alaska Packers,* the court provides no substantive look at another state's interest; because it has an interest, it is constitutional to apply its law.

Applications of minimal scrutiny

The choice of law only offends the 14th Amendment if the state has no significant contact or significant aggregation of conduct with the parties, transaction, or occurrence (*Allstate Ins. v. Hague*, 1981, Brennan). Constitutional to apply MN law because MN has enough contacts.

No contact violates the Constitution (*Phillips Petroleum Co. v. Shutts*, 1985, Rehnquist).

Unconstitutional for KS courts to apply KS law to claims with which KS had no significant contacts – would be arbitrary and unfair (full faith and credit).

Federal–State Conflicts

Erie doctrine

Federal courts with diversity jurisdiction apply the law of the state in which they sit.

Federal courts have no authority to apply rules of law drawn from some amorphous body of "general law."

Unconstitutional because federal courts have no delegated power to declare substantive laws.

Reasoning – prior law (*Swift*) prevented uniformity; impossible to determine general law *vs.* local law.

Erie R.R. Co. v. Tompkins (1938) interpreted the Federal Rules of Decision Act to require federal courts, in diversity actions, to apply state statutory and common law to substantive issues when there is no federal statute on point and federal law is procedural.

After *Erie*, federal courts in diversity follow the state supreme court predictive approach; predict how the state's highest court would rule if it heard the case.

The Rules of Decision Act 28 U.S.C. § 1652 states that in civil actions, the federal courts must apply the "law of the several states, except where the Constitution, or treaties of the U.S., or acts of Congress otherwise require or provide."

Under the Rules of Decision Act, the Constitution, treaties, and constitutional acts of congress always take precedence, where relevant, over state provisions; applies to proceedings in state and federal court.

In the absence of a controlling federal provision, the federal courts will be bound to follow state constitutions, statutes, and common law in a diversity action.

"Substantive" versus "Procedural" test – matters characterized as substantive would be governed by state law while procedural matters (concern the process by which the claims of rights are examined) would be governed by federal law.

The Supreme Court rejected the concept of federal common law in diversity actions.

Federal common law survives in matters which are exclusively within the purview of the federal courts such as Admiralty, Maritime, etc. (lawmaking power has not been granted to the states by the constitution, and there has been no congressional action to the contrary), in which case, it is controlling because of the supremacy clause of the Constitution.

The court applied the following rationale in invoking the Erie doctrine:

Uniformity of law sought under *Swift v. Tyson* never materialized and yielded inequitable administration of the law. Non-citizens gained a forum shopping advantage, which allowed them to evade potentially unfavorable state common-law rules (*Black & White Taxicab,* 1928 re-incorporated in another state for diversity and avoid an adverse decision in state court).

Sovereignty – the authority of the states to regulate their affairs was eroded by *Swift v. Tyson*.

Ascertaining the state law

Klaxon doctrine requires the federal court to apply the conflict-of-law rules of the state where the federal court sits.

Conflicts of law arise when the federal court is sitting in one state, and the cause of action arose in another, each with different laws.

When a case is transferred under § 1404 to another federal district court, the transferee court must apply the transferor court's substantive law and its conflict-of-law rules:

state constitutions or statutes are determinative, or

holdings on point by the highest court in the state.

When there is no holding on point, the federal court must decide what the state's highest court would do if confronted with the same issue.

Certification: some states permit, by statute, questions of law to be "certified" to the highest court in the state for a determination.

Some states allow courts to decide issues in controversy before them, considering:

time allocation,

abstract question removed from the case.

Abstention: a federal court can suspend its inquiry and require a plaintiff to bring the case in state court first if:

the state law is unsettled, and

interpretation will have serious public policy implications for the state.

Therefore, some states will not certify a case initially brought in federal court.

Limitation of state power in federal courts

The *Outcome Determinative test* (*Guaranty Trust Co. v. York*, 1945 – SC applied the NY statute of limitations rather than the federal so as not to bar litigation).

State rules control if the choice between state or federal requirements could be outcome determinative in the case.

Rationale: the result of a diversity case in a federal court should be substantially the same (so far as legal rules determine the outcome) as it would be in state court.

Contrasting substance and procedure is inadequate; any matter outcome-determinative would be substantive. The dilemma is that procedural matters can be outcome determinative.

When considering outcome determination, evaluate the rationale under *Erie*:

1) avoidance of inequitable administration of the law, and

2) prevention of forum shopping.

Statute of limitations is outcome determinative for *Erie* purposes.

The *Balancing test* (*Byrd v. Blue Ridge Rural Electric Cooperative, Inc.*) – the court applied a balancing test between the competing federal and state interests advanced by their respective procedural rules. The court held that the federal interest of a jury trial under the 7th Amendment was an overriding interest when compared to the state's workman's compensation regulations. The court considered:

state rights and obligations,

disruption to the federal system of distribution of functions,

outcome determinative.

The *Modified Outcome Determinative test* effectively builds a protective wall around the Federal Rules of Civil Procedure and removes them from the scope of the *Erie* doctrine.

In *Hanna v. Plumer* (1965), the court held in favor of service of process under the federal rules, which conflicted with service under state law.

Federal Rules of Civil Procedure supersede state procedure

The Rules arise under the Rules Enabling Act and thus supersede state procedural law they conflict with (supremacy clause).

A conflict may be the result of:

1) a direct collision between a federal rule and a state law, or

2) the federal rule may "occupy the same field" as the state law.

The Rules supersede conflicting state laws whenever they are on point and constitutional.

If there is no conflict, both federal and state rules may be applied.

A Rule is constitutional if it arises under the Rules Enabling Act and is rationally capable of being classified as procedural. If a federal rule arises under the Enabling Act, is on point, and is constitutional, it is binding.

A Rule may only be invalidated if the advisory committee, Supreme Court or Congress erred in promulgating it. No Federal Rule has been found invalid under the Act.

If a Rule is on point and conflicts with state law, the Rule supersedes.

Application of federal rules

Hanna does not overrule *Byrd* since references to *Erie* are only *dicta.*

Pure *Erie* cases (arising under the Rules of Decision Act) require the application of the outcome determinative or balancing test considering the rationale behind the *Erie* doctrine:

forum shopping, and

inequitable application of the law.

Privileges – under Rule 501, state-created privileges are substantive and outcome-determinative, there is no federal interest, and state policy should not be thwarted by diversity.

Walker v. Armco Steel (1980) – Rule 3, which provides that the filing of the complaint commences a civil action, does not affect the tolling of the statute of limitations.

The purpose of Rule 3 is to offer time parameters for federal procedural requirements (e.g., filing an answer); thus, there is no conflict between Rule 3 and the state statute of limitations.

Cases may turn on a narrow interpretation of the Rule. If a Rule is interpreted more broadly, it supplants state law.

Federal questions concerning state law

Congress may specify the Rule of Decision to be applied, superseding contrary state rules.

Federal courts have developed a specialized common law to decide cases where:

the subject matter must be governed by federal law,

there are no congressional enactments,

the issue is within federal law-making competence and not addressed by Congress,

there are vital federal interests and the necessity of a uniform national standard (federal interests may be inferred from related statutes).

If federal common law applies, there is no *Erie* problem because of the Supremacy Clause.

If Congress subsequently addresses the issue, the statute supersedes the earlier federal common-law rule.

A case based on federal common law is a "federal question," and a state court hearing a claim must apply the federal rule.

Similarly, a federal court sitting in diversity must apply the federal common law.

This rule applies to claims where the underlying basis of the action lies within the federal common law's scope. For example, a lawyer sues a defendant for inducing their client to fire them in a maritime case. This tort action is subject to federal common law since there is a need for uniformity in maritime affairs.

Federal law governs questions involving the rights of the U.S. arising under nationwide federal programs.

The rights and duties of the U.S. on commercial paper are included. State law governs disputes between private parties regarding commercial paper (e.g., conversion of U.S. bonds).

State law may be incorporated if there is little need for a special federal rule for uniformity. This is especially applicable in commercial transactions since states have adopted the UCC, and parties enter such transactions relying on state law.

International conflicts and foreign affairs

Foreign relations are within the authority of the executive branch of the federal government, and judicial interference is likely to frustrate national goals.

Act of state doctrine precludes the courts from questioning the validity of the actions of a foreign sovereign effective within its territory.

Foreign affairs are governed by federal law only (even if a state has enacted the doctrine in terms identical to federal decisions).

The doctrine has its underpinnings in comity and the constitutional separation of powers.

The doctrine only applies where the court would have to determine the validity of foreign government actions (mere embarrassment of the foreign government is insufficient).

District courts typically define the question as jurisdictional or as a choice-of-law problem.

Actions of foreign governments fall within the doctrine if:

taking of property (could be other action),

occurs within the sovereign's territory,

sovereignty is recognized at the time of the suit,

there is no treaty or additional unambiguous agreement on the subject.

A state cannot condition conveyance of real property to citizens of a foreign country upon a reciprocal right to American citizens since such a law intrudes upon foreign affairs.

A state law that is neutral on its face may result in a different outcome.

State action in the field may infringe on federal authority, or it may be meaningless since it has no effect.

State statutes prohibiting state pension fund investment in companies doing business in certain countries may prevail since the state is a market participant. However, some lower court have struck down such a statute.

Any party may invoke the act of state doctrine, but only a foreign sovereign can raise the defense of sovereign immunity (governed by statute).

For insurance policies, courts perform interest analysis (e.g., the grouping of contacts) to determine which law applies (basically a private matter). Courts generally apply the law of the insured risk to genuine conflicts.

Monetary conversion is determined as of the judgment date (e.g., NY rule).

Avoidance of doctrine – characterization of the action or nature of the law involved.

Cases with international scope apply the same choice-of-law rules as in interstate settings.

Foreign sovereign compulsion does not create a conflict of law issue; instead, it is a defense.

Legislative jurisdiction (jurisdiction to prescribe) is a consideration in international cases.

Treaties with foreign nations supersede local laws.

Recurring Problems of Conflict of Laws

Federalism for choice of laws

Erie doctrine: no federal common law (not bound by statute) in diversity cases, apply the substantive law (statutes and precedent) of the state where a court sits.

Erie doctrine does not apply in federal questions, except as governed by statutes or the Constitution.

There is no federal general common law; case law (judge-made law) delegates lawmaking authority to judges.

Federal common law exists by judges filling in the gaps (e.g., the Sherman Antitrust Act, Alien Tort Claims Act).

Implications on the choice of laws:

> *Klaxon* (1941) – federal court sitting in diversity does have to apply the choice-of-law regime of the state where they are sitting;
>
> *Swift v. Tyson* (1842) – common law contract case;
>
> Rules of Decision Act (1948) – a federal court applies the law of the state where no federal law exists (does not apply to judge-made law);
>
> Federal courts sitting in diversity need not apply the state's unwritten law, can develop common law interpretation.

Disadvantages

Forum shopping – discriminates against residents by non-residents.

No uniformity in common law – failed to create a center of gravity in federal common law.

There are differences in law, even within the same state.

Neither Congress nor federal courts have the power to declare the law for the states.

General lawmaking authority rests with the states unless there is an express grant of federal legislative authority.

Federal courts have no inherent lawmaking power unless authorized by Congress or courts.

The diversity clause does not empower Congress to make substantive law or delegate power to federal courts.

Guaranty Trust v. York (1945): York sued Guaranty Trust for self-interest. The statute of limitations barred the suit, but the federal court allowed suit; the Supreme Court reversed.

In equity, a federal court must use the statute of limitations of the state where it sits.

Outcome determinative test – if the result would change, use federal law; *Erie* uses state law.

A federal court in diversity is only another court of the state, but this was unworkable as a federal court would need to incorporate two sets of laws: one for federal and another for diversity.

Federal common law governs the claim preclusive effect of dismissal by a federal court sitting in diversity; no uniform federal rule.

The court must adopt a law that would be applied by state courts in the state in which the federal court sits.

Klaxon v. Senator Electrical (1941): NY substantive law (1st Restatement) was reversed by the Supreme Court.

Federal district court sitting in diversity must apply the law of the state where it sits and treat state choice-of-law questions like state substantive law questions.

Uniform administrability of the laws – there is no federal choice-of-law regime:

> prevents forum shopping- but federal courts in different states are not uniform, encouraging the plaintiff to bring suit in certain places,
>
> avoids renvoi (when a court is faced with a conflict of law and must consider the law of another state),
>
> disinterested forum – not overly bound by parochial rules.

Van Dusen v. Barrack (1964) – problems with *Klaxon*: defendant seeks to transfer to another court, and the transferee court must apply the state law that would have been applied if there is no change of venue.

The same rule applies if the plaintiff transfers the case (*Ferens v. John Deere*).

An act of Congress or the Supremacy Clause of the Constitution mandates enforcing U.S. law.

Testa v. Katt (1947): the Emergency Price Control Act – a buyer of goods may sue the seller in any court for not more than three times the overcharge and attorney's fees. The Rhode Island state court only awarded compensatory damages for the overcharge because the statute was penal and public policy exception not to enforce criminal statutes of foreign jurisdictions. The Supreme Court held that a state court must enforce a federal Act (supremacy) even if the state has a policy against enforcement.

A federal Act supersedes a countervailing policy of a state.

The U.S. does not bear the same relation to states as foreign jurisdictions.

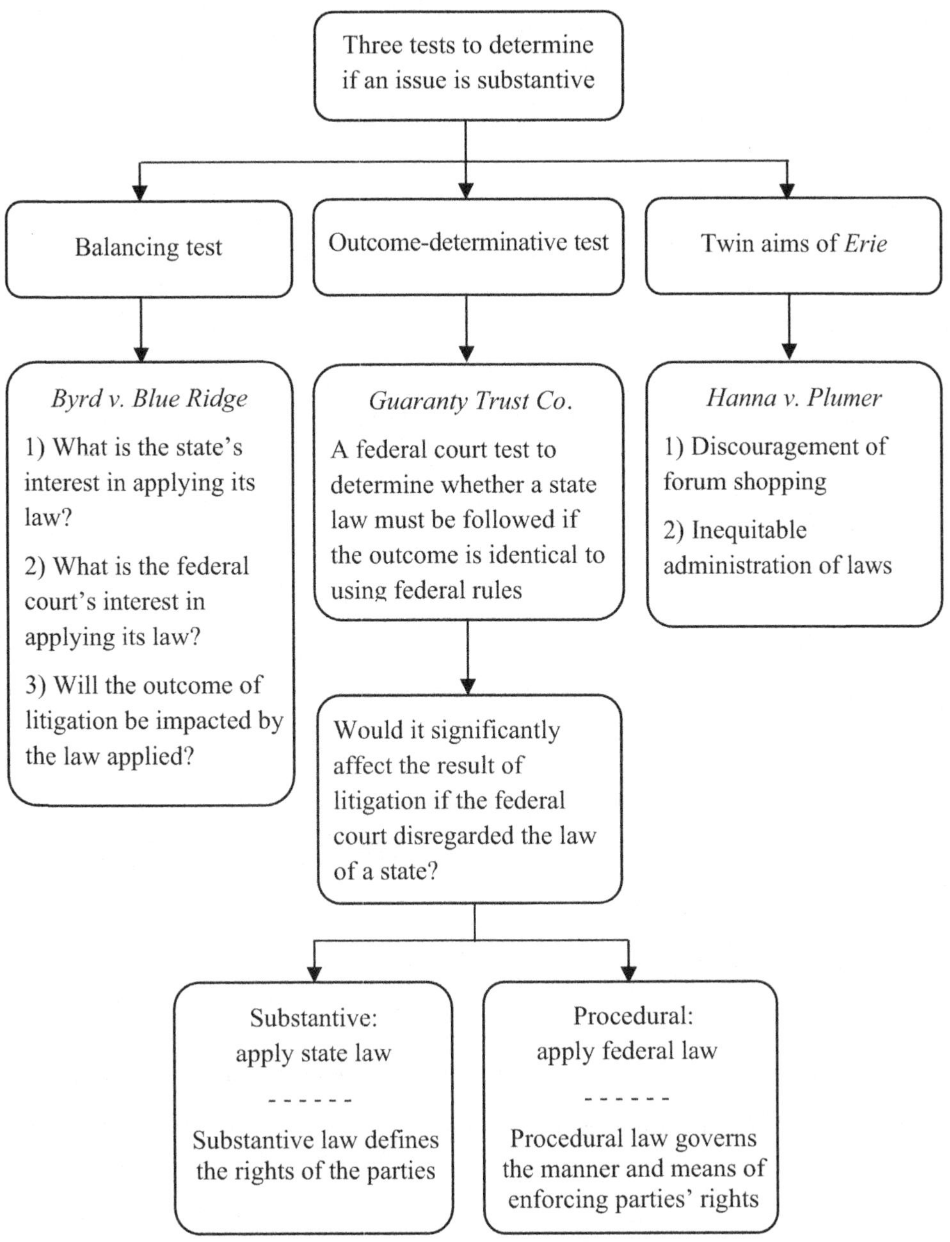

International conflicts

Full faith and credit does not apply between a foreign country and a U.S. state.

Limits of legislative jurisdiction in international law: jurisdiction to proscribe legislative jurisdiction recognizes states' authority to make substantive laws applicable to conduct relationships or status.

Territorial bases for jurisdiction over extraterritorial crimes under international law:

Territoriality – where the offense was committed,

Subjective – conduct occurs in the territory,

Objective – effects felt within a territory.

Protective jurisdiction is based on injury to the national interest. It has a narrow construction whereby the offenses are against the Secretary of State, the integrity of governmental functions (e.g., counterfeiting, espionage, passport fraud).

Universal jurisdiction is when the physical custody of the defendant that committed offenses impacts the entire world (e.g., privacy, state trade, hijacking, war crimes).

No jurisdiction if the exercise of authority is unreasonable.

Methods to define unreasonableness:

link of activity of the territory to the regulatory state,

connection.

The character of action to be regulated is important to the regulatory state:

justified expectation,

importance of regulations to the international political, economic, and legal system,

consistency of regulation with traditions of the international legal system,

when another state has intent in the regulatory Act,

likelihood of conflict with another state's regulation.

Comity (i.e., mutual recognition) reduces international friction.

Court must use legislative history, extra-statutory materials, canons of statutory construction.

Foley Brothers (1949) presumption – legislation of Congress, unless a contrary intent appears, is only meant to apply within the territorial jurisdiction of the U.S. and must be clearly stated:

congressional intent, and

reasonableness (comity) analysis.

Courts refrain from judging acts of a foreign government within their territory.

Territoriality – extraterritorial effects to a foreign state action.

Clear law – if clear local law prohibits the act, the doctrine does not apply. Not solely limited to government parties.

Abstention – a negative doctrine whereby courts do not adjudicate, but presume, the validity of foreign acts.

Full Faith and Credit for Foreign Judgments

Foreign judgments

Jurisdiction requirement: subject matter jurisdiction over the case and personal jurisdiction over the defendant or at least,

full and fair opportunity to challenge jurisdiction,

on the merits,

final adjudication.

Requirements of the judgment:

judgment must meet full faith and credit requirements, and

no valid defenses apply.

Equitable decrees and obligation to enforce sister state judgments

The settlement is within the meaning of the full faith and credit clause because of the court's significant involvement in implementing the judgment.

Congress shall have the power to approve and effect full faith and credit (i.e., judgments from the courts of sister states).

U.S. Constitution Article IV § 1 – full faith and credit shall be given in each state to the public acts, records, and judicial proceedings of every other state.

28 U.S.C. § 1738 – requires federal courts give full faith and credit to state court judgments.

The Supreme Court has consistently required state courts to grant full faith and credit to federal court judgments.

The doctrine promotes judicial efficiency and justice.

Enforcing a claim in a foreign jurisdiction required a final judgment in the original state and an action to enforce it in another.

A final judgment (*res judicata*) in the original state is entitled to full faith and credit (*preclusion*) in the subsequent state:

the original judgment must be valid (due process / personal jurisdiction),

the original judgment must be final (e.g., adjustments of alimony are not final).

Some states permit modifications of foreign alimony judgments by statute (or judicial creation) for public policy to prevent a defendant from eluding a support obligation so the state will not have to care for the aggrieved party.

If a judgment is modifiable (e.g., future alimony or child support), it is not a final judgment but will usually be enforced under principles of comity.

Judgments for amounts already accrued and in arrears are considered final judgments.

The original judgment must have been decided on the merits (i.e., judgment involves the substance of the plaintiff's claim). Default and consent judgments are on the merits.

Dismissal for lack of jurisdiction (e.g., improper venue, *forum non conveniens*) is not on the merits.

Majority view: dismissals based upon laches and running of the statutes of limitations are not on the merits.

In federal court, a judgment can be registered in any district, making it enforceable and alleviating the need for a separate suit.

Most states have adopted similar provisions.

Full faith and credit must be given to wrongly decided cases since the proper remedy is appeal through the state's appellate process culminating with a *writ of certiorari* to the Supreme Court.

Full faith and credit to judicial proceedings of other nations

The recognizing state determines whether the foreign nation court had jurisdiction and used fair procedures.

Federal common law considerations favor enforcing a foreign nation's judgment (*Hilton v. Guyot*) when the:

plaintiff and defendant are citizens of the foreign state,

defendant is a citizen of the foreign state,

plaintiff is a citizen of the foreign state, and judgment is for the defendant.

Reciprocity

Federal courts should recognize and enforce a foreign country's judgments if that country subjects an American judgment to similar treatment (*Hilton*).

Most states recognize foreign country judgments subject to the usual defenses and reject reciprocity (doctrine explicitly rejected by NY).

To avoid the majority rule, bring an action in a state that requires reciprocity and bring an enforcement action under full faith and credit.

Reciprocity is part of the federal common law and does not apply in diversity cases since the court was not deciding a federal question.

Reciprocity can be confined to a narrow holding – only when a foreign national prevails in a suit against a U.S. citizen.

Comity is the recognition one nation allows to the legislative, executive, or judicial acts of another government based upon mutual respect and cooperation among sovereign nations.

Limitations on full faith and credit

Full faith and credit does not apply to foreign nation judgments.

2nd Restatement of Conflicts § 103 Limitations on Full Faith and Credit: the court must have jurisdiction; otherwise, the judgment is not entitled to full faith and credit.

Full faith and credit does not oblige states to enforce (as opposed to recognizing) the judgments of sister states in the manner specified by that sister state's law.

Equitable judgment enforcement: full faith and credit does not mean the states must adopt the practices of other states regarding the time, manner, and mechanisms for enforcing judgments.

The enforcement measures do not travel with the sister state judgment as preclusive effects do; such measures remain subject to forum law control.

Exclusive jurisdiction over a federal cause of action granted by statute may partially repeal full faith and credit under 28 U.S.C. § 1738 (federal court recognition of a state court judgment).

A problem arises when a plaintiff brings a state cause of action in state court but cannot also assert their federal cause of action since Congress has granted the federal courts exclusive jurisdiction (e.g., antitrust, patent cases).

An award in one state should be entitled to full faith and credit, barring a second recovery in a sister state.

States need not respect a judgment affecting title to land located in their state when another state renders judgment.

A divorce decree issued in the original state that vests title to property located in a different state does not have to be recognized in that state for a quiet title action.

If a spouse brought an action to enforce the original judgment in another state, the outcome would likely be different since there is no reason not to enforce an equity decree.

Baker v. General Motors (US 1998) – exceptions to full faith and credit:

> an original judgment that purports to accomplish an official act within the exclusive province of another state (e.g., deeding of land),
>
> injunctions interfering with litigation over which the ordering state has no authority,
>
> if the plaintiff is held in contempt of the subsequent court (highly criticized opinion).

Limitations imposed by the state of the transaction

States determine the competency of their courts and are not bound by limitations on jurisdiction imposed by the law of a sister state.

State statutes that localize a transitory cause of action and grant exclusive jurisdiction to its local courts do not prohibit a sister state court from asserting jurisdiction.

The judgment from the sister state is entitled to full faith and credit, unless:

> anti-suit injunctions are based upon such a statute,
>
> a forum is not compelled to accept the jurisdiction of a cause of action created under a sister state's laws.

State administrative agency determinations that have not been judicially reviewed are not given issue preclusion effect.

Recognition of Foreign Judgments

Claim preclusion

Res judicata (claim preclusion) prohibits a second suit on a claim or cause of action, which was asserted in prior litigation and resulted in a valid, final judgment on the merits.

Claim preclusion prevents a party from relitigating an entire suit when:

1) final judgment on the first suit is entered,
2) the same cause of action as the first suit,
3) same subject matter and ultimate issue,
4) the second suit seeks relief for the same harm,
5) same parties or their privies,
6) successors in interest or holders of future interests, or
7) beneficiaries of actual parties.

Persons bound by *res judicata* are parties to the action and those in privity with them.

Privity by a person so closely related to a party that it is fair to bind them to the litigation (e.g., trustee and beneficiary of a trust, successive property owners regarding an easement).

Issue preclusion

Collateral estoppel (issue preclusion) prohibits relitigating issues decided in a prior proceeding regardless of whether the second proceeding is based upon the same cause of action.

In a second suit on a different cause of action, issues litigated and decided are precluded from relitigating if:

1) the issue was litigated in the first proceeding,
2) the issue was necessary to support the judgment of the first proceeding,
3) the party against whom collateral estoppel is asserted was a prior party or privy in the first proceeding,
4) the party had a full and fair opportunity to litigate the issue in the prior proceeding.

Federal law controls the preclusive effects of federal court judgments regardless of whether the court was exercising federal question or diversity jurisdiction (majority view).

If a defendant makes a limited appearance for an *in rem* or *quasi in rem* proceeding (e.g., foreclosed mortgage) in court and the parties litigate the merits, that court's findings on issues litigated preclude subsequent relitigating of those issues in a different court even though the first court lacked personal jurisdiction over the defendant.

If a defendant appears specially, and the court determines that it has personal jurisdiction, the defendant cannot claim a lack of jurisdiction to prevent full faith and credit in another court.

Similarly, subject matter jurisdiction issues are precluded if fully and fairly litigated.

Mutuality of estoppel

Claim and issue preclusion will not be applied to the detriment of strangers to the litigation since they were not provided notice and given the opportunity to be heard.

If a court with property-based jurisdiction exceeds its limited powers and purports to issue a personal judgment against a defendant, that judgment is not entitled to full faith and credit.

Unless it has personal jurisdiction over a debtor, the court cannot issue a deficiency judgment

A court with *in rem* jurisdiction is limited to issuing preclusive judgments regarding the *res* (i.e., item of real or personal property) only.

Class suits: a judgment is binding on members of the class whenever they may later bring suit on the same cause of action, if:

1) absent members of the class were adequately represented in the litigation, and
2) a reasonable number of the class were given adequate notice of the suit and had an opportunity to be heard.

Defenses to Recognition or Enforcement

Defenses against application of foreign law

Comity of nations – a court gives deference (not an obligation) to a foreign decision.

Requirements to recognize judgment – preconditions to acceptance of comity:

1) full and fair trial,
2) court of competent jurisdiction,
3) a trial conducted through regular proceedings,
4) adequate notice to defendant (English),
5) impartial justice between citizens and aliens.

There is no prejudice in a court of laws against foreign judgments; the difference between the foreign and U.S. systems is due process violation but will not block enforcement. This is a less demanding standard than an international measure of due process.

There must be no fraud in procuring the judgment and no reason for denying comity.

§ 4 Uniform Foreign Money Judgment Recognition Acts

Section 4 foreign judgments are entitled to full faith and credit if requirements are met.

The judgment must not be rendered under a system that did not provide impartial tribunals or procedures compatible with due process requirements.

Mandatory defenses – judgment will not be enforced when:

1) no personal jurisdiction over the defendant,
2) no subject matter jurisdiction.

Discretionary defenses – judgment may not be enforced when:

1) no notice within sufficient time,
2) judgment obtained by fraud,
3) violation of public policy,
4) the judgment conflicts with another final and conclusive judgment,
5) violation of an agreement between the parties,
6) inconvenient forum.

Notes for active learning

Nature of Original Proceedings

Foreign country judgments

Jurisdiction must have been proper, and fair procedures must have been used in the foreign country proceeding.

Apply the recognizing state's law – the state's idea of due process (e.g., minimum contacts, fair play, and substantial justice).

Defenses against a foreign nation judgment emanate from public policy, which is broader application than in domestic matters and international law that an American court cannot recognize (e.g., slavery).

State law determines the effect of foreign nation judgments on American courts.

Lack of personal or subject matter jurisdiction makes a judgment void and not entitled to full faith and credit. Challenges to jurisdictional determinations are made in the rendering state's appellate process and eventually by *writ* to the Supreme Court.

By bringing an action in a court, the plaintiff is submitting to the court's jurisdiction. Therefore, the judgment will have a preclusive effect against the plaintiff in an action in another court.

A mere recital of jurisdiction is conclusory and insufficient. The recital of jurisdictional facts upon which jurisdiction was based is not enough to preclude the issue.

Inconsistent judgments – full faith and credit must be accorded to a court judgment even if that judgment fails to give full faith and credit to a prior court judgment. This creates a last-in-time rule for the applicability of judgments.

When the third forum is also the first, the Supreme Court requires recognition of the second forum's judgment.

Lack of finality (common in domestic relations cases) – not entitled to full faith and credit.

Final judgments such as for payment of past alimony must be given effect in another court.

Accrued alimony is not yet reduced to a judgment if:

> the original court modifies alimony awards prospectively; accrued alimony is not modifiable and subject to enforcement in the subsequent court,
>
> the original court retrospectively modifies alimony.

Modifiable judgments are not final, but subsequent courts exercise discretion enforcing them.

The plaintiff is not disadvantaged if they are accorded due process.

Modifiable judgments eliminate the undue burden on the plaintiff of having to return to the original court to obtain a final judgment.

Extrinsic fraud could not have been addressed within the earlier trial (e.g., bribing a judge).

With extrinsic fraud, the defendant was deprived of the opportunity to litigate, and the subsequent court does not have to grant full faith and credit to a judgment obtained by fraud.

Intrinsic fraud (e.g., perjury of a witness) could have been addressed during litigation and is not a good defense to full faith and credit.

With intrinsic fraud, a collateral attack is not available regarding fraud that the resisting party had an opportunity to litigate in the original court.

If the original court's law allows a collateral attack, the subsequent court may address the issue by applying its procedural rules.

Full faith and credit may be denied for a judgment based on a cause of action that violates the forum's public policy.

For mistakes by the judge in the earlier trial, the proper remedy is an appeal.

Later judgment can be enforced even though it is inconsistent with a valid earlier one. The rule is to enforce the last judgment.

Defenses – nature of the original cause of action

Penal judgments are not entitled to full faith and credit and are narrowly defined:

the purpose is to punish rather than compensate, and

recovery is in favor of the state.

Penal damages do not include:

punitive damages if recovery favors an individual,

wrongful death awards even where the defendant's fault is the measure of recovery.

Judgments not entitled to full faith and credit:

a tort judgment in favor of a state's proprietary interests,

a tax judgment since the purpose is the generation of revenue.

Judgments based upon mistake of fact or law are nonetheless entitled to full faith and credit.

The subsequent court must recognize the other court's judgment even if the original court erroneously interpreted the subsequent court's law, and it has an interest in the activity (*Fauntleroy v. Lum* 1908 – judgment enforced a "futures" trading agreement illegal in the forum).

The forum can apply its statute of limitations barring action from enforcing a judgment even though shorter than the original court's statute of limitations. This is an exception to the rule applying at least as much credit to a judgment as the original forum.

The statute of limitations on enforcing foreign judgments can be shorter than the statute of limitations for domestic judgments if an action in the foreign state can revive the foreign judgment. The time limit begins on the date of the last foreign transaction.

A state cannot refuse to enforce a sister state judgment on the ground that the original action could not have been brought in the state in which enforcement is sought (e.g., lacked subject matter jurisdiction over the original cause of action).

The subsequent court is merely enforcing a judgment, and it is irrelevant that the claim could not have been brought there.

Notes for active learning

Family Law Judgments

Types of divorce

Ex parte divorce – only one of the spouses is validly domiciled, where the divorce is granted. The decree does not govern collateral matters (e.g., property, alimony, support, custody).

Bi-lateral divorce – one of the spouses is validly domiciled, where the divorce is granted, and each is subject to personal jurisdiction there.

Consent divorce – parties want out of the marriage and go somewhere to get divorced ("quickie divorce"). This divorce is not valid if neither spouse is domiciled in the jurisdiction that granted it.

Family law judgments

Termination of marital status (divorce decree) must have proper subject matter jurisdiction.

One spouse must be domiciled in the state rendering the divorce.

Divorce judgments: decree is valid as to the divorce.

The general rule is to give full faith and credit if:

proper jurisdiction,

a decree is valid in the sister state,

decree valid as to the divorce.

Jurisdiction is proper if at least one party is domiciled in the rendering state.

Procedural matters on divorce

The plaintiff bears the burden of proof.

Parties may introduce relevant evidence even if the evidence came into existence after the divorce was granted.

Any interested person who is not estopped can attack the divorce decree for lack of subject matter jurisdiction.

Estoppel for divorce

Estoppel applies to the challenger subject to personal jurisdiction in the earlier proceeding (spouse in a bi-lateral divorce cannot challenge divorce).

> The challenger played a meaningful role in the granting of the divorce, even without personal jurisdiction.
>
> The spouse remarried in reliance on the earlier divorce.
>
> Persons in privity with a party to the divorce include children.

Property awards (e.g., alimony, child support) must have personal jurisdiction over a spouse whose property rights are in issue.

Valid jurisdiction for determining child custody lies only in the child's home state.

Divisible divorce doctrine

Divisible divorce – the marriage is dissolved, but the incident issues (e.g., alimony, child custody, visitation) are reserved until a later proceeding.

This type of divorce is granted when the court has subject matter jurisdiction but lacks personal jurisdiction over the defendant (only one party domiciled in the state).

If the decree has some valid parts and others not, the valid parts hold, and remainder disregarded.

Relationship matrix

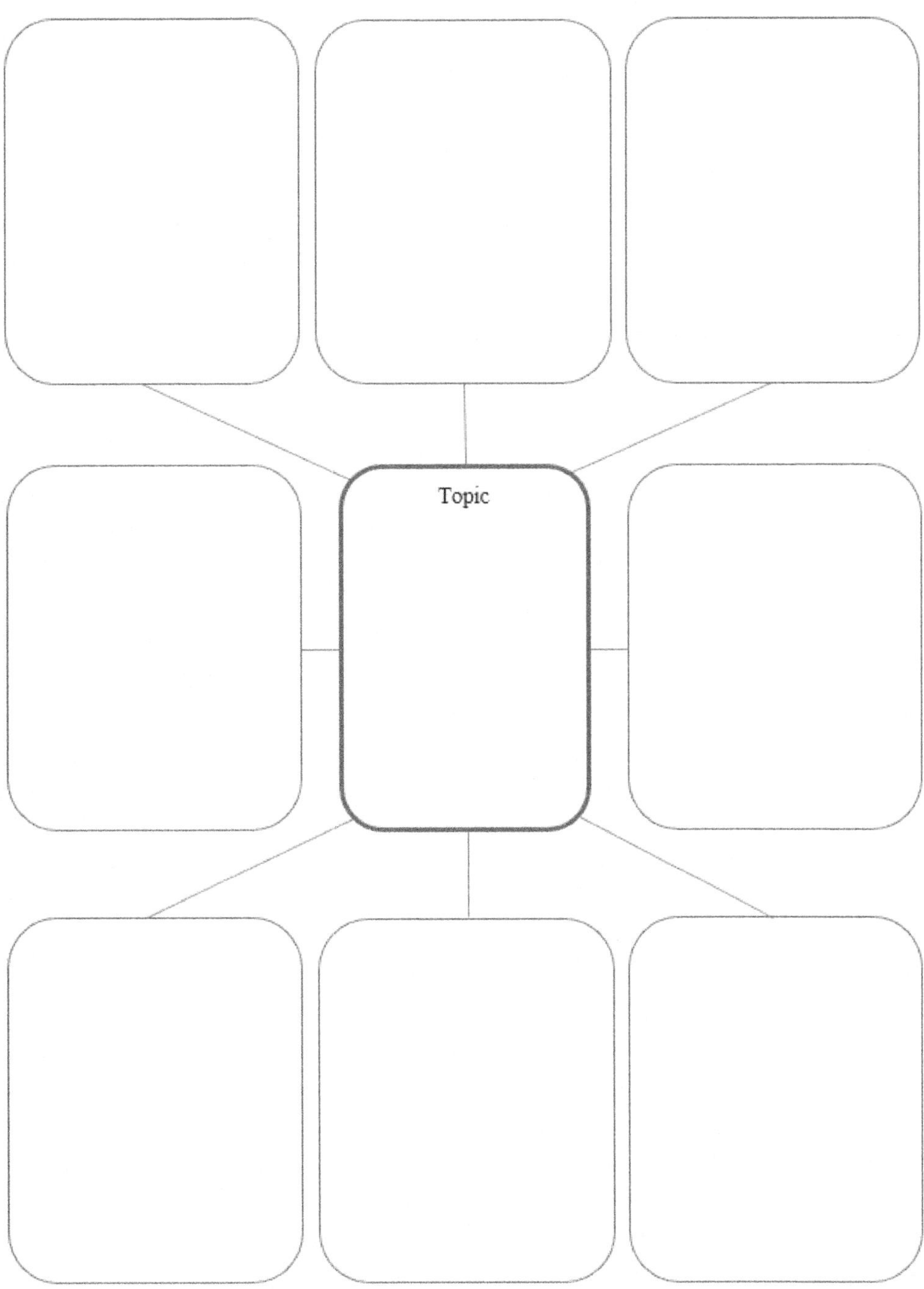

Notes for active learning

Family Law

Family Law is generally tested alone, though occasionally it encompasses conflict of laws. Several Family Law issues are tested frequently. Therefore, maximize your score by focusing on highly tested items such as child custody and support, alimony, and property division. Less frequently tested topics include marriage requirements, cohabitation, fault-based divorce, marital rape, tort immunity, privacy, and reproductive technology issues.

The Uniform Interstate Family Support Act (UIFSA) and the Uniform Child Custody Jurisdiction and Enforcement Act (UCCJEA) generally set the governing law on child support and child custody issues.

Getting Married

Contract to marry

There is no right to sue for breach of a contract to marry.

There is no right to sue in tort for deceit connected with breach of such a contract.

Antenuptial (prenuptial) agreement validity is frequently tested in domestic relations.

The validity of the antenuptial agreement is tested at the time it is executed.

The following must be satisfied before an antenuptial agreement is deemed valid.

1. The agreement must be in writing.
2. There must be full and fair disclosure of the financial status of each party.
3. Independent counsel should represent each party.
4. The agreement must comport with the requirements for the validity of contracts (e.g., consideration and absence of fraud, misrepresentation, or duress).
5. The agreement must contain a fair and reasonable provision as measured at the time of the execution for the party contesting the agreement.

There is no requirement that the antenuptial agreement approximates what a party might receive upon dissolution of a marriage if there were no agreement.

Validity of agreement at the time of divorce

The antenuptial agreement is tested at the time of the divorce to ensure that the agreement has the same vitality that the parties intended at the time of execution.

The term unconscionable is a more appropriate term than *fair and reasonable* to describe the standard at the time of the enforceability of the antenuptial agreement.

Again, the agreement is not tested against the amount awarded by the court in the absence of an agreement.

The agreement will not be unenforceable under this test unless, due to circumstances occurring during the marriage, enforcement of the agreement would leave the contesting spouse without sufficient property, maintenance, or appropriate employment for support.

Marriage ceremony necessary

Marriage requires a ceremony performed by a person authorized to conduct marriage ceremonies as a condition precedent to a valid marriage in the jurisdiction.

Irregularity in the procedure to obtain the license or lack of capacity in the person officiating will not invalidate the marriage if it is consummated with the party's full belief that there has been a valid marriage.

Common law marriages are invalid unless the state recognizes them under a conflict of law principles because they were validly contracted in a state which recognizes common-law marriages.

Age as an impediment to a valid marriage

A person authorized to solemnize marriages is not authorized to marry an individual under age 18 unless the marriage is authorized by a court order obtained after parental consent.

Parental consent can be dispensed with if the parent is absent or unfit.

If a person has entered a marriage pursuant to a marriage ceremony while under age 18, the marriage is valid if the parties continue to live as spouses after the party reaches 18.

Incestuous marriages

Consanguinity invalidates marriages between grandparent and grandchild, brother and sister, parent and child, uncle and niece, or aunt and nephew.

Affinity invalidates marriages between in-laws and step-relations within similar relationships.

First cousins are not prohibited from marrying.

Same-sex marriages

The Supreme Court held that statutes that limit marriage to a man and a woman are unconstitutional under the constitution's equal protection clause because there is no rational basis to limit a person's ability to marry only a person of the opposite sex.

There is a high likelihood that there will be questions on this issue.

Determine that the same-sex couple has complied with the legal procedures to be married.

Same-sex couples have the same rules concerning the ability to hold property as tenants by the entirety. The rules on the right of a spouse to inherit and other marriage and divorce incidents apply to legally married same-sex couples.

Lack of mental capacity

Marriage is not valid unless each party has the mental capacity to enter the relationship.

Each party must understand the nature of marrying and the duties imposed on individuals in the state of marriage.

A person under conservatorship, which would preclude their capacity to enter a contract, may nevertheless have the capacity to marry.

Prior marriage still in force

The termination of a prior valid marriage by annulment, death, or a valid divorce is required before a party can enter a new marriage.

Nevertheless, a marriage that is void because a prior marriage is still in force will be valid after the prior marriage is dissolved if:

> one of the parties to the subsequent marriage acted in good faith at the time of the ceremony,
>
> the parties continue to live together after the impediment is removed, and
>
> one of the spouses believes in good faith that they are validly married after removing the impediment.

Marriages contracted outside of the state

A marriage contracted outside of the state will be recognized as valid unless a resident marries in a foreign jurisdiction to avoid state marriage laws or unless the marriage would be against public policy (e.g., incestuous marriage).

An out-of-state or foreign marriage that fails to comply with the requirements for marriage in that jurisdiction but satisfies the requirements for a valid marriage where the parties live as spouses will be recognized as valid in the resident state.

Marriages by out-of-state residents

The statute provides that a party residing and intending to continue to reside in another state cannot contract a valid marriage in the state if the marriage would be invalid in such a state.

Notes for active learning

Separation and Divorce

Divorce – subject matter jurisdiction and venue

For a state to have jurisdiction to grant a divorce, one spouse must be domiciled there.

If the spouse who is currently domiciled in the state never lived with the other spouse in the state, the cause of action for divorce did not occur in the state, and the defendant spouse does not live in the state, the spouse domiciled in the state must be a resident for a prescribed period (e.g., at least a year) before the state has jurisdiction.

If the jurisdictional requirements are satisfied, the divorce defendant need not have contact with the state for the court to have jurisdiction to dissolve the marriage.

If these conditions are not satisfied and the state does not have jurisdiction, any decree of divorce issued by the state may be collaterally attacked by parties other than the spouses.

The venue for a divorce action is the probate and family court in the county of either party.

If either party still lives in the county where the parties last lived together as spouses, that county is the sole venue for the divorce action.

Personal jurisdiction; service of process

A court order affecting the property of a divorce defendant by alimony, child support, or division of property is not binding unless the state has personal jurisdiction over that defendant.

Jurisdiction is typically obtained when the defendant is served with process in the state or is domiciled in the state.

Bases of long-arm jurisdiction

If personal service or domicile is not available, the state has two provisions of the long-arm statute, which establishes personal jurisdiction over an out-of-state divorce defendant:

1) Living as one of the parties to a marriage (or former marriage) with the marital domicile of both parties within the state for at least one of the two years immediately preceding commencement, notwithstanding the subsequent departure of the defendant from the state.

2) Having previously been subject to the exercise of personal jurisdiction in the state, which resulted in a child support order, when the plaintiff and child continue to reside in the state, and the plaintiff seeks to enforce or modify the order.

Service of a divorce complaint may be made by procedures prescribed in the state's long-arm statute if the defendant is not a resident.

Service may be made by publication where the defendant's location is unknown.

Service by publication gives only *in rem* jurisdiction over the marriage and does not permit the entry of support orders against the defendant or marital property division.

Grounds for divorce

There are eight grounds for divorce: one no-fault ground and several based upon cause.

Most divorces are filed as no-fault divorces so that the technical issues relating to fault grounds for divorce rarely appear in questions and, therefore, will only be mentioned briefly.

Divorce *nisi* is a divorce judgment that becomes effective on a specified date unless during that period cause is shown for why the decree should not go into effect.

No-fault

The basis of no-fault divorce is the irretrievable breakdown of the marriage.

How an action for divorce based on the irretrievable breakdown of the marriage will proceed depends upon whether the parties have reached an agreement on such issues as custody, child support, alimony, and property division.

No-fault with an agreement

If the parties file a notarized separation agreement, the judge holds a hearing to determine if an irretrievable breakdown exists and if the agreement is fair and proper.

If the judge makes the required findings, a decree of divorce *nisi* is entered shortly (e.g., 30, 60 days after the hearing) and becomes final after the waiting period (e.g., 60, 90 days).

Thus, after the decree vests, each may remarry.

No-fault without an agreement

If the parties fail to file an agreement, the case is tried.

The judge must find an irretrievable breakdown of the marriage and determine alimony, disposition of the marital property, custody, and visitation at a trial

The trial cannot occur until a set time (30, 60, 0 days) after the complaint is filed, and a decree of divorce *nisi* will not occur until the judge enters the order.

After a statutory time, a decree *nisi* becomes a final decree of divorce.

Fault grounds for divorce

Depending on the jurisdiction, the fault grounds for divorce include adultery, impotence, desertion for at least one year preceding the filing of the complaint, gross and confirmed intoxication by use of liquor or drugs, nonsupport, sentence to confinement in a penal institution for five or more years, and cruel and abusive treatment.

When fault grounds are the basis for divorce, the most used is cruel and abusive treatment, which is the deliberate activity of one spouse, maliciously intended to harm the other spouse's health, which does harm the other spouse.

Affirmative defenses are available if the plaintiff files a complaint based upon fault:

1. Condonation – the plaintiff has forgiven the offense, and the couple has resumed marital relations;

2. Insanity;

3 Connivance – the plaintiff facilitated the breach by the defendant.

Temporary orders

While a divorce complaint is pending, the court can make temporary orders for custody, support, and marital domicile possession.

The court may require a spouse to vacate the marital home for a period.

Final decree – when effective

A divorce is not effective until there is a final decree.

The only decree that a probate judge can enter is a decree *nisi*.

The decree *nisi* ripens into a final decree after a statutory period.

During that statutory period, the parties remain married.

If one party dies during that period, the other has the right of a surviving spouse.

Final decree – either party may remarry

When the decree becomes final, either party may remarry.

Final decree – effect on wills

A divorce or annulment revokes provisions in a will for the former spouse, and the property passes as if the former spouse had predeceased the testator.

A divorce or annulment revokes the designation of the former spouse in a fiduciary capacity under the will.

If the testator remarries their former spouse, the will provisions are revived.

A legal separation does not terminate their marital status and does not revoke will provisions.

The Divorce Judgment

Independent separation and support agreements

Most divorce cases are settled, and the parties enter into a separation agreement that covers property division, alimony, custody visitation, and child support.

If the parties choose the separation agreement can survive the divorce decree as a contract between the parties

The property division and alimony provisions are enforceable as a contract, not subject to modification because of changed circumstances, and cannot be enforced by contempt.

However, those provisions in the separation agreement dealing with child support, visitation, and custody can be modified by the court in the future because of changed circumstances, and the parties cannot prevent such modification by contract.

A court can order additional alimony for a former spouse to prevent them from becoming a liability for government programs.

Divorce terms merged into the divorce decree

If there is no agreement, the judge decides the issues, or the parties agree that the agreement shall be merged into the court decree and have no further effect as an independent contract.

The final decree is modifiable for past due and future alimony, custody, and child support in the event of changed circumstances.

Failure to comply with the agreement shall be enforceable by contempt of court.

Agreements are presumed to survive the decree.

Division of property

In a divorce decree, a judge can divide the spouses' property or periodic alimony payments.

By statute, a spouse's estate, including property owned by that spouse before the marriage and property inherited from that spouse's family or part of a spouse's retirement plan, may be assigned to the other spouse.

A vested remainder interest in a trust is a marital interest subject to division, but a possibility of inheritance from a living person is not.

Factors affecting property division

In property division, a judge has great discretion but must consider the factors below.

If the judge refers to the appropriate criteria in their findings, they will likely be upheld on appeal.

In dividing property, the judge is required to consider the capacity of each spouse to earn a living after the divorce:

1) the length of the marriage (the longer the marriage, the more likely the assets will be split evenly),

2) conduct of the parties during the marriage (fault is a factor in a no-fault divorce),

3) age,

4) health,

5) occupation,

6) amount and sources of income,

7) vocational skills,

8) employability,

9) estate.

The less earning capacity, the more likely a spouse will be given income-producing assets.

The judge considers the current and future needs of the spouses:

1) liabilities and needs,

2) opportunities for the acquisition of future assets, and

3) present and future needs of dependent children.

The custodial parent is likely to be awarded the marital home to raise the children.

Timing of property division

An order dividing marital assets is a court's final order, which may not later be relitigated due to "changed circumstances."

A property division may be ordered after the decree becomes final if the issue was not litigated during the divorce hearing.

If one party to a marriage obtains an out-of-state divorce in which property division issues are not litigated, that party has a right to come back to the state to obtain a property division.

The assets subject to division are assets that the parties owned at the time of the divorce.

The court will consider the value of the assets subject to division at the time of the property division proceeding, not at the time of the divorce.

Enhancement in the value of those assets caused by the labor of one party after the divorce will not be subject to division.

Alimony

A court may award that one spouse pays periodic alimony to the other to support a spouse after the divorce.

The court uses the criteria outlined in determining property division to determine the amount of periodic alimony.

The award for periodic alimony is made in conjunction with the division of assets.

A dependent spouse will not need as generous an asset division if they are the beneficiary of a sizeable periodic alimony order.

If the obligation to pay periodic alimony is set forth in a separation agreement, the obligation terminates typically upon the recipient's remarriage.

Many agreements contain provisions terminating the agreement at such time as the recipient spouse is cohabiting even though the spouse has not remarried.

Unless it is specifically made to survive, a periodic alimony order terminates upon either spouse's death.

If the alimony award is in a separation agreement that is merged into the divorce decree, it is modifiable when there is a material change in the circumstances of the parties.

Enforcement of alimony

The court can require the spouse obligated for alimony to provide security for those payments.

Failure to make payments can be enforced in the probate court by a contempt decree.

Child Custody

Custody of minor children

While married, both parents of a minor child have custody unless the court finds them unfit.

If one parent dies, the surviving parent has sole custody unless found to be unfit.

The jurisdiction determines the custody arrangements for minor children if the state is the child's historic home state.

The state has jurisdiction if the child has been living in the state for more than a statutory time (e.g., six months), and one parent lives in the state, or if it does not appear that another state has jurisdiction to determine custodial arrangements.

The state has jurisdiction if it is necessary for the state court to assume jurisdiction to protect the child from abandonment, abuse, or neglect.

Separate support

Separate support is an action filed in the probate court by one spouse against the other spouse to establish judicial orders on the spouse and minor children's support, custody, and visitation without terminating the marriage.

A spouse may petition for a decree of separate support, whether the spouses are living apart.

Jurisdiction for separate support

Contact with the state is sufficient to establish jurisdiction under its long-arm statute is the jurisdiction prerequisite to filing a separate support action.

Since a separate support decree is based upon a valid marriage, that decree is an adjudication that the marriage is valid and can be used as collateral estoppel in any action challenging the marriage's validity.

Grounds and defenses

Nonsupport, desertion, or justifiable cause are grounds for separate support.

Compliance with a fair and reasonable separation agreement is a defense.

Effect of support decree

The separate support decree only makes temporary adjustments to the marital relationship in support, custody, and visitation.

It forbids a spouse from imposing restrictions on the other spouse's activity.

Unlike a divorce decree, it does not make permanent property divisions or transfer assets from one spouse to another.

However, the separate support decree can permit one spouse to exclusively occupy the property (e.g., marital home) owned by the other spouse.

A decree of separate support terminates the rights of the defendant spouse to intestacy or waiver of the will if the plaintiff spouse dies.

The prevailing spouse does not lose these rights if the losing spouse dies.

Legal custody *vs.* physical custody

If there are minor children of the marriage, the divorce agreement or decree must address custody and visitation rights.

There are two kinds of custody, legal and physical custody.

A parent having legal custody has the right to make significant decisions in a child's life (e.g., where they attend school).

In most divorce decrees, the parents share legal custody.

Physical custody deals with the parent with whom the child will live and makes the day-to-day decisions about a child's life.

Ordinarily, one parent is granted physical custody.

Right of parents to custody

Each parent has an equal right to legal and physical custody unless they are unfit.

A court decides between parents based upon the best interests of the child.

A child custody decree is always modifiable if the child's best interests change as they grow.

If the court determines that each parent is unfit to have custody, it has the discretion to award custody to third persons and apply the best-interest-of-the-child standard.

Visitation rights

When one parent is granted primary physical custody, the other parent is ordinarily granted visitation rights.

The nature and extent of those rights depend on conditions in the parents' lives (e.g., where they live while with the child, the demands on the child's time).

Grandparents' visitation rights

The probate court by statute may grant reasonable visitation rights to grandparents if it determines that such visitation is in the child's best interests.

Such visitation is not permissible if the child's parents are living and both objects.

Grandparent visitation orders are most granted when the child's parents are divorced, and the parent who is the child of the grandparents has died, leaving sole custody in the other parent.

Custodial parent establishing permanent residence out of state

The parent who has primary physical custody cannot establish a residence outside the state without the probate court's permission.

The non-custodial parent has the right to notice and to be heard on the matter.

If the custodial parent seeks to remove the child from the state to deprive the non-custodial parent of having a relationship with the child, the court will likely deny permission to leave the state.

If the custodial spouse seeks to relocate because of extended family proximity in the out-of-state location or improved job prospects, permission is likely to be granted.

Child support

Both parents must support the minor children of the marriage after a divorce.

By state statutes, generally, obligation extends until a child reaches age 21 if they live with one parent and 23 when in an educational program.

As an incident to a divorce decree or when the paternity of a child born out of wedlock has been established, the court will order the non-custodial parent to make child support payments to the custodial parent.

Most child support orders are set following formulae contained in established child support guidelines, which weigh such factors as:

1) the incomes of each parent,

2) the number of children to be supported, and

3) the other obligations of the custodial and noncustodial parents.

The parties can make child support arrangements outside of the guidelines if the court deems them reasonable.

If the court finds that one parent is deliberately earning substantially less than they reasonably could, it may base the child support order on earning potential rather than current income.

Right of father to contest paternity

During a divorce trial, a husband who does not believe that he is the father of a child born to his wife during the marriage can petition the court to order paternity tests.

If the finding at the time of the trial is conclusive that the husband is not the father, the court cannot order child support.

If a husband has paid child support and later learns that the child is not his biological child, he cannot recover the amounts paid.

Extraterritorial Recognition of Divorce Decrees and Orders

Constitutional basis for jurisdiction

Constitutional divorce jurisdiction is based upon the domicile of one of the parties.

One spouse initiates the extraterritorial divorce

If a spouse goes to a state where neither is domiciled and obtains a divorce decree, the decree is invalid because the rendering state lacked jurisdiction. The other spouse may bring a petition in the home state to have the decree declared invalid.

An out-of-state decree is presumptively valid until attacked.

If the non-contesting spouse has taken advantage of the decree, they may be estopped from attacking it.

Both spouses initiate the extraterritorial divorce

The domicile of one of the parties, an essential element of jurisdiction, was an issue that could have been litigated in the rendering state.

If the non-petitioning spouse enters an appearance in the foreign jurisdiction and does not contest its jurisdiction, they cannot collaterally attack the decree in their home state.

The doctrine of collateral estoppel prevents the issue of the jurisdiction from being relitigated.

A person who is not a party to the divorce cannot attack the validity of the foreign decree if collateral parties are not permitted to attack decrees in the rendering state.

Recognition of decrees of foreign countries

The state need not recognize the validity of foreign, as opposed to out-of-state decrees, but will find a spouse estopped from attacking a foreign decree if benefited from it.

Divisible divorce

States enforce valid divorce decrees rendered by sister states because of the full faith and credit clause.

If each party is domiciled in the state, enforcement of the foreign decree may be sought in the domicile state.

The state may modify foreign divorce order portions modifiable under state law (e.g., child support orders, custody orders, and alimony orders).

Enforcement of foreign child custody orders

Under the Uniform Child Custody Jurisdiction Act, the state will defer to a prior and continuing exercise of jurisdiction by a sister state despite the child's temporary presence in the state.

Dissolution and Annulment

Void marriages

Marriages prohibited for reasons of consanguinity (i.e., degree of relationship between family members), affinity, or the existence of a former marriage are void. No legal process is required to have them declared invalid (void).

Void marriages may be attacked by parties other than the participants in the marriage, even after the death of one of the married parties.

Parties may seek to have the marriage annulled even when it is void.

Children of a marriage void because of consanguinity or affinity are born out of wedlock.

Children of a void marriage, because a prior marriage is in force, are legitimate to the party capable of contracting the marriage if that party acted in good faith.

If the marriage is subsequently validated because the parties continue to live as a couple after the prior marriage is dissolved, the child becomes legitimate as to both parents.

Voidable marriages

An annulment is necessary to terminate marriages, which are invalid for reasons other than consanguinity, affinity, or the existence of a former marriage.

To terminate such an invalid marriage, an annulment must be sought during the lifetime of both spouses.

Grounds for annulment include lack of mental capacity, duress, and fraud going to the essence of the marriage contract.

A concealed pregnancy where the husband is not the father, concealed impotence, or lack of intent to perform customary marital duties constitutes fraud, which goes to the essence of the marriage contract.

After the annulment, the marriage is considered null and treated as if it never existed for most purposes.

Alimony payments from an earlier marriage will not be reinstated after the annulment.

Children of a voidable marriage are legitimate as to the party capable of contracting a voidable marriage because of the age or insanity of the other spouse.

Notes for active learning

Parent, Child and State

Termination of parental rights

Permanent termination of parental rights in the child must be based upon a finding of parental unfitness proved by *clear and convincing* evidence.

Rights and liabilities of minors

The age of majority (often 18) is when a person is free from parents' guardianship and can marry without parental consent, contract, and make a will.

Generally, torts committed while children are minors are not attributed to their parents.

A parent may be liable for their negligence concerning a tort committed by their child for allowing the child to use a dangerous instrumentality or for failing to restrain a child after learning of the child's propensity for harmful conduct.

Children may sue their parents in negligence since parent-child immunity has been abolished.

Legitimacy and paternity

Children born to or conceived by a woman while she is married are presumed to be the legitimate children of that woman and her spouse.

A child conceived by a married person is illegitimate as to the father if the lack of paternity is proven *beyond a reasonable doubt.*

DNA testing is admissible on this issue and resolves the question of paternity conclusively.

A child born out of wedlock is legitimized if their parents marry, and the father acknowledges the child.

There is little difference between a legitimate child's rights and an illegitimate child whose paternity is acknowledged.

An acknowledged illegitimate child is an heir of their mother and father.

Conclusiveness of divorce decree on paternity

If the husband allows a divorce decree to be entered, which includes a finding that he is the father and is ordered in the decree to support the child, and there is no evidence at trial that he is not the father, there is a judgment of paternity.

That judgment of paternity can be vacated during a specific time under Probate based on newly discovered evidence.

A husband will be bound by a long-standing divorce decree, which includes a paternity judgment, even if it is conclusively proven that he is not the father.

Rights of the biological father to establish paternity

A person claiming to be the biological father can petition the court to establish paternity.

A court does not need to proceed with such a petition if it determines no family relationship between the putative father and child.

Child support

Parents must support their child, whether legitimate or illegitimate until they reach the state's statutory age.

A court may extend this obligation if the child lives with and depends on one parent or if the child is enrolled in an educational program.

The obligation to support is incorporated into court orders when the parents are engaged in a divorce, separate support litigation or when the mother seeks support from the father of her illegitimate child.

If a person supports an illegitimate child in the mistaken belief that he is the father and does not insist on a paternity test and establishes a paternal bond with the child, the court can require them to continue supporting the child even if it is later determined that they are not the biological father.

Individuals who adopt children have the same support obligations as natural parents.

The court can continue a support order against the estate of a deceased parent.

Adoption

Who may adopt

A person over 18 may petition to adopt a younger person but cannot adopt a brother, sister, spouse, aunt, or uncle.

If married, the spouse of the adopting party must join the petition.

Consent for adoption

For the adoption to be granted, the adoptee must consent if over a statutory age.

If the adoptee is married, their spouse must consent.

The necessary consent is that of the natural parents or the mother if the child is illegitimate.

Consent of a parent may be waived if the adoptee is over statutory age or if the court considers adoption in the child's best interests.

Because the right of a parent to maintain a relationship with their natural child is a fundamental right, parental rights can be terminated, and an adoption permitted only upon a showing of parental unfitness.

In some jurisdictions, counsel must be provided in the adoption proceeding to an indigent nonconsenting parent who desires to contest the petition.

Effect of adoption

A person who has been adopted is a child of their adoptive parents for all purposes, including intestate distribution.

Not only do they take as an heir from the adoptive parents, but they take as a child of their adoptive parents in determining rights to inherit from the adoptive parent's relatives.

An adopted child loses their status as a child of their natural parents when determining their rights to inherit from them or their kindred.

The exception is that a child adopted by a spouse of a natural parent after the death of the other natural parent retains the right to inherit from the relatives of the deceased natural parent.

When an adopted child dies intestate and is not survived by issue, their heirs are determined as if they had been born to their adoptive parents.

Relationship matrix

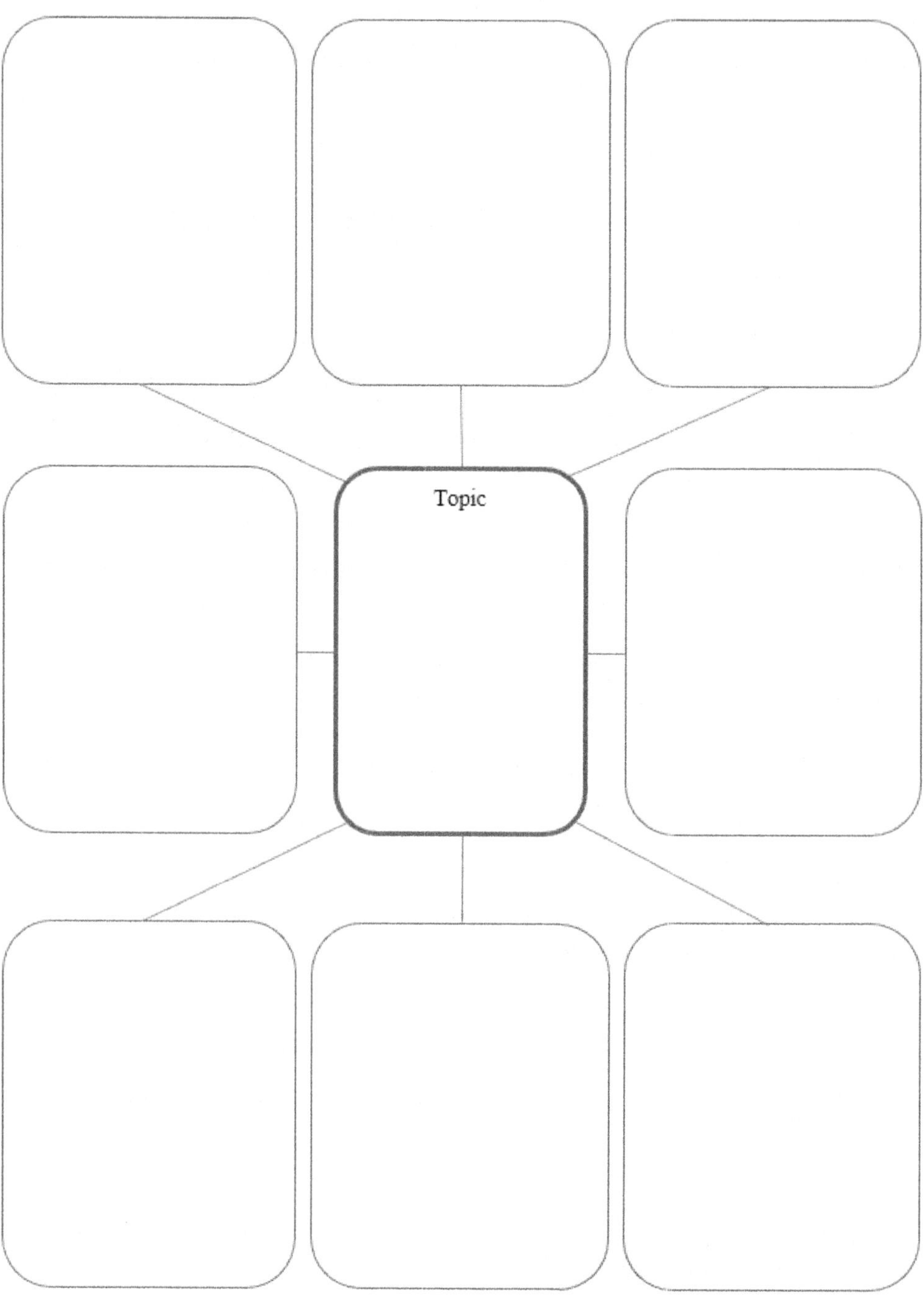

Notes for active learning

Notes for active learning

Trusts and Estates

Trusts and Estates are generally tested as a standalone subject and appear on the exam regularly. A question on wills or trusts will likely appear on the exam, but seldom both. Maximize your score by mastering the frequently tested Trusts and Estate items such as intestate succession, types of trusts (e.g., pour-over, discretionary, charitable), class gifts, future interests, validity and revocability of a will or trust.

Learn essential vocabulary to score more points on Trusts and Estates. Trusts definitions to know are settlor, beneficiary, trustee, testamentary trust, pour-over will, power of appointment, and rule of convenience. Wills definitions to know are ademption, codicil, descendant (or issue), devise or legacy (i.e., gift), disclaim, heirs, intestate, predecease, testate and testator.

The Probate Estate

Distribution of the estate

The law of wills, the rules of intestate distribution, and the laws governing estates' administration apply to the assets which are in the probate estate of the decedent.

The assets in the probate estate are held in the name of the decedent at the time of death.

The following property is not held solely in the decedent's name is not in the probate estate.

Partnership property

Partnership property, absent a specific provision in the partnership agreement, vests in the remaining partners at death.

The asset, which is in the estate of the deceased partner, is the right to an accounting of the value of the deceased's partnership assets.

Many partnership agreements modify this rule and permit the estate to remain as a partner or provide a mechanism whereby the deceased partner's interest is liquidated.

Property held in a fiduciary capacity

Property held by the decedent as a trustee (i.e., fiduciary) does not vest in the executor but must be turned over to the successor fiduciary.

Jointly-held property

Real and personal property held between the decedent and another as joint tenants or property held between the decedent and their spouse as tenants by the entirety passes directly to the surviving joint tenant. It is not part of the probate estate.

Completed gifts

An irrevocable gift made by the decedent during their lifetime, either outright or in trust, is vested in the donee or the trustee and is not part of the probate estate.

Causes of action – survival

Lawsuits pending and which survive death are assets of the probate estate.

Suits that survive death in which the decedent was a defendant can be prosecuted against the estate.

Contract actions and tort actions for personal injury survive death.

Intangible tort actions, such as libel, slander, and deceit, do not survive death. The estate cannot recover on such actions, nor is it liable for such actions brought because of actions of the decedent.

Causes of action – wrongful death actions

Actions to recover for the conscious pain and suffering and lost wages which the decedent suffered while living are assets of the probate estate.

Proceeds received from actions for wrongful death, while brought by the executor in the name of the decedent death actions, are not assets of the probate estate. These proceeds are distributed primarily to the surviving spouse and children per a statutory formula.

Life insurance and rights under pension plans

Insurance on the life of the decedent, even if the decedent was the owner of the life insurance policy, which is payable to a named beneficiary, is paid directly to the named beneficiary and is not an asset of the probate estate.

The decedent's pension plan proceeds, naming an individual as a beneficiary after the death of the decedent pass outside the probate estate.

Intestate Distribution of Estate

Complete and partial intestacy

Most exams have a question that requires applying the laws of descent and distribution.

The most common way for applying the law of intestacy is when an actor in a question dies without a will, and the examinee must determine how their estate should be distributed.

A complete or partial intestacy occurs when a will does not entirely dispose of the decedent's assets. This occurs if the will has no residuary clause or does not effectively dispose of the probate estate assets.

Even if an heir has been disinherited in the body of the will, they take by intestacy if the will fails to dispose of all assets.

The estate will be distributed by the intestacy law, where a will is declared invalid, and there is no prior will that governs the estate's distribution.

If a trust does not entirely dispose of its assets, which would occur when the final distribution is to the children or issue of a named beneficiary and that beneficiary does not have children or issue, the assets are disposed of by intestate distribution.

Intestate distribution laws are applied as if the settlor had died at the time when there was a failure of distribution, not at the time of the settlor's death.

Statutory disposition

The laws of intestate distribution apply to the net probate estate, which are assets remaining in the probate estate after the payment of debts, expenses of administration, funeral expenses, and taxes.

Spouse survives

Determining if a spouse survived the decedent presents two issues:

1) the person who claims the position of a surviving spouse must be validly married to the decedent and not divorced from the decedent when the decedent died, and

2) the person who was the spouse must survive the decedent. If their deaths were simultaneous, the simultaneous death act discussed below applies.

Spouse and issue survive

Issue includes the decedent's descendants whether, by blood or adoption, and includes children, grandchildren, great-grandchildren, etc.

If a surviving spouse and the decedent are survived by issue, that surviving spouse takes one-half of the net probate estate by intestacy.

The issue takes the other half per the rules for the distribution of the estate among the issue.

Spouse and kindred survive

If the decedent has a surviving spouse but no surviving descendants but is survived by kindreds (i.e., related persons to the decedent) such as parents, siblings, nieces, nephews, aunts, uncles, or cousins, the surviving spouse takes a statutory amount (e.g., the first $300,000) of the net probate estate and one-half of the remaining probate estate.

The kindred take half above the statutory amount.

For example, the decedent has a surviving spouse and a surviving mother and father, and the estate is $600,000. The surviving spouse takes $450,000 (statutory amount plus ½ in excess), and the mother and father take $75,000 each.

Spouse survives, but no issue or kindred survive

If a spouse survives without issue or kindred, the surviving spouse takes the entire probate estate.

Issue survive

If the decedent is survived by issue and there is no surviving spouse or the surviving spouse does not take their portion, the entire net probate estate is allocated to issue.

If children survive the decedent, that property reserved for issue passes in equal shares to the surviving children and to issue of any deceased child by right of representation.

If no children are surviving, the property is divided equally among grandchildren with a right of representation for the children of a deceased grandchild who is survived by issue.

No issue survive, but parents survive

If the decedent is not survived by issue, property not allocated to a surviving spouse is divided equally to the surviving parents.

No issue and no parents survive, but siblings or their issue survive

If there is no surviving issue or parents, property not allocated to a surviving spouse passes to the decedent's siblings, including half-siblings (i.e., persons with one parent in common with the decedent).

Issue of a deceased sibling, nephews, nieces, and their issue, take their deceased parent's share by right of representation as long as one sibling survives.

If there are no surviving siblings, property not allocated to a surviving spouse is inherited by nephews and nieces in equal shares with the issue of a deceased nephew or niece taking their parent's share by right of representation.

If those taking are in the same generation, they share equally; otherwise, they take equally in the older generation with children of deceased members of that generation taking their parent's share by right of representation.

No issue, parents, siblings, or their issue survive

If neither issue, parents, siblings, nor their issue survives, property not allocated to a surviving spouse passes in equal shares to the next of kin of the same degree of kindred.

The degree of kinship is determined by counting from the decedent up to the decedent's common ancestors and the next of kin and counting down to the next of kin.

For example, a first cousin is of the fourth degree of kindred because two degrees are used by counting to the common grandparent and two degrees counting down to the level of a cousin.

For example, a first cousin once removed is of the fifth degree of kindred.

For collateral kin of equal degree claim through different ancestors, those claiming the nearest ancestor are preferred.

Escheat

If a spouse and nor kindred survive, the property escheats to the state.

Additional rules of intestate distribution

A person adopted is a child of their adoptive parents for purposes of intestate distribution.

They take as an heir from their adoptive parents and the position of a child of their adoptive parents in determining their right to inherit from their adoptive parent's relatives.

An adopted child loses their status as a child of their natural parents when determining their right to inherit from them or their kindred.

The exception is that a child adopted by a spouse of a natural parent after the other natural parent dies retains the right to inherit from the relatives of the deceased natural parent.

When an adopted child dies intestate and is not survived by issue, their heirs are determined as if they had been born to their adoptive parents.

Half-blood

Children with one common parent are siblings for intestacy purposes and inherit an equal share with persons who have two common parents.

Children born out of wedlock

A child born out of wedlock is always a child of their mother for purposes of intestate succession, even if deemed an illegitimate child.

A child born out of wedlock is deemed a legitimate child of both parents for intestacy purposes if their parents have intermarried and the father has acknowledged them as his child or been adjudged as the father.

A child born out of wedlock who is illegitimate may inherit from and through their father:

1) if the father acknowledged paternity, or

2) if, during their lifetime or after death, the decedent has been adjudged in a judicial proceeding to be the father.

An illegitimate child may initiate a judicial proceeding to establish paternity after the decedent's death.

The descendants of a deceased illegitimate child may take their share by representation if paternity of the illegitimate has been acknowledged or established if paternity has not been acknowledged or judicially established, an illegitimate child cannot take as a child under intestacy laws.

If an illegitimate person dies intestate without issue, their mother or relatives are their heirs.

For their father and relatives to take by intestacy, the father–child relationship must be established by the father's acknowledgment of the child or through judicial proceedings.

Posthumous children

A child born to a married woman after her husband's death is a child of the deceased husband under intestacy laws.

The fatherhood of a child born out of wedlock after the father's death can be judicially established.

Limitation of rights of heir or legatee who kills testator

Some states have no statute which limits the rights of heir or legatees who kill the testator to inherit from their estate but imposes a constructive trust on the assets which such a person would receive and redistributes them to those who would inherit if the murderer predeceased the testator.

Notes for active learning

Execution of Wills

Contract to make a will

A contract to make a will containing specific provisions is valid if it is in writing.

The consideration for such a contract is often that the other party will make a reciprocal will.

If the testator violates their contractual obligation by executing a will that does not contain the provisions obligated by contract, the will executed is valid, but the person holding the contractual obligation can impress the estate with a constructive trust to dispose of the assets following the contractual obligation.

A critical issue in many questions is the devolution of the property after death and assesses whether an instrument described in the question is a valid will.

To intelligently discuss that issue, apply the following law.

Age for capacity to execute a will

A person must be eighteen years of age or older to execute a valid will.

Testamentary capacity

The testator must be of sound mind; that is, must understand in a general way:

1) the nature and extent of their property

2) the natural objects of their bounty; and

3) the nature of their act of making a will.

In a contest over the validity of a will, the will's proponent, usually the named executor, has the burden of proving that the testator was of sound mind when the will was executed.

The testator is presumed to be of sound mind until the opponents of the validity of the will introduce credible evidence that the testator lacked testamentary capacity.

The proponent of the will has the burden of persuasion on the issue and must prove capacity by a preponderance of the evidence.

In such a will contest, three classes of persons are competent to give an opinion on the soundness of the testator's mind when the will was executed:

1) witnesses to the will;

2) the testator's physician; and

3) a psychiatrist or other person who can qualify as an expert on sanity.

Other persons may testify in a will contest concerning facts upon which conclusions about the testator's sound mind can be based.

Testamentary intent

For a document to be a valid will, the testator must sign it with the understanding of making a will.

A document is ineffective as a will if the testator intends that it is a joke or solely designed to accomplish some purpose other than disposing of their property at death.

If the testator executes a will conditioned on some event occurring and it does not occur, the will is revoked.

The testator must generally know and approve the contents but need not know the technical details contained in it.

Written requirements for the execution of a valid will

A will must be entirely in writing.

A nuncupative will (an oral disposition of personal property) may be used only by a soldier in actual military service or a mariner at sea.

Oral wills are otherwise invalid.

Signature required by the testator or at their express direction

The writing must be signed by the testator or another in their presence and express direction.

If the testator intends the writing to be their signature executing the document, which they assert as their will, the testator may sign or make a mark on any part of the will.

Proper attestation

Holographic wills are entirely in the testator's handwriting and not valid unless attested or executed in a jurisdiction that recognizes the validity of unattested holographic wills.

The testator's signature must be properly attested to by two witnesses.

The testator need not sign the instrument in the presence of the witnesses.

If the testator does not sign in their presence, the testator must show their signature to each attesting witness, acknowledge that the signature is theirs, and ask them to sign the will as attesting witnesses in the testator's presence.

The will is valid even if a witness did not see the testator's signature if the witness could have seen it if they had wished.

The witnesses must know that they are witnessing a will but need not read it or be aware of its contents.

A competent witness can be any person of enough understanding when a subscribing witness, even if a minor.

A person who affixes the testator's signature to the will at their express direction may serve as a witness to the will.

A will is valid even if the witness is dead or incompetent when offered for probate.

The witness's signature can be proven by persons who saw them sign the will or identify the witness's signature.

At a probate proceeding where the validity of the will is in issue, the witness need not have a present memory of executing the will if they identify their signature as a subscribing witness.

Interested witnesses

A person who signs the will as one of the two necessary attesting witnesses and receives a legacy or devise under the will is an interested witness.

The fact that the witness was interested does not invalidate the will.

The legacy or devise to an interested witness or an interested witness's spouse is void.

If there are more than two witnesses to the will, the interested witness's signature is superfluous, and the legacy to that witness is valid.

If the witness is not named a legatee or devisee in the will but takes because of an anti-lapse statute's operation, their legacy is valid.

A witness is not considered an interested witness because they are named executor but receives no legacy of a will.

He does not forfeit their appointment as executor because they witnessed the will.

The signature of a person as a witness to a will who is an officer or director of a charity named a beneficiary of the will does not void that charity's legacy.

If a legacy is void because the legatee was a necessary witness to the will, that legacy is treated like a lapsed legacy. An alternative legatee takes, or if there is no alternative legatee, the residue is increased by the void legacy.

If the void legacy is the sole residuary legacy, or there is no residue clause in the will, the amount of the void disposition is distributed per the laws of intestacy.

If there is more than one residuary legatee, and the legacy to one of them is void because that residuary legatee was an interested witness, the residuary legatee is divided among the other residuary legatees proportionately unless the will indicates a contrary intent.

Codicils

Once a will has been validly executed, it cannot be altered or amended except by an instrument executed following the requirements for a valid will.

If the testator changes the content of the will on the face of the will by adding a new legatee or substituting one legatee for another, the changes are invalid, and the will, as initially executed, will be considered the testator's will.

An exception to this rule is the doctrine of partial revocation.

If the testator only crosses out a specific part of the will, that act is considered a partial revocation of that portion.

A will can be changed by a codicil (i.e., a document that alters an existing will) executed with the same formalities as a will.

A codicil modifies rather than replaces the will's provisions unless a contrary intent is clear.

A validly executed codicil republishes the will on the codicil's date.

A challenge to the original will cannot be sustained unless the challenge is also effective against the codicil.

A properly drafted codicil should explicitly refer to the will.

Conflict of laws as applied to wills

If the will is in writing and is signed, a will executed in conformity with either the law of the testator's domicile or the law of the place where it was executed will be recognized as a valid will by state court.

If the decedent who executed a will out of state dies domiciled in the state, the construction and legal effect of a disposition of personalty are governed by state law; and the disposition of real estate is governed by the law of its *situs* of that real estate.

A choice-of-law provision in a will specifying that a specific state's law will govern it will be recognized unless the law of a different state is contrary to public policy.

Notes for active learning

Revocation and Revival of Wills

Will revocation

Even if it is concluded that a will is valid, determine that it has not been revoked before using its provisions to dispose of the decedent's estate.

Events in the testator's life such as marriage and divorce occurring after the will is executed and before death revokes a will either wholly or partially.

The voluntary action of the testator may revoke a will in two ways.

Revocation by an instrument executed in the same manner

The testator can revoke a will by another instrument executed and attested to in the same manner as a will.

The instrument that frequently revokes a will is a subsequent will that typically contains language explicitly revoking prior wills and codicils.

The subsequent instrument may contain no dispositive language and only contain language revoking prior wills, in which case the intestacy laws would govern the estate's devolution.

If an instrument revokes part of a will, it is considered a codicil.

If the subsequent will is not valid, it does not revoke the earlier will.

Revocation by intentional destruction

The testator may revoke a will wholly or partially by performing a physical act on the will itself to revoke it in whole or in part.

Crossing out specific paragraphs of a will is a partial revocation of those sections.

If the testator, with intent to revoke a will, causes physical destruction of the paper by tearing or burning it, the entire will is revoked.

Defacing the will by writing canceled over the writing in the document revokes it.

An unwitnessed notation signed by the testator declaring the will revoked is not enough.

There is a presumption that a will that cannot be found was revoked.

That presumption can be rebutted by producing secondary evidence of its contents and showing that the testator did not intend its destruction.

The scrivener can testify to the contents of the will because the attorney-client privilege is inapplicable in probate proceedings dealing with a will's validity.

Intentional destruction of one of two duplicate wills constitutes a revocation.

Conditional or dependent relative revocation

If the revocation of a will occurred by a physical act conditioned upon the valid execution of a new will, the new will is not valid because it was improperly executed. The revocation is not valid, and the old will continues to be operative.

Revival of revoked wills

A will that has been revoked by a subsequent will is not automatically revived if the subsequent will is thereafter revoked.

If the testator's intent at the time they revoked the subsequent will is to reinstate a prior will, the court will revive the prior will.

Special Circumstances Affecting Intestate and Testate Distribution

Simultaneous death

The Uniform Simultaneous Death Act applies if the order of death of two or more individuals cannot be determined by affirmative proof.

If there is valid forensic evidence or eyewitness testimony that one person lived longer than the other, this Act does not apply.

The Act applies to the interpretation of the effect of wills and the application of intestacy laws.

Its Act's provisions are frequently tested in Wills' questions.

The mechanics of its operation should be committed to memory.

The basic principle of the Act is that in determining a person's estate whose death coincided, conclusively presume that the decedent survived the other person whose death coincided.

Thus, inconsistent facts are applied to the estate of each decedent.

The specific rules are:

1) A legatee or devisee in a will or a person entitled to take under the intestacy laws who died simultaneously is deemed to have predeceased the decedent whose estate is being distributed. Therefore, the rules of lapsed legacies apply.

2) If the two persons who died simultaneously held property as joint tenants or as tenants by the entirety, then for one half of the property, one joint tenant is deemed to have survived, and the second joint tenant is deemed to have survived for the other half.

Half of the jointly held property is considered an asset of the estate of each who died simultaneously. That estate is probated as if the holder of the other half of the joint tenancy has predeceased them.

3) The named beneficiary in an insurance policy predeceased the insured.

The insurance policy proceeds would thus be payable to the alternative beneficiary or the deceased's estate if there is no alternative beneficiary.

For a question involving simultaneous deaths, determine which assets, including jointly held assets, are in the estate of each decedent and determine how the estate is to be distributed as if the other person who died simultaneously had predeceased the decedent.

Advancement

Property which the decedent gives during their lifetime to an heir, with the intent that the gift satisfies wholly or partially the share to which the donee would be entitled from the donor's estate is an advancement.

The amount of the *inter-vivos* gift is added to the intestate estate. The larger amount is divided by the number of shares in the estate to determine each beneficiary's amount.

The amount of the advancement is deducted from the share of the heir who received it.

An *inter-vivos* gift is an advancement only if the donor describes the gift as an advancement in writing or if the donee acknowledges the gift as an advancement in writing.

The advancement is its fair market value at the date of the gift or the amount in which the donor states the value to be at the date of the gift.

Renunciation of property interests

A person may disclaim in whole or in part any interest passing to them as the result of the decedent's death by filing a signed disclaimer in probate court (and in the registry of deeds where disclaimed realty is located) within the statutory time (e.g., nine months) after the donee became entitled to the property.

Once filed, a disclaimer is irrevocable and becomes the property of the person who would have taken it if the disclaiming party had died immediately before the event, which entitled the disclaiming party to receive the property.

Limitations on testamentary dispositions

The decedent's right to make an effective testamentary disposition is limited by considerations of public policy set forth in statutes.

Spouse's elective share

In wills questions requiring to determine which individuals take which parts of the estate, always consider the rights of a surviving spouse to take an elective share and compare the size of that share to the amount which the surviving spouse would take under the will.

Property that the spouse receives as a surviving joint owner or from the proceeds of an insurance policy or through *inter-vivos* gifts does not count against their elective share.

A surviving spouse has a statutory right to waive the provisions of the will and claim the statutory elective share.

This right must be exercised by a writing filed in the Registry of Probate within the statutory time (e.g., six months) after the decedent's will has been allowed.

The spouse's elective share (calculated on the net probate estate) is computed by one of three formulae depending on the other heirs.

To file for an elective share, the person claiming to be the surviving spouse must be validly married to the person claiming to be the surviving spouse at the time of their death and not be a party against whom a separate support action has been filed.

If issue survive

If the decedent is survived by issue, the spouse takes one-third of the net probate estate.

If the amount of the net probate estate is more than $75,000 so that the elective share would exceed $25,000, the spouse receives only $25,000 outright and a life interest in the amount by which the one-third share exceeds $25,000.

The spouse receives a life estate in the portion of the estate, which is real property, and a life interest in a trust fund for the remaining amount in which they are entitled as a life interest.

If kin survive, but no issue survive

If the decedent is survived by kin but no issue, the spouse takes the first $25,000 of the net probate estate outright, plus the income from one-half of the remaining probate estate.

If no issue or kin survive

If the decedent is not survived by issue or kin, the spouse takes $25,000 outright plus one-half of the remaining probate estate outright.

If a spouse has deserted the decedent spouse, or in a case where the decedent spouse was living apart from the surviving spouse under a probate decree of separate support for a justifiable cause, the spouse has no right to waive the will.

The right to waive the will and take a statutory forced share is personal to the spouse and terminates if they die before waiving the will.

The will may not be waived by the executor of the surviving spouse's estate.

Acceptance of any benefits under the will bar the right to waive.

Property held in a revocable *inter vivos* trust where the decedent was settlor, sole trustee, and life income beneficiary is part of the probate estate for purposes of computing the amount of the estate to which the election statute applies.

Some states do not have a statute that calculates the amount to which the waiver statute applies by including jointly held property, completed *inter-vivos* gifts, proceeds of life insurance, and the value of property held in trust for the benefit of the deceased spouse.

When making the waiver-of-the-will calculation, not all states deduct the amounts contained in the above categories, which are now the property of the surviving spouse.

Children not mentioned in the will (pretermitted children)

In will fact patterns where the decedent is survived by a child or by the children of a deceased child, who is not mentioned in the will, consider the possibility that the child is pretermitted (i.e., not mentioned in the will) and has the right to claim their intestate share.

A child can be pretermitted whether born before or after the date when the will was executed.

There are three ways in which a testator can prevent a child or grandchild of a deceased child from being pretermitted.

1) He can leave the child or grandchild a legacy of any size.
2) The testator can indicate that the omission was intentional and not caused by mistake. The easiest way to show intent is to state that intent in the will.
3) He can make provisions for that child during their lifetime.

The terms "accident" or "mistake" do not refer to facts that led the testator to omit the child intentionally but instead to error or mistake in drafting and executing the will.

For example, if the testator says that they make no provision for Son because Son stole from them, Son is not a pretermitted child even if the testator was mistaken about the theft.

The executor and the persons who oppose the child's claim have the burden of showing that the omission was not caused by accident or mistake.

The pretermitted child must file a claim against the estate for their intestate share.

No pretermitted child can take a share in real property unless a claim is filed in the Registry of Probate within one year after approval of the executor's bond.

The intestate share paid to the pretermitted child is first paid out of the estate's residue and from devisees and legatees proportionally.

An illegitimate child cannot be a pretermitted child.

No limitations on charitable bequests

Some states have no statutory provisions limiting the proportion of an estate that may be left to charity nor limiting charitable bequests made in a will executed close to death.

Provisions in restraint of marriage

The testator cannot validly require that a legacy be forfeited if the beneficiary marries.

The testator can condition a testamentary disposition upon a legatee not marrying a person outside of their religion.

Courts are likely to construe a provision that appears to be an absolute restraint on marriage as a provision for a beneficiary's support while that beneficiary is single.

Such a provision in a trust which supports a beneficiary until that beneficiary is married would be upheld.

Notes for active learning

Interpretation and Construction of Wills

Incorporation by reference

A will may incorporate a document, even ones not executed with the formalities of a will if it:

1) was in existence when the will was executed and

2) is identified by clear and satisfactory proof as the paper referred to in the will.

The doctrine has been expanded by statute for revocable *inter vivos* trusts.

The dispositive provisions of an existing revocable *inter vivos* trust may be incorporated by reference into a will even though the trust is revocable or amendable.

If the trust is amended after the will is executed, the document incorporated into the will is the trust as amended.

The devise or bequest to the trustee of a revocable *inter vivos* trust lapses if the trust is revoked or terminated before the testator's death.

Facts of independent significance

A will may provide for the designation of a beneficiary or the amount of a disposition by reference to some future unattested act occurring after the execution of the will if the future act has some significance apart from the will.

For example, a bequest of "one week's wages to those persons in my employ at the date of my death" has two facts that control the recipients' identity and the amount they are to receive, which will be determined after the will has been executed.

Each of these two facts has significance outside of the will itself.

Alterations and interlineations

A new provision inserted after a will was duly executed is invalid, but the will remains valid.

For alterations to the text of the will, they are valid if made before the will was signed.

The proponents of the will have the burden of proving that the alterations were made before the will was signed.

If the testator has struck out a provision of the will after the will was signed, that provision is revoked because a will may be wholly or partially revoked by defacing the instrument itself.

Ambiguities

Extrinsic evidence to explain or contradict the terms of a will is inadmissible unless the will is ambiguous, even if the language of the will was contrary to the intent which the testator expressed orally.

Patent ambiguities

Patent ambiguities appear on the face of the will. For example, the same parcel of property is devised for two different beneficiaries in two separate paragraphs of the will. Extrinsic evidence is not admissible to resolve such ambiguity. The instrument is construed from its language alone or according to general rules of construction.

A mistake may cause the patent ambiguity in the *factum*, a mistake in the will itself, such as an inaccurate description of the property or an erroneous identification of legatee.

Usually, a will may not be corrected for a mistake in the *factum*.

The testator refers to a person (e.g., "my wife"), but the language does not accurately describe their legal relationship; the court will ignore the erroneous legal description.

Latent ambiguities

Latent ambiguities occur when there is no inconsistency in the language of the will itself, but extrinsic facts give rise to ambiguity.

For example, the will may devise $20,000 to Aunt Angela. The testator had two aunts named Angela because their mother and father each had a sister named Angela.

Where there is such a latent ambiguity, extrinsic evidence is admissible to aid in interpreting the will.

Construction of Terms for Relationship and Survivorship

Heirs and next of kin

The terms *heirs* and *next of kin* ordinarily mean persons who inherit by intestacy at the time of the decedent's death.

If the time for the interest of heirs or next of kin to vest is later, the terms include persons who would have been the decedent's heirs at that later date.

For example, if the testator devises a life estate "to my wife for life and then to my heirs," the heirs are those who would have taken if the testator had died at the time that the life estate in the testator's wife terminated.

Then living

The term *then living* requires that the person taking the remainder interest be alive when the prior estate terminates.

Adopted children

Unless a contrary intent plainly appears by the instrument's terms, adopted children are treated the same as natural children in construing the words "child," "grandchild," "issue," "heir," or "heir-at-law."

Construction of devises

If a will devises real estate and does not specify the quality of the estate conveyed, the devise is in fee simple or, if the testator cannot devise a fee simple, the greatest estate the testator could devise.

Exercise of a general power of appointment

The residuary clause of a will does not exercise a general power of appointment held by the testator unless it shows an intent to exercise that power.

If the general power of appointment is not exercised, the assets of the trust in which the power of appointment was held will go by way of the provisions of the trust controlling a default in the exercise of the power of appointment.

If there is no default provision, the property in the trust would go to the heirs of the settlor determined as of the time of the failure to exercise the power of appointment.

Notes for active learning

Changes in Property, Beneficiaries and Marital Status Before Death

While the will is executed during the testator's life, it does not become operative until death.

During that time, changes can occur in the testator's marital status, the testator's property, and the individuals who are beneficiaries of the will.

Each of these changes affects how the will disposes of property at the death of the decedent.

Classification of testamentary dispositions

Testamentary dispositions are classified per the assets of the estate available to pay them.

A specific devise or bequest disposes of an identified item of property owned by the testator and, except in extraordinary circumstances, can only be paid by delivering that asset.

A demonstrative bequest is a gift payable primarily from a specified source and, if that source is inadequate, the estate's general assets can be used to pay it.

A general or pecuniary bequest is payable from the estate's general assets rather than requiring distribution from specific assets.

A residuary disposition is a gift of whatever remains in the estate after claims and other dispositions have been satisfied.

Effect of change in assets between execution and death

The property, which is the subject of a specific bequest, is adeemed, and the beneficiary receives nothing if the testator does not own that asset at the time of death.

Specific bequests – ademption by extinction

An item purchased to replace the asset is not the subject of the specific bequest.

For real estate, which is subject to a binding purchase and sale agreement at the time of death, the doctrine of equitable conversion applies, and the asset of the estate is the right to the proceeds, not the real estate.

An exception to the ademption rule is if the testator's conservator or guardian sold the property.

In that example, the beneficiary is entitled to anything that remains of the proceeds of the sale.

Pecuniary bequests – ademption by satisfaction

If the testator gives a prospective legatee a gift before the will is executed, that gift will not be considered to have satisfied a bequest.

If a gift is received by a beneficiary from the testator after the will is executed, it will only be considered to have satisfied the bequest if the testator declared in writing that it was in satisfaction of the gift or unless the beneficiary acknowledged in writing that the gift was in satisfaction of the bequest.

The rule is like that of advancements for intestate shares.

Changes in securities

A legatee is only entitled to the number of shares of the security as has been bequeathed to them, providing that the testator owned that many shares at death.

The legatee is entitled to additional shares of security if the testator received them as a stock split or stock dividend from the original shares bequeathed.

The specific legatee is entitled to securities received in exchange for the bequeathed securities due to a merger, consolidation, reorganization, or similar action.

Encumbered property

The devisee of real property or the legatee of personal property takes the property subject to any mortgage or security interest at the time of death unless the will provides differently.

Lapse – changes in beneficiaries

Unless the will provides an alternative disposition if the named beneficiary predeceases the testator or unless the anti-lapse statute applies, a legacy or devise made to one who predeceases the testator lapses.

If the lapsed legacy is not a residuary, the amount of that legacy becomes part of the estate's residue and passes under the residuary clause.

If the lapsed legacy is the residuary legacy, the assets pass by intestacy.

The anti-lapse statute

When an anti-lapse statute is applicable, the legacy which was supposed to go to a deceased beneficiary is transferred to the issue of that deceased beneficiary provided that the testator has not shown a different intent.

The anti-lapse statute is only applicable when the deceased beneficiary is a blood relative of the testator.

A gift to the deceased child of a spouse does not pass by operation of the anti-lapse statute to the issue of that child.

For the anti-lapse statute to operate, the deceased relative must have been survived by issue, including adopted children.

The property passes to the issue per the law of intestate distribution discussed above.

For example, if the beneficiary were survived by two children and the two children of a deceased child, the children take one-third of the legacy. The remaining one-third would be split between the children of the deceased child.

The legacy is not paid under the will of the deceased relation.

If the deceased blood relative survived by issue dies before the execution of the will, the anti-lapse statute will still apply.

If there are two or more residuary legatees and one predeceases the testator, the remaining legatees take the residue, and nothing is distributed by intestacy.

If the deceased residuary legatee is a relation and is survived by issue, the anti-lapse statute applies, and the issue takes the deceased residuary legatee's share of the residue.

Class gifts – definition of a class

A class gift exists when a testator makes a gift to several persons, usually with the same relationship to the testator, such as "nephews and nieces."

The class may increase in number as additional persons are born and qualify as members of the class, or it may decrease as members of the class die before the time the gift is to be distributed.

Whether a group of beneficiaries is to be considered a class or to be considered individually is answered by determining the intent of the testator.

Time to determine membership

If the class gift is a legacy or devise to be paid at the time of the testator's death, membership in the class is determined at the testator's death.

Persons who have predeceased the testator, even if they were alive at the time of the will, are not members of the class.

Even if they bear an appropriate relationship to become class members, persons born after the testator's death are excluded.

If the class gift is payable at some time after the testator's death, the time for determining membership in the class is the time when the property is distributed to the class.

Unless there is a provision in the will that conditions the benefits of the class gift upon survivorship until distribution time, membership in the class does not decrease after the testator's death. However, it can increase with births after death but before distribution.

If distribution of the benefits of the class gift takes place over time (e.g., beneficiaries are eligible for distributions when they obtain a specific age), the rule of convenience, which can be overcome by expressing a contrary intent, closes class membership at the first distribution.

The anti-lapse applies to class gifts.

If the testator left the property 'to my brother for life and his children," the statute allows the issue of the testator's nephews and nieces who predeceased the testator to take.

However, if the provision were "to my brother for life and then to his children then living," the anti-lapse statute could not apply because there is a condition of survivorship.

Changes in marital status – marriage

Marriage after the date of the execution of the will revokes an entire will unless it appears from the will itself that it was made in contemplation of the marriage.

Unless such a testator makes a new will after marriage, their estate is distributed by intestacy laws.

A will revoked by marriage is not revived by divorce.

Changes in marital status – divorce

A divorce or annulment revokes provisions in a will for the former spouse, and the property passes as if the former spouse had predeceased the testator.

A divorce revokes the designation of the former spouse in a fiduciary capacity under the will.

If the testator remarries their former spouse, the provisions are revived.

A legal separation of spouses does not terminate their married status and does not revoke any provisions of a will.

The Distribution of The Estate After Death

The estate at the time of death

Most exam questions require explaining how the estate of the decedent is distributed at death.

The will, which was ambulatory until the time of death, becomes an operative instrument by the process of probate.

A petition to probate the decedent's last will and testament is filed by the executor in the probate (e.g., county) court of the decedent's domicile at the time of death.

The burden of proving that the will was validly executed, that it has not been revoked, and that the decedent was competent at the time of execution is on the proponent of the will.

The decree admitting the will to probate established the will as the decedent's probate estate's dispositive instrument.

The decree may be revoked if a later will is found or the will was a forgery.

The named executor is ordinarily appointed executor when the will is allowed, but the court has the discretion to appoint a different fiduciary if the named executor is unfit.

If there is no will, the probate process is known as administration.

The surviving spouse has the first claim on the fiduciary position of the administrator.

Children have the next right to the appointment as administrators.

The administrator performs duties like an executor and distributes the estate following the laws of intestacy.

Will contests

The decedent's heirs and beneficiaries of a prior will have standing to contest the validity of the will offered for probate on one or more of three grounds.

The heirs must be given notice of the petition for probate.

Legatees under prior wills should be given notice if their existence is known, but failure to notice prior legatees will not void the probate proceeding.

A testator may include a valid and enforceable provision in their will requiring any legatee who contests the will to forfeit any provisions made under the will.

A beneficiary petition for interpretation of a will does not challenge the validity of the will and therefore does not invoke an *in terrorem* clause.

Improper execution

If the will was improperly executed, it is invalid.

Improper execution will occur if the testator fails to sign the will in the presence of witnesses or acknowledge to them that the signature on the will is theirs or the statutory number of witnesses (e.g., one, two) fail to attest to the will.

The named executor has the burden of proving proper execution.

Lack of testamentary capacity

The validity of the will may be challenged if the decedent was under age 18 when the will was executed or if they were not of sound mind.

The burden is on the proponents to establish a sound mind once those challenging the will have produced credible evidence of an unsound mind.

Undue influence

A ground for challenging the will is that the testator was under undue influence at execution.

To constitute undue influence, coercion (mental, physical, or moral) must cause the desires of the person accused of using undue influence to be incorporated into the will rather than the desires of the testator.

Kindness or care for the decedent does not constitute undue influence if the testator responds by giving such person a substantial legacy.

If the person accused of exerting undue influence is in a fiduciary relationship to the testator and benefits themself, the court will likely find undue influence.

Legacies in favor of the scrivener of the will are particularly suspect.

The contestant bears the burden of proving undue influence.

Fraud in the inducement

Fraud, which deprives the testator of their right to make a will based upon the true state of affairs, is of two types, fraud in the inducement and fraud in the factum.

Fraud in the inducement is a knowingly false representation that causes the testator to make a different will than otherwise.

If successfully proven, fraud in the inducement will only void those provisions of the will, which were the product of that fraud, and the remaining portions of the will can be probated.

If the testator, in the absence of fraud, makes a mistake not having to do with the execution of the will, which induces them to dispose of property in a particular manner, the will is valid.

For example, a mistake about the value of one's property, or concerning how the decedent has been treated by one of their relatives, or whether the natural object of one's bounty is living or dead will not invalidate the will.

The test for determining whether the testator had sufficient mental capacity to create a valid trust is typically like that required to make a valid will. To have capacity, the settlor must have been at least 18 years old and must know the extent of their property and the natural objects of their bounty. The "natural objects" include family members such as spouses, children, and siblings.

Fraud in the *factum*

Fraud in the factum occurs when the decedent is defrauded that they are making a will or about the contents of the will.

For example, the decedent thinks they are signing a contract when the document is a will, or the decedent signs a will but does not know that there are beneficiaries in the will whom they did not want.

For it to be the basis to contest a will, the fraud must be operative when the will was executed.

The burden of proving fraud is on the contestant.

Fraud in the *factum* goes to whether the decedent knew that they were executing a will and voids the instrument.

Remedies for fraud and undue influence

A person objecting to a will based on fraud or undue influence must contest the validity of the will in probate and cannot maintain a separate action for constructive trust or tort damages.

If the fraud or undue influence prevented the execution of a will in favor of the plaintiff, they would maintain a tort action for interference with an advantageous relationship.

If the alleged wrongdoer benefited from their conduct by taking under the decedent's will, the remedy for the person who was left out of the will is to ask the court to impose a *constructive trust* upon the defendant's ill-gotten gains for the plaintiff's benefit.

A constructive trust is not an actual trust by the traditional definition; a constructive trust is a legal fiction remedy for unjust enrichment.

The constructive trust orders the unjustly enriched person to transfer the property to the intended party.

Other reasons for the invalidity of a will

The probate court, where the will is probated, is the forum to address other issues concerning the validity of the will, such as whether the will has been revoked or terminated by a subsequent marriage.

If the court determines that a will is invalid for any reason, prior wills may be probated since the provision in the invalid will revoking prior wills is invalid.

If there are no prior wills, the court treats the probate as an administration and distributes property by the laws of intestacy.

Issues altering the operation of the will

The probate court is the forum where the issues of pretermitted children and waiver of the will by a surviving spouse are determined.

Collection of the assets of the estate

Once appointed, the executor or administrator collects the estate assets and files an inventory.

Special rules affect the following assets.

Debts owed by the executor to the estate

Any debt which the executor owes to the estate is treated as paid.

The executor must account for that money in their final account.

If the executor cannot pay it and they filed a surety bond, the sureties must pay the amount the executor owed the estate.

Income from specifically bequeathed assets

Income-producing assets specifically devised or bequeathed carry the right to income from the date of death.

The executor is entitled to the income accrued to the decedent before death as a general asset of the estate.

Income accruing after death is paid to the beneficiaries of the specifically bequeathed assets.

Real estate – heirs or devisees normally have control

Real estate descends directly to the heirs or devisees, and the executor does not have the right to rents nor the responsibilities of management as soon as the will is allowed.

Executor may sell real estate to pay debts and expenses

If the estate's personal property assets are insufficient to pay debts and taxes of the estate, the executor has the power to petition the probate court to sell real estate to satisfy obligations.

To give good title to real estate during the first year after the death, a license from the probate court for the executor to sell with the assent of the devisees is necessary.

Powers and duties of a fiduciary

Unless the will or a probate court order confers greater authority, the executor or administrator has limited power.

The executor may expend money to protect and preserve estate assets and comply with the decedent's contractual obligations.

To liquidate the estate, the executor has the power to sell personal property.

If the estate is solvent, the executor or administrator can keep the assets that the decedent held and distribute assets in kind or partly in kind.

Standard of executor's obligations

An executor or administrator is a fiduciary and subject to fiduciary duties of care and loyalty

Liability of executor or administrator

An executor is not personally liable for contracts made by them in their capacity as an executor unless they failed to reveal their fiduciary capacity.

A creditor may hold the estate liable on such contracts.

The estate, but not the executor, is liable in tort due to control of the estate's property unless the executor is personally negligent.

To satisfy the duty of care, an executor must carry liability insurance on managed property.

Payment of debts and claims

The executor or administrator first uses the estate assets to pay debts and claims in the following order of priority.

A widow's allowance (payable immediately after death without regard to the estate's debts) to help the widow and minor children adjust to death has priority on the assets.

The amount is per minor child given with a limited amount for necessaries for the widow.

A widower would probably qualify for such an allowance.

The priorities for debts are in the following order:

1) expenses of administration;
2) necessary funeral expenses and expenses of last illness;
3) debts entitled to preference under laws of the United States;
4) taxes and excise duties;
5) wages (up to statutory amount) for labor performed within a year of death;
6) debts for necessaries furnished to the decedent or their family within 6 months of death;
7) all other debts.

If the assets are insufficient to satisfy one class in full, the debts abate pro-rata.

Priority of secured debts with collateral

A secured party, including a mortgagee, may seek repayment out of the security and is not subject to priorities except the extent to which the debt exceeds the collateral value.

Suits for services – claimant can testify

Since some states have no dead man rule, plaintiffs can testify to an oral contract with the deceased for services.

If the claim is for services rendered, only claims accruing during the last six years of the decedent's life are collectible because of the statute of limitations.

Claim to leave property by will

If the claim is that services were rendered in reliance on an oral promise to leave the property by will, the suit on the contract to leave the property by will is unenforceable because of the statute of frauds.

The plaintiff can sue the estate and collect damages in *quantum meruit* for the fair value of services rendered in reliance on the unenforceable oral promise.

The cause of action for a promise to leave the property by will does not accrue until the will becomes operative at the time of death.

The contract statute of limitations will not bar a claim for services rendered in reliance on the promise, and the plaintiff can collect for services rendered after the date of the promise if the estate is sued promptly.

Debts due to the executor

If the executor has a claim against the estate, they may collect it.

The beneficiaries have a right to contest the validity and amount under arbitration procedures established by the probate court.

Notice of claim filed against an estate

A creditor should make a claim by mailing a written statement of the claim to the executor within the statutory period (e.g., four months) after the executor or administrator has been appointed, describing the nature and extent of the claim.

Disallowance of claims

The executor or administrator has a statutory period (e.g., sixty days) after receipt to disallow the claim.

Failure to disallow gives that claim the status of an allowed claim and tolls the statute of limitations for suits against estates.

Payments during the statutory period

Because the executor or administrator does not know the number of claims against an estate, the executor should not pay claims within the statutory period (e.g., four months) from their appointment.

If the executor pays claims they have knowledge of after the statutory period, they are not personally liable to creditors who make a later claim, which would render the estate insolvent.

Statute of limitations for suits against the estate

Suits against the estate, except for the exceptions discussed hereafter, must be brought within the statutory period from the deceased's death.

Notes for active learning

Exceptions to One-Year Statute for Suits Against the Estate

The Supreme Court may permit a late-filed claim if it finds the claimant is not guilty of culpable neglect and that equity and justice require the waiver.

New assets in an estate

If new assets come into the estate more than one year after the decedent's death, creditors may sue for the new assets within six months after the executor receives them or four months after the creditor learns of them, whichever comes first.

Claim not yet accrued

If a claim is presented before the estate is fully administered but will not accrue during the one year, the court may order that sufficient assets be held to satisfy the claim when it matures, and the lawsuit need not be commenced until the cause of action accrues.

Claim satisfied out of insurance

If the claim is to be satisfied by an insurance policy or bond, the suit may be brought within the time limits of the ordinary statute of limitations if that suit is within three years of the date of death.

Tax returns

The executor is responsible for paying the federal estate tax and filing estate tax returns if the estate is large enough to require that a return be filed.

The executor must file fiduciary income tax returns to report the income earned by the estate.

Notes for active learning

Payment of Legacies and Distributive Shares

Payment to a spouse in intestacy without issue

The administrator must pay a statutory amount to the spouse first out of personalty and then from the realty in an intestate administration where a spouse, but no issue survives.

If the entire net probate estate is less than the statutory amount, the administrator can obtain a determination that the surviving spouse is entitled to the entire estate.

Time of the payment of legacies

Legacies are not payable until a statutory period (e.g., nine months) after the executor's appointment.

General or pecuniary legacies carry interest after the statutory period elapses.

A legacy to support a minor or widow instead of a dower bears interest from the date of death.

Income earned from the date of death from a bequeathed asset is paid to that beneficiary.

Legacies to executor, debtors, and creditors

A legacy to a person named as an executor ordinarily requires that the executor serves in that capacity to qualify for the legacy.

Whether a bequest left to a creditor of the estate is used to reduce the debt owed is determined by the intent of the testator.

The size of the bequest, the relationship between the creditor and testator, the character of the legacy, and the time the debt arose are relevant factors in making that determination.

If the testator is a creditor of the legatee, the executor has the right to offset the debt against the legacy unless the legatee shows that the testator intended to forgive the debt and grant a legacy.

If the statute of limitations barred the debt at the time of the execution of the will, there is a strong indication that the testator did not intend that it be collected.

Abatement of legacies

The testator has the power to specify the order in which legacies will abate where the assets are insufficient.

If the assets of the estate are insufficient to pay the creditors and legacies in the will, the order of abatement is:

1) residuary legacies;
2) general legacies which abate *pro-rata* if not enough assets exclusive of specific legacies to pay them in full;
3) specific legacies and devises that abate pro-rata if specific legacies and devises must be used to satisfy the estate's debts.

Legacies satisfying a legal obligation of 1) the testator, 2) a minor, 3) instead of dower, or 4) as the result of an ante-nuptial agreement, are entitled to priority over specific legacies and devises.

Completion of the Administration of the Estate

Filing account

Upon complete administration of the estate, the executor or administrator files a final account, showing inventory, income, expenses, and distributions.

Challenge to account

Heirs and other interested persons have a right to challenge the account.

If found deficient, the executor can be required to pay sums into the estate, and the sureties can be held liable if the executor defaults.

Finality of account

Once allowed, the executor is discharged and is subject to further challenge only if the allowance of the account was procured by fraud or manifest error.

Notes for active learning

Definition of a Trust

Trusts divide legal and equitable interests

A trust is an entity recognized by the law in which a trustee holds legal title to the property to benefit the beneficiaries who have an equitable interest in the trust property.

Separation of the legal and equitable title is an essential element of a trust.

If a sole trustee who holds the legal interest is identical to the sole beneficiary holding the equitable interests, there is a merger.

The trust is terminated, and the sole trustee/beneficiary owns the property outright.

An essential element of a trust is that the trustee stands in a fiduciary relationship with the beneficiaries concerning the trust property.

Distinguished from other relationships

Agency, debtor-creditor, and bailment distinguish between trust and other legal relationships.

The facts may be ambiguous in some questions, so discuss the law of trusts and analyze the facts under one of the following legal frameworks.

Agency

A trust is distinguished from an agency because an agent does not hold legal title to the principal's property.

Debtor–creditor

A trust is not a debtor–creditor relationship.

A creditor has a claim at law against the debtor for damages in the amount of the debt. In contrast, a trust beneficiary has an equitable interest in specific trust property and the benefit of the trustee's fiduciary obligations.

Bailment

A bailee only has a possessory interest, not title, in the property held for the bailee.

While the bailee has a duty to avoid negligence concerning the property and can be required to turn the property over to the bailor, there is no fiduciary duty between the bailor and bailee.

Notes for active learning

Voluntarily Created Trusts

Methods of trust creation

A voluntary trust is created when the settlor with the express or implied intent to create a trust performs the acts necessary to establish a trust.

The acts of the settlor may be donative or required by a contractual relationship.

The act which accompanies the creation of a trust is a *declaration* or *transfer*.

Trust creation by declaration

A trust is created by a declaration when the settler, orally or in writing, intends to hold property that they own in trust and hold it at least partially for others' benefit.

When a declaration creates a trust, the settlor is the trustee, and the settlor holds legal title to the property in their fiduciary capacity as trustee.

Trust creation by transfer

A trust can be created when the settlor transfers the legal title to their property to a third party and designates the beneficiaries who have the equitable title to the property.

Voluntary or donative trusts

A voluntary trust is created without consideration by declaration (or transfer).

A declaration needs communication of the intent to hold property in trust and does not need to comply with the formalities of a transfer.

Thus, an individual can make an effective gift in trust by declaring that they are holding property, which they own in trust, for the benefit of the donee of the gift without the need of delivery to complete the gift.

If a transfer is necessary to complete the creation of a voluntary trust, the settlor must comply with the delivery requirements for a donative transaction to be complete.

Personal property must be delivered to the trustee.

There must be execution and delivery of a deed to the trustee for a trust to be created by the transfer of real property

A voluntary declaration of trust requires a clear showing of intent to create a trust.

If the declaration of trust is oral, there must be notice to and acceptance by the beneficiary.

No notice to a beneficiary is needed with a written declaration of trust.

Trusts created by contract

If there is an obligation to create a trust by a contract supported by valid consideration and that obligation is specifically enforceable, the person who has agreed to create a trust can be required in equity to satisfy their obligation and transfer the property to a trust.

If the promise involves a trust where the *res* (body) of the trust is land, the contract will have to be enforceable under the statute of frauds.

Testamentary or *inter vivos* trusts

A testamentary trust is created in a will and becomes operational only at death.

An *inter vivos* trust becomes effective during the lifetime of the settlor.

Pour-over provisions for testamentary trusts

A trust created by the terms of a will is only valid if the will is valid and can only be amended by a subsequent will or a codicil.

Under the doctrine of incorporation by reference, the estate assets may be bequeathed or devised to an existing inter-vivos trust.

This trust is known as a pour-over trust.

By statute, if the trust is in existence when the will is executed, the trust can subsequently be amended by the testator in a manner that does not observe the formalities of executing a will. The assets poured into the trust will be governed by the terms of the amended trust.

An *inter vivos* trust is irrevocable unless the settlor expressly retained the power to revoke it.

If a settlor attempts to set up a trust that will only come into existence at their death, it must be created by an instrument executed with the formalities of a will.

If the trust is created during the lifetime of the testator, it will not be invalid because it did not comply with the formalities of wills even if the settlor is the sole trustee, the sole lifetime beneficiary, and retains the power to amend and revoke it.

Such a trust is the classic pour-over trust commonly used today.

Savings account trust

A common substitute for a testamentary disposition is a savings bank trust where the donor opens an account in their name in trust for the donee.

There must be a formal document setting forth the terms of the trust, or the donor must give notice to the beneficiary that the trust has been created.

Gifts to minors

The Transfers to Minors Act allows the registration of certain types of personal property in a custodian's name for a minor.

The custodian may make payments for the minor's use and benefit without court approval, and the property becomes the sole property of the minor upon reaching majority.

Notes for active learning

Required Elements of a Trust

For a private voluntary trust to be validly created, the following elements are necessary

Once created, a trust will not fail for lack of a trustee because the courts can always appoint a successor trustee if no trustee is named in the instrument.

Capacity of the settlor

The settlor must be of sufficient age and mental capacity.

If the trust is testamentary, the validity of the trust depends upon the validity of the will.

The capacity of the testator/settlor can be challenged in a will contest.

The creation of an *inter vivos* trust requires a present capacity of the settlor to declare that they are holding property in trust or conveying the trust property.

The settlor must convey the present intent to create a trust relationship where the legal title to the property is held by a trustee for the benefit of a beneficiary and must comply with the formalities of creating a trust by declaring themselves trustee or transferring the property to a trustee.

To create a trust, the language employed by the transferor settlor when transferring the property to a transferee must impose mandatory obligations on the transferee to hold the property in trust for the benefit of the trust beneficiaries.

If the transferor uses precatory language such as "wish," "hope," "request," or "desire" for the transferee's use of the property, they will not create a trust due to the lack of an enforceable obligation placed upon the transferee.

Where the circumstances show that the settlor did intend to impose mandatory duties, a court may construe precatory language as creating mandatory obligations on the transferee and therefore creating a trust.

In making that determination, the court may be more likely to find a trust if the settlor had an obligation to support the beneficiaries.

Necessity for writing

A testamentary trust is part of a will and must always be created by formally executed writings.

An *inter vivos* trust may be created orally if it involves only personal property.

An *inter vivos* trust containing land created by a settlor's declaration is valid only if the settlor has executed a writing indicating that they are holding the land in trust.

If the trust in land is created by transfer to the trustee, that transfer must be in writing.

If a purported settlor conveys land to a third person without indication that the third person holds the property in a trust, the transferee can carry out the terms of the trust that were given by the trustee orally or void any trust obligation.

An oral promise to hold proceeds from the sale of land in a trust is not within the Statute of Frauds and will be enforced when the trustee sells the property.

Trust property

There must be some identifiable trust property in which the settlor can declare that they hold in trust or with a present right to convey to a trustee.

Intangible property interests and contingent interests, which are more than mere expectancy, can be the subject of a trust.

Definite or ascertainable beneficiaries

For a private trust instead of a charitable trust discussed later, the beneficiaries must be identified or ascertainable.

The settlor may designate a definite and ascertainable class of persons as beneficiaries.

Valid trust purpose

A private express trust cannot be created for an illegal purpose or contrary to public policy.

If the trustee, in carrying out the terms of the trust, would be required to commit a tortious act or defraud creditors of the settlor, the trust is invalid.

Time restrictions

The Uniform Statutory Rule Against Perpetuities provides that the interest of the beneficiaries in the principal of a trust, or a special, testamentary, or contingent power of appointment is valid if it is certain to vest within the common-law rule period or does vest within 90 years after its creation.

The statute embodies a wait rule, which allows the non-vested property interest a grace period of 90 years to vest.

The statute has a reformation provision that allows a court on the petition of an "interested person" to modify an invalid disposition under the rule stated above so that it follows the grantor's intent as nearly as possible but does, in fact, vest within 90 years.

Defining Characteristics of Charitable Trusts

Charitable purpose

A legally recognized charitable purpose, such as the furtherance of health, religion, education, government, or the arts, is an essential characteristic of a charitable trust.

The settlor can create a charitable trust that does not set forth a defined charitable purpose but limits the trustees' activity to the furtherance of charitable purposes.

Indefinite class of beneficiaries

For a trust to qualify as charitable, there must be a public benefit, so the persons to be benefited must be members of an indefinite class.

If a defined class of beneficiaries such as a scholarship trust at a university for the settlor's descendants, the trust is not charitable.

If the class of beneficiaries is large such as the inhabitants of a specific town, the indefinite class of beneficiaries' test has been met.

Similarities to private trusts

A charitable trust may be created by any methods for creating an express trust, and there must be a settlor with the capacity to convey properly expressed intent, and a specific trust *res* (or *corpus*), and power of enforcement.

Notes for active learning

Limitations of Private Trusts Inapplicable to Charitable Trusts

Rule against perpetuities inapplicable

A charitable trust may continue indefinitely and is not subject to the rule against perpetuities or the rule against accumulations unless the accumulation is found to be unreasonable.

Failure of purpose

When some other change in circumstances renders it impracticable to administer the trust as provided by the settlor, or the charitable purpose intended by the settlor has or can no longer be accomplished, the doctrine of *cy pres* (as near as possible) may be applicable.

Instead of terminating the trust, the courts alter the trust's purpose to continue while following the settlor's original intent as possible.

Under the *cy pres* doctrine (i.e.., *amending a legal document*), a court may modify the trust's purpose and permit the trustee to use the trust *res* (body) for another charitable purpose, close to the settlor's original charitable intent.

If the trust instrument indicates that the *cy pres* doctrine is not applied, the trust *res* (i.e., body) reverts to the settlor or their estate.

Enforcing the trust

In a private trust, the beneficiaries have the power to enforce the provisions of the trust.

Since there are no defined beneficiaries in a charitable trust, the enforcement power is given by statute to the state's Attorney General.

Notes for active learning

Spendthrift Provisions

Protections for beneficiaries

A beneficiary's equitable interest in income or principal of the trust may be voluntarily assigned and may be subjected to the claims of judgment creditors of the beneficiary unless the terms of the trust provide otherwise.

The settlor may insert a spendthrift provision in a trust, which validly prohibits the beneficiary from transferring their interest in the trust before it is distributed to them.

Such a provision prevents the beneficiary's creditors from reaching the beneficiary's interest in the trust to satisfy their claims.

Once a beneficiary receives a distribution from the trust, creditors may reach that distribution.

A settlor cannot insert a spendthrift provision in a trust which protects their beneficial interest in the trust from creditors.

A discretionary trust, in which the beneficiary has no right to income until the trustee decides to pay it, will so protect the beneficiary's interest from creditors.

The settlor can give the trustee the discretionary power to pay income due to a specific beneficiary or accumulate it and provide that the trustee has the discretion to pay the income among several beneficiaries.

When those provisions are in place, neither the beneficiary nor their creditors can compel payment or funds from the trust.

Notes for active learning

Administration of the Trust by the Trustee

Appointment of the trustee

The settlor ordinarily has the power to select the trustee and provide for succession of trustees.

If the trustee refuses to serve or fails to qualify, the probate court has broad discretion in naming a trustee or appointing a successor trustee to fill a vacancy.

Resignation or removal of the trustee

Once a trustee is in office, they may resign if authorized by the trust instrument or with permission of all the beneficiaries or the probate court.

The probate court has the power to remove a trustee upon a petition filed by the beneficiaries for failing to perform their duties, breaching a fiduciary duty, or where there is hostility between the trustee and the beneficiaries.

Compensation of the trustee

A trustee is entitled to receive reasonable compensation for their services as a trustee.

A trustee is entitled to reimbursement for expenses occurring in the administration of the trust.

A trustee who is an attorney can render legal services to the trust and be paid separately for those services.

If the trust instrument does not allocate fees between income and principal, the court can determine the allocation.

Notes for active learning

Powers of the Trustee

The trustee has powers conferred by the trust instrument to manage the trust assets and distribute them to beneficiaries; the trustee may incorporate statutory optional fiduciary powers by reference.

Power of sale or contract

Without a specific grant of power, a trustee may sell and transfer personal property unless the trust instrument prohibits such sale.

The authority to sell or transfer real estate must be expressly granted in the trust.

Otherwise, the trust must obtain court approval to sell or transfer real estate.

A trustee has the power to enter contracts on behalf of the trust and further has the power to execute instruments that will accomplish or facilitate the exercise of their other powers.

Power to invest

A trustee has the power and duty to invest the trust property, make the property productive, and use reasonable care and skill to choose and manage investments.

Power of apportionment

If the trust provides that income is paid to one set of beneficiaries and principal to another set, the trust instrument sets the standards for apportionment of income and expenses.

Absent authority in the trust instrument, the trustee should pay ordinary expenses out of income and extraordinary expenses and those solely beneficial to the remainder interests out of principal.

The general rule provides that cash dividends are allocated to income and stock dividends to the principal.

Power to invade principal

The trust instrument can provide discretionary principal payments to income beneficiaries and usually set up a standard by which such payments should be made.

The discretion of the trustee to make such payments will rarely be disturbed by a court.

Unless there is power in the trust instrument to invade principal, a court will not permit principal payments to an income beneficiary if the instrument benefits a different principal beneficiary.

If an income beneficiary is the sole principal beneficiary upon a particular age, the court has the discretion to permit principal payment acceleration for circumstances not foreseen by the settlor.

Duties and Liabilities of the Trustee

Duty of loyalty and good faith

The highest fiduciary duty of loyalty is imposed upon a trustee.

The trustee must avoid conflicts of interest between their interests and the trusts and between the interests of others to whom the trustee owes a fiduciary duty and those of the trust.

When a conflict occurs, the trustee cannot enter a transaction on behalf of the trust unless the transaction is fair to the trust and the trust instrument authorizes them explicitly, or the trustee makes appropriate disclosure and receives permission from the court or beneficiaries.

If a beneficiary is not competent to act, guardian *ad litem* should be appointed and act on behalf of the incompetent beneficiaries.

If the trustee takes an action that affects life tenants and remaindermen, the trustee must act fairly to each group.

If the trustee purchases property in their individual capacity, which is an appropriate opportunity for the trust, a constructive trust can be imposed upon the property held by the trustee in their individual capacity.

A constructive trust can be imposed upon the property if the trustee purchases property from the trust without complying with their fiduciary obligations.

Duty of reasonable care and skill

The trustee must abide by the limitations imposed by the trust instrument for their powers of investment.

The trustee must exercise reasonable care and skill in managing the trust.

The trust instrument can authorize the trustee to take greater risks with trust investments and particularly authorize the trustee to retain the investments transferred initially to the trust even though the investment concentration would not be prudent for trust investment.

If the trustee exercises the required standard of care, they are not liable for mistakes in judgment.

Unless the trust instrument authorizes delegation explicitly, a trustee may not delegate their duties to others, except for ministerial (i.e., purely administrative) duties.

Even though a trustee can seek expert advice on matters concerning trust property, the trustee must supervise agents and make the final decision on actions suggested.

Trust property must not be commingled with the trustee's property.

Except when there is an authority to invest in a common trust fund, it should not be placed with funds from other trusts.

Duty to make property productive

The trustee may not keep unproductive property such as vacant land as an asset of the trust unless the trust instrument authorizes this or the beneficiary's consent for such an investment.

The trustee has a duty to sell the unproductive property and reinvest in productive assets.

Duty to account

The trustee has a duty to account to the beneficiaries, telling them how they managed the trust property, the income they are entitled to, and the amount of principal held in the trust.

Liability to third parties

A trustee is not personally liable for a contract, which they make in a disclosed capacity as a trust unless the contract expressly provides personal liability.

A trustee is not personally liable for torts committed during prudent administration of the trust unless there is a personal fault by the trustee.

The trust estate is liable for claims in tort or contract for obligations entered by the trustee or tort claims arising from the trust's property.

Termination of the Trust

Termination by the settlor

The settlor's unilateral action could terminate a trust if they reserved the power in the trust instrument to revoke it.

If the power is not reserved, the trust cannot be terminated by the settlor unless they obtain all the beneficiaries' consent, which must be of legal age and competent.

Termination after the settlor's death

Even if all the beneficiaries of a trust approve of its termination after the settlor's death, courts will not ordinarily terminate it before the time specified in the trust if such termination is contrary to the settlor's intent.

Where no material purpose of the settlor remains to be accomplished, the court may allow termination upon request of all the beneficiaries whose interests are vested and who are competent to consent.

If the trust is spendthrift or discretionary, the settlor's purpose in creating the trust has not been fulfilled, so it cannot be terminated even if all the beneficiaries desire such termination.

The trustee has no power to terminate the trust unless such power was expressly granted.

If the trustee has the power to distribute the principal of the trust, they can effectively terminate it by conveying the trust property to the beneficiaries per the terms of the trust.

Termination by the court

If an emergency or unforeseen circumstance (e.g., severe medical need) by a beneficiary causes the trust purpose to be impaired or frustrated, a court may terminate the trust even though the settlor's material purpose still exists, and beneficiaries do not consent.

Notes for active learning

Trusts Created by Operation of Law

There are two kinds of legal entities labeled as trusts, purchase money *resulting trusts* and *constructive trusts* created by operation of law, and do not fit the classic definition of trusts.

Each entity is important for exam purposes because candidates must be aware of the circumstances where they are operative and discuss them in their answers.

Resulting trusts – failure or inadequacy of express trust

If the settlor failed to create an express trust and has transferred the property to an individual whom they intended to act as a trustee or the settlor has transferred the property to the trustee above that needed to accomplish the purposes of the trust, that person holds the property for the settlor, heirs, or successors.

The trust is a resulting trust because it is presumed that, upon the failure of an express trust or the lack of need, the settlor intended the property be retained for their benefit.

If a trust were created because of a contractual obligation of the settlor, the trust could fail.

If the person intended to be benefited by the contractual obligation creating a trust becomes the legal owner of the property rather than a beneficiary, no resulting trust was created.

If the settlor used precatory language when they transferred property, so no trust exists, and the transferee of the property holds the property outright, and no resulting trust exists.

Purchase money conveyances

When one person pays consideration for the transfer of property, but the title is taken in the name of another person, and there is no donative intent on the part of the person paying the consideration, the person receiving the property holds it in a purchase money resulting trust.

If the person named who furnished the consideration has an obligation to support the person whose name title is taken, the presumption for a gift and no resulting trust arises.

The presumption of a gift arises where one spouse furnishes the consideration for the purchased property, and the title is taken in the name of the other spouse.

No such presumption of a gift occurs if a parent furnishes the consideration and title is taken in the name of an adult child

Even where there is a presumption of a gift, that presumption may be rebutted by clear and convincing evidence, and a resulting trust arises.

The statute of frauds does not apply to a resulting trust.

Proof of the intent not to make a gift and not to vest a beneficial interest in the grantee of the deed may be made by parol evidence.

A resulting trust must arise at the time of purchase from a third party.

If the person furnishing the consideration takes the title from the seller in their name and subsequently transfers property upon an oral promise of the grantee to hold the property in trust, no resulting trust is presumed.

If the person who did not take title paid only part of the purchase price, they might establish a resulting trust for a partial interest in the property if they show clear and convincing evidence that their payment was for a distinct interest in the property.

Constructive trusts

A court creates a constructive trust as an equitable remedy when there is no intention (express or presumed) to create a voluntary trust.

The equitable remedy is employed to avoid unjust enrichment where the legal title to the property was obtained:

1) by fraud,
2) in violation of a fiduciary or confidential relationship,
3) by testamentary devise or intestate succession when the titleholder promised the testator that they would hold the property in trust for the benefit of someone else.

When a court finds that a constructive trust has been established, it will order the person whose conduct caused the constructive trustee to transfer title to and possession of the property held in the constructive trust to its rightful owner.

The circumstances which give rise to a constructive trust may be proven by oral evidence.

Neither the statute of frauds nor the parol evidence rule prevents a constructive trust from arising.

Fraud

If the property is conveyed to a person who makes a promise to use the property for a specific purpose and that person had no intent of fulfilling that promise when the property was conveyed, a court will impose a constructive trust upon the property requiring the grantee to use it for the intended purpose.

If the constructive trust remedy is not available because the grantor cannot prove an express trust and that the conveyance was procured by fraudulent intent, the grantor can recover the fair market value of the land based on a failure of consideration.

Violation of fiduciary or confidential relationship

A constructive trust will be imposed upon the property that is obtained in violation of a fiduciary relationship, such as attorney and client, trustee and beneficiary, physician and patient, business partners, employer and employee, corporate director or officer, and corporation or accountant and client.

Abuse of the fiduciary relationship can be shown by evidence of self-dealing or using confidential information to the advantage of the recipient at the expense of the one who disclosed the information or corporate opportunity.

Family relationship alone does not create fiduciary relationships but can be a factor if establishing one.

A fiduciary relationship does not ordinarily exist between businesspersons in arm's length relationships, but a confidential or fiduciary relationship may exist between those in a business relationship; if there is a misuse of confidential information.

Secret trusts on testamentary transfers

If a decedent fails to make a will and dies intestate, an express trust cannot be established.

If a decedent makes a will benefit an individual in reliance upon the oral promise of the person benefited by the will or by the intestacy that they use the inheritance to benefit another person, an express trust cannot be established.

A court can impose a constructive trust on the inheritance and require that the legatee use the property for fulfilling the promise made to the testator.

Relationship matrix

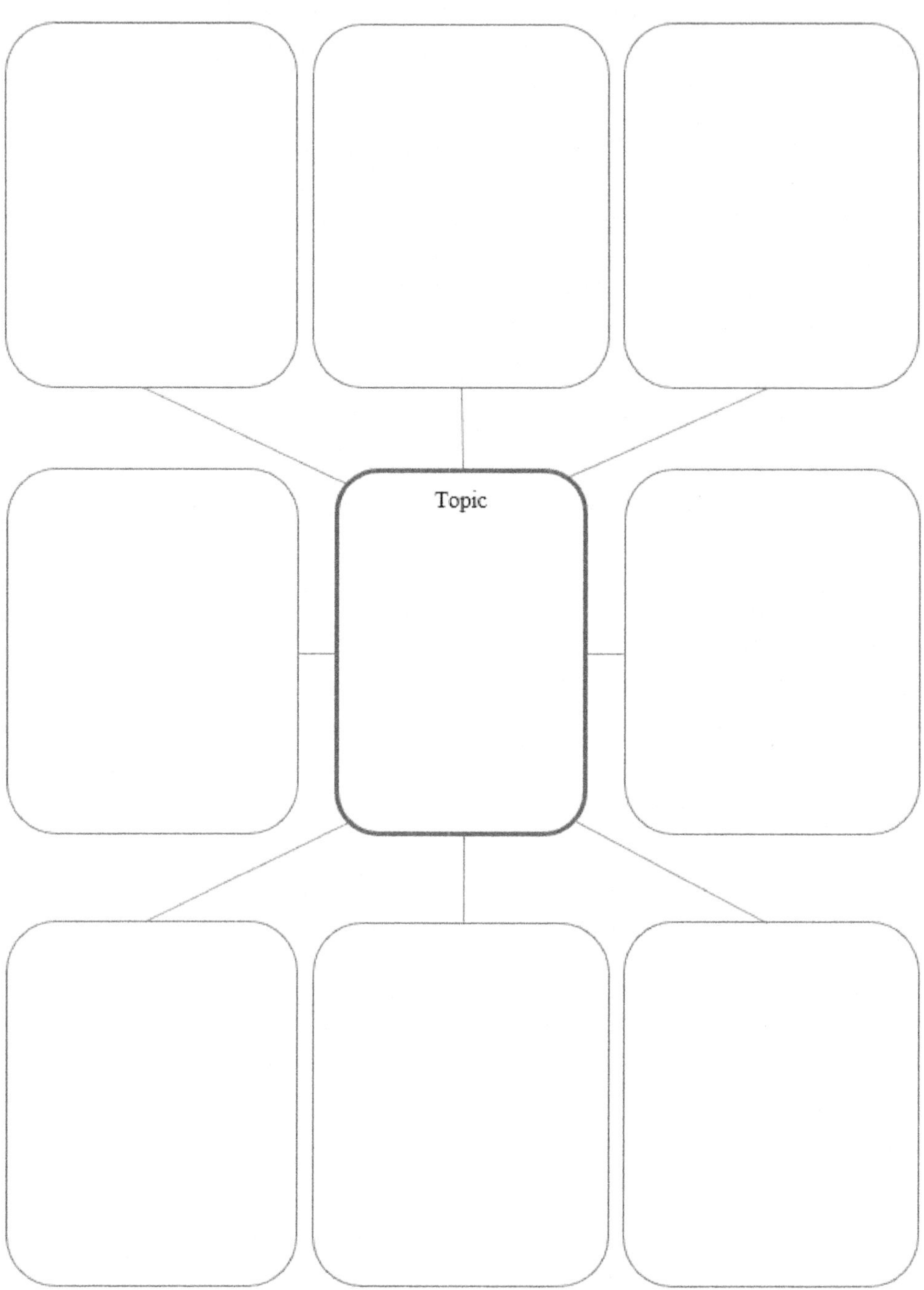

Notes for active learning

Notes for active learning

Secured Transactions

Secured Transactions is tested regularly as a standalone subject but may appear as a component of Contracts or Real Property. While specific items tested on Secured Transactions are somewhat predictable, they are challenging. The most tested items include classification of goods (e.g., consumer goods, inventory, equipment, farm products), security interest, attachment, perfection, and default. It is imperative to be familiar with the complex vocabulary.

For Secured Transaction questions, it is essential to understand the application of the Uniform Commercial Code Article 9. Per the National Conference of Bar Examiners (NCBE), assume that the Official Texts of Articles 1 and 9 of the UCC are adopted.

The Uniform Commercial Code (UCC) – Articles 1 and 9

History of the Uniform Commercial Code

The Uniform Law Commission (ULC), formed in 1892, promulgated uniform commercial laws.

The Uniform Negotiable Instruments Law, approved in 1896, was soon enacted in every state.

In 1940, the Uniform Law Commission drafted a comprehensive code to provide guidelines for commercial transactions.

In 1942, the ULC and the American Law Institute partnered to assemble the component commercial laws in a comprehensive Uniform Commercial Code (UCC) offered to the states for their consideration in 1951.

In 1953, Pennsylvania became the first state to adopt the UCC, and every other state had adopted the UCC within twenty years.

The UCC has been adopted, with some modifications, by every state and the District of Columbia, Guam, and the U.S. Virgin Islands.

UCC Article 1 – general provisions

Uniform Commercial Code (UCC) Article 1 contains definitions and general provisions applicable as default rules to transactions covered under other articles of the UCC.

Article 1 was revised in 2001, with a few minor amendments to harmonize with recent revisions of other UCC articles.

UCC Article 9 – Secured Transactions

The Uniform Commercial Code Article 9 provides a statutory framework that governs secured transactions, granting credit secured by personal property.

Each state maintains an office for filing financial statements to disclose security interests in encumbered property publicly.

A substantial revision to Article 9 was completed in 1998 and adopted in all states.

Secured transactions and UCC law

The law in the U.S. covers the creation and enforcement of a security interest.

A secured transaction happens when a person or business borrows money to acquire property, including real estate, vehicles, or business equipment.

A security interest exists when a borrower enters a contract that allows the lender (secured party) to take collateral the borrower owns if the borrower cannot repay the loan.

The term *security interest* is often used interchangeably with *lien* in the U.S.

Purpose of secured transactions

A security interest promotes economic security because it provides the lender with the promise of repayment. If the borrower defaults on the loan, the lender should recoup the loan amount by taking the agreed-upon asset used as collateral and selling it.

A security interest is particularly valuable in bankruptcy because secured creditors collect debts before creditors without a security interest.

Law governs secured transactions

A security interest generally is created with a security agreement, which is a contract governed by UCC Article 9 and state laws governing contracts.

Article 9 of the UCC governs voluntary and commercial transaction and creates an interest in personal property.

Real property secured transactions, such as for a real estate mortgage, are not governed by Article 9 but by real property laws that vary among states.

Fixtures include personal property attached to real property (e.g., furnace, kitchen cabinets).

Statutory liens arise from laws providing a right to retain property against its owner as security for obligations, governed by enabling statutes.

Creating security interests under Article 9

For a security interest to be enforceable against the debtor and third parties, value must be exchanged for the collateral.

UCC Article 9 sets forth three requirements:

1) the debtor must have rights in the collateral or the ability to convey rights in the collateral to a secured party, and either

2) the debtor must have "authenticated" a security agreement describing the collateral, or

3) the creditor must be in possession of the collateral.

When Article 9 requirements are satisfied, the security interest "attaches" to the collateral and becomes enforceable.

Usually, a borrower and lender sign a security agreement.

Such a security agreement usually includes:

1) a description of the borrower's collateral,

2) a description of the obligation it secures,

3) an identification of what constitutes a default,

4) rights of the creditor if the borrower defaults,

5) requirements of the debtor for the care of and insurance maintained on the collateral, and

6) other obligations of the parties to the transaction.

A statute of frauds within UCC Article 9 requires the security agreement be in writing.

An exception to this requirement be in writing is when a security interest is pledged.

A pledge is when a borrower gives the collateral to the lender in exchange for a loan (e.g., goods to a pawnbroker in exchange for a cash loan).

If a security agreement does not exist, and the security interest is not pledged, but the transaction appears to be an Article 9 transaction, the court may recognize it as such by applying the composite document rule.

The court will consider documents supporting the security agreement and create an enforceable security interest by reading the documents.

The parties must authenticate the documents specified by this rule; if this proves impossible, the security agreement fails.

Perfection

The perfection of a security agreement allows a secured party to prioritize the collateral over a third party, should the borrower default on the loan.

Perfection becomes important if other creditors have an interest in the secured property because a secured creditor's obligation will be satisfied before other liens; known as priority.

The creditor with the highest priority will be repaid before others if the borrower defaults and foreclosure occurs.

Three exceptions exist for filing for perfection:

automatic redemption,

possession, and

taking control of a deposit account.

The typical way to perfect a security interest is by filing a notice in a public office.

The filing of a public notice puts other creditors on notice of the attached security interest in the creditor's property.

The required filing most frequently is a financing statement.

For a financing statement to be valid, it must include:

1) the debtor's name,

2) the secured party's name or representative, and

3) a description of the property covered by the statement.

If any of the three elements are missing from a financing statement, the security interest will not be perfected.

A financing statement is valid for five years from the date it was filed and can be extended.

The United States does not have a central place for filing.

Each state has a UCC filing system; though the filing office varies from state to state, most commonly, it is the Secretary of State's office.

For the most part, each county in the U.S. has a real estate recording office where Article 9 fixture filings can be done.

Article 9 – Secured Transactions

Introduction to secured transactions

Article 9 addresses issues about the priority of parties concerning the collateral.

Issues concerning the foreclosure method of a security interest, the rights of the debtor when the secured party wants to foreclose the security interest, the rights of parties in bankruptcy, or the intricacies of exotic types of security interests have not been asked and will not be discussed.

An approach to priority problems

For Article 9, questions about the rights of the parties resolve the following issues.

1) Is the security interest of each claimant and other secured parties valid?
2) Have the various security interests attached? When did attachment occur?
3) Is the collateral consumer goods, business equipment, or business inventory?
4) Are any of the security interests purchase money security interests?
5) Has each security interest been perfected, and when was each perfected?
6) Has the property been acquired from the debtor by a good faith purchaser?
7) What priority rule applies to the claims of each party?

Creating the security interest by security agreement

A security agreement establishes a security interest.

A security agreement must be in writing and contain a statement that a security interest in collateral, described in the agreement, is created, and the debtor must sign it.

A security agreement can agree to give a security interest in property that the debtor will acquire in the future. Such an interest does not attach until the debtor obtains an interest in the property.

Creating the security interest by pledge

A pledge occurs when the secured party takes possession of the debtor's property with an oral or written agreement that the secured party will hold the property to secure a debt.

Notes for active learning

Attaching the Security Interest

Collateral for the security interest

Even if there is a security agreement or a pledge, a creditor has no security interest in a piece of collateral until that interest attaches to the collateral.

If a security interest has been properly created, the debtor must receive value, which is defined as consideration to support a contract.

Examples of "value" are:

1) a binding agreement by the secured party to extend credit, or

2) total or partial satisfaction of a pre-existing claim, or

3) the debtor's acceptance of delivery of the collateral per the pre-existing contract.

Debtor must have rights in the collateral

This issue does not arise if the debtor is the collateral owner.

The debtor may not yet acquire title to the collateral because:

1) it is being manufactured according to a purchase order,

2) the security interest would not arise until the goods are identified in the contract.

Identified goods during seller's insolvency

The buyer has a particular property interest in the goods, which entitles them to obtain identified goods (for which they made at least partial payment) upon the seller's insolvency.

This interest gives certain rights to:

1) specific performance, and

2) an insurable interest in the identified goods.

Notes for active learning

Collateral

Types of collateral

Bar exam questions under Article 9 rarely deal with sophisticated business arrangements in collateral, such as accounts receivable.

Bar exam questions generally deal with tangible personal property.

There are four important categories for a priority problem:

1) consumer goods,

2) machinery used in business (different rules for perfection),

3) business inventory,

4) collateral, which is attached to real estate, is a fixture.

Mortgagee *vs.* secured party

The rules for filing to perfect a security interest in such collateral against the owner and mortgagees of the real property are different from that of property not so affixed.

Special priority rules apply for mortgagees of real property.

The term *fixtures* is defined by law.

In most states, whether a chattel has become a fixture depends on the objective intent of the owner of the property.

Where the chattel is so affixed to the realty that its identity is lost, or where it cannot be removed without material injury to the realty itself, any security interest in the property as personalty is lost, and the owner of the real estate is the owner of the collateral.

If the property can be removed from the real estate without substantial damage, the secured party can preserve their security interest in the collateral with proper filing.

A fixture filing must be made to obtain priority over subsequent interests in real estate.

Notes for active learning

Perfected Security Interests

Notice by perfection

The perfection of a security interest is similar to the process of recording a mortgage.

Its purpose is to give notice to the world that the secured party has a security interest in specified collateral of the debtor to let other potential creditors know that the secured party has a claim on that collateral to satisfy its debt.

If a secured party fails to perfect its security interest, it risks losing its ability to exercise a secured party's rights in the collateral.

Perfection of a security interest established by pledge

Possession of the collateral by the secured party is sufficient to perfect a pledge.

No filing is required.

Perfection by filing

A security interest is protected by filing only if accomplished as prescribed by Article 9 and filed in the proper place.

Except where the Code provides a grace period, perfection occurs at the time of filing or when the property attaches, whichever is later.

Automatic perfection

An interest in consumer goods is automatically perfected as soon as the secured party's security interest attaches without filing or possession.

Certificates of title for motor vehicles – perfection

When a car is registered, a "certificate of title" is issued.

When dealing with the motor vehicle, the certificate of title determines who owns the car and the extent to which the named owner's title is subject to others' interests.

A security interest in an automobile used as consumer goods or equipment is perfected only by applying for a certificate of title, showing the security interest on it.

There is a ten-day grace period for perfecting a security interest on a motor vehicle that operates in the same manner as the grace period for a purchase money security interest.

Filing of a security interest

The primary object of the filing is to give interested parties notice of the security interest.

The filing requirement is satisfied if a security agreement or financing statement containing the following information is filed:

1) Name and address of the debtor and secured party.

2) Description of the collateral by items or types; must reasonably identify what is described.

3) Signature of only the debtor.

Minor errors will not affect the validity of the filing.

Amendments are permitted.

The proper place of filing a security interest is with the Secretary of State's office.

Characterizing the Status of Contesting Third Parties

Third-party claims to the collateral

Before applying the rules of priority, characterize the various parties' status.

In most questions, the parties fall into four groups:

1) general creditors of the debtor,
2) other secured creditors of the debtor,
3) creditors who have obtained a judicial lien against the debtor's property, and
4) transferees of the title to the property.

In general, to assert their rights, each of the types of parties must have no actual knowledge of another party's security interest when they gave credit or purchased the property.

The exception to this rule is the buyer in the ordinary course of business who takes free of a lien even if they knew about it.

General creditors

A *general creditor* has a claim (including a judgment) against the debtor but no lien against the property in question.

A secured party always prevails over a general creditor.

Lien creditors

A general creditor who obtains a pre-judgment or post-judgment lien of the property in issue is a lien creditor.

An assignee for the benefit of creditors and a trustee in bankruptcy is a lien creditor.

Their priority position for collateral is determined by the time they obtained the lien.

Other secured parties

Secured parties have security interests created under Article 9.

Rules for the priorities of secured parties are established by Article 9.

Transferees

Transferees have acquired the debtor's ownership in the collateral instead of persons with lesser interests, such as secured parties.

Buyer in the ordinary course of business

The Buyer in Ordinary Course of Business is the most important and favored party in the Commercial Code.

Section 1-201 defines the buyer in the ordinary course of business as:

> A person, who in good faith and without knowledge that the sale violates the ownership rights or security interests of a third party in the goods, buys in the ordinary course from a person in the business of selling goods of that kind but omits a pawnbroker.

"Buying" may be for cash or by an exchange of other property or on secured or unsecured credit and includes receiving goods or title under a pre-existing contract for sale.

This does not include a transfer in bulk or as security for the satisfaction of a money debt.

To disqualify the buyer, there must be knowledge not merely of the third party's interests but that the sale violates those interests.

Buyers of appliances, automobiles or other inventory from retailers are usually buyers in the ordinary course of business.

A retailer buying inventory from a wholesaler is a buyer in the ordinary course of business.

Owners of real estate to which the collateral is attached

Owners of real estate to which the collateral is attached, and their mortgagees, may have rights in the collateral if it can be characterized as real estate if the perfection of the security interest did not include a filing in the registry of deeds.

Priority Rules

Preparation to apply the priority rules

When presented with a priority problem, the first step is to take each party and apply the governing law to determine their status.

If the party is claiming rights as a secured party, determine if they have a valid security interest in the property, when and if attached, when was it perfected.

Check if the secured party has a purchase money security interest.

Check if the secured party knew a prior unperfected security interest when they perfected their interest.

If the title has been transferred from the person who initially granted the security interest, determine if the transferee was a *bona fide* purchaser.

Once these characterizations are completed, apply the following rules to determine priority.

Secured party *vs.* unsecured creditor

If the secured party has a valid security interest in the collateral, they prevail over an unsecured creditor, even if the secured party does not perfect.

Secured party *vs.* statutory lien creditor

Artisans who perform work on personal property (car repairman) have a lien on the property for the work performed if they retain possession.

That lien is superior to a secured party's lien, perfected before the statutory lien arose.

Secured party *vs.* lien creditor

A general creditor can become a lien creditor by suing the debtor and establishing a lien on the debtor's property.

That lien becomes equivalent to a perfected security interest when the creditor has a lien on the goods.

To determine whose lien has priority, compare the date of the secured party's interest with when the judicial lien was perfected.

A judicial lien is perfected when the sheriff takes possession.

The first party to achieve the perfected lien status prevails.

Notes for active learning

Purchase Money Secured Interest (PMSI)

Priority rules for a purchase money security interest

Purchase money security interests (PMSI) have special rules of priority.

A purchase money security interest arises if the security interest is in favor of:

1) seller of the collateral to secure all or part of its price; or

2) a person who, by making advances or incurring an obligation, gives value to enable the debtor to acquire rights in or the use of collateral if such value is so used.

"Grace period" for purchase money security interests

Where the security interest is a purchase money security interest, there is a ten-day grace period for filing the notice of a security interest.

If the interest is filed within ten days of the date the debtor comes into possession of the collateral, the filing reverts to the time the debtor took possession.

This reversion is good against only bulk transferees and lien creditors.

It does not apply to good faith purchasers.

Except for collateral in the form of inventory, a purchase money security interest prevails over other security interests, provided it is perfected within ten days of the time possession is given to the debtor.

First in time, first in right

Where there are two or more secured parties contesting rights in the same collateral, the basic rule is again first in time, first in right.

There are three rules to determine who is first in time.

1) If both security interests are perfected, the first to perfect by properly filing prevails.

   If a security agreement includes after-acquired property, no security interest in that property arises until the interest attaches when the debtor obtains possession.

   Filing, not attachment, determines priority.

   A creditor who obtained a security interest in the after-acquired property and perfected it by filing prevails over a non-purchase money security interest filed later.

2) If one security interest is perfected and the other not, the perfected security interest prevails.

3) If neither security interest is perfected, the person whose interest first attached will prevail, but since neither party has completed the filing necessary for perfection, either party can perfect first and prevail.

PMSI *vs.* non-PMSI – who perfected first

Where the collateral is anything other than inventory (e.g., machinery), the purchase money secured interest (PMSI) party prevails over other security interests in the collateral.

This includes against those who hold a security interest in after-acquired collateral and have previously perfected if the purchase money secured interest party perfects within 10 days after the debtor obtains possession.

If the purchase-money collateral is inventory, the purchase money security holder will not prevail against a previously perfected security interest in that inventory unless the party claiming under the purchase money security interest:

1) perfects before giving possession to the debtor, and

2) gives notice to other secured parties of record.

Secured Party *vs.* Transferees of the Collateral

General rule

A purchaser of the collateral who gives value and takes delivery without knowledge of an outstanding unperfected security interest prevails over the secured party.

This rule applies to a purchase money security interest sold during the ten-day grace period.

A person who purchases collateral where there is a perfected security interest owns the property subject to the security interest unless one of the following special rules applies:

Where a debtor has permission to sell the collateral

If the secured party gives the debtor permission to sell the collateral, the secured party's security interest is extinguished upon sale; the buyer and subsequent purchasers take free and clear and with the security interest.

For example, if the bank has a perfected lien on all refrigerators in the dealer's stock and gives the dealer the right to sell them free of the collateral, the buyer will prevail even if they knew of the lien and was not a purchaser in the ordinary course of the seller's business.

Consumer buyers

Consumer buyers take free and clear of unfiled security interests.

For example, a buyer gives the seller a purchase money security interest on a refrigerator they purchase as consumer goods. Seller does not file the security interest, but it is perfected under the rule of automatic perfection without filing for consumer goods. If the buyer later sells that refrigerator to another consumer, that consumer takes free of the perfected security interest.

Bona Fide Purchasers in Ordinary Course of Business

A buyer in the ordinary course of business buys from a seller of goods of that kind, in good faith and without knowledge that the sale violates others' interests.

The buyer takes free of other interests, even the interest of an owner of the property who merely deposited the property with the seller.

A buyer in the ordinary course takes free of security interests created by the seller, even though the security interests are filed or otherwise perfected even though the buyer in the ordinary course knew of the security interest.

Secured Party *vs.* Landlord of the Debtor

The secured party has the right to remove personal property, which has become a fixture, and sell it if they had perfected that interest by filing it following the ordinary filing rules and has also filed it in the registry of deeds where the land lies.

The secured party's rights in the collateral are superior to the landlord and the landlord's mortgage, even if the mortgage was filed before the security interest.

If the collateral is so entwined with the real estate that it is not possible to remove it without significant damage to the real estate, the landlord prevails.

UNIFORM COMMERCIAL CODE (UCC)

Annotated Sections

STERLING
Test Prep

Applicable Sections Table of Contents*

* *Abridged*

Applicable Sections Table of Contents *(continued)*

Applicable Sections Table of Contents *(continued)*

Applicable Sections Table of Contents *(continued)*

Applicable Sections Table of Contents *(continued)*

Applicable Sections Table of Contents *(continued)*

Applicable Sections Table of Contents *(continued)*

Applicable Sections Table of Contents *(continued)*

Applicable Sections Table of Contents *(continued)*

Applicable Sections Table of Contents *(continued)*

General Provisions of the Uniform Commercial Code

The following chapters are for reference.

The National Conference of Bar Examiners (NCBE) listed chapters for Article 1 and Article 9 (Secured Transactions) are included below.

§ 1-103. Construction of the UCC Promotes Purposes and Policies

The Uniform Commercial Code must be liberally construed and applied to promote its underlying purposes and policies, which are:

a) to clarify and modernize the law governing commercial transactions;

b) to permit the continued expansion of commercial practices through custom, usage, and agreement of the parties; and

c) to make uniform the law among the various jurisdictions.

Unless displaced by the provisions of the Uniform Commercial Code, the principles of law and equity, including the law merchant and the law relative to capacity to contract, principal and agent, estoppel, fraud, misrepresentation, duress, coercion, mistake, bankruptcy, and other validating or invalidating cause supplement its provisions.

§ 1-105. Severability

If any provision or clause of the Uniform Commercial Code or its application is held invalid, the invalidity does not affect other provisions or applications of the UCC, which can be given effect without the invalid provision or application, and to this end, the provisions of the UCC are severable.

§ 1-108. Electronic Signatures in Commerce Act

This article modifies and supersedes the federal Electronic Signatures in Global and National Commerce Act, 15 U.S.C. Section 7001 *et seq.*, except that nothing in this article modifies or supersedes that Act or authorizes electronic delivery of any of the notices described in that Act.

General Definitions and Principles of Interpretation

§ 1-201. General Definitions

Subject to definitions in other articles of the UCC that apply to articles or parts thereof:

Action, as a judicial proceeding, includes recoupment, counterclaim, set-off, suit in equity, and other proceeding in which rights are determined.

Aggrieved party means a party entitled to pursue a remedy.

Agreement means the bargain of the parties as found in their language or inferred from other circumstances, including course of performance, course of dealing, or usage of trade.

Bearer means a person in possession of a negotiable instrument, the document of title, or certificated security payable to the bearer or endorsed in blank.

Bill of lading means a document evidencing the receipt of goods for shipment issued by a person engaged in the business of transporting or forwarding goods.

Buyer in the ordinary course of business means a person that buys goods in good faith, without knowledge that the sale violates the rights of another in the goods, and in the ordinary course from a person, other than a pawnbroker, in the business of selling goods of that kind.

A person buys goods in the ordinary course if the sale to the person comports with the usual or customary practices in the business in which the seller is engaged or with the seller's own usual or customary practices.

A buyer in the ordinary course of business may buy for cash by exchanging other property or on secured or unsecured credit and may acquire goods or documents of title under a preexisting contract for sale.

Only a buyer that takes possession of the goods or has a right to recover the goods from the seller under Article 2 may be a buyer in the ordinary course of business.

Buyer in the ordinary course of business does not include a person that acquires goods in a transfer in bulk or as security for or in total or partial satisfaction of a money debt.

Contract means the total legal obligation resulting from the parties' agreement as determined by the Uniform Commercial Code as supplemented by any other applicable laws.

Creditor includes a general creditor, a secured creditor, a lien creditor, and any representative of creditors, including an assignee for the benefit of creditors, a trustee in bankruptcy, a receiver in equity, and an executor or administrator of an insolvent debtor.

Delivery, for an instrument, a document of title, or chattel paper, means voluntary transfer of possession.

Document of title includes bill of lading, dock warrant, dock receipt, warehouse receipt or order for the delivery of goods, and other document which in the regular course of business is treated as adequately evidencing that the person in possession of it is entitled to receive and dispose of the document and the goods it covers.

A document of the title must purport to be issued by or addressed to a bailee and purport to cover goods in the bailee's possession identified or fungible portions of an identified mass.

Fault means a default, breach, or wrongful act or omission.

Fungible good means: 1) goods of which any unit, by nature or usage of trade, is the equivalent of any other like unit; or 2) goods that by agreement are treated as equivalent.

Good faith means honesty and the observance of reasonable commercial standards of fair dealing.

Holder means 1) the person in possession of a negotiable instrument that is payable to the bearer or an identified person in possession, or 2) the person in possession of a document of title if the goods are deliverable to bearer or the order of the person in possession.

Insolvency proceeding includes an assignment for the benefit of creditors or proceedings intended to liquidate or rehabilitate the estate of the person involved.

Insolvent means:

1) having ceased to pay debts in the ordinary course of business other than as a result of *bona fide* dispute;
2) being unable to pay debts as they become due; or
3) being insolvent within the meaning of federal bankruptcy law.

Party (distinguished from "third party") means a person engaged in a transaction or agreed subject to the Uniform Commercial Code.

Present value means the amount as of a date certain of one or more sums payable in the future, discounted to the date certain by use of either an interest rate specified by the parties if that rate is not manifestly unreasonable at the time the transaction is entered into or, if an interest rate is not so specified, a commercially reasonable rate that considers the facts at the time the transaction is entered into.

Purchase means taking by sale, lease, mortgage, pledge, lien, security interest, issue or reissue, gift, or other voluntary transaction creating an interest in the property.

Record means information that is inscribed on a tangible medium or that is stored in an electronic or other medium and is retrievable in perceivable form.

Remedy means any remedial right to which an aggrieved party is entitled with or without resort to a tribunal.

Security interest means an interest in personal property or fixtures which secures payment or performance of an obligation.

Security interest includes any interest of a consignor and a buyer of accounts, chattel paper, a payment intangible, or a promissory note in a transaction subject to Article 9.

A seller or lessor may acquire a security interest by complying with Article 9.

Surety includes a guarantor or other secondary obligor.

Unauthorized signature means a signature made without actual, implied, or apparent authority. The term includes a forgery.

Warehouse receipt means a receipt issued by a person engaged in the business of storing goods for hire.

§ 1-202. Notice; Knowledge

A person has **notice** of a fact if the person:

1) has actual knowledge of it;

2) has received a notice or notification of it; or

3) from the facts and circumstances known to the person at the time in question, has reason to know that it exists.

Knowledge means actual knowledge. "Knows" has a corresponding meaning.

Discover, or **learn**, refer to knowledge rather than to reason to know.

A person **notifies** or **gives** a notice or notification to another person by taking such steps as may be reasonably required to inform the other person in the ordinary course, whether the other person comes to know of it.

A person **receives** a notice or notification when:

1) it comes to that person's attention; or

2) it is duly delivered in a form reasonable under the circumstances at the place of business through which the contract was made or at another location held out by that person as the place for receipt of such communications.

Notice or knowledge received by an organization is effective for a particular transaction from the time it is brought to the attention of the individual conducting that transaction or should have been brought to the individual's attention if the organization had exercised due diligence.

An organization exercises due diligence if it maintains reasonable routines for communicating significant information to the person conducting the transaction, and there is reasonable compliance with the routines.

Due diligence does not require an individual acting for the organization to communicate information unless the communication is part of the individual's regular duties or the individual has reason to know of the transaction and that the transaction would be materially affected by the information.

§ 1-203. Lease Distinguished from Security Interest

A transaction in the form of a lease creates a security interest if the consideration that the lessee is to pay the lessor for the right to possession and use of the goods is an obligation for the term of the lease and is not subject to termination by the lessee, and:

1) the original term of the lease is equal to or greater than the remaining economic life of the goods;

2) the lessee is bound to renew the lease for the remaining economic life of the goods or is bound to become the owner of the goods;

3) the lessee has an option to renew the lease for the remaining economic life of the goods for no additional consideration or nominal additional consideration upon compliance with the lease agreement; or

4) the lessee has an option to become the owner of the goods for no additional consideration or nominal additional consideration upon compliance with the lease agreement.

A lease transaction does *not* create a security interest merely because:

1) the present value of the consideration the lessee is obligated to pay the lessor for the right to possession and use of the goods is substantially equal to or is greater than the fair market value of the goods at the time the lease is entered into;

2) the lessee assumes the risk of loss of the goods;

3) the lessee agrees to pay, for the goods, taxes, insurance, filing, recording, or registration fees, or service or maintenance costs;

4) the lessee has an option to renew the lease or to become the owner of the goods;

5) the lessee has an option to renew the lease for a fixed rent that is equal to or greater than the reasonably predictable fair market rent for the use of the goods for the term of the renewal at the time the option is to be performed; or

6) the lessee has an option to become the owner of the goods for a fixed price that is equal to or greater than the predictable fair market value of the goods at the time the option is to be performed.

Additional consideration is nominal if it is less than the lessee's reasonably predictable cost of performing under the lease agreement if the option is not exercised.

Additional consideration is *not nominal* if:

1) when the option to renew the lease is granted to the lessee, the rent is stated to be the fair market rent for the use of the goods for the term of the renewal determined at the time the option is to be performed; or

2) when the option to become the owner of the goods is granted to the lessee, the price is stated to be the fair market value of the goods determined at the time the option is to be performed.

The "remaining economic life of the goods" and "reasonably predictable" fair market rent, fair market value, or cost of performing under the lease agreement must be determined regarding the facts and circumstances at the time the transaction is entered.

§ 1-303. Course of Performance, Course of Dealing, and Usage of Trade

A course of performance is a sequence of conduct between the parties to a particular transaction that exists if:

1) the agreement of the parties for the transaction involves repeated occasions for performance by a party; and

2) the other party, with knowledge of the nature of the performance and opportunity for objection to it, accepts the performance or acquiesces in it without objection.

A **course of dealing** is a sequence of conduct concerning previous transactions between the parties to a particular transaction that is regarded as establishing a common basis of understanding for interpreting their expressions.

A **usage of trade** is any practice or method of dealing having such regularity in a place, vocation, or trade for an expectation that it will be observed for the transaction in question.

If it is established that such a usage is embodied in a trade code or similar record, the interpretation of the record is a question of law.

A **course of performance** or **course of dealing** between the parties or **usage of trade** in the vocation or trade in which they are engaged or of which they are or should be aware is relevant in ascertaining the meaning of the parties' agreement, may give meaning to specific terms of the agreement, and may supplement or qualify the terms of the agreement.

A usage of trade applicable in the place in which part of the performance under the agreement is to occur may be so utilized as to that part of the performance.

The express terms of an agreement and applicable course of performance, course of dealing, or usage of trade must be construed whenever reasonable as consistent with each other.

If such a construction is unreasonable:

1) express terms prevail over course of performance, course of dealing, and usage of trade;

2) course of performance prevails throughout dealing and usage of trade; and

3) course of dealing prevails over usage of trade.

A course of performance is relevant to show a waiver or modification of any term inconsistent with the course of performance.

Evidence of a relevant usage of trade offered by one party is not admissible unless that party has given the other party notice to prevent unfair surprise to the other party.

§ 1-304. Obligation of Good Faith

Duties within the UCC impose an obligation of *good faith* in performance and enforcement.

§ 1-305. Remedies to be Liberally Administered

The remedies provided by the UCC must be liberally administered so the aggrieved party may be put in as good a position as if the other party had entirely performed.

Consequential, special damages or penal damages do not apply except as expressly provided in the UCC or by another rule of law.

Any right or obligation declared by the UCC is enforceable by action unless the provision declaring it specifies a different and limited effect.

§ 1-307. Prima Facie Evidence by Third-Party Documents

A document in due form purporting to be a bill of lading, certificate of insurance, inspector's certificate, or other document authorized by the contract to be issued by a third party is prima facie evidence of its authenticity and the facts stated in the document by the third party.

§ 1-308. Performance or Acceptance Under Reservation of Rights

A party with explicit reservation of rights performs or promises performance or assents to performance in a manner demanded by the other party does not prejudice the rights reserved; it does not apply to an accord and satisfaction.

Such words as **without prejudice**, **under protest**, or the like are sufficient.

§ 1-309. Option to Accelerate at-Will

A term providing that one party may accelerate payment or performance or additional collateral "at-will" or when the party "deems itself insecure" means that the party has the power to do so only if that party in good faith believes that the prospect of payment or performance is impaired.

The burden of establishing a lack of good faith is on the party against which the power has been exercised.

§ 1-310. Subordinated Obligations

An obligation may be issued as subordinated to the performance of another obligation of the person obligated, or a creditor may subordinate its right to performance of an obligation by agreement with either the person obligated, or another creditor of the person obligated.

Subordination does not create a security interest as against either the common debtor or a subordinated creditor.

Article 9 – Secured Transactions

§ 9-102. Definitions

Accession means goods physically united with other goods such that the identity of the original goods is not lost.

Account means a right to payment of a monetary obligation, whether or not earned by performance, (i) for property that has been or is to be sold, leased, licensed, assigned, or disposed of, (ii) for services rendered, (iii) for a policy of insurance issued, (iv) for a secondary obligation incurred, (v) for energy provided, (vi) for the use of a vessel under a contract, (vii) arising out of the use of a credit card, or (viii) as winnings in a game of chance by government.

The term includes health-care insurance receivables.

The term does *not* include

rights to payment evidenced by chattel paper or an instrument,

commercial tort claims,

deposit accounts,

investment property,

letter-of-credit rights or letters of credit, or

rights to payment for money or funds advanced or sold, other than rights arising out of the use of a credit or charge card or information contained on or for use with the card.

Account debtor means a person obligated on an account, chattel paper, or general intangible.

The term does not include persons obligated to pay a negotiable instrument, even if the instrument constitutes part of chattel paper.

Accounting, except as used in "accounting for," means a record:

(A) authenticated by a secured party;

(B) indicating the aggregate unpaid secured obligations as of a date not more than 35 days earlier or 35 days later than the date of the record; and

(C) identifying the components of the obligations in reasonable detail.

Agricultural lien means an interest in farm products:

(A) which secures payment or performance of an obligation for:

(i) goods or services furnished in connection with a debtor's farming operation; or

(ii) rent on real property leased by a debtor in connection with its farming operation;

(B) which is created by statute in favor of a person that:

(i) in the ordinary course of its business furnished goods or services to a debtor in connection with a debtor's farming operation; or

(ii) leased real property to a debtor in connection with the debtor's farming operation; and

(C) whose effectiveness does not depend on the person's possession of the personal property.

As-extracted collateral means oil, gas, or other minerals subject to a security interest that:

is created by a debtor having an interest in the minerals before extraction; and

attaches to the minerals as extracted.

Authenticate means to sign or intently adopt a record, to attach to with the record an electronic sound, symbol, or process.

Cash proceeds mean money, checks, or deposit accounts.

Certificate of title means a statute provides the security interest to be indicated on the certificate as a condition of the security interest obtaining priority over a lien creditor's rights concerning the collateral.

The term includes another record maintained as an alternative to a certificate of title by the governmental unit that issues certificates of title if a statute permits the security interest to be indicated on the record because of the security interest's obtaining priority over the rights of a lien creditor concerning the collateral.

Chattel paper means a record evidencing a monetary obligation and a security interest in specific goods, a lease of specific goods, or license of software used in the goods.

Monetary obligation means a monetary obligation secured by the goods or owed under a lease of the goods and includes a monetary obligation for software used in the goods.

The term monetary obligation does *not* include:

a) charters or other contracts involving the use or hire of a vessel or

b) records that evidence a right to payment arising from using a credit or charge card or information contained for use with the card.

If a transaction is evidenced by records that include an instrument or series of instruments, the group of records taken together constitutes chattel paper.

Collateral means the property subject to a security interest or agricultural lien.

The term includes:

(A) proceeds to which a security interest attaches;

(B) accounts, chattel paper, and promissory notes that have been sold; and

(C) goods that are subject of a consignment.

Commercial tort claim means a claim arising in tort for which:

(A) the claimant is an organization; or

(B) the claimant is an individual, and the claim:

(i) arose in the course of the claimant's business or profession; and

(ii) does not include damages arising out of personal injury to or the death of an individual.

Commodity account means an account maintained by a commodity intermediary in which a commodity contract is carried for a commodity customer.

Commodity contract means a commodity futures contract, an option on a commodity futures contract, a commodity option, or another contract if the contract or option is:

(A) traded on or subject to the rules of a board of trade that has been designated as a contract market for such a contract under federal commodities laws; or

(B) traded on a foreign commodity board of trade, exchange, or market and is carried on the books of a commodity intermediary for a commodity customer.

Commodity customer means a person for which a commodity intermediary carries a commodity contract on its books.

Commodity intermediary means a person:

(A) registered as a futures commission merchant under federal commodities law; or

(B) in the ordinary course of its business provides settlement services for a board of trade designated as a contract market according to federal commodities law.

Communicate means:

(A) to send a written or another tangible record;

(B) to transmit a record by any means agreed upon by the persons sending and receiving the record; or

(C) in the case of transmission of a record to or by a filing office, to transmit a record by any means prescribed by filing-office rule.

Consignee means a merchant to which goods are delivered in a consignment.

Consignment means a transaction, regardless of its form, in which a person delivers goods to a merchant for sale and:

(A) the merchant:

(i) deals in goods of that kind under a name other than the name of the person making delivery;

(ii) is not an auctioneer; and

(iii) is not generally known by its creditors to be substantially engaged in selling the goods of others;

(B) for each delivery, the aggregate value of the goods is $1,000 or more at delivery;

(C) the goods are not consumer goods before delivery; and

(D) the transaction does not create a security interest in an obligation.

Consignor means a person that delivers goods to a consignee in a consignment.

Consumer debtor means a debtor in a consumer transaction.

Consumer goods mean goods used or bought for use primarily for personal, family, or household purposes.

Consumer-goods transaction means a consumer transaction in which:

(A) an individual incurs an obligation primarily for personal, family, or household purposes; and

(B) a security interest in consumer goods secures the obligation.

Consumer obligor means an obligor who is an individual and who incurred the obligation as part of a transaction entered primarily for personal, family, or household purposes.

Consumer transaction means a transaction in which (i) an individual incurs an obligation primarily for personal purposes, (ii) a security interest secures the obligation, and (iii) the collateral is held primarily for personal purposes.

The term includes consumer-goods transactions.

Continuation statement means an amendment of a financing statement which:

(A) identifies, by file number, the initial financing statement to which it relates; and

(B) indicates that it is a continuation statement for, or that it is filed to continue the effectiveness of, the identified financing statement.

Debtor means:

(A) a person having an interest, other than a security interest in the collateral, whether or not the person is an obligor;

(B) a seller of accounts, chattel paper, payment intangibles, or promissory notes; or

(C) a consignee.

Deposit account means a demand, time, savings, passbook, or similar account maintained with a bank. The term does not include investment property or accounts evidenced by an instrument.

Document means a document of title or a receipt of the type described in Section 7-201(2).

Electronic chattel paper means chattel paper evidenced by a record consisting of information stored in an electronic medium.

Encumbrance means a right, other than an ownership interest, in real property. The term includes mortgages and other liens on real property.

Equipment means goods other than inventory, farm products, or consumer goods.

Farm products mean goods, other than standing timber, for which the debtor is engaged in a farming operation and which are:

(A) crops grown or to be grown, including:

(i) crops produced on trees, vines, and bushes; and

(ii) aquatic goods produced in aquacultural operations.

(B) livestock, born or unborn, including aquatic goods produced in aquacultural operations;

(C) supplies used or produced in a farming operation; or

(D) products of crops or livestock in their unmanufactured states.

Farming operation means raising, cultivating, propagating, fattening, grazing, or any other farming, livestock, or aquacultural operation.

File number means the number assigned to an initial financing statement.

Filing office means an office designated as the place to file a financing statement.

Filing-office rule means a rule adopted.

Financing statement means a record composed of an initial financing statement and any filed record relating to the initial financing statement.

Fixture filing means the filing of a financing statement covering goods that are to become fixtures.

The term includes the filing of a financing statement covering goods of a transmitting utility that are to become fixtures.

Fixture means goods that have become so related to real property that an interest in them arises under real property law.

General intangible means any personal property, other than accounts, chattel paper, commercial tort claims, deposit account, documents, goods, instruments, investment property, letters of credit, money, and oil, gas, or other minerals before extraction.

The term includes payment intangibles and software.

Good faith means honesty and using reasonable commercial standards of fair dealing.

Goods mean things that are movable when a security interest attaches.

The term includes (i) fixtures, (ii) standing timber that is to be cut and removed under a conveyance or contract for sale, (iii) the unborn young of animals, (iv) crops, even if the crops are produced on trees, vines, or bushes, and (v) manufactured homes.

The term goods includes a computer program embedded in goods and any supporting information provided in connection with a transaction relating to the program if:

> (i) the program is associated with the goods in such a manner that it customarily is considered part of the goods, or
>
> (ii) by becoming the owner of the goods, a person acquires a right to use the program in connection with the goods.

The term goods does not include a computer program embedded in goods that consist solely of the medium in which the program is embedded.

The term goods does not include accounts, chattel paper, commercial tort claims, deposit accounts, documents, general intangibles, instruments, investment property, letters of credit, money, or oil, gas, or other minerals before extraction.

Governmental unit means a subdivision, agency, department, county, parish, municipality, or another unit of the United States, a State, or a foreign country.

The term includes an organization having a separate corporate existence if the organization is eligible to issue debt with interest exempt from income taxation.

Health-care-insurance receivable means an interest in or claim under a policy of insurance which is a right to payment of a monetary obligation for health-care goods or services provided.

Instrument means a negotiable instrument or any other writing that evidences a right to the payment of a monetary obligation, is not itself a security agreement, and is of a type that in the ordinary course of business is transferred by delivery with any necessary endorsement.

The term does not include (i) investment property, (ii) letters of credit, or (iii) writings that evidence a right to payment arising from the use of a credit card.

Inventory means goods, other than farm products, which:

(A) are leased by a person as lessor;

(B) are held by a person for sale or lease or to be furnished under a contract of service;

(C) are furnished by a person under a contract of service; or

(D) consist of raw materials, work in process, or materials used or consumed in a business.

Investment property means security (certificated or uncertificated), security account, commodity contract, or commodity account.

Jurisdiction of organization (for a registered organization) means the jurisdiction under whose law the organization is organized.

Letter-of-credit right means a right to payment or performance under a letter of credit, whether the beneficiary has demanded or is at the time entitled to demand payment or performance.

The term does not include the right of a beneficiary to demand payment or performance under a letter of credit.

Lien creditor means:

(A) a creditor that has acquired a lien on the property involved by attachment, levy;

(B) an assignee for the benefit of creditors from the assignment;

(C) a trustee in bankruptcy from the date of the filing of the petition; or

(D) a receiver in equity from the time of appointment.

Manufactured home means a structure, transportable in one or more sections, which, in the traveling mode, is eight body feet or more in width or 40 body feet or more in length, or, when erected on site, is 320 or more square feet, and designed to be used as a dwelling when connected to the required utilities, and includes the plumbing, heating, air-conditioning, and electrical systems contained therein.

Manufactured-home transaction means a secured transaction:

(A) that creates a purchase-money security interest in a manufactured home, other than a manufactured home held as inventory; or

(B) in which a manufactured home, other than a manufactured home held as inventory, is the primary collateral.

Mortgage means a consensual interest in real property, including fixtures, which secures payment or performance of an obligation.

New debtor means a person that becomes bound as a debtor by a security agreement previously entered by another person.

New value means (i) money, (ii) money's worth in property, services, or new credit, or (iii) release by a transferee of an interest in property previously transferred to the transferee.

The term does not include an obligation substituted for another obligation.

Noncash proceeds mean proceeds other than cash proceeds.

Obligor means a person that, for an obligation secured by a security interest in an agricultural lien,

(1) owes payment or performance of the obligation,

(ii) has provided property other than the collateral to secure payment or another performance of the obligation, or

(iii) is otherwise accountable for payment or other performance of the obligation.

The term does not include issuers (nominated persons) under a letter of credit.

Original debtor means a person that, as a debtor, entered into a security agreement to which a new debtor has become bound.

Payment intangible means a general intangible under which the account debtor's principal obligation is monetary.

Proceeds mean the following property:

(A) whatever is acquired upon the sale, lease, license, exchange, or other disposition of collateral;

(B) whatever is collected on, or distributed on account of, collateral;

(C) rights arising out of collateral;

(D) to the extent of the value of collateral, claims arising out of the loss, nonconformity, or interference with the use of, defects or infringement of rights in, or damage to, the collateral; or

(E) to the extent of the value of the collateral and the extent payable to the debtor or the secured party, insurance payable because of the loss of, defects, or infringement of rights in, or damage to, the collateral.

Promissory note means an instrument evidencing a promise to pay a monetary obligation, does not evidence an order to pay, and does not contain an acknowledgment by a bank that the bank has received funds for the deposit.

Proposal means a record authenticated by a secured party, which includes the terms on which the secured party is willing to accept collateral in satisfaction of the obligation it secures.

Public-finance transaction means a secured transaction in connection with which:

(A) debt securities are issued;

(B) all or a portion of the securities issued have an initial stated maturity of at least 20 years; and

(C) the debtor, obligor, secured party, account debtor, or other person obligated on collateral, assignor or assignee of a secured obligation, or assignor or assignee of a security interest is a State government.

Public organic record means a record that is available to the public for inspection and is:

(A) a record consisting of the record initially filed with or issued by a State or the United States to form or organize an organization and any record filed with or issued by the State or the United States which amends or restates the initial record;

(B) an organic record of a business trust consisting of the record initially filed with a State and records filed with the State which amends the initial record, if a statute of the State governing business trusts requires that the record be filed with the State; or

(C) a record consisting of legislation enacted by the legislature of a State or the Congress which forms an organization, any record amending the legislation, and any record filed with or issued by the State or the United States which amends the name of the organization.

Pursuant to commitment means according to the secured party's obligation, whether a subsequent event of default or another event not within the secured party's control has relieved the secured party from its obligation.

Record, except as used in **for the record, of record, record or legal title**, and **record owner**, means information that is inscribed on a tangible medium or which is stored in an electronic medium and is retrievable in perceivable form.

Registered organization means an organization organized solely under the law of a single State or the United States by the filing of a public organic record with, or the enactment of legislation by the State or the United States.

The term registered organization includes a business trust that is formed under the law of a single State if a statute of the State governing business trusts requires that the business trust's organic record be filed with the State.

Secondary obligor means an obligor to the extent that:

(A) the obligor's obligation is secondary; or

(B) the obligor has a right of recourse for an obligation secured by collateral against the debtor, another obligor, or property of either.

Secured party means:

(A) a person in whose favor a security interest is created or provided for under a security agreement, whether or not any obligation to be secured is outstanding;

(B) a person that holds an agricultural lien;

(C) a consignor;

(D) a person to which accounts, chattel paper, payment intangibles, or promissory notes have been sold;

(E) a trustee, indenture trustee, agent, or another representative in whose favor a security interest or agricultural lien is created.

Security Agreement means an agreement that creates a security interest.

Send, in connection with a record or notification, means:

(A) to deposit in the mail, deliver for transmission, or transmit by other usual means of communication, with postage or cost of transmission provided for, addressed to any address reasonable under the circumstances; or

(B) to cause the record or notification to be received within the time, it would have been received if sent under subparagraph (A).

Software means a computer program and supporting information provided in connection with a transaction relating to the program. The term does not include a computer program included in the definition of goods.

Supporting obligation means a letter-of-credit right or secondary obligation that supports an account's payment or performance, chattel paper, an instrument, or investment property.

Tangible chattel paper means chattel paper evidenced by a record or records consisting of information that is inscribed on a tangible medium.

Termination statement means an amendment of a financing statement which:

(A) identifies, by its file number, the initial financing statement to which it relates; and

(B) indicates that it is a termination statement or the identified financing statement is no longer effective.

Transmitting utility means a person primarily engaged in the business of:

(A) operating a railroad, subway, street railway, or trolley bus;

(B) transmitting communications electrically, electromagnetically, or by light;

(C) transmitting goods by pipeline or sewer; or

(D) producing or transmitting electricity, gas, steam, or water.

§ 9-103. PMSI; Application of Payments; Burden of Establishing

Purchase-money collateral means goods or software that secures a purchase-money obligation incurred for that collateral.

Purchase-money obligation means an obligation of an obligor incurred as part of the price of the collateral or for value given to enable the debtor to acquire rights in the collateral.

Purchase-money security interest (PMSI) in goods

A security interest in goods is a purchase-money security interest:

1) to the extent that the goods are purchase-money collateral for that security interest;

2) if the security interest is in inventory that is or was purchase-money collateral, to the extent that the security interest secures a purchase-money obligation incurred for other inventory that the secured party holds a purchase-money security interest; and

3) to the extent that the security interest secures a purchase-money obligation incurred for software in which the secured party holds or held a purchase-money security interest.

Purchase-money security interest in software

A security interest in software is a purchase-money security interest to the extent that the security interest secures a purchase-money obligation incurred for goods in which the secured party holds a purchase-money security interest if:

1) the debtor acquired its interest in the software in an integrated transaction in which it acquired an interest in the goods; and

2) the debtor acquired its interest in the software for the principal purpose of using the software in the goods.

Consignor's inventory purchase-money security interest

The security interest of a consignor in goods the subject of a consignment is a purchase-money security interest in inventory.

Application of payment in non-consumer-goods transactions

In a transaction other than a consumer-goods transaction, if the extent to which a security interest is a purchase-money security interest depends on the application of a payment to an obligation, the payment must be applied:

1) following any reasonable method of application to which the parties agree;

2) in the absence of the parties' agreement to a reasonable method, following any intention of the obligor manifested at or before the time of payment; or

3) in the absence of an agreement to a reasonable method and a timely manifestation of the obligor's intention, in the following order:

(A) to obligations not secured; and

(B) if more than one obligation is secured, to obligations secured by purchase-money security interests in the order in which those obligations were incurred.

Purchase-money security interest status in non-consumer-goods

In a transaction other than a consumer-goods transaction, a purchase-money security interest does *not* lose its status as such, even if:

1) the purchase-money collateral secures an obligation that is not a purchase-money obligation;

2) the collateral that is not purchase-money collateral secures the purchase-money obligation; or

3) the purchase-money obligation has been renewed, refinanced, consolidated, or restructured.

Burden of proof in non-consumer-goods transactions

In a transaction other than a consumer-goods transaction, a secured party claiming a purchase-money security interest has the burden of proving the extent of the security interest is a purchase-money security interest.

Non-consumer-goods transactions; no inference.

The limitation of the rules is intended to leave to the court to determine the proper rules in consumer-goods transactions.

The court may not infer from that limitation the proper rule in consumer-goods transactions and may apply established approaches.

§ 9-104. Control of Deposit Account

Requirements for control. A secured party has control of a deposit account if:

1) the secured party is the bank with which the deposit account is maintained;

2) the debtor, secured party, and bank have agreed in an authenticated record that the bank will comply with instructions originated by the secured party directing the disposition of funds in the deposit account without further consent by the debtor; or

3) the secured party becomes the bank's customer for the deposit account.

Debtor's right to direct disposition

A secured party with control, even if the debtor retains the right to direct the disposition of funds from the deposit account.

§ 9-105. Control of Electronic Chattel Paper

General rule: a secured party controls electronic chattel paper if a system evidencing the transfer of interests in the chattel paper establishes the secured party as the person to which the chattel paper was assigned.

Specific facts: a system satisfies subsection (a) if the record comprising the chattel paper are created, stored, and assigned in such a manner that:

1) a single authoritative copy of the record exists which is unique, identifiable, and except as otherwise provided;

2) the authoritative copy identifies the secured party as the assignee of the record;

3) the authoritative copy is communicated to and maintained by the secured party or its designated custodian;

4) copies or amendments that add or change an identified assignee of the authoritative copy can be made only with the consent of the secured party;

5) each copy of the authoritative copy is readily identifiable as a copy that is not the authoritative copy; and

6) any amendment of the authoritative copy is readily identifiable as authorized or unauthorized.

§ 9-106. Control of Investment Property

A person has control of a certificated security, uncertificated security, or security entitlement.

Control of commodity contract

A secured party has control of a commodity contract if:

1) the secured party is the commodity intermediary with which the commodity contract is carried; or

2) the commodity customer, secured party, and commodity intermediary have agreed that the commodity intermediary will apply value distributed on the commodity contract as directed by the secured party without further consent by the commodity customer.

Effect of control of securities account or commodity account

A secured party controlling security entitlements or commodity contracts carried in a securities account or commodity account has control over the account.

§ 9-107. Control of Letter-of-Credit Right

A secured party has control of a letter-of-credit right to the extent of any right to payment or performance by the issuer if the issuer has consented to an assignment of proceeds of the letter of credit or as applicable under law.

§ 9-108. Sufficiency of Description

A description of personal or real property is sufficient, whether or not it is specific if it reasonably identifies what is described.

Examples of reasonable identification

A description of collateral reasonably identifies the collateral if it identifies the collateral by:

1) specific listing;

2) category;

3) except as otherwise provided, a type of collateral defined;

4) quantity;

5) computational or allocational formula or procedure; or

6) any other method if the identity of the collateral is determinable.

Generic description not sufficient

A description of collateral as "all the debtor's assets" or "all the debtor's personal property" or using words of similar import does not reasonably identify the collateral.

Investment property

A description of a security entitlement, securities account, or commodity account is enough if it describes:

1) the collateral by those terms or as investment property; or

2) the underlying financial asset or commodity contract.

When description by type insufficient

A description only by the type of collateral is an insufficient description of:

1) a commercial tort claim; or

2) in a consumer transaction, consumer goods, a security entitlement, a securities account, or a commodity account.

Applicability of Article 9

§ 9-109. Scope

Except as otherwise provided, this article applies to:

1) a transaction that creates a security interest in personal property or fixtures by contract;

2) an agricultural lien;

3) a sale of accounts, chattel paper, payment intangibles, or promissory notes;

4) a consignment.

A security interest in secured obligations

Applying this article to a security interest in a secured obligation is not affected by the fact that the obligation is itself secured by a transaction or interest to which this article does not apply.

Extent to which the article does not apply

This article does not apply if:

1) a statute, regulation, or treaty of the U.S. preempts this article;

2) another statute of the State expressly governs the creation, perfection, priority, or enforcement of a security interest created by a governmental unit of this State;

3) a statute or governmental unit of another State or a foreign country; or

4) the rights of a transferee beneficiary or nominated person under a letter of credit are independent and superior.

Inapplicability of article

This article does not apply to:

A landlord's lien, other than an agricultural lien;

A lien, other than an agricultural lien, given by statute or rule of law, but Section 9-333 applies to the priority of the lien;

A claim for wages, salary, or employee compensation;

A sale of accounts, chattel paper, payment intangibles, or promissory notes as part of a sale of the business.

An assignment of accounts, chattel paper, payment intangibles, or promissory notes which is for collection only;

An assignment of a right to payment under a contract to an assignee obligated to perform;

An assignment of a single account, payment intangible, or promissory note to an assignee for a preexisting indebtedness;

A transfer of an interest in or an assignment of a claim under a policy of insurance, other than an assignment by or to a healthcare provider of a healthcare-insurance receivable and any subsequent assignment of the right to payment;

Sections 9-315 and 9-322 apply to priorities in proceeds;

An assignment of a right represented by a judgment, other than a judgment taken on a right to payment that was collateral.

The creation or transfer of an interest in or lien on real property, including a lease or rents thereunder, except to the extent that provision is made for:

(A) liens on real property in Sections 9-203 and 9-308;

(B) fixtures in Section 9-334;

(C) fixture filings in Sections 9-501, 9-502, 9-512, and 9-519; and

(D) security agreements covering personal and real property.

§ 9-110. Security Interests Arising Under Article 2 or 2A

Before the debtor obtains possession of the goods:

1) the security interest is enforceable;

2) filing is not required to perfect the security interest;

3) the rights of the secured party after default by the debtor are governed by Article 2 or 2A; and

4) the security interest has priority over a conflicting security interest created by the debtor.

Validity of Security Agreements and Rights of Parties

§ 9-201. General Effectiveness of Security Agreement

A security agreement is effective according to its terms between the parties, against purchasers of the collateral, and creditors.

Applicable consumer laws and other laws

A transaction subject to this article is subject to applicable rule of law which establishes a different rule for consumers and insert a reference to (i) another statute or regulation that regulates the rates, charges, agreements, and practices for loans, credit sales, or other extensions of credit and (ii) any consumer-protection statute or regulation.

Other applicable law controls

In case of conflict between this article and a rule of law, statute, or regulation, the rule of law, statute, or regulation controls.

Failure to comply with a statute or regulation has only the effect the statute or regulation specifies.

Further deference to other applicable law

This article does not:

1) validate rate, charge, agreement, or practice that violates a rule of law, statute, or regulation described in subsection (b); or

2) extend the application of the rule of law, statute, or regulation to a transaction not otherwise subject to it.

§ 9-202. Title to Collateral Immaterial

The provisions of this article about rights and obligations apply whether title to collateral is in the secured party or the debtor.

§ 9-203. Attachment and Enforceability of Security Interest

A security interest attaches to collateral when it becomes enforceable against the debtor for the collateral unless an agreement expressly postpones the time of attachment.

Enforceability

A security interest is enforceable against the debtor and third parties for the collateral only if:

1) value has been given;

2) the debtor has rights in the collateral or the power to transfer rights in the collateral to a secured party; and

3) one of the following conditions is met:

(A) the debtor has authenticated a security agreement that describes the collateral and, if the security interest covers timber to be cut, a description of the land concerned;

(B) the collateral is not a certificated security and is in possession of secured party under debtor's security agreement;

(C) the collateral is a certificated security in registered form, and the security certificate has been delivered to the secured party; or

(D) the collateral is deposit accounts, electronic chattel paper, investment property, or letter-of-credit rights, and the secured party has control under the debtor's security agreement.

Other UCC provisions

Subsection (b) is subject to the security interest of a collecting bank, the security interest of a letter-of-credit issuer or nominated person, a security interest arising under Article 2 or 2A, and on security interests in investment property.

Bound by another's security agreement

A person becomes bound as debtor by a security agreement entered into by another person if, by operation of law other than this article or by contract:

1) the security agreement becomes effective to create a security interest in the person's property; or

2) the person becomes generally obligated for the obligations of the other person, including the obligation secured under the security agreement, and acquires or succeeds to all or substantially all the assets of the other person.

Effect of new debtor becoming bound

If a new debtor becomes bound as debtor by a security agreement entered by another person:

1) the agreement satisfies subsection (b)(3) for the existing or after-acquired property of the new debtor to the extent the property is described in the agreement; and

2) another agreement is not necessary to make a security interest in the property enforceable.

Proceeds and supporting obligations

The attachment of a security interest in collateral gives the secured party the rights to proceeds and is an attachment of a security interest in a supporting obligation for the collateral.

Lien securing payment rights

The attachment of a security interest in a right to payment or performance secured by a security interest on personal or real property is an attachment of a security interest in the security interest, mortgage, or another lien.

Security entitlement in a securities account

The attachment of a security interest in a securities account is an attachment of a security interest in the security entitlements carried in the securities account.

Commodity contracts in a commodity account

A security interest in a commodity account is an attachment of a security interest in the commodity contracts carried in the commodity account.

§ 9-204. After-Acquired Property; Future Advances

After-acquired collateral

A security agreement may create or provide for a security interest in after-acquired collateral.

After-acquired property clause not effective

A security interest does not attach under an after-acquired property clause to:

1) consumer goods, other than an accession as additional security unless the debtor acquires rights in them within ten days after the secured party gives value; or

2) a commercial tort claim.

Future advances and other value

A security agreement may provide that collateral secures, or that accounts, chattel paper, payment intangibles, or promissory notes are sold in connection with future advances or other value, whether or not the advances or value are given according to commitment.

§ 9-205. Use or Disposition of Collateral Permissible

Security interest not invalid or fraudulent

A security interest is not invalid or fraudulent against creditors solely because:

1) the debtor has the right or ability to:

(A) use, commingle, or dispose of all or part of the collateral, including returned or repossessed goods;

(B) collect, compromise, enforce, or deal with collateral;

(C) accept the return of collateral or make repossessions; or

(D) use, commingle, or dispose of proceeds; or

2) the secured party fails to require the debtor to account for proceeds or replace collateral.

Requirements of possession not relaxed

This section does not relax the requirements of possession if attachment, perfection, or enforcement of a security interest depends upon possession of the collateral by the secured party.

§ 9-206. Security Interest Arising in Purchase or Delivery of Financial Asset

A security interest in favor of a securities intermediary attaches to a person's security entitlement if:

1) the person buys a financial asset through the securities intermediary in a transaction in which the person is obligated to pay the purchase price to the securities intermediary at the time of the purchase; and

2) the securities intermediary credits the financial asset to the buyer's securities account before the buyer pays the securities intermediary.

Security interest secures an obligation to pay for a financial asset.

The security interest described secures the person's obligation to pay for the financial asset.

Security interest in payment against delivery

A security interest in favor of a person that delivers a certificated security or other financial asset represented by a writing attaches to the security or another financial asset if:

1) the security or another financial asset:

(A) in the ordinary course of business is transferred by delivery with any necessary indorsement or assignment; and

(B) is delivered under an agreement between persons in the business of dealing with securities or financial assets; and

2) the agreement calls for delivery against payment.

Security interest secures an obligation to pay for delivery.

The security interest secures an obligation to make payment for the delivery.

§ 9-207. Rights and Duties from Possession or Control

Duty of care when secured party in possession

A secured party shall use reasonable care (*duty of care*) in the custody and preservation of collateral in the secured party's possession.

For chattel paper or an instrument, reasonable care includes taking necessary steps to preserve rights against prior parties unless otherwise agreed.

Expenses, risks, duties, and rights of secured party in possession

If a secured party has possession of collateral:

1) reasonable expenses, including the cost of insurance and payment of taxes or other charges, incurred in the custody, preservation, use, or operation of the collateral are chargeable to the debtor and are secured by the collateral;

2) the risk of accidental loss or damage is on the debtor to the extent of a deficiency of adequate insurance coverage;

3) the secured party shall keep the collateral identifiable, but fungible collateral may be commingled; and

4) the secured party may use or operate the collateral:

(A) to preserve the collateral or its value;

(B) as permitted by order of a court having competent jurisdiction; or

(C) except in the case of consumer goods, in the manner and to the extent agreed by the debtor.

Duties and rights when secured party in possession or control

A secured party having possession of collateral or control of collateral:

1) may hold as additional security any proceeds, except money or funds, received from the collateral;

2) shall apply money or funds received from the collateral to reduce the secured obligation, unless remitted to the debtor; and

3) may create a security interest in the collateral.

§ 9-208. Additional Duties of Secured Party Having Control

This section applies when there is no outstanding secured obligation, and the secured party is not committed to incur obligations or give value.

Duties of secured party after receiving debtor demand

Within 10 days after receiving an authenticated demand by the debtor:

1) a secured party having control of a deposit account shall send to the bank with which the deposit account is maintained an authenticated statement that releases the bank from the obligation to comply with instructions originated by the secured party;

2) a secured party having control of a deposit account shall:

(A) pay the debtor the balance on deposit in the deposit account; or

(B) transfer the balance on deposit into a deposit account in the debtor's name;

3) a secured party, other than a buyer, having control of electronic chattel paper shall:

(A) communicate the authoritative copy of the electronic chattel paper to the debtor or its designated custodian;

(B) if the debtor designates a custodian that is the designated custodian with which the authoritative copy of the electronic chattel paper is maintained for the secured party, communicate to the custodian an authenticated record releasing the designated custodian from further obligation to comply with instructions originated by the secured party and instructing the custodian to comply with instructions originated by the debtor; and

(C) take appropriate action to enable the debtor or its designated custodian to make copies of or revisions to the authoritative copy, which add or change an identified assignee of the authoritative copy without the consent of the secured party.

4) a secured party having control of investment property shall send to the securities intermediary or commodity intermediary with which the security entitlement or commodity contract is maintained an authenticated record that releases the securities intermediary or commodity intermediary from further obligation to comply with entitlement orders or directions originated by the secured party;

5) a secured party having control of a letter-of-credit right shall send to each person having an unfulfilled obligation to pay or deliver proceeds of the letter of credit to the secured party an authenticated release from further obligation to pay or deliver proceeds of the letter of credit to the secured party.

§ 9-209. Duties of Secured Party If Account Debtor Notified of Assignment

Except as otherwise provided, this section applies if:

1) there is no outstanding secured obligation; and

2) the secured party is not committed to incur obligations or give value.

Duties of secured party after receiving debtor demand

Within 10 days after receiving an authenticated demand by the debtor, a secured party shall send to an account debtor that has received notification of an assignment to the secured party as assignee under Section 9-406(a) an authenticated record that releases the account debtor from further obligation to the secured party.

§ 9-210. Request for Accounting; Statement of Account

Request for an accounting means a record authenticated by a debtor requesting that the recipient provide an accounting of the unpaid obligations secured by collateral and reasonably identifying the transaction or relationship that is the subject of the request.

Request regarding a list of collateral means a record authenticated by a debtor requesting that the recipient approve or correct a list of what the debtor believes to be the collateral securing an obligation and reasonably identifying the transaction or relationship that is the subject of the request.

Request regarding a statement of account means a record authenticated by a debtor requesting that the recipient approve or correct a statement indicating what the debtor believes to be the aggregate amount of unpaid obligations secured by collateral as of a specified date and reasonably identifying the transaction or relationship subject to the request.

Duty to respond to requests

A secured party, other than a buyer of accounts, chattel paper, payment intangibles, or promissory notes or a consignor, shall comply with a request within 14 days after receipt:

1) in the case of a request for an accounting, by authenticating and sending the debtor an accounting; and

2) in the case of a request for a list of collateral or a request regarding a statement of account, by authenticating and sending the debtor an approval or correction.

Request regarding the list and type of collateral

A secured party that claims a security interest in a particular type of collateral owned by the debtor may comply with a request regarding a list of collateral by sending the debtor an authenticated record, including a statement to that effect within 14 days after receipt.

Request regarding the list of collateral; no interest claimed

A person that receives a request regarding a list of collateral, claims no interest in the collateral when it receives the request, and claimed an interest in the collateral at an earlier time shall comply with the request within 14 days after receipt by sending the debtor an authenticated record:

1) disclaiming any interest in the collateral; and

2) if known to the recipient, providing the name and mailing address of any assignee or successor to the recipient's interest in the collateral.

Request for accounting; no interest in obligation claimed

A person that receives a request for an accounting or a request regarding a statement of account, claims no interest in the obligations when it receives the request, and claimed an interest in the obligations at an earlier time shall comply with the request within 14 days after receipt by sending the debtor an authenticated record:

1) disclaiming any interest in the obligations; and

2) if known to the recipient, providing the name and mailing address of the assignee or successor to the recipient's interest in the obligations.

Charges for responses

A debtor is entitled without charge to one response to a request under this section during any six months.

The secured party may require payment not exceeding $25 for each additional response.

Validity of Security Agreements and Rights of Parties

§ 9-301. Perfection and Priority of Security Interests

The following rules determine the law governing perfection, the effect of perfection or nonperfection, and the priority of a security interest in collateral:

While a debtor is in a jurisdiction, the local law of that jurisdiction governs perfection, the effect of perfection or nonperfection, and the priority of a security interest in the collateral.

While collateral is in a jurisdiction, the local law of that jurisdiction governs perfection, the effect of perfection or nonperfection, and the priority of a possessory security interest in that collateral.

While negotiable documents, goods, instruments, or the tangible chattel paper is in a jurisdiction, the local law of that jurisdiction governs:

(A) the perfection of a security interest in the goods by filing a fixture filing;

(B) the perfection of a security interest in timber to be cut; and

(C) the effect of perfection or nonperfection and the priority of a nonpossessory security interest in the collateral.

The local law of the jurisdiction in which the wellhead or minehead is located governs perfection, the effect of perfection or nonperfection, and the priority of a security interest in as-extracted collateral.

§ 9-308. Continuity of Security Interest or Agricultural Lien Perfected

Perfection of security interest

A security interest is perfected if it has attached, and the applicable requirements for perfection have been satisfied.

A security interest is perfected when it attaches if the applicable requirements are satisfied before the security interest attaches.

Perfection of an agricultural lien

An agricultural lien is perfected if it has become effective, and the applicable requirements for perfection have been satisfied.

An agricultural lien is perfected when it becomes effective if the applicable requirements are satisfied before the agricultural lien becomes effective.

Continuous perfection by different methods

A security interest or agricultural lien is perfected continuously if it is originally perfected by one method under this article and is later perfected by another method, without an intermediate period when it was unperfected.

Supporting obligation

The perfection of a security interest in collateral perfects a security interest in a supporting obligation for the collateral.

Lien securing the right to payment

The perfection of a security interest in a right to payment or performance perfects a security interest in a security interest, mortgage on personal or real property securing the right.

Security entitlement carried in a securities account

The perfection of a security interest in a securities account perfects a security interest in the security entitlements carried in the securities account.

Commodity contracts carried in a commodity account

The perfection of a security interest in a commodity account perfects a security interest in the commodity contracts carried in the commodity account.

§ 9-309. Security Interest Perfected Upon Attachment

The following security interests are perfected when they attach:

1) a purchase-money security interest in consumer goods, except as provided for consumer goods subject to a statute or treaty.

2) an assignment of accounts or payment intangibles which does not by itself or in conjunction with other assignments to the same assignee transfer a significant part of the assignor's outstanding accounts or payment intangibles;

3) a sale of a payment intangible;

4) a sale of a promissory note;

5) a security interest created by the assignment of a health-care-insurance receivable to the provider of the health-care goods or services;

6) a security interest until the debtor takes possession of the collateral;

7) a security interest of a collecting bank;

8) a security interest of an issuer or nominated person;

9) a security interest arising in the delivery of a financial asset;

10) a security interest in investment property created by a broker or securities intermediary;

11) a security interest in a commodity contract or a commodity account created by a commodity intermediary;

12) an assignment for the benefit of creditors of the transferor and subsequent transfers by the assignee thereunder; and

13) a security interest created by an assignment of a beneficial interest in a decedent's estate.

§ 9-310. Security Interests and Agricultural Liens Without Filing Provisions

Except as otherwise provided, a financing statement must be filed to perfect security interests and agricultural liens.

Exceptions: filing not necessary

The filing of a financing statement is not necessary to perfect a security interest:

1) that is perfected under Section 9-308(d), (e), (f), or (g);

2) that is perfected under Section 9-309 when it attaches;

3) in property subject to a statute, regulation, or treaty;

4) in goods in possession of a bailee which is perfected;

5) in certificated securities, documents, goods, or instruments which is perfected without filing or possession;

6) in collateral in the secured party's possession;

7) in certificated security, which is perfected by delivery of the security certificate to the secured party;

8) in deposit accounts, electronic chattel paper, investment property, or letter-of-credit rights, which is perfected by control;

9) in proceeds that are perfected.

Assignment of perfected security interest

If a secured party assigns a perfected security interest or agricultural lien, a filing under this article is not required to continue the perfected status of the security interest against creditors of and transferees from the original debtor.

§ 9-311. Perfection Subject to Statutes, Regulations, And Treaties

Security interests subject to other laws

The filing of a financing statement is not necessary to perfect a security interest in property subject to:

1) a statute, regulation, or treaty of the U.S. whose requirements for a security interest obtains priority over the rights of a lien creditor for the property preempt;

2) any statute covering automobiles, trailers, mobile homes, boats, farm tractors, or the like, which provides for a security interest to be indicated on a certificate of title as a condition of perfection, and any non-UCC central filing statute; or

3) a statute of another jurisdiction that provides for a security interest to be indicated on a certificate of title as a condition of the security interest's obtaining priority over the rights of a lien creditor for the property.

Compliance with other law

Compliance with the requirements of a statute, regulation, or treaty for obtaining priority over the rights of a lien creditor is equivalent to the filing of a financing statement under this article.

A security interest in property subject to a statute, regulation, or treaty may be perfected only by compliance with those requirements.

A security interest so perfected remains perfected notwithstanding a change in the use or transfer of possession of the collateral.

Duration and renewal of perfection

Duration and renewal of perfection of a security interest perfected by compliance with the requirements prescribed by a statute, regulation, or treaty are governed by the statute, regulation, or treaty.

Inapplicability to certain inventory

During any period in which collateral subject to a statute specified is inventory held for sale or lease by a person or leased by that person as lessor, and that person is in the business of selling goods of that kind, this section does not apply to a security interest in that collateral.

§ 9-312. Perfection Without Filing or Transfer of Possession

The following section addresses perfection of Security Interests in Chattel Paper, Deposit Accounts, Documents, Goods Covered by Documents, Instruments, Investment Property, Letter-Of-Credit Rights, And Money; Perfection by Permissive Filing; Temporary Perfection Without Filing or Transfer of Possession.

Perfection by filing permitted

A security interest in chattel paper, negotiable documents, instruments, or investment property may be perfected by filing.

Control or possession of certain collateral

Except as otherwise provided for proceeds:

1) a security interest in a deposit account may be perfected only by control;

2) and except as otherwise provided, a security interest in a letter-of-credit right may be perfected only by control; and

3) a security interest in money may be perfected only by the secured party taking possession.

Goods covered by the negotiable document

Goods in possession of a bailee who issued a negotiable document covering the goods:

1) a security interest in the goods may be perfected by perfecting a security interest in the document; and

2) a security interest perfected in the document has priority over any security interest that becomes perfected in the goods by another method during that time.

Goods covered by the nonnegotiable document

While goods are in possession of a bailee that has issued a nonnegotiable document covering the goods, a security interest in the goods may be perfected by:

1) issuance of a document in the name of the secured party;

2) the bailee's receipt of the secured party's interest; or

3) filing as to the goods.

Temporary perfection: new value

A security interest in certificated securities, negotiable documents, or instruments is perfected without filing or the taking of possession for 20 days from the time it attaches to the extent that it arises for new value given under an authenticated security agreement.

Temporary perfection: goods or documents made available

A perfected security interest in a negotiable document or goods in possession of a bailee, other than one that has issued a negotiable document for the goods, remains perfected for 20 days without filing if the secured party makes available to the debtor the goods or documents representing the goods for:

1) ultimate sale or exchange; or

2) loading, unloading, storing, shipping, transshipping, manufacturing, processing, or otherwise dealing with them in a manner preliminary to their sale or exchange.

Temporary perfection: delivery of security certificate or instrument

A perfected security interest in a certificated security or instrument remains perfected for 20 days without filing if the secured party delivers the security certificate or instrument to the debtor for:

1) ultimate sale or exchange; or

2) presentation, collection, renewal, or registration of transfer.

Expiration of temporary perfection

After 20 days, perfection depends upon compliance with this article.

§ 9-313. Possession or Delivery Without Filing

Perfection by possession or delivery

A secured party may perfect a security interest in negotiable documents, goods, instruments, money, or tangible chattel paper by taking possession of the collateral.

A secured party may perfect a security interest in certificated securities by taking delivery of the certificated securities.

Goods covered by a certificate of title

For goods covered by a certificate of title issued by this State, a secured party may perfect a security interest in the goods by taking possession of the goods only in the circumstances described in Section 9-316(d).

Collateral in possession of a person other than the debtor

For collateral other than certificated securities and goods covered by a document, a secured party takes possession of collateral in possession of a person other than the debtor, the secured party, or a lessee of the collateral from the debtor in the ordinary course of the debtor's business, when:

1) the person in possession authenticates a record acknowledging that it holds the collateral for the secured party's benefit; or

2) the person takes possession of the collateral after
having authenticated a record acknowledging that it will hold possession of collateral for the secured party's benefit.

Time of perfection by possession; continuation of perfection

If perfection of a security interest depends upon possession of the collateral by a secured party, perfection occurs no earlier than the time the secured party takes possession and continues while the secured party retains possession.

Time of perfection by delivery; continuation of perfection

A security interest in a certificated security in registered form is perfected by delivery when delivery of the certificated security occurs and remains perfected until the debtor obtains possession of the security certificate.

Acknowledgment not required

A person in possession of collateral is not required to acknowledge that it holds possession for a secured party's benefit.

Effectiveness of acknowledgment; no duties or confirmation

If a person acknowledges possession for the secured party's benefit:

1) the acknowledgment is effective, even if the acknowledgment violates the rights of a debtor; and

2) unless the person otherwise agrees or law other than this article provides, the person does not owe a duty to the secured party and is not required to confirm the acknowledgment to another person.

Secured party's delivery to a person other than the debtor

A secured party having possession of collateral does not relinquish possession by delivering the collateral to a person other than the debtor or a lessee of the collateral from the debtor in the ordinary course of the debtor's business if the person was instructed before the delivery or is instructed contemporaneously with the delivery:

1) to possess the collateral for the secured party's benefit; or

2) to redeliver the collateral to the secured party.

Effect of delivery under subsection (h); no duties or confirmation

A secured party does not relinquish possession, even if a delivery under subsection (h) violates the rights of a debtor.

A person to which collateral is delivered does not owe a duty to the secured party and is not required to confirm the delivery to another person unless the person otherwise agrees or law other than this article otherwise provides.

§ 9-314. Perfection by Control

A security interest in investment property, deposit accounts, letter-of-credit rights, or electronic chattel paper may be perfected by control of the collateral.

Specified collateral: time of perfection by control; continuation of perfection

A security interest in deposit accounts, electronic chattel paper, or letter-of-credit rights is perfected by control when the secured party obtains control and remains perfected by control only while the secured party retains control.

Investment property: time of perfection by control; continuation of perfection

A security interest in investment property is perfected by control from the time the secured party obtains control and remains perfected by control until:

1) the secured party does not have control; and

2) one of the following occurs:

(A) if the collateral is a certificated security, the debtor has or acquires possession of the security certificate;

(B) if the collateral is an uncertificated security, the issuer has registered the debtor as the registered owner; or

(C) if the collateral is a security entitlement, the debtor is or becomes the entitlement holder.

§ 9-315. Secured Party's Rights on Disposition and In Proceeds

Disposition of collateral: continuation of security interest or agricultural lien; proceeds

1) a security interest or agricultural lien continues in collateral notwithstanding sale, lease, license, exchange, or other disposition thereof unless the secured party authorized the disposition free of the security interest or agricultural lien; and

2) a security interest attaches to identifiable proceeds of collateral.

When commingled proceeds identifiable

Proceeds commingled with other property are identifiable:

1) if the proceeds are goods, as provided by Section 9-336; and

2) if the proceeds are not goods, to the extent that the secured party identifies the proceeds by a method of tracing, including equitable principles, that is permitted under law other than this article for the commingled property of the type involved.

The perfection of a security interest in proceeds

A security interest in proceeds would be a perfected security interest if the security interest in the original collateral was perfected.

Continuation of perfection

A perfected security interest in proceeds becomes unperfected on the 21st day after the security interest attaches to the proceeds unless:

1) the following conditions are satisfied:

(A) a filed financing statement covers the original collateral;

(B) the proceeds are collateral in which a security interest may be perfected by filing in the office in which the financing statement has been filed; and

(C) the proceeds are not acquired with cash proceeds;

2) the proceeds are identifiable cash proceeds; or

3) the security interest in the proceeds is perfected other than under subsection (c) when the security interest attaches to the proceeds or within 20 days.

When perfected security interest in proceeds becomes unperfected

If a filed financing statement covers the original collateral, a security interest in proceeds remaining perfected under subsection (d)(1) becomes unperfected at the latter of:

1) when the effectiveness of the filed financing statement lapses or is terminated; or

2) the 21st day after the security interest attaches to the proceeds.

§ 9-316. Perfection Following Change in Governing Law

General rule: effect on the perfection of change in governing law

A security interest perfected according to the law of the jurisdiction designated remains perfected until the earliest of:

1) the time perfection would have ceased under the law of that jurisdiction;

2) the expiration of four months after a change of the debtor's location to another jurisdiction; or

3) the expiration of one year after a transfer of collateral to a person that thereby becomes a debtor and is in another jurisdiction.

Security interest perfected or unperfected under law of new jurisdiction

If a security interest described in subsection (a) becomes perfected under the law of the other jurisdiction before the earliest event described in that subsection, it remains perfected.

If the security interest does not become perfected under the law of the other jurisdiction before the earliest time or event, it becomes unperfected and is deemed never to have been perfected as against a purchaser of the collateral.

Possessory security interest in collateral moved to a new jurisdiction

A possessory security interest in collateral, other than goods covered by a certificate of title and as-extracted collateral consisting of goods, remains continuously perfected if:

1) the collateral is located in one jurisdiction and subject to a security interest perfected under the law of that jurisdiction;

2) thereafter the collateral is brought into another jurisdiction; and

3) upon entry into the other jurisdiction, the security interest is perfected under the law of the other jurisdiction.

Goods covered by a certificate of title from another state

A security interest in goods covered by a certificate of title which is perfected by a method under the law of another jurisdiction when the goods become covered by a certificate of title from the new state remains perfected until the security interest would have become unperfected under the law of the other jurisdiction had the goods not become so covered.

When security interest becomes unperfected against purchasers

A security interest described in subsection (d) becomes unperfected as against a purchaser of the goods for value and is deemed never to have been perfected as against a purchaser of the goods for value if the applicable requirements for perfection are not satisfied before the earlier of the:

1) time the security interest would have become unperfected under the law of the other jurisdiction had the goods not become covered by a certificate of title from this State; or

2) expiration of four months after the goods had become so covered.

Change in the jurisdiction of the bank, issuer, nominated person or intermediary

A security interest in deposit accounts, letter-of-credit rights, or investment property which is perfected under the law of the bank's jurisdiction, the issuer's jurisdiction, or the securities intermediary's jurisdiction, as applicable, remains perfected until the earlier of:

1) the time the security interest would have become unperfected under the law of that jurisdiction; or

2) the expiration of four months after a change of the applicable jurisdiction to another jurisdiction.

Effect on filed financing statement for changes in governing law

The following rules apply to collateral to which a security interest attaches within four months after the debtor changes to another jurisdiction:

1) A financing statement filed before the change according to the law of the jurisdiction designated is effective to perfect a security interest in the collateral if the financing statement would have been effective to perfect a security interest in the collateral had the debtor not changed its location.

2) If a security interest becomes perfected under the law of the other jurisdiction before the earlier of the time or the end of the period described in that subsection, it remains perfected.

If the security interest does not become perfected under the law of the other jurisdiction before the earlier of that time or the end of that period, it becomes unperfected and is deemed never to have been perfected as against a purchaser of the collateral.

Governing law changes on financing statements filed against the original debtor

If a financing statement naming an original debtor is filed under the jurisdiction and a new debtor is in another jurisdiction, the following apply:

1) The financing statement is effective to perfect a security interest in collateral acquired by the new debtor within four months, the new debtor becomes bound, if the financing statement would have been effective to perfect a security interest in the collateral had the collateral been acquired by the original debtor.

2) A security interest perfected by the financing statement and which becomes perfected under the law of the other jurisdiction before the earlier of the time the financing statement would have become ineffective under the law of the jurisdiction designated or the expiration of the four months remains perfected.

A security interest that is perfected by the financing statement, but which does not become perfected under the law of the other jurisdiction before the earlier time or event becomes unperfected and is deemed never to have been perfected as against a purchaser of the collateral.

§ 9-317. Priority Over Unperfected Interest or Agricultural Lien

Conflicting security interests and rights of lien creditors

A security interest or agricultural lien is subordinate to the rights of:

1) a person entitled to priority under Section 9-322; and

2) a person that becomes a lien creditor before the earlier of::

(A) the security interest or agricultural lien is perfected; or

(B) one of the conditions specified is met, and a financing statement covering the collateral is filed.

Buyers that receive delivery

A buyer, other than a secured party, of tangible chattel paper, documents, goods, or certificated security takes free of a security interest or agricultural lien if the buyer gives value and receives delivery of the collateral without knowledge of the security interest or agricultural lien and before it is perfected.

Lessees that receive delivery

A lessee of goods takes free of a security interest or agricultural lien if the lessee gives value and receives delivery of the collateral without knowledge of the security interest or agricultural lien and before it is perfected.

Licensees and buyers of certain collateral

A licensee of a general intangible or a buyer, other than a secured party, collateral other than tangible chattel paper, documents, goods, or certificated security takes free of a security interest if the licensee or buyer gives value without knowledge of the security interest and before it is perfected.

Purchase-money security interest

If a person files a financing statement for a purchase-money security interest within 20 days after the debtor receives delivery of the collateral, the security interest takes priority over the rights of a buyer, lessee, or lien creditor, which arise between the time the security interest attaches and the time of filing.

§ 9-322. Priorities Among Conflicting Interests on Same Collateral

Priority among conflicting security interests and agricultural liens in the same collateral is determined according to the following rules:

> 1) Conflicting perfected security interests and agricultural liens rank according to priority in time of filing or perfection.

Priority dates from the earlier of the time a filing covering the collateral is first made, or the security interest or agricultural lien is first perfected if there is no period after that when there is neither filing nor perfection.

> 2) A perfected security interest or agricultural lien has priority over a conflicting unperfected security interest or agricultural lien.
>
> 3) The first security interest or agricultural lien to attach or become effective has priority if conflicting security interests and agricultural liens are unperfected.

Time of perfection: proceeds and supporting obligations

1) the time of filing or perfection as to a security interest in collateral is the time of filing or perfection as to a security interest in proceeds; and

2) the time of filing or perfection as to a security interest in collateral supported by a supporting obligation is the time of filing or perfection as to a security interest in the supporting obligation.

Special priority rules: proceeds and supporting obligations

A security interest in collateral that qualifies for priority over a conflicting security interest has priority over a conflicting security interest in:

1) any supporting obligation for the collateral; and

2) proceeds of the collateral if:

(A) the security interest in proceeds is perfected;

(B) the proceeds are cash proceeds or of the same type as the collateral; and

(C) in the case of proceeds, all intervening proceeds are cash proceeds, proceeds of the same type as the collateral, or an account relating to the collateral.

First-to-file priority rule for certain collateral

If a security interest in chattel paper, deposit accounts, negotiable documents, instruments, investment property, or letter-of-credit rights is perfected by a method other than filing, conflicting perfected security interests in proceeds of the collateral rank according to priority in time of filing.

Priority under agricultural lien statute

A perfected agricultural lien on collateral has priority over a conflicting security interest in or agricultural lien on the same collateral if the statute creating the agricultural lien provides.

§ 9-323. Future Advances

When priority based on time of the advance

To determine the priority of a perfected security interest, perfection of the security interest dates from the time an advance is made to the extent that the security interest secures an advance that:

1) is made while the security interest is perfected only:

(A) under Section 9-309 when it attaches; or

(B) temporarily under Section 9-312; and

2) is not made according to a commitment entered before or while the security interest is perfected by a method other than under Section 9-309 or 9-312.

Lien creditor

A security interest is subordinate to the rights of a lien creditor to the extent that the security interest secures an advance made more than 45 days after the person becomes a lien creditor unless the advance is made:

1) without knowledge of the lien; or

2) according to a commitment without knowledge of the lien.

Buyer of receivables

Subsections do not apply to a security interest held by a secured party that is a buyer of accounts, chattel paper, payment intangibles, promissory notes, or a consignor.

Buyer of goods

A buyer of goods other than a buyer in the ordinary course of business takes free of a security interest to the extent that it secures advances made after the earlier of:

1) the time the secured party acquires knowledge of the buyer's purchase; or

2) 45 days after the purchase.

Advances made according to commitment: priority of buyer of goods

Subsection (d) does not apply if the advance is made according to a commitment entered without knowledge of the buyer's purchase and before the expiration of the 45 days.

Lessee of goods

A lessee of goods, other than a lessee in the ordinary course of business, takes the leasehold interest that is free of a security interest to the extent that it secures advances made after the earlier of:

1) the time the secured party acquires knowledge of the lease; or

2) 45 days after the lease contract becomes enforceable.

Advances made according to commitment: priority of lessee of goods

Subsection (f) does not apply if the advance is made according to a commitment entered without knowledge of the lease and before the expiration of the 45 days.

§ 9-324. Priority of Purchase-Money Security Interests

A perfected purchase-money security interest in goods other than inventory or livestock has priority over a conflicting security interest in the same goods, and a perfected security interest in its identifiable proceeds has priority if the purchase-money security interest is perfected when the debtor receives possession of the collateral or within 20 days.

Inventory purchase-money priority

A perfected purchase-money security interest in inventory has priority over a conflicting security interest in the same.

A perfected purchase-money security interest has priority over a conflicting security interest in chattel paper or instrument constituting proceeds of the inventory and in proceeds of the chattel paper.

A perfected purchase-money security interest has priority in identifiable cash proceeds of the inventory to the extent the identifiable cash proceeds are received on or before the delivery of the inventory to a buyer, if:

1) the purchase-money security interest is perfected when the debtor receives possession of the inventory;

2) the purchase-money secured party sends an authenticated notification to the holder of the conflicting security interest;

3) the holder of the conflicting security interest receives the notification within five years before the debtor receives possession of the inventory; and

4) the notification states that the person sending the notification has or expects to acquire a purchase-money security interest in the inventory of the debtor and describes the inventory.

Holders of conflicting inventory security interests to be notified

Subsections apply only if the holder of the conflicting security interest had filed a financing statement covering the same types of inventory:

1) if the purchase-money security interest is perfected by filing, before the date of the filing; or

2) if the purchase-money security interest is temporarily perfected without filing or possession before the beginning of the 20 days.

Livestock purchase-money priority

A perfected purchase-money security interest in livestock that is farm products has priority over a conflicting security interest in the same livestock, a perfected security interest in their identifiable proceeds and products in their unmanufactured states has priority, if:

1) the purchase-money security interest is perfected when the debtor receives possession of the livestock;

2) the purchase-money secured party sends an authenticated notification to the holder of the conflicting security interest;

3) the holder of the conflicting security interest receives the notification within six months before the debtor receives possession of the livestock; and

4) the notification states that the person sending the notification has or expects to acquire a purchase-money security interest in livestock of the debtor and describes the livestock.

Holders of conflicting livestock security interests to be notified

Subsections (d)(2) through (4) apply if the holder of the conflicting security interest had filed a financing statement covering the same types of livestock:

1) if the purchase-money security interest is perfected by filing, before the date of the filing; or

2) if the purchase-money security interest is temporarily perfected without filing or possession before the beginning of the 20 days.

Software purchase-money priority

A perfected purchase-money security interest in software has priority over a conflicting interest in the same collateral.

A perfected security interest in its identifiable proceeds has priority, to the extent that the purchase-money security interest in the goods in which the software was acquired has priority in the goods and proceeds of the goods.

Conflicting purchase-money security interests

A security interest securing an obligation incurred as all or part of the price of the collateral has priority over a security interest securing an obligation incurred for value given to enable the debtor to acquire rights in or the use of collateral; and in other cases, applies to the qualifying security interests.

§ 9-325. Priority of Security Interests in Transferred Collateral

Subordination of security interest in transferred collateral

A security interest created by a debtor is subordinate to a security interest in the same collateral created by another person if:

1) the debtor acquired the collateral subject to the security interest created by the other person;

2) the security interest created by the other person was perfected when the debtor acquired the collateral; and

3) there is no period after that when the security interest is unperfected.

Subsection (a) subordinates a security interest only if the security interest:

1) would have priority solely under Section 9-322(a) or 9-324; or

2) arose solely under Section 2-711(3) or 2A-508(5).

§ 9-326. Priority of Security Interests Created by New Debtor

Subordination of security interest created by a new debtor

A security interest created by a new debtor in which the new debtor has or acquires rights and is perfected solely by a filed financing statement that would be ineffective to perfect the security interest but for the application of Section 9-316(i)(1) or 9-508 is subordinate to a security interest in the collateral which is perfected other than by a filed financing statement.

Priority under other provisions; multiple original debtors

The other provisions determine the priority among conflicting security interests in the same collateral perfected by filed financing statements.

If the security agreements to which a new debtor became bound as debtor were not entered into by the original debtor, the conflicting security interests rank according to priority in time of the new debtor's having become bound.

§ 9-327. Priority of Security Interests in Deposit Accounts

Rules governing priority among conflicting security interests in the same deposit account:

1) A security interest held by a secured party having control of the deposit account has priority over a conflicting security interest.

2) A security interests perfected by control rank according to priority in time of obtaining control.

3) A security interest held by the bank with which the deposit account is maintained has priority over a conflicting security interest held by another secured party.

4) A security interest perfected by control has priority over a security interest held by the bank with the deposit account.

§ 9-328. Priority of Security Interests in Investment Property

Rules governing priority among conflicting security interests in the same investment property:

1) A security interest held by a secured party controlling investment property has priority over a security interest held by a secured party that does not have control of the investment property.

2) Except as otherwise provided, conflicting security interests held by secured parties, each of which has control rank according to priority in time of:

(A) if the collateral is a security, obtaining control;

(B) if the collateral is a security entitlement carried in a securities account and:

(i) if the secured party obtained control, the secured party becomes the person for which the securities account is maintained;

(ii) if the secured party obtained control under Section 8-106(d)(2), the securities intermediary's agreement to comply with the secured party's entitlement orders for security entitlements carried or to be carried in the securities account; or

(iii) if the secured party obtained control through another person under Section 8-106(d)(3), the time for priority would be based under this paragraph if the other person were the secured party; or

(C) if the collateral is a commodity contract with a commodity intermediary, the satisfaction of the requirement for control specified in Section 9-106(b)(2) for commodity contracts carried with the commodity intermediary.

3) A security interest held by a securities intermediary in a security entitlement or securities account maintained with the securities intermediary has priority over a conflicting security interest held by another secured party.

4) A security interest held by a commodity intermediary in a commodity contract or a commodity account maintained with the commodity intermediary has priority over a conflicting security interest held by another secured party.

5) A security interest in a certificated security in registered form perfected by taking delivery under Section 9-313(a) and not by control under Section 9-314 has priority over a conflicting security interest perfected by a method other than control.

6) Conflicting security interests created by a broker, securities intermediary, or commodity intermediary, perfected without control rank equally.

7) In all other cases, priority among conflicting security interests in investment property is governed by Sections 9-322 and 9-323.

§ 9-329. Priority of Security Interests in Letter-of-Credit Right

Rules governing priority among conflicting security interests in the same letter-of-credit right:

1) A security interest held by a secured party controlling the letter-of-credit right has priority over a conflicting security interest held by a secured party that does not have control.

2) Security interests perfected by control rank according to priority in time of obtaining control.

§ 9-331. Priority of Interests Under Other Articles; Under Article 8

Rights under Articles 3, 7, and 8 not limited

This article does not limit the rights of a holder in due course of a negotiable instrument, a holder to which a negotiable document of title has been duly negotiated, or a protected purchaser of a security.

These holders or purchasers take priority over an earlier security interest, even if perfected, to the extent provided in Articles 3, 7, and 8.

Protection under Article 8

This article does not limit the rights or impose liability to persons protected against the assertion of a claim under Article 8.

Filing does not constitute notice

Filing under this article does not constitute notice of a claim or defense to the holders, or purchasers, or persons described in subsections (a) and (b).

§ 9-333. Priority of Certain Liens Arising by Operation of Law

Possessory lien means an interest, other than a security interest or an agricultural lien:

1) which secures payment or performance of an obligation for services or materials furnished for goods by a person in the ordinary course of the person's business;

2) which is created by statute or law in favor of the person; and

3) whose effectiveness depends on the possession of the goods.

Priority of possessory lien

A possessory lien on goods has priority over a security interest in the goods unless the lien is created by a statute that expressly provides otherwise.

§ 9-334. Priority of Security Interests in Fixtures and Crops

A security interest under this article may be created in goods that are fixtures or may continue in goods that become fixtures.

A security interest does not exist under this article in ordinary building materials incorporated into an improvement on land.

Security interest in fixtures under real property law

This article does not prevent the creation of an encumbrance upon fixtures under real property law.

General rule: the subordination of security interest in fixtures

A security interest in fixtures is subordinate to a conflicting interest of an encumbrancer or owner of the related real property other than the debtor.

Fixtures purchase-money priority

A perfected security interest in fixtures has priority over a conflicting interest of an encumbrancer or owner of the real property if the debtor has an interest of record in or is in possession of the real property and:

1) the security interest is a purchase-money security interest;

2) the interest of the encumbrancer or owner arises before the goods become fixtures; and

3) the security interest is perfected by a fixture filing before the goods become fixtures or within 20 days after that.

Priority of security interest in fixtures over interests in real property

A perfected security interest in fixtures has priority over a conflicting interest of an encumbrancer or owner of the real property if:

1) the debtor has an interest of record in the real property or is in possession of the real property and the security interest:

(A) is perfected by a fixture filing before the interest of the encumbrancer or owner is of record; and

(B) has priority over any conflicting interest of a predecessor in title of the encumbrancer or owner.

2) before the goods become fixtures, the security interest is perfected by any method permitted by this article, and the fixtures are readily removable:

(A) factory or office machines;

(B) equipment that is not primarily used or leased for use in the operation of the real property; or

(C) replacements of domestic consumer appliances.

3) the conflicting interest is a lien on the real property obtained by legal or equitable proceedings after a method permitted by this article perfected the security interest; or

4) the security interest is created in a manufactured home in a manufactured-home transaction; and

Priority based on consent, disclaimer, or right to remove

A security interest in fixtures, whether or not perfected, has priority over a conflicting interest of an encumbrancer or owner of the real property if:

1) the encumbrancer has, in an authenticated record, consented to the security interest or disclaimed it in the goods as fixtures; or

2) the debtor has a right to remove the goods as against the encumbrancer or owner.

The priority of the security interest continues for a reasonable time if the debtor's right to remove the goods as against the encumbrancer or owner terminates.

Priority of construction mortgage

A mortgage is a construction mortgage to the extent that it secures an obligation incurred to construct an improvement on land, including the acquisition cost of the land if a recorded record of the mortgage so indicates.

Except as otherwise provided, a security interest in fixtures is subordinate to a construction mortgage if a record of the mortgage is recorded before the goods become fixtures and the goods become fixtures before the completion of the construction.

A mortgage has this priority to the same extent as a construction mortgage to the extent that it is given to refinance a construction mortgage.

Priority of security interest in crops

A perfected security interest in crops growing on real property has priority over a conflicting interest of an encumbrancer or owner of the real property if the debtor has an interest of record in or is in possession of the real property.

§ 9-335. Accessions

Accession means goods physically united with other goods so that the identity of the original goods is *not* lost.

Creation of security interest in an accession

A security interest may be created in an accession and continues in collateral as an accession.

Perfection of security interest

If a security interest is perfected when the collateral becomes an accession, the security interest remains perfected in the collateral.

Priority of security interest

Except as otherwise provided, the other provisions of this part determine the priority of a security interest in an accession.

Compliance with the certificate-of-title statute

A security interest in an accession is subordinate to a security interest in the whole, perfected by compliance with the requirements of a certificate-of-title statute.

Removal of accession after default

After default, a secured party may remove an accession from other goods if the security interest in the accession has priority over the claims of every person having an interest in the whole.

Reimbursement following removal

A secured party that removes an accession from other goods shall promptly reimburse any holder of a security interest in, or owner of, the whole or of the other goods, other than the debtor, for the cost of repair of physical injury to the whole or the other goods.

The secured party need not reimburse the holder or owner for diminution in value of the whole or the other goods caused by the absence of the accession removed or by any necessity for replacing it.

A person entitled to reimbursement may refuse permission to remove until the secured party gives adequate assurance for the performance of the obligation to reimburse.

§ 9-336. Commingled Goods

"Commingled goods" means goods physically united with other goods, so their identity is lost in a product or mass.

No security interest in commingled goods as such

A security interest does not exist in commingled goods as such.

A security interest may attach to a product or mass that results when goods become commingled goods.

Attachment of security interest to product or mass

If collateral becomes commingled, a security interest attaches to the product.

Perfection of security interest

If a security interest in collateral is perfected before the collateral becomes commingled, the security interest attached to the product is perfected.

Priority of security interest

Except as otherwise provided, the other provisions of this part determine the priority of a security interest that attaches to the product.

Conflicting security interests in product or mass

If more than one security interest attaches to the product or mass under subsection (c), the following rules determine priority:

1) A perfected security interest has priority over a security interest that is unperfected when the collateral becomes commingled goods.

2) If more than one security interest is perfected, the security interests rank equally in proportion to the value of the collateral at the time it became commingled goods.

§ 9-339. Priority Subject to Subordination

This article does not preclude subordination by agreement by a person entitled to priority.

Rights of Third Parties

§ 9-401. Alienability of Debtor's Rights

Whether a debtor's rights in collateral may be voluntarily or involuntarily transferred is governed by a law other than this article.

An agreement does not prevent the transfer

An agreement between the debtor and secured party, which prohibits a transfer of the debtor's rights in collateral or makes the transfer a default, does not prevent transfer.

§ 9-404. Rights Acquired by Assignee; Claims And Defenses Against Assignee

Assignee's rights subject to terms, claims, and defenses; exceptions

Unless an account debtor has made an enforceable agreement not to assert defenses or claims, the rights of an assignee are subject to:

1) terms of the agreement between the account debtor and assignor and any defense or claim in recoupment arising from the transaction that gave rise to the contract; and

2) the defense or claim of the account debtor against the assignor accrues before the account debtor receives a notification of the assignment authenticated by the assignor or the assignee.

Account debtor's claim reduces the amount owed to an assignee

The claim of an account debtor against an assignor may be asserted against an assignee only to reduce the amount the account debtor owes.

Rule for individual under other law

This section is subject to law other than this article which establishes a different rule for an account debtor who is an individual and who incurred the obligation primarily for personal, family, or household purposes.

Omission of the required statement in a consumer transaction

In a consumer transaction, if a record evidences the account debtor's obligation, and the law requires that the record include a statement about the account debtor's recovery against an assignee for claims and defenses against the assignor may not exceed amounts paid by the debtor, and the record does not include such a statement, the extent that a debtor against the assignor is determined as if the record included such a statement.

Inapplicability to healthcare insurance receivables

This does not apply to an assignment of a health-care-insurance receivable.

§ 9-405. Modification of Assigned Contract

Effect of modification on the assignee

A modification of or substitution for an assigned contract is effective against an assignee if made in good faith.

The assignee acquires corresponding rights under the modified or substituted contract.

The assignment may provide that the modification or substitution is a breach of contract by the assignor.

Applicability of subsection above

Subsection above applies to the extent that:

1) the right to payment or a part thereof under an assigned contract has not been fully earned by performance; or

2) the right to payment has been fully earned by performance, and the account debtor has not received notification of the assignment.

Rules for individuals under other law

This section is subject to law other than this article which establishes a different rule for an account debtor who is an individual and who incurred the obligation primarily for personal, family, or household purposes.

§ 9-406. Account Debtor Discharge; Notification; Restrictions on Assignment

Discharge of account debtor; effect of notification

An account debtor on an account, chattel paper, or payment may discharge its obligation by paying the assignor until, but not after, the debtor receives notification, authenticated by the assignor or the assignee, that the amount due has been assigned and that payment is to be made to the assignee.

After receiving notification, the account debtor may discharge its obligation by paying the assignee and may not discharge the obligation by paying the assignor.

When notification ineffective

Notification is ineffective:

1) if it does not reasonably identify the rights assigned;

2) to the extent that an agreement between an account debtor and a seller of an intangible payment limits the debtor's duty to pay other than the seller and the limitation is effective under the law; or

3) at the option of an account debtor, if the notification notifies the account debtor to make less than the full amount of installment or periodic payment to the assignee, even if:

(A) only a portion of the account, chattel paper, or payment intangible has been assigned to that assignee;

(B) a portion has been assigned to another assignee; or

(C) the account debtor knows that the assignment to that assignee is limited.

Proof of assignment

If requested by the account debtor, an assignee shall seasonably furnish reasonable proof that the assignment has been made.

Unless the assignee complies, the account debtor may discharge its obligation by paying the assignor, even if the account debtor has received a notification.

Term restricting assignment generally ineffective

A term in an agreement between an account debtor and an assignor or a promissory note is ineffective to the extent that it:

1) prohibits, restricts, or requires the consent of the account debtor obligated on the promissory note to the assignment or transfer of, or the creation, perfection, or enforcement of a security interest in, the account, chattel paper, payment intangible, or promissory note; or

2) provides that the assignment or transfer or the creation, attachment, perfection, or enforcement of the security interest may give rise to a default, breach, right of recoupment, claim, defense, termination, right of termination, or remedy under the account, chattel paper, payment intangible, or promissory note.

Legal restrictions on assignments were generally ineffective

A rule of law, statute, or regulation that prohibits, restricts, or requires the consent of a government, or official, or account debtor to the assignment or transfer of, or creation of a security interest in, an account or chattel paper is ineffective to the extent that the rule of law, statute, or regulation:

1) prohibits, restricts, or requires the consent of the government, governmental body or official, or account debtor to the assignment or transfer of, or the creation, attachment, perfection, or enforcement of a security interest in the account or chattel paper; or

2) provides that the creation, attachment, perfection, or enforcement of the security interest may give rise to a default, breach, right of recoupment, claim, defense, termination, right of termination, or remedy under the account or chattel paper.

Subsection (b)(3) not waivable

Except as otherwise provided, an account debtor may not waive or vary its option.

Rules for individuals under other law

This section is subject to law other than this article which establishes a different rule for an account debtor who is an individual and who incurred the obligation primarily for personal, family, or household purposes.

Inapplicability to healthcare insurance receivables

This section does not apply to an assignment of a healthcare insurance receivable.

Filing Office – Contents and Effectiveness of Financing Statement

§ 9-501. Filing Office

If the law of the State governs perfection of a security interest or agricultural lien, the office in which to file a financing statement to perfect the security interest or agricultural lien is:

1) the office designated for the filing or recording of a record of a mortgage on the related real property, if:

(A) the collateral is as-extracted or timber to be cut; or

(B) the financing statement is filed as a fixture filing, and the collateral is goods that are or are to become fixtures; or

2) the office duly authorized, in all other cases, including a case in which the collateral is goods that are or are to become fixtures, and the financing statement, is not filed as a fixture filing.

Filing office for transmitting utilities

The office in which to file a financing statement to perfect a security interest in collateral, including fixtures, of a transmitting utility, is the [state designated office].

The financing statement constitutes a fixture filing as to the collateral indicated in the financing statement, which is or is to become fixtures.

§ 9-512. Amendment of Financing Statement

Alternative A: Amendment of information in the financing statements

A person may add or delete collateral, continue, or terminate the effectiveness of, or otherwise amend the information provided in, a financing statement by filing an amendment that:

1) identifies, by its file number, the initial financing statement to which the amendment relates; and

2) if the amendment relates to an initial financing statement filed [or recorded] in a filing office.

Alternative B: Period of effectiveness not affected

The filing of an amendment does not extend the period for the financing statement.

Effectiveness of amendment adding collateral

A financing statement that is amended by an amendment adding collateral is effective as to the added collateral from the date of the filing of the amendment.

Effectiveness of amendment adding debtor

A financing statement that is amended by an amendment that adds a debtor is effective as to the added debtor only from the date of the filing of the amendment.

Certain amendments ineffective

An amendment is ineffective to the extent it:

1) purports to delete all debtors and fails to provide the name of a debtor to be covered by the financing statement; or

2) purports to delete all secured parties of record and fails to provide the name of a new secured party of record.

§ 9-513. Termination Statement

Consumer goods

A secured party shall cause the secured party of record for a financing statement to file a termination statement for the financing statement if the financing statement covers consumer goods and:

1) there is no obligation secured by the collateral covered by the financing statement and no commitment to advance, incur an obligation, or otherwise give value; or

2) the debtor did not authorize the filing of the initial financing statement.

Time for compliance

A secured party shall cause the secured party of record to file the termination statement:

1) within one month after there is no obligation secured by the collateral covered by the financing statement and no commitment to make an advance, incur an obligation, or otherwise give value; or

2) if earlier, within 20 days after the secured party receives an authenticated demand from a debtor.

Other collateral

Within 20 days after a secured party receives an authenticated demand from a debtor, the secured party shall cause the secured party of record for a financing statement to send the debtor a termination statement for the financing statement or file the termination statement in the filing office if:

1) except in the case of a financing statement covering accounts or chattel paper that has been sold or goods the subject of a consignment, there is no obligation secured by the collateral covered by the financing statement and no commitment to make an advance, incur an obligation, or otherwise give value;

2) the financing statement covers accounts or chattel paper that has been sold, but the account debtor or another person obligated has discharged their obligation;

3) the financing statement covers goods that were the subject of a consignment to the debtor but are not in the debtor's possession; or

4) the debtor did not authorize the filing of the financing statement.

Effect of filing termination statement

Upon filing a termination statement with the filing office, the financing statement to which the termination statement relates ceases to be effective.

The filing with the filing office of a termination statement relating to a financing statement indicates that the debtor is a transmitting utility and causes the financing statement's effectiveness to lapse.

§ 9-514. Assignment of Powers of Secured Party of Record

Assignment reflected on the initial financing statement

An initial financing statement may reflect an assignment of the secured party's power to authorize an amendment to the financing statement by providing the name and mailing address of the assignee as the name and address of the secured party.

Assignment of the filed financing statement

A secured party of record may assign of record all or part of its power to authorize an amendment to a financing statement by filing in the filing office an amendment of the financing statement which:

1) identifies, by its file number, the initial financing statement;

2) provides the name of the assignor; and

3) provides the name and mailing address of the assignee.

Assignment of record of mortgage

An assignment of record of a security interest in a fixture covered by a record of a mortgage which is effective as a financing statement filed as a fixture filing, may be made only by an assignment of record of the mortgage as provided by law.

§ 9-519. Maintaining Records; Communicating Record's Information

Filing office duties

For each record filed in a filing office, the filing office shall:

1) assign a unique number to the filed record;

2) create a record that bears the number with date and time of filing;

3) maintain the filed record for public inspection; and

4) index the filed record following subsections (c), (d), and (e).

File number

A file number [assigned after January 1, 2002,] must include a digit that:

1) is mathematically derived from the digits of the file number; and

2) aids the filing office in determining whether the file number includes a single-digit or transpositional error.

Indexing: general

The filing office shall:

1) index an initial financing statement by the name of the debtor and index filed records relating to the initial financing statement in a manner that associates with one another an initial financing statement and filed records relating to the initial financing statement; and

2) index a record that provides a name of a debtor which was not previously provided in the financing statement to which the record also relates according to the name that was not previously provided.

Indexing: real-property-related financing statement

If a financing statement is filed as a fixture filing or covers as-extracted collateral or timber to be cut, the filing office shall index it:

1) under the names of the debtor and of each owner of record shown on the financing statement as if they were the mortgagors under a mortgage of the real property described; and

2) to the extent that the law of this State provides for indexing of records of mortgages under the name of the mortgagee, under the name of the secured party as if the secured party were the mortgagee thereunder, or if indexing is by description as if the financing statement were a record of a mortgage of the real property described.

Indexing: real-property-related assignments

If a financing statement is filed as a fixture filing or covers as-extracted collateral or timber to be cut, the filing office shall index an assignment filed:

1) under the name of the assignor as grantor; and

2) to the extent that the State law provides for indexing a record of the assignment of a mortgage under the name of the assignee.

Alternative A: Retrieval and association capability

The filing office shall maintain a capability:

1) to retrieve a record by the name of the debtor and by the file number assigned to the initial financing statement to which the record relates; and

2) to associate and retrieve an initial financing statement and each filed record relating to the initial financing statement.

Alternative B: Retrieval and association capability

The filing office shall maintain a capability:

1) to retrieve a record by the name of the debtor and:

(A) if the filing office is described in Section 9-501(a)(1), by the file number assigned to the initial financing statement to which the record relates and the date [and time] that the record was filed [or recorded]; or

(B) if the filing office is described in Section 9-501(a)(2), by the file number assigned to the initial financing statement to which the record relates; and

2) to associate and retrieve an initial financing statement and each filed record relating to the initial financing statement.

[End of Alternatives]

Removal of debtor's name

The filing office may not remove a debtor's name from the index until one year after the effectiveness of a financing statement naming the debtor lapses for secured parties of record.

Timeliness of filing office performance

The filing office shall perform the acts required at the time and in the manner prescribed by the filing-office rule, but not later than two business days after the filing office receives the record in question.

Default and Enforcement of Security Interest

§ 9-601. Rights After Default; Judicial Enforcement

Rights of secured party after default

After default, a secured party has the rights provided in this part and, except as otherwise provided by the agreement of the parties.

A secured party:

1) may reduce a claim to judgment, or enforce the claim, security interest, or agricultural lien by available judicial procedure; and

2) if the collateral documents may proceed as to documents or goods they cover.

Rights and duties of the secured party in possession or control

A secured party in possession of collateral has the rights and duties.

Rights cumulative; simultaneous exercise

The rights are cumulative and may be exercised simultaneously.

Rights of debtor and obligor

Except as otherwise provided, after default, a debtor and an obligor have the rights provided in this part and by agreement of the parties.

Lien of levy after judgment

If a secured party has reduced its claim to judgment, the lien of any levy that may be made upon the collateral by an execution based upon the judgment relates to the earliest of:

1) the date of perfection of the security interest or agricultural lien in the collateral;

2) the date of filing a financing statement covering the collateral; or

3) any date specified in a statute under which the agricultural lien was created.

Execution sale

A sale according to an execution is a foreclosure of the security interest or agricultural lien by judicial procedure within the meaning of this section.

A secured party may purchase at the sale and thereafter hold the collateral free of other requirements of this article.

Consignor or buyer of certain rights to payment

This part imposes no duties upon a secured party that is a consignor or is a buyer of accounts, chattel paper, payment intangibles, or promissory notes.

§ 9-602. Waiver and Variance of Rights and Duties

To the extent that they give rights to a debtor or obligor and impose duties on a secured party, the debtor or obligor may not waive or vary the rules stated in the following listed sections:

1) use and operation of the collateral by the secured party;

2) requests for an accounting concerning a list of collateral and statement of account;

3) collection and enforcement of collateral;

4) application or payment of noncash proceeds, enforcement, or disposition;

5) require accounting for or payment of proceeds of collateral;

6) imposes upon a secured party that takes possession of collateral without judicial process the duty not to breach the peace;

7) the disposition of collateral;

8) calculation of a deficiency or surplus when a disposition is made to the secured party, a person related to the secured party, or a secondary obligor;

9) explanation of the calculation of a surplus or deficiency;

10) acceptance of collateral in satisfaction of obligation;

11) the redemption of collateral;

12) permissible waivers; and

13) the secured party's liability for failure to comply with this article.

§ 9-603. Agreed Standards Concerning Rights and Duties

The parties may determine by agreement the standards measuring the fulfillment of the rights of a debtor or obligor and the duties of a secured party if the standards are not manifestly unreasonable.

Agreed standards inapplicable to breach of peace.

§ 9-604. Procedure from Real Property or Fixtures

Personal and real property enforcement

If a security agreement covers personal and real property, a secured party may proceed:

1) under this part as to the personal property without prejudicing any rights to the real property; or

2) as to personal property and real property per the rights to real property, the other provisions of this part do not apply.

Enforcement for fixtures

Subject to subsection (c), if a security agreement covers goods that are or become fixtures, a secured party may proceed:

1) under this part; or

2) per the rights to real property, the other provisions of this part do not apply.

Removal of fixtures

If a secured party holding a security interest in fixtures has priority over owners and encumbrancers of the real property, the secured party, after default, may remove the collateral from the real property.

Injury caused by removal

A secured party that removes collateral shall promptly reimburse any encumbrancer or owner of the real property, other than the debtor, for the cost of repair of physical injury caused by the removal.

The secured party need not reimburse the encumbrancer or owner for diminution in value of the real property caused by the absence of the goods removed or by necessity of replacing them.

A person entitled to reimbursement may refuse permission to remove until the secured party gives adequate assurance for the performance of the obligation to reimburse.

§ 9-605. Unknown Debtor or Secondary Obligor

A secured party does not owe a duty based on status as a secured party:

1) to a person that is a debtor, unless the secured party knows:

(A) that the person is a debtor or obligor;

(B) the identity of the person; and

(C) how to communicate with the person; or

2) to a secured party or lienholder that has filed a financing statement against a person unless the secured party knows:

(A) that the person is a debtor; and

(B) the identity of the person.

§ 9-606. Time of Default for Agricultural Lien

A default occurs with an agricultural lien when the secured party becomes entitled to enforce the lien under the statute.

§ 9-607. Collection and Enforcement by Secured Party

Collection and enforcement generally

If so agreed, and in any event after default, a secured party:

1) may notify an account debtor or other person obligated on collateral to make a payment or otherwise render performance to or for the benefit of the secured party;

2) may take proceeds to which the secured party is entitled;

3) may enforce the obligations of an account debtor or other person obligated on collateral and exercise the rights of the debtor to the obligation of the account debtor or other person obligated on collateral to make the payment or render performance to the debtor, and to property that secures the obligations of the account debtor or other person obligated on the collateral;

4) if it holds a security interest in a deposit account perfected by control under, may apply the balance of the deposit account to the obligation secured by the deposit account; and

5) if it holds a security interest in a deposit account perfected by control, may instruct the bank to pay the balance of the account to or for the benefit of the secured party.

Nonjudicial enforcement of mortgage

If necessary to enable a secured party to exercise the right of a debtor to enforce a mortgage nonjudicially, the secured party may record in the office in which a record of the mortgage is recorded:

1) a copy of the security agreement that provides for a security interest in the obligation secured by the mortgage; and

2) the secured party's affidavit in recordable form stating that:

(A) a default has occurred for the obligation secured by the mortgage; and

(B) the secured party is entitled to enforce the mortgage nonjudicially.

Commercially reasonable collection and enforcement

A secured party shall proceed in a commercially reasonable manner if the secured party:

1) undertakes to collect from or enforce an obligation of an account debtor or other person obligated on collateral; and

2) is entitled to charge back uncollected collateral or otherwise to full or limited recourse against the debtor or a secondary obligor.

Expenses of collection and enforcement

A secured party may deduct from the collection's reasonable expenses of collection and enforcement, including reasonable attorney's fees and legal expenses incurred by the secured party.

Duties to the secured party not affected

This section does not determine whether an account debtor, bank, or other person obligated on collateral owes a duty to a secured party.

§ 9-608. Liability for Deficiency and Right to Surplus

Application of proceeds, surplus and deficiency

If a security interest or agricultural lien secures payment or performance of an obligation, the following rules apply:

1) A secured party shall apply or pay over for application the cash proceeds of collection or enforcement in the following order to:

(A) the reasonable expenses of collection and enforcement and, to the extent provided for by agreement and not prohibited by law, reasonable attorney's fees and legal expenses incurred by the secured party;

(B) the satisfaction of obligations secured by the security interest or agricultural lien under which the collection or enforcement is made; and

(C) the satisfaction of obligations secured by any subordinate security interest in the collateral subject to the security interest or agricultural lien under which the collection or enforcement is made if the secured party receives an authenticated demand for proceeds before distribution of the proceeds is completed.

2) If requested by a secured party, a holder of a subordinate security interest shall furnish reasonable proof of the interest or lien within a reasonable time.

Unless the holder complies, the secured party need not comply with the holder's demand under paragraph (1)(C).

3) A secured party need not apply or pay over for noncash proceeds of collection and enforcement unless the failure to do so would be commercially unreasonable.

A secured party that applies or pays over for application noncash proceeds shall do so in a commercially reasonable manner.

4) A secured party shall account to and pay a debtor for surplus, and the obligor is liable for the deficiency.

No surplus or deficiency in sales of certain rights to payment

If the underlying transaction is a sale of accounts, chattel paper, payment intangibles, or promissory notes, the debtor is not entitled to surplus, and the obligor is not liable for the deficiency.

§ 9-609. Secured Party's Right to Possession After Default

Possession; rendering equipment unusable; disposition on debtor's premises

After default, a secured party:

1) may take possession of the collateral; and

2) without removal, may render equipment unusable and dispose of collateral on a debtor's premises.

Judicial and nonjudicial process

A secured party may proceed:

1) according to judicial process; or

2) without judicial process, without breach of the peace.

Assembly of collateral

If so agreed, and in any event after default, a secured party may require the debtor to assemble the collateral and make it available to the secured party at a place to be designated by the secured party, which is reasonably convenient to each party.

§ 9-610. Disposition of Collateral After Default

Disposition after default

After default, a secured party may sell, lease, license, or otherwise dispose of the collateral in its present condition or following commercially reasonable preparation or processing.

Commercially reasonable disposition

Every aspect of a disposition of collateral, including the method, manner, time, place, and other terms, must be commercially reasonable.

If commercially reasonable, a secured party may dispose of collateral by public or private proceedings, by one or more contracts, as a unit or in parcels, and at any time and place and on any terms.

Purchase by the secured party

A secured party may purchase collateral:

1) at a public disposition; or

2) at a private disposition only if the collateral is customarily sold on a recognized market or the subject of standard price quotations.

Warranties on disposition

A contract for sale, lease, license, or other disposition includes the warranties relating to title, possession, and quiet enjoyment, which accompany a voluntary disposition of property of the kind subject to the contract.

Disclaimer of warranties

A secured party may disclaim or modify warranties under subsection (d):

1) in a manner that would be effective to disclaim or modify the warranties in a voluntary disposition of property of the kind subject to the contract of disposition; or

2) by communicating to the purchaser a record evidencing the contract for disposition and including an express disclaimer or modification of the warranties.

Record sufficient to disclaim warranties

A record is enough to disclaim warranties if it indicates "There is no warranty relating to title, possession, quiet enjoyment, or the like in this disposition" or uses words of similar import.

§ 9-611. Notification Before Disposition of Collateral

Notification date means the earlier of the date on which:

1) a secured party sends to the debtor and any secondary obligor an authenticated notification of disposition; or

2) the debtor and any secondary obligor waive the right to notification.

Notification of disposition required

A secured party that disposes of collateral shall send to the persons specified a reasonable authenticated notification of disposition.

Persons to be notified

To comply, the secured party shall send notification of disposition to:

1) the debtor;

2) any secondary obligor; and

3) if the collateral is other than consumer goods:

(A) any person from which the secured party has received, before the notification date, an authenticated notification of a claim of an interest in the collateral;

(B) any other secured party or lienholder that, 10 days before the notification date, held a security interest perfected by the filing of a financing statement that:

(i) identified the collateral;

(ii) was indexed under the debtor's name as of that date; and

(iii) was filed in the office in which to file a financing statement against the debtor covering the collateral as of that date; and

(C) another secured party that, 10 days before the notification date, held a security interest in the collateral perfected by compliance with a statute, regulation, or treaty.

Subsection inapplicable: perishable collateral; recognized market

Subsection does not apply if the collateral is perishable or threatens to decline speedily in value or is of a type customarily sold on a recognized market.

Compliance with subsection (c)(3)(B)

A secured party complies with the requirement for notification prescribed:

1) not later than 20 or earlier than 30 days before the notification date, the secured party requests, in a commercially reasonable manner, information concerning financing statements indexed under the debtor's name in the office indicated; and

2) before the notification date, the secured party:

(A) did not receive a response to the request for information; or

(B) received a response to the request for information and sent an authenticated notification of disposition to each secured party or other lienholder named in that response whose financing statement covered the collateral.

§ 9-612. Notification Timeliness Before Disposition of Collateral

Reasonable time is a question of fact

Whether notification is sent within a reasonable time is a question of fact.

10-day period sufficient in non-consumer transactions

In a transaction other than a consumer transaction, a notification of disposition is sent after default and ten days or more before the earliest time of disposition outlined in the notification is sent within a reasonable time before the disposition.

§ 9-613. Notification Form and Content Before Disposition of Collateral

The following rules apply:

1) A notification of disposition is enough if the notification:

(A) describes the debtor and the secured party;

(B) describes the collateral subject to the disposition;

(C) states the method of intended disposition;

(D) states that debtor is entitled to an accounting of the indebtedness and states the charge for an accounting; and

(E) states the time and place of a public disposition or the time after which any other disposition is to be made.

2) Whether the contents of a notification that lacks any of the information specified are nevertheless enough a question of fact.

3) The contents of a notification providing substantially the information specified in paragraph (1) are sufficient, even if the notification includes: (A) information not specified by that paragraph; or (B) minor errors that are not seriously misleading.

4) A particular phrasing of the notification is not required.

5) The following form of notification and the form appearing in Section 9-614(3) each provides enough information:

SAMPLE

NOTIFICATION OF DISPOSITION OF COLLATERAL

To: [Name of debtor or obligor]

From: [Name, address, and telephone number of the secured party]

Name of Debtor(s): [Include only if debtor(s) are not an addressee]

[For a public disposition:]

We will sell [or lease or license] the [describe collateral] to the highest qualified bidder in public as follows:

Day and Date: ________ Time: ________ Place: ________

[For a private disposition:]

We will sell [or lease or license] the [describe collateral] privately sometime after [day and date].

You are entitled to an accounting of the unpaid indebtedness secured by the property that we intend to dispose of for a charge of $ ____.

You may request an accounting by calling us.

[End of Form]

§ 9-614. Notification Before Disposition: Consumer-Goods Transactions

In a consumer-goods transaction, the following rules apply:

1) A notification of disposition must provide the following:

(A) the information specified in Section 9-613(1);

(B) a description of liability for a deficiency of the person to which the notification is sent;

(C) a telephone number for which the amount that must be paid to the secured party to redeem the collateral; and

(D) a telephone number or mailing address for information about the disposition and the obligation secured is available.

2) A particular phrasing of the notification is not required.

3) The following form of notification, when completed, provides enough information:

SAMPLE

NOTICE OF OUR PLAN TO SELL PROPERTY

[Name and address of secured party] [Date]

[Name and address of obligor who is also a debtor]

Subject: [Identification of Transaction]

We have your [collateral] because you broke promises in our agreement.

[For a public disposition:]

We will dispose of [describe collateral] at public sale.

The sale will be held as follows:

Date: _____ Time: _____ Place: _____

You may attend the sale and bring bidders if you want.

[For a private disposition:]

We will sell dispose of [describe collateral] at a private sale after [date].

The money that we get from the sale (after paying our costs) will reduce the amount you owe. If we get less money than owed, you may still owe the difference. If we get more money than you owe, you will get the extra money unless we must pay it to someone else.

You can get the property back at any time before we sell it by paying us the full amount you owe (not just the past due payments), including our expenses. To learn the exact amount you must pay, call us at [telephone number].

If you want us to explain to you in writing how we have figured the amount owed us, you may call us at [number] or write us at [secured party's address] and request a written explanation. We charge $ 50 for the explanation if we sent another explanation within the last six months.

If you need more information about the sale, call us at [telephone number] or write to us at [secured party's address].

We are sending this notice to the following other people who have an interest in [describe collateral] or who owe money under your agreement:

[Names of other debtors and obligors, if any]

[End of form]

§ 9-615. Proceeds; Liability for Deficiency and Right to Surplus

Application of proceeds

A secured party shall apply or pay over for application the cash proceeds of disposition in the following order to:

1) the reasonable expenses of retaking, holding, preparing for disposition, processing, and disposing of, and, to the extent provided for by agreement and not prohibited by law, reasonable attorney's fees and legal expenses incurred by the secured party;

2) the satisfaction of obligations secured by the security interest or agricultural lien under which the disposition is made;

3) the satisfaction of obligations secured by a subordinate security interest in or another subordinate lien on the collateral if:

(A) the secured party receives from the holder of the subordinate security interest a demand for proceeds before distribution of the proceeds is completed; and

(B) in a case in which a consignor has an interest in the collateral, the subordinate security interest is senior to the interest of the consignor; and

4) a secured party that is a consignor of the collateral if the secured party receives from the consignor an authenticated demand for proceeds before distribution of the proceeds is completed.

Proof of subordinate interest

If requested by a secured party, a holder of a subordinate security interest shall furnish reasonable proof of the interest or lien within a reasonable time.

Application of noncash proceeds

A secured party need not apply or pay the noncash proceeds of disposition unless the failure to do so would be commercially unreasonable.

A secured party that applies or pays over for application noncash proceeds shall do so in a commercially reasonable manner.

Surplus or deficiency if obligation secured

If the security interest under which a disposition is made secures payment or performance of an obligation, after making the payments:

1) the secured party shall pay a debtor for surplus; and

2) the obligor is liable for deficiency.

No surplus or deficiency in sales of certain rights to payment

If the underlying transaction is a sale of accounts, chattel paper, payment intangibles, or promissory notes:

1) the debtor is not entitled to surplus; and

2) the obligor is not liable for deficiency.

Surplus or deficiency in disposition to a person related to the secured party

The surplus or deficiency following disposition is calculated based on the proceeds that would have been realized in a disposition complying with this part to a transferee other than the secured party, a person related to the secured party, or a secondary obligor if:

1) the transferee in the disposition is the secured party, a person related to the secured party, or a secondary obligor; and

2) the amount of proceeds of the disposition is significantly below the range of proceeds that a complying disposition to a person other than the secured party, a person related to the secured party, or a secondary obligor would have brought.

Cash proceeds received by the junior secured party

A secured party that receives cash proceeds of a disposition in good faith and without knowledge that the receipt violates the rights of the holder of a security interest that is not subordinate to the security interest or agricultural lien under which the disposition is made:

1) takes the cash proceeds free of the security interest or other liens;

2) is not obligated to apply the proceeds of the disposition to the satisfaction of obligations secured by the security interest; and

3) is not obligated to pay the holder of the security for surplus.

§ 9-616. Calculation of Surplus or Deficiency

Explanation means a writing that:

(A) states the amount of the surplus or deficiency;

(B) how the secured party calculated the surplus or deficiency;

(C) states that future debits, credits, charges, including additional credit service charges or interest, and expenses may affect the amount of the surplus or deficiency; and

(D) provides a telephone number or mailing address from which additional information concerning the transaction is available.

Request means a record:

(A) authenticated by a debtor or consumer obligor;

(B) requesting that the recipient explain; and

(C) sent after disposition of the collateral.

Explanation of calculations

In a consumer-goods transaction in which the debtor is entitled to a surplus or a consumer obligor is liable for a deficiency, the secured party shall:

1) send an explanation to the debtor or consumer obligor, as applicable, after the disposition and:

> (A) before or when the secured party accounts to the debtor and pays surplus or first makes written demand on the consumer obligor after the disposition for payment of the deficiency; and
>
> (B) within 14 days after receipt of a request; or

2) in the case of a consumer obligor who is liable for a deficiency, within 14 days after receipt of a request, send to the consumer obligor a record waiving the secured party's right to a deficiency.

Required information

To comply, a writing must provide the information in the following order:

1) the aggregate amount of obligations secured by the security interest under which the disposition was made, and, if the amount reflects a rebate of unearned interest or credit service charge, an indication of that fact, calculated as of a specified date:

(A) if the secured party takes or receives possession of the collateral after default, not more than 35 days before the secured party takes or receives possession; or

(B) if the secured party takes or receives possession of the collateral before default or does not take possession of the collateral, not more than 35 days before the disposition;

2) the amount of proceeds of the disposition;

3) the aggregate amount of the obligations after deducting proceeds;

4) the amount, in the aggregate or by type, and types of expenses, including expenses of retaking, holding, preparing for disposition, processing, and disposing of the collateral, and attorney's fees secured by the collateral which is known to the secured party and relates to the current disposition;

5) the amount and types of credits, including interest or credit service charges, to which the obligor is entitled; and

6) the amount of the surplus or deficiency.

Substantial compliance

A particular phrasing of the explanation is not required.

An explanation complying substantially with the requirements, even if it includes minor errors that are not seriously misleading.

Charges for responses

A debtor or consumer obligor is entitled without charge to one response to a request under this section during any six-month period in which the secured party did not send to the debtor or consumer obligor an explanation.

The secured party may require payment of a charge not exceeding $25 for each additional response.

§ 9-617. Rights of Transferee of Collateral

Effects of disposition

A secured party's disposition of collateral after default:

1) transfers to a transferee for value all of the debtor's rights in the collateral;

2) discharges the security interest; and

3) discharges subordinate security interests or subordinate liens.

Rights of good-faith transferee

A transferee that acts in good faith takes free of the rights and interests, even if the secured party fails to comply with this article or the requirements of any judicial proceeding.

Rights of another transferee

If a transferee does not take free of the rights and interests, the transferee takes the collateral subject to:

1) the debtor's rights in the collateral;

2) the security interest or agricultural lien under which the disposition is made; and

3) any other security interest.

§ 9-618. Rights and Duties of Certain Secondary Obligors

A secondary obligor acquires the rights and becomes obligated to perform the duties of the secured party after the secondary obligor:

1) receives an assignment of secured obligation from the secured party;

2) receives a transfer of collateral from the secured party and agrees to accept the rights and assume the duties of the secured party; or

3) is subrogated to the rights of a secured party for the collateral.

Effect of assignment, transfer, or subrogation

An assignment, transfer, or subrogation described in subsection (a):

1) is not a disposition of collateral; and

2) relieves the secured party of further duties under this article.

§ 9-619. Transfer of Record or Legal Title

Transfer statement means a record authenticated by a secured party stating:

1) the debtor has defaulted in connection with an obligation secured by specified collateral;

2) the secured party has exercised its post-default remedies concerning the collateral;

3) that, because of the exercise, a transferee has acquired the rights of the debtor in the collateral; and

4) the name and address of the secured party, debtor, and transferee.

Effect of transfer statement

A transfer statement entitles the transferee to the transfer of record of all rights of the debtor in the collateral specified in the statement in any official filing, recording, registration, or certificate-of-title system covering the collateral.

If a transfer statement is presented with the applicable fee and request form to the official or office responsible for maintaining the system, the office shall:

1) accept the transfer statement;

2) promptly amend its records to reflect the transfer; and

3) if applicable, issue a new appropriate certificate of title in the name of the transferee.

No relief of secured party's duties transfer without disposition

A transfer of the record or legal title to collateral to a secured party or otherwise is not of itself a disposition of collateral under this article and does not relieve the secured party of its duties under this article.

§ 9-620. Acceptance of Collateral in Satisfaction; Compulsory Disposition

Conditions to acceptance in satisfaction

A secured party may accept collateral in satisfaction of the obligation it secures only if:

1) the debtor consents to the acceptance;

2) the secured party does not receive a notification of objection to the proposal authenticated by:

(A) a person to which the secured party was required to send a proposal; or

(B) any other person, other than the debtor, holding an interest in the collateral subordinate to the security interest;

3) if the collateral is consumer goods, the collateral is not in possession of the debtor when the debtor accepts; and

4) subsection (e) does not require the secured party to dispose of the collateral, or the debtor waives the requirement.

Purported acceptance is ineffective

A purported acceptance of collateral under this section is ineffective unless:

1) the secured party consents to the acceptance in an authenticated record or sends a proposal to the debtor.

Debtor's consent

A debtor consents to an acceptance of collateral in partial satisfaction of the obligation it secures only if the debtor agrees to the terms of the acceptance in a record authenticated after default.

A debtor consents to an acceptance of collateral in satisfaction of the obligation it secures only if the debtor agrees to the terms of the acceptance in a record authenticated after default or the secured party:

(A) sends to the debtor after default a proposal that is unconditional or subject only to a condition that collateral not in possession of the secured party be preserved or maintained;

(B) in the proposal, proposes to accept collateral in satisfaction of the obligation it secures; and

(C) does not receive a notification of objection authenticated by the debtor within 20 days after the proposal is sent.

Effectiveness of notification

Notification of objection must be received by the secured party:

1) in the case of a person to which the proposal was sent within 20 days after notification was sent to that person; and

2) in other cases: within 20 days of the last notification, or if a notification was not sent before the debtor consents to acceptance.

Mandatory disposition of consumer goods

A secured party that has taken possession of collateral shall dispose of the collateral within the time specified if:

1) 60 percent of the cash price has been paid in the case of a purchase-money security interest in consumer goods; or

2) 60 percent of the principal amount has been paid in the case of a non-purchase-money security interest in consumer goods.

Compliance with mandatory disposition requirement

The secured party shall dispose of the collateral:

1) within 90 days after taking possession; or

2) within any longer period to which the debtor and secondary obligors have agreed in an agreement to that effect entered and authenticated after default.

No partial satisfaction in a consumer transaction

A secured party may not accept collateral in a consumer transaction in partial satisfaction of the obligation it secures.

§ 9-621. Notification of Proposal to Accept Collateral

Persons to which proposal to be sent

A secured party that desires to accept collateral in full or partial satisfaction of the obligation it secures shall send its proposal to:

1) any person from which the secured party had received, before the debtor consented to the acceptance, an authenticated notification of a claim in the collateral;

2) any other secured party or lienholder that, ten days before the debtor consented to the acceptance, held a security interest in the collateral perfected by the filing of a financing statement that:

(A) identified the collateral;

(B) was indexed under the debtor's name as of that date; and

(C) was filed in the office in which to file a financing statement against the debtor covering the collateral as of that date; and

3) any other secured party that, 10 days before the debtor consented to the acceptance, held a security interest in the collateral perfected by compliance with a statute, regulation, or treaty.

Proposal to be sent to the secondary obligor in partial satisfaction

A secured party that desires to accept collateral in partial satisfaction of the obligation it secures shall send its proposal to any secondary obligor in addition to the persons described in subsection (a).

§ 9-622. Effect of Acceptance of Collateral

A secured party's acceptance of collateral in full or partial satisfaction of the obligation it secures:

1) discharges the obligation to the extent consented to by the debtor;

2) transfers to the secured party all debtor's rights in the collateral;

3) discharges the security interest or agricultural lien that is the subject of the debtor's consent and any subordinate security interest or another subordinate lien; and

4) terminates any other subordinate interest.

Discharge of subordinate interest, notwithstanding noncompliance

A subordinate interest is discharged or terminated, even if the secured party fails to comply with this article.

§ 9-623. Right to Redeem Collateral

Persons that may redeem

A debtor, secondary obligor, or other secured party or lienholder may redeem the collateral.

Requirements for redemption

To redeem the collateral, a person shall tender:

1) fulfillment of obligations secured by the collateral; and

2) the reasonable expenses and attorney's fees.

When redemption may occur

A redemption may occur at any time before a secured party:

1) has collected collateral;

2) has disposed of collateral; or

3) has accepted collateral in satisfaction of the obligation it secures.

§ 9-624. Waiver

Waiver of disposition notification

A debtor or secondary obligor may waive the right to notification of disposition of collateral only by an agreement to that effect entered and authenticated after default.

Waiver of mandatory disposition

A debtor may waive the right to require disposition of collateral only by an agreement to that effect entered and authenticated after default.

Waiver of redemption right

Except in a consumer-goods transaction, a debtor or secondary obligor may waive the right to redeem collateral only by an agreement to that effect entered and authenticated after default.

§ 9-625. Remedies for Secured Party's Failure Complying with Article

Judicial orders concerning noncompliance

If a secured party is not proceeding following this article, a court may order or restrain collection, enforcement, or disposition of collateral on appropriate terms and conditions.

Damages for noncompliance

A person is liable for damages caused by a failure to comply with this article.

Loss caused by a failure to comply may include loss resulting from the debtor's inability to obtain, or increased costs of, alternative financing.

Persons are entitled to recover statutory damages in a consumer-goods transaction.

At the time of failure, a debtor or holder of a security interest may recover damages.

If the collateral is consumer goods, a debtor or obligor when a secured party failed to comply may recover for that failure.

Recovery for an amount not less than the credit service charge plus 10 percent of the principal amount of the obligation or the time-price differential plus 10 percent of the cash price.

Recovery when deficiency eliminated or reduced

A debtor whose deficiency is eliminated may recover for the loss of surplus.

A debtor or secondary obligor whose deficiency is eliminated or reduced may not otherwise recover for noncompliance with the provisions of this part relating to the collection, enforcement, disposition, or acceptance.

Statutory damages: noncompliance with specified provisions.

In addition to damages recoverable, the debtor, consumer obligor, or person named as a debtor in a filed record, as applicable, may recover $500 in each case from a person that:

1) fails to comply with Section 9-208, 9-209 and 9-616(b);

2) files a record of no entitlement under Section 9-509(a);

3) fails to cause the secured party of record to file or send a termination statement;

4) fails to comply and whose failure is part of a pattern or consistent with a practice of noncompliance.

Statutory damages: noncompliance with Section 9-210

A debtor or consumer obligor may recover damages and $500 in each case from a person that, without reasonable cause, fails to comply with a request.

A recipient of a request which never claimed an interest in the collateral or obligations that are the subject of a request under that section has a reasonable excuse for failure to comply with the request within the meaning of this subsection.

Limitation of security interest: noncompliance with Section 9-210

If a secured party fails to comply with a request regarding a collateral list or a statement of account, the secured party may claim a security interest only as shown in the list or statement included in the request against a person reasonably misled by the failure.

§ 9-626. Deficiency or Surplus Is in Issue

Applicable rules if the amount of deficiency or surplus in an issue

In an action arising from a transaction, other than a consumer transaction, in which the amount of a deficiency or surplus is in issue, these rules apply:

1) A secured party need not prove compliance with the provisions of this part relating to the collection, enforcement, disposition, or acceptance unless the debtor or a secondary obligor places the secured party's compliance in the issue.

2) If the secured party's compliance is placed in issue, the secured party has the burden of establishing that the collection, enforcement, disposition, or acceptance was conducted following this part.

3) If a secured party fails to prove that the collection, enforcement, disposition, or acceptance was conducted per the provisions of this part relating to the collection, enforcement, disposition, or acceptance, the liability of a debtor or a secondary obligor for a deficiency is limited to an amount by which the sum of the secured obligation, expenses, and attorney's fees exceeds the greater of:

(A) the proceeds of the collection, enforcement, disposition, or acceptance; or

(B) the proceeds that would have been realized had the noncomplying secured party proceeded following the provisions of this part relating to the collection, enforcement, disposition, or acceptance.

4) The amount of proceeds that would have been realized is equal to the sum of the secured obligation, expenses, and attorney's fees unless the secured party proves that the amount is less than that sum.

5) If a deficiency or surplus is calculated, the debtor or obligor has the burden of establishing that the amount of proceeds of the disposition is significantly below the range of prices that a complying disposition to a person other than the secured party, a person related to the secured party, or a secondary obligor would have brought.

Non-consumer transactions with no inference

The limitation of the rules to transactions other than consumer transactions is intended to leave to the court the determination of the proper rules in consumer transactions.

The court may not infer from that limitation the nature of the proper rule in consumer transactions and may continue to apply established approaches.

§ 9-627. Determination of Commercially Reasonable Conduct

No preclusion of commercial reasonableness

The fact that a greater amount could have been obtained by a collection, enforcement, disposition, or acceptance at a different time or in a different method from that selected by the secured party is not sufficient to preclude the secured party from establishing that the collection, enforcement, disposition, or acceptance was commercially reasonable.

Commercially reasonable dispositions

Disposition of collateral is made in a commercially reasonable manner if:

1) in the usual manner on any recognized market;

2) at a price in a recognized market at the time of the disposition; or

3) otherwise in conformity with reasonable commercial practices among dealers in the type of property subject to disposition.

Approval by the court or on behalf of creditors

A collection, enforcement, disposition, or acceptance is commercially reasonable if it has been approved:

1) in a judicial proceeding;

2) by a *bona fide* creditors' committee;

3) by a representative of creditors; or

4) by an assignee for the benefit of creditors.

§ 9-628. Limitation on Liability for Secondary Obligor

Limitation of liability of a secured party for noncompliance

Unless a secured party knows that a person is a debtor or obligor, knows the identity of the person, and knows how to communicate with the person:

The secured party is not liable to the person, secured party, or lienholder that has filed a financing statement against the person for failure to comply with this article; and

The secured party's failure to comply with this article does not affect the liability of the person for a deficiency.

Limitation of liability based on status as a secured party

A secured party is not liable because of its status as a secured party:

1) to the debtor or obligor unless the secured party knows:

(A) that the person is a debtor or obligor;

(B) the identity of the person; and

(C) how to communicate with the person; or

2) to a secured party or lienholder that has filed a financing statement against a person unless the secured party knows:

(A) that the person is a debtor; and

(B) the identity of the person.

Limitation of liability in non-consumer-goods transactions

A secured party is not liable, and a person's liability for a deficiency is not affected because of an act or omission arising out of the secured party's reasonable belief that a transaction is not a consumer-goods transaction if the secured party's belief is based on reasonable reliance on:

1) a debtor's representation concerning the purpose for which collateral was to be used, acquired, or held; or

2) an obligor's representation concerning the purpose for which a secured obligation was incurred.

Limitation of multiple liabilities for statutory damages

A secured party is not liable more than once for one secured obligation.

Relationship matrix

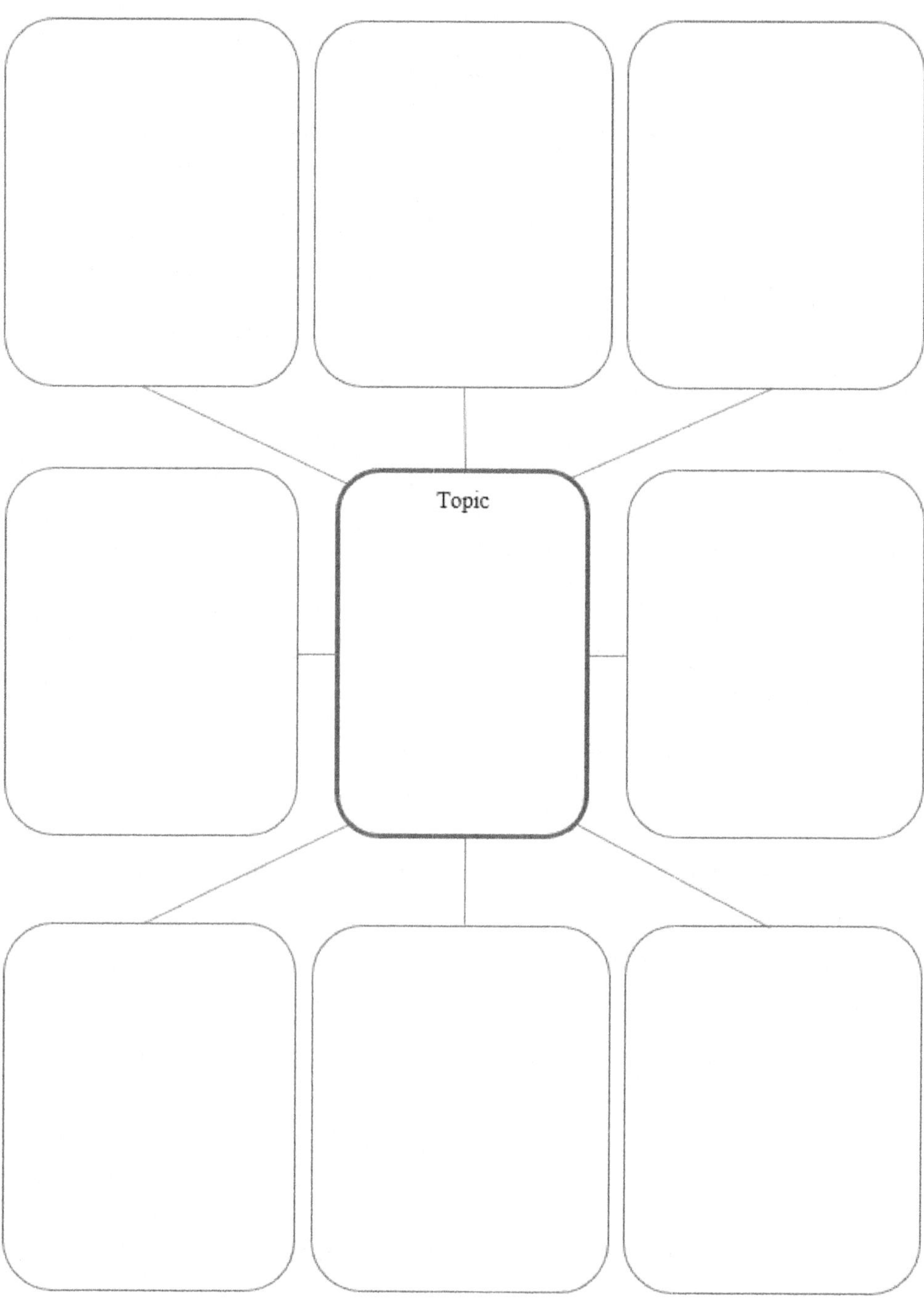

Notes for active learning

Notes for active learning

Appendix

STERLING
Test Prep

Overview of American Law

Overview of American Law

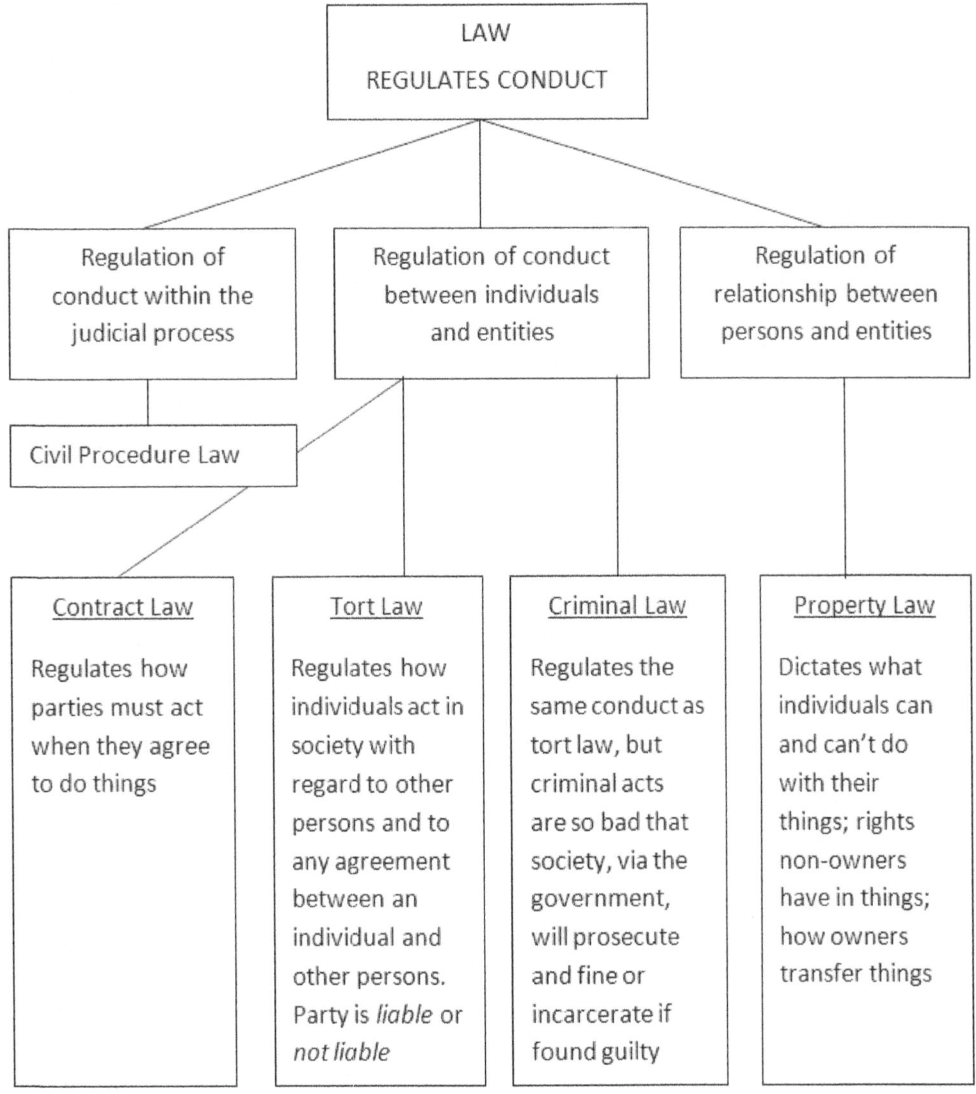

U.S. Court Systems – Federal and State Courts

There are two kinds of courts in the USA – federal courts and state courts.

Federal courts are established under the U.S. Constitution by Congress to decide disputes involving the Constitution and laws passed by Congress. A state establishes state and local courts (within states, local courts are established by cities, counties, and other municipalities).

Jurisdiction of federal and state courts

The differences between federal courts and state courts are defined by jurisdiction.[1] Jurisdiction refers to the kinds of cases that a particular court is authorized to hear and adjudicate (i.e., the pronouncement of a legally binding judgment upon the parties to the dispute).

Federal court jurisdiction is limited to the types of cases listed in the Constitution and specifically provided by Congress. For the most part, federal courts only hear:

- cases in which the United States is a party[2];
- cases involving violations of the U.S. Constitution or federal laws (under federal-question jurisdiction[3]);
- cases between citizens of different states if the amount in controversy *exceeds* $75,000 (under diversity jurisdiction[4]); and
- bankruptcy, copyright, patent, and maritime law cases.

State courts, in contrast, have broad jurisdiction, so the cases individual citizens are likely to be involved in (e.g., robberies, traffic violations, contracts, and family disputes) are usually heard and decided in state courts. The only cases state courts are not allowed to hear are lawsuits against the United States and those involving certain specific federal laws: criminal, antitrust, bankruptcy, patent, copyright, and some maritime law cases.

In many cases, both federal and state courts have jurisdiction whereby the plaintiff (i.e., the party initiating the suit) can choose whether to file their claim in state or federal court.

Criminal cases involving federal laws can be tried only in federal court, but most criminal cases involve violations of state law and are tried in state court. Robbery is a crime, but what law makes it is a crime? Except for certain exceptions, state laws, not federal laws, make robbery a crime. There are only a few federal laws about robbery, such as the law that makes it a federal crime to rob a bank whose deposits are insured by a federal agency. Examples of other federal crimes are the transport of illegal drugs into the country or across state lines and using the U.S. mail system to defraud consumers.

Crimes committed on federal property (e.g., national parks or military reservations) are prosecuted in federal court.

Federal courts may hear cases concerning state laws if the issue is whether the state law violates the federal Constitution. Suppose a state law forbids slaughtering animals outside of certain limited areas. A neighborhood association brings a case in state court against a defendant who sacrifices chickens in their backyard. When the court issues an order (i.e., an injunction[5]) forbidding the defendant from further sacrifices, the defendant challenges the state law in federal court as an unconstitutional infringement of religious freedom.

Some conduct is illegal under both federal and state laws. For example, federal laws prohibit employment discrimination, and the states have added additional legal restrictions. A person can file their claim in either federal or state court under federal law or federal and state laws. A case that only involves a state law can be brought only in state court.

Appeals for review of actions by federal administrative agencies are federal civil cases.

For example, if the Environmental Protection Agency, over the objection of area residents, issued a permit to a paper mill to discharge water used in its milling process into the Scenic River, the residents may appeal and have the federal court of appeals review the agency's decision.

[1] *jurisdiction* – 1) the legal authority of a court to hear and decide specific types of case; 2) the geographic area over which the court has the authority to decide cases.

[2] *parties* – the plaintiff and the defendant in a lawsuit.

[3] *federal-question jurisdiction* – the federal district courts' authorization to hear and decide cases arising under the Constitution, laws, or treaties of the United States.

[4] *diversity jurisdiction* – the federal district courts' authority to hear and decide civil cases involving plaintiffs and defendants who are citizens of different states (or U.S. citizens and foreign nationals) and meet specific statutory requirements.

[5] *injunction* – a judge's order that a party takes or refrain from taking a particular action. An injunction may be preliminary until the outcome of a case is determined or permanent.

Organization of the federal courts

Congress has divided the country into 94 federal judicial districts, with each having a U.S. district court. The U.S. district courts are the federal trial courts -- where federal cases are tried, witnesses testify, and juries serve.

Each district has a U.S. bankruptcy court, which is part of the district court that administers the U.S. bankruptcy laws.

Congress uses state boundaries to help define the districts. Some districts cover an entire state, like Idaho. Other districts cover just part of a state, like the Northern District of California. Congress placed each of the ninety-four districts in one of twelve regional circuits whereby each circuit has a court of appeals. The losing party can petition the court of appeals to review the case to determine if the district judge applied the law correctly.

There is a U.S. Court of Appeals for the Federal Circuit, whose jurisdiction is defined by subject matter rather than geography. It hears appeals from certain courts and agencies, such as the U.S. Court of International Trade, the U.S. Court of Federal Claims, and the U.S. Patent and Trademark Office, and certain types of cases from the district courts (mainly lawsuits claiming that patents have been infringed).

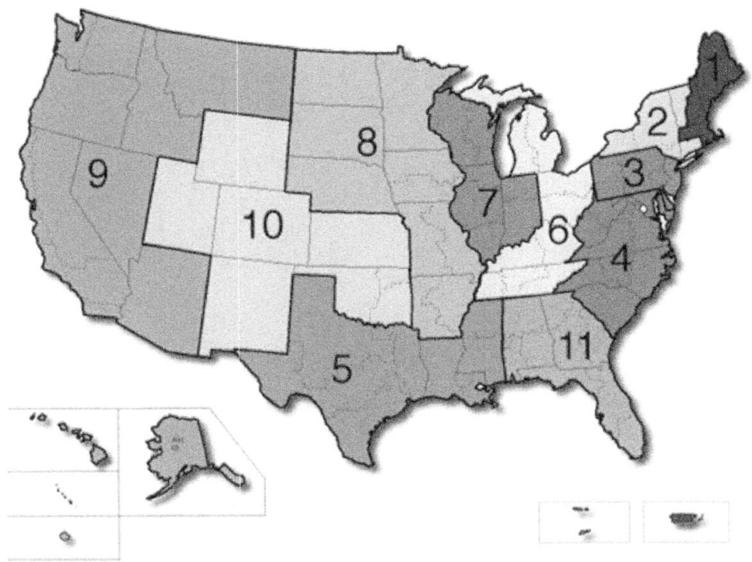

Twelve regional federal circuits

The Supreme Court in Washington, D.C., is the highest court in the nation. The losing party can petition in a case in the court of appeals (or, sometimes, in a state supreme court), can petition the Supreme Court to hear an appeal.

Unlike a court of appeals, the Supreme Court does not have to hear the case. The Supreme Court hears only a small percentage of the cases it is asked to review.

Notes for active learning

How Civil Cases Move Through the Federal Courts

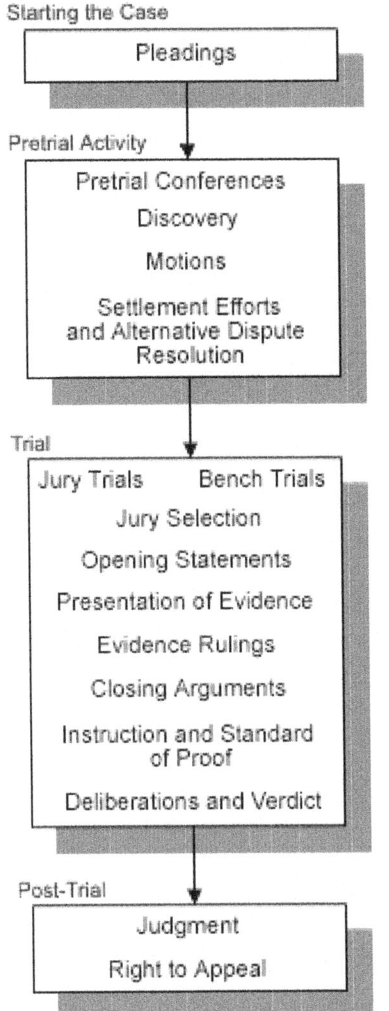

A federal civil case begins when a person, or their legal representative, files a paper with the clerk of the court that asserts another person's wrongful act injured the person. In legal terminology, the plaintiff files a *complaint* against the defendant.

The defendant files an *answer* to the complaint. These written statements of the party's positions are called pleadings. In some circumstances, the defendant may file a *motion* instead of an answer; the motion asks the court to take some action, such as dismiss the case or require the plaintiff to explain more clearly what the lawsuit is about.

Jury trials

In a jury trial, the jury decides what happened, and to apply the legal standards, the judge tells them to apply to reach a verdict. The plaintiff presents evidence supporting its view of the case, and the defendant presents evidence rebutting the plaintiff's evidence or supporting its view of the case. From these presentations, the jury must decide what happened and applied the law to those facts.

The jury never decides what law applies to the case; that is the role of the judge. For example, in a discrimination case where the plaintiff alleged that their workplace was hostile, the judge tells the jury the legal standard for a hostile environment.

The jury would have to decide whether the plaintiff's description of events was true and whether those events met the legal standard. A trial jury, or petit jury, may consist of six to twelve jurors in a civil case.

Bench trials

If the parties agree not to have a *jury trial* and leave the fact-finding to the judge, the trial is a *bench trial.* In bench and jury trials, the judge ensures the correct legal standards are followed.

In contrast to a jury trial, the judge decides the facts and renders the verdict in a *bench trial.*

For example, in a discrimination case in which the plaintiff alleged a hostile environment, the judge would determine the legal standard for a hostile environment and decide whether the plaintiff's description of events was true and whether those events met the legal standard.

Some kinds of cases always have bench trials. For example, there is never a jury trial if the plaintiff is seeking an injunction, an order from the judge that the defendant does, or stop doing something, as opposed to monetary damages.

Some statutes provide that a judge must decide the facts in certain types of cases.

Jury selection

A jury trial begins with the selection of jurors. Citizens are selected for jury service through a process set out in laws passed by Congress and in the federal rules of procedure.

First, citizens are called to court to be available to serve on juries. These citizens are selected at random from sources, in most districts, lists of registered voters, which may be augmented by other sources, such as lists of licensed drivers in the judicial district.

The judge and the lawyers choose who will serve on the jury.

To choose the jurors, the judge and sometimes the lawyers ask prospective jurors questions to determine if they will decide the case fairly, a process known as *voir dire.*

The lawyers may request that the judge excuse jurors they think may not be impartial, such as those who know a party in the case or who have had an experience that might make them favor one side over the other. These requests for rejecting jurors are *challenges for cause.*

The lawyers may request that the judge excuse a certain number of jurors without reason; these requests are *peremptory challenges.*

Instructions and standard of proof

Following the closing arguments, the judge gives instructions to the jury, explaining the relevant law, how the law applies to the case, and what questions the jury must decide.

How sure do jurors have to be before they reach a verdict? One important instruction the judge gives the jury is the standard of proof they must follow in deciding the case.

The courts, through their decisions, and Congress, through statutes, have established standards by which facts must be proven in criminal and civil cases.

In civil cases, to decide for the plaintiff, the jury must determine by a *preponderance of the evidence* that the defendant failed to perform a legal duty and violated the plaintiff's rights. A preponderance of the evidence means that, based on the evidence, the evidence favors the plaintiff more (even if only slightly) than it favors the defendant.

If the evidence in favor of the plaintiff could be placed on one side of a scale and that in favor of the defendant on the other, the plaintiff would win if the evidence in favor of the plaintiff was heavy enough to tip the scale. If the two sides were even, or if the scale tipped for the defendant, the defendant would win.

Judgment

In civil cases, if the jury (or judge) decides in favor of the plaintiff, the result usually is that the defendant must pay the plaintiff money or damages. The judge orders the defendant to pay the decided amount. Sometimes the defendant is ordered to take some specific action that will restore the plaintiff's rights. If the defendant wins the case, there is nothing more the trial court needs to do as the case is disposed of and the defendant is held not liable.

Right to appeal

The losing party in a federal civil case has a right to appeal the verdict to the U.S. court of appeals (i.e., Federal Circuit Courts) and ask the court to review the case to determine whether the trial was conducted properly. The losing party in the state trial court has a right to appeal the verdict to the state court of appeal.

The grounds for appeal usually are that the federal district (or state) judge made an error, either in the procedure (e.g., admitting improper evidence) or interpreting the law. The government may appeal in civil cases, as any other party may. Neither party may appeal if there was no trial -- parties settled their civil case out of court.

Notes for active learning

How Criminal Cases Move Through the Federal Courts

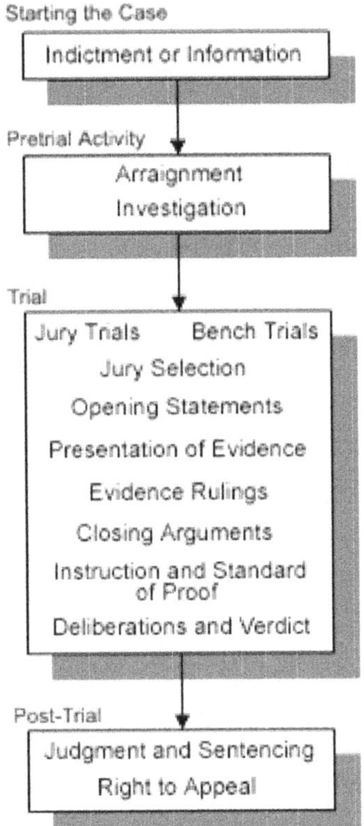

Indictment or information

A criminal case formally begins with an indictment or information, which is a formal accusation that a person committed a crime.

An indictment may be obtained when a lawyer (i.e., prosecutor) for the executive branch of the U.S. government (i.e., U.S. attorney or assistant U.S. attorney) present evidence to a federal grand jury that, according to the government, indicates a person committed a crime.

The U.S. attorney tries to convince the grand jury that there is enough evidence to show that the person probably committed the crime and should be formally accused. If the grand jury agrees, it issues an indictment.

A grand jury is different from a trial jury or petit jury.

A grand jury determines whether the person may be tried for a crime; a petit jury listens to the evidence presented at the trial and determines whether the defendant is guilty.

Petit is French for "small"; petit juries usually consist of twelve jurors in criminal cases.

Grand is French for "large"; grand juries have from sixteen to twenty-three jurors.

Grand jury indictments are most often used for *felonies* (i.e., punishable by imprisonment of more than a year or by death) such as bank robberies or sales of illegal drugs.

Grand jury indictments are not necessary to prosecute *misdemeanors* (i.e., less serious than a felony but more serious than an infraction) and are necessary for felonies.

For lesser crimes, the U.S. attorney issues an *information* that substitutes for an indictment. For example, speeding on a highway in a national park is a misdemeanor.

An information is used when a defendant waives an indictment by a grand jury.

Arraignment

After the grand jury issues the indictment, the accused (i.e., defendant) is summoned to court or arrested (if not already in custody). The next step is an arraignment, a proceeding in which the defendant is brought before a judge, told of the charges they are accused of, and asked to plead guilty or not guilty. If the defendant's plea is guilty, a time is set for the defendant to return to court to be sentenced.

If the defendant pleads "not guilty," the time is set for the trial.

A defendant may enter a plea bargain with the prosecution--usually by agreeing to plead guilty to some but not all charges or lesser charges. The prosecution drops the remaining charges.

About nine out of ten defendants in criminal cases plead guilty.

Investigation

In a criminal case, a defense lawyer conducts a thorough investigation before trial, interviewing witnesses, visiting the crime scene, and examining physical evidence. An important part of this investigation is determining whether the evidence the government plans to use to prove its case was obtained legally.

The Fourth Amendment to the Constitution forbids unreasonable searches and seizures. To enforce this protection, the Supreme Court has decided that illegally seized evidence cannot be used at trial for most purposes.

For example, if the police seize evidence from a defendant's home without a search warrant, the lawyer for the defendant can ask the court to exclude the evidence from use at trial. The court holds a hearing to determine whether the search was unreasonable.

If the court rules that key evidence was seized illegally and cannot be used, the government often drops the charges against the defendant.

If the government has a strong case and the court ruled that the evidence was obtained legally, the defendant may decide to plead guilty rather than go to trial, where a conviction is likely.

Deliberations and verdict

After receiving its instructions from the judge, the jury retires to the jury room to discuss the evidence and reach a verdict (a decision on the factual issues). A criminal jury verdict must be unanimous; all jurors must agree that the defendant is guilty or not guilty.

If the jurors cannot agree, the judge declares a mistrial, and the prosecutor must decide whether to ask the court to dismiss the case or have it presented to another jury.

Judgment and sentencing

In federal criminal cases, if the jury (or judge, if there is no jury) decides that the defendant is guilty, the judge sets a date for a sentencing hearing. In federal criminal cases, the jury does not decide whether the defendant will go to prison or for how long; the judge does.

In federal death penalty cases, the jury does decide whether the defendant will receive a death sentence. Sentencing statutes passed by Congress control the judge's sentencing decision. Additionally, judges use Sentencing Guidelines, issued by the U.S. Sentencing Commission, as a source of advice as to the proper sentence. The guidelines consider the nature of the offense and the offender's criminal history.

A presentence report, prepared by one of the court's probation officers, provides the judge with information about the offender and the offense, including the sentence recommended by the guidelines. After determining the sentence, the judge signs a judgment, including the plea, the verdict, and sentence.

Right to appeal

A defendant who is found guilty in a federal criminal trial has a right to appeal the decision to the U.S. court of appeals, that is, ask the court of appeals to review the case to determine whether the trial was conducted properly. The grounds for appeal are usually that the district judge is said to have made an error, either in a procedure (admitting improper evidence, for example) or interpreting the law.

A defendant who pled guilty may not appeal the conviction.

A defendant who pled guilty may have the right to appeal their sentence.

The government may not appeal if a defendant in a criminal case is found not guilty because the Double Jeopardy Clause of the Fifth Amendment to the Constitution provides that no person shall "be twice put in jeopardy of life or limb" for the same offense.

This reflects society's belief that, even if a subsequent trial might finally find a defendant guilty, it is not proper for the government to harass an acquitted defendant through repeated retrials.

However, the government may sometimes appeal a sentence.

Notes for active learning

How Civil and Criminal Appeals Move Through the Federal Courts

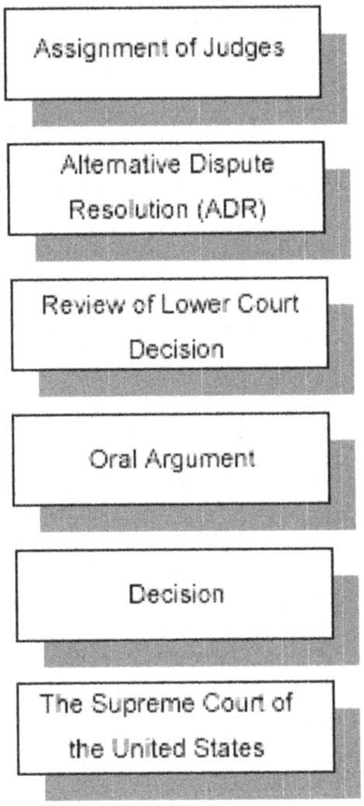

Assignment of Judges

Alternative Dispute Resolution (ADR)

Review of Lower Court Decision

Oral Argument

Decision

The Supreme Court of the United States

Assignment of judges

The courts of appeals usually assign cases to a panel of three judges. The panel decides the case for the entire court. Sometimes, when the parties request it or a question of unusual importance, the judges on the appeals court assemble *en banc* (a rare event).

Review of a lower court decision

In making its decision, the panel reviews key parts of the record. The record consists of the documents filed in the case at trial and the transcript of the trial proceedings. The panel learns about the lawyers' legal arguments from the lawyers' briefs.

Briefs are written documents that each side submits to explain its case and tell why the court should decide in its favor.

Oral argument

If the court permits oral argument, the lawyers for each side have a limited amount of time (typically between 15 to 30 minutes) to argue (i.e., advocate and explain) their case to the judges (or justices at the highest court in the jurisdiction) in a formal courtroom session. The judges (or justices for the highest court in the jurisdiction) frequently question the attorneys about the relevant law as it applies to the facts and issues in the case before them.

A court of appeals differs from the federal trial courts. There are no jurors, witnesses, or court reporters. The lawyers for each side, but not the parties, are usually present in the courtroom.

Decision

After the submission of briefs and oral arguments, the judges discuss the case privately, consider relevant *precedents* (court decisions from higher courts in prior cases with similar facts and legal issues), and reach a decision. Courts are required to follow precedents.

For example, a U.S. court of appeals must follow the U.S. Supreme Court's decisions; a district court must follow the decisions of the U.S. Supreme Court and the decisions of the court of appeals of its circuit.

Courts are influenced by decisions they are not required to follow, such as the decisions of other circuits. Courts follow precedent unless they set forth reasons for the diversion.

At least two of the three judges on the panel must agree on a decision. One judge who agrees with the decision is chosen to write an opinion, which announces and explains the decision.

If a judge on the panel disagrees with the majority's opinion, the judge may write a dissent, giving reasons for disagreeing.

Many appellate opinions are published in books of opinions, called reporters. The opinions are read carefully by other judges and lawyers looking for precedents to guide them in their cases.

The accumulated judicial opinions make up a body of law known as *case law*, which is usually an accurate predictor of how future cases will be decided.

For decisions that the judges believe are important to the parties and contribute little to the law, the appeals courts frequently use short, unsigned opinions that often are not published.

If the court of appeals decides that the trial judge incorrectly interpreted the law or followed incorrect procedures, it reverses the district court's decision.

For example, the court of appeals could hold that the district judge allowed the jury to base its decision on evidence that never should have been admitted, and thus the defendant cannot be guilty.

Most of the time, courts of appeals uphold, rather than the reverse, district court decisions.

Sometimes when a higher court reverses the decision of the district court, it sends the case back (i.e., *remand* the case) to the lower court for another trial.

For example, *Miranda v. Arizona* case (1966), the Supreme Court ruled 5-4 that Ernesto Miranda's confession could not be used as evidence because he had not been advised of his right to remain silent or of his right to have a lawyer present during questioning.

However, the government did have other evidence against him. The case was remanded for a new trial, in which the improperly obtained confession was not used as evidence, but the other evidence convicted Miranda.

The Supreme Court of the United States

The Supreme Court is the highest in the nation. It is a different kind of appeals court; its major function is not correcting errors made by trial judges but clarifying the law in cases of national importance or when lower courts disagree about interpreting the Constitution or federal laws.

The Supreme Court does not have to hear every case that it is asked to review. Each year, losing parties ask the Supreme Court to review about 8,000 cases.

Almost all cases come to the Court as a *petition for writ of certiorari*. The court selects only about 80 to 120 of the most significant cases to review with oral arguments.

Supreme Court decisions establish a precedent for interpreting the Constitution and federal laws; holdings that state and federal courts must follow.

The power of judicial review makes the Supreme Court's role in our government vital. Judicial review is the power of a court when deciding a case to declare that a law passed by a legislature or action by the executive branch is invalid because it is inconsistent with the Constitution.

Although district courts, courts of appeals, and state courts can exercise the power of judicial review, their decisions about federal law are always subject, on appeal, to review by the Supreme Court.

When the Supreme Court declares a law unconstitutional, its decision can only be overruled by a later decision of the Supreme Court or Amendment to the Constitution.

Seven of the twenty-seven Amendments to the Constitution have invalidated the decisions of the Supreme Court. However, most Supreme Court cases do not concern the constitutionality of laws, but the interpretation of laws passed by Congress.

Although Congress has steadily increased the number of district and appeals court judges over the years, the Supreme Court has remained the same size since 1869. It consists of a Chief Justice and eight associate justices.

Like the federal court of appeals and federal district judges, the Supreme Court justices are appointed by the President with the Senate's *advice and consent.*

Unlike the judges in the courts of appeals, Supreme Court justices never sit on panels. Absent recusal, nine justices hear cases, and a majority ruling decides cases.

The Supreme Court begins its annual session, or term, on the first Monday of October. The term lasts until the Court has announced its decisions in cases where it has heard an argument that term—usually late June or early July.

During the term, the Court, sitting for two weeks at a time, hears oral arguments on Monday through Wednesday and holds private conferences to discuss the cases, reach decisions, and begin preparing the written opinions that explain its decisions.

Most decisions and opinions are released in the late spring and early summer.

Standards of review for federal courts

Standard of review	*De novo*	Clearly erroneous	Abuse of discretion
Type of decision under review	Question of the law	Question of fact	Discretionary action
Lower-court decision maker	Trial judge	Trial judge	Trial judge
Deference given to lower court	No deference	Substantial deference	Extreme deference
Party typically benefitted	Appellant	Appellee	Appellee
Definition	An appellate court reviews the legal question anew and independently, without regard to the conclusions reached by the trial court. "When *de novo* review is compelled, no form of appellate deference is acceptable." *Salve Regina College v. Russell,* (1991).	A finding is 'clearly erroneous' when although there is evidence to support it, the reviewing court on the entire evidence is left with the definite and firm conviction that a mistake has been committed. *United States v. United States Gypsum Co.,* (1948) "If the district court's account of the evidence is plausible in light of the record viewed in its entirety, the court of appeals may not reverse it even though convinced that had it been sitting as the trier of fact, it would have weighed the evidence differently. When there are two permissible views of the evidence, the factfinder's choice between them cannot be clearly erroneous." *Anderson v. Bessemer City,* (1985).	Generally, an abuse of discretion only occurs where no reasonable person could take the view adopted by the trial court. If reasonable persons could differ, no abuse of discretion can be found. *Harrington v. DeVito,* (7th Cir.1981) Under the abuse of discretion standard, a trial court's decision will not be disturbed unless the appellate court has a definite and firm conviction that the lower court made a clear error of judgment or exceeded the bounds of permissible choice in the circumstances. We will not alter a trial court's decision unless it can be shown that the court's decision was an arbitrary, capricious, whimsical, or manifestly unreasonable judgment. *Wright v. Abbott Laboratories, Inc.,* (10th Cir. 2001)
Examples	Motions for summary judgment, constitutional questions, statutory interpretation	Questions regarding who did what, where, and when; questions of intent and motive; questions of ultimate fact (such as negligence)	Rule 11 sanctions, attorney's fees, courtroom management, motions to compel, injunctions, and temporary restraining orders.

The Constitution of the United States (*a transcription*)

THE U.S. NATIONAL ARCHIVES & RECORDS ADMINISTRATION
www.archives.gov

The following text is a transcription of the Constitution as it was inscribed by Jacob Shallus on parchment (the document on display in the Rotunda at the National Archives Museum.) The spelling and punctuation reflect the original.

The Constitution of the United States: A Transcription

The following text is a transcription of the Constitution as it was inscribed by Jacob Shallus on parchment (displayed in the Rotunda at the National Archives Museum.) The authenticated text of the Constitution can be found on the website of the Government Printing Office.

We the People of the United States, in Order to form a more perfect Union, establish Justice, insure domestic Tranquility, provide for the common defence, promote the general Welfare, and secure the Blessings of Liberty to ourselves and our Posterity, do ordain and establish this Constitution for the United States of America.

Article. I

Section. 1.

All legislative Powers herein granted shall be vested in a Congress of the United States, which shall consist of a Senate and House of Representatives.

Section. 2.

The House of Representatives shall be composed of Members chosen every second Year by the People of the several States, and the Electors in each State shall have the Qualifications requisite for Electors of the most numerous Branch of the State Legislature.

No Person shall be a Representative who shall not have attained to the Age of twenty five Years, and been seven Years a Citizen of the United States, and who shall not, when elected, be an Inhabitant of that State in which he shall be chosen.

Representatives and direct Taxes shall be apportioned among the several States which may be included within this Union, according to their respective Numbers, which shall be determined by adding to the whole Number of free Persons, including those bound to Service for a Term of Years, and excluding Indians not taxed, three fifths of all other Persons. The actual Enumeration shall be made within three Years after the first Meeting of the Congress of the United States, and within every subsequent Term of ten Years, in such Manner as they shall by Law direct. The Number of Representatives shall not exceed one for every thirty Thousand, but each State shall have at Least one Representative; and until such enumeration shall be made, the State of New Hampshire shall be entitled to chuse three, Massachusetts eight, Rhode-Island and Providence

Plantations one, Connecticut five, New-York six, New Jersey four, Pennsylvania eight, Delaware one, Maryland six, Virginia ten, North Carolina five, South Carolina five, and Georgia three.

When vacancies happen in the Representation from any State, the Executive Authority thereof shall issue Writs of Election to fill such Vacancies.

The House of Representatives shall chuse their Speaker and other Officers; and shall have the sole Power of Impeachment.

Section. 3.

The Senate of the United States shall be composed of two Senators from each State, chosen by the Legislature thereof, for six Years; and each Senator shall have one Vote.

Immediately after they shall be assembled in Consequence of the first Election, they shall be divided as equally as may be into three Classes. The Seats of the Senators of the first Class shall be vacated at the Expiration of the second Year, of the second Class at the Expiration of the fourth Year, and of the third Class at the Expiration of the sixth Year, so that one third may be chosen every second Year; and if Vacancies happen by Resignation, or otherwise, during the Recess of the Legislature of any State, the Executive thereof may make temporary Appointments until the next Meeting of the Legislature, which shall then fill such Vacancies.

No Person shall be a Senator who shall not have attained to the Age of thirty Years, and been nine Years a Citizen of the United States, and who shall not, when elected, be an Inhabitant of that State for which he shall be chosen.

The Vice President of the United States shall be President of the Senate, but shall have no Vote, unless they be equally divided.

The Senate shall chuse their other Officers, and also a President pro tempore, in the Absence of the Vice President, or when he shall exercise the Office of President of the United States.

The Senate shall have the sole Power to try all Impeachments. When sitting for that Purpose, they shall be on Oath or Affirmation. When the President of the United States is tried, the Chief Justice shall preside: And no Person shall be convicted without the Concurrence of two thirds of the Members present.

Judgment in Cases of Impeachment shall not extend further than to removal from Office, and disqualification to hold and enjoy any Office of honor, Trust or Profit under the United States: but the Party convicted shall nevertheless be liable and subject to Indictment, Trial, Judgment and Punishment, according to Law.

Section. 4.

The Times, Places and Manner of holding Elections for Senators and Representatives, shall be prescribed in each State by the Legislature thereof; but the Congress may at any time by Law make or alter such Regulations, except as to the Places of chusing Senators.

The Congress shall assemble at least once in every Year, and such Meeting shall be on the first Monday in December, unless they shall by Law appoint a different Day.

Section. 5.

Each House shall be the Judge of the Elections, Returns and Qualifications of its own Members, and a Majority of each shall constitute a Quorum to do Business; but a smaller Number may adjourn from day to day, and may be authorized to compel the Attendance of absent Members, in such Manner, and under such Penalties as each House may provide.

Each House may determine the Rules of its Proceedings, punish its Members for disorderly Behaviour, and, with the Concurrence of two thirds, expel a Member.

Each House shall keep a Journal of its Proceedings, and from time to time publish the same, excepting such Parts as may in their Judgment require Secrecy; and the Yeas and Nays of the Members of either House on any question shall, at the Desire of one fifth of those Present, be entered on the Journal.

Neither House, during the Session of Congress, shall, without the Consent of the other, adjourn for more than three days, nor to any other Place than that in which the two Houses shall be sitting.

Section. 6.

The Senators and Representatives shall receive a Compensation for their Services, to be ascertained by Law, and paid out of the Treasury of the United States. They shall in all Cases, except Treason, Felony and Breach of the Peace, be privileged from Arrest during their Attendance at the Session of their respective Houses, and in going to and returning from the same; and for any Speech or Debate in either House, they shall not be questioned in any other Place.

No Senator or Representative shall, during the Time for which he was elected, be appointed to any civil Office under the Authority of the United States, which shall have been created, or the Emoluments whereof shall have been encreased during such time; and no Person holding any Office under the United States, shall be a Member of either House during his Continuance in Office.

Section. 7.

All Bills for raising Revenue shall originate in the House of Representatives; but the Senate may propose or concur with Amendments as on other Bills.

Every Bill which shall have passed the House of Representatives and the Senate, shall, before it become a Law, be presented to the President of the United States; If he approves he shall sign it, but if not he shall return it, with his Objections to that House in which it shall have originated, who shall enter the Objections at large on their Journal, and proceed to reconsider it. If after such Reconsideration two thirds of that House shall agree to pass the Bill, it shall be sent, together with the Objections, to the other House, by which it shall likewise be reconsidered, and if approved by two thirds of that House, it shall become a Law. But in all such Cases the Votes of both Houses shall be determined by yeas and Nays, and the Names of the Persons voting for and against the Bill shall be entered on the Journal of each House respectively. If any Bill shall not be returned by the President within ten Days (Sundays excepted) after it shall have been presented to him, the Same shall be a Law, in like Manner as if he had signed it, unless the Congress by their Adjournment prevent its Return, in which Case it shall not be a Law.

Every Order, Resolution, or Vote to which the Concurrence of the Senate and House of Representatives may be necessary (except on a question of Adjournment) shall be presented to the President of the United States; and before the Same shall take Effect, shall be approved by him, or being disapproved by him, shall be repassed by two thirds of the Senate and House of Representatives, according to the Rules and Limitations prescribed in the Case of a Bill.

Section. 8.

The Congress shall have Power To lay and collect Taxes, Duties, Imposts and Excises, to pay the Debts and provide for the common Defence and general Welfare of the United States; but all Duties, Imposts and Excises shall be uniform throughout the United States;

To borrow Money on the credit of the United States;

To regulate Commerce with foreign Nations, and among the several States, and with the Indian Tribes;

To establish an uniform Rule of Naturalization, and uniform Laws on the subject of Bankruptcies throughout the United States;

To coin Money, regulate the Value thereof, and of foreign Coin, and fix the Standard of Weights and Measures;

To provide for the Punishment of counterfeiting the Securities and current Coin of the United States;

To establish Post Offices and post Roads;

To promote the Progress of Science and useful Arts, by securing for limited Times to Authors and Inventors the exclusive Right to their respective Writings and Discoveries;

To constitute Tribunals inferior to the Supreme Court;

To define and punish Piracies and Felonies committed on the high Seas, and Offences against the Law of Nations;

To declare War, grant Letters of Marque and Reprisal, and make Rules concerning Captures on Land and Water;

To raise and support Armies, but no Appropriation of Money to that Use shall be for a longer Term than two Years;

To provide and maintain a Navy;

To make Rules for the Government and Regulation of the land and naval Forces;

To provide for calling forth the Militia to execute the Laws of the Union, suppress Insurrections and repel Invasions;

To provide for organizing, arming, and disciplining, the Militia, and for governing such Part of them as may be employed in the Service of the United States, reserving to the States respectively, the Appointment of the Officers, and the Authority of training the Militia according to the discipline prescribed by Congress;

To exercise exclusive Legislation in all Cases whatsoever, over such District (not exceeding ten Miles square) as may, by Cession of particular States, and the Acceptance of Congress, become the Seat of the Government of the United States, and to exercise like Authority over all Places purchased by the Consent of the Legislature of the State in which the Same shall be, for the Erection of Forts, Magazines, Arsenals, dock-Yards, and other needful Buildings;—And

To make all Laws which shall be necessary and proper for carrying into Execution the foregoing Powers, and all other Powers vested by this Constitution in the Government of the United States, or in any Department or Officer thereof.

Section. 9.

The Migration or Importation of such Persons as any of the States now existing shall think proper to admit, shall not be prohibited by the Congress prior to the Year one thousand eight hundred and eight, but a Tax or duty may be imposed on such Importation, not exceeding ten dollars for each Person.

The Privilege of the Writ of Habeas Corpus shall not be suspended, unless when in Cases of Rebellion or Invasion the public Safety may require it.

No Bill of Attainder or ex post facto Law shall be passed.

No Capitation, or other direct, Tax shall be laid, unless in Proportion to the Census or enumeration herein before directed to be taken.

No Tax or Duty shall be laid on Articles exported from any State.

No Preference shall be given by any Regulation of Commerce or Revenue to the Ports of one State over those of another: nor shall Vessels bound to, or from, one State, be obliged to enter, clear, or pay Duties in another.

No Money shall be drawn from the Treasury, but in Consequence of Appropriations made by Law; and a regular Statement and Account of the Receipts and Expenditures of all public Money shall be published from time to time.

No Title of Nobility shall be granted by the United States: And no Person holding any Office of Profit or Trust under them, shall, without the Consent of the Congress, accept of any present, Emolument, Office, or Title, of any kind whatever, from any King, Prince, or foreign State.

Section. 10.

No State shall enter into any Treaty, Alliance, or Confederation; grant Letters of Marque and Reprisal; coin Money; emit Bills of Credit; make any Thing but gold and silver Coin a Tender in Payment of Debts; pass any Bill of Attainder, ex post facto Law, or Law impairing the Obligation of Contracts, or grant any Title of Nobility.

No State shall, without the Consent of the Congress, lay any Imposts or Duties on Imports or Exports, except what may be absolutely necessary for executing it's inspection Laws: and the net

Produce of all Duties and Imposts, laid by any State on Imports or Exports, shall be for the Use of the Treasury of the United States; and all such Laws shall be subject to the Revision and Controul of the Congress.

No State shall, without the Consent of Congress, lay any Duty of Tonnage, keep Troops, or Ships of War in time of Peace, enter into any Agreement or Compact with another State, or with a foreign Power, or engage in War, unless actually invaded, or in such imminent Danger as will not admit of delay.

Article. II

Section. 1.

The executive Power shall be vested in a President of the United States of America. He shall hold his Office during the Term of four Years, and, together with the Vice President, chosen for the same Term, be elected, as follows

Each State shall appoint, in such Manner as the Legislature thereof may direct, a Number of Electors, equal to the whole Number of Senators and Representatives to which the State may be entitled in the Congress: but no Senator or Representative, or Person holding an Office of Trust or Profit under the United States, shall be appointed an Elector.

The Electors shall meet in their respective States, and vote by Ballot for two Persons, of whom one at least shall not be an Inhabitant of the same State with themselves. And they shall make a List of all the Persons voted for, and of the Number of Votes for each; which List they shall sign and certify, and transmit sealed to the Seat of the Government of the United States, directed to the President of the Senate. The President of the Senate shall, in the Presence of the Senate and House of Representatives, open all the Certificates, and the Votes shall then be counted. The Person having the greatest Number of Votes shall be the President, if such Number be a Majority of the whole Number of Electors appointed; and if there be more than one who have such Majority, and have an equal Number of Votes, then the House of Representatives shall immediately chuse by Ballot one of them for President; and if no Person have a Majority, then from the five highest on the List the said House shall in like Manner chuse the President. But in chusing the President, the Votes shall be taken by States, the Representation from each State having one Vote; A quorum for this Purpose shall consist of a Member or Members from two thirds of the States, and a Majority of all the States shall be necessary to a Choice. In every Case, after the Choice of the President, the Person having the greatest Number of Votes of the Electors shall be the Vice President. But if there should remain two or more who have equal Votes, the Senate shall chuse from them by Ballot the Vice President.

The Congress may determine the Time of chusing the Electors, and the Day on which they shall give their Votes; which Day shall be the same throughout the United States.

No Person except a natural born Citizen, or a Citizen of the United States, at the time of the Adoption of this Constitution, shall be eligible to the Office of President; neither shall any Person be eligible to that Office who shall not have attained to the Age of thirty five Years, and been fourteen Years a Resident within the United States.

In Case of the Removal of the President from Office, or of his Death, Resignation, or Inability to discharge the Powers and Duties of the said Office, the Same shall devolve on the Vice President, and the Congress may by Law provide for the Case of Removal, Death, Resignation or Inability, both of the President and Vice President, declaring what Officer shall then act as President, and such Officer shall act accordingly, until the Disability be removed, or a President shall be elected.

The President shall, at stated Times, receive for his Services, a Compensation, which shall neither be encreased nor diminished during the Period for which he shall have been elected, and he shall not receive within that Period any other Emolument from the United States, or any of them.

Before he enters on the Execution of his Office, he shall take the following Oath or Affirmation:—"I do solemnly swear (or affirm) that I will faithfully execute the Office of President of the United States, and will to the best of my Ability, preserve, protect and defend the Constitution of the United States."

Section. 2.

The President shall be Commander in Chief of the Army and Navy of the United States, and of the Militia of the several States, when called into the actual Service of the United States; he may require the Opinion, in writing, of the principal Officer in each of the executive Departments, upon any Subject relating to the Duties of their respective Offices, and he shall have Power to grant Reprieves and Pardons for Offences against the United States, except in Cases of Impeachment.

He shall have Power, by and with the Advice and Consent of the Senate, to make Treaties, provided two thirds of the Senators present concur; and he shall nominate, and by and with the Advice and Consent of the Senate, shall appoint Ambassadors, other public Ministers and Consuls, Judges of the supreme Court, and all other Officers of the United States, whose Appointments are not herein otherwise provided for, and which shall be established by Law: but the Congress may by Law vest the Appointment of such inferior Officers, as they think proper, in the President alone, in the Courts of Law, or in the Heads of Departments.

The President shall have Power to fill up all Vacancies that may happen during the Recess of the Senate, by granting Commissions which shall expire at the End of their next Session.

Section. 3.

He shall from time to time give to the Congress Information of the State of the Union, and recommend to their Consideration such Measures as he shall judge necessary and expedient; he may, on extraordinary Occasions, convene both Houses, or either of them, and in Case of Disagreement between them, with Respect to the Time of Adjournment, he may adjourn them to such Time as he shall think proper; he shall receive Ambassadors and other public Ministers; he shall take Care that the Laws be faithfully executed, and shall Commission all the Officers of the United States.

Section. 4.

The President, Vice President and all civil Officers of the United States, shall be removed from Office on Impeachment for, and Conviction of, Treason, Bribery, or other high Crimes and Misdemeanors.

Article III

Section. 1.

The judicial Power of the United States, shall be vested in one supreme Court, and in such inferior Courts as the Congress may from time to time ordain and establish. The Judges, both of the supreme and inferior Courts, shall hold their Offices during good Behaviour, and shall, at stated Times, receive for their Services, a Compensation, which shall not be diminished during their Continuance in Office.

Section. 2.

The judicial Power shall extend to all Cases, in Law and Equity, arising under this Constitution, the Laws of the United States, and Treaties made, or which shall be made, under their Authority;—to all Cases affecting Ambassadors, other public Ministers and Consuls;—to all Cases of admiralty and maritime Jurisdiction;—to Controversies to which the United States shall be a Party;—to Controversies between two or more States;—between a State and Citizens of another State,—between Citizens of different States,—between Citizens of the same State claiming Lands under Grants of different States, and between a State, or the Citizens thereof, and foreign States, Citizens or Subjects.

In all Cases affecting Ambassadors, other public Ministers and Consuls, and those in which a State shall be Party, the supreme Court shall have original Jurisdiction. In all the other Cases before mentioned, the supreme Court shall have appellate Jurisdiction, both as to Law and Fact, with such Exceptions, and under such Regulations as the Congress shall make.

The Trial of all Crimes, except in Cases of Impeachment, shall be by Jury; and such Trial shall be held in the State where the said Crimes shall have been committed; but when not committed within any State, the Trial shall be at such Place or Places as the Congress may by Law have directed.

Section. 3.

Treason against the United States, shall consist only in levying War against them, or in adhering to their Enemies, giving them Aid and Comfort. No Person shall be convicted of Treason unless on the Testimony of two Witnesses to the same overt Act, or on Confession in open Court.

The Congress shall have Power to declare the Punishment of Treason, but no Attainder of Treason shall work Corruption of Blood, or Forfeiture except during the Life of the Person attainted.

Article. IV

Section. 1.

Full Faith and Credit shall be given in each State to the public Acts, Records, and judicial Proceedings of every other State. And the Congress may by general Laws prescribe the Manner in which such Acts, Records and Proceedings shall be proved, and the Effect thereof.

Section. 2.

The Citizens of each State shall be entitled to all Privileges and Immunities of Citizens in the several States.

A Person charged in any State with Treason, Felony, or other Crime, who shall flee from Justice, and be found in another State, shall on Demand of the executive Authority of the State from which he fled, be delivered up, to be removed to the State having Jurisdiction of the Crime.

No Person held to Service or Labour in one State, under the Laws thereof, escaping into another, shall, in Consequence of any Law or Regulation therein, be discharged from such Service or Labour, but shall be delivered up on Claim of the Party to whom such Service or Labour may be due.

Section. 3.

New States may be admitted by the Congress into this Union; but no new State shall be formed or erected within the Jurisdiction of any other State; nor any State be formed by the Junction of two or more States, or Parts of States, without the Consent of the Legislatures of the States concerned as well as of the Congress.

The Congress shall have Power to dispose of and make all needful Rules and Regulations respecting the Territory or other Property belonging to the United States; and nothing in this Constitution shall be so construed as to Prejudice any Claims of the United States, or of any particular State.

Section. 4.

The United States shall guarantee to every State in this Union a Republican Form of Government, and shall protect each of them against Invasion; and on Application of the Legislature, or of the Executive (when the Legislature cannot be convened), against domestic Violence.

Article. V

The Congress, whenever two thirds of both Houses shall deem it necessary, shall propose Amendments to this Constitution, or, on the Application of the Legislatures of two thirds of the several States, shall call a Convention for proposing Amendments, which, in either Case, shall be valid to all Intents and Purposes, as Part of this Constitution, when ratified by the Legislatures of three fourths of the several States, or by Conventions in three fourths thereof, as the one or the other Mode of Ratification may be proposed by the Congress; Provided that no Amendment which may be made prior to the Year One thousand eight hundred and eight shall in any Manner affect the first and fourth Clauses in the Ninth Section of the first Article; and that no State, without its Consent, shall be deprived of its equal Suffrage in the Senate.

Article. VI

All Debts contracted and Engagements entered into, before the Adoption of this Constitution, shall be as valid against the United States under this Constitution, as under the Confederation.

This Constitution, and the Laws of the United States which shall be made in Pursuance thereof; and all Treaties made, or which shall be made, under the Authority of the United States, shall be the supreme Law of the Land; and the Judges in every State shall be bound thereby, any Thing in the Constitution or Laws of any State to the Contrary notwithstanding.

The Senators and Representatives before mentioned, and the Members of the several State Legislatures, and all executive and judicial Officers, both of the United States and of the several States, shall be bound by Oath or Affirmation, to support this Constitution; but no religious Test shall ever be required as a Qualification to any Office or public Trust under the United States.

Article. VII

The Ratification of the Conventions of nine States, shall be sufficient for the Establishment of this Constitution between the States so ratifying the Same.

The Word, "the," being interlined between the seventh and eighth Lines of the first Page, The Word "Thirty" being partly written on an Erazure in the fifteenth Line of the first Page, The Words "is tried" being interlined between the thirty second and thirty third Lines of the first Page and the Word "the" being interlined between the forty third and forty fourth Lines of the second Page.

Attest William Jackson Secretary, done in Convention by the Unanimous Consent of the States present the Seventeenth Day of September in the Year of our Lord one thousand seven hundred and Eighty seven and of the Independance of the United States of America the Twelfth In witness whereof We have hereunto subscribed our Names, G°. Washington, *Presidt and deputy from Virginia*

Delaware
Geo: Read
Gunning Bedford jun
John Dickinson
Richard Bassett
Jaco: Broom

Maryland
James McHenry
Dan of St Thos. Jenifer
Danl. Carroll

Virginia
John Blair
James Madison Jr.

North Carolina
Wm. Blount
Richd. Dobbs Spaight
Hu Williamson

South Carolina
J. Rutledge
Charles Cotesworth Pinckney
Charles Pinckney
Pierce Butler

Georgia
William Few
Abr Baldwin

New Hampshire
John Langdon
Nicholas Gilman

Massachusetts
Nathaniel Gorham
Rufus King

Connecticut
Wm. Saml. Johnson
Roger Sherman

New York
Alexander Hamilton

New Jersey
Wil: Livingston
David Brearley
Wm. Paterson
Jona: Dayton

Pensylvania
B Franklin
Thomas Mifflin
Robt. Morris
Geo. Clymer
Thos. FitzSimons
Jared Ingersoll
James Wilson
Gouv Morris

Enactment of the Bill of Rights of the United States of America (1791)

The first ten Amendments to the Constitution make up the Bill of Rights. Written by James Madison in response to calls from several states for greater constitutional protection for individual liberties, the Bill of Rights lists specific prohibitions on governmental power. The Virginia Declaration of Rights, written by George Mason, strongly influenced Madison.

One of the contention points between Federalists and Anti-Federalists was the Constitution's lack of a bill of rights that would place specific limits on government power.

Federalists argued that the Constitution did not need a bill of rights because the people and the states kept powers not explicitly given to the federal government.

Anti-Federalists held that a *bill of rights* was necessary to safeguard individual liberty.

Madison, then a member of the U.S. House of Representatives, went through the Constitution itself, making changes where he thought most appropriate.

Several Representatives, led by Roger Sherman, objected that Congress had no authority to change the wording of the Constitution. Therefore, Madison's changes were presented as a list of amendments that would follow Article VII.

The House approved 17 amendments. Of these 17, the Senate approved 12. Those 12 were sent to the states for approval in August of 1789. Of those 12 proposed amendments, 10 were quickly ratified. Virginia's legislature became the last to ratify the Amendments on December 15, 1791. These Amendments are the Bill of Rights.

The Bill of Rights is a list of limits on government power. For example, what the Founders saw as the natural right of individuals to speak and worship freely was protected by the First Amendment's prohibitions on Congress from making laws establishing a religion or abridging freedom of speech.

Another example is the natural right to be free from the government's unreasonable intrusion in one's home was safeguarded by the Fourth Amendment's warrant requirements.

Other precursors to the Bill of Rights include English documents such as the Magna Carta[1], the Petition of Rights, the English Bill of Rights, and the Massachusetts Body of Liberties.

The Magna Carta illustrates Compact Theory[1] as well as initial strides toward limited government. Its provisions address individual rights and political rights. Latin for "Great Charter," the Magna Carta was written by Barons in Runnymede, England, and forced on the King.

Although the protections were generally limited to the prerogatives of the Barons, the Magna Carta embodied the general principle that the King accepted limitations on his rule. These included the fundamental acknowledgment that the king was not above the law.

Included in the Magna Carta are protections for the English church, petitioning the king, freedom from the forced quarter of troops and unreasonable searches, due process and fair trial protections, and freedom from excessive fines. These protections can be found in the First, Third, Fourth, Fifth, Sixth, and Eighth Amendments to the Constitution.

The Magna Carta is the oldest compact in England. The Mayflower Compact, the Fundamental Orders of Connecticut, and the Albany Plan are examples from the American colonies.

The Articles of Confederation was a compact among the states, and the Constitution creates a compact based on a federal system between the national government, state governments, and the people. The Hayne-Webster Debate focused on the compact created by the Constitution.

[1] Philosophers including Thomas Hobbes, John Locke, and Jean-Jacques Rousseau theorized that peoples' condition in a "state of nature" (that is, outside of society) is one of freedom, but that freedom inevitably degrades into war, chaos, or debilitating competition without the benefit of a system of laws and government. They reasoned, therefore, that for their happiness, individuals willingly trade some of their natural freedom in exchange for the protections provided by the government.

The Bill of Rights: Amendments I–X

Amendment I

Congress shall make no law respecting an establishment of religion, or prohibiting the free exercise thereof; or abridging the freedom of speech, or of the press; or the right of the people peaceably to assemble, and to petition the government for a redress of grievances.

Amendment II

A well regulated militia, being necessary to the security of a free state, the right of the people to keep and bear arms, shall not be infringed.

Amendment III

No soldier shall, in time of peace be quartered in any house, without the consent of the owner, nor in time of war, but in a manner to be prescribed by law.

Amendment IV

The right of the people to be secure in their persons, houses, papers, and effects, against unreasonable searches and seizures, shall not be violated, and no warrants shall issue, but upon probable cause, supported by oath or affirmation, and particularly describing the place to be searched, and the persons or things to be seized.

Amendment V

No person shall be held to answer for a capital, or otherwise infamous crime, unless on a presentment or indictment of a grand jury, except in cases arising in the land or naval forces, or in the militia, when in actual service in time of war or public danger; nor shall any person be subject for the same offense to be twice put in jeopardy of life or limb; nor shall be compelled in any criminal case to be a witness against himself, nor be deprived of life, liberty, or property, without due process of law; nor shall private property be taken for public use, without just compensation.

Amendment VI

In all criminal prosecutions, the accused shall enjoy the right to a speedy and public trial, by an impartial jury of the state and district wherein the crime shall have been committed, which district shall have been previously ascertained by law, and to be informed of the nature and cause of the accusation; to be confronted with the witnesses against him; to have compulsory process for obtaining witnesses in his favor, and to have the assistance of counsel for his defense.

Amendment VII

In suits at common law, where the value in controversy shall exceed twenty dollars, the right of trial by jury shall be preserved, and no fact tried by a jury, shall be otherwise reexamined in any court of the United States, than according to the rules of the common law.

Amendment VIII

Excessive bail shall not be required, nor excessive fines imposed, nor cruel and unusual punishments inflicted.

Amendment IX

The enumeration in the Constitution, of certain rights, shall not be construed to deny or disparage others retained by the people.

Amendment X

The powers not delegated to the United States by the Constitution, nor prohibited by it to the states, are reserved to the states respectively, or to the people.

Constitutional Amendments XI–XXVII

AMENDMENT XI

Passed by Congress March 4, 1794. Ratified February 7, 1795.

Note: Article III, section 2, of the Constitution was modified by amendment 11.

The Judicial power of the United States shall not be construed to extend to any suit in law or equity, commenced or prosecuted against one of the United States by Citizens of another State, or by Citizens or Subjects of any Foreign State.

AMENDMENT XII

Passed by Congress December 9, 1803. Ratified June 15, 1804.

Note: A portion of Article II, section 1 of the Constitution was superseded by the 12th amendment.

The Electors shall meet in their respective states and vote by ballot for President and Vice-President, one of whom, at least, shall not be an inhabitant of the same state with themselves; they shall name in their ballots the person voted for as President, and in distinct ballots the person voted for as Vice-President, and they shall make distinct lists of all persons voted for as President, and of all persons voted for as Vice-President, and of the number of votes for each, which lists they shall sign and certify, and transmit sealed to the seat of the government of the United States, directed to the President of the Senate; -- the President of the Senate shall, in the presence of the Senate and House of Representatives, open all the certificates and the votes shall then be counted; -- The person having the greatest number of votes for President, shall be the President, if such number be a majority of the whole number of Electors appointed; and if no person have such majority, then from the persons having the highest numbers not exceeding three on the list of those voted for as President, the House of Representatives shall choose immediately, by ballot, the President. But in choosing the President, the votes shall be taken by states, the representation from each state having one vote; a quorum for this purpose shall consist of a member or members from two-thirds of the states, and a majority of all the states shall be necessary to a choice. [And if the House of Representatives shall not choose a President whenever the right of choice shall devolve upon them, before the fourth day of March next following, then the Vice-President shall act as President, as in case of the death or other constitutional disability of the President. --]* The person having the greatest number of votes as Vice-President, shall be the Vice-President, if such number be a majority of the whole number of Electors appointed, and if no person have a majority, then from the two highest numbers on the list, the Senate shall choose the Vice-President; a quorum for the purpose shall consist of two-thirds of the whole number of Senators, and a majority of the whole number shall be necessary to a choice. But no person constitutionally ineligible to the office of President shall be eligible to that of Vice-President of the United States.

**Superseded by section 3 of the 20th Amendment.*

AMENDMENT XIII

Passed by Congress January 31, 1865. Ratified December 6, 1865.

Note: A portion of Article IV, section 2, of the Constitution was superseded by the 13th amendment.

Section 1.
Neither slavery nor involuntary servitude, except as a punishment for crime whereof the party shall have been duly convicted, shall exist within the United States, or any place subject to their jurisdiction.

Section 2.
Congress shall have power to enforce this article by appropriate legislation.

AMENDMENT XIV

Passed by Congress June 13, 1866. Ratified July 9, 1868.

Note: Article I, section 2, of the Constitution was modified by section 2 of the 14th amendment.

Section 1.
All persons born or naturalized in the United States, and subject to the jurisdiction thereof, are citizens of the United States and of the State wherein they reside. No State shall make or enforce any law which shall abridge the privileges or immunities of citizens of the United States; nor shall any State deprive any person of life, liberty, or property, without due process of law; nor deny to any person within its jurisdiction the equal protection of the laws.

Section 2.
Representatives shall be apportioned among the several States according to their respective numbers, counting the whole number of persons in each State, excluding Indians not taxed. But when the right to vote at any election for the choice of electors for President and Vice-President of the United States, Representatives in Congress, the Executive and Judicial officers of a State, or the members of the Legislature thereof, is denied to any of the male inhabitants of such State, being twenty-one years of age,* and citizens of the United States, or in any way abridged, except for participation in rebellion, or other crime, the basis of representation therein shall be reduced in the proportion which the number of such male citizens shall bear to the whole number of male citizens twenty-one years of age in such State.

Section 3.
No person shall be a Senator or Representative in Congress, or elector of President and Vice-President, or hold any office, civil or military, under the United States, or under any State, who, having previously taken an oath, as a member of Congress, or as an officer of the United States, or as a member of any State legislature, or as an executive or judicial officer of any State, to support the Constitution of the United States, shall have engaged in insurrection or rebellion against the same, or given aid or comfort to the enemies thereof. But Congress may by a vote of two-thirds of each House, remove such disability.

Section 4.
The validity of the public debt of the United States, authorized by law, including debts incurred for payment of pensions and bounties for services in suppressing insurrection or rebellion, shall not be questioned. But neither the United States nor any State shall assume or pay any debt or obligation incurred in aid of insurrection or rebellion against the United States, or any claim for the loss or emancipation of any slave; but all such debts, obligations and claims shall be held illegal and void.

Section 5.
The Congress shall have the power to enforce, by appropriate legislation, the provisions of this article.

**Changed by section 1 of the 26th Amendment.*

AMENDMENT XV

Passed by Congress February 26, 1869. Ratified February 3, 1870.

Section 1.
The right of citizens of the United States to vote shall not be denied or abridged by the United States or by any State on account of race, color, or previous condition of servitude.

Section 2.
The Congress shall have the power to enforce this article by appropriate legislation.

AMENDMENT XVI

Passed by Congress July 2, 1909. Ratified February 3, 1913.

Note: Article I, section 9, of the Constitution was modified by amendment 16.

The Congress shall have power to lay and collect taxes on incomes, from whatever source derived, without apportionment among the several States, and without regard to any census or enumeration.

AMENDMENT XVII

Passed by Congress May 13, 1912. Ratified April 8, 1913.

Note: Article I, section 3, of the Constitution was modified by the 17th Amendment.

The Senate of the United States shall be composed of two Senators from each State, elected by the people thereof, for six years; and each Senator shall have one vote. The electors in each State shall have the qualifications requisite for electors of the most numerous branch of the State legislatures.

When vacancies happen in the representation of any State in the Senate, the executive authority of such State shall issue writs of election to fill such vacancies: *Provided*, That the legislature of any State may empower the executive thereof to make temporary appointments until the people fill the vacancies by election as the legislature may direct.

This amendment shall not be so construed as to affect the election or term of any Senator chosen before it becomes valid as part of the Constitution.

AMENDMENT XVIII

Passed by Congress December 18, 1917. Ratified January 16, 1919. Repealed by Amendment 21.

Section 1.
After one year from the ratification of this article the manufacture, sale, or transportation of intoxicating liquors within, the importation thereof into, or the exportation thereof from the United States and all territory subject to the jurisdiction thereof for beverage purposes is hereby prohibited.

Section 2.
The Congress and the several States shall have concurrent power to enforce this article by appropriate legislation.

Section 3.
This article shall be inoperative unless it shall have been ratified as an amendment to the Constitution by the legislatures of the several States, as provided in the Constitution, within seven years from the date of the submission hereof to the States by the Congress.

AMENDMENT XIX

Passed by Congress June 4, 1919. Ratified August 18, 1920.

The right of citizens of the United States to vote shall not be denied or abridged by the United States or by any State on account of sex.

Congress shall have power to enforce this article by appropriate legislation.

AMENDMENT XX

Passed by Congress March 2, 1932. Ratified January 23, 1933.

Note: Article I, section 4, of the Constitution was modified by section 2 of this Amendment. In addition, a portion of the 12th Amendment was superseded by section 3.

Section 1.
The terms of the President and the Vice President shall end at noon on the 20th day of January, and the terms of Senators and Representatives at noon on the 3d day of January, of the years in which such terms would have ended if this article had not been ratified; and the terms of their successors shall then begin.

Section 2.
The Congress shall assemble at least once in every year, and such meeting shall begin at noon on the 3d day of January, unless they shall by law appoint a different day.

Section 3.
If, at the time fixed for the beginning of the term of the President, the President elect shall have died, the Vice President elect shall become President. If a President shall not have been chosen before the time fixed for the beginning of his term, or if the President elect shall have failed to qualify, then the Vice President elect shall act as President until a President shall have qualified; and the Congress may by law provide for the case wherein neither a President elect nor a Vice President elect shall have qualified, declaring who shall then act as President, or the manner in which one who is to act shall be selected, and such person shall act accordingly until a President or Vice President shall have qualified.

Section 4.
The Congress may by law provide for the case of the death of any of the persons from whom the House of Representatives may choose a President whenever the right of choice shall have devolved upon them, and for the case of the death of any of the persons from whom the Senate may choose a Vice President whenever the right of choice shall have devolved upon them.

Section 5.
Sections 1 and 2 shall take effect on the 15th day of October following the ratification of this article.

Section 6.
This article shall be inoperative unless it shall have been ratified as an amendment to the Constitution by the legislatures of three-fourths of the several States within seven years from the date of its submission.

AMENDMENT XXI

Passed by Congress February 20, 1933. Ratified December 5, 1933.

Section 1.
The eighteenth article of amendment to the Constitution of the United States is hereby repealed.

Section 2.
The transportation or importation into any State, Territory, or possession of the United States for delivery or use therein of intoxicating liquors, in violation of the laws thereof, is hereby prohibited.

Section 3.
This article shall be inoperative unless it shall have been ratified as an amendment to the Constitution by conventions in the several States, as provided in the Constitution, within seven years from the date of the submission hereof to the States by the Congress.

AMENDMENT XXII

Passed by Congress March 21, 1947. Ratified February 27, 1951.

Section 1.
No person shall be elected to the office of the President more than twice, and no person who has held the office of President, or acted as President, for more than two years of a term to which some other person was elected President shall be elected to the office of the President more than once. But this Article shall not apply to any person holding the office of President when this Article was proposed by the Congress, and shall not prevent any person who may be holding the office of President, or acting as President, during the term within which this Article becomes operative from holding the office of President or acting as President during the remainder of such term.

Section 2.
This article shall be inoperative unless it shall have been ratified as an amendment to the Constitution by the legislatures of three-fourths of the several States within seven years from the date of its submission to the States by the Congress.

AMENDMENT XXIII

Passed by Congress June 16, 1960. Ratified March 29, 1961.

Section 1.
The District constituting the seat of Government of the United States shall appoint in such manner as the Congress may direct:

A number of electors of President and Vice President equal to the whole number of Senators and Representatives in Congress to which the District would be entitled if it were a State, but in no event more than the least populous State; they shall be in addition to those appointed by the States, but they shall be considered, for the purposes of the election of President and Vice President, to be electors appointed by a State; and they shall meet in the District and perform such duties as provided by the twelfth article of amendment.

Section 2.
The Congress shall have power to enforce this article by appropriate legislation.

AMENDMENT XXIV

Passed by Congress August 27, 1962. Ratified January 23, 1964.

Section 1.
The right of citizens of the United States to vote in any primary or other election for President or Vice President, for electors for President or Vice President, or for Senator or Representative in Congress, shall not be denied or abridged by the United States or any State by reason of failure to pay any poll tax or other tax.

Section 2.
The Congress shall have power to enforce this article by appropriate legislation.

AMENDMENT XXV

Passed by Congress July 6, 1965. Ratified February 10, 1967.

Note: Article II, section 1, of the Constitution was affected by the 25th amendment.

Section 1.
In case of the removal of the President from office or of his death or resignation, the Vice President shall become President.

Section 2.
Whenever there is a vacancy in the office of the Vice President, the President shall nominate a Vice President who shall take office upon confirmation by a majority vote of both Houses of Congress.

Section 3.
Whenever the President transmits to the President pro tempore of the Senate and the Speaker of the House of Representatives his written declaration that he is unable to discharge the powers and duties of his office, and until he transmits to them a written declaration to the contrary, such powers and duties shall be discharged by the Vice President as Acting President.

Section 4.
Whenever the Vice President and a majority of either the principal officers of the executive departments or of such other body as Congress may by law provide, transmit to the President pro tempore of the Senate and the Speaker of the House of Representatives their written declaration that the President is unable to discharge the powers and duties of his office, the Vice President shall immediately assume the powers and duties of the office as Acting President.

Thereafter, when the President transmits to the President pro tempore of the Senate and the Speaker of the House of Representatives his written declaration that no inability exists, he shall resume the powers and duties of his office unless the Vice President and a majority of either the principal officers of the executive department or of such other body as Congress may by law provide, transmit within four days to the President pro tempore of the Senate and the Speaker of the House of Representatives their written declaration that the President is unable to discharge the powers and duties of his office. Thereupon Congress shall decide the issue, assembling within forty-eight hours for that purpose if not in session. If the Congress, within twenty-one days after receipt of the latter written declaration, or, if Congress is not in session, within twenty-one days after Congress is required to assemble, determines by two-thirds vote of both Houses that the President is unable to discharge the powers and duties of his office, the Vice President shall continue to discharge the same as Acting President; otherwise, the President shall resume the powers and duties of his office.

AMENDMENT XXVI

Passed by Congress March 23, 1971. Ratified July 1, 1971.

Note: Amendment 14, section 2, of the Constitution was modified by section 1 of the 26th amendment.

Section 1.
The right of citizens of the United States, who are eighteen years of age or older, to vote shall not be denied or abridged by the United States or by any State on account of age.

Section 2.
The Congress shall have power to enforce this article by appropriate legislation.

AMENDMENT XXVII

Originally proposed Sept. 25, 1789. Ratified May 7, 1992.

No law, varying the compensation for the services of the Senators and Representatives, shall take effect, until an election of Representatives shall have intervened

States' Rights Under the U.S. Constitution

Selective incorporation under the 14th Amendment

The U.S. Constitution has Articles and Amendments that established constitutional rights.

The provisions in the Bill of Rights (i.e., the first ten Amendments to the Constitution) were initially binding upon only the federal government.

In time, most of these provisions became binding upon the states through *selective incorporation* into the *due process clause* of the 14th Amendment (i.e., reverse incorporation).

When a provision is made binding on a state, a state can no longer restrict the rights guaranteed in that provision.

The 1st Amendment guarantees the freedoms of speech, press, religion, and assembly.

The 5th Amendment protects the right to grand jury proceedings in federal criminal cases.

The 6th Amendment guarantees a right to confront witnesses (i.e., Confrontation Clause).

The right to confront witnesses was not *selectively incorporated* into the due process clause of the 14th Amendment and is not binding upon the states.

Therefore, persons involved in state criminal proceedings as a defendant have no federal constitutional right to grand jury proceedings.

Whether an individual has a right to a grand jury becomes a question of state law.

The 10th Amendment, which is part of the Bill of Rights, was ratified on December 15, 1791. It states the Constitution's principle of federalism by providing that powers not granted to the federal government by the Constitution, nor prohibited to the States, are reserved to the States or the people.

Federalism in the United States

Federalism in the United States is the evolving relationship between state governments and the federal government.

The American government has evolved from a system of dual federalism to associative federalism.

In "Federalist No. 46," James Madison wrote that the states and national government "are in fact but different agents and trustees of the people, constituted with different powers."

Alexander Hamilton, in "Federalist No. 28," suggested that both levels of government would exercise authority to the citizens' benefit: "If their [the peoples'] rights are invaded by either, they can make use of the other as the instrument of redress."[3]

Because the states were preexisting political entities, the U.S. Constitution did not need to define or explain federalism in one section, but it often mentions the rights and responsibilities of state governments and state officials in relation to the federal government.

The federal government has certain *express powers* (also called *enumerated powers*), which are powers spelled out in the Constitution, including the right to levy taxes, declare war, and regulate interstate and foreign commerce.

Also, the *Necessary and Proper Clause* gives the federal government the *implied power* to pass any law "necessary and proper" to execute its express powers.

Enumerated powers of the Federal Government are contained in Article I, Section 8 of the U.S. Constitution.

Other powers—the *reserved powers*—are reserved to the people or the states under the 10th Amendment. The Supreme Court decision significantly expanded the power delegated to the federal government in *McCulloch v. Maryland* (1819) and the 13th, 14th and 15th, Amendments to the Constitution following the Civil War.

Comprehensive Glossary of Legal Terms

Over 2,100 essential legal terms defined and explained. An excellent reference source for law students, practitioners and readers seeking an understanding of legal vocabulary and its application.

Landmark U.S. Supreme Court Cases: Essential Summaries

Learn important constitutional cases that shaped American law. Understand how the evolving needs of society intersect with the U.S. Constitution. Short summaries of seminal Supreme Court cases focused on issues and holdings.

Visit our Amazon store

Frank J. Addivinola, Ph.D., J.D., L.LM., MBA

The lead author and chief editor of this preparation guide is Dr. Frank Addivinola. With his outstanding education, professional training, legal and business experience, and university teaching, Dr. Addivinola lent his expertise to develop this book.

Attorney Frank Addivinola is admitted to practice law in several jurisdictions. He has served as an academic advisor and mentor for students and practitioners.

Dr. Addivinola holds an undergraduate degree from Williams College. He completed his Masters at Harvard University, Masters in Biotechnology at Johns Hopkins University, Masters in Technology Management and MBA at the University of Maryland University College, J.D. and L.LM. from Suffolk University, and Ph.D. in Law and Public Policy from Northeastern University.

During his extensive teaching career, Dr. Addivinola taught university courses in Introduction to Law and developed law coursebooks. He received several awards for community service, research, and presentations.

Made in the USA
Monee, IL
23 April 2022

95271382R00450